W9-CTB-998

5 STEPS TO A 5™

# AP Chemistry

## 2023

# 5 STEPS TO A 5™

# AP Chemistry

## 2023

John T. Moore, EdD
Richard H. Langley, PhD

McGraw Hill

New York Chicago San Francisco Athens London Madrid
Mexico City Milan New Delhi Singapore Sydney Toronto

Copyright © 2022, 2021, 2019, 2018, 2017, 2016 by McGraw Hill. All rights reserved. Printed in the United States of America. Except as permitted under the United States Copyright Act of 1976, no part of this publication may be reproduced or distributed in any form or by any means, or stored in a database or retrieval system, without the prior written permission of the publisher.

2 3 4 5 6 7 8 9 LHS 27 26 25 24 23 22 (Cross-Platform Prep Course only)
2 3 4 5 6 7 8 9 LHS 27 26 25 24 23 22 (Elite Student Edition)

ISBN 978-1-264-48179-8 (Cross-Platform Prep Course only)
MHID 1-264-48179-9

e-ISBN 978-1-264-48306-8 (e-book Cross-Platform Prep Course only)
e-MHID 1-264-48306-6

ISBN 978-1-264-48356-3 (Elite Student Edition)
MHID 1-264-48356-2

e-ISBN 978-1-264-48414-0 (e-book Elite Student Edition)
e-MHID 1-264-48414-3

McGraw Hill, the McGraw Hill logo, *5 Steps to a 5*, and related trade dress are trademarks or registered trademarks of McGraw Hill and/or its affiliates in the United States and other countries and may not be used without written permission. All other trademarks are the property of their respective owners. McGraw Hill is not associated with any product or vendor mentioned in this book.

*AP, Advanced Placement Program,* and *College Board* are registered trademarks of the College Board, which was not involved in the production of, and does not endorse, this product.

McGraw Hill products are available at special quantity discounts to use as premiums and sales promotions or for use in corporate training programs. To contact a representative, please visit the Contact Us pages at www.mhprofessional.com.

McGraw Hill is committed to making our products accessible to all learners. To learn more about the available support and accommodations we offer, please contact us at accessibility@mheducation.com. We also participate in the Access Text Network ("http://www.accesstext.org" www.accesstext.org), and ATN members may submit requests through ATN.

## Cross-Platform Prep Course

### Single User License Terms and Conditions

Access to the digital content included with this book is governed by the McGraw Hill License Agreement outlined below. By using this digital content you agree to the terms of that license.

**DURATION OF LICENSE.** Access to the Cross-Platform Prep Course will expire one year from your initial login.

Your purchase of this McGraw Hill product, including its access code through a retail store is subject to the refund policy of that store.

The Content is a copyrighted work of McGraw Hill and McGraw Hill reserves all rights in and to the Content. The Work is © 2022 by McGraw Hill, LLC.

**RESTRICTIONS ON TRANSFER.** The user is receiving only a limited right to use the Content for user's own internal and personal use, dependent on purchase and continued ownership of this Cross-Platform product. The user may not reproduce, forward, modify, create derivative works based upon, transmit, distribute, disseminate, sell, publish, or sublicense the Content or in any way commingle the Content with other third party content, without McGraw Hill's consent.

**LIMITED WARRANTY.** The McGraw Hill Content is provided on an "as is" basis. Neither McGraw Hill nor its licensors make any guarantees or warranties of any kind, either express or implied, including, but not limited to, implied warranties of merchantability or fitness for a particular purpose or use as to any McGraw Hill Content or the information therein or any warranties as to the accuracy, completeness, currentness, or results to be obtained from, accessing or suing the McGraw Hill content, or any material referenced in such content or any information entered into licensee's product by users or other persons and/or any material available on or that can be accessed through the licensee's product (including via any hyperlink or otherwise) or as to non-infringement of third party rights. Any warranties of any kind, whether express or implied, are disclaimed. Any material or data obtained through use of the McGraw Hill content is at your own discretion and risk and user understands that it will be solely responsible for any resulting damage to its computer system or loss of data.

Neither McGraw Hill nor its licensors shall be liable to any subscriber or to any user or anyone else for any inaccuracy, delay, interruption in service, error, or omission, regardless of cause, or for any damage resulting therefrom.

In no event will McGraw Hill or its licensors be liable for any indirect, special, or consequential damages, including but not limited to, lost time, lost money, lost profits or good will, whether in contract, tort, strict liability or otherwise, and whether or not such damages are foreseen or unforeseen with respect to any use of the McGraw Hill content.

# CONTENTS


Preface xiii
Acknowledgments xiv
About the Authors xiv
Introduction: The Five-Step Program xv

STEP 1 **Set Up Your Study Program**

**1 What You Need to Know About the AP Chemistry Exam 3**
Background of the Advanced Placement Program 3
Who Writes the AP Chemistry Exam? 4
The AP Grades and Who Receives Them 4
Reasons for Taking the AP Chemistry Exam 4
Questions Frequently Asked About the AP Chemistry Exam 5

**2 How to Plan Your Time 11**
Three Approaches to Preparing for the AP Chemistry Exam 11
Calendar for Each Plan 14

STEP 2 **Determine Your Test Readiness**

**3 Take a Diagnostic Exam 19**
Getting Started: The Diagnostic Exam 20
AP Chemistry Final Practice Exam, Section I (Multiple Choice) 21
Answers and Explanations for Final Practice Exam, Section I (Multiple Choice) 34
AP Chemistry Final Practice Exam, Section II (Free Response) 41
Answers and Explanations for Final Practice Exam, Section II (Free Response) 47
Scoring and Interpretation 56

STEP 3 **Develop Strategies for Success**

**4 How to Approach Each Question Type 59**
Multiple-Choice Questions 59
Free-Response Questions 62

STEP 4 **Review the Knowledge You Need to Score High**

**5 Basics 69**
Units and Measurements 70
Dimensional Analysis—the Factor Label Method 71
The States of Matter 72
Phase Diagrams 72
The Structure of the Atom 74
Oxidation Numbers 82
Nomenclature Overview 83
Experiments 89
Common Mistakes to Avoid 89
Review Questions 90

Answers and Explanations 92
Free-Response Question 94
Answer and Explanation 94
Rapid Review 95

**6 Stoichiometry 97**
Moles and Molar Mass 98
Percent Composition and Empirical Formulas 98
Introduction to Reactions 100
Reaction Stoichiometry 100
Limiting Reactants 102
Percent Yield 103
Molarity and Solution Calculations 104
Experiments 104
Common Mistakes to Avoid 105
Review Questions 105
Answers and Explanations 108
Free-Response Question 112
Answer and Explanation 113
Rapid Review 114

**7 Spectroscopy, Light, and Electrons 117**
The Nature of Light 118
Spectroscopy and the Electromagnetic Spectrum 119
Beer–Lambert Law 120
Wave Properties of Matter 121
Atomic Spectra 121
Atomic Orbitals 122
Photoelectron (Photoemission) Spectroscopy (PES) 124
Experiments 124
Common Mistakes to Avoid 124
Review Questions 125
Answers and Explanations 127
Free-Response Question 128
Answer and Explanation 129
Rapid Review 130

**8 Bonding 131**
Lewis Electron-Dot Structures 132
Ionic and Covalent Bonding 132
Molecular Geometry—VSEPR 136
Valence Bond Theory 139
Molecular Orbital Theory 140
Resonance 142
Bond Length, Strength, and Magnetic Properties 143
Structure of Metals and Alloys 143
Experiments 145
Common Mistakes to Avoid 145
Review Questions 146
Answers and Explanations 148
Free-Response Question 149

Answer and Explanation 150
Rapid Review 151

**9 Solids, Liquids, and Intermolecular Forces 153**
Structures and Intermolecular Forces 154
The Liquid State 156
The Solid State 157
Relationship of Intermolecular Forces to Phase Changes 159
Potential Energy 160
Experiments 161
Common Mistakes to Avoid 161
Review Questions 161
Answers and Explanations 164
Free-Response Question 165
Answer and Explanation 166
Rapid Review 166

**10 Gases 169**
Kinetic Molecular Theory 170
Gas Law Relationships 171
Experiments 181
Common Mistakes to Avoid 183
Review Questions 184
Answers and Explanations 186
Free-Response Question 188
Answer and Explanation 189
Rapid Review 190

**11 Solutions 191**
Concentration Units 192
Electrolytes and Nonelectrolytes 194
Colligative Properties 195
Colloids 197
Composition of Mixtures 198
Separation of Solutions and Mixtures Chromatography 199
Experiments 200
Common Mistakes to Avoid 201
Review Questions 201
Answers and Explanations 204
Free-Response Questions 206
Answers and Explanations 207
Rapid Review 207

**12 Reactions and Periodicity 209**
AP Exam Format 210
General Aspects of Chemical Reactions and Equations 210
General Properties of Aqueous Solutions 212
Precipitation Reactions 213
Oxidation–Reduction Reactions 214
Coordination Compounds 218
Acid–Base Reactions 219
Experiments 223

Common Mistakes to Avoid 223
Review Questions 224
Answers and Explanations 226
Free-Response Question 228
Answer and Explanation 229
Rapid Review 229

**13 Kinetics 231**
How Reactions Occur—Collision Model 232
Rates of Reaction 233
Integrated Rate Laws 236
Reaction Energy Profile 238
Activation Energy 239
Reaction Mechanisms 239
Steady-State Approximation 240
Multistep Reaction Energy Profile 240
Catalysts 240
Experiments 242
Common Mistakes to Avoid 242
Review Questions 243
Answers and Explanations 246
Free-Response Question 248
Answer and Explanation 249
Rapid Review 250

**14 Thermodynamics 253**
Energy Diagrams 254
Heat Transfer and Thermal Equilibrium 254
Calorimetry 255
Energy of Phase Changes 257
Introduction to Enthalpy of Reaction 258
Bond Enthalpies 259
Laws of Thermodynamics 260
Hess's Law 260
Enthalpies of Formation 262
Thermodynamics and Equilibrium 265
Thermodynamic and Kinetic Control 265
Coupled Reactions 265
Experiments 266
Common Mistakes to Avoid 266
Review Questions 267
Answers and Explanations 270
Free-Response Question 272
Answer and Explanation 272
Rapid Review 273

**15 Equilibrium 275**
Equilibrium Expressions 277
Magnitude of the Equilibrium Constant 277
Properties of the Equilibrium Constant 278
Calculating Equilibrium Concentrations 279

Representations of Equilibrium 281
Le Châtelier's Principle 282
Solubility Equilibria 285
Common-Ion Effect 287
pH and Solubility 287
Free Energy of Dissolution 288
Other Equilibria 289
Experiments 289
Common Mistakes to Avoid 289
Review Questions 290
Answers and Explanations 292
Free-Response Question 295
Answer and Explanation 296
Rapid Review 298

**16 Acids and Bases 299**
Acid–Base Equilibrium 300
$K_a$—the Acid Dissociation Constant 302
$K_w$—the Water Dissociation Constant 303
Molecular Structure of Acids and Bases 304
pH 305
$K_b$—the Base Dissociation Constant 306
Acidic/Basic Properties of Salts 308
Buffers 309
Acid–Base Reactions and Buffers 311
Titration Equilibria 312
Experiments 317
Common Mistakes to Avoid 317
Review Questions 318
Answers and Explanations 321
Free-Response Question 323
Answer and Explanation 324
Rapid Review 324

**17 Electrochemistry 327**
Redox Reactions 328
Electrochemical Cells 328
Quantitative Aspects of Electrochemistry 335
Nernst Equation 336
Electrolysis and Faraday's Law 338
Experiments 338
Common Mistakes to Avoid 338
Review Questions 339
Answers and Explanations 342
Free-Response Question 344
Answer and Explanation 344
Rapid Review 345

*Additional Review and Applications*

**18 Nuclear Chemistry 349**
Nuclear Reactions 350

Natural Radioactive Decay Modes 350
Nuclear Stability 352
Nuclear Decay Calculations 352
Mass–Energy Relationships 353
Common Mistakes to Avoid 354
Review Questions 354
Answers and Explanations 356
Free-Response Question 356
Answer and Explanation 357
Rapid Review 358

**19 Organic Chemistry 359**
Hydrocarbons 360
Structural Isomerism 360
Common Functional Groups 361
Acid–Base Chemistry 361
Experiments 363
Common Mistakes to Avoid 364
Review Questions 364
Answers and Explanations 365
Free-Response Questions 366
Answers and Explanations 366
Rapid Review 368

**20 Experimental Investigations 369**
Experiment 1: Spectroscopy 370
Experiment 2: Spectrophotometry 373
Experiment 3: Gravimetric Analysis 374
Experiment 4: Titration 375
Experiment 5: Chromatography 377
Experiment 6: Determination of the Type of Bonding in Solid Samples 378
Experiment 7: Stoichiometry 378
Experiment 8: Redox Titration 379
Experiment 9: Chemical and Physical Changes 381
Experiment 10: Kinetics 381
Experiment 11: Rate Laws 382
Experiment 12: Calorimetry 383
Experiment 13: Chemical Equilibrium—Le Châtelier's Principle 384
Experiment 14: Acid–Base Titrations 385
Experiment 15: Buffer pH 385
Experiment 16: The Capacity of a Buffer 386
Common Mistakes to Avoid 387
Review Questions 387
Answers and Explanations 391
Free-Response Questions 394
Answers and Explanations 397
Rapid Review 401

**STEP 5 Build Your Test-Taking Confidence**
**AP Chemistry Practice Exam 1 405**
AP Chemistry Practice Exam 1, Section I (Multiple Choice) 407

Answers and Explanations for Exam 1, Section I (Multiple Choice) 420
AP Chemistry Practice Exam 1, Section II (Free Response) 426
Answers and Explanations for Exam 1, Section II (Free Response) 432

**AP Chemistry Practice Exam 2 439**
AP Chemistry Practice Exam 2, Section I (Multiple Choice) 441
Answers and Explanations for Exam 2, Section I (Multiple Choice) 453
AP Chemistry Practice Exam 2, Section II (Free Response) 459
Answers and Explanations for Exam 2, Section II (Free Response) 463

**Appendixes**
Pre-AP Diagnostic Exam 473
SI Units 493
Balancing Redox Equations Using the Ion–Electron Method 495
Common Ions 499
Bibliography 502
Websites 502
Glossary 503
Avoiding "Stupid" Mistakes on the Free-Response Section 512
Exam Resources 515

# PREFACE

Welcome to the AP Chemistry Five-Step Program. The fact that you are reading this preface suggests that you will be taking the AP Exam in chemistry. The AP Chemistry Exam is constantly evolving and so this guide has evolved. We have updated the book to match the new AP Chemistry Exam. The new exam has an emphasis on sets—a series of questions that refer to the same given information, along with changes in the free-response portion.

The AP Chemistry Exam and other standardized chemistry exams certainly aren't easy, but the rewards are worth it—college credit, a good preparation for college chemistry, and the satisfaction of a job well done. You will have to work and study hard to do well, but throughout this book we will help you master the material and get ready for the exam.

Both of us have many years of experience in teaching introductory general chemistry at the university level. John Moore is the author of *Chemistry for Dummies*, and he and Richard "Doc" Langley have also written *Chemistry for the Utterly Confused*, a guide for college/high school students. Each of us has certain skills and experiences that will be of special help in presenting the material in this book. Richard has also taught high school science, and John has years of experience teaching chemistry to both public school teachers and students. Both of us have been graders for the AP Chemistry Exam free-response questions for years (20+ years for Richard and a few less for John) and have firsthand knowledge of how the exam is graded and scored. We have tried not only to make the material understandable but also to present the problems in the format of the AP Chemistry Exam. We will let you know about common student errors along the way. By faithfully working the problems you will increase your familiarity with the exam format, so that when the time comes to take the exam there will be no surprises.

Use this book in addition to your regular chemistry text. We have outlined three different study programs to prepare you for the exam. If you choose the yearlong program, use it as you are taking your AP Chemistry course. It will provide additional problems in the AP format. If you choose one of the other two programs, use it with your chemistry textbook also; but you may need to lean a little more on this review book. Either way, if you put in the time and effort, you will do well.

Now it's time to start. Read the Introduction: The Five-Step Program; Chapter 1, What You Need to Know About the AP Chemistry Exam; and Chapter 2, How to Plan Your Time. Then take the Pre-AP Diagnostic Exam in the appendixes. Your score will show how well you understand the material right now and point out weak areas that may need a little extra attention. Use the review exams at the end of the chapters to check your comprehension. Also, pay attention to the free-response questions. That is where you can really shine, and they are worth almost as much as the multiple-choice part. Use the Rapid Reviews to brush up on the important points in the chapters. Just before taking the exam, review the section on avoiding "stupid" mistakes at the back of this book. Then take the AP Chemistry Final Practice Exam in Chapter 3. Keep this book handy—it is going to be your friend for the next few weeks or months.

Good luck—but remember that luck favors the prepared mind.

# ACKNOWLEDGMENTS

The authors would like to thank Grace Freedson, who believed in our abilities and gave us this project. Many thanks also to Anya Kozorez, whose production talents moved this project along. A really big thanks to Mindy Wurtz for her insights and suggestions. Many thanks to our colleagues at the AP Chemistry readings for their helpful suggestions.

# ABOUT THE AUTHORS

John Moore grew up in the foothills of western North Carolina. He attended the University of North Carolina–Asheville, where he received his bachelor's degree in chemistry. He earned his master's degree in chemistry from Furman University in Greenville, South Carolina. After a stint in the US Army he decided to try his hand at teaching. In 1971, he joined the faculty of Stephen F. Austin State University in Nacogdoches, Texas. In 1985 he started back to school part time, and in 1991 he received his doctorate in science education from Texas A&M University. In 2003 his first book, *Chemistry for Dummies*, was published.

Richard Langley grew up in southwestern Ohio. He attended Miami University in Oxford, Ohio, where he earned bachelor's degrees in chemistry and mineralogy and a master's degree in chemistry. He next went to the University of Nebraska in Lincoln, where he received his doctorate in chemistry. He took a postdoctoral position at Arizona State University in Tempe, Arizona, then became a visiting assistant professor at the University of Wisconsin–River Falls. He first joined Stephen F. Austin State University in Nacogdoches, Texas, in 1982.

The authors are coauthors of *Chemistry for the Utterly Confused, Must Know Chemistry for High School, Biochemistry for Dummies*, and *Organic Chemistry II for Dummies.*

Both authors are graders for the free-response portion of the AP Chemistry Exam. In fact, between them, they have almost forty years of AP grading experience and estimate that together they have graded more than 150,000 exams.

# INTRODUCTION: THE FIVE-STEP PROGRAM

## The Basics

Not too long ago, you enrolled in AP Chemistry. A curiosity about chemistry, encouragement from a respected teacher, or the simple fact that it was a requirement may have been your motivation. No matter what the reason, you find yourself flipping through a book that promises to help you culminate this experience with the highest of honors, a 5 in AP Chemistry. Yes, it is possible to achieve this honor without this book. There are many excellent teachers of AP Chemistry out there who teach, coax, and otherwise prepare their students into getting a 5 every year. However, for most students preparing for the exam, the benefits of buying this book far outweigh its cost.

The key to doing well on the Advanced Placement (AP) Chemistry Exam is to outline a method of attack and not to deviate from this method. We will work with you to make sure you take the best path toward the test. You will need to focus on each step, and this book will serve as a tool to guide your steps. But do not forget—no tool is useful if you do not use it.

## Organization of the Book

This book conducts you through the five steps necessary to prepare yourself for success on the exam. These steps will provide you with the skills and strategies vital to the exam, and the practice that will lead you toward the perfect 5.

First, we start by introducing the basic five-step plan used in this book. Then in Chapter 1, we will give you some background information about the AP Chemistry Exam. Next, in Chapter 2, we present three different approaches to preparing for the exam. In the appendixes you will find the Pre-AP Diagnostic Exam and in Chapter 3, we give you an opportunity to evaluate your knowledge with diagnostic exam. The results of these exams will allow you to customize your study. In Chapter 4, we offer you a multitude of tips and suggestions about the different types of questions on the AP Chemistry Exam. Many times good test-taking practices can help raise your score.

Since the volume of the material to be mastered can be intimidating, Chapters 5 to 20 present a comprehensive review of the material that you will cover in an AP Chemistry course. This is review material, but since not all this material appears in every AP Chemistry class, it will also help to fill in the gaps in your chemistry knowledge. You can use it in conjunction with your textbook if you are currently taking AP Chemistry, or you can use it as a review of the concepts you covered. At the end of each chapter, you will find both a multiple-choice and free-response exam for you to test yourself. The answers and explanations are included. This will also help you identify any topics that might require additional study.

After these content chapters, there are two complete chemistry practice exams, including multiple-choice and free-response questions. The answers and explanations are included. These exams will allow you to test your skills. The multiple-choice questions will provide you with practice on questions similar to those asked on past AP Exams. These are not the exact questions, but ones that will focus you on the key AP Chemistry topics. There are also examples of free-response questions; there are fewer of these since they take much longer to answer. After you take an exam, you should review each question. Ask yourself, why was this question present? Why do I need to know this? Make sure you check your answers against the explanations. If necessary, use the index to locate a particular topic and reread the review material. In Step 5 we suggest that you take the Final Practice Exam in Chapter 3, identify those areas that need additional study, and review the appropriate material. Then take the second exam and use the results to guide your additional study.

Finally, in the appendixes you will find additional resources to aid your preparation. These include:

- The Pre-AP Diagnostic Exam
- A tip sheet on how to avoid "stupid" mistakes and careless errors
- Common conversions
- How to balance redox equations
- A list of common ions
- A bibliography
- Several useful websites
- A glossary of terms related to AP Chemistry
- A table of half-reactions for use while answering free-response questions
- A table of equations and abbreviations for use while answering free-response questions
- A periodic table for use when answering any exam questions

# The Five-Step Program

## Step 1: Set Up Your Study Program

In Step 1, you will read a brief overview of the AP Chemistry Exams, including an outline of the topics. You will also follow a process to help determine which of the following preparation programs is right for you:

- Full school year: September through May
- One semester: January through May
- Six weeks: Basic training for the exam

## Step 2: Determine Your Test Readiness

Step 2 and the Pre-AP Diagnostic Exam will provide you with ways to assess your current level of understanding. These exams will let you know about your current level of preparedness and on which areas you should focus your study. Much of this material is considered to be "prior knowledge," which is material you should know before taking an AP Chemistry course. This will not appear directly on the AP Exam; however, you will need to know this material to understand many of the questions.

- Take the diagnostic exams slowly and analyze each question. Do not worry about how many questions you get right. Hopefully, this exam will boost your confidence.
- Review the answers and explanations following each exam, so that you see what you do and do not yet fully understand.

### Step 3: Develop Strategies for Success

Step 3 provides strategies that will help you do your best on the exam. These strategies cover both the multiple-choice and free-response sections of the exam. Some of these tips are based upon experience in writing questions, and others have been gleaned from our years of experience reading (grading) the AP Chemistry Exams.

- Learn how to read and analyze multiple-choice questions.
- Learn how to answer multiple-choice questions.
- Learn how to plan and write answers to the free-response questions.

### Step 4: Review the Knowledge You Need to Score High

Step 4 encompasses most of this book. In this step, you will learn or review the material you need to know for the test. Your results on the diagnostic exam will let you know on which material you should concentrate your study. Concentrating on some material does not mean you can ignore the other material. You should review all the material, even what you already know.

There is a lot of material here, enough to summarize a yearlong experience in AP Chemistry and highlight the, well, highlights. Some AP courses will have covered more material than yours; some will have covered less. But the bottom line is that if you thoroughly review this material, you will have studied all that is on this exam and what appears on other standardized chemistry exams and you will have significantly increased your chances of scoring well. This edition gives new emphasis to some areas of chemistry to bring your review more in line with the revised AP Chemistry Exam format. For example, there is more discussion of reactions and the laboratory experience. Each chapter contains a short exam to monitor your understanding of the current chapter.

### Step 5: Build Your Test-Taking Confidence

In Step 5, you will complete your preparation by testing yourself on practice exams. This section contains *two* complete chemistry exams, solutions, and sometimes more important, advice on how to avoid the common mistakes. Be aware that these practice exams are *not* reproduced questions from actual AP Chemistry Exams, but they mirror both the material tested by AP and the way in which it is tested.

## The Graphics Used in This Book

To emphasize particular skills and strategies, we use several icons throughout this book. An icon in the margin will alert you to pay particular attention to the accompanying text. We use these four icons:

This icon highlights an especially important concept or fact that you should not pass over.

This icon calls your attention to a strategy that you may want to try.

This icon indicates a tip that you might find useful.

This icon points to material that is not directly tested on the AP Chemistry Exam but may be required by your teacher in high school, on other standardized chemistry exams, and certainly by your college teacher. Although you won't find this specific content on the AP Exam, knowing it will improve your understanding of chemistry, helping you to better grasp the material that is directly tested on the exam.

**Boldfaced** words indicate terms that are included in the glossary at the end of this book.

***UPDATE***

Just as this book was being prepared, for publication the College Board announced that beginning in Spring 2023, calculators may be used on all parts of the AP Chemistry exam. So please ignore any directions on test questions in this study guide that say, "no calculators." However, don't ignore our tips on rounding off and estimation. Many times these skills allow you to determine the correct answer faster than by using a calculator.

STEP 1

# Set Up Your Study Program

CHAPTER 1 What You Need to Know About the AP Chemistry Exam
CHAPTER 2 How to Plan Your Time

CHAPTER 1

# What You Need to Know About the AP Chemistry Exam

**IN THIS CHAPTER**

**Summary:** Learn what topics are on the test, how the ETS scores the test, and basic test-taking information.

KEY IDEA

**Key Ideas**

- Most colleges will award credit for a score of 4 or 5.
- Multiple-choice questions account for half of your final score.
- Points are not deducted for incorrect answers to multiple-choice questions. You should try to eliminate incorrect answer choices and then guess; there is no penalty for guessing.
- Free-response questions account for half of your final score.
- There is a conversion of your composite score on the two test sections to a score on the 1 to 5 scale.

## Background of the Advanced Placement Program

The College Board began the Advanced Placement program in 1955 to construct standard achievement exams that would allow highly motivated high school students the opportunity to receive advanced placement as first-year students in colleges and universities in the United States. Today, there are 38 courses and exams with more than 4.2 million students from every state in the nation and from foreign countries taking the annual exams in May.

The AP programs are for high school students who wish to take college-level courses. In our case, the AP Chemistry course and exam involve high school students in college-level chemistry studies.

## Who Writes the AP Chemistry Exam?

A group of college and high school chemistry instructors known as the AP Development Committee creates the AP Chemistry Exam. The committee's job is to ensure that the annual AP Chemistry Exam reflects what is taught in college-level chemistry classes at high schools.

This committee writes a large number of multiple-choice questions, which are pretested and evaluated for clarity, appropriateness, and range of possible answers.

The free-response essay questions that make up Section II go through a similar process of creation, modification, pretesting, and final refinement, so that the questions cover the necessary areas of material and are at an appropriate level of difficulty and clarity. The committee also makes a great effort to construct a free-response exam that will allow for clear and equitable grading by the AP readers.

It is important to remember that the AP Chemistry Exam undergoes a thorough evaluation after the yearly administration of the exam. This way, the College Board can use the results to make course suggestions and to plan future tests.

## The AP Grades and Who Receives Them

Once you have taken the exam and it has been scored, your test will be graded with one of five numbers by the College Board:

- A 5 indicates that you are extremely well qualified.
- A 4 indicates that you are well qualified.
- A 3 indicates that you are adequately qualified.
- A 2 indicates that you are possibly qualified.
- A 1 indicates that you are not qualified to receive college credit.

A grade report, consisting of a grade of 1 to 5, will be sent to you in July. You will also indicate the college(s) to which you want your AP score sent at the time of the exam. The report that the college receives contains your score for every AP Exam you took that year and the grades you received in prior years, except for any that you request withheld. In addition, your scores will be sent to your high school.

## Reasons for Taking the AP Chemistry Exam

Why put yourself through a year of intensive study, pressure, stress, and preparation? Only you can answer that question. Following are some of the reasons that students have indicated to us for taking the AP Exam:

- Because colleges look favorably on the applications of students who elect to enroll in AP courses
- To receive college credit or advanced standing at their colleges or universities
- To compare themselves with other students across the nation
- For personal satisfaction
- Because they love the subject
- So that their families will be proud of them
- To gain experience taking standardized tests

There are other reasons, but no matter what they are, the primary reason for your enrolling in the AP Chemistry course and taking the exam in May is to feel good about yourself and the challenges that you have met.

While there may be some idealistic motivators, let's face it: most students take the exam because they are seeking college credit. This means you are closer to graduation before you even start attending classes. Even if you do not score high enough to earn college credit, the fact that you elected to enroll in AP courses tells admission committees that you are a high achiever and serious about your education.

## Questions Frequently Asked About the AP Chemistry Exam

### What Is Going to Appear on the Exam?

This is an excellent question. The College Board, having consulted with those who teach chemistry, develops a curriculum that covers material that college professors expect to cover in their first-year classes. Based upon this outline of topics, the multiple-choice exams are written such that those topics are covered in proportion to their importance to the expected chemistry understanding of the student. Confused? Suppose that faculty consultants agree that environmental issues are important to the chemistry curriculum, maybe to the tune of 10 percent. If 10 percent of the curriculum in an AP Chemistry course is devoted to environmental issues, you can expect roughly 10 percent of the multiple-choice exam to address environmental issues. Remember, this is just a guide and each year the exam differs slightly in the percentages.

### How Is the Advanced Placement Chemistry Exam Organized?

Table 1.1 summarizes the format of the AP Chemistry Exam.

**Table 1.1**

| SECTION | NUMBER OF QUESTIONS | TIME LIMIT |
|---|---|---|
| I. Multiple-Choice Questions | 60 | 90 minutes |
| II. Free-Response Questions | | 105 minutes |
| Long Questions | 3 | 20–25 minutes per question |
| Short Questions | 4 | 3–10 minutes per question |

The exam is a two-part exam designed to take about three hours. The first section has 60 multiple-choice questions. You will have 90 minutes to complete this section.

The second part of the exam is the free-response section. You will begin this section after you have completed and turned in your multiple-choice scan sheet. There will be a break before you begin the second section. The length of this break will vary from school to school. You will not be able to go back to the multiple-choice questions later.

You will receive a test booklet for the free-response section of the test. You will have 105 minutes to answer seven questions. These questions may cover any of the material in the AP Chemistry course. The free-response section consists of two parts. In both parts, you may use a calculator. There will probably be two lab questions—one an experimental design question and the other an analysis of data or observations. There will be two questions involving representations of molecules—one involving a conversion between different types of representations and the other requiring an analysis or creation of an atomic or molecular view explaining a representation. Finally, there will be a quantitative question involving reasoning to solve a problem.

### Who Grades My AP Chemistry Exam?

Every June a group of chemistry teachers gathers for a week to assign grades to your hard work. Each of these "Faculty Consultants" spends a day or so in training on a question. Each reader becomes an expert on that question, and because each exam book is anonymous, this process provides a very consistent and unbiased scoring of that question. During a typical day of grading, there is a selection of a random sample of each reader's scores for cross-checking by other experienced "Table Leaders" to ensure that the graders maintain a level of consistency throughout the day and the week. Statistical analysis of each reader's scores on a given question ensure that they are not giving scores that are significantly higher or lower than the mean scores given by other readers of that question. All these measures ensure consistency and fairness for your benefit.

### Will My Exam Remain Anonymous?

Absolutely. Even if your high school teacher happens to read your booklet, there is virtually no way he or she will know it is you. To the reader, each student is a number, and to the computer, each student is a bar code.

### What About That Permission Box on the Back?

The College Board uses some exams to help train high school teachers so that they can help the next generation of chemistry students to avoid common mistakes. If you check this box, you simply give permission for your exam to be used in this way. Even if you give permission, no one will ever know it is your exam.

### How Is My Multiple-Choice Exam Scored?

You will place your answers to the multiple-choice questions on a scan sheet. The scan sheet is computer graded. The computer counts the number of correct responses. There is no penalty for incorrect answers or for leaving an answer blank (however, you should never do this).

The following is the weighting used for the various chemical units and topics:

| | |
|---|---|
| Unit 1—Atomic Structure/Properties | 7–9% |
| Unit 2—Molecular and Ionic Compounds Structures/Properties | 7–9% |
| Unit 3—Intermolecular Forces/Properties | 18–22% |
| Unit 4—Chemical Reactions | 7–9% |
| Unit 5—Kinetics | 7–9% |
| Unit 6—Thermodynamics | 7–9% |
| Unit 7—Equilibrium Principles | 7–9% |
| Unit 8—Acids and Bases | 11–15% |
| Unit 9—Applications of Thermodynamics | 7–9% |

### AP Units and Chapter Correlation

The AP chemistry course is divided into nine units, as shown above. The following is a list of the topics in the AP Curriculum correlated with the chapters in this book where they originally appear. These topics are distributed throughout Chapters 5 through 17 in this book and apply to both the multiple-choice and the free-response questions. The order is not the same as given in this list in order to facilitate learning. In addition, some topics may appear in more than one place. The unit/chapter correlation for each unit will also be repeated in the introduction to the unit. Many of these topics are also reviewed in Chapter 20. You may wish to go to the AP website for a fuller description of each of the topics.

| Unit | Topic | Chapter |
|---|---|---|
| Unit 1 | Atomic Structure and Properties | |
| 1.1 | Moles and Molar Mass | 6 |
| 1.2 | Mass Spectroscopy of Elements | 5 |
| 1.3 | Elemental Composition of Pure Substances | 6 |
| 1.4 | Composition of Mixtures | 11 |
| 1.5 | Atomic Structure and Electron Configuration | 5 and 7 |
| 1.6 | Photoelectron Spectroscopy | 7 |
| 1.7 | Periodic Trends | 5 |
| 1.8 | Valence Electrons and Ionic Compounds | 5 and 12 |
| Unit 2 | Molecular and Ionic Compounds Structure and Properties | |
| 2.1 | Types of Chemical Bonds | 8 |
| 2.2 | Intramolecular Force and Potential Energy | 9 |
| 2.3 | Structure of Ionic Solids | 9 |
| 2.4 | Structure of Metals and Alloys | 8 |
| 2.5 | Lewis Diagrams | 8 |
| 2.6 | Resonance and Formal Charge | 8 |
| 2.7 | VSEPR and Bond Hybridization | 8 |
| Unit 3 | Intermolecular Forces and Properties | |
| 3.1 | Intermolecular Forces | 9 |
| 3.2 | Properties of Solids | 9 |
| 3.3 | Solids, Liquids, and Gases | 5 |
| 3.4 | Ideal Gas Law | 10 |
| 3.5 | Kinetic Molecular Theory | 10 |
| 3.6 | Deviation from Ideal Gas Law | 10 |
| 3.7 | Solutions and Mixtures | 6, 11, 12 |
| 3.8 | Representations of Solutions | 6 |
| 3.9 | Separation of Solutions and Mixtures Chromatography | 11 |
| 3.10 | Solubility | 11 |
| 3.11 | Spectroscopy and the Electromagnetic Spectrum | 7 |
| 3.12 | Photoelectric Effect | 5 |
| 3.13 | Beer–Lambert Law | 7 |
| Unit 4 | Chemical Reactions | |
| 4.1 | Introduction for Reactions | 6 |
| 4.2 | Net Ionic Equations | 12 |
| 4.3 | Representations of Reactions | 11 |
| 4.4 | Physical and Chemical Changes | 12 |
| 4.5 | Stoichiometry | 6 |
| 4.6 | Introduction to Titration | 12 |
| 4.7 | Types of Chemical Reactions | 12 |
| 4.8 | Introduction to Acid–Base Reactions | 12 |
| 4.9 | Oxidation–Reduction (Redox) Reactions | 12 |
| Unit 5 | Kinetics | |
| 5.1 | Reaction Rates | 13 |
| 5.2 | Introduction to Rate Law | 13 |

| | | |
|---|---|---|
| 5.3 | Concentration Changes Over Time | 13 |
| 5.4 | Elementary Reactions | 13 |
| 5.5 | Collision Model | 13 |
| 5.6 | Reaction Energy Profile | 13 |
| 5.7 | Introduction to Reaction Mechanisms | 13 |
| 5.8 | Reaction Mechanism and Rate Law | 13 |
| 5.9 | Steady-State Approximation | 13 |
| 5.10 | Multistep Reaction Energy Profile | 13 |
| 5.11 | Catalysis | 13 |
| Unit 6 Thermodynamics | | |
| 6.1 | Endothermic and Exothermic Processes | 14 |
| 6.2 | Energy Diagrams | 14 |
| 6.3 | Heat Transfer and Thermal Equilibrium | 14 |
| 6.4 | Heat Capacity and Calorimetry | 14 |
| 6.5 | Energy of Phase Changes | 14 |
| 6.6 | Introduction to Enthalpy of Reaction | 14 |
| 6.7 | Bond Enthalpies | 14 |
| 6.8 | Enthalpy of Formation | 14 |
| 6.9 | Hess's Law | 14 |
| Unit 7 Equilibrium | | |
| 7.1 | Introduction to Equilibrium | 15 |
| 7.2 | Direction of Reversible Reactions | 15 |
| 7.3 | Reaction Quotient and Equilibrium Constant | 15 |
| 7.4 | Calculating the Equilibrium Constant | 15 |
| 7.5 | Magnitude of the Equilibrium Constant | 15 |
| 7.6 | Properties of the Equilibrium Constant | 15 |
| 7.7 | Calculating Equilibrium Concentrations | 15 |
| 7.8 | Representations of Equilibrium | 15 |
| 7.9 | Introduction to Le Châtelier's Principle | 15 |
| 7.10 | Reaction Quotient and Le Châtelier's Principle | 15 |
| 7.11 | Introduction to Solubility Equilibria | 15 |
| 7.12 | Common-Ion Effect | 15 |
| 7.13 | pH and Solubility | 15 |
| 7.14 | Free Energy of Dissolution | 15 |
| Unit 8 Acids and Bases | | |
| 8.1 | Introduction to Acids and Bases | 16 |
| 8.2 | pH and pOH of Strong Acids and Bases | 16 |
| 8.3 | Weak Acid and Base Equilibria | 16 |
| 8.4 | Acid–Base Reactions and Buffers | 16 |
| 8.5 | Acid–Base Titrations | 16 |
| 8.6 | Molecular Structure of Acids and Bases | 16 |
| 8.7 | pH and $pK_a$ | 16 |
| 8.8 | Properties of Buffers | 16 |
| 8.9 | Henderson–Hasselbalch Equation | 16 |
| 8.10 | Buffer Capacity | 16 |
| Unit 9 Applications of Thermodynamics | | |
| 9.1 | Introduction to Entropy | 14 |
| 9.2 | Absolute Entropy and Entropy Change | 14 |
| 9.3 | Gibbs Free Energy and Thermodynamic Favorability | 14 |

| | | |
|---|---|---|
| 9.4 | Thermodynamic and Kinetic Control | 14 |
| 9.5 | Free Energy and Equilibrium | 14 |
| 9.6 | Coupled Reactions | 14 |
| 9.7 | Galvanic (Voltaic) and Electrolytic Cells | 17 |
| 9.8 | Cell Potential and Free Energy | 17 |
| 9.9 | Cell Potential Under Nonstandard Conditions | 17 |
| 9.10 | Electrolysis and Faraday's Law | 17 |

## How Is My Free-Response Exam Scored?

You are required to answer seven free-response questions. The point totals will vary depending on whether it is a long question or a short one. There are three long-answer questions, and they count 10 points each. In addition, there are four short-answer questions counting 4 points each.

## So How Is My Final Grade Determined and What Does It Mean?

Your total composite score for the exam is found by adding the value from the multiple-choice section to the score from the free-response section and rounding that sum to the nearest whole number.

Keep in mind that the total composite scores needed to earn a 5, 4, 3, 2, or 1 change each year. A committee of AP, College Board, and Educational Testing Service (ETS) directors, experts, and statisticians determines these cutoffs. The same exam that is given to AP Chemistry high school students is given to college students. The various college professors report how the college students fared on the exam. This provides information for the chief faculty consultant on where to draw the lines for a 5, 4, 3, 2, or 1 score. A score of 5 on this AP Exam is set to represent the average score received by the college students who scored an A on the exam. A score of 3 or 4 is the equivalent of a college grade B, and so on.

## How Do I Register and How Much Does It Cost?

If you are enrolled in AP Chemistry in your high school, your teacher will provide all these details. You do not have to enroll in the AP course to register for and complete the AP Exam. When in doubt, the best source of information is the College Board's website: www.collegeboard.org.

Students who demonstrate financial need may receive a refund to help offset the cost of testing. There are also several optional fees that are necessary if you want your scores rushed to you or if you wish to receive multiple grade reports.

## What Should I Do the Night Before the Exam?

Last-minute cramming of massive amounts of material will not help you. It takes time for your brain to organize material. There is some value to a last-minute review of material. This may involve looking over the Rapid Review portions of a few (not all) chapters or looking through the Glossary. The night before the test should include a light review and various relaxing activities. **A full night's sleep is one of the best preparations for the test.**

## What Should I Bring to the Exam?

Here are some suggestions:

- Several pencils and an eraser that does not leave smudges.
- Black- or blue-colored pens for use on the free-response section.
- A watch so that you can monitor your time. You never know if the exam room will or will not have a clock on the wall. Make sure you turn off the beep that goes off on the hour.

- A calculator that you have used during your preparation for the exam. Do not bring a new or unfamiliar calculator.
- Your school code.
- Your photo identification and social security number.
- Tissues.
- Your quiet confidence that you are prepared and ready to rock and roll.

### What Should I NOT Bring to the Exam?

TIP

It's probably a good idea to leave the following items at home:

- A smartphone, cell phone, or any other electronic communication device.
- Books, a dictionary, study notes, flash cards, highlighting pens, correction fluid, a ruler, or any other office supplies.
- Portable music of any kind.
- Clothing with any chemistry on it.
- Panic or fear. It's natural to be nervous, but you can comfort yourself that you have used this book and that there is no room for fear on your exam.

You should:

- Allow plenty of time to get to the test site.
- Wear comfortable clothing.
- Eat a light breakfast and/or lunch.
- Remind yourself that you are well prepared and that the test is an enjoyable challenge and a chance to share your knowledge.
- Be proud of yourself!
- Review the tip sheet on avoiding "stupid" mistakes at the back of this book.

Once test day comes, there is nothing further you can do. Do not worry about what you could have done differently. It is out of your hands, and your only job is to answer as many questions correctly as you possibly can. The calmer you are, the better your chances of doing well.

CHAPTER 2

# How to Plan Your Time

**IN THIS CHAPTER**

**Summary:** The right preparation plan for you depends on your study habits and the amount of time you have before the test.

**Key Idea**

✪ Choose the study plan that's right for you.

## Three Approaches to Preparing for the AP Chemistry Exam

You are the best judge of your study habits. You should make a realistic decision about what will work best for you. Good intentions and wishes will not prepare you for the exam. Decide what works best for you. Do not feel that you must follow one of these schedules exactly; you can fine-tune any one of them to your own needs. Do not make the mistake of forcing yourself to follow someone else's method. Look at the following descriptions and see which best describes you. This will help you pick a prep mode.

**You're a full-year prep student if:**

1. You are the kind of person who likes to plan for everything very far in advance.
2. You arrive very early for appointments.
3. You like detailed planning and everything in its place.
4. You feel that you must be thoroughly prepared.
5. You hate surprises.

If you fit this profile, consider **Plan A.**

**You're a one-semester prep student if:**

1. You are always on time for appointments.
2. You are willing to plan ahead to feel comfortable in stressful situations but are OK with skipping some details.
3. You feel more comfortable when you know what to expect, but a surprise or two is good.

If you fit this profile, consider **Plan B.**

**You're a six-week prep student if:**

1. You get to appointments at the last second.
2. You work best under pressure and tight deadlines.
3. You feel very confident with the skills and background you learned in your AP Chemistry class.
4. You decided late in the year to take the exam.
5. You like surprises.

If you fit this profile, consider **Plan C.**

Look now at Table 2.1 and the following calendars for plans A, B, and C. Choose the plan that will best suit your particular learning style and timeline. For best results, choose a plan and stick with it.

STRATEGY

If your instructor covers the chapters in a different order, feel free to adjust the order of the chapters to meet the alternate schedule.

STRATEGY

**Table 2.1 General Outline of Three Different Study Plans**

| Month | PLAN A (Full School Year) | PLAN B (One Semester) | PLAN C (Six Weeks) |
|---|---|---|---|
| | Pre-AP Diagnostic Exam in Appendix | Pre-AP Diagnostic Exam in Appendix | Pre-AP Diagnostic Exam in Appendix |
| September–October | Introduction to material and Chapter 5 | Introduction to material | Introduction to material and Chapters 1–4 |
| November | Chapters 6–7 | | |
| December | Chapters 8–9 | | |
| January | Chapters 10–11 | Chapters 5–7 | |
| February | Chapters 12–13 | Chapters 8–10 | |
| March | Chapters 14–16 | Chapters 11–14 | |
| April | Chapters 17–20;<br><br>Chapter 3 Exam<br>Review Exam<br>Practice Exam 1<br>Review Exam | Chapters 15–20;<br><br>Chapter 3 Exam<br>Review Exam<br>Practice Exam 1<br>Review Exam | Skim Chapters 5–14 & all Rapid Reviews;<br>Chapter 3 Exam<br>Review Exam<br>Practice Exam 1<br>Review Exam |
| May | Review everything; Practice Exam 2<br>Review Exam | Review everything; Practice Exam 2<br>Review Exam | Skim Chapters 15–20; Practice Exam 2<br>Review Exam |

## Calendar for Each Plan

### Plan A: You Have a Full School Year to Prepare

The main reason for you to use this book is as a preparation for the AP Chemistry Exam as well as other standardized chemistry exams. However, this book can fill other roles. It can broaden your study of chemistry, help your analytical skills, and enhance your scientific-writing abilities. These will aid you in a college course in chemistry. Use this plan to organize your study during the coming school year.

**SEPTEMBER–OCTOBER** (Check off the activities as you complete them.)

— Determine the student mode (A, B, or C) that applies to you.
— Carefully read Chapters 1, 2, and 4 of this book. You should highlight material that applies specifically to you.
— Take Pre-AP Diagnostic Exam in the Appendix.
— Pay close attention to your walk-through of the Pre-AP Diagnostic Exam.
— Look at the AP and other websites.
— Skim the review chapters in Step 4 of this book. (Reviewing the topics covered in this section will be part of your yearlong preparation.)
— Buy a few color highlighters.
— Look through the entire book. You need to get some idea of the layout, and break it in. Highlight important points.
— Have a clear picture of your school's AP Chemistry curriculum.
— Use this book as a supplement to your classroom experience.

**NOVEMBER** (The first 10 weeks have elapsed.)

— Read and study Chapter 5, Basics.
— Read and study Chapter 6, Stoichiometry.
— Read and study Chapter 7, Spectroscopy, Light, and Electrons.

**DECEMBER**

— Read and study Chapter 8, Bonding.
— Read and study Chapter 9, Solids, Liquids, and Intermolecular Forces.
— Review Chapters 5–7.

**JANUARY** (20 weeks have elapsed.)

— Read and study Chapter 10, Gases.
— Read and study Chapter 11, Solutions.
— Review Chapters 5–10.

**FEBRUARY**

— Read and study Chapter 12, Reactions and Periodicity.
— Read and study Chapter 13, Kinetics.
— Review Chapters 5–11.
— Evaluate your weaknesses and refer to the appropriate chapters. You may wish to retake part of the Diagnostic Exam.

**MARCH** (30 weeks have now elapsed.)

— Read and study Chapter 14, Thermodynamics.
— Read and study Chapter 15, Equilibrium.
— Read and study Chapter 16, Acids and Bases.
— Read and study Chapter 17, Electrochemistry.
— Review Chapters 5–13.

**APRIL**

— Take the Chapter 3 Diagnostic Exam and review your results during the first week of April.
— Evaluate your strengths and weaknesses. Review the appropriate chapters to correct any weaknesses.
— Complete Practice Exam 1 around April 15.
— Score the exam and analyze your mistakes.
— Read and study Chapter 18, Nuclear Chemistry.
— Read and study Chapter 19, Organic Chemistry.
— Read and study Chapter 20, Experimental Investigations.
— Review Chapters 5–17.

**MAY** (first 2 weeks) (THIS IS IT!)

— Review Chapters 5–20—all the material!
— Take Practice Exam 2.
— Score the exam and analyze your mistakes.
— Review the tip sheet on avoiding "stupid" mistakes.
— Get a good night's sleep before the exam. Fall asleep knowing you are well prepared.

GOOD LUCK ON THE TEST!

## Plan B: You Have One Semester to Prepare

This approach uses the assumption that you have completed at least one semester of AP Chemistry. This calendar begins in midyear and prepares you for the mid-May exam.

**JANUARY–FEBRUARY**

— Take Pre-AP Diagnostic Exam in the Appendix.
— Pay close attention to your walk-through of the Pre-AP Diagnostic Exam.
— Read Chapters 1, 2, and 4 in this book.
— Pay careful attention to the Diagnostic Exam.
— Pay close attention to your walk-through of the Diagnostic Exam.
— Read and study Chapter 5, Basics.
— Read and study Chapter 6, Stoichiometry.
— Read and study Chapter 7, Spectroscopy, Light, and Electrons.
— Read and study Chapter 8, Bonding.
— Read and study Chapter 9, Solids, Liquids, and Intermolecular Forces.
— Evaluate your strengths and weaknesses.
— Study appropriate chapters to correct your weaknesses.

**MARCH** (10 weeks to go.)

— Read and study Chapter 10, Gases.
— Review Chapters 5–7.
— Read and study Chapter 11, Solutions.
— Read and study Chapter 12, Reactions and Periodicity.
— Review Chapters 8–10.
— Read and study Chapter 13, Kinetics.
— Read and study Chapter 14, Thermodynamics.

**APRIL**

— Take the Chapter 3 Diagnostic Exam and review your results during the first week of April.
— Take Practice Exam 1 in the first week of April.
— Evaluate your strengths and weaknesses.
— Study appropriate chapters to correct your weaknesses.
— Read and study Chapter 15, Equilibrium.
— Read and study Chapter 16, Acids and Bases.
— Review Chapters 5–10.
— Read and study Chapter 17, Electrochemistry.
— Read and study Chapter 18, Nuclear Chemistry.
— Review Chapters 11–14.
— Complete Practice Exam 1 around April 15.
— Score the exam and analyze your mistakes.
— Read and study Chapter 19, Organic Chemistry.
— Read and study Chapter 20, Experimental Investigations.

**MAY** (first 2 weeks) (THIS IS IT!)

— Review Chapters 5–20—all the material!
— Take Practice Exam 2.
— Score the exam and analyze your mistakes.
— Review the tip sheet on avoiding "stupid" mistakes at the back of this book.
— Get a good night's sleep before the exam. Fall asleep knowing you are well prepared.

GOOD LUCK ON THE TEST!

## Plan C: You Have Six Weeks to Prepare

This approach is for students who have already studied most of the material that may be on the exam. The best use of this book for you is as a specific guide toward the AP Chemistry Exam. There are time constraints to this approach, as the exam is only a short time away. The plan is designed to take you through your final review. This is not the best time to try to learn new material.

**APRIL 1–15**

— Take Pre-AP Diagnostic Exam in the Appendix.
— Pay close attention to your walk-through of the Pre-AP Diagnostic Exam.
— Skim Chapters 1, 2, and 4.
— Go over Chapter 5.
— Skim Chapters 6–9.
— Carefully go over the Rapid Review sections of Chapters 5–9.
— Take the Chapter 3 Diagnostic Exam and review your results during the first week of April.
— Skim and highlight the Glossary.

**APRIL 15–MAY 1**

— Complete Practice Exam 1 around April 15.
— Score the exam and analyze your mistakes.
— Skim Chapters 10–14.
— Carefully go over the Rapid Review sections of Chapters 10–14.
— Carefully go over the Rapid Review sections of Chapters 5–9 again.
— Continue to skim and highlight the Glossary.

**MAY** (first 2 weeks) (THIS IS IT!)

— Skim Chapters 15–20.
— Carefully go over the Rapid Reviews for Chapters 15–20.
— Complete Practice Exam 2.
— Score the exam and analyze your mistakes.
— Review the tip sheet on avoiding "stupid" mistakes at the back of this book.
— Get a good night's sleep before the exam. Fall asleep knowing that you are well prepared.

GOOD LUCK ON THE TEST!

STEP 2

# Determine Your Test Readiness

CHAPTER 3 Take a Diagnostic Exam

CHAPTER 3

# Take a Diagnostic Exam

IN THIS CHAPTER

**Summary:** The AP Exam writers assume that you are bringing a certain level of knowledge to your AP Chemistry class. The AP Chemistry Exam does not test this "prior knowledge" directly, but it is still necessary to understand this material before taking the exam. For example, it is assumed that you already know that if you dissolve a strong electrolyte, such as solid $NaNO_3$, in water, then you also know that the solution contains no $NaNO_3(aq)$ but $Na^+(aq)$ and $NO_3^-(aq)$. The following sample problem is another example.

**Sample Problem:** Given the following chemical equation:

$$AgNO_3(aq) + K_3PO_4(aq) \rightarrow Ag_3PO_4(s) + KNO_3(aq)$$

what is the $Ag^+(aq)$ concentration present after mixing 10.00 mL of a 0.1000 *M* $AgNO_3$ solution with 5.00 mL of a 0.1000 *M* $K_3PO_4$ solution? The $K_{sp}$ of $Ag_3PO_4$ is $1.4 \times 10^{-16}$.

The prior knowledge needed here is that you need to balance the equation before solving the problem.

There is a Pre-AP Diagnostic Exam in the Appendix for your benefit. It will test your understanding of the knowledge you should bring to your AP class. This exam will let you know where you need to spend most of your study time preparing for each topic. This does not mean you can skip the review of other topics; you should always review all topics. The exam has only multiple-choice questions and not a mixture of multiple-choice and free-response questions like you will see on the AP Exam.

The Pre-AP Diagnostic Exam will give you an idea of where you are in terms of your preparation for your AP class. The questions have been written to approximate the coverage of material that you will see on the AP Exam. However, there will be a few questions on content that will not be directly tested on the AP Exam; these questions refer to basic chemistry knowledge that your teacher (and the exam writers) will expect you to know and that you will need to know before taking the AP Chemistry Exam. Once you are done with the exam, check your work against the given answers, which also indicate where you can find the corresponding material in the book.

This final Diagnostic Practice Exam below will be the final one that you will take a few days before taking the AP Exam. By this point you have reviewed the material and have taken two practice exams. This exam is your last opportunity to spot your weaknesses. Take it as if it were the "real" AP Chemistry exam, allowing the same time, with or without a calculator as directed in the instructions, and so on. After you take the exam, score it, and note your weaknesses. Review those topics and look over anything else about which you are uneasy. Then review the part of Chapter 1 on What Should I Bring to the Exam? Be sure to get a good night's sleep and earn that 5!

**Key Ideas**

- Answer questions that approximate the coverage of topics on the AP Exam.
- Check your work against the given answers.
- Determine your areas of strength and weakness.
- Highlight the topics to which you must give special attention.

---

*This practice exam is designed for you to take after you have completed your initial study for the AP Exam and before you begin your final study. Make sure you follow these guidelines as to when you will take this exam. The AP Exam is a timed exam; keep this in mind as you prepare. When taking the various tests presented in this book, you should follow the AP Exam rules as closely as possible. Anyone can improve his or her score by using notes, books, or unlimited time. You will have none of these on the AP Exam, so resist the temptation to use them on practice exams. Carefully time yourself, do not use other materials, and use a calculator only when expressly allowed to do so. After you have finished an exam, you may use other sources to go over questions you missed or skipped. We have seen many students get into trouble because the first time they attempted a test under "test conditions" was on the test itself.*

*Make notes concerning the questions you did not understand well (even if you got the correct answer). Use these notes to help you during your final review.*

## Getting Started: The Diagnostic Exam

The following questions refer to different chapters in the book. Remember that it is not necessary to get the correct answer (though it would be nice). You will have time later to work on getting the correct answer. The problems you have trouble with will help direct your studying as you prepare for the AP Exam. If you have trouble (even if you got the correct answer), it indicates that you should spend additional time reviewing the topic. While answering these questions, you may use a calculator and periodic table. For each question, simply circle the letter of your choice, and for each question you have difficulty with, circle the question number.

Some people will wish to repeat some or all questions on this exam before taking the AP Exam.

## AP Chemistry Final Practice Exam, Section I (Multiple Choice)

**Time—1 hour and 30 minutes**

**NO CALCULATOR MAY BE USED WITH SECTION I**

Answer the following questions in the time allowed. You may use the periodic table in the back of the book.

| COMPOUND | BOILING POINT (°C) | MOLAR MASS ($g\ mol^{-1}$) |
|---|---|---|
| $CH_3F$ | −78.4 | 34.0 |
| $CH_3Cl$ | −24.0 | 50.5 |
| $CH_3Br$ | 3.5 | 94.9 |
| $CH_3I$ | 42.4 | 141.9 |

1. Which of the following best explains why the boiling point of $CH_3F$ is lower than the other three compounds in the table above?

(A) It is the lightest of the four.
(B) Larger molecules get tangled and cannot escape each other.
(C) It has weaker hydrogen bonds.
(D) It is a more symmetrical molecule.

2. The Dumas method is a simple procedure for the determination of the molar mass of a gas. In this procedure the mass of a gas is divided by the moles of gas determined from the ideal gas equation ($n = PV/RT$). The molar masses of some compounds, such as formic acid, HCOOH, illustrated above, show a significant deviation from the "correct" values. Why does the presence of dimers as illustrated make it unlikely to obtain an accurate molar mass of acids, such as formic acid?

(A) Formic acid, like all acids, will lose a hydrogen ion, so the molar mass is that of the formate ion, $HCOO^-$, which is less than that of formic acid.
(B) Formic acid is a liquid at room temperature, and its boiling point is too high to get accurate results.
(C) Acids are too reactive to give accurate results.
(D) The presence of strong intermolecular forces (hydrogen bonding) makes the gas nonideal; therefore the ideal gas law is not applicable.

3. In which of the following groups are the species listed correctly in order of increasing electron affinity?

(A) Sr, Ca, Ba
(B) Se, Tc, Ba
(C) Mn, Fe, Ni
(D) Cl, Br, I

**Use the following information to answer questions 4–10.**

For many years, the nitrogen content of food and other substances has been determined by the Kjeldahl method. There are many variations in the method, but the general procedure is as follows: Initially, the sample with a catalyst is heated in boiling sulfuric acid, to convert all the nitrogen present into ammonium sulfate (or ammonium hydrogen sulfate). The sulfuric acid is cooled, diluted, and excess strong base added (for example, NaOH). The strong base neutralizes the remaining sulfuric acid and converts the ammonium ion to ammonia gas. The reactions are:

$$2\ NaOH(aq) + H_2SO_4(aq) \rightarrow Na_2SO_4(aq) + 2\ H_2O(l)$$

$$(NH_4)_2SO_4(aq) + 2\ NaOH(aq) \rightarrow 2\ NH_3(g) + Na_2SO_4(aq) + 2\ H_2O(aq)$$

The strong base must be added quickly and the system immediately sealed to prevent the loss of any ammonia gas. The container is heated to drive all remaining ammonia from the solution. The expelled ammonia gas is trapped in excess aqueous hydrochloric acid.

$$NH_3(g) + HCl(aq) \rightarrow NH_4Cl(aq)$$

Finally, the quantity of ammonia generated is determined by back-titrating the excess hydrochloric acid with standard sodium hydroxide.

$$NaOH(aq) + HCl(aq) \rightarrow NaCl(aq) + H_2O(l)$$

A food chemist wishes to use the Kjeldahl method to determine the percent of nitrogen in a sample of dog food. The nitrogen in the dog food is primarily in protein. The chemist weighs three separate samples of dog food into three separate flasks. She then adds a small quantity of selenium to serve as a catalyst and 25 mL of concentrated sulfuric acid. In a fume hood, she heats each of the flasks to boiling (338°C) and lets the samples digest until the samples have dissolved completely.

One by one, she adds the samples to the flask on the left in the figure below. She then pipettes 50.00 mL of standard 0.1000 *M* HCl into the flask at the right of the figure. With everything ready, she temporarily opens the flask on the left and quickly adds excess NaOH solution and closes the flask. Then she heats the left flask until it begins to boil. She boils the flask for 20 minutes and dismantles the apparatus. She stoppers the right-hand flask and sets it aside while she repeats the procedure on the remaining two samples.

Once all three samples have been treated, she titrates each with standard 0.1000 *M* NaOH using phenolphthalein as the indicator.

The chemist completes the following data table in her lab book.

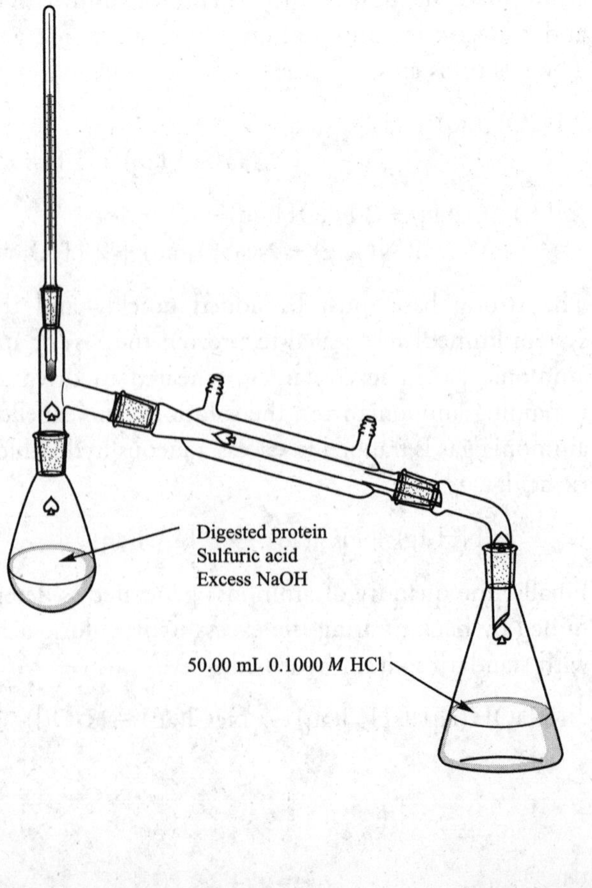


| | SAMPLE 1 | SAMPLE 2 | SAMPLE 3 |
|---|---|---|---|
| Mass of flask plus dog food sample | 175.433 g | 175.734 g | 179.42 g |
| Mass of empty flask | 175.245 g | 175.544 g | 179.215 g |
| Final volume of standard NaOH in buret | 41.52 mL | 41.62 mL | 41.02 mL |
| Initial volume of standard NaOH in buret | 0.25 mL | 0.35 mL | 0.47 mL |

**4.** What type of reaction generated the ammonia gas?

(A) neutralization
(B) combination
(C) decomposition
(D) combustion

**5.** Why must the liquid in the right flask be dilute acid?

(A) Dilute acid is necessary to neutralize the excess sodium hydroxide formed.
(B) Dilute acid captures the ammonia gas.
(C) Dilute acid causes the reaction to go to completion.
(D) Dilute acid is easier to handle than many other liquids.

**6.** Would it be possible to use this procedure to determine the percent of sulfur (as sulfur dioxide) in the dog food?

(A) Yes, because sulfur dioxide is volatile.
(B) No, because sulfur dioxide is not volatile.
(C) Yes, because sulfur dioxide is a base like ammonia.
(D) No, because sulfur dioxide is not a base like ammonia.

**7.** The flask on the right initially contained $5.000 \times 10^{-3}$ mole of HCl. How does this value relate to the moles of ammonia plus the moles of NaOH used in the titration?

(A) The moles HCl = moles NaOH.
(B) The moles HCl = moles $NH_3$ + moles NaOH.
(C) The moles HCl = moles $NH_3$.
(D) The relationship is unknown.

**8.** Approximately how many moles of ammonia gas formed from sample 1?

(A) 0.002 mole
(B) 0.004 mole
(C) 0.005 mole
(D) 0.001 mole

**9.** If the sample were pure nitrogen, approximately how many moles of ammonia gas would form from sample 3?

(A) 0.040 mole
(B) 0.025 mole
(C) 0.015 mole
(D) 0.150 mole

**10.** Would it be possible to substitute acetic acid, $HC_2H_3O_2$, for the hydrochloric acid?

(A) No, because acetic acid is a weak acid and weak acid–base reactions are not efficient.
(B) Yes, because the identity of the acid is irrelevant.
(C) No, because ammonia will not dissolve in an acetic acid solution.
(D) No, because acetic acid is volatile.

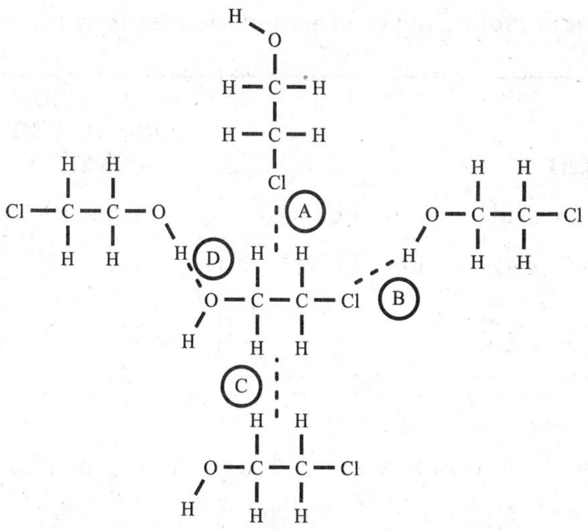


**11.** A small region in a sample of liquid $C_2H_4ClOH$ is illustrated above. The lettered (A, B, C, and D) dashed lines represent intermolecular forces influencing the central molecule. Which of the following sets places the intermolecular forces in order of decreasing strength?

(A) D > B > A > C
(B) B > D > A > C
(C) D > B > C > A
(D) D > A > B > C

**12.** A bottle of wine is claimed to be 50 years old. If the age is correct, the bottle is expected to sell for a minimum of $100,000 at auction. A syringe was inserted through the cork of the bottle and a small sample of wine was removed. Analysis of the wine sample indicated that a small amount of natural radioactive tritium, $^{3}H$, was present. If the bottle was really 50 years old, about how much of the original tritium should remain? The half-life of tritium is 12.33 years.

(A) 25%
(B) 12%
(C) 6%
(D) 50%

**Use the following information for questions 13–15.**

| ACID | FORMULA | $K_a$, ACID DISSOCIATION CONSTANT |
|---|---|---|
| Iodic acid | $HIO_3$ | $1.7 \times 10^{-1}$ |
| Chloroacetic acid | $HC_2H_2ClO_2$ | $1.4 \times 10^{-3}$ |
| Benzoic acid | $C_6H_5COOH$ | $6.2 \times 10^{-5}$ |
| Phenol | $C_6H_5OH$ | $1.0 \times 10^{-10}$ |

**13.** A buffered solution with a pH near 5 is needed for an experiment. Using the above information, which of the combinations would be the best choice to prepare the buffer?

(A) $HIO_3 + KIO_3$
(B) $HC_2H_2ClO_2 + KC_2H_2ClO_2$
(C) $C_6H_5OH + C_6H_5OK$
(D) $C_6H_5COOH + C_6H_5COOK$

**14.** A student wishes to measure the pH of a 0.10 *M* solution of the sodium salt of each of the acids in the table. The salts chosen were $NaIO_3$, $NaC_2H_2ClO_2$, $C_6H_5COONa$, and $C_6H_5ONa$, respectively. Which of the four salt solutions will have the highest pH?

(A) $NaIO_3$
(B) $NaC_2H_2ClO_2$
(C) $C_6H_5COONa$
(D) $C_6H_5ONa$

**15.** Which of the acids in the table would be the easiest to titrate with a weak base like ammonia ($K_b = 1.8 \times 10^{-5}$)?

(A) $HIO_3$
(B) $HC_2H_2ClO_2$
(C) $C_6H_5COOH$
(D) $C_6H_5OH$

**Use the following information to answer questions 16–20.**

pH versus volume of titrant added

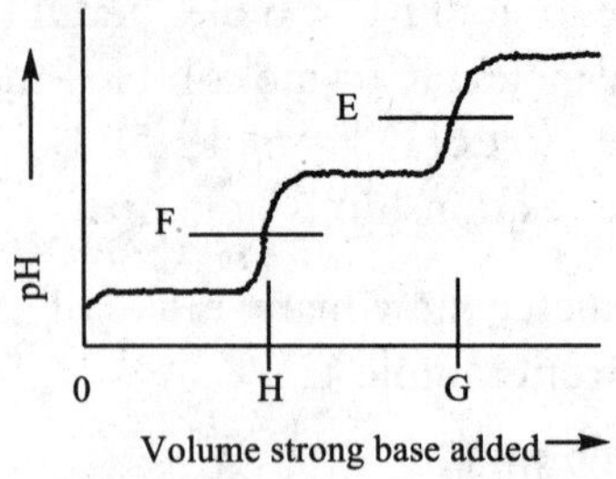


$H_2C_4H_2O_4$ $K_{a1} = 1.2 \times 10^{-2}$ $K_{a2} = 5.9 \times 10^{-7}$

$pK_{a1} = 1.92$ $pK_{a2} = 6.23$

Maleic acid, $H_2C_4H_2O_4$, is a weak diprotic acid. The titration curve shown above is an idealized graph for a diprotic acid. On this graph, E and F represent the pH at the endpoints with the possibility that E may shift slightly and either E or F may not be present. H is the volume of base required to titrate the first hydrogen ion and G is the quantity of base necessary to titrate both hydrogen ions. G is double H.

**16.** What is the approximate pH at ½ H?

(A) 7
(B) 2
(C) 4
(D) Impossible to predict

**17.** If G is less than twice H, what would this indicate?

(A) There is an acidic contaminant.
(B) There is a basic contaminant.
(C) The indicator was added too late.
(D) The maleic acid is synthetic.

**18.** Which of the following bases would be the best choice for the titration?

(A) $Mg(OH)_2$
(B) $Na_2CO_3$
(C) $NH_3$
(D) $Ba(OH)_2$

**19.** In the titration of a sample of maleic acid with standard NaOH, what is the approximate value of F?

(A) < 7
(B) > 7
(C) = 7
(D) unknown

**20.** The titration of many diprotic acids will not work as well as indicated by the idealized titration curve illustrated earlier. Maleic acid is a good candidate for this type of titration (determining both end-points). Why is maleic acid a good candidate?

(A) $K_{a2}$ and $K_{a1}$ are sufficiently close together.
(B) Maleic acid reacts more rapidly than do other acids.
(C) Maleic acid reacts more slowly than do other reactions.
(D) $K_{a2}$ and $K_{a1}$ are sufficiently far apart.

**21.** Which of the following CANNOT behave as both a Brønsted base and a Brønsted acid?

(A) $HC_2O_4^-$
(B) $HSO_4^-$
(C) $HPO_4^{2-}$
(D) $SO_3^{2-}$

**22.** A student mixes 100.0 mL of 0.100 *M* sodium oxalate, $Na_2C_2O_4$, solution with 100.0 mL of 0.100 *M* silver nitrate solution, $AgNO_3$. A white precipitate immediately forms, and the silver ion concentration drastically decreases. Correctly place the concentrations of the remaining ions in order of decreasing concentration.

(A) $[Na^+] > [C_2O_4^{2-}] > [NO_3^-]$
(B) $[C_2O_4^{2-}] > [NO_3^-] > [Na^+]$
(C) $[Na^+] > [NO_3^-] > [C_2O_4^{2-}]$
(D) $[NO_3^-] > [Na^+] > [C_2O_4^{2-}]$

**23.** A chemistry student wishes to determine the molar mass of a volatile liquid. She adds a small quantity of the volatile liquid into a weighed flask and covers the opening with aluminum foil. With a pin, she punches a small hole in the aluminum foil. She then clamps the flask to a ring stand and lowers the flask into a bath of boiling water (temperature measured with a thermometer). After all the liquid has evaporated, she quickly removes the flask from the water bath and cools the flask so that the vapor remaining in the flask condenses. Once the flask has cooled, she dries and reweighs the flask. The mass of the starting material remaining in the flask is determined by subtracting the mass of the empty flask from the mass of the flask with the condensed vapor. She then empties the flask and refills it with water. Once filled she uses a graduated cylinder to determine the volume of water, and hence of the flask, present. What other information is needed to finish the experiment?

(A) the heat of vaporization of the volatile liquid
(B) the original mass of the volatile liquid
(C) the mass of the displaced water
(D) the barometric pressure

$H_2O(l) \rightarrow H_2(g) + 1/2\ O_2(g)$ $\quad \Delta H° = +300$ kJ

$CO_2(g) \rightarrow C(s) + O_2(g)$ $\quad \Delta H° = +400$ kJ

$C_2H_2(g) + 5/2\ O_2(g) \rightarrow H_2O(l) + 2\ CO_2(g)$ $\quad \Delta H° = -1{,}300$ kJ

**24.** Using the information given above, calculate the enthalpy change for the following reaction:

$$2\ C(s) + H_2(g) \rightarrow C_2H_2(g)$$

(A) 500 kJ
(B) −200 kJ
(C) −500 kJ
(D) 200 kJ

**25.** The solubility of calcium hydroxide, $Ca(OH)_2$, in water is 0.173 g/100 mL $H_2O$ at 20°C, and 0.121 g/100 g $H_2O$ at 60°C. Which of the following conclusions may be related to this?

(A) The heat of solution of calcium hydroxide is exothermic.
(B) The hydration energies of calcium ions and hydroxide ions are very low.
(C) The heat of solution for calcium hydroxide is endothermic.
(D) The solution is not an ideal solution.

**Use the information on the containers in the following diagram to answer questions 26–28.**

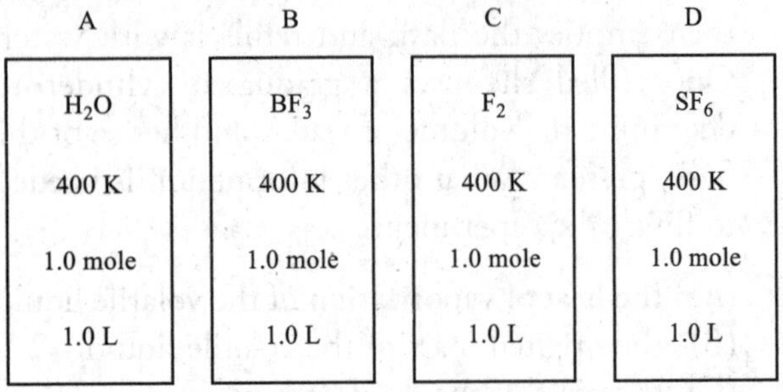


Approximate molar masses: $H_2O = 18\ g\ mol^{-1}$, $BF_3 = 68\ g\ mol^{-1}$, $F_2 = 38\ g\ mol^{-1}$, $SF_6 = 146\ g\ mol^{-1}$

**26.** Under the conditions indicated, in which of the gas samples is the average velocity of the molecules about half that of water, $H_2O$?

(A) $SF_6$
(B) $F_2$
(C) $BF_3$
(D) They are all at the same temperature; therefore, they have the same average velocity.

**27.** Which of the four gases will probably show the least deviation from ideal behavior?

(A) $F_2$
(B) $H_2O$
(C) $BF_3$
(D) $SF_6$

**28.** Container C develops a small leak. Which of the following variables would change?

(A) moles, temperature, and pressure
(B) moles and pressure
(C) temperature and pressure
(D) moles and temperature

**29.** At high temperatures, ammonia decomposes to the elements. At a certain temperature, the specific rate constant, $k$, for this first-order reaction is $3.5 \times 10^{-3}\ s^{-1}$. What mass of a 0.100-g sample of starting material will remain after 400 s?

(A) 0.0500 g
(B) 0.0250 g
(C) 0.0125 g
(D) 0.00625 g

**Use the information on the containers in the following diagram to answer questions 30–34 concerning the following equilibrium:**

$$2\ C_2H_4(g) + O_2(g) \leftrightarrows 2\ CH_3CHO(g)$$

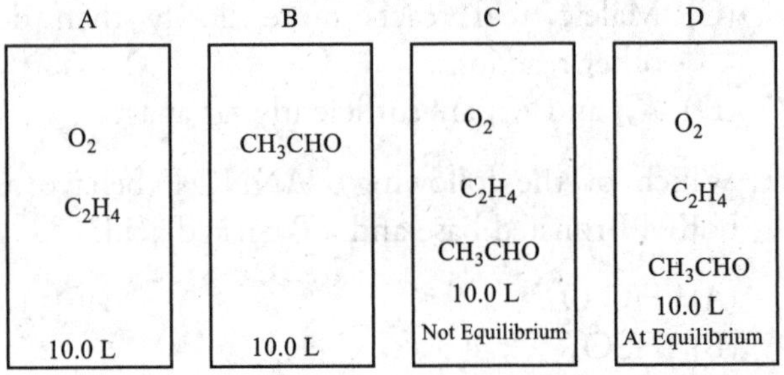


**30.** Container A initially contained 0.25 mole of $O_2$ and 0.60 mole of $C_2H_4$ and then comes to equilibrium. At equilibrium, there is 0.30 mole of $C_2H_4$ in the flask. What is the value of $K_c$, the equilibrium constant, for the reaction?

(A) 0.10
(B) 10
(C) 0.010
(D) 100

**31.** A 1.00-mole sample of $CH_3CHO$ is placed in container B and the system is allowed to go to equilibrium. What can be said about the relative rates of reaction with respect to the various components?

(A) The rate of $C_2H_4(g)$ formation is numerically equal to the rate of $CH_3CHO$ loss.
(B) The rate of $O_2(g)$ is numerically equal to the rate of $CH_3CHO$ loss.
(C) The rate of $C_2H_4(g)$ formation is half the rate of $O_2(g)$ formation.
(D) The rate of $O_2(g)$ formation is equal to the rate of $C_2H_4(g)$ formation.

**32.** The mixture in container D is in equilibrium. Which of the following is true?

(A) The rates of the forward and reverse reactions are equal to zero.
(B) The rate of the forward reaction is equal to the rate of the reverse reaction.
(C) The pressure in the system is increasing.
(D) The pressure in the system is decreasing.

**33.** The mixture in container A goes to equilibrium. If the initial moles of $C_2H_4(g)$ is twice the initial moles of $O_2(g)$, which of the following is true?

(A) Both reactants are limiting; therefore, the reaction will continue until there are zero moles of $C_2H_4$ and $O_2$ remaining.
(B) The total pressure of the system decreases until the system reaches equilibrium.
(C) The total pressure of the system increases until the system equals equilibrium.
(D) There is insufficient information.

**34.** As the mixture in container B approaches equilibrium, the partial pressure of $CH_3CHO$ gas decreases by 1.0 atm. Assuming there is no change in temperature, what is the net change in the total pressure of the system?

(A) +1.0 atm
(B) +0.50 atm
(C) −1.0 atm
(D) −0.50 atm

**Use the information on standard reduction potentials in the following table to answer questions 35–39.**

| | |
|---|---|
| $F_2(g) + 2\ e^- \rightarrow 2\ F^-(aq)$ | +2.87 |
| $Ag^+(aq) + 1\ e^- \rightarrow Ag(s)$ | +0.80 |
| $O_2(g) + 2\ H_2O(l) + 4\ e^- \rightarrow 4\ OH^-(aq)$ | +0.40 |
| $AgCl(s) + 1\ e^- \rightarrow Ag(s) + Cl^-(aq)$ | +0.22 |
| $Sn^{2+}(aq) + 2\ e^- \rightarrow Sn(s)$ | −0.14 |
| $NO_2^-(aq) + 5\ H_2O(l) + 6\ e^- \rightarrow NH_3(aq) + 7\ OH^-(aq)$ | −0.15 |
| $Cr^{3+}(aq) + 3\ e^- \rightarrow Cr(s)$ | −0.74 |
| $2\ H_2O(l) + 2\ e^- \rightarrow H_2(g) + 2\ OH^-(aq)$ | −0.83 |
| $Al^{3+}(aq) + 3\ e^- \rightarrow Al(s)$ | −1.66 |
| $Cs^+(aq) + 1\ e^- \rightarrow Cs(s)$ | −2.91 |

**35.** A student constructs an electrolysis cell with two inert electrodes in an aqueous solution that is 1.0 *M* in cesium nitrite, $CsNO_2$, and 1.0 *M* in cesium hydroxide, CsOH. As the cell operates, an odorless gas evolves from one electrode and a gas with a distinctive odor evolves from the other electrode. Choose the correct statement from the following list.

(A) The odorless gas is oxygen.
(B) The odorless gas is the result of reduction.
(C) The gas with the distinctive odor is the result of oxidation.
(D) The odorless gas evolves at the negative electrode.

**36.** Another student constructs a galvanic cell involving a tin, Sn, electrode in a 1.0 *M* tin(II) chloride, $SnCl_2$, solution and a chromium, Cr, electrode in a 1.0 *M* chromium(III) sulfate, $Cr_2(SO_4)_3$, solution. What is the cell potential?

(A) +0.60 V
(B) −0.60 V
(C) +0.88 V
(D) 0.00 V

**37.** Another student attempted to prepare an electrolysis cell to produce aluminum metal, Al, from an aqueous solution of aluminum chloride, $AlCl_3$, using a 6.0 V battery. The cathode compartment of the electrolysis contained 1.0 *M* aluminum chloride, and the anode compartment contained 1.0 *M* calcium chloride, $CaCl_2$. The student was unsuccessful. Why was the student unable to produce aluminum metal?

(A) The voltage from the battery was insufficient to force the reaction to occur.
(B) Reduction of chloride ions occurred in preference to reduction of aluminum ions.
(C) Aluminum chloride solutions do not conduct electricity.
(D) Reduction of water occurred in preference to reduction of aluminum ions.

**38.** Which of the substances in the table would be capable of reducing the aluminum ions in solid aluminum chloride, $AlCl_3$, to aluminum metal? Assume the cell potentials in the table also apply to the solid state.

(A) Cr(s)
(B) Cs(s)
(C) Ag(s)
(D) none

**39.** A student constructs a galvanic cell that has a chromium, Cr, electrode in a compartment containing a 1.0 *M* chromium(III) nitrate, $Cr(NO_3)_3$, solution and a silver, Ag, electrode in a compartment containing 1.0 *M* silver nitrate, $AgNO_3$, solution. A salt bridge containing a 1.0 *M* potassium chloride, KCl, solution connects the two compartments. The student used the following two half-reactions from the table:

$Ag^+(aq) + 1\ e^- \rightarrow Ag(s)$ +0.80

$Cr^{3+}(aq) + 3\ e^- \rightarrow Cr(s)$ −0.74

When the student measures the cell potential, the value is far from the ideal predicted value. What is the cause of this discrepancy?

(A) The initial concentrations should have been lower than 1.0 *M*.
(B) The initial concentrations should have been higher than 1.0 *M*.
(C) The potassium chloride in the salt bridge interfered with the reaction.
(D) The student did not allow the cell to come to equilibrium.

**Use the information on the acids in the following diagram to answer questions 40–41.**

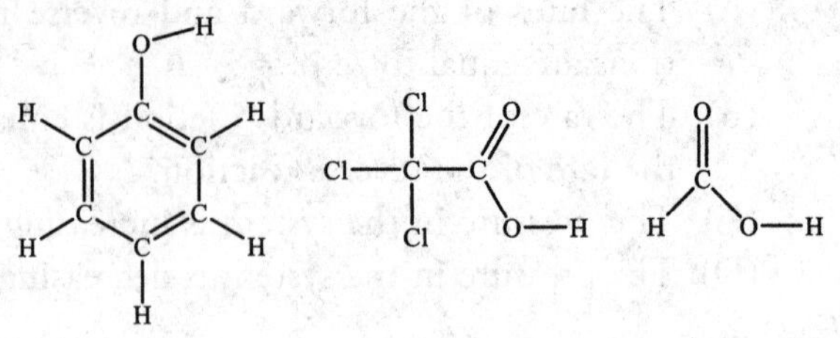

| | Phenol | Trichloroacetic Acid | Formic Acid |
|---|---|---|---|
| $K_a$ | $1.0 \times 10^{-10}$ | $2.0 \times 10^{-1}$ | $1.8 \times 10^{-4}$ |
| $pK_a$ | 10.0 | 0.70 | 3.75 |

**40.** Sample solutions of each of the three acids shown above were titrated with 0.10 *M* sodium hydroxide, NaOH. Each of the acid solutions had a concentration of 0.10 *M*. Which of the acid titrations had the highest pH at the endpoint?

(A) formic acid
(B) phenol
(C) trichloroacetic acid
(D) They all had a pH of 7 at the endpoint.

**41.** A student prepares three buffer solutions. Each solution is 1.0 *M* in one of the acids in the table and 1.0 *M* in its corresponding sodium salt. Which of the solutions has the greatest buffer capacity with respect to added NaOH and why?

(A) The phenol buffer does because it is the strongest acid.
(B) The trichloroacetic acid buffer does because it is the strongest acid.
(C) The formic acid buffer does because it donates both of its hydrogen atoms.
(D) All are the same.

**42.** Sulfurous acid is an unstable acid in solution, which decomposes to water and gaseous sulfur dioxide. The sulfur dioxide will escape from the solution. The decomposition of the acid lowers its concentration over time. What effect will the decomposition of one-third of the acid have on the agreement between the endpoint of the titration and the equivalence point during a titration with standard sodium hydroxide?

(A) The endpoint would remain near the ideal equivalence point.
(B) The endpoint would be before the ideal equivalence point.
(C) The endpoint would be after the ideal equivalence point.
(D) It is impossible to determine.

**43.** Three 20.00 mL samples of approximately 0.10 *M* *p*-cresol, $CH_3C_6H_4OH$, $K_a = 6.7 \times 10^{-11}$ were removed from a container and placed in separate 250 mL flasks. The samples were titrated with standard 0.1025 *M* sodium hydroxide, NaOH, solution. Thymolphthalein was the acid–base indicator used in the titration. The samples required 21.75, 22.38, and 31.75 mL to reach the endpoint. Which of the following might explain why the third sample required significantly more of the base to reach the endpoint?

(A) The indicator was added too soon.
(B) The wrong indicator was used.
(C) There was an acid contaminating the unclean flask.
(D) There was a base contaminating the unclean flask.

**44.** During the study of the reaction AB → A + B, a chemist constructs several graphs. The graph [AB] of versus time and the graph of ln [AB] versus time both give a curved line; however, the graph of 1/[AB] versus time gives a straight line. This implies the rate law is

(A) Rate = $k$[AB]
(B) Rate = $k[AB]^0$
(C) Rate = $k[AB]^2$
(D) Rate = $k[AB]^{-1}$

**45.** The photoelectron spectrum of boron has three peaks. One peak is less intense than the other two. Which peak is the less intense peak?

(A) the 2p peak
(B) the 2s peak
(C) the 1s peak
(D) the 1p peak

| COMPOUND | FORMULA | MOLAR MASS ($g\ mol^{-1}$) | BOILING POINT (°C) |
|---|---|---|---|
| Pentane | $C_5H_{12}$ | 72.1 | 36.1 |
| Diethyl amine | $(C_2H_5)_2NH$ | 73.1 | 55.5 |
| Methyl propyl ether | $CH_3$-O-$C_3H_7$ | 74.1 | 39.1 |
| Diethyl ether | $(C_2H_5)_2O$ | 74.1 | 34.5 |

**46.** According to the data in the table above, which of the compounds has the strongest intermolecular forces?

(A) pentane
(B) diethyl amine
(C) methyl propyl ether
(D) diethyl ether

**Use the following information to answer questions 47 and 48.**

| METAL | ION | IONIC RADIUS (pm) (CUBIC ENVIRONMENT) | MELTING POINT OF FLUORIDE (°C) |
|---|---|---|---|
| Sodium | $Na^+$ | 132 | 996 |
| Cadmium | $Cd^{2+}$ | 124 | 1110 |
| Lanthanum | $La^{3+}$ | 130 | 1493 |

47. Each of the ions in the table form stable fluorides (NaF, $CdF_2$, and $LaF_3$). Lanthanum fluoride, $LaF_3$, has a melting point higher than that of the other fluorides. Which of the following is the best explanation of why this is true?

(A) Lanthanum is a lanthanide element, and the melting points of these elements are always high.
(B) There is more fluorine in the formula $LaF_3$ than in the other formulas.
(C) Lanthanum had the highest charge; therefore, it has the highest lattice energy.
(D) Alkali metals like sodium and transition metals like cadmium tend to have low melting points.

48. The lithium ion, $Li^+$, is smaller than the sodium ion. Predict how the melting point of lithium fluoride, LiF, compares to that of sodium fluoride?

(A) It is higher because smaller ions have a higher lattice energy.
(B) It is the same because the charges are the same.
(C) It is lower because smaller ions have a smaller lattice energy.
(D) It is impossible to predict because there is insufficient information in the problem.

49. During the investigation of a chemical reaction by a chemistry student, he was able to determine that the reaction was nonspontaneous at 1 atm and 298 K. However, he learned that cooling the system with dry ice (–78°C) caused the reaction to become spontaneous. Which of the following combinations must apply to this reaction?

(A) $\Delta H < 0$, $\Delta S < 0$, and $\Delta G = 0$
(B) $\Delta H > 0$, $\Delta S < 0$, and $\Delta G > 0$
(C) $\Delta H < 0$, $\Delta S < 0$, and $\Delta G > 0$
(D) $\Delta H > 0$, $\Delta S > 0$, and $\Delta G > 0$

50. A 0.060 *M* solution of a weak acid has a pH of 2.0. What is the ionization constant, $K_a$ for this acid?

(A) $2.0 \times 10^{-1}$
(B) $1.7 \times 10^{-1}$
(C) $5.0 \times 10^{-3}$
(D) $2.0 \times 10^{-3}$

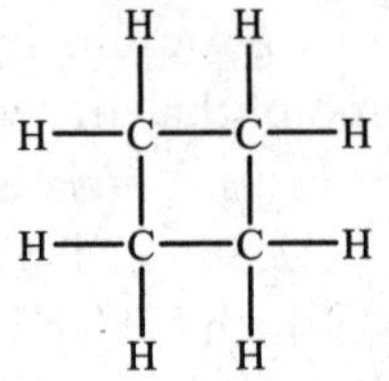

51. Cyclobutane, shown above, is a relatively unstable compound. As seen in the diagram, the four carbon atoms form the corners of a square and each carbon atom has two hydrogen atoms attached to complete an octet of electrons around the carbon atoms. Based upon this structure, why is cyclopropane a relatively unstable compound?

(A) The bonds do not match the angles.
(B) Compounds that have identical atoms bonded to each other are relatively unstable.
(C) There is no resonance to stabilize the compound.
(D) Hydrocarbon compounds are relatively unstable in general.

**52.** A chemist has a 500 mL beaker with 0.0010 mole of sodium cyanide, NaCN, on the bottom. She adds 250 mL of water and 0.0010 mole of hydrochloric acid. She then tests the solution and finds that it conducts electricity. Which of the following best represents the major species in the beaker after the addition of the acid?

(A)

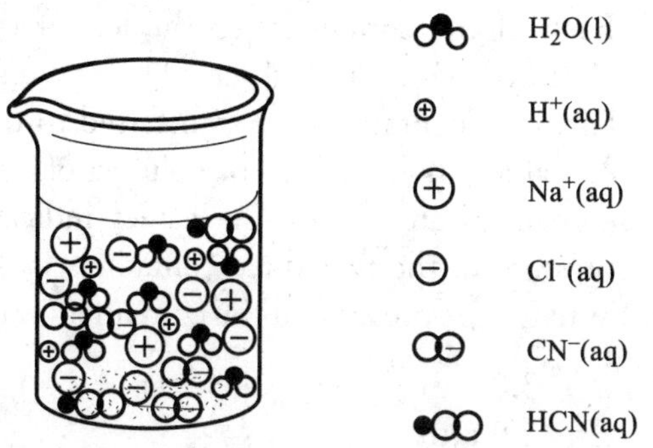


(B)

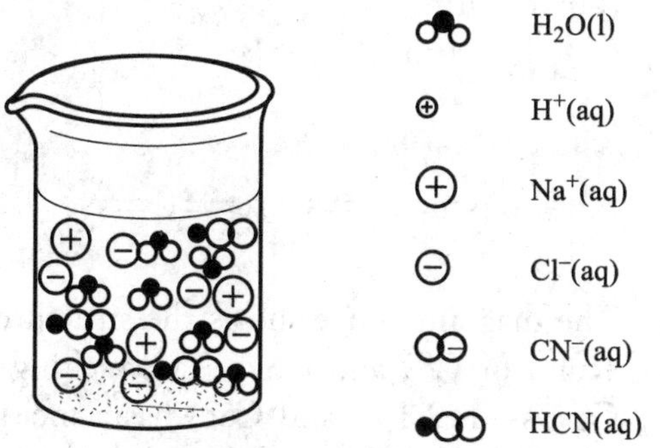


(C)

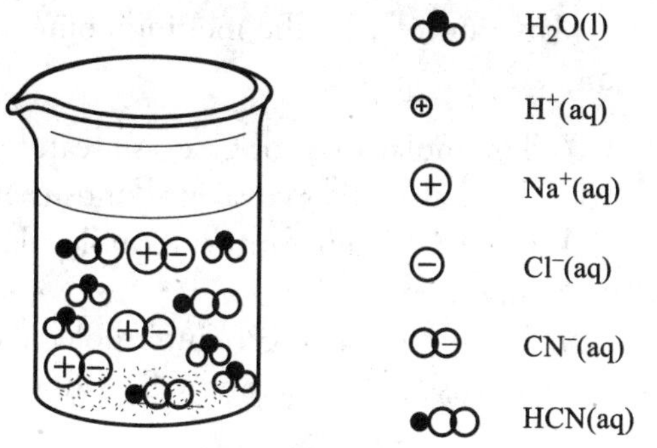


(D)

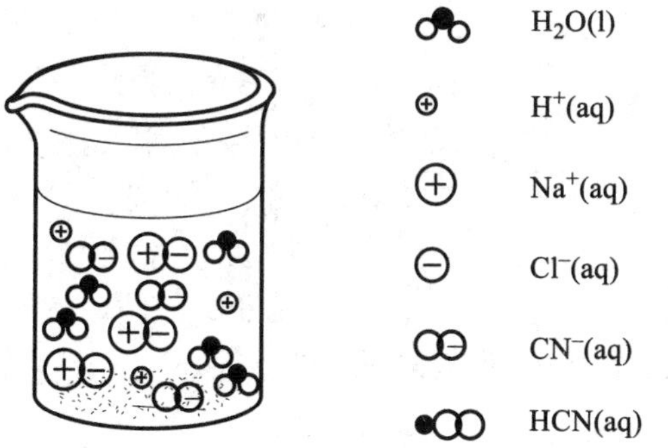


**53.** A dilute aqueous solution of hydrochloric acid, HCl, is heated to the boiling point. Which of the following best represents this system?

(A)

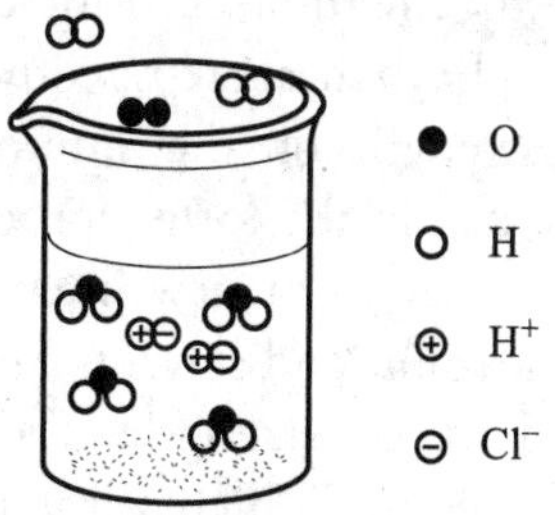


(B)

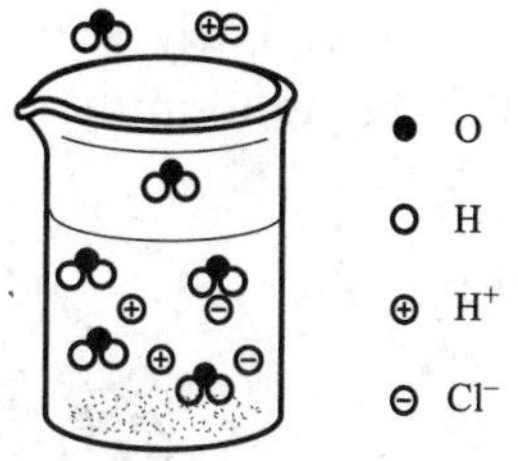


(C)

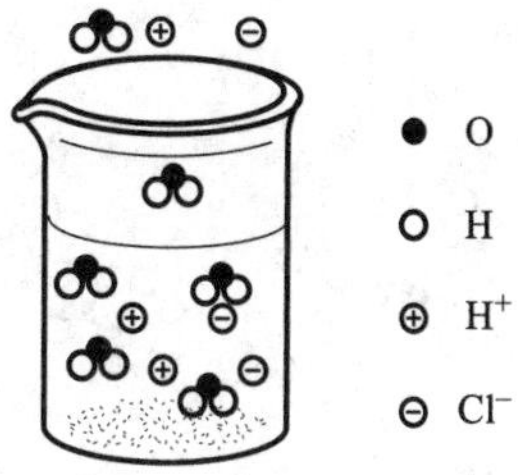


(D)

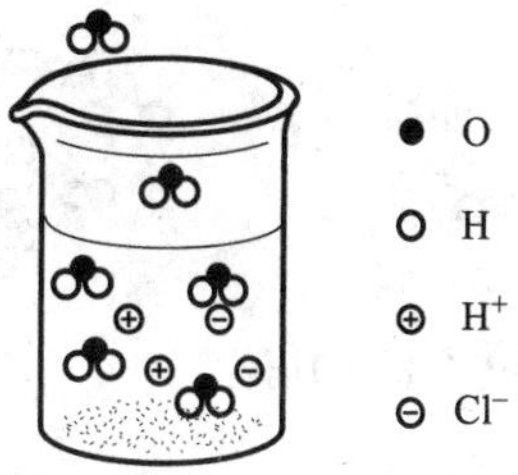


$$Cr_2O_7^{2-}(aq) + H^+(aq) + S^{2-}(aq) \rightarrow Cr^{3+}(aq) + S(s) + H_2O(l)$$

**54.** What is the coefficient of $H^+$ when the above reaction is balanced?

(A) 2
(B) 14
(C) 18
(D) 6

55. There are three steps in the formation of a solution. It is necessary to overcome the intermolecular forces present within the solute. It is also necessary to overcome the intermolecular forces present within the solvent. Both these steps require energy related to the strength of the intermolecular forces. The final step in the formation of a solution involves the creation of new intermolecular forces between the solute and solvent. This energy release is related to the strength of the intermolecular forces created. Which of the following illustrates a situation most likely to release the greatest amount of energy to form the new intermolecular forces?

(A) $LiF(s) + H_2O(l)$

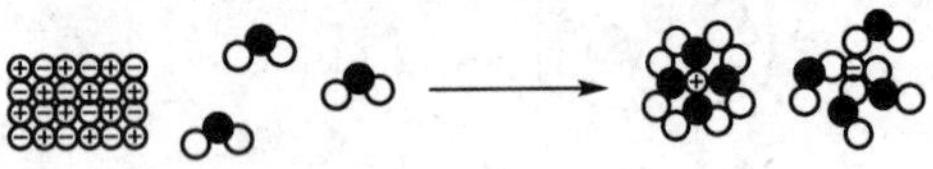

(B) $CH_3CH_2OH(l) + H_2O(l)$

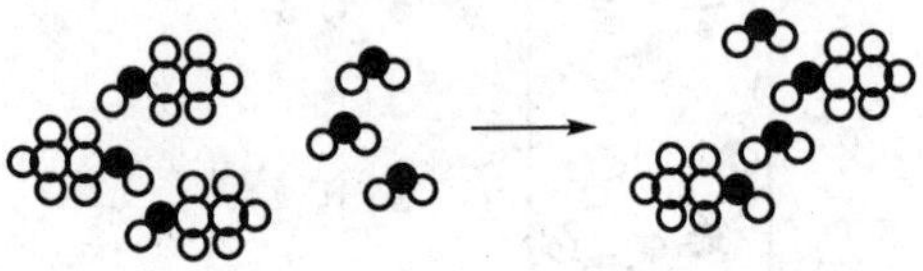

(C) $CCl_4(l) + Cl_2(g)$

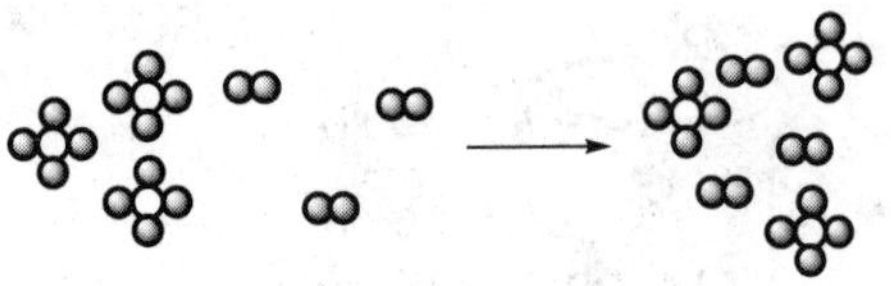

(D) $CCl_4(l) + CH_3CH_2OH(l)$

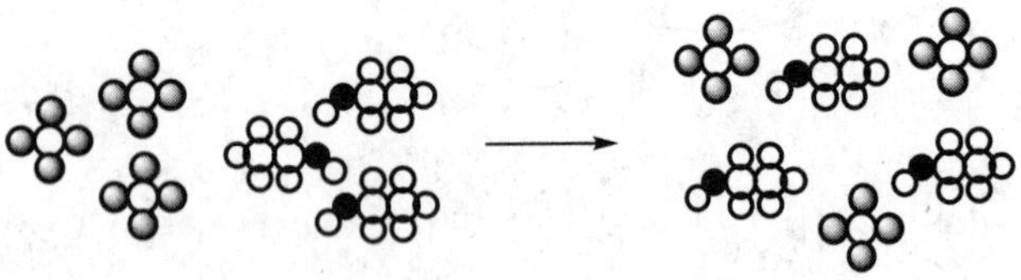

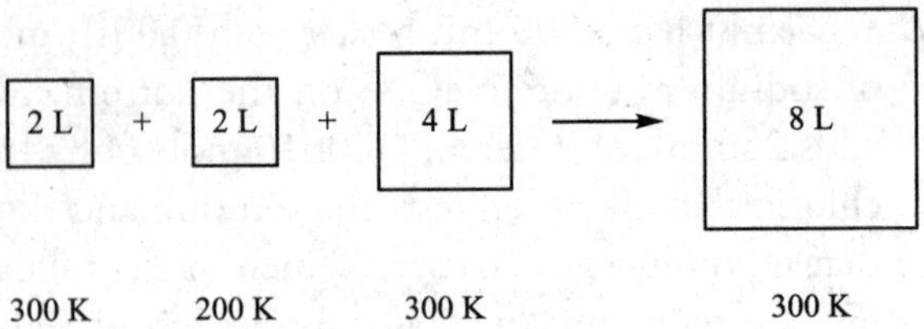


56. Each of the containers to the left of the arrow are filled with an ideal gas. The contents in the left three containers are transferred to the empty container on the right. The volumes of the original containers are exactly the values indicated. The pressure in the first three containers is 0.75 atm. What is the pressure in the container on the right?

(A) 3.0 atm
(B) 4.0 atm
(C) 1.1 atm
(D) 0.50 atm

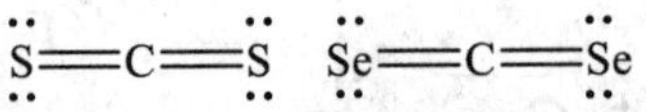

57. The diagram above shows the structure of molecules of $CS_2$ and $CSe_2$. The melting point of $CS_2$ is −112.1°C and $CSe_2$ has a melting point of −43.7°C. Which of the following is the best explanation of why the melting point of $CSe_2$ is higher?

(A) The molar mass of $CSe_2$ is greater.
(B) $CS_2$ has weaker covalent bonds than $CSe_2$.
(C) Only $CS_2$ can form intermolecular dipole-dipole forces.
(D) $CSe_2$ has stronger intermolecular forces because it is polar and $CS_2$ is not.

$N_2O(g) + NO(g) \leftrightarrows N_2(g) + NO_2(g)$ $\Delta H = -139$ kJ

**58.** The above reaction was the subject of a kinetics experiment. The reaction was shown to obey the rate law Rate = $k[N_2O][NO]$. Which of the following is the most likely to illustrate an effective collision?

(A) 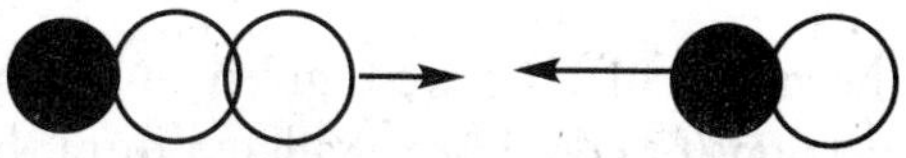

(B) 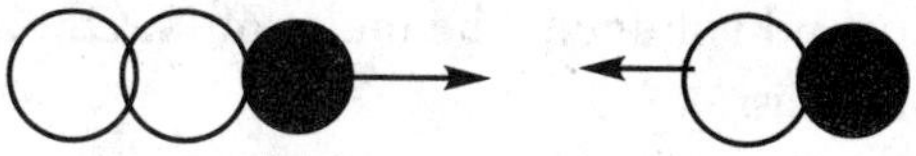

(C) 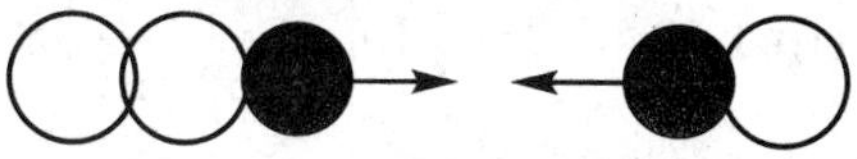

(D) 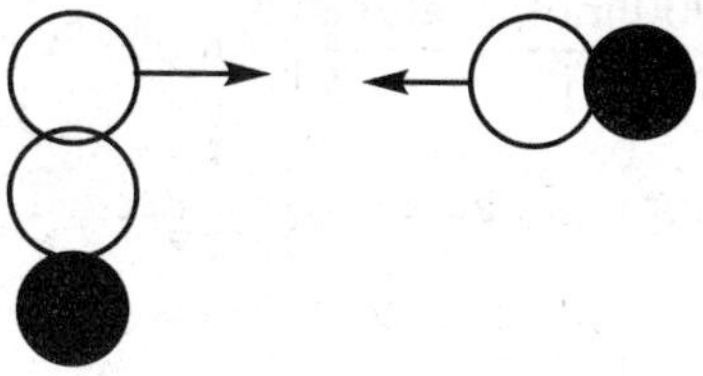

$$CHCl_3(g) + Cl_2(g) \rightarrow CCl_4(g) + HCl(g)$$

The proposed mechanism for the above reaction is as follows:

Step 1: $Cl_2(g) \leftrightarrows 2\ Cl(g)$ (fast) $k_1$

Step 2: $CHCl_3(g) + Cl(g) \rightarrow CCl_3(g) + HCl(g)$ (slow) $k_2$

Step 3: $CCl_3(g) + Cl(g) \rightarrow CCl_4(g)$ (fast) $k_3$

**59.** What is the rate law expression for this reaction?

(A) Rate = $k[CHCl_3][Cl]$
(B) Rate = $k[CHCl_3][Cl_2]^{1/2}$
(C) Rate = $k[Cl_2]$
(D) Rate = $k\left(\dfrac{[CCl_4]\,[HCl]}{[CHCl_3]\,[Cl_2]}\right)$

**60.** A 20.0-g sample of chromium metal was heated to 75.0°C. This sample was clamped in contact with a 25.00-g sample of beryllium metal originally at 25.0°C. The final temperature of the two metals was 34.9°C, and no heat was lost to the surroundings. What is one possible conclusion from this experiment?

(A) The heat lost by X was greater than the heat gained by Y.
(B) The metals have different heat capacities.
(C) The heat lost by X was less than the heat gained by Y.
(D) The final temperature was incorrectly determined, as it should be the average (50.0°C).

**STOP. End of AP Chemistry Final Practice Exam, Section I (Multiple Choice).**

# › Answers and Explanations for Final Practice Exam, Section I (Multiple Choice)

1. **A**—The boiling points are related to the strength of the intermolecular forces. For all four compounds dipole–dipole forces and London dispersion forces are present. If dipole–dipole forces were the primary factor, the sequence of boiling points should be the reverse of what is shown with $CH_3F$ having the highest boiling point. London dispersion forces depend upon the number of electrons present. The number of electrons present in the molecule increases with the boiling point, which indicates that, for these molecules, London dispersion forces are the key. You covered this material when you worked through Chapter 9.

2. **D**—Strong hydrogen bonds (dotted lines) hold two molecules of formic acid together. Ideal gases have no intermolecular forces. Therefore, the ideal gas law used in experiment is invalid because of the presence of strong intermolecular forces. You covered this in Chapters 8 and 9.

3. **C**—Increasing ionization energy applies to an element higher in a column on the periodic table, or in a position farther to the left in a period on the periodic table. Note, this type of explanation is unacceptable on the free-response portion of the AP Exam, where your explanation would require additional information such as a discussion of radii and effective nuclear charges. You covered this in Chapter 12.

4. **A**—The reaction is neutralization reaction between the ammonium ion (acid) and the sodium hydroxide (base). You saw the different types of reactions in Chapter 12.

5. **B**—Since ammonia is a base, it will react with the acid. The ammonia is captured by its reaction with the dilute acid; otherwise, part of the ammonia would escape.

6. **D**—The procedure works because the gas (ammonia) is a base that will react with the acid. Sulfur dioxide is an acidic oxide; therefore, it will neither react with nor be trapped by the dilute acid.

7. **B**—Both reactions with HCl have 1:1 stoichiometry, so moles acid = moles base. The ammonia first reacts with some of the Hcl, then the NaOH reacts with the remainder.

8. **D**—The moles of HCl ($5.000 \times 10^{-3}$) – moles NaOH titration ($4.127 \times 10^{-3}$) = moles $NH_3$ ($8.73 \times 10^{-4}$).

The moles of HCl were given in the preceding question (or could be calculated from the molarity and volume). The moles of NaOH are calculated as:

$$((41.52-0.25)\ \text{mL})\left(\frac{1\ \text{L}}{1{,}000\ \text{mL}}\right)\times$$

$$\left(\frac{0.1000\ \text{mole NaOH}}{\text{L}}\right)=\text{moles NaOH}$$

Only an approximate answer is needed.

It is easier to calculate the answer by simple rounding as:

$$((41.52-0.25)\ \text{mL})\left(\frac{1\ \text{L}}{1{,}000\ \text{mL}}\right)\times$$

$$\left(\frac{0.1000\ \text{mol NaOH}}{\text{L}}\right)$$

$$=(40\ \text{mL})\left(\frac{0.1000\ \text{mol NaOH}}{1{,}000\ \text{mL}}\right)$$

$$\approx(0.0400)\left(\frac{0.1000\ \text{mol NaOH}}{1}\right)$$

$$=0.00400\ \text{mole}$$

0.005000 mole HCl – 0.00400 mole NaOH ≈ 0.00100 mole

This was covered in Chapter 6. It is not necessary to write down everything when taking the multiple-choice portion of the exam; however, we have seen numerous wrong answers from people not writing down their steps. There is ample room for you to write the steps in the exam booklet.

**9. C**—The mole–mole ratio between N and $NH_3$ is 1:1. The mass of sample 2 is (179.425 − 179.215) g = 0.210 g N. Convert this to moles and use the mole–mole ratio to determine the moles of ammonia:

$$(0.210\ \text{g N})\left(\frac{1\ \text{mol N}}{14.0\ \text{g N}}\right)\left(\frac{1\ \text{mol NH}_3}{1\ \text{mol N}}\right)$$

$$= 1.50 \times 10^{-2}\ \text{moles NH}_3$$

Only an approximate answer is needed.

It is easier to calculate the answer by simply rounding as (and factoring out a 7):

$$(0.21\ \text{g N})\left(\frac{1\ \text{mol N}}{14\ \text{g N}}\right)\left(\frac{1\ \text{mol NH}_3}{1\ \text{mol N}}\right)$$

$$= (0.030\ \text{g N})\left(\frac{1\ \text{mol N}}{2.0\ \text{g N}}\right)\left(\frac{1\ \text{mol NH}_3}{1\ \text{mol N}}\right)$$

$$= 1.5 \times 10^{-2}\ \text{moles NH}_3$$

**10. A**—Sulfur dioxide gas is soluble in water and, while less soluble in dilute acid, some would still dissolve to give an erroneous volume (smaller).

**11. A**—The intermolecular forces in order of decreasing strength are: D = hydrogen bonding (strongest), B = dipole–dipole force, A = dipole–induced dipole force, and C = London dispersion force (weakest). If you have trouble here, you should go back to where you covered intermolecular forces the first time you covered the AP material (Chapter 9).

**12. C**—The decay reaction is first-order and 50 years amounts to about four half-lives. After one half-life, 50% would remain. Another half-life would reduce this by one-half to 25%, a third half-life would reduce the remaining material by 12.5%, and the fourth half-life would reduce the amount remaining to 6.26%. The closest answer is (C). Note, this is not a nuclear chemistry problem; it is a kinetics problem. Do not be misled by the presence of a radioactive substance; all radioactive substances follow first-order kinetics (Chapter 13).

**13. C**—The best choice to prepare the buffer is the one where the $pK_a$ is closest to the desired pH. It is possible to estimate the $pK_a$ for an acid (without a calculator) by taking the negative of the exponent for the different $K_a$ values. This gives 1 for $HIO_3$, 3 for $HC_2H_2ClO_2$, 5 for $C_6H_5COOH$, and 10 for $C_6H_5OH$. The $C_6H_5COOH$ has the value closest to the desired pH. It would not be a good choice since the $pK_a$ is so far from the pH; however, it is the best choice. Note that the formulas of the acids are irrelevant to this set of questions; only the $K_a$ values are needed to answer these questions. This shows that if you do not know the formula of a substance in a question, you can still do the problem.

**14. D**—These are salts of a weak acid and a strong base. The anion in such salts undergo hydrolysis. The hydrolysis of an anion (conjugate base) yields hydroxide ion (increases the pH). This hydrolysis is a $K_b$ equilibrium. The smaller the $K_a$ of the acid, the larger the $K_b$ of the conjugate base. A larger $K_b$ means a stronger base and the higher the pH.

**15. A**—In order to get good results when titrating a weak base, it is important to use as strong an acid as possible to get a sharp endpoint. $HIO_3$ is the strongest acid in the table.

**16. B**—The position ½ H is halfway to the first equivalence point. This is in the first buffer region of the titration. The pH at the halfway point is equal to $pK_a$ (= −log $K_a$). The value of $pK_a$ is 1.92. You covered this in Chapter 16.

**17. A**—To reach H, it is necessary to convert all the ascorbic acid to the hydrogen ascorbate ion, which means the moles of hydrogen ascorbate ion formed must equal the moles of ascorbic acid originally present. The moles of hydrogen ascorbate ion formed would require the same number of moles of base as that required to convert the ascorbic acid to hydrogen ascorbate. Equal moles would mean equal volumes added. If G is not twice H, there must be some contaminant present to react with the base.

**18. D**—In any acid–base titration, it is always easier to use a strong base (and a strong acid). Barium hydroxide, $Ba(OH)_2$, is the only strong base among the choices. You covered the reasons for this in Chapter 16.

**19. B**—The titration of a weak acid with a strong base always has an equivalence point above 7. A pH = 7 occurs in the titration of a strong acid with a strong base.

**20. D**—The $K_a$ values differ by a factor of over 20,000, which is great enough to distinguish the two equivalence points. Acid–base reactions, including maleic acid, are normally very fast reactions.

**21. D**—All the substances can behave as Brønsted bases (accept a hydrogen ion), because they are the conjugate bases of weak acids. Only D cannot behave as an acid (donate a hydrogen ion), because it has no hydrogen ion to donate.

**22. C**—Initially, doubling the volume will result in halving the concentrations (0.0500 *M*). Next, consider the reaction. The balanced equation is: $Na_2C_2O_4(aq) + 2\ AgNO_3(aq) \rightarrow Ag_2C_2O_4(s) + 2\ NaNO_3(aq)$. The silver ion is the limiting reagent (check this for yourself using a calculator—if you do not recall how to determine the limiting reagent, take the Diagnostic Exam in the Appendix of this book), so very little $Ag^+(aq)$ remains in solution (due to its $K_{sp}$, there must be a $K_{sp}$ because there was a precipitate). The precipitation of silver oxalate reduces the oxalate concentration from 0.0500 *M*. The nitrate does not change (soluble), remaining 0.0500 *M*. Since two sodium ions (soluble) are formed per sodium oxalate, after mixing the sodium ion concentration was 0.100 *M* and does not change (soluble). The concentrations are $Na^+ = 0.100\ M$, $NO_3^- = 0.0500\ M$, and $C_2O_4^{2-} < 0.0500\ M$ (there is no need to calculate the actual value; however, you should be able to use the procedure seen the first time you covered this material.) (The fact that neither the oxalate nor the nitrate ion separate is considered prior knowledge information that you learned before starting AP Chemistry.)

**23. D**—This is the Dumas method. To determine the molar mass of the gas it is necessary to know the mass of the gas (determined) and the moles of the gas. The ideal gas equation is necessary to determine the number of moles of gas present. To use the equation, it is necessary to know the temperature (measured), volume (determined = volume from graduated cylinder), and pressure of the gas. The pressure of the gas is equal to the barometric pressure, which still needs to be determined.

**24. D**—This is a Hess's law problem, requiring you to manipulate the given equations to produce the desired equation. It is possible to begin with any of the given equations. Take the given equations in order. Reverse the first equation, double the second equation, and reverse it (doubles the $\Delta H°$ and reverses the sign), and reverse the third equation (reverses the sign of $\Delta H°$). The results are:

$H_2(g) + 1/2\ O_2(g) \rightarrow H_2O(l)$ (−300 kJ)

$2\ C(s) + 2\ O_2(g) \rightarrow 2\ CO_2(g)$ (−800 kJ)

$H_2O(l) + 2\ CO_2(g) \rightarrow C_2H_2(g) + 5/2\ O_2(g)$ (+1300 kJ)

Add the three equations together and cancel any species appearing on opposite sides of the reaction arrow. The (2 + 1/2) $O_2(g)$ on the reactant side cancels the 5/2 $O_2(g)$ on the product side. The $H_2O(l)$ on the product cancels the $H_2O(l)$ on the reactant side. Finally, the 2 $CO_2(g)$ on each side cancel. The only substances not cancelled are: $H_2(g)$, 2 C(s), and $C_2H_2(g)$. If you get anything not identical to equation sought, you made an error.

**25. A**—Since the compound is less soluble in hot water, the solution process must be exothermic. Exothermic processes shift toward the starting materials (solid calcium hydroxide) at higher temperatures. This is an application of Le Châtelier's principle to a solubility equilibrium.

**26. C**—The gases are all at the same temperature; therefore their average kinetic energies are the same. Since kinetic energy is equal to ½ $mv^2$, ½ $m_1v_1^2$ = ½ $m_2v_2^2$, the subscripts refer to two different gases. Setting $m_1 = 18$ g mol$^{-1}$ and $v_2$ = ½ $v_1$ gives: ½ $18v_1^2$ = ½ $m_2$(½ $v_1)^2$; this leads to: $18v_1^2 = m_2\ (1/4\ v_1^2)$. Rearranging and canceling $v_1$ yields $m^2 = 4(18) = 72$ g mol$^{-1}$. The molar mass of $BF_3$ is the closest to this value.

**27. A**—The smaller the molecule and the less polar (more nonpolar) the gas is, the smaller the deviation from ideal gas behavior. While water is the smallest, it is extremely polar. The next largest molecule is $F_2$, which is nonpolar. This is an application of the kinetic molecular theory you covered in Chapter 10.

**28. A**—Escaping gas would decrease the number of moles. Less gas remaining in the container would mean less pressure. The faster moving gas molecules would escape faster, lowering the average velocity of those remaining in the container. A lower average velocity means a lower temperature.

**29. C**—It is necessary to use the half-life relationship for first-order kinetics. This relationship is $t_{1/2} = 0.693/k$, and $t_{1/2} = \left(\frac{0.693}{3.5 \times 10^{-3}\ \text{s}^{-1}}\right) = 198$ s. To save time on the exam you can approximate (no calculator) this equation as $t_{1/2} = \left(\frac{0.7}{0.0035}\right)$ or $\left(\frac{70}{0.35}\right)$ or $\left(\frac{2 \times 35}{0.35}\right) = 200$ s. If the half-life is ≈ 200 s, then the time (400 s) is equivalent to about two half-lives, so one-fourth of the sample should remain. Remaining mass $= \frac{0.0500\ \text{g}}{4} = 0.0250$ g.

**30. D**—The loss of 0.30 mol of $C_2H_4$ means that 0.15 mol of $O_2$ reacted (leaving 0.10 mol) and 0.30 mol of $CH_3CHO$ formed. Dividing all the moles by the volume gives the molarity: $[C_2H_2] = 0.030\ M$, $[O_2] = 0.010\ M$, and $[CH_3CHO] = 0.030\ M$. Next enter the values into the mass action expression:

$$K_c = \frac{[CH_3CHO]^2}{[O_2][C_2H_2]^2} = \frac{[0.030]^2}{[0.010][0.030]^2} = \frac{1}{[0.010]}$$
$$= 100$$

**31. A**—Based upon the stoichiometry of the reaction, $C_2H_4(g)$ will form at the same rate as $CH_3CHO(g)$ disappears, while the rate of $O_2(g)$ formation will equal half the rate of $CH_3CHO(g)$ loss. The numerical values are the same; however, the rates have opposite signs.

**32. B**—At equilibrium, there is no net change because the forward and reverse reactions are going at the same rate. At equilibrium, the forward and reverse reactions will be going at the same rate and the pressure will not be changing.

**33. B**—As the reaction approaches equilibrium, there is a net decrease in the number of moles of gas present. A decrease in the number of moles of gas will lead to a decrease in pressure. If the system is in equilibrium, there must be some of the reactants and products present (nothing can be 0).

**34. B**—The loss of 1.0 atm of $CH_3CHO(g)$, based on stoichiometry, leads to the formation of 1.0 atm of $C_2H_4(g)$ and 00.5 atm of $O_2(g)$; therefore, the net change is (−1.0 + 1.0 + 0.50) atm = 0.50 atm.

**35. A**—Oxygen (odorless) evolves at the anode (positive) and ammonia (distinctive odor) evolves at the cathode (negative). From the choices given, the only gas with a distinctive odor that could form is ammonia, $NH_3$. For this reason, the nitrite ion half-reaction must be the cathode reaction. The anode half-reaction must be the reverse of one of the reactions in the table. The only one of the half-reactions given that generates an odorless gas is the one involving oxygen, $O_2$. Do not forget, as you saw in Chapter 17, that an electrolysis cell is nonspontaneous with a negative cell potential. The cesium half-reaction will not occur under the conditions in this cell.

**36. A**—The tin electrode is the cathode (−0.14 V), and the chromium electrode is the anode (reverse sign, +0.74 V). Cell voltage = (−0.14 + 0.74) V = +0.60 V. The standard voltage of a galvanic cell is always positive, so you would know you made a mistake if you reversed the wrong half-reaction.

**37. D**—The formation of aluminum metal is a reduction and must occur in the cathode compartment. It is necessary to consider all possible half-reactions that might occur during electrolysis. Of the half-reactions listed, only the reduction of water and the reduction of aluminum ions are applicable to this experiment. For any electrolysis, the half-reaction requiring the least amount of energy will take place. So, while it is possible to reduce both water and the aluminum ion, the reduction potential for water is lower (requiring less energy), so water will reduce in preference to aluminum ion.

**38. B**—In order for substance A to reduce substance B, substance A must be a stronger reducing agent than substance B. Aluminum is a strong reducing agent as indicated by the large negative potential in the table (−1.66 V). The only substance in the table that has a more negative potential is cesium, Cs (−2.91 V).

**39. C**—Silver appears twice in the list of half-reactions, once in the simple reduction of silver ions and once in the reduction of silver chloride, AgCl. The AgCl half-reaction clearly shows that this compound is a solid. This solid will form as the silver ion in the silver nitrate solution reacts with chloride ion from the potassium chloride in the salt bridge. The formation of solid silver chloride will alter the concentration of the silver ion, which leads to a change in the cell potential.

**40. B**—The weakest acid (smallest $K_a$) will have the highest pH at the endpoint. Do not worry about the structures of the acids; the $K_a$ is the key. While you do not need to know organic chemistry for the AP Exam, such molecules may still appear as examples of other chemistry topics.

**41. D**—The buffer capacity only depends on the number of moles present. All three solutions have the same number of moles.

**42. B**—Less acid would require less than the ideal amount of base to reach the endpoint. Therefore, the endpoint would occur too soon.

**43. C**—An acid contaminant must be present, and the excess acid would require additional base to titrate this acid in addition to the *p*-cresol. Do not be distracted by the "OH" in phenol—it has a $K_a$; therefore, it must be an acid. The key is to recognize the principles (an acid has a $K_a$, and in situations like this, all acids will behave the same). The use of an organic compound is irrelevant as you are being asked about acid–base reactions, not organic chemistry.

**44. C**—Since only the plot of 1/[AB] versus time yielded a straight line, this implies that the reaction is second-order in AB. If the reaction were first-order, the graph of ln [AB] versus time would have given a straight line. If the reaction were a different order, a different graph would give a straight line. You were first introduced to this material in Chapter 13.

**45. C**—The electron configuration of boron is $1s^22s^22p^1$. The 1s and 2s orbitals both contain two electrons; thus, they should be equally intense. The 2p orbital with only one electron (half that of the other orbitals) should have less (half) the intensity. Note that answer (D) is impossible as there is no such thing as a 1p orbital; therefore, it cannot be the answer.

**46. B**—The compound with the highest boiling point has the strongest intermolecular forces. This is only valid if the molar masses are similar, which they are in the problem. Do not be distracted by the name of the compound or its formula.

**47. C**—The melting points of ionic materials depend upon the lattice energy. The higher the lattice energy, the higher the melting point is. Lattice energies depend upon the sizes of the ions and the magnitude of the charge. All three metal ions are approximately the same size; therefore, the size factor is minimal. This leaves the magnitude of the charge, and lanthanum, with the largest charge, which should have the highest lattice energy. Lattice energy was introduced to you in Chapter 9.

**48. A**—The lattice energy depends upon both the charge and the size of the ions involved. The greater the charge is, the greater the lattice energy will be (higher melting point). There is an inverse relationship between the lattice energy and the size of the ion. Therefore, the smaller the ion is, the greater the lattice energy will be (higher melting point).

**49. A**—The key relationship is $\Delta G = \Delta H - T\Delta S$. If the reaction is nonspontaneous at 1 atm and 298 K, then $\Delta G > 0$ under these conditions. For this reaction to become spontaneous ($\Delta G < 0$) at a lower temperature the reaction must be impeded by entropy (entropy was negative). If the entropy were negative, the enthalpy must also be negative, or the reaction could never be spontaneous. You covered these relationships in Chapter 14.

**50. D**—Enter the information into the $K_a$ expression. A pH of 2.0 means that $[H^+] = 10^{-2.0}\,M$ or $1.0 \times 10^{-2}$.

$K_a = \dfrac{[H^+][A^-]}{[HA]}$; $[H^+] = [A^-] = 1.0 \times 10^{-2}$, $[HA] = 0.060 - 1.0 \times 10^{-2} = 0.05$; therefore, $K_a = \dfrac{[1.0 \times 10^{-2}][1.0 \times 10^{-2}]}{[0.05]} = 0.002 = 2 \times 10^{-3}$. As always, on the multiple-choice part of the exam (no calculator), you must estimate.

**51. A**—A carbon atom with four single bonds should be tetrahedral. Tetrahedral atoms have an ideal bond angle of 109.5°. However, the carbon atoms in cyclobutane are at the corners of a square, where the ideal angle is 90°. The discrepancy between the two ideal bond angles leads to the relative instability of cyclobutane. This is a VSEPR problem, not an organic chemistry problem. Organic compounds serve as many good examples, such as this one, which do not involve organic chemistry.

**52. B**—The reaction is:

$$NaCN(s) + HCl(aq) \rightarrow NaCl(aq) + HCN(aq)$$

The only species existing in solution in relatively large amounts are $H_2O$, $Na^+$, $Cl^-$, and HCN. The mole ratio is 1:1 and since equal moles of both reactants are added, both reactants are limiting. The NaCl formed is a strong electrolyte and will be completely dissociated in solution (making the solution conducting). The HCN is a weak acid, which means that very little dissociates and in solution, it exists primarily as unionized molecules.

**53. B**—This answer shows the hydrogen ions and chloride ions as separate ions in solution, which is a property of strong electrolytes. Molecules of hydrogen chloride are present in the gas phase. The water molecules are present in both the liquid and gas phase. Other diagrams incorrectly show water decomposing, HCl molecules in solution, and hydrogen chloride vaporizing as separate ions.

**54. B**—The balanced equation is:

$$Cr_2O_7^{2-}(aq) + 14\ H^+(aq) + 3\ S^{2-}(aq) \rightarrow 2\ Cr^{3+}(aq) + 3\ S(s) + 7\ H_2O(l)$$

**55. A**—In diagram A, the forces forming are ion-dipole forces. In diagram B, the forces forming are hydrogen bonding. In diagram C, the forces forming are London dispersion forces. In diagram D, the forces forming are dipole-induced dipole forces. The strongest forces forming are ion–dipole forces. The strongest interaction forming will release the greatest amount of energy.

**56. C**—There are several ways of solving this problem. One way is to determine the moles present in the original containers, which must be the same as in the final container. In each case, moles = $n = PV/RT$. Numbering the containers from left to right as 1, 2, 3, and 4 gives (followed by estimating):

$$n_4 = n_1 + n_2 + n_3$$

$$n_1 + n_2 + n_3 = \left(\frac{(0.75\text{ atm})(2\text{ L})}{\left(0.08206\,\frac{L\cdot\text{atm}}{\text{mol K}}\right)(300\text{ K})}\right) + \left(\frac{(0.75\text{ atm})(2\text{ L})}{\left(0.08206\,\frac{L\cdot\text{atm}}{\text{mol K}}\right)(200\text{ K})}\right) + \left(\frac{(0.75\text{ atm})(4\text{ L})}{\left(0.08206\,\frac{L\cdot\text{atm}}{\text{mol K}}\right)(300\text{ K})}\right)$$

$$= \left(\frac{1.5}{(0.08206)(300)}\right) + \left(\frac{1.5}{(0.08206)(200)}\right) + \left(\frac{3.0}{(0.08206)(300)}\right)$$

$$= \left(\frac{4.5}{(0.08206)(300)}\right) + \left(\frac{1.5}{(0.08206)(200)}\right)$$

$$= \left(\frac{1.5}{(0.08206)(100)}\right) + \left(\frac{0.75}{(0.08206)(100)}\right)$$

$$= \left(\frac{1}{8.206}\right)(1.5 + 0.75)\text{ mol}$$

$$P_4 = n_4 RT/V$$

$$= \frac{\left(\left(\frac{1}{8.206}\right)(2.25)\right)\left(0.08206\,\frac{L\cdot\text{atm}}{\text{mol K}}\right)(300\text{ K})}{8\,L}$$

$$= \frac{(0.0225\text{ mol})(\text{atm})(300)}{8\text{ L}} = 0.84\text{ atm}$$

Extra detail is given in this solution. On the exam, it is not necessary to write out all these steps. Take shortcuts.

**57. A**—Stronger intermolecular forces lead to higher melting points. Both molecules are nonpolar; therefore, the key intermolecular forces are London dispersion forces. The greater molar mass of $CSe_2$ leads to stronger London dispersion forces. This illustrates why comparisons should only be made between molecules of similar molecular masses.

**58. B**—The rate law shows that the rate law is first order in each of the reactants. The reaction involves the transfer of an oxygen atom from $N_2O$ to NO to form $NO_2$, leaving an $N_2$. To form $NO_2$, the N from the NO must bond to the O from $N_2O$. To form the new NO bond, the N from NO must come in contact with the O of $N_2O$.

**59. B**—Only the slow step in a mechanism leads to the rate law. The $CHCl_3$ goes into the mechanism. However, the other substance (Cl) in the slow step is an intermediate and cannot be in the final answer. The intermediate, Cl, must be replaced with a reactant; since Cl is ½ $Cl_2$, the chlorine goes into the rate law as $[Cl_2]^{1/2}$. Answer (D) contains an equilibrium constant expression, which does not apply to kinetics problems like this one.

**60. B**—The heat lost must be identical to the heat gained (Law of Conservation of Energy). For the final temperature to be the average, the metals would need to have equal specific heats. The masses given in the problem are the same, and it is extremely unlikely that two different metals would have the same specific heat.

**STOP. End of AP Chemistry Final Practice Exam, Section I (Multiple Choice).**

# › AP Chemistry Final Practice Exam, Section II (Free Response)

**Time—1 hour and 45 minutes**

Answer the following questions in the time allowed. You may use a calculator and the resources at the back of the book. Write the answers on separate sheets of paper.

| Compound | $K_{sp}$ |
|---|---|
| LiF | $3.8 \times 10^{-3}$ |
| $BaF_2$ | $1.1 \times 10^{-6}$ |
| $MgF_2$ | $6.5 \times 10^{-9}$ |
| $SrF_2$ | $2.5 \times 10^{-9}$ |
| $CaF_2$ | $4.0 \times 10^{-11}$ |
| $CrF_3$ | $2.0 \times 10^{-11}$ |
| $CeF_3$ | $8.0 \times 10^{-16}$ |

***Question 1***

Use the $K_{sp}$ data given above to answer the following questions.

A chemist is investing the chemistry of metal fluoride compounds. Some of her data are in the $K_{sp}$ table given above. In addition to this information, she knows that sodium fluoride, NaF, is soluble in water and that hydrofluoric acid, HF, has $K_a = 6.8 \times 10^{-4}$ at 25°C.

(a) (i) Write a balanced chemical equation for the dissolution equilibrium of barium fluoride, $BaF_2$, in water.
  (ii) Write the $K_{sp}$ relationship for the dissolution equilibrium of barium fluoride.
  (iii) What is the concentration of fluoride ions in a saturated solution of barium fluoride?

(b) What is the solubility of strontium fluoride, $SrF_2$, in a 0.10 *M* strontium nitrate, $Sr(NO_3)_2$, solution?

(c) (i) How does the solubility of magnesium fluoride, $MgF_2$, in 1.0 *M* nitric acid compare to its solubility in pure water?
  (ii) Explain your answer to part (c) (i).

(d) Which of the following will produce a higher fluoride ion concentration in solution, calcium fluoride, $CaF_2$, or chromium(III) fluoride, $CrF_3$? What is the fluoride ion concentration for each of these two compounds?

(e) Write a balanced net ionic equation for the addition of a sodium fluoride solution to a cerium(III) nitrate, $Ce(NO_3)_3$ solution. Recall that sodium fluoride, NaF, is soluble in water.

*Question 2*

$$2\ ClO_2(aq) + 2\ OH^-(aq) \rightarrow ClO_3^-(aq) + ClO_2^-(aq) + H_2O(l)$$

A series of experiments were conducted to study the above reaction. The initial concentrations and rates are reported in the table below.

| | INITIAL CONCENTRATION (mole $L^{-1}$) | | INITIAL RATE OF FORMATION OF $ClO_3^-$ (*M* $min^{-1}$) |
|---|---|---|---|
| **EXPERIMENT** | **[$ClO_2$]** | **[$OH^-$]** | |
| 1 | 0.030 | 0.030 | 0.373 |
| 2 | 0.045 | 0.030 | 0.840 |
| 3 | 0.045 | 0.045 | 1.261 |

(a) (i) Determine the order of the reaction with respect to each reactant. Make sure you explain your reasoning.

(ii) What is the rate law for the reaction?

(b) Determine the value of the rate constant, making sure the units are included.

(c) Calculate the initial rate of disappearance of $ClO_2$ in experiment 1.

(d) The following has been proposed as a mechanism for this reaction.

Step 1: $ClO_2(aq) + ClO_2(aq) \rightarrow Cl_2O_4(aq)$

Step 2: $Cl_2O_4(aq) + OH^-(aq) \rightarrow ClO_3^-(aq) + HClO_2(aq)$

Step 3: $HClO_2(aq) + OH^-(aq) \rightarrow ClO_2^-(aq) + H_2O(l)$

Which step is the rate-determining step? Show that this mechanism is consistent with both the rate law for the reaction and with the overall stoichiometry.

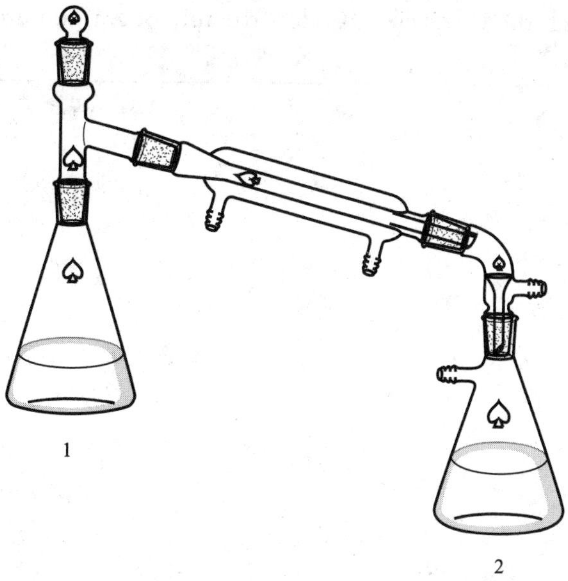


*Question 3*

A student wishes to analyze a sample of ammonium chloride, $NH_4Cl$, contaminated with sodium chloride, NaCl. She constructs the apparatus shown above to carry out this analysis. She weighs 1.032 g of sample into flask 1 and dissolves the solid in 50 mL of water. Then she adds 50.00 mL of 0.2000 *M* sulfuric acid, $H_2SO_4$, to flask 2. In the next step, she quickly adds an excess of concentrated sodium hydroxide, NaOH, solution to flask 1 and quickly seals the system. She then heats flask 1 to boiling and distills over about 25 mL of water to flask 2; during this process all the ammonia, $NH_3$, generated in flask 1 is transferred to flask 2. After the distillation is complete, she disassembles the apparatus and adds a small amount of Congo red indicator to flask 2 and titrates the solution in flask 2 with standard sodium hydroxide solution. The titration requires 39.35 mL of 0.1500 *M* sodium hydroxide solution to reach the endpoint.

Information on indicators:

| | pH Range | $pK_a$ | Color Change |
|---|---|---|---|
| Congo red | 3.0–5.2 | 4.1 | Bluish-violet → Red |
| Phenolphthalein | 8.2–10.0 | 9.3 | Colorless → Pink |

(a) (i) Calculate the moles of sulfuric acid originally in flask 2.
(ii) Calculate the moles of sulfuric acid reacting with the sodium hydroxide solution.
(iii) Calculate the moles of ammonia that reacted with the sulfuric acid.

(b) (i) Calculate the mass of ammonium chloride in the sample. (Molar mass of ammonium chloride = 53.50 g $mol^{-1}$.)
(ii) Calculate the percent ammonium chloride in the sample.

(c) (i) Strong acid–strong base titrations commonly use phenolphthalein as an indicator. Give a good reason why the student chose to use Congo red instead. The $pK_a$ of the ammonium ion is 9.25.
(ii) A second student used phenolphthalein in place of Congo red and got significantly different results. Was the second student's percent higher or lower than the student using Congo red? What was the cause of this discrepancy?

(d) In the box below, sketch the Lewis electron-dot structure of ammonium chloride.

***Question 4***

The following equipment is available for the determination of the enthalpy of solution (molar) for an unknown salt, AX. Assume the salt is soluble in water.

| | | | |
|---|---|---|---|
| analytical balance | thermometer | beaker(s) | support stand and clamp |
| stoppers | glass tubing | hot plate | graduated cylinder |
| test tube(s) | stopwatch | wire gauze | flask(s) |
| buret | pH meter | pipette(s) | polystyrene cups |

(a) Which of the above equipment is necessary for the determination of the enthalpy of solution?

(b) List the measurements necessary to determine the enthalpy of solution for the unknown salt.

(c) List what additional information is necessary to determine the enthalpy of solution.

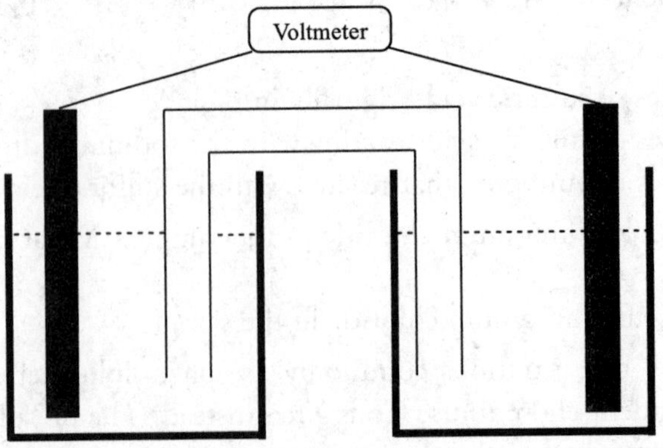


***Question 5***

The above schematic is one form of a galvanic cell. The electrode on the left is platinum metal in a solution that is 1.0 *M* in iron(II) sulfate, $FeSO_4$, and 1.0 *M* in iron(III) chloride, $FeCl_3$. The electrode on the right is either pure silver metal or silver metal, with a coating of solid silver chloride, AgCl, depending upon the experiment. In either case, the silver electrode is in a 1.0 *M* silver nitrate, $AgNO_3$, solution. The salt bridge contains 2.0 *M* potassium nitrate. The potentially important half-reactions are:

| | $E°$ |
|---|---|
| $Ag^+(aq) + e^- \rightarrow Ag(s)$ | +0.7994 V |
| $AgCl(s) + e^- \rightarrow Ag(s) + Cl^-(aq)$ | +0.224 V |
| $Fe^{3+}(aq) + e^- \rightarrow Fe^{2+}(aq)$ | +0.771 V |
| $Fe^{3+}(aq) + 3\,e^- \rightarrow Fe(s)$ | −0.036 V |
| $Fe^{2+}(aq) + 2\,e^- \rightarrow Fe(s)$ | −0.440 V |

(a) In the first experiment, a pure silver electrode was used. The voltmeter indicated the predicted voltage. Write an equation for the cell reaction.

(b) In the second experiment, a silver electrode coated with silver chloride was used. A 2.0 *M* solution of potassium chloride, KCl, was substituted for the potassium nitrate in the salt bridge. When connected, the voltmeter showed a voltage markedly different from the predicted value. Write the cell reaction for this experiment? What caused the voltage to deviate from the predicted value?

(c) When a cell is not standard, it is necessary to adjust the cell voltage to reflect the variation from standard conditions. Show the mathematical relationship necessary to calculate the nonstandard cell potential for the cell in part (b). There is no need to enter the numerical values or to calculate an answer.

***Question 6***

I II

Fulminates, $ONC^-$, salts of the extremely unstable fulminic acid, HOCN, are used in detonators for other explosives. Two resonance structures for the fulminate ion are shown above.

(a) Explain which of the two resonance forms is the more stable. The explanation must be justified with formal charges.

(b) The cyanate ion, $OCN^-$, is isomorphous with the fulminate ion, except that the carbon and nitrogen atoms exchange places. Like the fulminate ion, the cyanate ion has more than one resonance form. In each of the boxes below, draw a different resonance form of the cyanate ion.

| O C N | O C N |
|---|---|

$$2\,NaClO_3(aq) + SO_2(g) + H_2SO_4(aq) \rightarrow 2\,ClO_2(g) + 2\,NaHSO_4(aq)$$

(c) It is possible to prepare chlorine dioxide, $ClO_2$, by the above reaction. The best results occur when sodium chloride, NaCl, is added as a catalyst. This major industrial chemical is used directly or indirectly as a bleach. The observed bond angle is 118°. Explain the observed bond angle.

***Question 7***

A student in Denver, Colorado, used the following reaction to generate oxygen gas in a gas generator:

$$2\,H_2O_2(aq) \rightarrow 2\,H_2O(l) + O_2(g)$$

The reaction is catalyzed by the presence of iron(III) ions from a small amount of iron(III) chloride. The gas generator was connected by a tube to an inverted flask, filled with water, in a water bath. The gas displaced most of the water by the time the reaction ended. The flask was sealed while still inverted in the water bath. The flask was turned upright still containing the oxygen gas and the liquid water that had not been expelled. A graduated cylinder was used to measure the volume of water remaining in the flask. The flask was then refilled with water and a graduated cylinder was used to determine the total volume of the flask. The difference between the two volumes was the volume of oxygen in the flask. The volume of the sample was 375 mL at 26°C, and the pressure in the room was 635 mm Hg. The vapor pressure of water at 26°C is 25 mm Hg.

A second student conducted a similar experiment under identical conditions beginning with the following reaction:

$$Na_2SO_3(aq) + H_2SO_4(aq) \rightarrow Na_2SO_4(aq) + H_2O(l) + SO_2(g)$$

The second student's results were dramatically different from those of the first student (not as good), indicating that there was something drastically different.

(a) How many grams of oxygen are in the flask? Show all calculations.

(b) How many hydrogen atoms were in the oxygen gas in the flask after the reaction ended?

(c) What is the most likely reason why the second student did not get good results? Explain your reasoning.

**STOP. End of AP Chemistry Final Practice Exam, Section II (Free Response).**

# › Answers and Explanations for Final Practice Exam, Section II (Free Response)

***Question 1***

(a) (i) $BaF_2(s) \leftrightarrows Ba^{2+}(aq) + 2\ F^-(aq)$

You get 1 point for this answer. The equilibrium arrow and the ionic charges must be present.

(ii) $K_{sp} = [Ba^{2+}][F^-]^2$

You get 1 point for this answer. The charges must be included, and the fluoride ion concentration must be squared. You can still get 1 point if your expression correctly utilizes a wrong answer from part (a) (i).

(iii) $K_{sp} = [Ba^{2+}][F^-]^2 = 1.1 \times 10^{-6}$

Setting $[Ba^{2+}] = x$ and $[F^-] = 2x$ and inserting into the mass-action expression gives:

$$(x)(2x)^2 = 4x^3 = 1.1 \times 10^{-6}.$$

Solving for $x$ gives $x = 6.5 \times 10^{-3}$, and $[F^-] = 2x = 1.3 \times 10^{-2}\ M$.

You get 2 points for the correct $[F^-]$. If your only mistake was forgetting to double the $F^-$, you get 1 point. You can still get 1 point if you correctly used your wrong answer from part (a) (ii).

(b) Strontium nitrate is soluble in water (obviously because you are given a solution), which separates into strontium and nitrate ions. The strontium ion concentration is 0.10 $M$ and it is a common ion affecting the equilibrium.

$$K_{sp} = [Sr^{2+}][F^-]^2 = 2.5 \times 10^{-9}$$

Setting $[Sr^{2+}] = 0.10 + x$ and $[F^-] = 2x$ and inserting into the mass-action expression gives: $(0.10 + x)(2x)^2 = 2.5 \times 10^{-9}$. Assuming $x$ is much smaller than 0.10 allows a simplification of the calculation to $(0.10)(2x)^2 = 0.4\,x^2 = 2.5 \times 10^{-9}$.

Solving for $x$ gives $x = 7.9 \times 10^{-5}\ M$, which leads to $[F^-] = 2x = 1.6 \times 10^{-4}\ M$.

You get 1 point for the correct $[F^-]$.

(c) (i) Magnesium fluoride is more soluble in nitric acid than in pure water.

You get 1 point for this answer.

(ii) Hydrofluoric acid is a weak acid ($K_a = 6.8 \times 10^{-4}$); therefore, according to Le Châtelier's principle, the solubility equilibrium will be displaced to the right as fluoride ions combine with hydrogen ions from the nitric acid to form unionized hydrofluoric acid. The reactions are:

$$MgF_2(s) \leftrightarrows Mg^{2+}(aq) + 2\ F^-(aq) \text{ and } H^+(aq) + F^-(aq) \rightarrow HF(aq)$$

You get 1 point for this answer.

(d) If the two compounds have the same stoichiometry, the larger $K_{sp}$ would generate the higher fluoride ion concentration. However, this is not the case, so it is necessary to calculate the fluoride ion concentration for each.

$$K_{sp} = [Ca^{2+}][F^-]^2 = 4.0 \times 10^{-11}$$

Setting $[Ca^{2+}] = x$ and $[F^-] = 2x$, and inserting into the mass-action expression gives:

$$(x)(2x)^2 = 4x^3 = 4.0 \times 10^{-11}$$

Solving for $x$ gives $x = 2.15 \times 10^{-4}$, and $[F^-] = 2x = 4.3 \times 10^{-4}$ $M$.

$$K_{sp} = [Cr^{3+}][F^-]^3 = 2.0 \times 10^{-11}$$

Setting $[Cr^{3+}] = x$ and $[F^-] = 3x$, and inserting into the mass-action expression gives:

$$(x)(3x)^3 = 27x^4 = 2.0 \times 10^{-11}.$$

Solving for $x$ gives $x = 9.28 \times 10^{-4}$, and $[F^-] = 3x = 2.8 \times 10^{-3}$ $M$ (more soluble).

You get 1 point for doing the calculations and showing $CrF_3$ is more soluble and 1 additional point for two correct answers.

(e) It is easier to begin with the balanced molecular equation:

$$3\ NaF(aq) + Ce(NO_3)_3(aq) \rightarrow CeF_3(s) + 3\ NaF(aq)$$

Converting the molecular equation to a complete ionic equation:

$$3\ Na^+(aq) + 3\ NO_3^-(aq) + Ce^{3+}(aq) + 3\ NO_3^-(aq) \rightarrow CeF_3(s) + 3\ Na^+(aq) + 3\ NO_3^-(aq)$$

The ionic compounds NaF and $Ce(NO_3)_3$ should be separated into their ions since you are supplied with solutions, which means they must be soluble, and the sodium nitrate is also shown in the ionic form since you are told it is soluble in water. There is a $K_{sp}$ for $CeF_3$ given in the table; therefore, it does not separate into ions.

Removing the spectator ions ($Na^+$ and $NO_3^-$) from the complete ionic equation leaves the net ionic equation:

$$Ce^{3+}(aq) + 3\ F^-(aq) \rightarrow CeF_3(s)$$

You get 1 point for this answer.

Total your points for the different parts. There is a maximum of 10 points possible. Subtract 1 point if all answers did not have the correct number of significant figures. You covered this material with the Solubility Equilibria in Chapter 15.

***Question 2***

(a) (i) This part of the problem begins with a generic rate equation: Rate = $k[ClO_2]^m[OH^-]^n$. It is necessary to begin by determining the values of the exponents, the orders ($m$ and $n$). It does not matter which is determined first. We will begin with $ClO_2$; therefore, then it is necessary to pick two experiments from the table where the $ClO_2$ concentration changes, but the $OH^-$ concentration does not change. This would be experiments 1 and 2. Experiment 2 has 1.5 times the concentration of $ClO_2$ as experiment 1. This factor (1.5) times the $ClO_2$ concentration has increased the rate by 2.25 times. The relationship between the concentration ($\times$ 1.5) and the rate ($\times 2.25 = \times 1.5^2$) indicates that the order for $ClO_2$ is 2 (= $m$). Moving the other reactant, using experiments 2 and 3 (only the $OH^-$ concentration changes), we see that increasing the concentration by a factor of 1.5 increases the rate by the same factor. Thus, the order for $OH^-$ is 1 (= $n$). Give yourself 1 point for each order you got correct if you explained how you determined the order. The detail does not need to be in as much detail as given here.

(ii) Entering the orders from part (i) into the generic rate law gives: Rate = $k[ClO_2]^2[OH^-]^1$, which is usually simplified to: Rate = $k[ClO_2]^2[OH^-]$. Give yourself 1 point if you got this correct. If one or both of your orders from part (i) is incorrect, but you entered your answers correctly here, you still get 1 point for part (ii).

(b) Any one of the three experiments may be used to calculate the rate constant. If the problem asked for an average rate constant, you would need to calculate a value for each of the experiments and then average the values.

The rate law should be rearranged to: $k = \frac{\text{Rate}}{[ClO_2]^2\,[OH^-]}$. Then enter the appropriate values into this rearranged equation. Using experiment 1 as an example:

$$k = \frac{0.373\ M\ \text{min}^{-1}}{[0.030\ M]^2[0.030\ M]} = 1.3814 \times 10^4\ M/M^3\text{min} = 1.4 \times 10^4\ /M^2\text{min}$$

The answer could also be reported as $1.4 \times 10^4\ L^2/mol^2min$. You should not forget that $M$ = mol/L. Give yourself 1 point for the correct numerical value, unless you ended with the wrong number of significant figures. Give yourself 1 point for the correct units. If your rate law from part (a) (ii) was incorrect, but you used it correctly, you can still earn 1 or both points.

(c) The rate is based upon $ClO_3^-$; therefore, it is necessary to convert to $ClO_2$. The coefficients from the equation say that for every mole of $ClO_3^-$ that forms, two moles of $ClO_2$ reacted. Thus the rate of $ClO_2$ is twice the rate of $ClO_3^-$. Do not forget that since $ClO_3^-$ is forming, it has a positive rate, and since $ClO_2$ is reacting it has a negative rate. This gives:

$$\frac{-2\ \Delta[ClO_2]}{\Delta t} = \frac{\Delta[ClO_3^-]}{\Delta t}$$

Rearranging and plugging in the rate from experiment 1 gives:

$$\frac{\Delta[ClO_2]}{\Delta t} = -0.5\ (0.373\ \text{mol/L min}) = -0.186\ M\ \text{min}^{-1}$$

Give yourself 2 points if you got the entire answer correct. You get only 1 point if the sign is incorrect or the units are missing. If you got the significant figures wrong, deduct 1 point.

(d) The rate-determining step must match the rate law. One approach is to determine the rate law for each step in the mechanism. This gives:

Step 1: Rate = $k[ClO_2]^2$

Step 2: Rate = $k[Cl_2O_4][OH^-] = k[ClO_2]^2[OH^-]$

Step 3: Rate = $k[HClO_2][OH^-] = k[ClO_2][OH^-]^2$

The $Cl_2O_4$ and $[HClO_2]$ in steps 2 and 3 are intermediates. An intermediate cannot appear in the rate law; therefore, the $[Cl_2O_4]$ and $[HClO_2]$ will need to be replaced with reactants. In the far-right side of steps 2 and 3, this conversion from intermediate to reactant has been performed. Step 2 gives a rate-law matching the one derived in part (a). Give yourself 1 point if you picked step 2, or if you picked a step with a rate-law that matches your wrong answer for part (a). Give yourself 1 more point if you explained the substitution of reactants for intermediates.

To see if the stoichiometry is correct, simply add the three steps together and cancel the intermediates (materials that appear on both sides of the reaction arrow).

Step 1: $ClO_2(aq) + ClO_2(aq) \rightarrow Cl_2O_4(aq)$

Step 2: $Cl_2O_4(aq) + OH^-(aq) \rightarrow ClO_3^-(aq) + HClO_2(aq)$

Step 3: $HClO_2(aq) + OH^-(aq) \rightarrow ClO_2^-(aq) + H_2O(l)$

Total: $2\ ClO_2(aq) + Cl_2O_4(aq) + 2\ OH^-(aq) + HClO_2(aq) \rightarrow$
$Cl_2O_4(aq) + ClO_3^-(aq) + HClO_2(aq) + ClO_2^-(aq) + H_2O(l)$

After removing the intermediates ($Cl_2O_4$ and $HClO_2$):

$$2\ ClO_2(aq) + 2\ OH^-(aq) \rightarrow ClO_3^-(aq) + ClO_2^-(aq) + H_2O(l)$$

As this matches the original reaction equation, the mechanism fulfills the overall stoichiometry requirement. Give yourself 1 point if you have done this.

The total is 10 points for this question. You saw most of the material when you first went through the material in the Kinetics chapter (Chapter 13).

***Question 3***

(a) (i) The moles of sulfuric acid originally present in 50.00 mL of 0.2000 *M* $H_2SO_4$:

$$\left(\frac{0.2000 \text{ mol } H_2SO_4}{L}\right)(50.00 \text{ mL})\left(\frac{1 \text{ L}}{1{,}000 \text{ mL}}\right) = 0.01000 \text{ mol } H_2SO_4 \text{ (4 significant figures)}$$

(You can simplify this calculation as $\left(\frac{0.2000 \text{ mol } H_2SO_4}{1{,}000 \text{ mL}}\right)(50.00 \text{ mL}) = 0.01000 \text{ mol } H_2SO_4$

You get 1 point for this answer.

(ii) You need the balanced chemical equation for the reaction:

$$H_2SO_4(aq) + 2\ NaOH(aq) \rightarrow Na_2SO_4(aq) + 2\ H_2O(l)$$

The titration required 39.35 mL of 0.1500 *M* NaOH, and the calculation is:

$$\left(\frac{0.1500 \text{ mol NaOH}}{L}\right)(39.35 \text{ mL})\left(\frac{1 \text{ L}}{1{,}000 \text{ mL}}\right)\left(\frac{1 \text{ mol } H_2SO_4}{2 \text{ mol NaOH}}\right) = 0.002951 \text{ mol } H_2SO_4$$

(4 significant figures)

You get 1 point for this answer.

(iii) You need the balanced chemical equation for the reaction:

$$2\ NH_3(aq) + H_2SO_4(aq) \rightarrow (NH_4)_2SO_4\ (aq)$$

The moles of $H_2SO_4$ involved in this reaction is the moles originally present (0.01000 mole) minus the moles reacting with the NaOH (0.002951 mole).

$$(0.01000 - 0.002951)\text{mol } H_2SO_4\left(\frac{2 \text{ mol } NH_3}{1 \text{ mol } H_2SO_4}\right) = 0.0141 \text{ mol } NH_3 \text{ (3 significant figures)}$$

You get 1 point for this answer. If you miscalculated either of the preceding two answers but use your results correctly in this step, you still earn this point. The subtraction step resulted in the loss of one significant figure.

(b) (i) $(0.0141 \text{ mol } NH_3)\left(\frac{1 \text{ mol } NH_4Cl}{1 \text{ mol } NH_3}\right)\left(\frac{53.50 \text{ g } NH_4Cl}{1 \text{ mol } NH_4Cl}\right) = 0.754 \text{ g } NH_4Cl$ (3 significant figures)

You get 1 point for this answer.

(ii) $\frac{0.754 \text{ g } NH_4Cl}{1.032 \text{ g sample}} \times 100\% = 73.1\% \ NH_4Cl$ (3 significant figures)

You get 1 point for this answer. If you got the wrong result for part (b) (i), but used it correctly here, you still get the point.

(c) (i) The sodium hydroxide solution will react with not only the hydrochloric acid but also the ammonium ion. The Congo red endpoint is below where the ammonium ion begins to react (as noted from the p$K_a$); therefore, Congo red is a better measure of the amount of HCl reacting than phenolphthalein, which gives an endpoint after at least some of the ammonium ion has reacted.

You get 1 point for this answer.

(ii) The percent will be lower. It will be necessary to use more sodium hydroxide solution to reach the endpoint, making it appear that less ammonia reacted with the $H_2SO_4$. If there were less ammonia, then the percentage would be lower.

You get 1 point for predicting the percent will be lower and 1 point for the explanation.

(d)

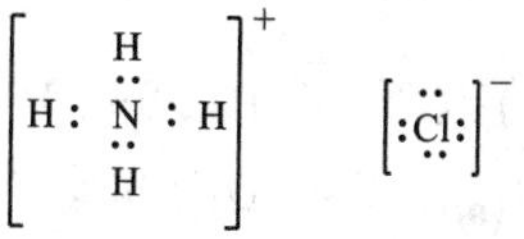

You get 1 point for having an octet on the nitrogen and an octet on the chlorine with no additional electrons shown.

You get 1 point for showing an ionic structure with no hint of a covalent bond between the ammonium ion and the chloride ion. The brackets are not essential but are present here as an aid to stress that these are ions with no covalent (electron-sharing).

Total your points. There is a maximum of 10 possible points. Subtract 1 point if any of your answers does not have the correct number of significant figures.

### *Question 4*

(a) Analytical balance, thermometer, polystyrene cup, support stand and clamp, beakers, or flasks.

You must have these five items to get 1 point. There is no deduction if you have an additional item. You do not get the point if you list any item that is not on the list.

(b) The values needed are the masses of the sample and water, and the temperature change. These require the following measurements:

There are two ways to determine the masses (your choice), and you only need to use one.

Using the balance

1. Determine the mass of an empty beaker or flask; then redetermine the mass after the unknown solid has been added to the beaker or flask.

   Determine the mass of an empty polystyrene cup; then redetermine the mass after a quantity of water has been added to the cup.

2. Place an empty beaker or flask on the balance and tare the balance; then add the unknown solid and read the mass off the balance.

   Place an empty polystyrene cup on the balance and tare the balance; then add water and read the mass of the balance.

Using the thermometer

Place the thermometer in the water (in the cup) and record the initial temperature.

Leave the thermometer in the water and add the unknown solid. Wait until the temperature stops changing and record the final temperature.

The use of the balance is worth 1 point. The use of the thermometer is worth 1 point. Statements such as "Measure the temperature change" earn no credit.

(c) The specific heat of water is needed, and the molar mass of the unknown solid are needed.

This complete list is worth 1 point.

Total your points. There are 4 possible points. We have seen students taking the AP Exam have trouble with a problem like this because they described the procedure instead of listing only the measurements. This is a "Laboratory" question, which will appear at least once on the free-response portion of the exam. You covered the basic principles necessary for the question in Chapter 20.

***Question 5***

(a) To get the cell reaction, the correct two half-reactions are needed. Since a pure silver electrode is present, it is necessary to use the silver half-reaction that does not contain chloride. There is no iron metal present; therefore, neither of the two iron half-reactions containing iron metal can be used. The two half-reactions must be:

$$Ag^+(aq) + e^- \rightarrow Ag(s) \qquad +0.7994\ V$$

$$Fe^{3+}(aq) + e^- \rightarrow Fe^{2+}(aq) \qquad +0.771\ V$$

The iron half-reaction has a lower standard potential, so it should be changed from a reduction to an oxidation (reversed) before it is added to the silver half-reaction. Both half-reactions involve one electron; therefore, the two may be simply added.

$$Ag^+(aq) + e^- \rightarrow Ag(s) \qquad +0.7994\ V$$

$$Fe^{2+}(aq) \rightarrow Fe^{3+}(aq) + e^- \qquad -0.771\ V$$

Cell reaction $\quad Ag^+(aq) + Fe^{2+}(aq) \rightarrow Fe^{3+}(aq) + Ag(s)$

You get 1 point for the correct equation.

(b) To get the cell reaction, the correct two half-reactions are needed. Since a silver electrode with AgCl is present, it is necessary to use the silver half-reaction. There is no iron metal present; therefore, neither of the two iron half-reactions containing iron metal can be used. The two half-reactions must be:

$$AgCl(s) + e^- \rightarrow Ag(s) + Cl^-(aq) \qquad +0.224\ V$$

$$Fe^{3+}(aq) + e^- \rightarrow Fe^{2+}(aq) \qquad +0.771\ V$$

The silver chloride half-reaction has a lower standard potential, so it should be changed from a reduction to an oxidation (reversed) before it is added to the iron half-reaction. Both half-reactions involve one electron; therefore, the two may be simply added.

$$Ag(s) + Cl^-(aq) \rightarrow AgCl(s) + e^- \qquad -0.224\ V$$

$$Fe^{3+}(aq) + e^- \rightarrow Fe^{2+}(aq) \qquad +0.771\ V$$

Cell reaction $\quad Ag(s) + Cl^-(aq) + Fe^{3+}(aq) \rightarrow Fe^{2+}(aq) + AgCl(s)$

You get 1 point for the correct equation.

As indicated by the silver chloride half-reaction, AgCl is a solid (precipitate). Some chloride ions will diffuse from the salt bridge and react with the silver ions present in the silver nitrate solution. This reaction will precipitate some of the silver ion from the solution. Precipitation of some of the silver ion from the solution will alter the concentration from standard (1 *M*). Any change from standard will alter the voltage.

You get 1 point for this explanation. Simply saying the cell is not standard does not earn this point.

(c) If the cell is not standard, it is necessary to use the Nernst equation to make the adjustment. The equation is present in the exam booklet (in the back of this book).

$$E_{cell} = E^\circ_{cell} - \left(\frac{RT}{nF}\right)\ln Q = E^\circ_{cell} - \left(\frac{0.0592}{n}\right)\log Q \text{ at } 25°C$$

$$Q = \frac{[C]^c[D]^d}{[A]^a[B]^b}, \text{ where aA + bB} \rightarrow \text{cC + dD}$$

Using the cell reaction from (b), it is only necessary to determine $Q$.

$$Q = \frac{[Fe^{2+}]}{[Cl^-][Fe^{3+}]}$$

You get 1 point for the correct setup for $Q$. $Q$ cannot contain any solids (Ag or AgCl).

Total your points; there are 4 points possible. This is normally one of the last topics covered in an AP Chemistry course, so you may need to go back to the last few class lectures to clarify any difficulties you had with this question. You also covered this material when you first went through Chapter 17 in this book.

***Question 6***

(a) Here are the two Lewis structures with formal charges included. (There may be other Lewis structures; however, you are specifically told to deal with these two.) While not specifically required, you should calculate the formal charge for each of the six atoms, and it will simplify your justification if you include your answers as indicated below. Recall that for an atom, the formal charge equals the number of valance electrons minus the number of electrons in lone pairs minus one-half the electrons involved in bonding pairs to that atom. (You may wish to confirm your understanding of formal charges by confirming the formal charges shown below.)

I II

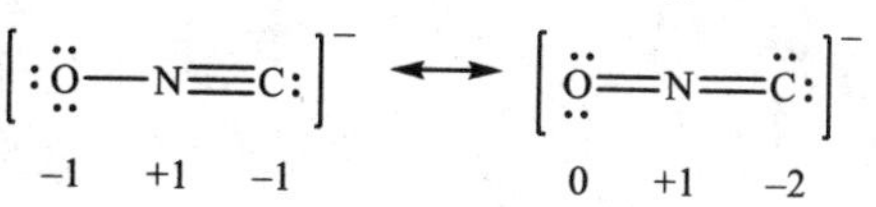

Structure I is the more stable structure. The presence of a −2 formal charge indicates that Structure II is less stable.

You get 1 point for the correct choice including the formal charge argument. Any mention of another structure is irrelevant. Any justification based upon the bonding is irrelevant; besides, both structures contain two σ bonds and two π bonds. In both structures, all the atoms have a complete octet of electrons.

(b) There are three reasonable resonance forms, which are pictured below. Other forms are either incorrect or different views of the forms shown below. You need to reproduce any two of them. In all structures all atoms obey the octet rule (failure to do this is a common reason for a structure being incorrect). The exact placement of the lone pairs is irrelevant if they are on the appropriate atoms. The square brackets are optional. Make sure that you do not accidently draw two views of the same structure. The only bonding schemes are (left to right): [1 and 3], [2 and 2], and [3 and 1].

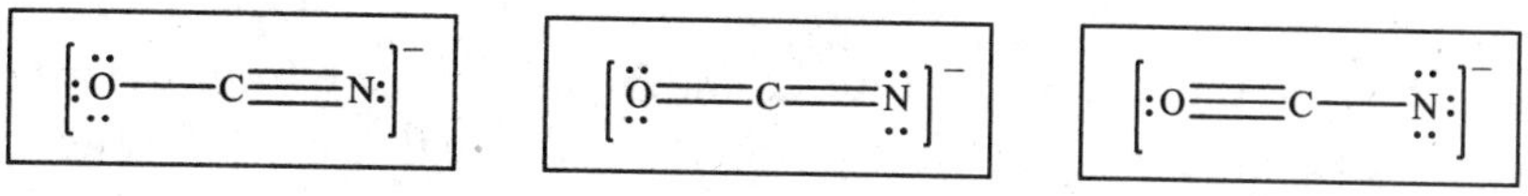

You get 1 point for each correct Lewis structure for a maximum of 2 points. Refrain from including all three structures in your answer, because if one is wrong, you may lose a point.

(c) The simplest/easiest way to explain the bond angle is to begin with a Lewis structure and utilize VSEPR. The Lewis structure is:

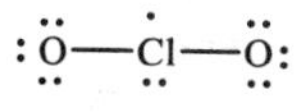

This is an odd electron atom molecule (19 valence electrons); therefore, the less electronegative element (Cl) will probably not have an octet. Chlorine is the central atom and the placement of four electron groups around it would normally lead to a bond angle of 109.5° ($sp^3$ hybridized). However, the lone electron will not repel as efficiently as a pair of electrons. The less effective repulsion allows the bond angle to increase to the observed 118°.

An alternate explanation is that the chlorine atom is $sp^2$ hybridized with the lone electron in an unhybridized p orbital. In this explanation, the angle is slightly less than the ideal 120° because of the presence of the lone pair. In this situation, the lone electron does not influence the angle.

You get 1 point for either explanation.

Total your points for the problem. There is a maximum of 4 possible points. Much of the material in this problem is based upon pre-AP material, with the final answers being based upon the additional understanding you gained by taking an AP Chemistry course.

***Question 7***

(a) The quickest way to answer this question is to use the ideal gas equation. The values necessary for this calculation are:

$P_{total}$ = 635 mm Hg

$P_{oxygen}$ = 635 – 25 = 610 mm Hg (Dalton's law)

$P$ = 610 mm Hg/760 mm Hg = 0.803 atm (The 760 mm Hg = 1 atm is in the exam booklet and in the back of this book.)

$V$ = 375 mL = 0.375 L

$T$ = 26°C = 299 K

$R$ = 0.08206 L atm $mol^{-1}$ $K^{-1}$ (given in the exam booklet and in the back of this book)

$n = PV/RT$ (rearranged from $PV = nRT$, which is in the exam booklet and in the back of this book)

$$= \frac{(0.803 \text{ atm})(0.375 \text{ L})}{(0.08206 \text{ L atm mol}^{-1}\text{ K}^{-1})(299 \text{ K})} = 0.01227 \text{ mol } O_2 \text{ (unrounded)}$$

$$\text{Mass} = (0.01227 \text{ mol } O_2)\left(\frac{32.0 \text{ g } O_2}{1 \text{ mol } O_2}\right) = 0.393 \text{ g } O_2 \text{ (rounded to 3 significant figures)}$$

Give yourself 1 point for using Dalton's law to determine the partial pressure of oxygen. Give yourself 1 point for the correct answer (no deduction for rounding differently). You must include ALL parts of the calculation (including "="). There is no deduction for combining steps. You cannot get this point if you did not subtract the vapor pressure of water from the total pressure. If you went directly through 22.4 L $mole^{-1}$, you receive 0 points because the conditions are not STP.

If you used a different approach and got the correct answer, you can still earn 1 point.

(b) The hydrogen atoms in the flask present in the water molecules are from the vapor pressure of water. This calculation also utilizes the ideal gas equation to calculate the moles of water present. These moles are then converted to moles of hydrogen atoms, which are converted to hydrogen atoms through Avogadro's number.

The variables used in part (a) are the same here except it is necessary to use only the vapor pressure of water.

$$P_{water} = \frac{25 \text{ mm Hg}}{760 \text{ mm Hg}} = 0.0329 \text{ atm (extra significant figure)}$$

$$n = PV/RT = \frac{(0.0329 \text{ atm})\ (0.375 \text{ L})}{(0.08206 \text{ L atm mol}^{-1}\text{ K}^{-1})\ (299 \text{ K})} = 5.028 \times 10^{-4} \text{ mol } H_2O \text{ (extra significant figures)}$$

Number of H atoms $= (5.028 \times 10^{-4}\ \text{mol H}_2\text{O})\left(\dfrac{2\ \text{mol H}}{1\ \text{mol H}_2\text{O}}\right)\left(\dfrac{6.022 \times 10^{23}\ \text{H atoms}}{1\ \text{mol H}}\right) = 6.1 \times 10^{20}$ H atoms (correct significant figures)

Give yourself 1 point for the correct answer (no deduction for rounding variations).

(c) Unlike oxygen gas, sulfur dioxide gas is soluble in water because it, like many nonmetal oxides, is capable of reacting with water to form an acid (acid anhydride). Oxygen is only slightly soluble in water.

Give yourself 1 point for indicating the problem is the solubility of sulfur dioxide in water.

Total your points for this question. There are 4 points possible. Deduct 1 point if you reported the wrong number of significant figures in any answer.

## Scoring and Interpretation

After finishing and scoring this diagnostic exam, you need to analyze your results. During this analysis, the key is not whether you got the question correct or not, but how well you understood the question. First, you should pay attention to any area where you had difficulty (even if you got the correct answer). This should not be limited to unfamiliar material, which you will no doubt see. Determine where this material is covered in the book. Plan on spending additional time on the chapters/sections in question. There may be some material that you do not recognize simply because it was not covered in your class. Save your results for comparison whenever you retake this exam.

If you did not do as well as you would have liked, don't panic. There is plenty of time for you to prepare for the exam. This diagnostic exam is a guide to allow you to know which path you need to follow as you prepare for the AP Exam. This exam is not intended to be a predictor of your success.

As stated earlier, it may be useful for you to retake this exam before you start your final review. When doing so, focus on the areas where you did not improve as much as you would like.

You are about to begin your 5 Steps to a 5. Remember, this test is to help you organize your study plan and not to predict your results on the exam.

Good luck!

STEP 3

# Develop Strategies for Success

CHAPTER 4 How to Approach Each Question Type

CHAPTER 4

# How to Approach Each Question Type

IN THIS CHAPTER

**Summary:** Use these question-answering strategies to raise your AP score.

KEY IDEA

**Key Ideas**

*Multiple-Choice Questions*

- Read the question carefully.
- Try to answer the question yourself before reading the answer choices.
- Drawing a picture can help.
- Don't spend too much time on any one question.
- In-depth calculations are not necessary; approximate the answer by rounding.

*Free-Response Questions*

- Write clearly and legibly.
- Be consistent from one part of your answer to another.
- Draw a graph if one is required.
- If the question can be answered with one word or number, don't write more.
- If a question asks "how," tell "why" as well.

---

## Multiple-Choice Questions

STRATEGY

Because you are a seasoned student accustomed to the educational testing machine, you have surely participated in more standardized tests than you care to count. You probably know some students who always seem to ace the multiple-choice questions, and some students who would rather set themselves on fire than sit for another round of "bubble trouble."

We hope that, with a little background and a few tips, you might improve your scores on this important component of the AP Chemistry Exam.

First, the background. Every multiple-choice question has three important parts:

1. The **stem** is the basis for the actual question. Sometimes this comes in the form of a fill-in-the-blank statement, rather than a question.

   Example: The mass number of an atom is the sum of the atomic number and ________.

   Example: What two factors lead to real gases deviating from the predictions of Kinetic Molecular Theory?

2. The **correct answer option**. Obviously, this is the one selection that best completes the statement or responds to the question in the stem. Because you have purchased this book, you will select this option many, many times.

3. **Distracter options**. Just as it sounds, these are the incorrect answers intended to distract anyone who decided not to purchase this book. You can locate this person in the exam room by searching for the individual who is repeatedly smacking his or her forehead on the desktop.

Students who do well on multiple-choice exams are so well prepared that they can easily find the correct answer, but other students do well because they are perceptive enough to identify and avoid the distracters. Much research has been done on how best to study for, and complete, multiple-choice questions. You can find some of this research by using your favorite Internet search engine, but here are a few tips that many chemistry students find useful.

1. *Let's be careful out there.* You must carefully read the question. This sounds obvious, but you would be surprised how tricky those test developers can be. For example, rushing past, and failing to see, the use of a negative can throw a student.

   Example: Which of the following is *not* true of the halogens?
   **a.** They are nonmetals.
   **b.** They form monatomic anions with a –1 charge.
   **c.** In their standard states they may exist as solids, liquids, or gases.
   **d.** All may adopt positive oxidation states.
   **e.** They are next to the noble gases on the periodic table.

   A student who is going too fast and ignores the negative ***not*** might select option (a), because it is true, and it was the first option that the student saw.

   You should be very careful about the wording. It is easy to skip over small words like "not," "least," or "most." You must make sure you are answering the correct question. Many students make this type of mistake—do not add your name to the list.

2. *See the answer, be the answer.* Many people find success when they carefully read the question and, before looking at the alternatives, visualize the correct answer. This allows the person to narrow the search for the correct option and identify the distracters. Of course, this visualization tip is most useful for students who have used this book to thoroughly review the chemistry content.

Example: When Robert Boyle investigated gases, he found the relationship between pressure and volume to be ____________.

Before you even look at the options, you should know what the answer is. Find that option, and then quickly confirm to yourself that the others are indeed wrong.

3. *Never say never.* Words like "never" and "always" are absolute qualifiers. If these words are in one of the choices, it is rarely the correct choice.

   Example: Which of the following is true about a real gas?
   **a.** There are never any interactions between the particles.
   **b.** The particles present always have negligible volumes.

   If you can think of any situation where the statements in (a) and (b) are untrue, then you have discovered distracters and can eliminate these as valid choices.

4. *Easy is as easy does.* It's exam day and you're all geared up to set this very difficult test on its ear. Question number one looks like a no-brainer. Of course! The answer is 7, choice (c). Rather than smiling at the satisfaction that you knew the answer, you doubt yourself. Could it be that easy? Sometimes they *are* just that easy.
5. *Sometimes, a blind squirrel finds an acorn.* Should you guess? Try to eliminate one or more answers before you guess. Then pick what you think is the best answer. You are not penalized for guessing, so don't leave an answer blank.
6. *Draw it, nail it.* Many questions are easy to answer if you do a quick sketch in the margins of your test book. Hey, you paid for that test book; you might as well use it.

   Example: The rate of the reverse reaction will be slower than the rate of the forward reaction if the relative energies of the reactants and products are:

| | *Reactant* | *Product* |
|---|---|---|
| **a.** | High | Equal to the reactants |
| **b.** | Low | Equal to the reactants |
| **c.** | High | Higher than the reactants |
| **d.** | Low | Higher than the reactants |
| **e.** | High | Lower than the reactants |

   These types of question are particularly difficult because the answer requires two ingredients. The graph that you sketch in the margin will speak for itself.

7. *Come back, Lassie, come back!* Pace yourself. If you do not immediately know the answer to a question, skip it. You can come back to it later. You have approximately 90 seconds per question. You can get a good grade on the test even if you do not finish all the questions. If you spend too much time on a question, you may get it correct; however, if you go on, you might get several questions correct in the same amount of time. The more questions you read, the more likely you are to find the ones for which you know the answers. You can help yourself on this timing by practice.

   Times are given for the various tests in this book; if you try to adhere strictly to these times, you will learn how to pace yourself automatically.

8. *Timing is everything, kid.* You have about 90 seconds for each of the 60 questions. Keep an eye on your watch as you pass the halfway point. If you are running out of time and you have a few questions left, skim them for the easy (and quick) ones so that the rest of your scarce time can be devoted to those that need a little extra reading or thought.

9. *Think!* But do not try to outthink the test. The multiple-choice questions are straightforward—do not overanalyze them. If you find yourself doing this, pick the simplest answer. If you know the answer to a "difficult" question, give yourself credit for preparing well; do not think that it is too easy and that you missed something. There are easy questions and difficult questions on the exam.

10. *Change is good?* You should change answers only as a last resort. You can mark your test so you can come back to a questionable problem later. When you come back to a problem, make sure you have a definite reason for changing the answer.
    Other things to keep in mind:
    - Take the extra half of a second required to fill in the bubbles clearly.
    - Don't smudge anything with sloppy erasures. If your eraser is smudgy, ask the proctor for another.
    - Absolutely, positively, check that you are bubbling the same line on the answer sheet as the question you are answering. We suggest that every time you turn the page you double-check that you are still lined up correctly.

## Free-Response Questions

You will have 105 minutes to complete Section II, the free-response part of the AP Chemistry Exam. There will be a total of seven free-response questions (FRQs) of two different types. Three questions will be of the long type. Plan on spending a maximum of 20–25 minutes per question on these three. You will be given some information (the question stem), and then you will have several questions to answer related to that stem. These questions will be, for the most part, unrelated to each other. You might have a lab question, an equilibrium constant question, and so on. But all these questions will be related to the original stem. The other type of free-response question will be the short type. There will be four of these. Plan on allowing 3–10 minutes per question.

There are several kinds of questions that are fair game in the free-response section (Section II). One category is quantitative. You might be asked to analyze a graph or a set of data and answer questions associated with this data. In many cases you will be required to perform appropriate calculations.

Another category of questions will be ones that refer to a laboratory setting/experiment. These lab questions tend to fall into two types: analysis of observations/data or the design of experiments. In the first type you might be given a set of data, for instance, kinetics data, and then be required to determine the order of reaction and/or the rate constant using that set of data. In the second type you might be asked to design a laboratory procedure given a set of equipment/reagents to accomplish a certain task, such as separation of certain metal ions in a mixture. You must use the equipment given, but you do not have to use all the equipment.

The third category of questions on the exam involves questions related to representations of atoms or molecules. These representations might include such things as Lewis structures, ball-and-stick models, or space-filling models. You might be asked to take one and convert it to another or to choose a particular representation that is the most useful in describing certain observations.

STRATEGY

Your score on the free-response questions amounts to one-half of your grade and, as long-time readers of essays, we assure you that there is no other way to score highly than to know your stuff. While you can guess on a multiple-choice question and have a one-quarter chance of getting the correct answer, there is no room for guessing in this section. There are, however, some tips that you can use to enhance your FRQ scores.

1. *Easy to read—easy to grade.* Organize your responses around the separate parts of the question and clearly label each part of your response. In other words, do not hide your answer; make it easy to find and easy to read. It helps you and it helps the reader to see where you are going. Trust us: helping the reader can never hurt. Which leads us to a related tip: write in English, not Sanskrit! Even the most levelheaded and unbiased reader has trouble keeping his or her patience while struggling with bad handwriting. (We have actually seen readers waste almost 10 minutes using the Rosetta Stone to decipher a paragraph of text that was obviously written by a time-traveling student from the Egyptian Empire.)
2. *Consistently wrong can be good.* The free-response questions are written in several parts. If you are looking at an eight-part question, it can be scary. However, these questions are graded so that you can salvage several points even if you do not correctly answer the first part. The key thing for you to know is that you must be consistent, even if it is consistently wrong. For example, you may be asked to draw a graph showing a phase diagram. Following sections may ask you to label the triple point, critical point, normal boiling point, and vapor pressure—each determined by the appearance of your graph. So let's say you draw your graph, but you label it incorrectly. Obviously, you are not going to receive that point. However, if you proceed by labeling the other points correctly in your *incorrect* quantity, you would be surprised how forgiving the grading rubric (grading guide) can be.
3. *Have the last laugh with a well-drawn graph.* There are some points that require an explanation (i.e., "Describe how . . ."). Not all free-response questions require a graph, but a garbled paragraph of explanation can be saved with a perfect graph that tells the reader you know the answer to the question. This does not work in reverse. A picture is worth a thousand words.
4. *If I say draw, you had better draw.* There are what readers call "graphing points," and these cannot be earned with a well-written paragraph. For example, if you are asked to draw a Lewis structure, certain points will be awarded for the picture, and only the picture. A delightfully written and entirely accurate paragraph of text will not earn the graphing points. You also need to label graphs clearly. You might think that a downward-sloping line is obviously a decrease, but some of those graphing points will not be awarded if lines and points are not clearly, and accurately, identified.
5. *Give the answer, not a dissertation.* There are some parts of a question where you are asked to simply "identify" something. This type of question requires a quick piece of analysis that can literally be answered in one word or number. That point will be given if you provide that one word or number whether it is the only word you write or the fortieth. For example, you may be given a table that shows how a reaction rate varies with concentration. Suppose the correct rate is 2. The point is given if you say "2," "two," and maybe even "ii." If you write a novel concluding with the word "two," you will get the point, but you have wasted precious time. On an exam like the AP Exam the question said to create a list. The list needed less than 10 words. Most students used a full page to answer the question, which obviously led to time problems later in the exam. This brings us to . . .

6. *Welcome to the magic kingdom.* If you surround the right answer to a question with a paragraph of chemical wrongness, you will usually get the point, so long as you say the magic word. The only exception is a direct contradiction of the right answer. For example, suppose that when asked to "identify" the maximum concentration, you spend a paragraph describing how the temperature may change the solubility and the gases are more soluble under increased pressure, and then say the answer is two. You get the point! You said the "two" and "two" was the magic word. However, if you say that the answer is two, but that it is also four, but on Mondays, it is six, you have contradicted yourself and the point will not be given.

7. *"How" really means "how" and "why."* Questions that ask how one variable is affected by another—and these questions are legion—require an explanation, even if the question doesn't seem to specifically ask how *and* why. For example, you might be asked to explain how effective nuclear charge affects the atomic radius. If you say that the "atomic radius decreases," you may have received only one of two possible points. If you say that this is "because effective nuclear charge has increased," you can earn the second point.

8. *Read the question carefully.* The free-response questions tend to be long (multipart) questions. If you do not fully understand one part of the question, you should go on to the next part. The parts tend to be stand-alone. If you make a mistake in one part, you will not be penalized for the same mistake a second time.

9. *Budget your time carefully.* Spend 1 to 2 minutes reading the question and mentally outlining your response. You should then spend the next 3 to 5 minutes outlining your response. Finally, you should spend about 15 minutes answering the question. A common mistake is to overdo the answer. The question is worth a limited number of points. If your answer is twice as long, you will not get more points. You will lose time you could spend on the remainder of the test. Make sure your answers go directly to the point. There should be no deviations or extraneous material in your answer.

10. *Make sure you spend some time on each section.* Grading of the free-response questions normally involves a maximum of 1 to 3 points for each part. You will receive only a set maximum number of points. Make sure you make an attempt to answer each part. You cannot compensate for leaving one part blank by doubling the length of the answer to another part.

    You should make sure the grader is able to find the answer to each part. This will help ensure that you get all the points you deserve. There will be at least a full page for your answer. There will also be questions with multiple pages available for the answer. You are not expected to use all of these pages. In some cases, the extra pages are there simply because of the physical length of the test. The booklet has a certain number of pages.

11. *Outlines are very useful.* They not only organize your answer, but they also can point to parts of the question you may need to reread. Your outline does not need to be detailed—just a few keywords to organize your thoughts. As you make the outline, refer to the question; this will take care of any loose ends. You do not want to miss any important points. You can use your outline to write a well-organized answer to the question. The grader is not marking on how well you wrote your answer, but a well-written response makes it easier for the grader to understand your answer and to give you all the points you deserve.

12. *Grading depends on what you get right in your answer.* If you say something that is wrong, it is not counted against you. Always try to say something. This will give you a chance for some partial credit. Do not try too hard and negate something you have already said. The grader needs to know what you mean; if you say something and negate it later, there will be doubt.

13. *Do not try to outthink the test.* There will always be an answer. For example, in a reaction question, "no reaction" will not be a choice. If you find yourself doing this, pick the simplest answer. If you know the answer to a "difficult" question, give yourself credit for preparing well; do not think that it is too easy and that you missed something. There are easy questions and difficult questions on the exam.

    *Questions concerning experiments will be incorporated into both the multiple-choice and free-response questions. This means that you will need to have a better understanding of the experiments to discuss not only the experiment itself but also the underlying chemical concepts.*

14. *Be familiar with all the suggested experiments.* It may be that you did not perform a certain experiment, so carefully review any that are unfamiliar in Chapter 20. You may not have done this particular experiment; however, you may have done a similar experiment. For example, ALL titrations have certain details in common. Discuss these experiments with your teacher.

15. *Be familiar with the equipment.* Be familiar not only with the name of the equipment used in the experiment but how it is used properly. For example, the correct use of a buret involves reading of the liquid meniscus.

16. *Be familiar with the basic measurements required for the experiments.* For example, in a calorimetry experiment you do not *measure* the change in temperature, you *calculate* it. You measure the initial and final temperatures. You will not receive credit for saying that you *measured* the change in temperature.

17. *Be familiar with the basic calculations involved in each experiment.* Review the appropriate equations given on the AP Exam. Know which ones may be useful in each experiment. Also, become familiar with simple calculations that might be used in each experiment. These include calculations of moles from grams, temperature conversions, and so on.

18. *Other things to keep in mind:*

    - Begin every free-response question with a reading period. Use this time well to jot down some quick notes to yourself, so that when you actually begin to respond, you will have a nice start.
    - The questions are written in logical order. If you find yourself explaining part **C** before responding to part **B**, back up and work through the logical progression of topics.
    - Abbreviations are your friends. You can save time by using commonly accepted abbreviations for chemical variables and graphical curves. With practice, you will get more adept at their use. There are several abbreviations present in the additional information supplied with the test. If you use any other abbreviations, make sure you define them. Do not invent "new" abbreviations without defining them.

STEP 4

# Review the Knowledge You Need to Score High


CHAPTER 5 Basics
CHAPTER 6 Stoichiometry
CHAPTER 7 Spectroscopy, Light, and Electrons
CHAPTER 8 Bonding
CHAPTER 9 Solids, Liquids, and Intermolecular Forces
CHAPTER 10 Gases
CHAPTER 11 Solutions
CHAPTER 12 Reactions and Periodicity
CHAPTER 13 Kinetics
CHAPTER 14 Thermodynamics
CHAPTER 15 Equilibrium
CHAPTER 16 Acids and Bases
CHAPTER 17 Electrochemistry

# CHAPTER 5

# Basics

**IN THIS CHAPTER**

In this chapter, the following AP topics are covered:

1.2 Mass Spectroscopy of Elements
1.5 Atomic Structure and Electron Configuration
1.7 Periodic Trends
1.8 Valence Electrons and Ionic Compounds
3.3 Solids, Liquids, and Gases
3.12 Photoelectric Effect

**Summary:** This chapter on basic chemical principles should serve as a review if you have had a pre-AP chemistry course in school. We assume (and we all know about assumptions) that you know about such things as the scientific method, elements, compounds, and mixtures. We may mention elementary chemistry topics like this, but we will not spend a lot of time discussing them. When you are using this book, have your textbook handy. If we mention a topic and it doesn't sound familiar, go to your textbook, and review it in depth. We will be covering topics that are on the AP Exam plus some information considered to be prior knowledge. We have found in our years of grading that while prior knowledge does not appear directly on the AP Exam, some errors that students make are related to the student missing some prior knowledge. There is a lot of good information in your text that is not covered on the AP Exam, so if you want more, read your text.

**Keywords and Equations**

KEY IDEA

This section of each chapter will contain the mathematical equations and constants that are supplied to you on the AP Exam. We have tried to use, as much as possible, the exact format that is used on the test.

| | | | |
|---|---|---|---|
| $T$ = temperature | $n$ = number of moles | $m$ = mass | $P$ = pressure |
| $V$ = volume | $D$ = density | $v$ = velocity | $\mathbf{M}$ = molar mass |
| $t$ = time (seconds) | | | |

electron charge, $e = -1.602 \times 10^{-19}$ coulomb
Avogadro's number $= 6.022 \times 10^{23}$ mol$^{-1}$

$D = \frac{m}{V}$  $K = °C + 273$

# Units and Measurements

Almost all calculations in chemistry involve both a number and a unit. One without the other is useless. Every time you complete a calculation, be sure that your units have canceled and that the desired unit is written with the number. **Always show your units!** Many students have lost points on the AP Exam because they missed a conversion since they did not write their units down.

## Units

The system of units used in chemistry is the SI system (Système International), which is related to the metric system. There are base units for length, mass, etc., and decimal prefixes that modify the base unit. Since most of us do not tend to think in these units, it is important to be able to convert back and forth from the English system to the SI system. These three conversions are useful ones, although knowing the others might allow you to simplify your calculations:

| | |
|---|---|
| mass: | 1 pound = 0.4536 kg (453.6 g) |
| volume: | 1 quart = 0.9464 dm$^3$ (0.9464 L) |
| length: | 1 inch = 2.54 cm (exact) |

As shown above, the SI unit for volume is the cubic meter (m$^3$), but most chemists use the liter (L, which is equal to 1 cubic decimeter [dm$^3$]) or milliliter (mL). The appendixes list the SI base units and prefixes, as well as some English–SI equivalents.

Many times, especially in working with gases, chemists use the Kelvin scale. Water freezes at 273.15 K and boils at 373.15 K. To convert from Celsius to kelvin:

$$K = °C + 273.15$$

**Absolute zero** is 0 K and is the point at which all molecular motion ceases.

The density of a substance is commonly calculated in chemistry. The **density (*D*)** of an object is calculated by dividing the mass of the object by its volume. (Some authors will use a lowercase *d* to represent the density term; be prepared for either.) Since density is independent of the quantity of matter (a big piece of gold and a little piece have the same density), it can be used for identification purposes. The most common units for density in chemistry are g/cm$^3$ or g/mL.

## Measurements

We deal with two types of numbers in chemistry—exact and measured. Exact values are just that—exact, by definition. There is no uncertainty associated with them. There are exactly 12 items in a dozen and 144 in a gross. Measured values, like the ones you deal with in the lab, have uncertainty associated with them because of the limitations of our measuring instruments. When those measured values are used in calculations, the answer must reflect that combined uncertainty by the number of significant figures that are reported in the final answer. The more significant figures reported, the greater the certainty in the answer.

The measurements used in calculations may contain varying numbers of significant figures, so carry as many as possible until the end and then round off the final answer. The least precise measurement will determine the significant figures reported in the final answer. Determine the number of significant figures in each *measured* value (not the exact ones) and then, depending on the mathematical operations involved, round off the final answer to the correct number of significant figures. Here are the rules for determining the number of significant figures in a measured value:

KEY IDEA

1. All nonzero digits (1, 2, 3, 4, etc.) are significant.
2. Zeroes between nonzero digits are significant.
3. Zeroes to the left of the first nonzero digit are not significant.
4. Zeroes to the right of the last nonzero digit are significant if there is a decimal point present, but not significant if there is no decimal point.

Rule 4 is a convention that many of us use, but some teachers or books may use alternative methods.

By these rules, 230,500. would contain 6 significant figures, but 230,500 would contain only 4.

Another way to determine the number of significant figures in a number is to express it in scientific (exponential) notation. The number of digits shown is the number of significant figures. For example, $2.305 \times 10^{-5}$ would contain 4 significant figures. You may need to review exponential notation.

In determining the number of significant figures to be expressed in the final answer, the following rules apply:

KEY IDEA

1. For addition and subtraction problems, the answer should be rounded off to the same number of decimal places as the measurement with the fewest decimal places.
2. For multiplication and division problems, round off the answer to the same number of significant figures in the measurement with the fewest significant figures.

TIP

**Remember:** carry as many numbers as possible throughout the calculation and only round off the final answer.

**The use of an improper number of significant figures may lower your score on the AP Exam.**

## Dimensional Analysis—the Factor Label Method

Dimensional analysis, sometimes called the factor label (or unit conversion) method, is a method for setting up mathematical problems. Mathematical operations are conducted with the units associated with the numbers, and these units are canceled until only the unit of the desired answer is left. This results in a setup for the problem. Then the mathematical operations can efficiently be conducted to yield the answer, which is rounded off to the correct number of significant figures. For example, to determine the number of centimeters in 2.3 miles:

First, write down the initial data as a fraction:

$$\frac{2.3 \text{ mi}}{1}$$

Convert from miles to feet:

$$\frac{2.3\ \text{mi}}{1} \times \frac{5{,}280\ \text{ft}}{1\ \text{mi}}$$

Convert from feet to inches:

$$\frac{2.3\ \text{mi}}{1} \times \frac{5{,}280\ \text{ft}}{1\ \text{mi}} \times \frac{12\ \text{in}}{1\ \text{ft}}$$

Finally, convert from inches to centimeters:

$$\frac{2.3\ \text{mi}}{1} \times \frac{5{,}280\ \text{ft}}{1\ \text{mi}} \times \frac{12\ \text{in}}{1\ \text{ft}} \times \frac{2.54\ \text{cm}}{1\ \text{in}}$$

The answer will be rounded off to 2 significant figures based upon the 2.3 miles, since all the other numbers are exact:

$$\frac{2.3\ \text{mi}}{1} \times \frac{5{,}280\ \text{ft}}{1\ \text{mi}} \times \frac{12\ \text{in}}{1\ \text{ft}} \times \frac{2.54\ \text{cm}}{1\ \text{in}} = 3.7015 \times 10^5\ \text{cm} = 3.7 \times 10^5\ \text{cm}$$

Remember: the units must cancel!
Also: make sure that the answer is legible and reasonable!

## The States of Matter

Matter can exist in one of three states: solid, liquid, or gas. A **solid** has both a definite shape and a definite volume. At the molecular level, the particles that make up a solid are close together and many times are locked into a very regular framework called a crystal lattice. Molecular motion exists, but it is slight.

A **liquid** has a definite volume but no definite shape. It conforms to the container in which it is placed. The particles are moving much more than in the solid. There are usually clumps of particles moving relatively freely among other clumps.

A **gas** has neither definite shape nor volume. It expands to fill the container in which it is placed. The particles move rapidly with respect to each other and act basically independently of each other. Later we will see the gas laws (Chapter 10). These laws apply only to gases; many students have lost points on the AP Exam by applying gas laws to other states of matter.

We will indicate the state of matter that a particular substance is in by a parenthetical s, l, or g. Thus, $H_2O(s)$ would represent solid water (ice), while $H_2O(g)$ would represent gaseous water (steam). For a more detailed discussion of solids, liquids, and gases see Chapters 9 and 10.

## Phase Diagrams

ENRICHMENT

The equilibrium that exists between a liquid and its vapor is just one of several that can exist between states of matter. As seen in your pre-AP course, a **phase diagram** is a graph representing the relationship of a substance's states of matter to temperature and pressure. The diagram allows us to predict which state of matter a substance will assume at a certain combination of temperature and pressure. Figure 5.1, on the next page, shows a general

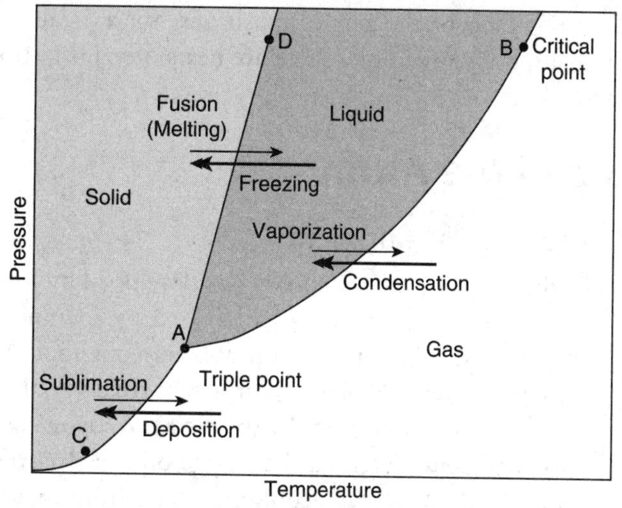


**Figure 5.1 A phase diagram.**

form of the phase diagram. This discussion is a quick review of phase diagrams. A review of this prior knowledge would have helped students on some of the tests we have graded.

Note that the diagram has three general areas corresponding to the three states of matter—solid, liquid, and gas. The line from A to C represents the solid's change in vapor pressure with changing temperature, for the sublimation equilibrium. The A-to-D line represents the variation in the melting point with varying pressure. The A-to-B line represents the variation of a liquid's vapor pressure with varying pressure. The B point shown on this phase diagram is called the **critical point** of the substance, the point beyond which the gas and liquid phases are indistinguishable from each other. At or beyond this critical point, no matter how much pressure is applied, the gas cannot be condensed into a liquid. Point A is the substance's **triple point**, the combination of temperature and pressure at which all three states of matter can exist together. The phase diagram for water is shown in Figure 5.2.

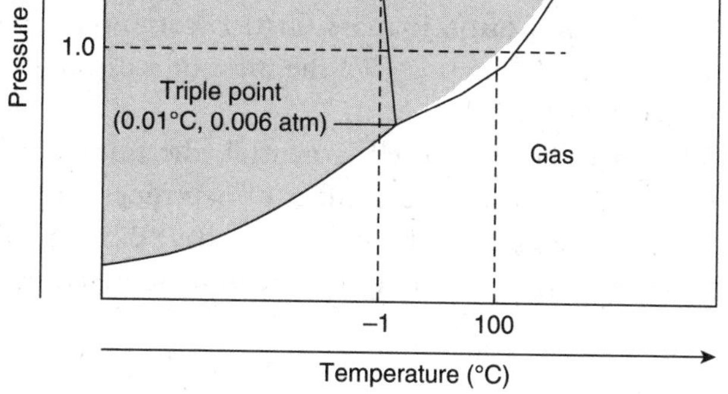


**Figure 5.2 Phase diagram for $H_2O$.**

For each of the phase transitions, there is an associated enthalpy change or heat of transition. For example, there are heats of vaporization, fusion, sublimation, and so on.

# The Structure of the Atom

## Historical Development

The first modern atomic theory was developed by John Dalton and first presented in 1808. Dalton used the term **atom** (first used by Democritus) to describe the tiny, indivisible particles of an element. Dalton also thought that atoms of an element are the same and atoms of different elements are different. In 1897, J. J. Thompson discovered the existence of the first subatomic particle, the **electron**, by using magnetic and electric fields. In 1909, Robert Millikan measured the charge on the electron in his oil drop experiment (electron charge = $-1.6022 \times 10^{-19}$ coulombs), and from that he calculated the mass of the electron.

In 1910, Ernest Rutherford was investigating atomic structure by shooting positively charged alpha particles at a thin gold foil. Most of the particles passed through with no deflection, but a few were slightly deflected, and occasionally an alpha particle was deflected back toward the alpha source. Rutherford concluded from this scattering experiment that the atom was mostly empty space where the electrons were, and that there was a dense core of positive charge at the center of the atom that contained most of the atom's mass. He called that dense core the **nucleus**.

## Subatomic Particles

Our modern theory of the atom describes it as an electrically neutral sphere with a tiny nucleus at the center, which holds the positively charged protons and the neutral neutrons. The negatively charged electrons move around the nucleus in complex paths, all of which compose the **electron cloud.** Table 5.1 summarizes the properties of the three fundamental subatomic particles:

**Table 5.1 The Three Fundamental Subatomic Particles**

| NAME | SYMBOL | CHARGE | MASS (amu) | MASS (g) | LOCATION |
|---|---|---|---|---|---|
| proton | $p^+$ | 1+ | 1.007 | $1.673 \times 10^{-24}$ | nucleus |
| neutron | $n^0$ | 0 | 1.009 | $1.675 \times 10^{-24}$ | nucleus |
| electron | $e^-$ | 1– | $5.486 \times 10^{-4}$ | $9.109 \times 10^{-28}$ | outside nucleus |

Many teachers and books omit the charges on the symbols for the proton and neutron.

The **amu (atomic mass unit)** is commonly used for the mass of subatomic particles and atoms. An amu is 1⁄12 the mass of a carbon-12 atom, which contains 6 protons and 6 neutrons (C-12).

Since the atom itself is neutral, the number of electrons must equal the number of protons. However, the number of neutrons in an atom may vary. Atoms of the same element (same number of protons) that have differing numbers of neutrons are called **isotopes**. A specific isotope of an element can be represented by the following symbolization:

$$^{A}_{Z}X$$

*X* represents the element symbol taken from the periodic table. *Z* is the **atomic number** of the element, the number of protons in the nucleus. *A* is the **mass number**, the sum of the protons and neutrons. By subtracting the atomic number (p) from the mass number (p + n), the number of neutrons may be determined. For example, $^{238}_{92}U$ (U-238) contains 92 protons, 92 electrons, and (238 – 92) 146 neutrons.

## Electron Shells, Subshells, and Orbitals

According to the current atomic model, the electrons in an atom are arranged in various energy levels or shells. The lower the number of the shell, the lower the energy. Within the shells, the electrons are grouped in **subshells** of slightly different energies. The number associated with the shell is equal to the number of subshells found at that energy level. For example, energy level 2 (shell 2) has two subshells. The subshells are denoted by the symbols s, p, d, f, etc., and correspond to differently shaped volumes of space in which the probability of finding the electrons is high. The electrons in a specific subshell may be distributed among volumes of space of equal energies called **orbitals.** There is one orbital for an s subshell, three for a p, five for a d, seven for an f, etc. Only two electrons may occupy an orbital. Table 5.2 summarizes the shells, subshells, and orbitals in an atom. Chapter 7 on Spectroscopy, Light, and Electrons has a discussion of the origin of this system.

**Table 5.2 Summary of Atomic Shell, Subshells, and Orbitals for Shells 1–4**

| SHELL (ENERGY LEVEL) | SUBSHELL | NUMBER OF ORBITALS | ELECTRON CAPACITY |
|---|---|---|---|
| 1 | s | 1 | 2 shell total |
| 2 | s | 1 | 2 |
| | p | 3 | 6 |
| | | | 8 shell total |
| 3 | s | 1 | 2 |
| | p | 3 | 6 |
| | d | 5 | 10 |
| | | | 18 shell total |
| 4 | s | 1 | 2 |
| | p | 3 | 6 |
| | d | 5 | 10 |
| | f | 7 | 14 |
| | | | 32 shell total |

## Energy-Level Diagrams

The information above can be shown in graph form as an energy-level diagram, as shown in Figure 5.3:

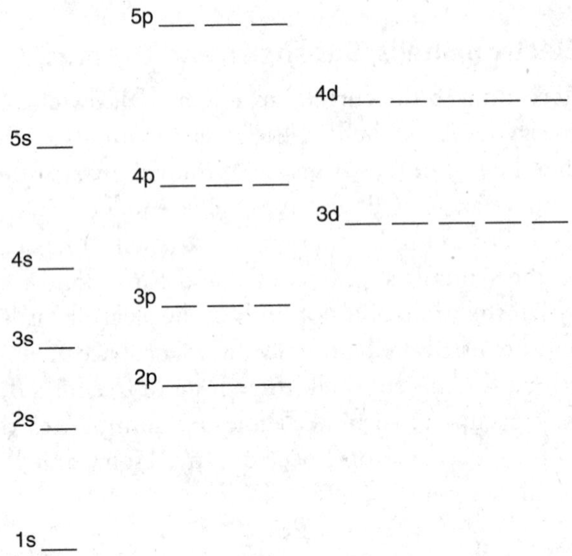


**Figure 5.3 Energy-level diagram of an atom.**

Be sure to fill the lowest energy levels first (**Aufbau principle**) when using the diagram in Figure 5.3. In filling orbitals having equal energy, electrons are added to the orbitals to half fill them all before any pairing occurs (**Hund's rule**). Sometimes it is difficult to remember the relative energy position of the orbitals. Notice that the 4s fills before the 3d. Figure 5.4 may help you remember the pattern in filling.

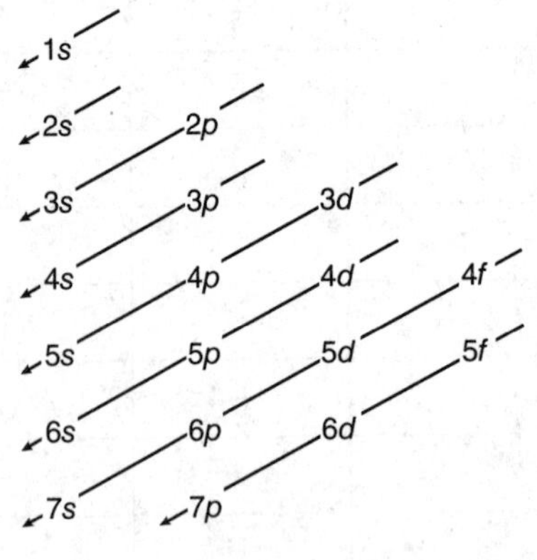


**Figure 5.4 Orbital filling pattern.**

Following these rules, the energy-level diagram for silicon (Z = 14) can be written as shown in Figure 5.5.

Although this filling pattern conveys a lot of information, it is bulky. A shorthand method for giving the same information has been developed—the electronic configuration.

## Electronic Configurations

The **electronic configuration** is a condensed way of representing the pattern of electrons in an atom. Using the Aufbau build-up pattern that was used in writing the energy-level diagram, consecutively write the number of the shell (energy level), the type of orbital (s, p, d, etc.), and then the number of electrons in that orbital shown as a superscript. For example, $1s^2 2s^1$ would indicate that there are two electrons in the s orbital in energy level (shell) 1, and one electron in the s orbital in energy level 2. Looking at the energy-level diagram for silicon in Figure 5.5, the electronic configuration would be written as:

$$\text{silicon: } 1s^2\ 2s^2 2p^6\ 3s^2\ 3p^2$$

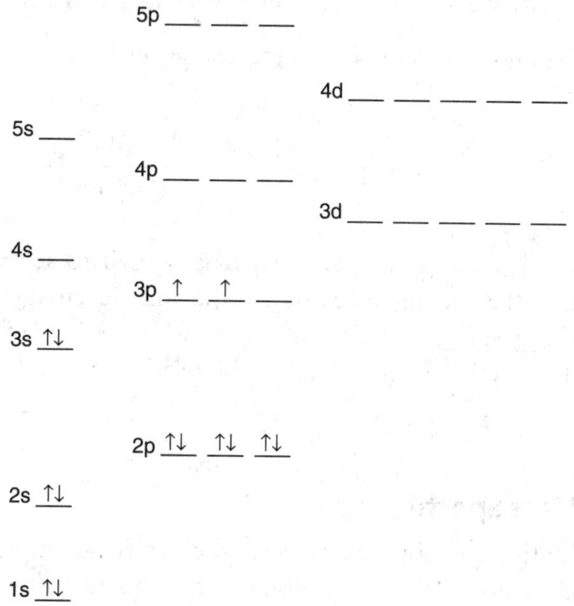


**Figure 5.5 Energy-level diagram for silicon.**

The sum of all the superscripts should be equal to the number of electrons in the atom (the atomic number, Z). Electronic configurations can also be written for cations and anions.

## The Photoelectric Effect

The photoelectric effect is the emission of electrons caused when electromagnetic radiation is absorbed by matter. Albert Einstein proposed a theory to explain this phenomena in 1905. This explanation used the concept that electromagnetic radiation consists of quantized packets of energy known as photons. This explanation was a significant step in the development of quantum mechanics. Photoelectron spectroscopy is a related phenomenon.

Electrons are emitted from matter when photons with a certain minimum amount of energy are absorbed. The minimum energy required is the binding energy, which is the energy "holding" the electron in the material. A photon with less energy cannot drive the electron out of the solid. A photon with more energy not only drives the electron out, but any energy greater than the binding energy is converted to kinetic energy.

Example:
It requires 545 kJ mol$^{-1}$ for platinum, Pt, metal to emit electrons via the photoelectric effect. What is the maximum kinetic energy of the emitted electrons if x-rays with a wavelength of 100 nm are used to emit the electrons?

Solution:
It is necessary to determine the energy needed to emit a single electron (one photon). The calculation is a simple conversion to get to joules:

$$E_{\text{needed}} = \left(\frac{545\ \text{kJ}}{\text{mol}}\right)\left(\frac{10^3}{\text{k}}\right)\left(\frac{1\ \text{mol}}{6.022\ \times\ 10^{23}}\right) = 9.05 \times 10^{-19}\ \text{J}$$

Next, determine the energy available from a 100-nm photon. It is possible to use the equation $E = \frac{hc}{\lambda}$ to determine this energy, which is faster than using $c = \lambda\nu$ to find $\nu$, and then using $E = h\nu$ to find the energy available.

$$E_{\text{available}} = \frac{hc}{\lambda} = \frac{(6.63\times10^{-34}\ \text{J s})(3.00\times10^{8}\ \text{m/s})}{(100\ \text{nm})}\left(\frac{\text{n}}{10^{-9}}\right) = 1.99 \times 10^{-18}\ \text{J}$$

The energy available is partially used to account for the photoelectric effect ($E_{\text{needed}}$) and the remainder must be the kinetic energy. In equation form, this is: $E_{\text{available}} = E_{\text{needed}} + E_{\text{kinetic}}$. This is in accord with the Law of Conservation of Energy. To determine the kinetic energy, rearrange the relationship and enter the appropriate values.

$$E_{\text{kinetic}} = E_{\text{available}} - E_{\text{needed}} = 1.99 \times 10^{-18}\ \text{J} - 9.05 \times 10^{-19}\ \text{J} = 1.08 \times 10^{-18}\ \text{J}$$

## Mass Spectroscopy

During the nineteenth century, chemists attempted to determine the atomic mass of the elements as they were discovered. This was done through various techniques involving gravimetric analysis. There were some problems with the procedure, because the chemists could not always be sure of the purity of the samples.

In the early twentieth century, the mass spectrometer was developed. This instrument increased the accuracy of the atomic masses of the elements. Early research confirmed that most elements consisted of a collection of different isotopes and, in most cases, the atomic mass is a weighted average of the masses of the different elements of an element. A weighted average is unnecessary in some cases because a few elements consist of only one isotope. Some examples of these monoisotopic elements are F, Na, Al, P, I, Cs, and Au. The most natural isotope, 10, is present in tin.

All elements have several known isotopes. Some of the isotopes may be stable and some may be radioactive. In addition, some isotopes are natural and other isotopes are artificial. Most natural occurring elements have at least one stable isotope. All artificial isotopes are radioactive.

To determine the atomic mass of an element, it is necessary to vaporize atoms of an element and ionize the atoms. The mass spectrometer, through magnetic and/or electrical fields, is able to separate the ions formed by mass and determine the mass accurately. The greater the number of ions of a particular mass the greater the percentage of that isotope.

If the isotopes of the halogens are examined, the observations are (skipping the very radioactive astatine) shown in Figure 5.6. The mass spectrometer shows that all natural iodine atoms are iodine-127 and all natural fluorine atoms are fluorine-19. Elemental

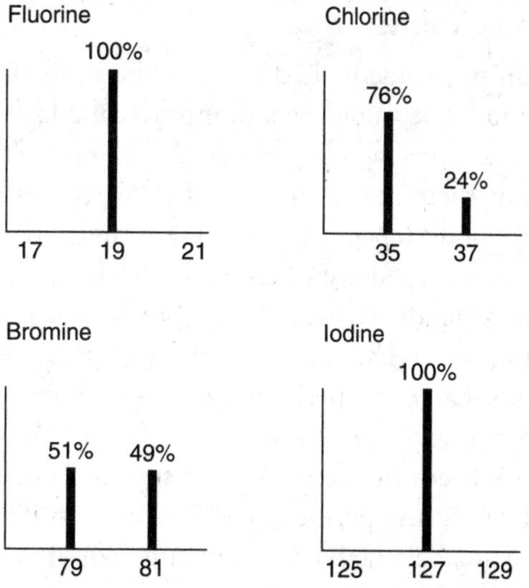


**Figure 5.6 Mass spectra of the halogens.**

chlorine is 76% chlorine-35 and 24% chlorine-37. Elemental bromine is 51% bromine-79 and 49% bromine 81. The atomic mass of fluorine and iodine are close to whole numbers; however, the masses are not exact partly because of the choice of carbon-12 as the reference for atomic masses and, especially in the case of iodine, the mass defect, which increases for larger nuclei. The atomic masses of chlorine, 35.453, and bromine, 79.904, are the weighted averages of the isotopes. The value for chlorine is closer to 35 because there is more chlorine-35 than chlorine-37. The nearly equal abundances of the bromine isotopes yield an average halfway between the two isotopes.

Mass spectroscopy has other uses besides determining atomic masses. The instrument is useful in determining the structures of compounds. If a volatile compound is introduced into the instrument, it is possible to ionize the molecules in a manner similar to ionizing atoms when determining atomic masses. However, molecules have another option. Molecules may fragment with the masses of the various fragments being determined. These fragments may be pieced together to determine the structure of the original compound. Figure 5.7 illustrates this procedure utilizing a simplified spectrum of ethanol, $C_2H_6O$.

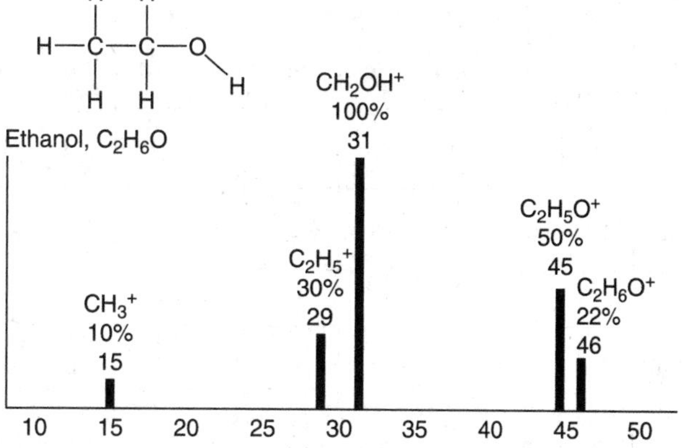


**Figure 5.7 A simplified mass spectrum of ethanol (pictured) with the peak assignments.**

## Periodic Table

If chemistry students had to learn the individual properties of the 100+ elements that are now known, it would be a monumental and frustrating task. Early scientists had to do just that. Then several scientists noticed trends in the properties of the elements and began grouping them in various ways. In 1871, a Russian chemist, Dmitri Mendeleev, introduced the first modern periodic table. He arranged the elements in terms of increasing atomic mass. He then arranged columns so that elements that had similar properties were in the same column. Mendeleev was able to predict the existence and properties of elements that were then unknown. Later, when they were discovered, Mendeleev's predictions were remarkably accurate. Later the periodic table was rearranged to sequence the elements by increasing atomic number, not mass. The result is the modern periodic table shown in Figure 5.8.

TIP

This is not the periodic table supplied on the AP Exam. The one in this book has additional family and period labels. Become familiar with these labels so that you can effectively use the unlabeled table on the exam. You may wish to add labels to the table supplied with the AP Exam.

KEY IDEA

Each square on this table represents a different element and contains three bits of information. The first is the element symbol. You should become familiar with the symbols of the commonly used elements. Second, the square lists the atomic number of the element, usually centered above the element. This integer represents the number of protons in the element's nucleus. The atomic number will always be a whole number. Third, the square lists the element's mass, normally centered underneath the element symbol. This number is usually not a whole number, because it is the weighted average (taking into consideration abundance) of all the masses of the naturally occurring isotopes of that element. The mass number can never be less than the atomic number.

The Periodic Table

Key:
Atomic number
**Symbol**
Atomic weight (mean relative mass)

| 1 | 2 | | 3 | 4 | 5 | 6 | 7 | 8 | 9 | 10 | 11 | 12 | 13 | 14 | 15 | 16 | 17 | 18 |
|---|---|---|---|---|---|---|---|---|---|---|---|---|---|---|---|---|---|---|
| 1<br>**H**<br>1.008 | | | | | | | | | | | | | | | | | | 2<br>**He**<br>4.002602(2) |
| 3<br>**Li**<br>6.94 | 4<br>**Be**<br>9.012182(3) | | | | | | | | | | | | 5<br>**B**<br>10.81 | 6<br>**C**<br>12.011 | 7<br>**N**<br>14.007 | 8<br>**O**<br>15.999 | 9<br>**F**<br>18.9984032(5) | 10<br>**Ne**<br>20.1797(6) |
| 11<br>**Na**<br>22.98976928(2) | 12<br>**Mg**<br>24.3050(6) | | | | | | | | | | | | 13<br>**Al**<br>26.9815386(2) | 14<br>**Si**<br>28.085 | 15<br>**P**<br>30.973762(2) | 16<br>**S**<br>32.06 | 17<br>**Cl**<br>35.45 | 18<br>**Ar**<br>39.948(1) |
| 19<br>**K**<br>39.0983(1) | 20<br>**Ca**<br>40.078(4) | | 21<br>**Sc**<br>44.955912(6) | 22<br>**Ti**<br>47.867(1) | 23<br>**V**<br>50.9415(1) | 24<br>**Cr**<br>51.9961(6) | 25<br>**Mn**<br>54.938045(5) | 26<br>**Fe**<br>55.845(2) | 27<br>**Co**<br>58.933195(5) | 28<br>**Ni**<br>58.6934(4) | 29<br>**Cu**<br>63.546(3) | 30<br>**Zn**<br>65.38(2) | 31<br>**Ga**<br>69.723(1) | 32<br>**Ge**<br>72.63(1) | 33<br>**As**<br>74.92160(2) | 34<br>**Se**<br>78.96(3) | 35<br>**Br**<br>79.904(1) | 36<br>**Kr**<br>83.798(2) |
| 37<br>**Rb**<br>85.4678(3) | 38<br>**Sr**<br>87.62(1) | | 39<br>**Y**<br>88.90585(2) | 40<br>**Zr**<br>91.224(2) | 41<br>**Nb**<br>92.90638(2) | 42<br>**Mo**<br>95.96(2) | 43<br>**Tc**<br>[97.91] | 44<br>**Ru**<br>101.07(2) | 45<br>**Rh**<br>102.90550(2) | 46<br>**Pd**<br>106.42(1) | 47<br>**Ag**<br>107.8682(2) | 48<br>**Cd**<br>112.411(8) | 49<br>**In**<br>114.818(3) | 50<br>**Sn**<br>118.710(7) | 51<br>**Sb**<br>121.760(1) | 52<br>**Te**<br>127.60(3) | 53<br>**I**<br>126.90447(3) | 54<br>**Xe**<br>131.293(6) |
| 55<br>**Cs**<br>132.9054519(2) | 56<br>**Ba**<br>137.327(7) | 57–70<br>* | 71<br>**Lu**<br>174.9668(1) | 72<br>**Hf**<br>178.49(2) | 73<br>**Ta**<br>180.94788(2) | 74<br>**W**<br>183.84(1) | 75<br>**Re**<br>186.207(1) | 76<br>**Os**<br>190.23(3) | 77<br>**Ir**<br>192.217(3) | 78<br>**Pt**<br>195.084(9) | 79<br>**Au**<br>196.966569(4) | 80<br>**Hg**<br>200.59(2) | 81<br>**Tl**<br>204.38 | 82<br>**Pb**<br>207.2(1) | 83<br>**Bi**<br>208.98040(1) | 84<br>**Po**<br>[209] | 85<br>**At**<br>[210] | 86<br>**Rn**<br>[222] |
| 87<br>**Fr**<br>[223.02] | 88<br>**Ra**<br>[226.03] | 89–102<br>** | 103<br>**Lr**<br>[262.11] | 104<br>**Rf**<br>[265.12] | 105<br>**Db**<br>[268.13] | 106<br>**Sg**<br>[271.13] | 107<br>**Bh**<br>[270] | 108<br>**Hs**<br>[277.15] | 109<br>**Mt**<br>[276.15] | 110<br>**Ds**<br>[281.16] | 111<br>**Rg**<br>[280.16] | 112<br>**Cn**<br>[285.17] | 113<br>**Nh**<br>[284.18] | 114<br>**Fl**<br>[289.19] | 115<br>**Mc**<br>[288.19] | 116<br>**Lv**<br>[293] | 117<br>**Ts**<br>[294] | 118<br>**Og**<br>[294] |

| | | | | | | | | | | | | | | |
|---|---|---|---|---|---|---|---|---|---|---|---|---|---|---|
| *lanthanoids | 57<br>**La**<br>138.90547(7) | 58<br>**Ce**<br>140.116(1) | 59<br>**Pr**<br>140.90765(2) | 60<br>**Nd**<br>144.242(3) | 61<br>**Pm**<br>[144.91] | 62<br>**Sm**<br>150.36(2) | 63<br>**Eu**<br>151.964(1) | 64<br>**Gd**<br>157.25(3) | 65<br>**Tb**<br>158.92535(2) | 66<br>**Dy**<br>162.500(1) | 67<br>**Ho**<br>164.93032(2) | 68<br>**Er**<br>167.259(3) | 69<br>**Tm**<br>168.93421(2) | 70<br>**Yb**<br>173.054(5) |
| **actinoids | 89<br>**Ac**<br>[227.03] | 90<br>**Th**<br>232.03806(2) | 91<br>**Pa**<br>231.03588(2) | 92<br>**U**<br>238.02891(3) | 93<br>**Np**<br>[237.05] | 94<br>**Pu**<br>[244.06] | 95<br>**Am**<br>[243.06] | 96<br>**Cm**<br>[247.07] | 97<br>**Bk**<br>[247.07] | 98<br>**Cf**<br>[251.08] | 99<br>**Es**<br>[252.08] | 100<br>**Fm**<br>[257.10] | 101<br>**Md**<br>[258.10] | 102<br>**No**<br>[259.10] |

**Figure 5.8 The periodic table.**

## Arrangement of Elements

There are several important groupings of elements on the periodic table that may be of use. One system involves putting the elements into three main groups—metals, nonmetals, and metalloids (semimetals). Look at Figure 5.8. Notice the heavy, stair-stepped line starting at boron (B) and going downward and to the right. The elements to the left of that line (except for H, Ge, and Sb) are classified as metals. **Metals** are normally solids (mercury being an exception), shiny, and good conductors of heat and electricity. They can be hammered into thin sheets (malleable) and extruded into wires (ductile). Chemically, metals tend to lose electrons in reactions, to form cations.

Elements bordering the stair-stepped line (B, Si, Ge, As, Sb, Te) are classified as metalloids. **Metalloids** have properties of both metals and nonmetals. Their unusual electrical properties make them valuable in the semiconductor and computer industry.

The rest of the elements, to the right of the metalloids, are called nonmetals. **Nonmetals** have properties that are often the opposite of metals. Some are gases, are poor conductors of heat and electricity, are neither malleable nor ductile, and tend to gain electrons in their chemical reactions to form anions.

Another way to group the elements on the periodic table is in terms of periods and groups (families). **Periods** are the horizontal rows, which have consecutive atomic numbers. The periods are numbered from 1 to 7. Elements in the same period do not have similar properties in terms of reactions.

The vertical columns on the periodic table are called **groups** or **families**. They may be labeled in one of two ways. An older and still widely used system is to label each group with a number and a letter, A or B. The groups that are labeled with an A are called the main-group elements, while the B groups are called the **transition elements**. Two other horizontal groups, the **inner transition elements**, have been pulled out of the main body of the periodic table. The number at the top of the main-group families indicates the number of **valence** (outermost shell) **electrons** in that element. **Valence electrons** are normally considered to be only the s and p electrons in the outermost energy level. The transition elements (B groups) are filling d orbitals, while the inner transition elements are filling f orbitals.

Four main-group families are given special names, which you should remember:

KEY IDEA

| | |
|---|---|
| 1A group (Group 1) | alkali metals |
| 2A group (Group 2) | alkaline earth metals |
| 7A group (Group 17) | halogens |
| 8A group (Group 18) | noble gases |

Another way to label the groups is to consecutively number the groups from left to right, 1–18.

## Trends in Periodic Properties

Trends are useful on the multiple-choice portion of the AP Exam, but simply stating a trend will **not** be sufficient on the free-response portion of the exam. You must give the reason behind the trend. For example, "higher on the periodic table" is a trend, but not a reason. Many students have lost points on the AP Exam by listing a trend instead of explaining why the trend exists.

The overall attraction an electron experiences is due to the **effective nuclear charge**. This attraction is related to the positive nuclear charge interacting with the negative electrons. Electrons between the nucleus and the electron under consideration interfere with, or shield, that electron from the full nuclear charge. This shielding lessens the nuclear charge. Within a period, the shielding is nearly constant; however, the effective nuclear charge will increase with an increasing number of protons (atomic number). Within the same family or group, as the atomic number increases so does the shielding, resulting in a relatively constant effective nuclear charge.

The size of an atom is generally determined by the number of energy levels occupied by electrons. This means that as we move from top to bottom within a group, the size of the atom increases due to the increased number of shells containing electrons. As we move from left to right within a period (within the same valence shell), the atomic size decreases somewhat owing to the increased effective nuclear charge on the electrons. This increased attraction is related to the increasing number of protons within the nucleus. The size of a cation is smaller than the neutral atom, because in many cases an entire energy shell has been removed, while an anion is larger than the corresponding neutral atom since the nuclear attraction is being distributed over additional electrons. As the number of electrons changes so will the electron–electron repulsion. The greater the electron–electron repulsion, the larger the species becomes, and vice versa.

The **ionization energy (IE)** is the energy needed to completely remove an electron from an atom. It may be expressed in terms of 1 atom or a mole of atoms. Energy is required in this process to overcome the attraction of the nucleus for the electrons. There are two factors affecting the magnitude of the ionization energy. One is the size of the atom. The smaller the atom, the more energy is needed to overcome the effective nuclear charge.

Therefore, ionization energy tends to decrease from top to bottom within a group, since the valence electrons (the first ones to be lost) are farther away from the nucleus.

The other factor is the magnitude of the effective nuclear charge. The greater the effective nuclear charge, the more energy is required to remove the electron. Since the effective nuclear charge increases from left to right within a period, the ionization energies will also increase from left to right. The increased effective nuclear charge results in the atom becoming slightly smaller, which also leads to a greater nuclear attraction for the electrons.

The ionization energy for the removal of a second electron is greater in all cases than the first, because the electron is being pulled away from a positively charged ion and the attraction is greater than from a neutral atom.

The **electron affinity (EA)** is the energy change that results from adding an electron to an atom or ion. The trends in electron affinity are not quite as regular as size or ionization energy trends. In general, electron affinity increases from left to right within a period (owing to the increased effective nuclear charge) and decreases from top to bottom within a group owing to increased atomic or ionic size. Noble gases are an exception—they have no EA.

Do not forget that the trends mentioned in this section may help you on the multiple-choice portion of the AP exam. However, it is the underlying reasons that you need for the free-response portion.

## Oxidation Numbers

**Oxidation numbers** are bookkeeping numbers that allow chemists to do things like balance redox equations. Don't confuse oxidation numbers with the charge on an ion. Oxidation numbers are assigned to elements in their natural state or in compounds using the following rules:

KEY IDEA

- The oxidation number of an element in its elemental form (i.e., $H_2$, Au, Ag, $N_2$) is zero.
- The oxidation number of a monatomic ion is equal to the charge on the ion. The oxidation number of $Mg^{2+}$ is +2.

- The sum of all the oxidation numbers of all the elements in a neutral molecule is zero. The sum of all the oxidation numbers in a polyatomic ion is equal to the charge on the ion.
- The alkali metal ions have an oxidation number of +1 in all their compounds.
- The alkaline earth metals have an oxidation number of +2 in all their compounds.
- The oxidation number of a hydrogen atom in a compound is +1, except it is –1 when combined with metals or boron in binary compounds.
- The oxidation number of halogens in their compounds is –1 except when combined with another halogen above them on the periodic table, or with oxygen.
- The oxidation number of an oxygen atom is –2 in compounds, except for peroxides, in which it is –1.

Determine the oxidation number of the sulfur atom in sulfuric acid, $H_2SO_4$. The sum of all the oxidation numbers must equal zero, since this is a neutral compound. The oxidation numbers of hydrogen (+1) and oxygen (–2) are known, so the oxidation number of the sulfur atom can be determined:

$$\underset{H_2SO_4}{2(+1) + ? + 4(-2) = 0}$$

The oxidation number of the sulfur atom in this compound must be +6.

# Nomenclature Overview

This overview covers some of the rules for naming simple inorganic compounds. There are additional rules, and some exceptions to these rules. The first part of this overview discusses the rules for deriving a name from a chemical formula. In many cases, the formula may be determined from the name by reversing this process. The second part examines situations in which additional information is needed to generate a formula from the name of a compound. The transition metals present some additional problems; therefore, there is a section covering transition metal nomenclature and coordination compounds.

## Binary Compounds

Binary compounds are compounds that consist of only two elements. Some binary compounds have special names, and these special names supersede any of the rules given below. $H_2O$ is water, $NH_3$ is ammonia, and $CH_4$ is methane. All other binary compounds have a name with a suffix *ide*. Binary compounds may be subdivided into metal type, nonmetal type, and acid type.

(a) **Metal type.** These binary compounds begin with metals. The metal is given first in the formula. In general, metals are the elements on the left-hand side of the periodic table, and the nonmetals are on the right-hand side. Hydrogen, a nonmetal, is an exception to this generalization.

First name the metal, then name the nonmetal with the suffix *ide.* Examples:

| **Formula** | **Name** |
|---|---|
| $Na_2O$ | sodium oxide |
| $MgCl_2$ | magnesium chloride |

The ammonium ion ($NH_4^+$) is often treated as a metal, and its compounds are named under this rule. Thus, $NH_4Cl$ is named ammonium chloride.

**(b) Nonmetal type.** These binary compounds have formulas that begin with a nonmetal. Prefixes are used to indicate the number of each atom present. No prefixes are used for hydrogen. Naming the compounds can best be explained using the following examples:

| Formula | Name |
|---|---|
| $CO$ | carbon monoxide |
| $SO_3$ | sulfur trioxide |
| $P_4O_{10}$ | tetraphosphorus decaoxide |

Carbon monoxide is one of the very few cases where the prefix *mono* is used. In general, you should not use *mono* in any other compound.

Some of the prefixes used to denote the numbers of atoms in a compound are listed below:

| Number of atoms | Prefix |
|---|---|
| 1 | mono |
| 2 | di |
| 3 | tri |
| 4 | tetra |
| 5 | penta |
| 6 | hexa |
| 7 | hepta |
| 8 | octa |
| 9 | nona |
| 10 | deca |

On many occasions the terminal *a* or *o* is dropped for oxides, so they read as pentoxide, heptoxide, or monoxide.

In normal nomenclature, the nonmetal prefixes are not used if a metal is present. One of the few exceptions to this is $MnO_2$, sometimes called manganese dioxide.

**(c) Acid type.** These binary compounds have formulas that begin with hydrogen. If the compound is not in solution, the naming is similar to that of the metal type.

If the compound is dissolved in $H_2O$, indicated by (*aq*), the compound takes on the prefix *hydro* and the suffix *ic*. If the compound is not in solution, the state of matter should be shown as follows:

$$HCl(g),\ HF(l)$$

If the formula has no designation of phase or water, either name may be used. Examples for naming these compounds are:

| Formula | Name |
|---|---|
| $HCl(g)$ | hydrogen chloride |
| $H_2S(g)$ | hydrogen sulfide |
| $HCl(aq)$ | *hydro*chlor*ic* acid |
| $H_2S(aq)$ | *hydro*sulfur*ic* acid |
| $HCl$ | hydrogen chloride or *hydro*chlor*ic* acid |
| $H_2S$ | hydrogen sulfide or *hydro*sulfur*ic* acid |

HCN (hydrocyanic acid) is named using these rules. However, in this case, it does not matter if the phase or water is indicated.

## Ternary Compounds

**Ternary compounds** are those containing three or more elements. If the first element in the formula is hydrogen, it is usually classified as an acid. If the formula contains oxygen in addition to the hydrogen, the compound is usually classified as an oxyacid. In general, if the first element in the formula is not hydrogen, the compound is classified as a salt.

Ternary acids are usually named with the suffixes *ic* or *ous*. The exceptions are the acids derived from ions with an *ide* suffix (see HCN in the preceding section). These acids undergo many reactions to form salts, compounds of a metal, and the ion of an acid. The ions from the acids $H_2SO_4$ and $HNO_3$ are $SO_4^{2-}$, $NO_3^-$. If an acid name has the suffix *ic*, the ion of this acid has a name with the suffix *ate*. If an acid name has the suffix *ous*, the ion has a name with the suffix *ite*. Salts have the same suffixes as the suffixes of the ions. The difference between the acid with a suffix *ic* and the acid with the suffix *ous* can many times be determined by visual inspection of the formula. The acid with the suffix *ous* usually has one fewer oxygen atom than the acid with the suffix *ic*. Examples:

| Formula | Name of the acid | Formula | Name of the acid |
|---|---|---|---|
| $H_2SO_4$ | sulfuric acid | $HNO_3$ | nitric acid |
| $H_2SO_3$ | sulfurous acid | $HNO_2$ | nitrous acid |

When the ternary compound is not an acid, the first element is usually a metal. In these cases, the name of the compound is simply the name of the metal followed by the name of the ion. The ammonium ion is treated as a metal in these cases.

The following are examples:

| Acid formula | Acid name | Ion name | Salt formula | Salt name |
|---|---|---|---|---|
| $H_2SO_4$ | sulfuric acid | sulfate ion | $Na_2SO_4$ | sodium sulfate |
| $H_2SO_3$ | sulfurous acid | sulfite ion | $Na_2SO_3$ | sodium sulfite |
| $HNO_3$ | nitric acid | nitrate ion | $KNO_3$ | potassium nitrate |
| $HNO_2$ | nitrous acid | nitrite ion | $KNO_2$ | potassium nitrite |
| $H_3PO_4$ | phosphoric acid | phosphate ion | $(NH_4)_3PO_4$ | ammonium phosphate |

## Writing Formulas

To write the formula from the name of a binary compound containing only nonmetals, write the symbols for the separate atoms with the prefixes converted to subscripts.

In all compounds, the total charge must be zero. There are NO exceptions. Thus, to determine the formula in those cases where no prefixes are given, it is necessary to have some idea what the individual charges are. The species with the positive charge is listed and named first; this is followed by the species with the negative charge. Subscripts may be needed to make sure the sum of the charges (valances) will equal zero. Examples:

1. Magnesium oxide

$$Mg^{2+}O^{2-} = +2 - 2 = 0$$

This gives MgO.

2. Sodium oxide

$$Na^{1+}O^{2-} = +1 - 2 = -1; \text{ thus a subscript is needed}$$
$$Na_2^{2(1+)}O^{2-} = 2(+1) - 2 = 0$$

This gives $Na_2O$.

**3.** Aluminum oxide

$$Al^{3+}O^{2-} = +3 - 2 = -1\text{; thus a subscript is needed}$$

$$Al_2{}^{2(3+)}O_3{}^{3(2-)} = 2(+3) + 3(-2) = 0$$

This gives $Al_2O_3$.

If a polyatomic ion must be increased to achieve zero charge, parentheses should be used. An example of this is shown as:

$$NH_4{}^{+}SO_4{}^{2-} = +1 - 2 = -1$$

$$(NH_4)_2{}^{2(1+)}SO_4{}^{2-} = 2(+1) - 2 = 0$$

This gives $(NH_4)_2SO_4$.

One way of predicting the values of the subscripts is to crisscross the valences. This is not a rule of nomenclature, but for practice purposes in this exercise it will be referred to as the crisscross rule. It works most of the time and therefore is worth considering. Example:

$Al^{3+}O^{2-}$ Crisscross the 2 from the oxygen charge to the aluminum and the 3 from the aluminum charge to the oxygen.

$Al_2{}^{3+}O_3{}^{2-}$

TIP

If the crisscross rule is applied, you should reduce the formula if possible. For example:

$Mn^{4+}O^{2-}$ crisscrosses to $Mn_2O_4$, which reduces to $MnO_2$.

If a formula is given, the crisscross rule can be reversed to give the valences:

$$Al_2O_3$$

$$Al_2{}^{3+}O_3{}^{2-}$$

As a first approximation, the valences of the representative elements can be predicted from their position on the periodic table. Hydrogen and the metals have positive charges beginning with +1 on the left and increasing by one as you proceed to the right on the periodic table (skipping the transition metals). Nonmetals begin with 0 in the rightmost column of the periodic table and decrease by 1 as you move to the left on the periodic table. Metalloids may be treated as metals or nonmetals. Examples are:

$$Na^{+}\ Mg^{2+}\ Al^{3+}\ Si^{4+}\ P^{3-}\ S^{2-}\ Cl^{-}\ Ar^{0}$$

## Transition Metals

Many transition metals and the group of six elements centered around lead on the periodic table commonly have more than one valence. The valence of these metals in a compound must be known before the compound can be named. Modern nomenclature rules indicate the valence of one of these metals with a Roman numeral suffix (Stock notation). Older nomenclature rules used different suffixes to indicate the charge. Examples:

**1.** $FeCl_3$
$Fe^{3+}Cl_3{}^{1-}$ (crisscross rule)

The compound is named iron(III) chloride or ferric chloride.

**2.** $FeCl_2$

If chloride is –1, two chloride ions are –2. Fe has a valence of +2, to give a total charge of zero. The name is iron(II) chloride or ferrous chloride.

**3.** $MnO_2$

$Mn^{4+}$ (found previously)
The name would be manganese(IV) oxide, although it is often named manganese dioxide.

The Roman numeral suffix is part of the name of the metal. Thus iron(III) is one word.

Stock notation should be used for all metals that have a variable valence. This includes almost all the transition elements and the elements immediately around lead on the periodic table. Stock notation is often omitted for Zn, Cd, and Ag, as they do not have variable valences.

The valences of some common metals and acids are listed in the appendixes.

## Coordination Compounds

**Coordination compounds** contain a complex. In general, a complex may be recognized because it is enclosed in square brackets [ ]. The square brackets are omitted when the actual structure of the complex is uncertain.

A complex is composed of a central atom, normally a metal, surrounded by atoms or groups of atoms called ligands. One way of forming a complex is illustrated below:

$$Ni^{2+}(g) + 6\ H_2O(l) \rightarrow [Ni(H_2O)_6]^{2+}(aq)$$

In this reaction, the metal behaves as a Lewis acid and accepts a pair of electrons from the Lewis base (ligand). In this case, the ligand is water, with the oxygen atom donating one of its lone pairs to the nickel. The oxygen atom is called the donor atom. In this complex, there are six donor atoms.

A complex may be ionic or neutral. An ionic complex is called a complex ion. A neutral complex is a type of coordination compound. The only difference in naming coordination compounds or complex ions is that anionic complex ions have an *ate* suffix.

A coordination compound may contain more than one complex ion or material that is not part of the complex, but it must have an overall neutral charge. Examples of coordination compounds are: $[Pt(NH_3)_2Cl_2]$, $K_2[Mn(C_2O_4)_3]$, and $[Ni(H_2O)_6]SO_4$.

When writing formulas, the metal (central atom) is *always* listed first within the brackets. However, when writing names, the metal name is *always* given last. Any material not listed within the brackets is named separately.

Examples:

| | |
|---|---|
| $[Ru(NH_3)_5(N_2)]Cl_2$ | coordination compound |
| $[Ru(NH_3)_5(N_2)]^{2+}$ | complex ion (cationic) |
| $[PtNH_3Cl_2(C_5H_5N)]$ | coordination compound |
| $[IF_6]^-$ | complex ion (anionic) (the name must end in *ate*) |
| $K[IF_6]$ | coordination compound (same *ate* ending) |

If everything in the formula is enclosed within one set of brackets, the entire name will be one word. If there is material outside the brackets, this outside material is named separately.

Just as with simpler compounds, cations are always named before anions. Thus, a cationic complex would be the first word in the name, and an anionic complex would be the last word in a name (with an *ate* ending).

Examples:

| | |
|---|---|
| $[Ni(H_2O)_4Cl_2]$ | tetraaquadichloronickel(II) |
| $[Co(NH_3)_6]Cl_3$ | hexaamminecobalt(III) chloride |
| $K_2[PtCl_4]$ | potassium tetrachloroplatinate(II) |

When naming a complex, or when writing the formula for a complex, the ligands are listed alphabetically. Again, do not forget that metals are first in the formula and last in the name.

The names of anionic ligands always end in an *o*, and neutral ligands basically remain unchanged. Two common exceptions in the case of neutral ligands are $NH_3$ = ammine (note the double *m*) and $H_2O$ = aqua. Other common ligands and their names are listed in the appendixes.

Multiple identical ligands have prefixes added to designate the number of such ligands:

| | | | | | |
|---|---|---|---|---|---|
| 2 | di- | 5 | penta- | 8 | octa- |
| 3 | tri- | 6 | hexa- | 9 | nona- |
| 4 | tetra- | 7 | hepta- | 10 | deca- |

Examples:

| | |
|---|---|
| $[Co(NH_3)_6]Cl_3$ | hexaamminecobalt(III) chloride |
| $[Cr(NO)_4]$ | tetranitrosylchromium(0) |

If the ligand name contains a prefix or begins with a vowel (except ammine and aqua), alternative prefixes should be used:

| | | | | | |
|---|---|---|---|---|---|
| 2 | bis- | 5 | pentakis- | 8 | octakis- |
| 3 | tris- | 6 | hexakis- | 9 | nonakis- |
| 4 | tetrakis- | 7 | heptakis- | 10 | decakis- |

When using the alternative prefixes, it is common practice to enclose the name of the ligand within parentheses. Either type of prefix is added after the ligands have been alphabetized.

Examples:

| | |
|---|---|
| $[Cr(en)_3]Cl_3$ | Tris(ethylenediamine)chromium(III) chloride |
| $K_2[Ge(C_2O_4)_3]$ | Potassium tris(oxalato)germanate |

Anionic complexes always have names ending in *ate*. This will require a change in the name of the metal. Thus, aluminum would become aluminate, and zinc would become zincate. The only exceptions to this are some of the metals whose symbols are based on Latin or Greek names. These exceptions are:

| **Metal (Greek or Latin name)** | **Symbol** | **Anionic name** |
|---|---|---|
| copper (cuprum) | Cu | cuprate |
| silver (argentum) | Ag | argentate |
| gold (aurum) | Au | aurate |
| iron (ferrum) | Fe | ferrate |
| tin (stannum) | Sn | stannate |
| lead (plumbum) | Pb | plumbate |

Examples:

$K[Au(CN)_4]$ potassium tetracyanoaurate(III)

$(NH_4)_2[PbCl_6]$ ammonium hexachloroplumbate(IV)

If the metal ion may exist in more than one oxidation state, this oxidation state should be listed, in Roman numerals, *immediately* after the name of the metal ion. The Roman numeral is enclosed in parentheses and is considered part of the same word, and not a separate grouping. If the metal occurs in only one oxidation state, no such indicator is used. This notation is the Stock system discussed earlier.

## Experiments

STRATEGY

Experiments involving the basic material covered in this chapter have been placed in the in-depth chapters throughout the remainder of this book.

## Common Mistakes to Avoid

TIP

Between the two of us, we have 70+ years of teaching experience. We've seen a lot of student mistakes. We will try to steer you clear of the most common ones.

1. Always show your units in mathematical problems.
2. No degree sign is used for kelvin.
3. Only consider measured values for significant figures.
4. When considering whether or not zeroes to the right of the last nonzero digit are significant, pay attention to whether or not there is a decimal point.
5. Round off only your final answer, not intermediate calculations.
6. In working problems, be sure that your units cancel.
7. If you are solving for cm, for example, be sure you end up with cm and not 1/cm.
8. Make sure your answer is a reasonable one.
9. Don't confuse the mass number ($A$) with the atomic number ($Z$).
10. When determining valence electrons, only the s and p electrons are considered.
11. Don't put more than 2 electrons in any individual orbital.
12. Always fill the lowest energy levels first.
13. Half filled orbitals of equal energy before pairing up the electrons.
14. In writing the electronic configuration of an atom, make sure you use the correct filling order (Aufbau principle).
15. Don't confuse the periods with the groups on the periodic table.
16. Don't confuse ionization energy with electron affinity.
17. Don't confuse oxidation numbers with ionic charge.
18. In naming compounds, don't confuse metal and nonmetal type binary compounds. Prefixes are used only with nonmetal types.
19. Be careful when using the crisscross rule to reduce the subscripts to their lowest whole-number ratio.
20. Be sure to report the proper number of significant figures. Never do a calculator dump (write down a long series of numbers from your calculator's display).
21. Simply knowing a periodic trend will allow you to pick the correct multiple-choice answer; however, you should be prepared to explain the trend in free-response questions.

## › Review Questions

Here are questions you can use to review the content of this chapter and practice for the AP Chemistry Exam. First are 26 multiple-choice questions primarily designed to test your background. Most of these questions test "prior knowledge" to remind you of the basics. Following those is a four-part free-response question like the ones in Section II of the exam. To make these questions an even more authentic practice for the actual exam, time yourself following the instructions provided.

### Multiple-Choice Questions

Answer the following questions in 40 minutes. You may not use a calculator. You may use the periodic table and the equation sheet at the back of this book.

**1.** Which of the following usually exists as a monatomic anion in most of its compounds?

(A) Fe
(B) Ne
(C) F
(D) Na

**2.** A magnesium compound has the general formula $MgXO_3$. X may be which of the following elements?

(A) C
(B) Cl
(C) P
(D) Na

**3.** Which of the following elements may occur in the greatest number of different oxidation states?

(A) C
(B) F
(C) O
(D) Ca

**4.** Choose the group that does NOT contain isotopes of the same element.

| GROUP | | NUMBER OF PROTONS | NUMBER OF NEUTRONS |
|---|---|---|---|
| (A) | Atom I | 18 | 18 |
| | Atom II | 18 | 19 |
| (B) | Atom I | 25 | 30 |
| | Atom II | 25 | 31 |
| (C) | Atom I | 37 | 42 |
| | Atom II | 37 | 41 |
| (D) | Atom I | 82 | 126 |
| | Atom II | 81 | 126 |

**5.** Which of the following groups has the species correctly listed in order of increasing radius?

(A) $Mg^{2+}$, $Ca^{2+}$, $Ba^{2+}$
(B) $K^+$, $Na^+$, $Li^+$
(C) $Br^-$, $Cl^-$, $F^-$
(D) Na, Mg, Al

**6.** Which of the following elements has the lowest electronegativity?

(A) C
(B) K
(C) Al
(D) I

**7.** Choose the ion with the largest ionic radius.

(A) $F^-$
(B) $Al^{3+}$
(C) $K^+$
(D) $I^-$

**8.** What is the name of the energy change when a gaseous atom, in the ground state, adds an electron?

(A) ionization energy
(B) sublimation energy
(C) atomization energy
(D) electron affinity

9. The following ionization energies are reported for element *X*. (All the values are in kJ $mol^{-1}$.)

| FIRST | SECOND | THIRD | FOURTH | FIFTH |
|---|---|---|---|---|
| 500 | 4,560 | 6,910 | 9,540 | 13,400 |

Based on the above information, the most likely identity of *X* is:

(A) Mg
(B) Cl
(C) Al
(D) Na

10. In general, as the atomic number increases within a period, the atomic radius:

(A) decreases
(B) increases
(C) first decreases and then increases
(D) does not change

11. Which of the following elements is a reactive gas?

(A) chlorine
(B) gold
(C) sodium
(D) radon

12. Which of the following elements is an unreactive metal?

(A) fluorine
(B) gold
(C) potassium
(D) argon

13. Which of the following represents the correct formula for potassium trisoxalatoferrate(III)?

(A) $P_3[Fe(C_2O_4)_3]$
(B) $K_3[Fe(C_2O_4)_3]$
(C) $KFe_3(C_2O_4)_3$
(D) $K_3[Fe_3(C_2O_4)_3]$

14. Which of the following substances will produce a colorless aqueous solution?

(A) $Zn(NO_3)_2$
(B) $CuSO_4$
(C) $K_2Cr_2O_7$
(D) $Co(NO_3)_2$

15. Which of the following compounds is the most likely to be ionic?

(A) $CH_4$
(B) $SiO_2$
(C) $Cs_2S$
(D) $XeF_2$

16. If the name of a binary compound, a compound containing only two elements, contains a multiplying prefix, such as *di-* or *tri-*, then the compound is most likely:

(A) ionic
(B) molecular
(C) metallic
(D) unstable

17. What is the symbol for the element that forms a protective oxide coating?

(A) K
(B) Ga
(C) Al
(D) Mg

18. Which of the following elements is important in the semiconductor industry to improve the conductivity of germanium, Ge?

(A) K
(B) Ga
(C) Al
(D) Mg

19. Which of the following aqueous solutions is blue?

(A) $CuSO_4$
(B) $Cr_2(SO_4)_3$
(C) $NiSO_4$
(D) $ZnSO_4$

20. To separate two substances by fractional crystallization, the two substances must differ in which of the following?

(A) solubility
(B) specific gravity
(C) vapor pressure
(D) viscosity

**21.** Bromine forms a series of acids like the series formed by chlorine. Which of the following series of bromine acids list the acids in order of increasing amount of oxygen present?

(A) bromous acid, hypobromous acid, perbromic acid, bromic acid
(B) bromous acid, bromic acid, hypobromous acid, perbromic acid
(C) perbromic acid, bromic acid, bromous acid, hypobromous acid
(D) hypobromous acid, bromous acid, bromic acid, perbromic acid

**22.** What should you do if you spill sulfuric acid on the countertop?

(A) Neutralize the acid with vinegar.
(B) Sprinkle solid NaOH on the spill.
(C) Neutralize the acid with $NaHCO_3$ solution.
(D) Neutralize the acid with an Epsom salt ($MgSO_4$) solution.

**23.** Which of the following can be achieved by using a visible-light spectrophotometer?

(A) running a flame test to determine if $Na^+$ or $K^+$ is in a solution
(B) finding the concentration of a $KMnO_4$ solution
(C) detecting the presence of isolated double bonds
(D) measuring the strength of a covalent bond

**24.** You have an aqueous solution of NaCl. The simplest method for separating NaCl from the solution is:

(A) evaporating the solution to dryness
(B) centrifuging the solution
(C) filtering the solution
(D) electrolyzing the solution

**25.** Which of the following anion/acid name pairs is incorrect?

(A) fluoride/fluoric acid
(B) nitrate/nitric acid
(C) sulfite/sulfurous acid
(D) sulfide/hydrosulfurous acid

**26.** A book has a mass of 2.7 kg on the earth. The same book weighs 6.0 pounds. The book is transported to the moon, where the gravity is 1/6 that on the surface of the earth. The book now weighs 1.0 pound. What is the mass of the book on the moon?

(A) The mass will be 0.45 kg.
(B) The mass will be 16 kg.
(C) The mass will be the same as on the earth.
(D) There is no way to know what the mass is.

## › Answers and Explanations

**1. C**—Most of the other elements are metals. Metals usually form monatomic cations. Neon, Ne, a noble gas, normally does not form ions. Fluorine, the only nonmetal, forms anions.

**2. A**—This question checks your prior knowledge of nomenclature. The element cannot be another metal (Na). The polyatomic ion must be $XO_3^{2-}$. Of the choices, only carbon gives a polyatomic ion with this general formula. The carbonate ion has the formula $CO_3^{2-}$. The polyatomic ions formed by the other nonmetals present are the chlorate ion, $ClO_3^-$, and the phosphite ion, $PO_3^{3-}$, neither of which has the charge necessary (−2).

**3. A**—Based on their positions on the periodic table:

| | |
|---|---|
| C | +4 to −4 |
| F | −1 and 0 (element) |
| O | −2 to 0 |
| Ca | +2 and 0 |

**4. D**—Isotopes MUST have the same number of protons, which makes D the correct answer. Different isotopes of an element have different numbers of neutrons.

**5. A**—All the others are listed in order of decreasing radius. Ions in the same column and with the same charge increase in size when going down a column the same as atoms. Atoms in the same row increase in size toward the left side. This argument is not adequate for the free-response portion of the exam, where explanations are needed instead of referring to trends.

**6. B**—In general, the element farthest from F on the periodic table will have the lowest electronegativity. There are exceptions, but you normally do not need to concern yourself with exceptions on the AP Exam.

**7. D**—The very large iodine atom (near the bottom of the periodic table) gains an electron to make it even larger. This reasoning is not adequate for the free-response portion of the exam.

**8. D**—The definition of electron affinity is the energy change when a ground-state gaseous atom adds an electron. Definitions will not appear directly on the AP Exam; however, if you do not know a definition, you may not understand a question.

**9. D**—The more electrons removed, the higher the values should be. The large increase between the first and second ionization energies indicates a change in electron shell. The element *X* has only 1 valence electron. This is true for Na. For the other elements, the numbers of valence electrons are as follows: Mg, 2; Cl, 7; and Al, 3.

**10. A**—An increase in the number of protons in the nucleus has a greater attraction (greater effective nuclear charge) for the electrons being added in the same energy level. Thus, the electrons are pulled closer to the nucleus, and the size slightly decreases. This thought process should be used on the free-response portion of the AP exam; however, simply remembering that radii decrease across a period is adequate for most multiple-choice questions.

**11. A**—The only other gas is radon (D), and it is inert. B and C are metals.

**12. B**—Potassium is a metal on the left side of the periodic table. Metals on the left side of the periodic table are very reactive. Argon (D) and fluorine (A) are gases, not metals.

**13. B**—*Ferrate(III)* means $Fe^{3+}$, while *trisoxalato* means $(C_2O_4)_3^{6-}$; three potassium atoms are needed to balance the charge. This is another chance to check your nomenclature.

**14. A**—B is blue; C is orange; and D is pink to red.

**15. C**—This is the only choice containing both a metal and a nonmetal. Compounds containing a metal and a nonmetal are usually ionic. The other compounds, which contain a nonmetal or metalloid and a nonmetal, are usually molecular (covalent).

**16. B**—Prefixes are commonly used when naming molecular compounds. Some examples are carbon dioxide, $CO_2$, and dibromine trioxide, $Br_2O_3$.

**17. C**—Aluminum forms a protective oxide coating.

**18. B**—Gallium, adjacent to Ge on the periodic table, is one of the elements that will improve the conductivity of germanium. The result is a p-type semiconductor.

**19. A**—B is purple; C is green; and D is colorless.

**20. A**—Fractional crystallization works because the less soluble material separates first.

**21. D**—The acids are hypobromous acid, $HBrO$; bromous acid, $HBrO_2$; bromic acid, $HBrO_3$; perbromic acid, $HBrO_4$.

**22. C**—Adding a weak base solution, such as $NaHCO_3$, which will not only neutralize the acid but help disperse the heat, is the best choice.

**23. B**—A solution containing a colored substance is necessary. A $KMnO_4$ solution is intense purple.

**24. A**—Separating materials in solution is normally not simple; therefore, removing the solvent through evaporation is the best choice.

**25. A**—Fluoride, $F^-$, yields hydrofluoric acid, HF. B refers to $NO_3^-$ and $HNO_3$. C refers to $SO_3^{2-}$ and $H_2SO_3$. D refers to $S^{2-}$ and $H_2S$.

**26. C**—Weight depends upon the mass of an object and gravitational attraction. Weight varies as gravity varies. Mass, on the other hand, does not depend on gravity. Mass is fixed, which is why there is a Law of Conservation of Mass but not a Law of Conservation of Weight.

## › Free-Response Question

*Both authors have been AP free-response graders for years. Here is a free-response question for practice.*

You have 10 minutes to answer the following question. You may use a calculator and the tables in the back of the book.

**Question**

Use the periodic table and other information concerning bonding and electronic structure to explain the following observations.

(a) The radii of iron cations are less than those of iron atoms, and $Fe^{3+}$ is smaller than $Fe^{2+}$.
(b) Write the electron configurations of Fe, $Fe^{2+}$, and $Fe^{3+}$.
(c) When moving across the periodic table from Li to Be to B, the first ionization energy increases from Li to Be, then drops for B. The first ionization energy of B is greater than that of Li.
(d) The electron affinity of F is higher than the electron affinity of O.
(e) The following observations have been made about the lattice energy and ionic radii of the compounds listed below. Compare NaF to CaO, and then compare CaO to BaO. All solids adopt the same crystal structure.

| Compound | Ionic radius of cation (pm) | Ionic radius of anion (pm) | Lattice energy (kJ/mole) |
|---|---|---|---|
| NaF | 116 | 119 | 911 |
| CaO | 114 | 126 | 3,566 |
| BaO | 149 | 126 | 3,202 |

## › Answer and Explanation

Notice that all the answers are very short. Do not try to fill all the space provided on the exam. You score points by saying specific things, not by the amount of material. The graders look for certain keywords or phrases. The answers should not contain statements that contradict each other; otherwise, there may be a penalty. Contradictions most commonly occur when the student tries to say too much. On the AP Exam, the different parts of the free-response questions tend to be more diverse than this one, as this question focuses only on this chapter, whereas the AP free-response questions focus on the entire course.

(a) The observed trend of radii is Fe > $Fe^{2+}$ > $Fe^{3+}$. There is an increase in the effective nuclear charge in this series. As electrons are removed, the repulsion between the remaining electrons decreases. The decrease in electron repulsion leads to an increase in the effective nuclear charge. The greater the effective nuclear charge, the greater the attraction of the electrons toward the nucleus and the smaller the atom or ion becomes.

Give yourself 1 point for the effective nuclear charge and give yourself 1 point for the remainder of the discussion.

(b) The electron configurations are Fe $1s^22s^22p^63s^23p^64s^23d^6$, $Fe^{2+}$ $1s^22s^22p^63s^23p^63d^6$, and $Fe^{3+}$ $1s^22s^22p^63s^23p^63d^5$. It is possible to condense the configurations to Fe $[Ar]4s^23d^6$, $Fe^{2+}$ $[Ar]3d^6$, and $Fe^{3+}$ $[Ar]3d^5$. Do not forget that electrons from the outer shell are always removed first. For iron, the outer shell is 4.

Give yourself 1 point for each correct electron configuration.

(c) When moving across a period on the periodic table, the value of the effective nuclear charge increases with atomic number. This causes a general increase from Li to Be to B. DO NOT use the argument that ionization energies increase to the right on the periodic table unless you also discuss effective nuclear charge.

The even higher value of Be (greater than B) is due to the increased stability of the electron configuration of Be. Beryllium has a filled s subshell. Filled subshells have an increased stability, and additional energy is required to pull an electron away.

Give yourself 0 points if you say that the ionization energy increases to the right on the periodic table. This is an observation, not an explanation. The effective nuclear charge argument is worth 1 point. Give yourself 1 more point for the filled subshell discussion.

On the AP Exam, this will most likely be a question involving PES (photoelectron spectroscopy), which we have not covered yet.

(d) The effective nuclear charge in F is greater than the effective nuclear charge in O. This causes a greater attraction of the electrons. DO NOT use the argument that electron affinity increases to the right on the periodic table unless you also discuss effective nuclear charge.

You get 1 point for the effective nuclear charge answer.

(e) Because all these solids adopt the same structure, the structure is irrelevant. The sizes of the anions are similar; thus, anion size arguments are not important. Two factors, other than structure and anion size, are important here. The two compounds with the highest lattice energies contain divalent ions (+2 or −2), whereas NaF contains univalent ions (+1 or −1). The higher the charge is, the greater the attraction between the ions is. The lattice energy increases as the attraction increases.

The difference between the CaO and BaO values occurs because the larger the ion is, the lower the attraction is (greater separation). The lower attraction leads to a lower lattice energy.

You get 1 point for correctly discussing the charges. A correct size argument will get you 1 more point.

Total your points. There are 10 points possible.

## ❯ Rapid Review

Here is a brief review of the most important points in the chapter. If something sounds unfamiliar, study it in the chapter and your textbook.

- Know the metric measurement system and some metric/English conversions.
- The density of a substance is mass per unit volume.
- Know how to determine the number of significant figures in a number, the rules for how many significant figures are to be shown in the final answer, and the round-off rules.
- Know how to set up problems using the factor label method.
- Know the differences between a solid, a liquid, and a gas at both the macroscopic and microscopic levels.
- Know the three basic subatomic particles—proton, neutron, and electron—their symbols, mass in amu, and their location.

- Isotopes are atoms of the same element that have differing numbers of neutrons.
- Electrons are located in energy levels called shells. Shells are divided into subshells, and there are orbitals for each subshell.
- Know the electron capacity of each orbital (always 2).
- Be able to write both the energy-level diagram and the electronic configuration of an atom or ion by applying both the Aufbau build-up principle and Hund's rule.
- Know how the modern periodic table was developed, including the differences between Mendeleev's table and the current table.
- Periods are the horizontal rows on the periodic table; the elements have properties unlike the other members of the period.
- Groups or families are the vertical rows on the periodic table; the elements have similar properties.
- Know the properties of metals, nonmetals, and metalloids and which elements on the periodic table belong to each group.
- Valence electrons are outer-shell electrons.
- The 1A family is known as the alkali metals; the 2As are the alkaline earth metals; the 7As are the halogens; and the 8As are the noble gases.
- Know why atoms get larger as we go from top to bottom in a group and slightly smaller as we move from left to right on the periodic table. Remember that on the free-response section, simply quoting a trend is not answering the question. This is true for all trends.
- Ionization energy is the energy it takes to remove an electron from a gaseous atom or ion. Ionization energy trends to decrease from top to bottom and increases from left to right on the periodic table. Much the same trend is noted for electron affinity, the energy change that takes place when an electron is added to a gaseous atom or ion. The trends depend on the size of the atom or ion and its effective nuclear charge. As trends they may help you on multiple-choice questions, but they are less likely to help on the free-response questions.
- Oxidation numbers are bookkeeping numbers. Know the rules for assigning oxidation numbers.
- Be able to name binary metal type and nonmetal type compounds, as well as ternary compounds, oxyacids, simple coordination compounds, etc.

CHAPTER 6

# Stoichiometry

**IN THIS CHAPTER**

In this chapter, the following AP topics are covered:

1.1 Moles and Molar Mass
1.3 Elemental Composition of Pure Substances
3.7 Solutions and Mixtures
3.8 Representations of Solutions
4.1 Introduction for Reactions
4.5 Stoichiometry

**Summary:** The previous chapter on chemical reactions discussed reactants and products in terms of individual atoms and molecules. But an industrial chemist is not interested in the number of molecules being produced; she or he is interested in kilograms or pounds or tons of products being formed per hour or day. How many kilograms of reactants will it take? How many kilograms of products will be formed? These are the questions of interest. A production chemist is interested primarily in the macroscopic world, not the microscopic one of atoms and molecules. Even a chemistry student working in the laboratory will not be weighing out individual atoms and molecules but measuring large numbers of them in grams. There must be a way to bridge the gap between the microscopic world of individual atoms and molecules, and the macroscopic world of grams and kilograms. There is—it is called the mole concept, and it is one of the central concepts in the world of chemistry.

**Keywords and Equations**

KEY IDEA

Avogadro's number = $6.022 \times 10^{23}$ $mol^{-1}$
Molarity, $M$ = moles solute per liter solution
$n$ = moles
$\boldsymbol{M}$ = molar mass
$m$ = mass

$$n = \frac{m}{\boldsymbol{M}}$$

## Moles and Molar Mass

The **mole** (**mol**) is the amount of a substance that contains the same number of particles as atoms in exactly 12 grams of carbon-12. This number of particles (atoms or molecules or ions) per mole is called **Avogadro's number** and is numerically equal to $6.022 \times 10^{23}$ particles. (While this value is important to the understanding of chemistry, you will probably never see this value directly on the AP Chemistry Exam or any other standardized exam.) The mole is simply a term that represents a certain number of particles, like a dozen or a pair. That relates moles to the microscopic world, but what about the macroscopic world? The mole also represents a certain mass of a chemical substance. That mass is the substance's atomic or molecular mass expressed in grams. In Chapter 5, the Basics chapter, we described the atomic mass of an element in terms of atomic mass units (amu). This was the mass associated with an individual atom. Then we described how one could calculate the mass of a compound by simply adding together the masses, in amu, of the individual elements in the compound. This is still the case, but at the macroscopic level the unit of grams is used to represent the quantity of a mole. Thus, the following relationships apply:

KEY IDEA

$$6.022 \times 10^{23} \text{ particles} = 1 \text{ mol}$$
$$= \text{atomic (molecular, formula) mass in grams}$$

The mass in grams of one mole of a substance is the **molar mass.**

The relationship above gives a way of converting from grams to moles to particles, and vice versa. If you have any one of the three quantities, you can calculate the other two. This becomes extremely useful in working with chemical equations, as we will see later, because the coefficients in the balanced chemical equation are not only the number of individual atoms or molecules at the microscopic level but also the number of moles at the macroscopic level.

How many moles are present in $1.50 \times 10^{29}$ helium atoms?

Answer:

$$(1.50 \times 10^{29} \text{ He atoms})\left(\frac{1 \text{ mol He atoms}}{6.022 \times 10^{23} \text{ He atoms}}\right) = 2.49 \times 10^{5} \text{ mol He}$$

## Percent Composition and Empirical Formulas

If the formula of a compound is known, it is a simple task to determine the percent composition of each element in the compound. For example, suppose you want to calculate the percentage of hydrogen and oxygen in water, $H_2O$. First calculate the molecular mass of water:

$$1 \text{ mol } H_2O = 2 \text{ mol H} + 1 \text{ mol O}$$

Substituting the masses involved:

$$1 \text{ mol } H_2O = 2\ (1.0079 \text{ g/mol}) + 16.00 \text{ g/mol} = 18.0158 \text{ g/mol}$$

(intermediate calculation—don't worry about significant figures yet)

Percentage hydrogen = [mass H/mass $H_2O$] × 100%

$$= \frac{2(1.0079 \text{ g/mol})}{18.0158 \text{ g/mol}} \times 100\%$$

$$= 11.19\% \text{ H}$$

Percentage oxygen = [mass O/mass $H_2O$] × 100%

$$= \left(\frac{(16.00 \text{ g/mol})}{18.0158 \text{ g/mol}}\right) \times 100\%$$

$$= 88.81\% \text{ O}$$

Compare this to the percent composition of hydrogen peroxide, $H_2O_2$, which is 5.93% H and 94.07% O. (You may want to prove these numbers for yourself.)

As a good check, add the percentages together. They must sum to 100% or be very close to it.

Determine the mass percent of each of the elements in cane sugar, $C_{12}H_{22}O_{11}$. Formula mass (FM) = 342.34 amu

Answer:

$$\%\text{C} = \frac{(12 \text{ C atoms})(12.01 \text{ amu/atom})}{(342.34 \text{ amu})} \times 100\% = 42.10\%$$

$$\%\text{H} = \frac{(22 \text{ H atoms})(1.01 \text{ amu/atom})}{(342.34 \text{ amu})} \times 100\% = 6.49\%$$

$$\%\text{O} = \frac{(11 \text{ O atoms})(16.00 \text{ amu/atom})}{(342.34 \text{ amu})} \times 100\% = 51.41\%$$

Total = 100.00%

The total is a check. It should be *very* close to 100%. (You may wish to prove to yourself that the significant figures are correct.)

In the problems above, the percentage data was calculated from the chemical formula, but the empirical formula can be determined if the percent compositions of the various elements are known. The **empirical formula** tells us what elements are present in the compound and the simplest whole-number ratio of elements. The data may be in terms of percentage, or mass, or even moles. But the procedure is still the same: convert each component to moles, divide each by the smallest number, and then use an appropriate multiplier if needed. The empirical formula mass can then be calculated. If the actual molecular mass is known, dividing the molecular mass by the empirical formula mass gives an integer (rounded if needed) that is used to multiply each of the subscripts in the empirical formula. This gives the **molecular (actual) formula**, which tells which elements are in the compound and the actual number of each. (Note: The percent composition of the empirical formula is identical to the percent composition of the molecular formula.)

For example, a sample of an unstable gas was analyzed and found to contain 2.70 g of carbon and 15.95 g of chlorine. The molar mass of the gas was determined to be about 160 g/mol. What are the empirical and molecular formulas of this gas?

Answer:

$$(2.70 \text{ g C})\left(\frac{1 \text{ mol C}}{12.01 \text{ g C}}\right) = 0.225 \text{ mol C} \qquad \left(\frac{0.225}{0.225}\right) = 1 \text{ C}$$

$$(15.95 \text{ g Cl})\left(\frac{1 \text{ mol Cl}}{35.45 \text{ g Cl}}\right) = 0.4499 \text{ mol Cl} \qquad \left(\frac{0.4449}{0.225}\right) = 2 \text{ Cl}$$

$$\therefore \text{ Empirical formula} = \text{CCl}_2$$

The molecular formula may be determined by dividing the actual molar mass of the compound by the empirical molar mass. In this case, the empirical molar mass is about 83 g/mol. Thus $\left(\frac{160\text{ g/mol}}{83\text{ g/mol}}\right) = 1.936$ which, to one significant figure, is 2. Therefore, the molecular formula is twice the empirical formula—$C_2Cl_4$.

Be sure to use as many significant digits as possible in the molar masses. Failure to do so may give you erroneous ratio and empirical formulas. Note that the multiplier (2 in this example) must be an integer.

## Introduction to Reactions

Matter undergoes many types of changes. Simplistically, these changes may be labelled as **physical changes** or **chemical changes**. In principle, all physical changes are reversible. For example, a simple change in temperature may cause water to undergo a physical change from solid ice to liquid water or vice versa. However, if you grind some salt into a fine powder, a physical change occurs, but it is one that is not easy to reverse. While these two examples are very different, these physical changes and others are characterized by no change in the composition of the substance. Water is $H_2O$, no matter if it is ice, liquid water, or steam. Interconversion of the phases of water are known as phase changes. The properties may change during a physical change but not the composition.

Chemical changes involve a change in composition and usually cannot be reversed. For example, you cannot revers the chemical change that occurs when you burn a lump of charcoal. A chemical change may involve one substance such as in Priestley's discovery by decomposing mercury(II) oxide to the mercury and oxygen by heating. Other chemical changes, often called chemical reactions, involve multiple substances. For example, the interactions of substance from food and from the air to keep you alive. In a chemical change, the conversion of substances to other substances (possibly accompanied by a phase change) may be accompanied by production of heat and/or light. Chemical changes may be described symbolically by a chemical equation. In Chapter 15, Equilibrium, you will see that some chemical changes are reversible.

The Law of Conservation of Mass is obeyed by both physical and chemical changes.

## Reaction Stoichiometry

As we have discussed previously, the balanced chemical equation not only indicates which chemical species are the reactants and the products but also indicates the relative ratio of reactants and products. Consider the balanced equation of the initial step in the Ostwald process—the burning of ammonia:

$$4\ NH_3(g) + 5\ O_2(g) \rightarrow 4\ NO(g) + 6\ H_2O(g)$$

This balanced equation can be read as: *4 ammonia molecules react with 5 oxygen molecules to produce 4 nitrogen oxide molecules and 6 water molecules.* But as indicated previously, the coefficients can stand not only for the number of atoms or molecules (microscopic level), but they can also stand for the number of *moles* of reactants or products. The equation can also be read as: *4 moles ammonia react with 5 moles oxygen to produce 4 moles nitrogen oxide and 6 moles water.* And if the number of moles is known, the number of grams or molecules can be calculated. This is **stoichiometry**, the calculation of the amount (mass, moles, particles) of one substance in a chemical reaction using another substance. The coefficients in a balanced chemical equation define the mathematical relationship between the reactants and products, and this allows the conversion from moles of one chemical species in the reaction to another.

STRATEGY

Consider the Ostwald process above. How many moles of ammonia are necessary to react completely with 15.0 mol of oxygen?

Before any stoichiometry calculation can be done, you must have a balanced chemical equation!

You are starting with moles of oxygen and want moles of ammonia, so we'll convert from moles of oxygen to moles of ammonia by using the ratio of moles of oxygen to moles of ammonia as defined by the balanced chemical equation:

$$\frac{15.0 \text{ mol } O_2}{1} \times \frac{4 \text{ mol } NH_3}{5 \text{ mol } O_2} = 12.0 \text{ mol } NH_3$$

The ratio of 4 mol $NH_3$ to 5 mol $O_2$ is called the stoichiometric ratio and comes from the balanced chemical equation.

Suppose you also wanted to know how many moles of nitrogen oxide would form from the complete reaction of 15.0 mol of oxygen. Just change the stoichiometric ratio:

$$\frac{15.0 \text{ mol } O_2}{1} \times \frac{4 \text{ mol NO}}{5 \text{ mol } O_2} = 12.0 \text{ mol NO}$$

Notice that this new stoichiometric ratio also came from the balanced chemical equation.

Suppose instead of moles you had grams and wanted an answer in grams. How many grams of ammonia would react with 85.0 g of oxygen gas?

TIP

In working problems that involve something other than moles, you will still need moles. And you will need the balanced chemical equation.

In this problem we will convert from grams of oxygen to moles of oxygen to moles of ammonia using the correct stoichiometric ratio, and finally to grams of ammonia. And we will need the molar mass of $O_2$ (32.00 g/mol) and ammonia (17.03 g/mol):

$$\frac{85.0 \text{ g } O_2}{1} \times \frac{1 \text{ mol } O_2}{32.00 \text{ g } O_2} \times \frac{4 \text{ mol } NH_3}{5 \text{ mol } O_2} \times \frac{17.03 \text{ g}}{1 \text{ mol } NH_3} = 36.2 \text{ g } NH_3$$

As an alternative, you could have calculated the number of ammonia molecules reacted if you had gone from moles of ammonia to molecules (using Avogadro's number):

$$\frac{85.0 \text{ g } O_2}{1} \times \frac{1 \text{ mol } O_2}{32.00 \text{ g } O_2} \times \frac{4 \text{ mol } NH_3}{5 \text{ mol } O_2} \times \frac{6.022 \times 10^{23} \text{ molecules } NH_3}{1 \text{ mol } NH_3}$$

$$= 1.28 \times 10^{24} \text{ molecules } NH_3$$

In the following reaction, 25.0 g of $H_2$ and excess Na are combined to produce NaH. How many grams of NaH will form?

$$2 \text{ Na(s)} + H_2\text{(g)} \rightarrow 2 \text{ NaH(s)}$$

$$\text{Answer: } (25.0 \text{ g } H_2)\left(\frac{1 \text{ mol } H_2}{2.02 \text{ g } H_2}\right)\left(\frac{2 \text{ mol NaH}}{1 \text{ mol } H_2}\right)\left(\frac{24.00 \text{ g NaH}}{1 \text{ mol NaH}}\right) = 594 \text{ g NaH}$$

## Limiting Reactants

In the examples above, one reactant was present in excess. One reactant was completely consumed, and some of the other reactant was left over. The reactant that is used up first is called the **limiting reactant** (LR). This reactant really determines the amount of product being formed. How is the limiting reactant determined? You can't assume it is the reactant in the smallest amount, since the reaction stoichiometry must be considered. There are generally two ways to determine which reactant is the limiting reactant:

1. Each reactant, in turn, is assumed to be the limiting reactant, and the amount of product that would be formed is calculated. The reactant that yields the *smallest* amount of product is the limiting reactant. The advantage of this method is that you get to practice your calculation skills; the disadvantage is that you must do more calculations.
2. The moles of reactant per coefficient of that reactant in the balanced chemical equation is calculated. The reactant that has the smallest mole-to-coefficient ratio is the limiting reactant. This is the method that many people use.

Let us consider the Haber reaction. Suppose that 25.0 g of nitrogen and 10.0 g of hydrogen react according to the following equation. Calculate the number of grams of ammonia that could be formed.

First, write the balanced chemical equation:

$$N_2(g) + 3\ H_2(g) \rightarrow 2\ NH_3(g)$$

Next, convert the grams of each reactant to moles:

$$\frac{25.0\ g\ N_2}{1} \times \frac{1\ mol\ N_2}{28.01\ g\ N_2} = 0.892\ mol\ N_2$$

$$\frac{10.0\ g\ H_2}{1} \times \frac{1\ mol\ H_2}{2.02\ g\ H_2} = 4.95\ mol\ H_2$$

Divide each by the coefficient in the balanced chemical equation. The smaller is the limiting reactant:

For $N_2$: 0.892 mol $N_2/1$ = 0.892 mol/coefficient *limiting reactant*
For $H_2$: 4.95 mol $H_2/3$ = 1.65 mol/coefficient

Note that even though there were fewer grams of hydrogen, it was not the limiting reagent. Finally, base the stoichiometry of the reaction on the limiting reactant:

$$\frac{25.0\ g\ N_2}{1} \times \frac{1\ mol\ N_2}{28.01\ g\ N_2} \times \frac{2\ mol\ NH_3}{1\ mol\ N_2} \times \frac{17.03\ g}{1\ mol\ NH_3} = 30.4\ g\ NH_3$$

**Anytime the quantities of more than one reactant are given, it is probably an LR problem.**

Let's consider another case. To carry out the following reaction: $As_2O_3(s) + 3H_2O(l) \rightarrow 2H_3AsO_3(aq)$, 125 g of $As_2O_3$ and 50.0 g of $H_3O$ were supplied. How many grams of $H_3AsO_3$ may be produced?

Answer:

1. Convert to moles:

$$(125\ g\ As_2O_3)\left(\frac{1\ mol\ As_2O_3}{197.84\ g\ As_2O_3}\right) = 0.632\ mol\ As_2O_3$$

$$(50.0\ g\ H_2O)\left(\frac{1\ mol\ H_2O}{18.02\ g\ H_2O}\right) = 2.77\ mol\ H_2O$$

2. Find the limiting reactant:

$$\frac{0.632\ \text{mol}}{1\ \text{mol}} = 0.632\ \text{mol As}_2\text{O}_3$$

$$\frac{2.77\ \text{mol}}{3\ \text{mol}} = 0.923\ \text{mol H}_2\text{O}$$

The 1 mol and the 3 mol come from the balanced chemical equation. The 0.6320 is smaller, so this is the LR.

3. Finish using the number of moles of the LR:

$$(0.632\ \text{mol As}_2\text{O}_3)\left(\frac{2\ \text{mol H}_3\text{AsO}_3}{1\ \text{mol As}_2\text{O}_3}\right)\left(\frac{125.95\ \text{g H}_3\text{AsO}_3}{1\ \text{mol H}_3\text{AsO}_3}\right) = 159\ \text{g}$$

## Percent Yield

In the preceding problems, the amount of product calculated based on the limiting-reactant concept is the maximum amount of product that could be formed from the given quantity of reactants. This maximum amount of product formed is called the **theoretical yield**. However, rarely is the amount that is actually formed (the **actual yield**) the same as the theoretical yield. Normally it is less. There are many reasons for this, but the principal reason is that most reactions do not go to completion; they establish an equilibrium system (see Chapter 15, Equilibrium, for a discussion of chemical equilibrium). For whatever reason, not as much as expected is formed. The efficiency of the reaction can be judged by calculating the percent yield. The **percent yield (% yield)** is the actual yield divided by the theoretical yield, and the result is multiplied by 100% to generate percentage:

$$\%\ \text{yield} = \frac{\text{actual yield}}{\text{theoretical yield}} \times 100\%$$

Consider the problem in which it was calculated that 40.3 g $NH_3$ could be formed. Suppose that reaction was carried out, and only 34.7 g $NH_3$ was formed. What is the percent yield?

$$\%\ \text{yield} = \frac{34.7\ \text{g}}{40.3\ \text{g}} \times 100\% = 86.1\%$$

Let's consider another percent yield problem in which a 45.0-g sample of barium oxide is heated with excess hydrogen bromide to produce water and 35.2 g of barium bromide. What is the percent yield of barium bromide?

$$\text{BaO(s)} + 2\text{HBr(g)} \rightarrow \text{BaBr}_2\text{(aq)} + \text{H}_2\text{O(l)}$$

Answer:

$$(45.0\ \text{g BaO})\left(\frac{1\ \text{mol BaO}}{153.3\ \text{g BaO}}\right)\left(\frac{1\ \text{mol BaBr}_2}{1\ \text{mol BaO}}\right)\left(\frac{297.10\ \text{g BaBr}_2}{1\ \text{mol BaBr}_2}\right) = 87.2\ \text{g BaBr}_2$$

The theoretical yield is 87.2 g.

$$\%\ \text{yield} = \frac{35.2\ \text{g BaBr}_2}{87.2\ \text{g BaBr}_2} \times 100\% = 40.4\%$$

**Note**: All the units except % must cancel. This includes canceling g $BaBr_2$ with g $BaBr_2$, not simply g.

## Molarity and Solution Calculations

We discuss solutions further in Chapter 11 Solutions, but solution stoichiometry is so common on the AP Exam that we will discuss it here briefly also. **Solutions** are homogeneous mixtures composed of a **solute** (substance present in smaller amount) and a **solvent** (substance present in larger amount). If sodium chloride is dissolved in water, the NaCl is the solute and the water the solvent.

One important aspect of solutions is their **concentration**, the amount of solute dissolved in the solvent. There are numerous concentration units, some of which we will mention in Chapter 11. In this chapter, we will focus on molarity and how it relates to stoichiometry. **Molarity** (*M*) is defined as the moles of solute per liter of solution:

$$M = \frac{\text{moles solute}}{\text{liters of solution}}$$

Let's start with a simple example of calculating molarity. A solution of KCl contains 59.12 g of this compound in 200.0 mL of solution. Calculate the molarity of KCl.

Answer:

$$\frac{(59.12\text{ g KCl})\left(\dfrac{1\text{ mol KCl}}{74.55\text{ g KCl}}\right)}{(200.0\text{ mL})\left(\dfrac{1\text{ L}}{1{,}000\text{ mL}}\right)} = 3.965\text{ M KCl}$$

Knowing the volume of the solution and the molarity allows you to calculate the moles or grams of solute present.

Next, let's see how we can use molarity to calculate moles. How many moles of sodium ions are in 0.200 L of a 0.20 *M* sodium sulfate solution?

Answer:

$$\left(\frac{0.20\text{ mol }Na_2SO_4}{\text{L}}\right)(0.200\text{ L})\left(\frac{2\text{ mol }Na^+}{1\text{ mol }Na_2SO_4}\right) = 0.080\text{ mol }Na^+$$

Stoichiometry problems (including limiting-reactant problems) involving solutions can be worked in the same fashion as before, except that the volume and molarity of the solution must first be converted to moles.

If 32.50 mL of a 0.1100 *M* NaOH solution is required to titrate 50.00 mL of a phosphoric acid solution, what is the concentration of the acid? The reaction is:

$$2NaOH\ (aq) + H_3PO_4(aq) \rightarrow Na_2HPO_4(aq) + 2H_2O\ (l)$$

Answer:

$$\frac{(32.50\text{ mL})\left(\dfrac{(0.1100\text{ mol NaOH})(1\text{ mol }H_3PO_4)}{(1{,}000\text{ mL})(2\text{ mol NaOH})}\right)}{(50.00\text{ mL})\left(\dfrac{(1\text{ L})}{(1{,}000\text{ mL})}\right)} = 0.03575\ M\ H_3PO_4$$

## Experiments

STRATEGY

Stoichiometry experiments must involve moles. They nearly always use a balanced chemical equation. Measurements include initial and final masses, and initial and final volumes. Calculations may include the difference between the initial and final values (on the

AP Exam you can never measure a difference). Using the formula mass and the mass in grams, moles may be calculated (not measured). Moles may also be calculated from the volume of a solution and its molarity.

Once the moles have been calculated (they are never measured), the experiment will be based on further calculations using these moles.

## Common Mistakes to Avoid

1. Avogadro's number is $6.022 \times 10^{23}$ (not $10^{-23}$).
2. Be sure to know the difference between molecules and moles.
3. In empirical formula problems, be sure to get the lowest ratio of whole numbers.
4. In stoichiometry problems, be sure to use the *balanced chemical equation.*
5. The stoichiometric ratio comes from the *balanced chemical equation.*
6. When in doubt, convert to moles.
7. In limiting-reactant problems, don't consider just the number of grams or even moles to determine the limiting reactant. Use the mol/coefficient ratio.
8. The limiting reactant is a reactant, a chemical species to the left of the reactant arrow.
9. *Use the balanced chemical equation.*
10. Percent yield is the actual yield of a substance divided by the theoretical yield of the same substance multiplied by 100%. (Normally the actual yield is given, and the theoretical yield is calculated.)
11. Molarity is moles of *solute* per liter of *solution,* not solvent.
12. Be careful when using Avogadro's number—use it when you need or have the number of atoms, ions, or molecules.

## ❯ Review Questions

Use these questions to review the content of this chapter and practice for the AP Chemistry Exam. First are 20 multiple-choice questions similar to what you will encounter in Section I of the AP Chemistry Exam. Included are questions designed to help you review prior knowledge. Following those is a long free-response question like the ones in Section II of the exam. To make these questions an even more authentic practice for the actual exam, time yourself following the instructions provided.

### Multiple-Choice Questions

Answer the following questions in 30 minutes. You may not use a calculator. You may use the periodic table and the equation sheet at the back of this book.

1. How many milliliters of 0.100 $M$ $H_2SO_4$ are required to neutralize 50.0 mL of 0.200 $M$ KOH?

(A) 25.0 mL
(B) 30.0 mL
(C) 20.0 mL
(D) 50.0 mL

2. A sample of oxalic acid, $H_2C_2O_4$, is titrated with standard sodium hydroxide, NaOH, solution. A total of 45.20 mL of 0.1200 $M$ NaOH is required to completely neutralize 20.00 mL of the acid. What is the concentration of the acid?

(A) 0.2712 $M$
(B) 0.1200 $M$
(C) 0.1356 $M$
(D) 0.2400 $M$

**3.** A solution is prepared by mixing 50.0 mL of 0.20 *M* arsenic acid, $H_3AsO_4$, and 50.0 mL of 0.20 *M* sodium hydroxide, NaOH. Which anion is present in the highest concentration?

(A) $HAsO_4^{2-}$
(B) $OH^-$
(C) $H_2AsO_4^-$
(D) $Na^+$

**4.** $14\ H^+(aq) + 6\ Fe^{2+}(aq) + Cr_2O_7^{2-}(aq) \rightarrow 2\ Cr^{3+}(aq) + 6\ Fe^{3+}(aq) + 7\ H_2O(l)$

This reaction is used in the titration of an iron solution. What is the concentration of the iron solution if it takes 45.20 mL of 0.1000 *M* $Cr_2O_7^{2-}$ solution to titrate 50.00 mL of an acidified iron solution?

(A) 0.5424 *M*
(B) 0.1000 *M*
(C) 1.085 *M*
(D) 0.4520 *M*

**5.** Which of the following best represents the balanced net ionic equation for the reaction of silver carbonate with concentrated hydrochloric acid? Silver ions have a 1+ charge. In this reaction, all silver compounds are insoluble.

(A) $2\ AgCO_3(s) + 4\ H^+(aq) + Cl^-(aq) \rightarrow Ag_2Cl(s) + CO_2(g) + 2\ H_2O(l)$
(B) $Ag_2CO_3(s) + 2\ H^+(aq) + 2\ Cl^-(aq) \rightarrow 2\ AgCl(s) + CO_2(g) + H_2O(l)$
(C) $AgCO_3(s) + 2\ H^+(aq) \rightarrow Ag^+(aq) + CO_2(g) + H_2O(l)$
(D) $Ag_2CO_3(s) + 4\ Cl^-(aq) \rightarrow 2\ AgCl_2(s) + CO_3^{2-}(aq)$

**6.** Vanadium forms several oxides. In which of the following oxides is the vanadium-to-oxygen mass ratio 2.39:1.00?

(A) VO
(B) $V_2O_3$
(C) $V_3O_4$
(D) $VO_2$

**7.** A student takes a beaker containing 25.0 mL of 0.10 *M* magnesium nitrate, $Mg(NO_3)_2$, and adds, with stirring, 25.0 mL of a 0.10 *M* potassium hydroxide, KOH. A white precipitate of magnesium hydroxide immediately forms. Which of the following correctly indicates the relative concentrations of the other ions' concentrations?

(A) $[K^+] > [Mg^{2+}] > [NO_3^-]$
(B) $[Mg^{2+}] > [NO_3^-] > [K^+]$
(C) $[K^+] > [NO_3^-] > [Mg^{2+}]$
(D) $[NO_3^-] > [K^+] > [Mg^{2+}]$

**8.** Sodium sulfate forms several hydrates. A sample of a hydrate is heated until all the water is removed. What is the formula of the original hydrate if it loses 43% of its mass when heated?

(A) $Na_2SO_4\ H_2O$
(B) $Na_2SO_4\ 2H_2O$
(C) $Na_2SO_4\ 6H_2O$
(D) $Na_2SO_4\ 8H_2O$

**9.** $3\ Cu(s) + 8\ HNO_3(aq) \rightarrow 3\ Cu(NO_3)_2(aq) + 2\ NO(g) + 4\ H_2O(l)$

Copper metal reacts with nitric acid according to the above equation. A 0.30-mole sample of copper metal and 10.0 mL of 12 *M* nitric acid are mixed in a flask. How many moles of NO gas will form?

(A) 0.060 mole
(B) 0.030 mole
(C) 0.010 mole
(D) 0.20 mole

**10.** Gold(III) oxide, $Au_2O_3$, can be decomposed to gold metal, Au, plus oxygen gas, $O_2$. How many moles of oxygen gas will form when 221 g of solid gold(III) oxide is decomposed? The formula mass of gold(III) oxide is 442 g/mole.

(A) 0.250 mole
(B) 0.500 mole
(C) 0.750 mole
(D) 1.00 mole

**11.** Which of the following is the correct net ionic equation for the reaction of nitrous acid, $HNO_2$, with sodium hydroxide, NaOH?

(A) $HNO_2(aq) + OH^-(aq) \rightarrow NO_2^-(aq) + H_2O(l)$
(B) $HNO_2(aq) + Na^+(aq) \rightarrow NaNO_2(s) + H^+(aq)$
(C) $HNO_2(aq) + NaOH(aq) \rightarrow NaNO_2(s) + H_2O(l)$
(D) $H^+(aq) + OH^-(aq) \rightarrow H_2O(l)$

**12.** $2\ KMnO_4(aq) + 5\ H_2C_2O_4(aq) + 3\ H_2SO_4(aq) \rightarrow K_2SO_4(aq) + 2\ MnSO_4(aq) + 10\ CO_2(g) + 8\ H_2O(l)$

How many moles of $MnSO_4$ are produced when 1.0 mole of $KMnO_4$, 5.0 moles of $H_2C_2O_4$, and 3.0 moles of $H_2SO_4$ are mixed?

(A) 4.0 moles
(B) 5.0 moles
(C) 2.0 moles
(D) 1.00 mole

**13.** When the following equation is balanced, it is found that 1.00 mole of $C_8H_{18}$ reacts with how many moles of $O_2$?

____ $C_8H_{18}(g)$ + ____ $O_2(g) \rightarrow$ ____ $CO_2(g)$ + ____ $H_2O(g)$

(A) 12.5 moles
(B) 10.0 moles
(C) 25.0 moles
(D) 37.5 moles

**14.** $Ca(s) + 2\ H_2O(l) \rightarrow Ca(OH)_2(aq) + H_2(g)$

Calcium reacts with water according to the above reaction. What volume of hydrogen gas, at 25°C and 1.00 atm, is produced from 0.200 mole of calcium?

(A) 4.48 L
(B) 4.89 L
(C) 3.36 L
(D) 0.410 L

**15.** $2\ CrO_4^{2-}(aq) + 3\ SnO_2^{2-}(aq) + H_2O(l) \rightarrow 2\ CrO_2^-(aq) + 3\ SnO_3^{2-}(aq) + 2\ OH^-(aq)$

How many moles of $OH^-$ form when 50.0 mL of 0.100 *M* $CrO_4^{2-}$ is added to a flask containing 50.0 mL of 0.100 *M* $SnO_2^{2-}$?

(A) 0.100 mole
(B) $6.66 \times 10^{-3}$ mole
(C) $3.33 \times 10^{-3}$ mole
(D) $5.00 \times 10^{-3}$ mole

**16.** A solution containing 0.20 mole of KBr and 0.20 mole of $MgBr_2$ in 2.0 L of water is provided. How many moles of $Pb(NO_3)_2$ must be added to precipitate all the bromide as insoluble $PbBr_2$?

(A) 0.10 mole
(B) 0.50 mole
(C) 0.60 mole
(D) 0.30 mole

**17.** Cycloalkanes are hydrocarbons with the general formula $C_nH_{2n}$, where $n \geq 3$. If a 0.560-g sample of any alkene is combusted in excess oxygen, how many moles of water will form?

(A) 0.0400 mole
(B) 0.600 mole
(C) 0.0200 mole
(D) 0.400 mole

**18.** For which of the following substances is the formula mass the same for both the empirical and molecular formulas?

(A) $H_2C_2O_4$
(B) $C_6H_{12}O_6$
(C) $CO_2$
(D) $H_2O_2$

**19.** How many grams of $Ti_2(SO_4)_3$ are necessary to make 500.0 mL of a solution that is 0.1000 M $Ti^{3+}$?

(A) 38.393 g
(B) 9.598 g
(C) 17.42 g
(D) 19.20 g

**20.** A chemist performs the following reaction: $Mg(s) + I_2(s) \rightarrow MgI_2(s)$

She begins with 2.30 grams of Mg and 26.0 grams of $I_2$ and produces 2.63 g of $MgI_2$.

Which of the following will lead to more $MgI_2$ being produced?

(A) Adding $I_2(s)$
(B) Increasing the pressure
(C) Adding Mg(s)
(D) Decreasing the temperature

## 〉Answers and Explanations

It is possible to simplify the calculations by replacing the definition of molarity $\left(\frac{\text{mol}}{\text{L}}\right)$ with the equivalent expression $\left(\frac{\text{mol}}{1{,}000\text{ mL}}\right)$.

**1. D**—The reaction is $H_2SO_4(aq) + 2\ KOH(aq) \rightarrow K_2SO_4(aq) + 2\ H_2O(l)$. The calculation is:

$$(50.0\text{ mL base})\left(\frac{0.200\text{ mol base}}{1{,}000\text{ mL}}\right)\left(\frac{1\text{ mol acid}}{2\text{ mol base}}\right)\left(\frac{1{,}000\text{ mL}}{0.100\text{ mol acid}}\right) = 50.0\text{ mL}$$

This calculation simplifies to $(50.0\text{ mL base})\left(\frac{\cancel{0.200}\text{ mol base}}{\cancel{1{,}000}\text{ mL}}\right)\left(\frac{\cancel{1{,}000}\text{ mL}}{\cancel{0.200}\text{ mol acid}}\right)$

Make sure you understand why the simplified calculation works. If you did not balance the equation, you probably used the wrong mole ratio and obtained 100.0 mL.

**2. C**—The reaction is $H_2C_2O_4(aq) + 2\ NaOH(aq) \rightarrow Na_2C_2O_4(aq) + 2\ H_2O(l)$.

As in question 1, if you do not balance the equation, you get the wrong mole–mole ratio. The calculation is:

$$(45.20\text{ mL base})\left(\frac{0.1200\text{ mol base}}{1{,}000\text{ mL}}\right)\left(\frac{1\text{ mol acid}}{2\text{ mol base}}\right)\left(\frac{1}{20.00\text{ mL acid}}\right)\left(\frac{1{,}000\text{ mL}}{\text{L}}\right)$$

$= 0.1356\ M$ acid

As always, round the values to get an estimate and pick the closest answer.

**3. C**—Moles acid $= (50.0\text{ mL})\left(\frac{0.20\text{ mol acid}}{1{,}000\text{ mL}}\right) = 0.0100$ mole

Moles base $= (50.0\text{ mL})\left(\frac{0.20\text{ mol base}}{1{,}000\text{ mL}}\right) = 0.0100$ mole

Answer B cannot be correct because the base is the limiting reagent.
There is enough base to react completely with only one of the ionizable hydrogen ions from the acid. This leaves $H_2AsO_4^-$. The net ionic equation is:

$$H_3AsO_4(aq) + OH^-(aq) \rightarrow H_2AsO_4^-(aq) + H_2O(l)$$

Answer D cannot be correct because it is a cation.

**4. A**— The balanced chemical equation is given, and the calculation is:

$$\left(45.20\text{ mL } Cr_2O_7^{2-}\right)\left(\frac{0.1000\text{ mol } Cr_2O_7^{2-}}{1{,}000\text{ mL } Cr_2O_7^{2-}}\right)\left(\frac{6\text{ mol } Fe^{2+}}{1\text{ mol } Cr_2O_7^{2-}}\right)\left(\frac{1}{50.00\text{ mL}}\right)\left(\frac{1{,}000\text{ mL}}{\text{L}}\right)$$

$= 0.5424\ M$

This is a perfect example of where simplification is important. Change the above calculation to:

$$(45.20\text{ mL } \cancel{Cr_2O_7^{2-}})\left(\frac{0.1000\text{ mol } \cancel{Cr_2O_7^{2-}}}{1{,}000\text{ mL } \cancel{Cr_2O_7^{2-}}}\right)\left(\frac{6\text{ mol } Fe^{2+}}{1\text{ mol } \cancel{Cr_2O_7^{2-}}}\right)\left(\frac{1}{50.00\ \cancel{\text{mL}}}\right)\left(\frac{1{,}000\ \cancel{\text{mL}}}{\text{L}}\right)$$

$= 0.5424\ M$

This becomes:

$$(45.20)\left(\frac{0.1000}{\cancel{1,000}}\right)\left(\frac{6\ \text{mol Fe}^{2+}}{1}\right)\left(\frac{1}{50.00}\right) = 0.5424\ M$$

Next, round and simplify to:

$$(\cancel{50})\left(\frac{0.1000}{1}\right)\left(\frac{6\ \text{mol Fe}^{2+}}{1}\right)\left(\frac{1}{\cancel{50.00}}\right)\left(\frac{1}{\text{L}}\right) = 0.6\ M$$

It is unnecessary to write everything shown here; you need only write/do the final calculation.

Since the 45.20 was rounded up, the answer is slightly high; therefore, pick the closest answer that is slightly lower.

5. **B**—The question states that in this reaction, all silver compounds are insoluble, which means that $Ag^+$ is not a possible product since it must come from a compound. Silver carbonate is insoluble, and its formula should be written as $Ag_2CO_3$. Hydrochloric acid is a strong acid, so it should be written as separate $H^+$ and $Cl^-$ ions. Silver chloride, AgCl, is insoluble, and carbonic acid, $H_2CO_3$, quickly decomposes to $CO_2$ and $H_2O$. Answers C and D are not balanced.

6. **C**—Begin by dividing each value in the given ratio by the atomic mass of the element:

$$\text{V: } \frac{2.39}{50.94} = 0.0469;\ \text{O: } \frac{1.00}{16.0} = 0.0625$$

Divide by the smaller value (0.0469):

$$\frac{0.0469}{0.0469} = 1 \text{ and } \frac{0.0625}{0.0469} = 1.33$$

It is necessary to have a whole-number ratio. The value 1.33 is too far from a whole number to round; therefore, it is necessary to multiply by the smallest value leading to a whole number. Multiplying both by 3 gives 3 V and 4 O, which corresponds to answer C.

7. **D**—The doubling of the volume will result in halving the concentrations ($Mg^{2+}$ = 0.050 *M*, $NO_3^-$ = 0.10 *M*, $K^+$ = 0.050 *M*, and $OH^-$ = 0.050 *M*). The reaction is:

$$Mg(NO_3)_2(aq) + 2\ KOH(aq) \rightarrow Mg(OH)_2(s) + 2\ KNO_3(aq)$$

After the reaction, some of the magnesium remains (the remainder precipitated, leaving < 0.050 *M*), the potassium does not change (soluble, so still 0.050 *M*), and there are two nitrate ions (soluble, so still 0.10 *M*) per magnesium nitrate.

8. **C**—The calculation is a percent composition calculation. This technically should be done for all four answers; however, you probably will not need more than two. For answer C, the calculation is:

$$\frac{(6\ \text{mol H}_2\text{O})\left(\frac{18\ \text{g H}_2\text{O}}{\text{mol H}_2\text{O}}\right)}{(1\ \text{mol Na}_2\text{SO}_4\cdot 6\text{H}_2\text{O})\left(\frac{250\ \text{g Na}_2\text{SO}_4\cdot 6\text{H}_2\text{O}}{1\ \text{mol Na}_2\text{SO}_4\cdot 6\text{H}_2\text{O}}\right)} \times 100\% = 43\%$$

The numerator gives the mass of the water molecules present, and the denominator is from the molar mass of the formula. The percentages for the other compounds are 11% (A), 20% (B), and 50% (D). As in other calculations, rounding will simplify the work. As an alternative, it is possible to solve this problem using an empirical formula calculation based on 43% $H_2O$ and (100 – 43)% = 57% $Na_2SO_4$. In this case, assume 100 g of sample (which makes the percentages equal to the grams present):

$$(43\text{ g } H_2O)\left(\frac{1\text{ mol } H_2O}{18\text{ g } H_2O}\right) = 2.4\text{ mol } H_2O$$

$$(57\text{ g } Na_2SO_4)\left(\frac{1\text{ mol } Na_2SO_4}{142\text{ g } Na_2SO_4}\right) = 0.40\text{ mol } Na_2SO_4$$

Dividing each of the moles by the smaller value (0.40 mol) gives 1 $Na_2SO_4$ for 6 $H_2O$.

**9. B**—Calculate the moles of acid to compare to the 0.30 mole of Cu:

$$(10.0\text{ mL})\left(\frac{12\text{ mol } HNO_3}{1{,}000\text{ mL}}\right) = 0.12\text{ mole } HNO_3$$

The acid is the limiting reactant, because 0.30 mole of copper requires 0.80 mole of acid. Use the limiting reactant to calculate the moles of NO formed:

$$(0.12\text{ mol } HNO_3)\left(\frac{2\text{ mol NO}}{8\text{ mol } HNO_3}\right) = 0.030\text{ mole } HNO_3$$

**10. C**—The balanced chemical equation is $2\ Au_2O_3(s) \rightarrow 4\ Au(s) + 3\ O_2(g)$.

$$(221\text{ g } Au_2O_3)\left(\frac{1\text{ mol } Au_2O_3}{442\text{ mol } Au_2O_3}\right)\left(\frac{3\text{ mol } O_2}{2\text{ mol } Au_2O_3}\right) = 0.750\text{ mol } O_2$$

Note the 2:1 relationship between the formula mass and the mass of reactant.

**11. A**—The molecular equation is $HNO_2(aq) + NaOH(aq) \rightarrow NaNO_2(aq) + H_2O(l)$.

Nitrous acid is a weak acid; as such, it should remain as $HNO_2$. Sodium hydroxide is a strong base, so it will separate into $Na^+$ and $OH^-$ ions. Any sodium compound that might form is soluble and will yield $Na^+$ ions. The sodium ions are spectator ions and are left out of the net ionic equation. Answer D only works for a strong acid and a strong base.

**12. D**—The $KMnO_4$ is the limiting reagent (2.0 moles of $KMnO_4$ are required to react with the given amounts of the other reactants). Each mole of $KMnO_4$ will produce a mole of $MnSO_4$.

**13. A**—The balanced equation is $2\ C_8H_{18}(g) + 25\ O_2(g) \rightarrow 16\ CO_2(g) + 18\ H_2O(g)$. The calculation is:

$$(1.00\text{ mol } C_8H_{18})\left(\frac{25\text{ mol } O_2}{2\text{ mol } C_8H_{18}}\right) = 12.5\text{ mole } O_2$$

**14. B**—Use the ideal gas equation ($PV = nRT$) and rearrange to isolate the volume:

$$V = \frac{nRT}{P} = \frac{\left[(0.200 \text{ mol Ca})\left(\frac{1 \text{ mol H}_2}{1 \text{ mol Ca}}\right)\right](0.08206 \text{ L atm mol}^{-1} \text{ K}^{-1})(298 \text{ K})}{(1.00 \text{ atm})}$$

$$= 4.89 \text{ L H}_2$$

Answer D is the result of not converting from °C to K. Answer A is the result of using 22.4 L $\text{mol}^{-1}$ when you are not at STP.

**15. C**—There are $(50.0 \text{ mL})\left(\frac{0.100 \text{ mol}}{1{,}000 \text{ mL}}\right) = 5.00 \times 10^{-3}$ mol of $CrO_4^{2-}$ and an equal number of moles of $SnO_2^{2-}$. Thus, $SnO_2^{2-}$ is the limiting reactant (larger coefficient in the balanced reaction).

$$(5.00 \times 10^{-3} \text{ mol SnO}_2^{2-})\left(\frac{2 \text{ mol OH}^-}{3 \text{ mol SnO}_2^{2-}}\right) = 3.33 \times 10^{-3} \text{ mole OH}^-$$

**16. D**—The volume of water is irrelevant. 0.20 mole of KBr will require 0.10 mole of $Pb(NO_3)_2$, and 0.20 mole of $MgBr_2$ will require 0.20 mole of $Pb(NO_3)_2$. Total the two yields to get the final answer.

**17. A**—One mole of a cycloalkane, $C_nH_{2n}$, will form $n$ moles of water.

$$C_nH_{2n}(g) + 1.5\, O_2(g) \rightarrow n\, CO_2(g) + \text{n}\, H_2O(g)$$

It is possible to determine the value of $n$ by dividing the mass of the cycloalkane by the empirical formula mass ($CH_2$ = 14 g/mole). This gives:

$$(0.560 \text{ g C}_n\text{H}_{2n})\left(\frac{1 \text{ mol C}_n\text{H}_{2n}}{14.0 \text{ g C}_n\text{H}_{2n}}\right)\left(\frac{n \text{ mol H}_2\text{O}}{n \text{ mol C}_n\text{H}_{2n}}\right) = 0.0400 \text{ mole H}_2\text{O}$$

**18. C**—For the formula mass of the empirical formula to be the same as that of the molecular formula, the two formulas must be the same. All the molecular formulas except $CO_2$ can be simplified to give an empirical formula that is different from the molecular formula.

**19. B**—The molar mass of $Ti_2(SO_4)_3$ is

$$(2 \text{ mol Ti})\left(\frac{47.867 \text{ g Ti}}{1 \text{ mol Ti}}\right) + (3 \text{ mol S})\left(\frac{32.065 \text{ g S}}{1 \text{ mole S}}\right) + (12 \text{ mol O})\left(\frac{15.999 \text{ g O}}{1 \text{ mol O}}\right)$$

$$= 383.927 \text{ g Ti}_2(\text{SO}_4)_3$$

Since you are not allowed to use a calculator, rounding simplifies everything:

$$(2 \text{ mol Ti})\left(\frac{50 \text{ g Ti}}{1 \text{ mol Ti}}\right) + (3 \text{ mol S})\left(\frac{32 \text{ g S}}{1 \text{ mole S}}\right) + (12 \text{ mol O})\left(\frac{16 \text{ g O}}{1 \text{ mol O}}\right) = 388 \text{ g Ti}_2(\text{SO}_4)_3$$

(Since the rounded answer is slightly higher, using it will produce an answer that is too high.)

To determine the necessary grams:

$$\left(\frac{383.927 \text{ g Ti}_2(\text{SO}_4)_3}{1 \cancel{\text{mol Ti}_2(\text{SO}_4)_3}}\right)\left(\frac{1 \cancel{\text{mol Ti}_2(\text{SO}_4)_3}}{2 \cancel{\text{mol Ti}^{3+}}}\right)\left(\frac{0.1000 \cancel{\text{mol Ti}^{3+}}}{\cancel{\text{L}}}\right)(500.0 \cancel{\text{mL}})\left(\frac{1 \cancel{\text{L}}}{1{,}000 \cancel{\text{mL}}}\right)$$

$= 9.598175 \text{ g Ti}_2(\text{SO}_4)_3$ (correct unit, all other units cancelled as shown)

(Using the rounded molar mass gives 9.7 g.)

The 17.42 g answer comes if you accidently read Ti as Tl in the formula (we have seen many variations of this on actual exams).

The 19.20 g answer comes if you skip the 2 in the formula (second step in the calculation). We see students doing this on the exam when they do not bother to write out the units while working problems. A similar answer results if you forget to include the volume of the solution.

The 38.393 answer comes from an incorrect volume conversion (dividing 1,000 by 500.0, another error we have seen on exams we have graded, mainly because there were no units written).

**20. C**—The quantities of more than one reactant are given; therefore it is necessary to determine which reactant is limiting. To determine the limiting reactant, it is necessary to convert the mass of the reactants to moles:

$$\text{moles Mg} = 2.30\text{ g Mg}\left(\frac{1\text{ mol Mg}}{24.305\text{ g Mg}}\right) = 0.0946\text{ mole Mg}$$

$$\text{moles } I_2 = 26.0\text{ g } I_2\left(\frac{1\text{ mol } I_2}{253.808\text{ g } I_2}\right) = 0.102\text{ mole } I_2$$

Instead of doing the calculations shown, rounding might help. Noticing that the masses given are slightly below 0.1 mole for the Mg and slightly above 0.1 mole for $I_2$, is really all that is necessary. Since the reaction has 1:1 stoichiometry, the reactant with the fewer moles (Mg) is limiting.

Adding more limiting reactant (Mg) will increase the yield.

Adding more excess reactant ($I_2$) will not increase the yield.

Increasing the pressure is irrelevant since no gases are involved.

Decreasing the temperature may result in it taking longer before the reaction goes to completion, but it will not change the yield.

## › Free-Response Question

You have 15 minutes to answer the following question. You may use a calculator and the tables in the back of the book.

**Question**

The analysis of a sample of a monoprotic acid found that the sample contained 40.0% C and 6.71% H. The remainder of the sample was oxygen.

(a) Determine the empirical formula of the acid. Show all work.

(b) A 0.2720-g sample of the acid, HA, was titrated with standard sodium hydroxide, NaOH, solution. Determine the molecular weight of the acid if the sample required 45.00 mL of 0.1000 *M* NaOH for the titration. Show all work.

(c) A second sample of HA was placed in a flask. The flask was placed in a hot water bath until the sample vaporized. It was found that 1.18 g of vapor occupied 300.0 mL at 100°C and 1.00 atm. Determine the molecular weight of the acid. Show all work.

(d) Using your answer from part (a), determine the molecular formula for part (b) and for part (c).

(e) Account for any differences in the molecular formulas determined in part (d).

## Answer and Explanation

(a) The percent oxygen (53.3%) is determined by subtracting the carbon and the hydrogen from 100%. Assuming there are 100 g of sample gives the grams of each element as being numerically equivalent to the percent. Dividing the grams by the molar mass of each element gives the moles of each.

$$\text{For C: } (40.0 \text{ g C})\left(\frac{1 \text{ mol C}}{12.01 \text{ g C}}\right) = 3.33 \qquad \text{C} = 1$$

$$\text{For H: } (6.71 \text{ g H})\left(\frac{1 \text{ mol H}}{1.008 \text{ g H}}\right) = 6.66 \qquad \text{H} = 2$$

Divide each of these by the smallest (3.33)

$$\text{For O: } (53.3 \text{ g O})\left(\frac{1 \text{ mol O}}{16.00 \text{ g O}}\right) = 3.33 \qquad \text{O} = 1$$

This gives the empirical formula $CH_2O$.

You get 1 point for correctly determining any of the elements and 1 point for getting the complete empirical formula correct if you show your work. The symbols do not need to be in the order shown here.

(b) Using HA to represent the monoprotic acid, the balanced equation for the titration reaction is:

$$\text{HA(aq)} + \text{NaOH(aq)} \rightarrow \text{NaA(aq)} + \text{H}_2\text{O(l)}$$

The moles of acid may then be calculated:

$$(45.00 \text{ mL NaOH})\left(\frac{0.1000 \text{ mol NaOH}}{1000 \text{ mL}}\right)\left(\frac{1 \text{ mol HA}}{1 \text{ mol NaOH}}\right) = 4.500 \times 10^{-3} \text{ mole HA}$$

The molecular mass is:

$$\frac{0.2720 \text{ g HA}}{4.500 \times 10^{-3} \text{ mol HA}} = 60.44 \text{ g/mol}$$

You get 1 point for the correct number of moles of HA (or NaOH) and 1 point for the correct final answer, if you show your work.

(c) There are several methods to solve this problem. One way is to use the ideal gas equation, as done here. The equation and the value of $R$ are in the exam booklet. First, find the moles: $n = PV/RT$. Do not forget that you MUST change temperature to kelvin.

$$n = \frac{(1.00 \text{ atm})(300.0 \text{ mL})}{(0.08206 \text{ L atm mol}^{-1} \text{ K}^{-1})(373 \text{ K})}\left(\frac{1 \text{ L}}{1000 \text{ mL}}\right)$$

$$n = 9.80 \times 10^{-3} \text{ mole HA}$$

The molecular mass is:

$$\frac{1.18 \text{ g HA}}{9.80 \times 10^{-3} \text{ mol HA}} = 120 \text{ g/mol}$$

You get 1 point for getting any part of the calculation correct and 1 point for getting the correct final answer, if you show your work. If you used a different method and got the correct results you will still get credit.

(d) The approximate formula mass from the empirical ($CH_2O$) formula is:

$$12 + 2(1) + 16 = 30 \text{ g/mol}$$

For part (b): $\frac{60.44 \text{ g/mol}}{30 \text{ g/mol}} = 2$

Molecular formula = 2 × empirical formula = $C_2H_4O_2$

For part (c): $\frac{120 \text{ g/mol}}{30 \text{ g/mol}} = 4$

Molecular formula = 4 × empirical formula = $C_4H_8O_4$

You get 1 point for each correct molecular formula. If you got the wrong answer in part (a), you could still get credit for one or both molecular formulas if you used the part (a) value correctly.

(e) The one formula is double the formula of the other. Thus, the smaller molecule dimerizes (forms a pair) to produce the larger molecule.

You get 1 point for pointing to any relationship between the two formulas. You get 1 point if you note the second formula is two of the lighter molecules added together.

Total your points. There are 10 points possible.

## › Rapid Review

- The mole is the amount of substance that contains the same number of particles as exactly 12 g of carbon-12.
- Avogadro's number is the number of particles per mole, $6.022 \times 10^{23}$ particles.
- A mole is also the formula (atomic, molecular) mass expressed in grams.
- If you have any one of the three—moles, grams, or particles—you can calculate the others.
- The empirical formula indicates which elements are present and the lowest whole-number ratio.
- The molecular formula tells which elements are present and the actual number of each.
- Be able to calculate the empirical formula from percent composition data or quantities from chemical analysis.
- Stoichiometry is the calculation of the amount of one substance in a chemical equation by using another substance from the equation.

- *Always use the balanced chemical equation* in reaction stoichiometry problems.
- Be able to convert from moles of one substance to moles of another, using the stoichiometric ratio derived from the *balanced chemical equation.*
- In working problems that involve a quantity other than moles, sooner or later it will be necessary to convert to moles.
- The limiting reactant is the reactant that is used up first.
- Be able to calculate the limiting reactant using the mol/coefficient ratio.
- Percent yield is the actual yield (how much was actually formed in the reaction) divided by the theoretical yield (the maximum possible amount of product formed) times 100%.
- A solution is a homogeneous mixture composed of a solute (species present in smaller amount) and a solvent (species present in larger amount).
- Molarity is the number of moles of solute per liter of solution. Don't confuse molarity, *M* or [ ], with moles, *n* or mol.
- Be able to work reaction stoichiometry problems using molarity.
- *Always use the balanced chemical equation* in reaction stoichiometry problems.
- Watch your units. The mass of one substance will not cancel the mass of another substance. The moles of one substance will never cancel the moles of a different substance. A mole ratio is required.

CHAPTER 7

# Spectroscopy, Light, and Electrons

**IN THIS CHAPTER**

In this chapter, the following AP topics are covered:

1.5 Atomic Structure and Electron Configuration
1.6 Photoelectron Spectroscopy
3.11 Spectroscopy and the Electromagnetic Spectrum

**Summary:** In the development of the model of the atom, it was thought initially that all subatomic particles obeyed the laws of classical physics—that is, they were tiny bits of matter behaving like macroscopic pieces of matter. Later, however, it was discovered that this particle view of the atom could not explain many of the observations being made. About this time, the dual particle/wave model of matter began to gain favor. It was discovered that in many cases, especially when dealing with the behavior of electrons, describing some of their behavior in terms of waves explained the observations much better. Thus, the quantum mechanical model of the atom was born.

**Keywords and Equations**

KEY IDEA

Planck's constant, $h = 6.626 \times 10^{-34}$ J s

Speed of light, $c = 2.998 \times 10^{8}$ m s$^{-1}$

| | | |
|---|---|---|
| $E$ = energy | $\nu$ = frequency | $\lambda$ = wavelength |
| $m$ = mass | $E = h\nu$ | $c = \lambda\nu$ |

# The Nature of Light

Light is a part of the **electromagnetic spectrum**—radiant energy composed of gamma rays, X-rays, ultraviolet light, visible light, and so on. Figure 7.1 shows the electromagnetic spectrum.

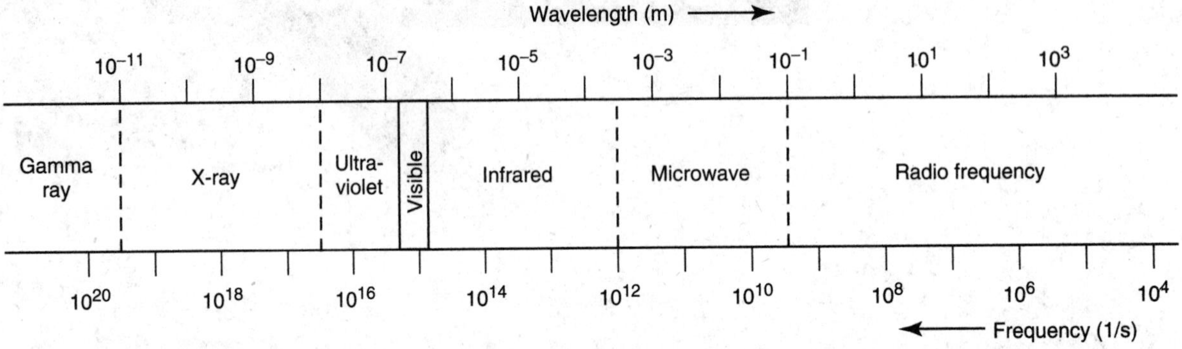


**Figure 7.1 The electromagnetic spectrum.**

The energy of the electromagnetic spectrum moves through space as waves that have three associated variables—frequency, wavelength, and amplitude. The **frequency,** $\nu$, is the number of waves that pass a point per second. **Wavelength** ($\lambda$) is the distance between two identical points on a wave. **Amplitude** is the height of the wave and is related to the intensity (or brightness, for visible light) of the wave. Figure 7.2 shows the wavelength and amplitude of a wave.

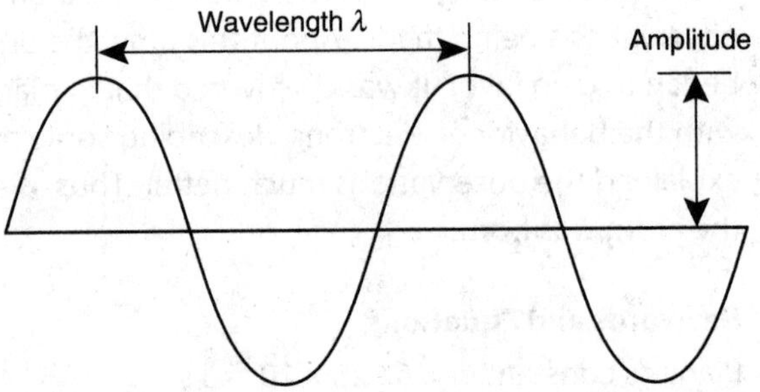


**Figure 7.2 Wavelength and amplitude of a wave.**

The energy associated with a certain frequency of light is related by the equation:

$E = h\nu$, where $h$ is Planck's constant = $6.626 \times 10^{-34}$ J s

In developing the quantum mechanical model of the atom, it was found that the electrons can have only certain distinct quantities of energy associated with them, and that for an electron in an atom to change its energy it must absorb or emit a certain amount of energy. The energy that is emitted or absorbed is really the difference in the two energy states and can be calculated by:

$$E = h\nu$$

All electromagnetic radiation travels at about the same speed in a vacuum, $2.998 \times 10^8$ m $s^{-1}$. This constant is called the **speed of light (*c*)**. The product of the frequency and the wavelength is the speed of light:

$$c = \nu\lambda$$

Let's apply some of the relationships. What wavelength of radiation has photons of energy $5.32 \times 10^{-19}$ J?

Answer:
Rearranging the equations:

$$E = h\nu \quad \text{and} \quad c = \nu\lambda$$

gives:

$$\nu = \frac{E}{h} \quad \text{and} \quad \lambda = \frac{c}{\nu}$$

Insert the appropriate values:

$$\nu = \frac{E}{h} = \frac{5.32 \times 10^{-19}\ \text{J}}{6.626 \times 10^{-34}\ \text{J s}} = 8.03 \times 10^{14}\text{s}^{-1}$$

Then:

$$\lambda = \frac{c}{\nu} = \frac{2.998 \times 10^{8}\ \text{ms}^{-1}}{8.03 \times 10^{17}\ \text{s}^{-1}} = 3.73 \times 10^{-7}\ \text{m}$$

This answer could have been calculated more quickly by combining the original two equations to give:

$$\lambda = \frac{hc}{E}$$

While this equation does not appear on the exam, it can save time by combining the two equations given on the exam into one calculation.

## Spectroscopy and the Electromagnetic Spectrum

Information about a substance may be determined by spectroscopy. There are a number of spectroscopic methods, each of which supplies different information. Some of the methods, and their uses, are in Table 7.1. Depending on the region of the electromagnetic spectrum, the absorption or emission of radiation results in a transition between the ground state and an excited state or vice versa.

In addition to the structural information from the methods mentioned in the table, it is possible to obtain information on the concentration of a species. The greater the concentration, the higher the percentage of radiation absorbed.

**Table 7.1 Some spectroscopic methods and their uses.**

| TYPE OF ELECTROMAGNETIC RADIATION | METHOD | INFORMATION AVAILABLE |
|---|---|---|
| Gamma rays | Mössbauer spectroscopy | Information concerning the nuclei of atoms |
| X-rays | Photoelectron spectroscopy | Information on the inner electrons |
| Ultraviolet-visible | Electronic spectroscopy | Information on the valance electrons |
| Infrared | Infrared spectroscopy | Information on chemical bonds |
| Microwave | Microwave spectroscopy | Information on the rotation of gaseous molecules |
| Radio (plus a magnetic field) | Nuclear magnetic resonance | Information on the structure of molecules |

## Beer–Lambert Law

In general, the concentration of a chemical may be related to the amount of radiation absorbed through the **Beer–Lambert law**, or simply Beer's law. In addition to the concentration, it is necessary to know the thickness (pathlength), through which the light passes, and the molar absorptivity, which depends upon the transition being observed and the wavelength of the radiation. The Beer–Lambert law is normally expressed by the following equation:

$$A = \varepsilon bc$$

$A$ is the amount of radiation absorbed (as an alternative, the percent of light transmitted can be measured). The symbol $\varepsilon$ is the molar absorptivity, $b$ is the pathlength, and $c$ is the concentration of the absorbing species. For a particular experiment, the molar absorptivity and the pathlength are fixed. A commonly used instrument for observing Beer's law is a spectrophotometer. A specially calibrated test tube, called a cuvette, holds the sample. Using the cuvette fixes the pathlength to the diameter of the cuvette. The wavelength to be absorbed can be adjusted, and normally, the wavelength chosen is the one with the greatest molar absorptivity for the transition of interest. The amount of radiation absorbed is measured, and the concentration calculated. However, the concentration is usually not calculated directly but determined through the preparation of a calibration curve.

A calibration curve is prepared by measuring the absorbance of several solutions of known concentration and plotting the observed absorbances versus concentration. Any concentration unit may be used, and, in most cases, the most convenient unit is chosen. Figure 7.3 shows a calibration curve for solutions containing the permanganate ion, $MnO_4^-$. Over the limited region shown in the calibration curve, the graph is linear. Care must be taken when using the graph not to go beyond the region experimentally shown to be linear. For example, this graph is not useful for a solution with an absorbance of 0.800 or

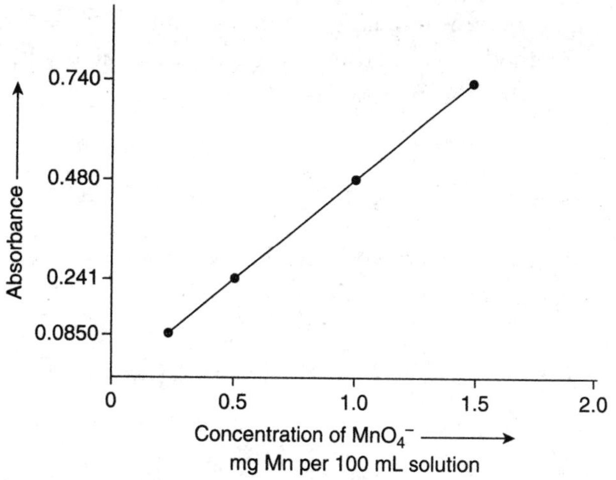


**Figure 7.3 A calibration curve for $MnO_4^-$ at 545 nm. The region shown is from 0.200 mg Mn per 100 mL to 1.50 mg Mn per 100 mL.**

higher, or below 0.850. At very low or very high concentrations the calibration curve is not linear. Deviations at low concentrations are the result of the concentration of the absorbing species being too low to result in a statistically significant probability of absorbing a photon of ration. When the concentration is too high, not every absorbing species will have a chance to absorb a photon because some of the species will be behind the ones that do absorb photons.

## Wave Properties of Matter

The concept that matter possesses both particle and wave properties was first postulated by de Broglie in 1925. He introduced the equation $\lambda = \frac{h}{mv}$, which indicates a mass ($m$) moving with a certain velocity ($v$) would have a specific wavelength ($\lambda$) associated with it. (Note that this $v$ is the velocity, not $\nu$ the frequency.) If the mass is very large (a locomotive), the associated wavelength is insignificant. However, if the mass is very small (an electron), the wavelength is measurable. The denominator may be replaced with the momentum of the particle ($p = mv$).

## Atomic Spectra

Late in the nineteenth century, scientists discovered that when the vapor of an element was heated it gave off a **line spectrum**, a series of fine lines of colors, instead of a continuous spectrum like a rainbow. This was used in the developing quantum mechanical model as evidence that the energy of the electrons in an atom was **quantized**; that is, there could only be certain distinct energies (lines) associated with the atom. Niels Bohr developed the first modern atomic model for hydrogen using the concepts of quantized energies. The Bohr model postulated a **ground state** for the electrons in the atom, an energy state of lowest energy, and an **excited state**, an energy state of higher energy. For an electron to go from its ground state to an excited state, it must absorb a certain amount of energy (a quantum). If the electron dropped back from that excited state to its ground state, that same amount of energy would be emitted. Bohr's model also allowed scientists to develop a method of calculating the energy associated with a specific energy level for the electron in the hydrogen atom:

$$E_n = \frac{-2.178 \times 10^{-18}}{n^2} \text{ joule}$$

where $n$ is the energy state. This equation can then be modified to calculate the energy difference between any two energy levels:

$$\Delta E = -2.18 \times 10^{-18}\,\text{J}\left(\frac{1}{n_{\text{final}}^2} - \frac{1}{n_{\text{initial}}^2}\right)$$

## Atomic Orbitals

Bohr's model worked well for hydrogen, the simplest atom, but didn't work very well for any others. In the early 1900s, Schrödinger developed a more involved model and set of equations that better described atoms by using quantum mechanical concepts. His model introduced a mathematical description of the electron's motion called a **wave function** or **atomic orbital**. Squaring the wave function (orbital) gives the volume of space in which the probability of finding the electron is high. This is commonly referred to as the **electron cloud**.

Schrödinger's equation required the use of three **quantum numbers** to describe each electron within an atom, corresponding to the orbital size, shape, and orientation in space. It was also found that a quantum number concerning the spin of the electron was needed.

ENRICHMENT

The first quantum number is the **principal quantum number (*n*)**. It describes the energy (related to size) of the orbital and relative distance from the nucleus. The allowed (by the mathematics of the Schrödinger equation) values are positive integers (1, 2, 3, 4, etc.). The smaller the value of $n$, the closer the orbital is to the nucleus. The number $n$ is sometimes called the atom's **shell**.

The second quantum number is the **angular momentum quantum number (*l*)**. Its value is related to the principal quantum number and has allowed values of 0 up to $(n - 1)$. For example, if $n = 3$, then the possible values of $l$ would be 0, 1, and 2 $(3 - 1)$. This value of $l$ defines the shape of the orbital:

- If $l = 0$, the orbital is called an s orbital and has a spherical shape with the nucleus at the center of the sphere. The greater the value of $n$, the larger the sphere.
- If $l = 1$, the orbital is called a p orbital and has two lobes of high electron density on either side of the nucleus. This makes for an hourglass or dumbbell shape.
- If $l = 2$, the orbital is a d orbital and can have a variety of shapes.
- If $l = 3$, the orbital is an f orbital, with more complex shapes.

Figure 7.4 shows the shapes of the s, p, and d orbitals. These are sometimes called **sublevels** or **subshells**.

The third quantum number is the **magnetic quantum number ($m_l$)**. It describes the orientation of the orbital around the nucleus. The possible values of $m_l$ depend on the value of the angular momentum quantum number, $l$. The allowed values for $m_l$ are $-l$ through zero to $+l$. For example, for $l = 2$ the possible values of $m_l$ would be $-2, -1, 0, +1, +2$. This is why, for example, if $l = 1$ (a p orbital), then there are three p orbitals corresponding to $m_l$ values of $-1, 0, +1$. This is also shown in Figure 7.4.

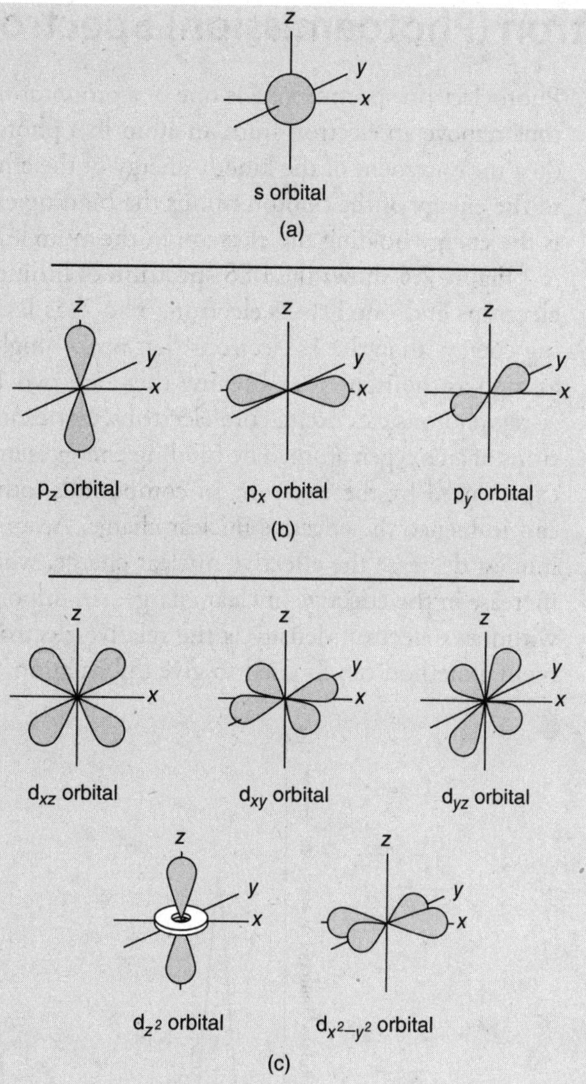


**Figure 7.4 The shapes of the s, p, and d atomic orbitals.**

The fourth quantum number, the spin quantum number ($m_s$), indicates the direction the electron is spinning. There are only two possible values for $m_s$, + ½ and −½.

The quantum numbers for the six electrons in carbon would be:

| QUANTUM NUMBER | FIRST ELECTRON | SECOND ELECTRON | THIRD ELECTRON | FOURTH ELECTRON | FIFTH ELECTRON | SIXTH ELECTRON |
|---|---|---|---|---|---|---|
| $n$ | 1 | 1 | 2 | 2 | 2 | 2 |
| $l$ | 0 | 0 | 0 | 0 | 1 | 1 |
| $m_l$ | 0 | 0 | 0 | 0 | 1 | 0 |
| $m_s$ | +½ | −½ | +½ | −½ | +½ | +½ |

Therefore, the electron configuration of carbon is $1s^2 2s^2 2p^2$.

## Photoelectron (Photoemission) Spectroscopy (PES)

Photoelectron spectroscopy is one of a group of related techniques where high-energy photons remove an electron from an atom in a photoelectric effect process. The method relies on a measurement of the kinetic energy of the emitted electron. The kinetic energy is equal to the energy of the photon minus the binding energy of the electron. The binding energy is the energy holding the electron in the atom and can be rather difficult to measure.

Figure 7.5 shows the PES spectrum of lithium. Lithium has three electrons; two are 1s electrons and one is a 2s electron. The 2s is less tightly bound (right peak—lower binding energy) than the 1s electrons (left peak—higher binding energy). The left peak is twice as high as the right peak because there are two 1s electrons compared to one 2s electron. X-ray photons can excite core electrons. For example, it is possible to focus on the 1s electrons of an oxygen atom. The binding energy is in part related to the effective nuclear charge experienced by the electron. In compounds, other atoms bonded to the atom of interest can influence the effective nuclear charge. Atoms donating electron density to the atom of interest decrease the effective nuclear charge, while electron-withdrawing atoms lead to an increase in the effective nuclear charge. An important factor in whether an atom donates or withdraws electron density is the relative electronegativity of the two atoms. This experimental method can be used to give information on which atoms are bonded to each other.

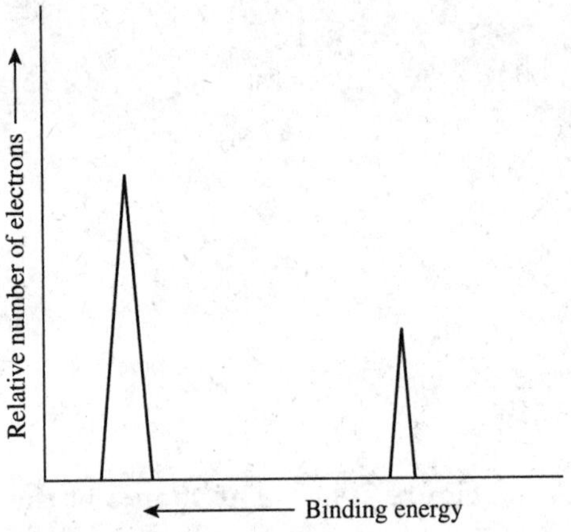


**Figure 7.5 PES spectrum of lithium.**

## Experiments

STRATEGY

No experimental questions related to this chapter have appeared on the AP Exam in recent years.

## Common Mistakes to Avoid

TIP

1. Be sure not to confuse wavelength and frequency.
2. The speed of light is $3.0 \times 10^8$ m/s. The exponent is positive.
3. The value of $n$ is never zero.
4. The values of $l$ and $m_l$ include zero.
5. Do not confuse velocity ($v$) and frequency ($\nu$).
6. The units of Planck's constant are J s, not J/s.

# ❯ Review Questions

Use these questions to review the content of this chapter and practice for the AP Chemistry Exam. First are 20 multiple-choice questions similar to what you will encounter in Section I of the AP Chemistry Exam. There are questions included to review prior knowledge of material. Following those is a long free-response question like the ones in Section II of the exam. To make these questions an even more authentic practice for the actual exam, time yourself following the instructions provided.

## Multiple-Choice Questions

Answer the following questions in 30 minutes. You may not use a calculator. You may use the periodic table and the equation sheet at the back of this book.

**1.** Which of the following represents the electron arrangement for the least reactive element of the four?

(A) 1s $\underline{\uparrow}$ 2s $\underline{\uparrow\downarrow}$
(B) 1s $\underline{\uparrow\downarrow}$ 2s $\underline{\uparrow}$
(C) [Kr] 5s $\underline{\uparrow\downarrow}$ 4d $\underline{\uparrow}\,\underline{\uparrow}\,\underline{\ \ }\,\underline{\ \ }\,\underline{\ \ }$
(D) 1s $\underline{\uparrow\downarrow}$ 2s $\underline{\uparrow\downarrow}$ 2p $\underline{\uparrow\downarrow}\,\underline{\uparrow\downarrow}\,\underline{\uparrow\downarrow}$

**2.** Which of the following might refer to a transition element?

(A) 1s $\underline{\uparrow}$ 2s $\underline{\uparrow\downarrow}$
(B) 1s $\underline{\uparrow\downarrow}$ 2s $\underline{\uparrow}$
(C) [Kr] 5s $\underline{\uparrow\downarrow}$ 4d $\underline{\uparrow}\,\underline{\uparrow}\,\underline{\ \ }\,\underline{\ \ }\,\underline{\ \ }$
(D) 1s $\underline{\uparrow\downarrow}$ 2s $\underline{\uparrow\downarrow}$ 2p $\underline{\uparrow\downarrow}\,\underline{\uparrow\downarrow}\,\underline{\uparrow\downarrow}$

**3.** Which of the following electron arrangements refers to the most chemically reactive element of the four?

(A) 1s $\underline{\uparrow}$ 2s $\underline{\uparrow\downarrow}$
(B) 1s $\underline{\uparrow\downarrow}$ 2s $\underline{\uparrow}$
(C) [Kr] 5s $\underline{\uparrow\downarrow}$ 4d $\underline{\uparrow}\,\underline{\uparrow}\,\underline{\ \ }\,\underline{\ \ }\,\underline{\ \ }$
(D) 1s $\underline{\uparrow\downarrow}$ 2s $\underline{\uparrow\downarrow}$ 2p $\underline{\uparrow\downarrow}\,\underline{\uparrow\downarrow}\,\underline{\uparrow\downarrow}$

**4.** Which of the following electron arrangements represents an atom in an excited state?

(A) 1s $\underline{\uparrow}$ 2s $\underline{\uparrow\downarrow}$
(B) 1s $\underline{\uparrow\downarrow}$ 2s $\underline{\uparrow}$
(C) [Kr] 5s $\underline{\uparrow\downarrow}$ 4d $\underline{\uparrow}\,\underline{\uparrow}\,\underline{\ \ }\,\underline{\ \ }\,\underline{\ \ }$
(D) 1s $\underline{\uparrow\downarrow}$ 2s $\underline{\uparrow\downarrow}$ 2p $\underline{\uparrow\downarrow}\,\underline{\uparrow\downarrow}\,\underline{\uparrow\downarrow}$

**5.** The ground-state configuration of $Fe^{2+}$ is which of the following?

(A) $1s^22s^22p^63s^23p^63d^54s^1$
(B) $1s^22s^22p^63s^23p^63d^6$
(C) $1s^22s^22p^63s^23p^63d^64s^2$
(D) $1s^22s^22p^63s^23p^63d^84s^2$

**6.** Which of the following contains only atoms that are diamagnetic in their ground state?

(A) Kr, Ca, and P
(B) Ne, Be, and Zn
(C) Ar, K, and Ba
(D) He, Sr, and C

**7.** Which of the following is the electron configuration of a halogen?

(A) $1s^21p^62s^22p^3$
(B) $1s^22s^22p^63s^23p^64s^23d^{10}4p^65s^24d^1$
(C) $1s^22s^22p^63s^23p^63d^3$
(D) $1s^22s^22p^5$

**8.** Which of the following is a possible configuration for a transition metal atom?

(A) $1s^21p^62s^22p^3$
(B) $1s^22s^22p^63s^23p^64s^23d^{10}4p^65s^24d^1$
(C) $1s^22s^22p^63s^23p^63d^3$
(D) $1s^22s^22p^5$

**9.** The following are some electron configurations reported by four students. Which of the following electron configurations is not possible?

(A) $1s^22s^32p^3$
(B) $1s^22s^22p^63s^23p^64s^23d^{10}4p^6$
(C) $1s^22s^22p^63s^23p^63d^3$
(D) $1s^22s^22p^5$

**10.** Which of the following is a possible configuration for a transition metal ion?

(A) $1s^2 1p^6 2s^2 2p^3$
(B) $1s^2 2s^2 2p^6 3s^2 3p^6 4s^2 3d^{10} 4p^6 5s^2 4d^1$
(C) $1s^2 2s^2 2p^6 3s^2 3p^6 3d^3$
(D) $1s^2 2s^2 2p^5$

**11.** If all the electrons are present in pairs, a substance is said to be diamagnetic. If there is at least one electron by itself in an orbital, a substance is said to be paramagnetic. In which of the following groups are all atoms diamagnetic?

(A) Be, O, and N
(B) Mg, Se, and Xe
(C) Kr, Be, and Zn
(D) At, Sn, and Ba

**12.** Which of the following explains why oxygen atoms, in their ground state, are paramagnetic?

(A) Pauli exclusion principle
(B) electron shielding
(C) Hund's rule
(D) Heisenberg uncertainty principle

**13.** An atomic orbital can hold no more than two electrons; this is a consequence of which of the following?

(A) Pauli exclusion principle
(B) electron shielding
(C) Hund's rule
(D) Heisenberg uncertainty principle

**14.** Why does the 4s orbital fill before the 3d orbital starts to fill?

(A) Pauli exclusion principle
(B) electron shielding
(C) Hund's rule
(D) Heisenberg uncertainty principle

**15.** Calcium reacts with element *X* to form an ionic compound. If the ground-state electron configuration of *X* is $1s^2 2s^2 2p^4$, what is the simplest formula for this compound?

(A) Ca$X$
(B) Ca$X_2$
(C) $Ca_4X_2$
(D) $Ca_2X_2$

**16.** In 1927, Clinton Davisson and Lester Germer experimentally confirmed what was known as the de Broglie hypothesis by observing the diffraction of electrons. This led to general acceptance of the de Broglie equation. Which of the following best explains the diffraction of electrons?

(A) Pauli exclusion principle
(B) Hund's rule
(C) the wave properties of matter
(D) Heisenberg uncertainty principle

**17.** How many peaks are expected in the photoelectron spectrum (PES) of aluminum?

(A) 4
(B) 3
(C) 2
(D) 5

**18.** Which peak is expected to be the most intense in the photoelectron spectrum (PES) of chlorine?

(A) 3s
(B) 2p and 3p will be equally intense
(C) 2p
(D) 3p

**19.** The Beer's law equation is $A = \varepsilon bc$. $A$ is the absorbance of the solution; what is the meaning of the other terms?

(A) $\varepsilon$ = molar absorptivity, $b$ = Beer's constant, and $c$ = concentration
(B) $\varepsilon$ = molar absorptivity, $b$ = path length, and $c$ = concentration
(C) $\varepsilon$ = extinction coefficient, $b$ = path length, and $c$ = speed of light
(D) $\varepsilon$ = extinction coefficient, $b$ = Beer's constant, and $c$ = speed of light

**20.** Determine the wavelength of light with and energy of $9.98 \times 10^{-19}$ J.

(A) $1.99 \times 10^{-7}$ m
(B) $5.03 \times 10^{6}$ m
(C) $4.51 \times 10^{23}$ m
(D) $1.98 \times 10^{-43}$ m

# Answers and Explanations

**1. D**—This configuration represents a noble gas (neon). The outer s and p orbitals are filled. C is the electron configuration of Zr. A and B are both Li, with A being an excited state and B being the ground state. See questions 2–4.

**2. C**—Transition elements have partially filled d orbitals. This configuration is for the metal zirconium, Zr.

**3. B**—The single electron in the s orbital indicates that this is the very reactive alkali metal lithium.

**4. A**—The 1s orbital is not filled. One indication of excited states is one or more inner orbitals being unfilled.

**5. B**—The electron configuration for iron is $1s^2 2s^2 2p^6 3s^2 3p^6 3d^6 4s^2$. To produce an iron(II) ion, the two 4s electrons are removed first.

**6. B**—The elements that are normally diamagnetic are those in the same columns of the periodic table as Be, Zn, and He because all the electrons are paired. Atoms in all other columns are normally paramagnetic.

**7. D**—Halogens have a valence shell with $s^2p^5$.

**8. B**—Transition metals have partially filled d orbitals ($d^{1-10}$), along with an $s^1$ or $s^2$. C represents a transition metal ion, not an atom.

**9. A**—A $2s^3$ configuration is not possible as s orbitals cannot accommodate more than two electrons.

**10. C**—The outer s-electrons are not present in most transition metal ions; however, d electrons may be present. C could be $V^{2+}$, $Cr^{3+}$, or $Mn^{4+}$ (among other choices). B is a Y atom.

**11. C**—Atoms with only completely filled shells or subshells are diamagnetic; all others are paramagnetic. From the choices given, the elements with complete shells or subshells are Be, Mg, Xe, Kr, Zn, and Ba. Only one answer consists of atoms from this group. It might be helpful to consult the periodic table, as these elements are in groups 2, 12, and 18. All odd atomic number atoms are paramagnetic.

**12. C**—The four electrons in the oxygen 2p orbitals are arranged with one pair and two unpaired electrons with spins parallel. This makes the oxygen atom paramagnetic. This arrangement is due to Hund's rule.

**13. A**—The Pauli exclusion principle restricts the number of electrons that can occupy a single orbital.

**14. B**—The d orbitals are shielded more efficiently than the s orbitals. Thus, the less-shielded d orbitals do not fill as readily as s orbitals with similar energy.

**15. A**—Calcium will form a +2 ion ($Ca^{2+}$), and *X* will need to gain two electrons to fill its outer shell and become a –2 ion ($X^{2-}$). The simplest formula for a compound containing a +2 ion and a –2 ion would be Ca*X*. The other answers involve different charges or a formula that has not been simplified.

**16. C**—Diffraction is a wave phenomenon; therefore, the observation of diffraction proves the wave properties of electrons (matter).

**17. D**—The first step is to determine the complete electron configuration of aluminum, which is $1s^2 2s^2 2p^6 3s^2 3p^1$.

In the electron configuration of Al there are five different types of orbitals being used (1s, 2s, 2p, 3s, and 3p). Five types of orbitals means five peaks.

**18. C**—The first step is to determine the complete electron configuration of chlorine, which is $1s^2 2s^2 2p^6 3s^2 3p^5$.

There are five types of orbitals so there will be five peaks. The most intense peak is the one with the most electrons (2p). The 3p orbital, with only five electrons, will be 5/6 times as intense as the 2p with 6 electrons.

**19. B**—These are listed on the equation sheet accompanying the exam. While it is possible to find these terms on the equation sheet with the exam, on a timed exam, distractions such as looking for items can lead to running out of time on the exam and not completing the exam.

**20. A**—The AP Exam gives two equations for use in the question. These questions are: $E = h\nu$ and $c = \lambda\nu$. The constants are also listed. The constants are $h = 6.626 \times 10^{-34}$ J s and $c = 2.998 \times 10^8$ m s$^{-1}$.

Using these equations requires each to be rearranged to $\nu = E/h$ and $\lambda = c/\nu$. The frequency calculated from the first of these equations is entered into the second to get the wavelength. The first calculation is

$$\nu = E/h = \frac{9.98 \times 10^{-19}\ \text{J}}{6.626 \times 10^{-34}\ \text{J s}} = 1.506 \times 10^{15}\ \text{s}^{-1}$$

(unrounded)

Entering this calculated frequency into the second equation gives

$$\lambda = c/\nu = \frac{2.998 \times 10^{8}\ \text{m s}^{-1}}{1.506 \times 10^{15}\ \text{s}^{-1}} = 1.99 \times 10^{-7}\ \text{m}$$

To save time on the exam, it will help if you combine the two equations before you begin calculating, this combined equation is $\lambda = hc/E$ (you should prove to yourself that this is the correct rearranged equation)

Using the combined equation

$$\lambda = hc/E = \frac{(6.626 \times 10^{-34}\ \text{J s})(2.998 \times 10^{8}\ \text{m s}^{-1})}{(9.98 \times 10^{-19}\ \text{J})}$$

$$= 1.99 \times 10^{-7}\ \text{m}$$

This saves doing two calculations and avoids the possibility of miscopying the answer from the first calculation into the second equation.

However, do not forget, you need to be able to do this without a calculator. With no calculation and the time constraints on a timed exam, it will help to round as much as possible. Rounding gives

$$\lambda = hc/E = \frac{(7 \times 10^{-34}\ \cancel{\text{J}}\,\cancel{\text{s}})(3 \times 10^{8}\ \text{m}\ \cancel{\text{s}^{-1}})}{(1 \times 10^{-18}\ \cancel{\text{J}})}$$

$$= \frac{(7 \times 3)(10^{-26}\ \text{m})}{(1 \times 10^{-18})} = 2 \times 10^{-7}\ \text{m}$$

Note, you are calculating a wavelength; therefore, your answer MUST have a length unit (m). The $5.03 \times 10^{6}$ m answer comes by calculating through using the inverse of both rearranged equation. If you had written and watched all your units, you would have caught this because your answer would have m$^{-1}$ as the unit, which is not a length unit.

The $4.51 \times 10^{23}$ m answer comes by calculating through using the inverse of the first rearranged equation and the correct second equation. In this case, the calculation gives the units m s$^2$, which is again not a length unit and obviously wrong (easily caught if you kept track of your units).

The $1.98 \times 10^{-43}$ m answer comes when the two equations were incorrectly rearranged to $\nu = Eh$ and $\lambda = c\nu$. In this case, the calculation gives the units m J$^2$, which is again not a length unit and obviously wrong (easily caught if you kept track of your units).

## › Free-Response Question

You have 15 minutes to answer the following question. You may use a calculator and the tables in the back of the book.

### Question

(a) The bond energy of fluorine is 159 kJ mol$^{-1}$.

i. Determine the energy, in J, of a photon of light needed to break an F–F bond.

ii. Determine the frequency of this photon in s$^{-1}$.

(b) Barium imparts a characteristic green color to a flame. The wavelength of this light is 551 nm. Determine the energy involved in kJ/mol.

## › Answer and Explanation

(a) If you do not remember them, several of the equations are given on the AP Exam and in the back of this book. In addition, the values of Planck's constant, Avogadro's number, and the speed of light are necessary. These constants are also given on the exam.

i. This is a simple conversion problem:

$$\left(\frac{159\text{ kJ}}{\text{mol}}\right)\left(\frac{1\text{ mol}}{6.022\times10^{23}}\right)\left(\frac{1{,}000\text{ J}}{1\text{ kJ}}\right)=2.64\times10^{-19}\text{ J}$$

Give yourself 1 point if you got this answer. If you got the wrong units (not J), you made a mistake.

ii. This part requires the equation $E = h\nu$. (This equation is given on the equation page of the AP Exam.)

$$\nu=\frac{E}{h}=\frac{2.64\times10^{-19}\text{ J}}{6.626\times10^{-34}\text{ J s}}=3.98\times10^{14}\text{ s}^{-1}$$

Give yourself 1 point for this answer. If you got the wrong answer in the preceding part but used it correctly here (in place of the $2.64\times10^{-19}$ J), you still get 1 point. If you got the wrong units (not $s^{-1}$), you made a mistake. You should realize that $s \neq s^{-1}$.

(b) This can be done as a one-step or two-step problem. The AP test booklet gives you the equations to solve this directly as a two-step problem. The two equations are $c = \lambda\nu$ and $E = h\nu$. This method will be followed here. The two equations may be combined to produce an equation ($E = hc/\lambda$) that will allow you to do the problem in one step (you can use the alternate one-equation method for practice and as a comparison).

Using $c = \lambda\nu$:

$$\nu=\frac{c}{\lambda}=\left(\frac{2.998\times10^{8}\text{ m s}^{-1}}{551\text{ nm}}\right)\left(\frac{1\text{ nm}}{10^{-9}\text{ m}}\right)=5.44\times10^{14}\text{ s}^{-1}$$

If you got the wrong units (not $s^{-1}$), you made a mistake. You should realize that $s \neq s^{-1}$.
Using $E = h\nu$:

$$E=(6.626\times10^{-34}\text{ J s})(5.44\times10^{14}\text{s}^{-1})\left(\frac{1\text{ kJ}}{1{,}000\text{ J}}\right)\left(\frac{6.022\times10^{23}}{\text{mol}}\right)$$
$$=2.17\times10^{2}\text{ kJ/mol}$$

The information in the first two parentheses is a plug-in into the equation. The third parentheses include a unit conversion from joules to kilojoules. The final parentheses convert from photons to moles.

Give yourself 1 point for each of these answers. If you did the problem as a one-step problem, give yourself 2 points if you got the final answer correct or 1 point if you left out any of the conversions. We have seen numerous students lose points on the AP Exam because they either did not write the units or did not pay attention to the units they had. If the units are wrong, there is something else wrong with your answer. In many cases on the exams we have graded, students have thrown away points because of inconsistent units.

Total your points. There are 4 points possible. Subtract 1 point if any answer does not have the correct number of significant figures.

## › Rapid Review

- Know the general regions of the electromagnetic spectrum.
- The frequency, $\nu$, is defined as the number of waves that pass a point per second.
- The wavelength, $\lambda$, is the distance between two identical points on a wave.
- The energy of light is related to the frequency by $E = h\nu$.
- The product of the frequency and wavelength of light is the speed of light: $c = \nu\lambda$.
- An orbital or wave function is a quantum mechanical, mathematical description of the electron.
- If all electrons in an atom are in their lowest possible energy level, then the atom is said to be in its ground state.
- If any electrons in an atom are in a higher energy state, then the atom is said to be in an excited state.
- The energy of an atom is quantized, existing in only certain distinct energy states.
- Quantum numbers are numbers used in Schrödinger's equation to describe the orbital size, shape, and orientation in space and the spin of an electron.
- The principal quantum number, $n$, describes the size of the orbital. It must be a positive integer. It is sometimes referred to as the atom's shell.
- The angular momentum quantum number, $l$, defines the shape of the electron cloud. If $l = 0$, it is an s orbital; if $l = 1$, it is a p orbital; if $l = 2$, it is a d orbital; if $l = 3$, it is an f orbital, etc.
- The magnetic quantum number, $m_l$, describes the orientation of the orbital around the nucleus. It can be integer values ranging from $-l$ through 0 to $+l$.
- The spin quantum number, $m_s$, describes the spin of the electron and can only have values of +½ and –½.
- Be able to write the quantum numbers associated with the first 20 electrons.

# CHAPTER 8

# Bonding

**IN THIS CHAPTER**

In this chapter, the following AP topics are covered:

2.1 Types of Chemical Bonds
2.4 Structure of Metals and Alloys
2.5 Lewis Diagrams
2.6 Resonance and Formal Charge
2.7 VSEPR and Bond Hybridization

**Summary:** The difference between elements and compounds was discussed in Chapter 5, Basics. But what are the forces holding together a compound? What is the difference in bonding between table salt and sugar? What do these compounds look like in three-dimensional space?

Compounds have a certain fixed proportion of elements. The periodic table often can be used to predict the type of bonding that might exist between elements. While there are exceptions, the following general guidelines normally apply:

KEY IDEA

metal + nonmetal → ionic bonds
nonmetal + nonmetal → covalent bonds
metal + metal → metallic bonding

Compounds exist in each category. In the ionic bonding category are substances like NaCl. A covalent example is $H_2O$. Examples in the metallic category are less well known, but materials such as $MgNi_2$ qualify. Metallic bonding in alloys are better-known examples of combinations with two or more metals.

We will discuss two types of bonding, ionic and covalent, in some depth. Suffice it to say that metallic bonding is a bonding situation between metals in which the valence electrons are donated to a vast electron pool (sometimes called a "sea of electrons") so that the valence electrons are free to move throughout the entire metallic solid. One consequence of this free movement of electrons is that metals conduct electricity.

The basic concept that drives bonding is related to the stability of the noble gas family (the group 8A or group 18 elements). Their extreme stability (lower energy state) is a consequence of these elements having a filled valence shell, a full complement of eight valence electrons. (Helium is an exception. Its valence shell, the 1s, is filled with two electrons.) This is called the octet rule. During chemical reactions, atoms tend to lose, gain, or share electrons in order to achieve a filled valence shell, to complete their octet. By completing their valence shell in this fashion, they become isoelectronic, having the same number and arrangement of electrons, as the closest noble gas. Note: the nearest noble gas is the one with the closest atomic number. For example, both sodium and fluorine are "next" to neon.

There are numerous exceptions to the octet rule; for example, some atoms may have more than an octet, and their compounds may have one or more atoms with less than an octet.

KEY IDEA

**Keywords and Equations**

There are no keywords or equations on the AP Exam specific to this chapter.

# Lewis Electron-Dot Structures

The Lewis electron-dot symbol is a way of representing the element and its valence electrons. The chemical symbol is written, which represents the atom's nucleus and all inner-shell electrons. The valence, or outer-shell, electrons are represented as dots surrounding the atom's symbol. Take the valence electrons, distribute them as dots one at a time around the four sides of the symbol, and then pair them up until all the valence electrons are distributed. Figure 8.1 shows the Lewis symbol for several different elements. In general, Lewis electron-dot structures do not work for the transition or inner transition metals.

The Lewis symbols will be used in the discussion of bonding, especially covalent bonding, and will form the basis of the discussion of molecular geometry.

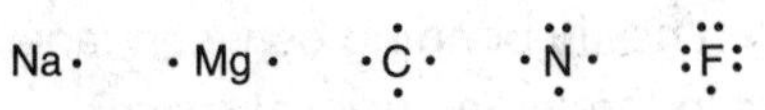


**Figure 8.1 Lewis electron-dot symbols for selected elements.**

# Ionic and Covalent Bonding

## Ionic Bonding

**Ionic bonding** results from the transfer of electrons from a metal to a nonmetal with the formation of cations (positively charged ions) and anions (negatively charged ions). The attraction of the opposite charges forms the **ionic bond**. The metal loses electrons to form a cation (the positive charge results from having more protons than electrons), and the nonmetal becomes an anion by gaining electrons (it now has more electrons than protons). This is shown in Figure 8.2 for the reaction of sodium and chlorine to form sodium chloride.

The number of electrons to be lost by the metal and gained by the nonmetal is determined by the number of electrons lost or gained by the atom to achieve a full octet. There is a rule of thumb that an atom can gain or lose one or two and, on rare occasions, three electrons, but not more than that. Sodium has one valence electron in energy

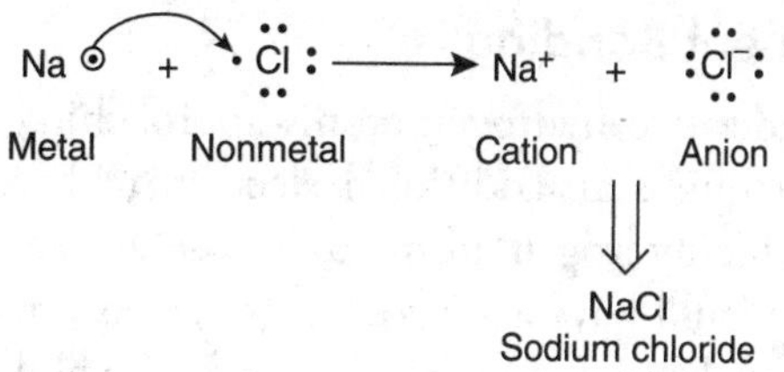


**Figure 8.2 Formation of sodium chloride.**

level 3, and chlorine has seven valence electrons in energy level 3. As shown in Figure 8.2, the lone sodium valence electron goes to the chlorine to produce ions.

If sodium loses the one electron from the valence shell, there are no electrons in that shell, and the highest energy electrons are now in energy level 2. Level 2 for the sodium ion now has an octet of electrons. In general, this is indicated with a Lewis-dot structure that has no electrons. Chlorine, having seven valence electrons, needs to gain one more to complete its octet. So, when an electron is transferred from sodium to chlorine, the outer shell of chlorine goes from seven to eight electrons. Thus, the transfer of one electron completes an octet for both elements.

If magnesium, with two valence electrons to be lost, reacts with chlorine (which needs one additional electron), then magnesium will donate one valence electron to each of *two* chlorine atoms, forming the ionic compound magnesium chloride, $MgCl_2$. Make sure the formula has the lowest whole-number ratio of elements.

If aluminum, with three valence electrons to be lost, reacts with oxygen, which needs two additional electrons to complete its octet, then the lowest common factor between 3 and 2 must be found; this value is 6. Two aluminum atoms would each lose three electrons (total of six electrons lost) to three oxygen atoms, which would each gain two electrons (total six electrons gained). The total number of electrons lost must equal the total number of electrons gained.

TIP

Another way of deriving the formula of the ionic compound is the **crisscross rule**. In this technique the cation and anion are written side by side. The numerical value of the superscript charge on the cation (without the sign) becomes the subscript on the nonmetal in the compound, and the superscript charge on the anion becomes the subscript on the metal in the compound. Figure 8.3 illustrates the crisscross rule for the reaction between aluminum and oxygen.

**Figure 8.3 Using the crisscross rule.**

If magnesium reacts with oxygen, then automatic application of the crisscross rule would lead to the formula $Mg_2O_2$, which is incorrect because the subscripts are not in the lowest whole-number ratio. This is a shortcoming of the crisscross rule that one must always consider. This means that $Mg_2O_2$ must be simplified to MgO. For the same reason, lead(IV) oxide (containing $Pb^{4+}$ and $O^{2-}$) would have the formula $PbO_2$ and not $Pb_2O_4$. Make sure the formula has the lowest whole-number ratio of elements.

Ionic bonding may also involve polyatomic ions. The polyatomic ion(s) replace(s) one or both monatomic ions, and while the formula may look more complicated, the polyatomic ion behaves like the smaller monatomic ion.

## Covalent Bonding

Consider two hydrogen atoms approaching each other. Both have only one electron, and each requires an additional electron to become isoelectronic with the nearest noble gas, He. One hydrogen atom could lose an electron; the other could gain that electron. One atom would have achieved its noble gas arrangement; but the other, the atom that lost its electron, has moved farther away from stability. The formation of the very stable $H_2$ cannot be explained by the loss and gain of electrons. In this situation, like that between any two nonmetals, electrons are shared, not lost, and gained. No ions are formed. It is a covalent bond that holds the atoms together. **Covalent bonding** is the sharing of one or more *pairs* of electrons. The covalent bonds in a **molecule** often are represented by a dash, which represents a shared *pair* of electrons. These covalent bonds may be single bonds, one pair of shared electrons as in H–H; double bonds, two shared pairs of electrons, $H_2C{=}CH_2$; or triple bonds, three shared pairs of electrons, N≡N. For the representative elements, three shared pairs are the maximum number of pairs shared between two atoms. The same driving force forms a covalent bond as an ionic bond—establishing a stable (lower energy) electron arrangement. In the case of the covalent bond, it is accomplished through sharing electrons.

In the hydrogen molecule, the electrons are shared equally. Each hydrogen nucleus has one proton equally attracting the bonding pair of electrons. A bond like this is called a **nonpolar covalent bond**. In cases where the two atoms involved in the covalent bond are not the same, the attraction is not equal, and the bonding electrons are pulled toward the atom with the greater attraction. The bond becomes a **polar covalent bond**, with the atom that has the greater attraction taking on a partial negative charge and the other atom a partial positive charge. Consider for example, HF(g). The fluorine has a greater attraction for the bonding pair of electrons and so takes on a partial negative charge at the expense of the hydrogen, which takes on a partially positive charge. Many times, in addition to using a single line to indicate the covalent bond, an arrow is used with the arrowhead pointing toward the atom that has the greater attraction for the electron pair and a cross at the opposite end:

$$^{\delta+}\mathrm{H}-\mathrm{F}^{\delta-}$$

$$+\!\!\!\longrightarrow$$

The **electronegativity (EN)** is a measure of the attractive force that an atom exerts on a bonding pair of electrons. Electronegativity values are tabulated. In general, electronegativities increase from left to right on the periodic table, except for the noble gases, and decrease going from top to bottom. This means that fluorine has the highest electronegativity of any element. If the difference in the electronegativities of the two elements involved in the bond is great (>1.7), the bond is considered mostly ionic in nature. If the difference is slight (<0.4), it is mostly nonpolar covalent. Anything in between these two extremes is polar covalent. Many times the electronegativities of the transition and inner transition metals are exceptions to the general trend trends observed for the representative elements.

Many times the Lewis structure will be used to indicate the bonding pattern in a covalent compound. In Lewis formulas, the valence electrons that are not involved in bonding are shown as dots surrounding the element symbols (never between two atoms), while a bonding pair of electrons is represented as a dash. There are several ways of deriving the Lewis structure, but here is one that works well for those compounds that obey the octet rule.

**Draw the Lewis structural formula for $CH_4O$.**
First, write a general framework for the molecule. In this case, the carbon must be bonded to the oxygen, because hydrogen can form only one bond. Hydrogen is *never* central. Remember: **carbon forms four bonds.**

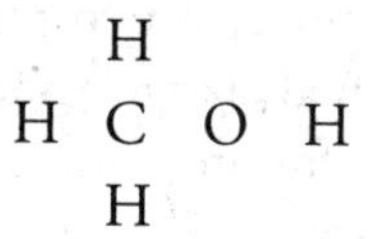

To determine where all the electrons are to be placed, apply the $N - A = S$ rule, where:

$N$ = sum of valence electrons needed for each atom. The two allowed values are two for hydrogen and eight for all other elements.
$A$ = sum of all available valence electrons
$S$ = # of electrons shared and $S/2$ = # bonds

For $CH_4O$, we would have:

| | 1 C | 4 H | 1 O | |
|---|---|---|---|---|
| $N$ | 8 | 4 (2) = 8 | 8 | = 24 |
| $A$ | 4 | 4 (1) = 4 | 6 | = 14 |

$S = N - A = 24 - 14 = 10$ bonds $= S/2 = 10/2 = 5$

Place the electron pairs, as dashes, between the adjacent atoms in the framework and then distribute the remaining available electrons so that each atom has its full octet, eight electrons—bonding or nonbonding, shared or not—for every atom except hydrogen, which gets two. Figure 8.4 shows the Lewis structural formula of $CH_4O$. (You should check to make sure you can locate the A = 14 electrons.)

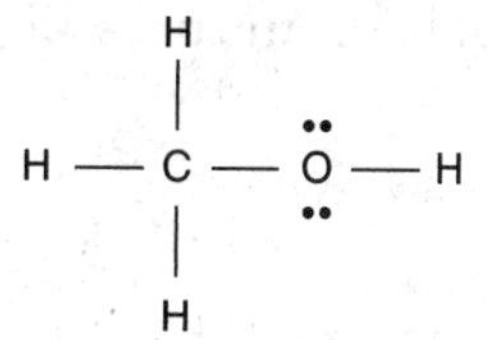

**Figure 8.4 Lewis structure of $CH_4O$.**

Note: $CH_4O$ is an organic compound, and while organic chemistry is not an AP topic, organic compounds make excellent examples and may appear on the AP Chemistry Exam in the form seen here.

Lewis structures may also be written for polyatomic anions or cations. The $N - A = S$ rule can be used, but if the ion is an anion, extra electrons equal to the magnitude of the negative charge must be added to the electrons available. If the ion is a cation, electrons must be subtracted.

As we have mentioned previously, there are many exceptions to the octet rule. In these cases, the $N - A = S$ rule does not apply, as illustrated by the following example.

Draw the Lewis structure for $XeF_4$.

Answer:

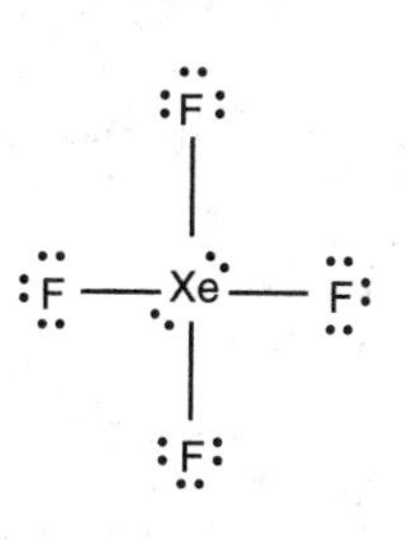

Each of the fluorine atoms will have an additional three pairs of electrons. Only the four fluorine atoms have their octets.

The process just outlined will usually result in the correct Lewis structure. However, there will be cases when more than one structure may seem to be reasonable. One way to eliminate inappropriate structures is by using the formal charge.

There is a formal charge associated with each atom in a Lewis structure. To determine the formal charge for an atom, enter the number of electrons for *each* atom into the following relationship:

$$\text{Formal charge} = (\text{number of valence electrons}) - (\text{number of nonbonding electrons} - \tfrac{1}{2}\ \text{number of bonding electrons})$$

A formal charge of zero for each atom in a molecule is a very common result for a favorable Lewis structure. In other cases, a favorable Lewis structure will follow the rules below. The formal charges are:

1. Small numbers, preferably 0.
2. No like charges are adjacent to each other, but unlike charges are close together.
3. The more electronegative element(s), the lower the formal charge(s) will be.
4. The total of the formal charges equals the charge on the ion or 0 for a compound.

Now we will apply this formal-charge concept to the cyanate ion $OCN^-$. We chose this example because many students incorrectly write the formula as $CNO^-$, and then try to use this as the atomic arrangement in the Lewis structure. Based on the number of electrons needed, the carbon, needing the most electrons, should be the central atom. We will work this example using both the incorrect atom arrangement and the correct atom arrangement. Notice that in both structures all atoms have a complete octet.

| | $[\underset{..}{\ddot{O}}::N::\ddot{C}:]^-$ | $[\underset{..}{\ddot{O}}::C::\ddot{N}:]^-$ |
|---|---|---|
| Number of valence electrons | 6  5  4 | 6  4  5 |
| – Number of nonbonding electrons | –4  –0  –4 | –4  –0  –4 |
| – $\frac{1}{2}$ Number of bonding electrons | –2  –4  –2 | –2  –4  –2 |
| Formal charges | 0  +1  –2 | 0  0  –1 |

The formal charges make the OCN arrangement the better choice.

## Molecular Geometry—VSEPR

The shape of a molecule has quite a bit to do with its reactivity and physical properties. This is especially true in biochemical processes, where slight changes in shape in three-dimensional space might make a certain molecule inactive or cause an adverse side effect. One way to predict the shape of molecules is the **VSEPR theory** (valence-shell electron-pair repulsion theory). The basic idea behind this theory is that the valence electron pairs surrounding a central atom, whether involved in bonding or not, will try to move as far away from each other as possible to minimize the repulsion between the like charges. Two geometries can be determined; the *electron-group geometry,* in which all electron pairs surrounding a nucleus are considered, and *molecular geometry,* in which the nonbonding electrons become "invisible" and only the geometry of the atomic nuclei is considered. For the purposes of geometry, double and triple bonds count the same as single bonds. To determine the geometry:

KEY IDEA

1. Write the Lewis electron-dot formula of the compound.
2. Determine the number of electron-pair groups surrounding the central atom(s). Remember that double and triple bonds are treated as a single group.
3. Determine the geometric shape that maximizes the distance between the electron groups. This is the geometry of the electron groups.
4. Mentally allow the nonbonding electrons to become invisible. They are still there and are still repelling the other electron pairs, but we don't "see" them. The molecular geometry is determined by the remaining arrangement of atoms (as determined by the bonding electron groups) around the central atom.

KEY IDEA

Figure 8.5, on the next page, shows the electron-group and molecular geometry for two to six electron pairs.

For example, let's determine the electron-group and molecular geometry of carbon dioxide, $CO_2$, and water, $H_2O$. At first glance, one might imagine that the geometry of these two compounds would be similar, since both have a central atom with two groups attached. Let's see if that is true.

First, write the Lewis structure of each. Figure 8.6 shows the Lewis structures of these compounds. Don't forget a correct Lewis-dot structure may be drawn with more than one "geometry"; these shapes may or may not be related to the true shape of the molecule.

Next, determine the electron-group geometry of each. For carbon dioxide, there are two electron groups around the carbon, so it would be linear. For water, there are four electron pairs around the oxygen—two bonding and two nonbonding electron pairs—so the electron-group geometry would be tetrahedral.

Finally, mentally allow the nonbonding electron pairs to become invisible and describe what is left in terms of the molecular geometry. For carbon dioxide, all groups are involved in bonding, so the molecular geometry is also linear. However, water has two nonbonding pairs of electrons, so the remaining bonding electron pairs (and hydrogen nuclei) are in a bent arrangement. If you had drawn the Lewis-dot structure as H–O–H (linear), it would not alter the fact that the water molecule is bent.

This determination of the molecular geometry of carbon dioxide and water also accounts for the fact that carbon dioxide does not possess a dipole and water has one, even though both are composed of polar covalent bonds. Carbon dioxide, because of its linear shape, has partial negative charges at both ends and a partial charge in the middle. To possess a dipole, one end of the molecule must have a positive charge and the other a negative end. Water, because of its bent shape, satisfies this requirement. Carbon dioxide does not.

| Total Electron Pairs | Electron-Group Geometry | Bonding Pairs | Nonbonding Pairs (Lone Pairs) | | Molecular Geometry |
|---|---|---|---|---|---|
| 2 |  Linear | 2 | 0 | 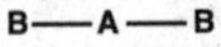 | Linear |
| 3 | 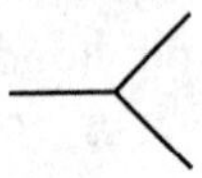 Trigonal planar | 3 | 0 | 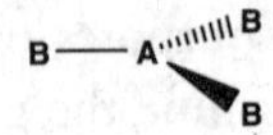 | Trigonal planar |
| | | 3 | 1 |  | Bent |
| 4 | 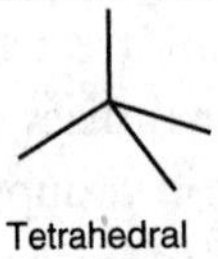 Tetrahedral | 4 | 0 | 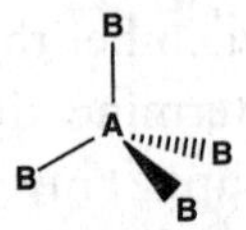 | Tetrahedral |
| | | 3 | 1 | 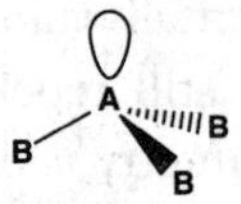 | Trigonal pyramidal |
| | | 3 | 2 | 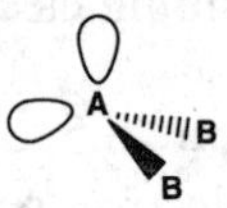 | Bent |
| 5 | 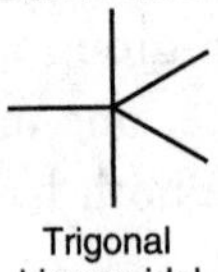 Trigonal bipyramidal | 5 | 0 |  | Trigonal bipyramidal |
| | | 4 | 1 | 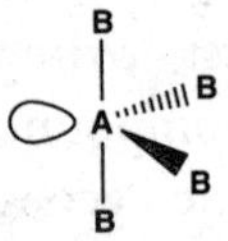 | Irregular tetrahedral (see-saw) |
| | | 3 | 2 | 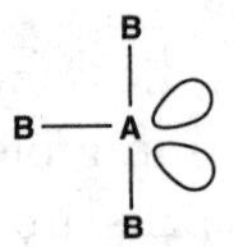 | T-shaped |
| | | 3 | 2 |  | Linear |
| 6 | 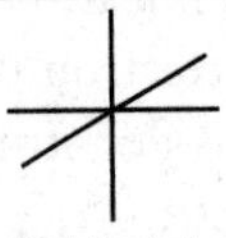 Octahedral | 6 | 0 | 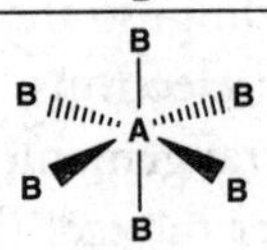 | Octahedral |
| | | 5 | 1 | 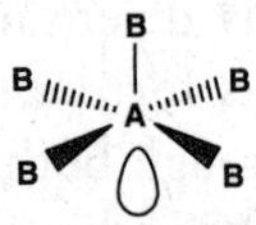 | Square pyramidal |
| | | 4 | 2 | 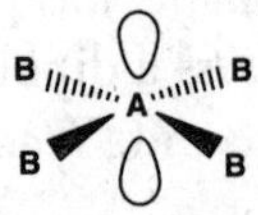 | Square planar |

**Figure 8.5 Electron-group and molecular geometry.**

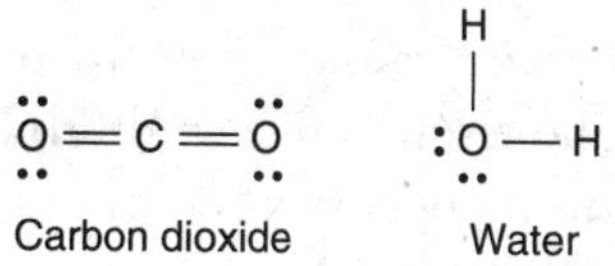


**Figure 8.6 Lewis structures of carbon dioxide and water.**

# Valence Bond Theory

The VSEPR theory is only one way in which the molecular geometry of molecules may be determined. Another way involves the valence bond theory. The **valence bond theory** describes covalent bonding as the mixing of atomic orbitals to form a new kind of orbital, a hybrid orbital. **Hybrid orbitals** are new atomic orbitals formed as a result of mixing the original atomic orbitals of the atoms involved in the covalent bond. The number of hybrid orbitals formed is the same as the number of atomic orbitals mixed, and the type of hybrid orbital formed depends on the types of atomic orbital mixed. Figure 8.7 shows the hybrid orbitals resulting from the mixing of s, p, and d orbitals.

KEY IDEA

*sp hybridization* results from the overlap of an s orbital with one p orbital. Two sp hybrid orbitals are formed with a bond angle of 180°. This is a linear orientation.

*$sp^2$ hybridization* results from the overlap of an s orbital with two p orbitals. Three $sp^2$ hybrid orbitals are formed with a trigonal planar orientation and a bond angle of 120°.

One place this type of bonding occurs is in the formation of the carbon-to-carbon double bond, as will be discussed later.

*$sp^3$ hybridization* results from the mixing of one s orbital and three p orbitals, giving four $sp^3$ hybrid orbitals with a tetrahedral geometric orientation. This $sp^3$ hybridization is found in carbon when it forms four single bonds.

| | Linear | Trigonal planar | Tetrahedral | Trigonal bipyramidal | Octahedral |
|---|---|---|---|---|---|
| **Atomic orbitals mixed** | one s<br>one p | one s<br>two p | one s<br>three p | one s<br>three p<br>one d | one s<br>three p<br>two d |
| **Hybrid orbitals formed** | two sp | three $sp^2$ | four $sp^3$ | five $sp^3d$ | six $sp^3d^2$ |
| **Unhybridized orbitals remaining** | two p | one p | none | four d | three d |

**Orientation**

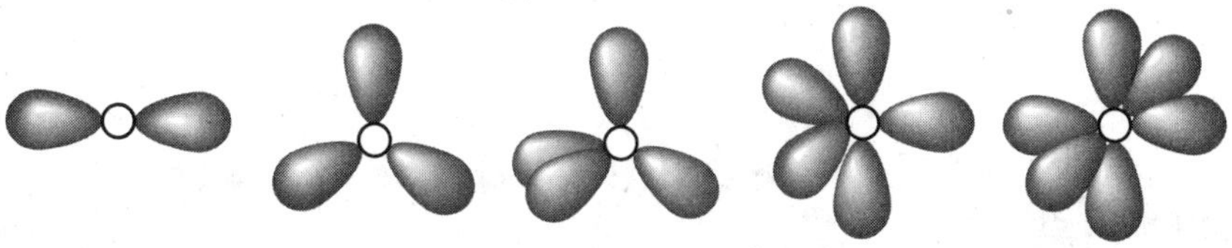

**Figure 8.7 Hybridization of s, p, and d orbitals.**

ENRICHMENT

*$sp^3d$ hybridization* results from the blending of an s orbital, three p orbitals, and one d orbital. The result is five $sp^3d$ orbitals with a trigonal bipyramidal orientation. This type of bonding occurs in compounds like $PCl_5$. Note that this hybridization is an exception to the octet rule.

*$sp^3d^2$ hybridization* occurs when one s, three p, and two d orbitals are mixed, giving an octahedral arrangement. $SF_6$ is an example. Again, this hybridization is an exception to the octet rule. If one starts with this structure and one of the bonding pairs becomes a lone pair, then a square pyramidal shape results, while two lone pairs give a square planar shape.

Figure 8.8 shows the hybridization that occurs in ethylene, $H_2C{=}CH_2$. Each carbon atom has $sp^2$ hybridization. On each carbon, two of the hybrid orbitals have overlapped with an s orbital on a hydrogen atom to form a carbon-to-hydrogen covalent bond. The third $sp^2$ hybrid orbital has overlapped with the $sp^2$ hybrid on the other carbon to form a carbon-to-carbon covalent bond. Note that the remaining p orbital on each carbon that has not undergone hybridization is also overlapping above and below a line joining the carbons. In ethylene, there are two types of bonds. In **sigma ($\sigma$) bonds,** the overlap of the orbitals occurs on a line between the two atoms involved in the covalent bond. In ethylene, the C–H bonds and one of the C–C bonds are sigma bonds. In **pi ($\pi$) bonds,** the overlap of orbitals occurs above and below a line through the two nuclei of the atoms involved in the bond. A double bond always is composed of one sigma and one pi bond. A carbon-to-carbon triple bond results from the overlap of a sp hybrid orbital and two p orbitals on one carbon, with the same on the other carbon. In this situation, there will be one sigma bond (overlap of the sp hybrid orbitals) and two pi bonds (overlap of two sets of p orbitals).

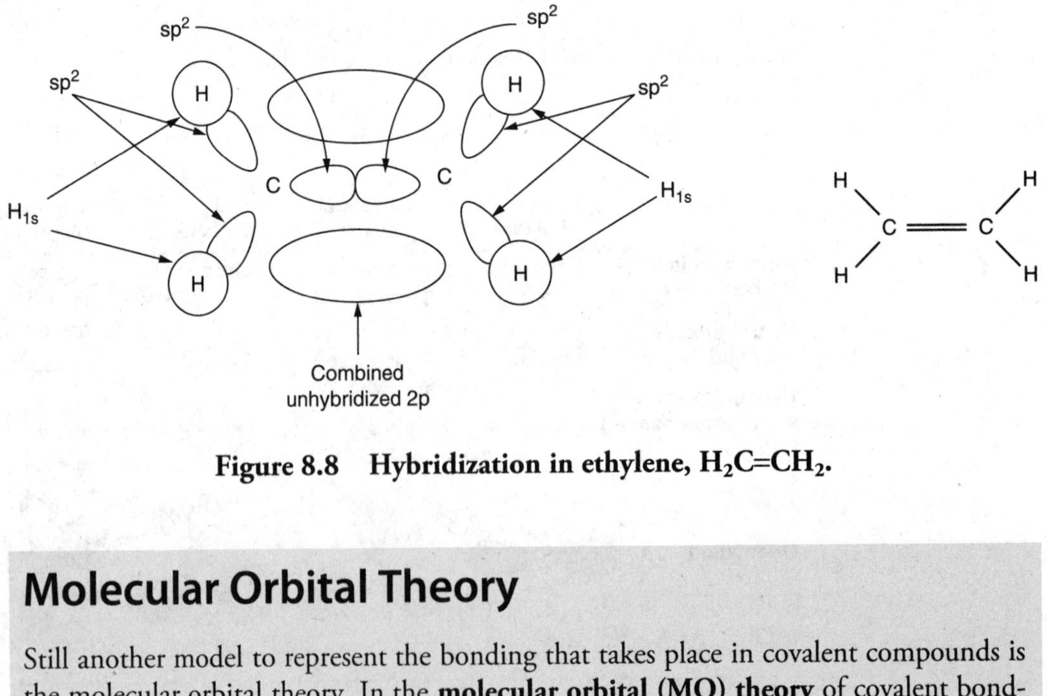


**Figure 8.8 Hybridization in ethylene, $H_2C{=}CH_2$.**

ENRICHMENT

## Molecular Orbital Theory

Still another model to represent the bonding that takes place in covalent compounds is the molecular orbital theory. In the **molecular orbital (MO) theory** of covalent bonding, atomic orbitals (AOs) on the individual atoms combine to form orbitals that encompass the entire molecule. These are called molecular orbitals (MOs). These molecular orbitals have definite shapes and energies associated with them. When two atomic orbitals are added, two molecular orbitals are formed, one bonding and one antibonding.

The bonding MO is of lower energy than the antibonding MO. In the molecular orbital model, the atomic orbitals are added together to form the molecular orbitals. Then the electrons are added to the molecular orbitals, following the rules used previously when filling orbitals: lowest-energy orbitals get filled first, maximum of two electrons per orbital, and half-fill orbitals of equal energy before pairing electrons (see Chapter 5). When s atomic orbitals are added, one sigma bonding ($\sigma$) and one sigma antibonding ($\sigma^*$) molecular orbital are formed. Figure 8.9 shows the molecular orbital diagram for $H_2$.

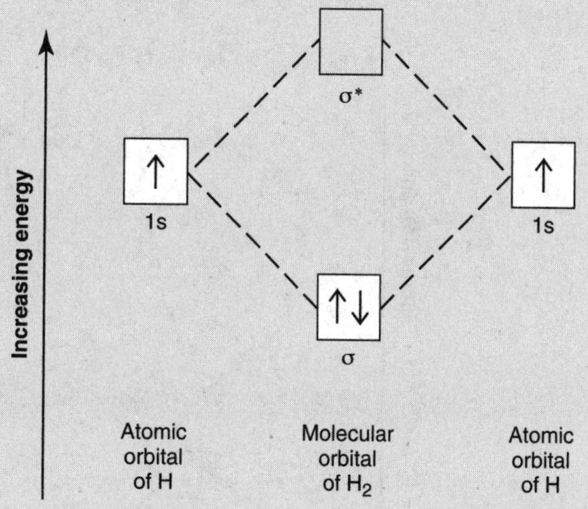


**Figure 8.9 Molecular orbital diagram of $H_2$.**

Note that the two electrons (one from each hydrogen) have both gone into the sigma bonding MO. The bonding situation can be calculated in the molecular orbital theory by calculating the MO bond order. The MO bond order is the number of electrons in bonding MOs minus the number of electrons in antibonding MOs, divided by 2. For $H_2$ in Figure 8.9 the bond order would be $(2 - 0)/2 = 1$. A stable bonding situation exists between two atoms when the bond order is greater than zero. The larger the bond order, the stronger the bond.

When two sets of p orbitals combine, one sigma bonding and one sigma antibonding MO are formed, along with two bonding pi MOs and two pi antibonding ($\pi$) MOs. Figure 8.10 shows the MO diagram for $O_2$. For the sake of simplicity, the 1s orbitals of each oxygen and the MOs for these electrons are not shown, just the valence-electron orbitals.

KEY IDEA

The bond order for $O_2$ would be $(10 - 6)/2 = 2$. (Don't forget to count the bonding and antibonding electrons at energy level 1.) Unlike VSEPR or valence bond theory, MO theory predicts that the oxygen molecule has two unpaired electrons (the two highest energy electrons). Experimental observations demonstrate the oxygen molecules have two unpaired electrons each. MO theory is the only one of the three theories to give the correct answer.

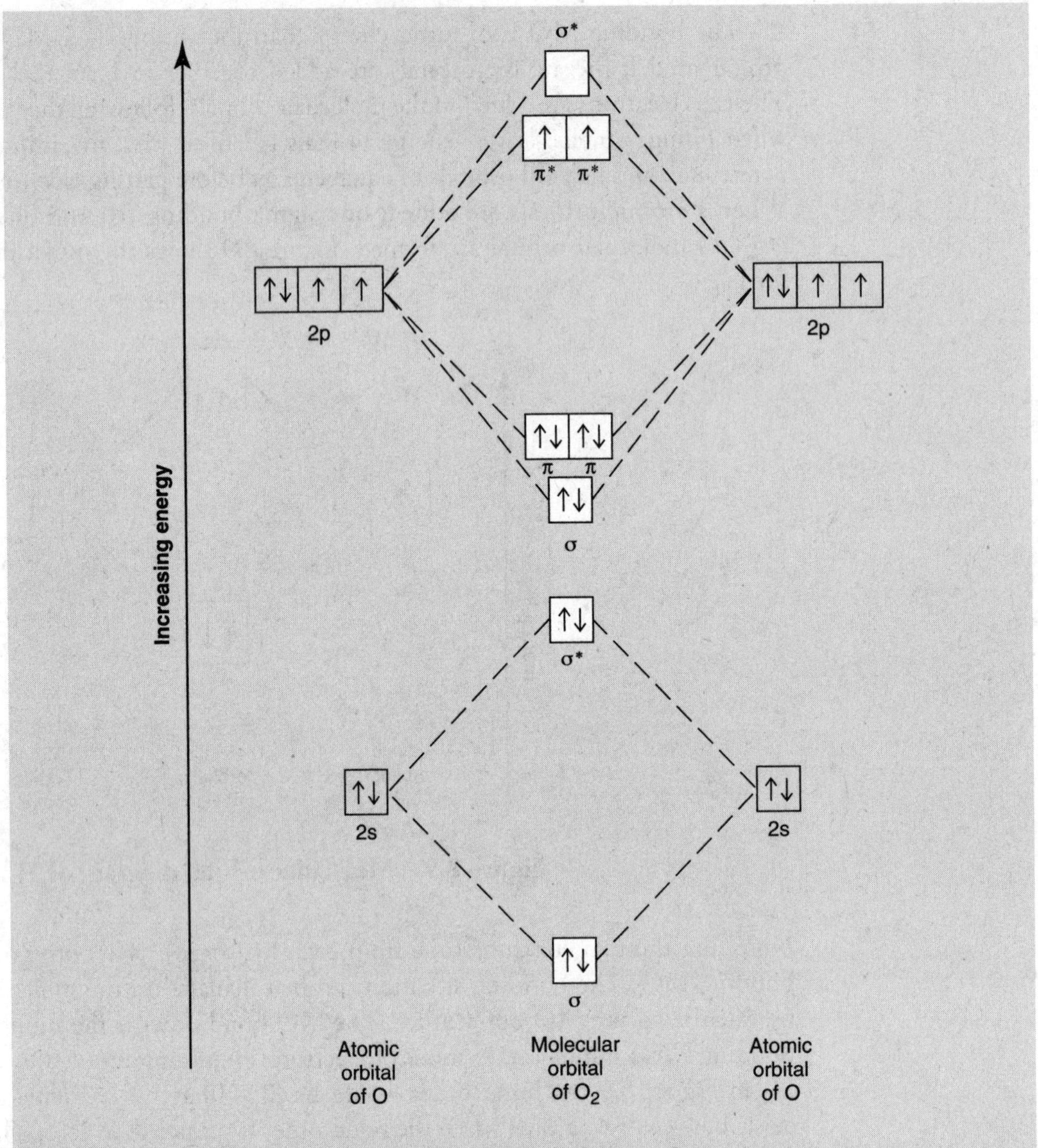


**Figure 8.10 MO diagram of $O_2$.**

## Resonance

TIP

Sometimes when writing the Lewis structure of a compound, more than one possible structure is generated for a given molecule. The nitrate ion, $NO_3^-$, is a good example. Three possible Lewis structures can be written for this polyatomic anion, differing in which oxygen is double bonded to the nitrogen. None truly represents the actual structure of the nitrate ion; that would require an average of all three Lewis structures. **Resonance** theory is used to describe this situation. Resonance occurs when more than one Lewis structure can be written for a molecule (without rearranging the atoms). The individual structures are called resonance structures (or forms) and are written with a two-headed arrow (↔) between them. Figure 8.11 shows the three resonance forms of the nitrate ion.

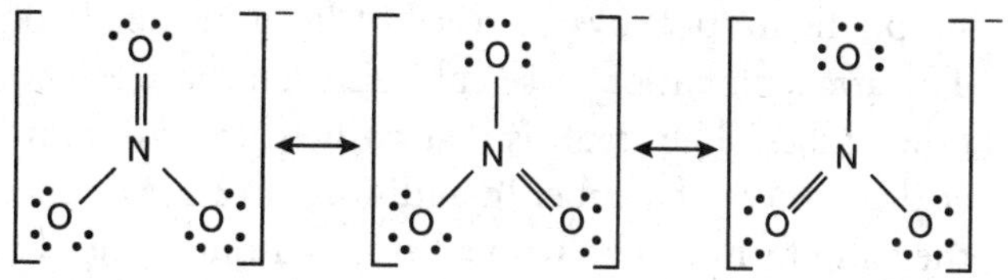


**Figure 8.11 Resonance structures of the nitrate ion, $NO_3^-$.**

Again, let us emphasize that the actual structure of the nitrate is not any of the three shown. Neither is it flipping back and forth among the three. It is an average of all three. All the bonds are the same, intermediate between single bonds and double bonds in strength and length.

# Bond Length, Strength, and Magnetic Properties

The length and strength of a covalent bond is related to its bond order. The greater the bond order, the shorter and stronger the bond. Diatomic nitrogen, for example, has a short, extremely strong bond due to its nitrogen-to-nitrogen triple bond.

One of the advantages of the molecular orbital model is that it can predict some of the magnetic properties of molecules. If molecules are placed in a strong magnetic field, they exhibit one of two magnetic behaviors—attraction or repulsion. **Paramagnetism**, the attraction to a magnetic field, is due to the presence of unpaired electrons; **diamagnetism**, the slight repulsion from a magnetic field, is due to the presence of only paired electrons. Look at Figure 8.10, the MO diagram for diatomic oxygen. Note that it does have two unpaired electrons in the $\pi_{2p}^*$ antibonding orbitals. Thus, one would predict, based on the MO model, that oxygen should be paramagnetic, and that is exactly what is observed in the laboratory.

# Structure of Metals and Alloys

Approximately 80 percent of the elements are metals. There are three basic structures adopted by most metals. One of these basic structures is body-centered cubic. One of the metals adopting this structure is lithium. The structure of lithium is pictured in Figure 8.12. In the structure of lithium, there are eight lithium atoms at the corners of a cube with an additional lithium atom in the center of the cube. The structure is more intricate than this

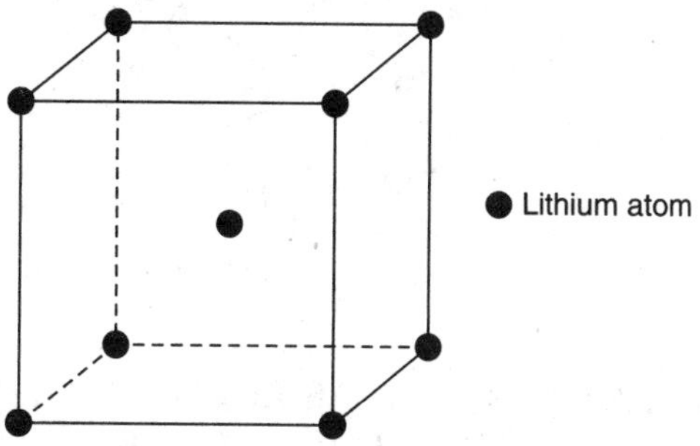


**Figure 8.12 The body-centered cubic structure of lithium metal.**

simple figure portrays. A piece of lithium metal consists of these cubes stacked together. The arrangement of these cubes is such that each corner of each cube is a corner of seven other cubes. The result is that corner lithium atom is surrounded by eight lithium atoms at the corners of a cube. In addition, if one examines the atoms at the center of the cubes, they also form a cube with a lithium atom at the center of a cube.

All the lithium atoms have the same electronegativity, and if they were not metal atoms, one would assume covalent bonding. However, covalent will not work. If we look at the lithium atom in the center of the cube, it is bonded to the eight corners. If these were covalent bonds, 16 electrons would be necessary. However, lithium atoms only have one valence electron, which gives a total of nine for the cube. Nine electrons are far less than the 16 required by covalent bonds. Compared to the bonding in covalent compounds, metals are electron deficient. Metallic bonding does not have localized bonds like covalent bonding has. One view of metallic bonding is to consider the metal nuclei and core electrons to be in fixed positions with the valence electrons freely moving. The freely moving electrons serve as a "glue" to keep the atoms together. The freely moving electrons are often referred to as a "sea of electrons."

The other metal structures are similar except that each atom is surrounded by 12 neighbors instead of 8.

When more than one type of metal atom is present, there are two possible results. (A few nonmetallic atoms may also work.) An intermetallic compound may form. An intermetallic compound, like any compound, has a fixed composition. The more common situation is for an alloy to form. An alloy is a solution, and as such behaves like all other solutions. Solutions may be unsaturated, saturated, or supersaturated. The solvent and solute may be miscible (able to mix in any proportion). Alloys exhibit all these characteristics.

There are two broad categories of alloys. One category is the interstitial alloys. The other category is the substitutional alloys. Some alloys may be a mixture of both types. The different types of metal alloys are illustrated in Figure 8.13.

Interstitial alloys form when a metal "dissolves" small atoms. These small atoms, such as boron, carbon, and hydrogen, fit into the spaces between the metal atoms. These spaces

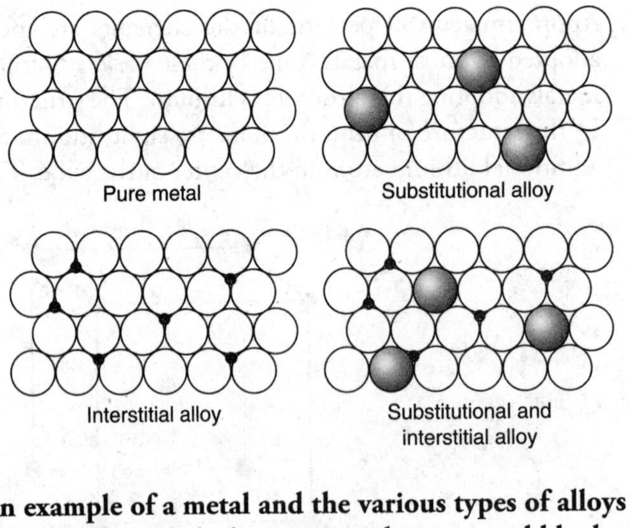


**Figure 8.13 An example of a metal and the various types of alloys that metal may form. The metal could be nickel, the interstitial atoms could be hydrogen, and the substitutional atom could be cobalt.**

are "interstitial holes." The metal atoms generally remain in or near their original positions. Many of these compounds are commercially important. For example, many metal hydrides are useful for the storage of hydrogen. Some of these metal hydrides can store more hydrogen per unit volume than an equal volume of liquid hydrogen. Most steel contains some interstitial carbon for added strength. Many interstitial hydrides are nonstoichiometric (no definite formula). For example, the maximum amount of hydrogen that can dissolve in palladium metal gives the formula $PdH_{0.7}$.

Substitutional alloys occur when one metal atom substitutes for another. Normally the atoms need to be close to the same size (the radii should not differ by more than 15%). If the radii differ by more than 15%, there may be limited dissolution of one metal into another. The radii used are metallic radii, not atomic radii, or ionic radii. For example, manganese will dissolve in iron as observed in most steels.

## Experiments

STRATEGY

There have been no experimental questions concerning this material on recent AP Chemistry Exams.

## Common Mistakes to Avoid

TIP

1. Remember that metals + nonmetals form ionic bonds, while the reaction of two nonmetals forms a covalent bond. And finally, the reaction between two metals forms a metallic bond. While there are exceptions to these predictions, do not expect them to appear on the AP Chemistry Exam.
2. The octet rule does not always work, but for the representative elements, it works the majority of the time. Hydrogen will always be an exception because it aims to get two electrons.
3. Atoms that lose electrons form cations; atoms that gain electrons form anions.
4. In writing the formulas of ionic compounds, make sure the subscripts are in the lowest ratio of whole numbers.
5. When using the crisscross rule, be sure the subscripts are reduced to the lowest whole-number ratio.
6. When using the $N - A = S$ rule in writing Lewis structures, be sure you add electrons to the $A$ term for a polyatomic anion and subtract electrons for a polyatomic cation.
7. In the $N - A = S$ rule, only the *valence* electrons are counted.
8. In using the VSEPR theory, when going from the electron-group geometry to the molecular geometry, start with the electron-group geometry; make the nonbonding electrons mentally invisible; and then describe what is left.
9. When adding electrons to the molecular orbitals, remember to begin with the lowest energy first. On orbitals with equal energies, half-fill and then pair up.
10. When writing Lewis structures of polyatomic ions, don't forget to show the charge.
11. When you draw resonance structures, you can move only electrons (bonds). Never move the atoms.
12. When answering questions, the stability of the noble-gas configurations is a result, not an explanation. Your answers will require an explanation, i.e., lower-energy state.

# › Review Questions

Use these questions to review the content of this chapter and practice for the AP Chemistry Exam. First are 20 multiple-choice questions similar to what you will encounter in Section I of the AP Chemistry Exam. The multiple-choice portion also includes questions designed to help you review prior knowledge. Following those is a long free-response question like the ones in Section II of the exam. To make these questions an even more authentic practice for the actual exam, time yourself following the instructions provided.

## Multiple-Choice Questions

Answer the following questions in 30 minutes. You may not use a calculator. You may use the periodic table and the equation sheet at the back of this book.

**1.** VSEPR predicts an $SbF_5$ molecule will be which of the following shapes?

(A) tetrahedral
(B) trigonal bipyramidal
(C) square pyramid
(D) trigonal planar

**2.** The shortest bond would be present in which of the following substances?

(A) $I_2$
(B) CO
(C) $CCl_4$
(D) $O_2^{2-}$

**3.** Which of the following does NOT have one or more $\pi$ bonds?

(A) $H_2O$
(B) $HNO_3$
(C) $O_2$
(D) $N_2$

**4.** Which of the following is nonpolar?

(A) $IF_5$
(B) $IF_3$
(C) $SiF_4$
(D) $SeF_4$

**5.** Resonance structures are necessary to describe the bonding in which of the following?

(A) $H_2O$
(B) $ClF_3$
(C) $HNO_3$
(D) $CH_4$

**For questions 6 and 7, pick the best choice from the following:**

(A) ionic bonds
(B) hybrid orbitals
(C) resonance structures
(D) van der Waals attractions

**6.** An explanation of the equivalent bond lengths of the nitrite ion is:

**7.** Most organic substances have low melting points. This may be because, in most cases, the intermolecular forces are:

**8.** Which of the following has more than one unshared pair of valence electrons on the central atom?

(A) $BrF_5$
(B) $NF_3$
(C) $IF_7$
(D) $ClF_3$

**9.** Which of the following groups contains only elements that can exceed an octet in at least some of their compounds?

(A) Sb, Br, N
(B) As, I, Si
(C) C, S, Bi
(D) O, Te, Ge

**10.** The only substance listed below that contains ionic, $\sigma$, and $\pi$ bonds is:

(A) $Ca_3P_2$
(B) $CO_2$
(C) $CaCO_3$
(D) $NH_3$

**11.** The electron pairs point toward the corners of which geometrical shape for a molecule with $sp^2$ hybrid orbitals?

(A) trigonal planar
(B) octahedron
(C) trigonal bipyramid
(D) trigonal pyramid

**12.** Regular tetrahedral molecules or ions include which of the following?

(A) $SF_4$
(B) $NH_4^+$
(C) $XeF_4$
(D) $ICl_4^-$

**13.** Which of the following molecules or ions has the greatest number of unshared electrons around the central atom?

(A) $SO_2$
(B) $NO_3^-$
(C) $KrF_2$
(D) $SF_4$

**14.** Which of the following molecules is the least polar?

(A) $PH_3$
(B) $CH_4$
(C) $H_2O$
(D) $NO_2$

**15.** Which of the following molecules is the most polar?

(A) $NH_3$
(B) $N_2$
(C) $CH_3I$
(D) $BF_3$

**16.** Each of the following processes involves breaking bonds, and most involve forming new bonds. Which of the following processes involves breaking an ionic bond?

(A) $H_2(g) + I_2(g) \rightarrow 2\ HI(g)$
(B) $2\ KCl(s) \rightarrow 2\ K(g) + Cl_2(g)$
(C) $Ca(s) \rightarrow Ca(g)$
(D) $2\ C_8H_{18}(g) + 25\ O_2(g) \rightarrow 16\ CO_2(g) + 18\ H_2O(g)$

**17.** Which of the following sets of bonds is listed in order of increasing covalent character?

(A) Na–Cl < Al–Cl < P–Cl < Cl–Cl
(B) Na–Cl < P–Cl < Cl–Cl < Al–Cl
(C) P–Cl < Cl–Cl < Al–Cl < Na–Cl
(D) Al–Cl < Na–Cl < P–Cl < Cl–Cl

**18.** Which of the following molecules does NOT contain one or more $\pi$ bonds?

(A) $CO_2$
(B) $SF_6$
(C) CO
(D) $SO_3$

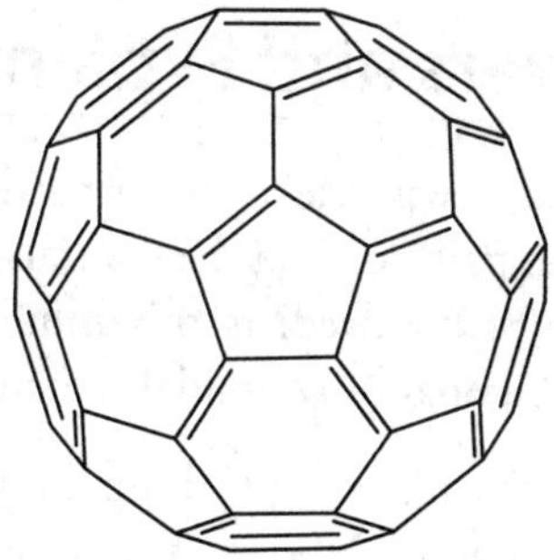

**19.** The above diagram illustrates a portion of a molecule of buckminsterfullerene (a "Bucky ball"). The corners are carbon atoms. Each carbon atom has four covalent bonds, allowing it to follow the octet rule. The structure also shows many single and double bonds. Carbon–carbon double bonds are shorter than carbon–carbon single bonds. In an analysis of the structure of buckminsterfullerene, all carbon–carbon bonds are found to be the same length and not a combination of short double bonds and longer single bonds. Which of the following best explains this observation?

(A) VSEPR
(B) resonance
(C) hybridization
(D) experimental error

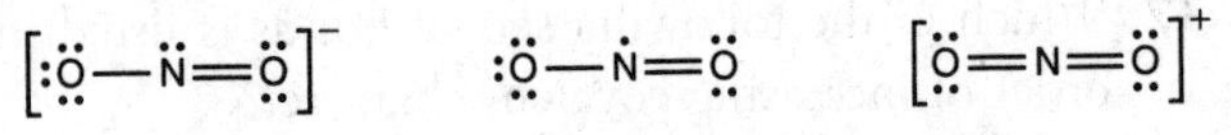

20. There are three nitrogen-oxygen species known with a 1:2 nitrogen-to-oxygen ratio. The Lewis electron-dot diagrams for these three nitrogen oxygen species are shown in the above diagram. Which of the three has the largest bond angle?

(A) $NO_2^-$
(B) $NO_2$
(C) $NO_2^+$
(D) All have a 180° angle.

## › Answers and Explanations

1. **B**—The Lewis (electron-dot) structure has five bonding pairs around the central Sb and no lone pairs. VSEPR predicts this number of pairs to give a trigonal bipyramidal structure.

2. **B**—All bonds except those in CO are single bonds. The CO bond is a triple bond. Triple bonds are shorter than double bonds, which are shorter than single bonds. Drawing Lewis structures might help you answer this question.

3. **A**—Answers B through D contain molecules with double or triple bonds. Double and triple bonds contain $\pi$ bonds. Water has only single ($\sigma$) bonds. If any of these are not obvious to you, draw a Lewis structure.

4. **C**—Use VSEPR; only the tetrahedral $SiF_4$ is nonpolar. The other materials form square pyramidal ($IF_5$), T-shaped ($IF_3$), and irregular tetrahedral ($SeF_4$) shapes and are therefore polar.

5. **C**—All other answers involve species containing only single bonds. Substances without double or triple bonds seldom need resonance structures.

6. **C**—Resonance causes bonds to have the same average length.

7. **D**—Many organic molecules are nonpolar. Nonpolar substances are held together by weak van der Waals attractions.

8. **D**—Lewis structures are required. You may not need to draw all of them. A and B have one unshared pair, whereas C does not have an unshared pair. D has two unshared pairs of electrons.

9. **B**—For an atom to exceed an octet of electrons, it must be in the third period or lower on the periodic table. The elements N, C, and O are in the second period; therefore, the answers containing these elements contain an element that cannot exceed an octet. Only answer B is limited to elements that can exceed an octet.

10. **C**—The ionic bonds are present in the calcium compounds (eliminating all but A and C). The phosphide ion, $P^{3-}$, has no internal bonding (eliminating A); however, the carbonate ion, $CO_3^{2-}$, has both $\sigma$ and $\pi$ bonds.

11. **A**—This hybridization requires a geometrical shape with three corners. B is for six pairs. C is for five pairs. D has four pairs.

12. **B**—One or more Lewis structures may help you. A is an irregular tetrahedron (see-saw); C and D are square planar.

13. **C**—Draw the Lewis structures. The number of unshared pairs are as follows: (A) 1; (B) 0; (C) 3; (D) 1.

14. **B**—All molecules are polar except B.

**15. A**—Drawing one or more Lewis structures may help you. Only A and C are polar. Only the ammonia has hydrogen bonding, which is very, very polar.

**16. B**—Calcium is a metal; therefore, the process shown is breaking metallic bonds. All the species in A and D are covalently bonded molecules. Potassium chloride, KCl, is an ionic compound, and separating the ions involves breaking ionic bonds.

**17. A**—Increasing covalent character means decreasing electronegativity difference. Chlorine is a constant, so the electronegativity differences of concern are all relative to chlorine. The most covalent would be a bond with an electronegativity difference of 0, which occurs when chlorine is bonded to chlorine (Cl–Cl). In general, the covalent character will decrease (ionic character will increase) when moving from chlorine to the left on the periodic table. The Na–Cl bond would be the most ionic (least covalent). Only answer A has the bonds in the correct order.

**18. B**—The $SF_6$ molecule has six $\sigma$ bonds and no $\pi$ bonds. The other three molecules have double or triple bonds. All double bonds are a combination of an $\sigma$ bond and a $\pi$ bond, and all triple bonds are a combination of one $\sigma$ bond and two $\pi$ bonds.

**19. B**—The process of resonance tends to equalize the lengths of the bonds involved.

**20. C**—Just looking at the Lewis structures can be misleading. You should use VSEPR to predict the bond angles. The ion $NO_2^+$ is a linear species (bond angle 180°) because there are no lone electron pairs on the nitrogen atom.

The other two molecules are bent species (bond angle < 180°) due to the lone electron (≈134°) or pair of electrons (≈118°) on the nitrogen. The presence of resonance does not alter the result.

## › Free-Response Question

You have 15 minutes to answer the following question. You may use a calculator and the tables in the back of the book.

### Question

Answer the following questions about structure and bonding.

(a) Which of the following tetrafluoride compounds is polar? Use Lewis electron-dot structures to explain your conclusions.

$SiF_4$ $SF_4$ $XeF_4$

(b) Rank the following compounds in order of increasing melting point. Explain your answer. Lewis electron-dot structures may aid you.

$SnF_2$ $SeF_2$ $KrF_2$

(c) Use Lewis electron-dot structures to show why the carbon–oxygen bonds in the oxalate ion ($C_2O_4^{2-}$) are all equal.

(d) When $PCl_5$ is dissolved in a polar solvent, the solution conducts electricity. Explain why. Use an appropriate chemical equation to illustrate your answer. Hint: there are no $P^{5+}$ ions present.

## › Answer and Explanation

(a) Sulfur tetrafluoride is the only one of the three compounds that is polar.

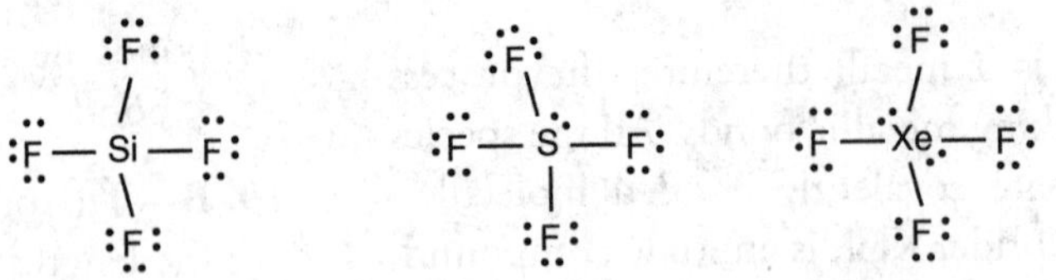

$SiF_4$: four bonding pairs and no lone pairs Tetrahedral

$SF_4$: four bonding pairs and one lone pair. Seesaw

$XeF_4$: four bonding pairs and two lone pairs. Square planar

You get 1 point if you correctly predict only $SF_4$ to be polar, and 1 point for having a correct Lewis structure for $SF_4$. You get 1 point each for a correct Lewis structure for $SiF_4$ and $XeF_4$.

(b) The order is $KrF_2 < SeF_2 < SnF_2$.

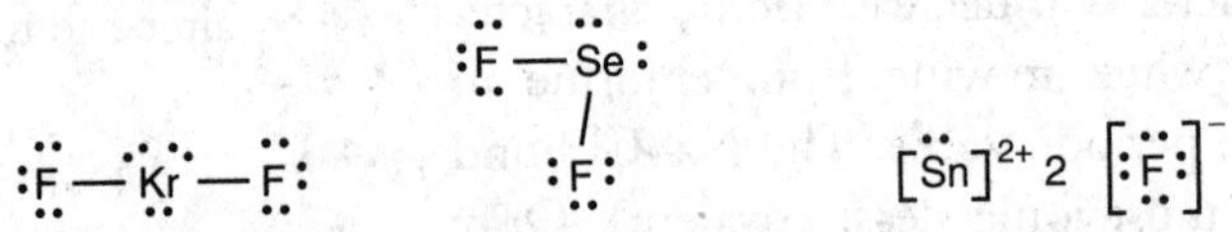

$KrF_2$: two bonding pairs and three nonbonding pairs

$SeF_2$: two bonding pairs and two nonbonding pairs

$SnF_2$: ionic

The Lewis structure indicates that $KrF_2$ is nonpolar. Thus, it has only very weak London dispersion forces between the molecules. $SeF_2$ is polar, and the molecules are attracted by dipole–dipole attractions, which are stronger than London (higher melting point). $SnF_2$ has the highest melting point because of the presence of strong ionic bonds.

You get 1 point for the order and 1 point for the discussion.

(c) It is possible to draw the following resonance structures for the oxalate ion. The presence of resonance equalizes the bonds.

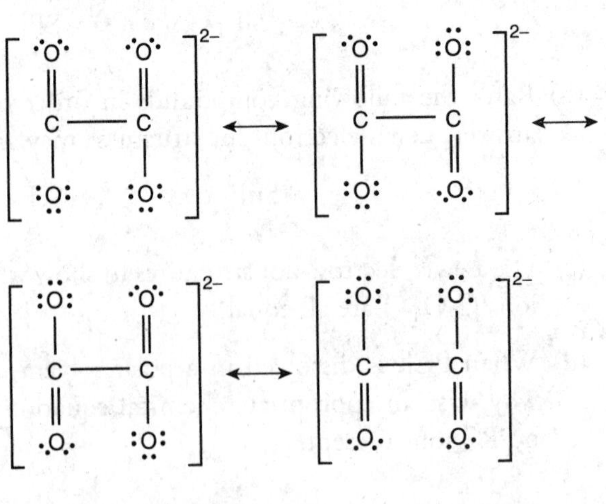

You get 1 point for any correct Lewis structure for $C_2O_4^{2-}$ and 1 point for showing or discussing resonance.

(d) $PCl_5$ must ionize (be an electrolyte). There are several acceptable equations, all of which must indicate the formation of ions. Here are two choices:

$$2\ PCl_5 \leftrightarrows PCl_4^+ + PCl_6^- \quad \text{or} \quad PCl_5 \leftrightarrows PCl_4^+ + Cl^-$$

You get 1 point for the explanation and 1 point for any *balanced* equation showing the formation of ions unless the equation contains $P^{5+}$ ions.

Total your points. There are 10 points possible.

## ❯ Rapid Review

- Compounds are pure substances that have a fixed proportion of elements.
- Metals react with nonmetals to form ionic bonds, and nonmetals react with other nonmetals to form covalent bonds.
- The Lewis electron-dot structure is a way of representing an element and its valence electrons.
- Atoms tend to lose, gain, or share electrons to achieve the same electronic configuration as (become isoelectronic to) the nearest noble gas.
- Atoms are generally most stable when they have a complete octet (eight electrons).
- Ionic bonds result when a metal loses electrons to form cations and a nonmetal gains those electrons to form an anion.
- Ionic bonds can also result from the interaction of polyatomic ions.
- The attraction of the opposite charges (anions and cations) forms the ionic bond.
- The crisscross rule can help determine the formula of an ionic compound.
- In covalent bonding two atoms share one or more electron pairs.
- If the electrons are shared equally, the bond is a nonpolar covalent bond, but unequal sharing results in a polar covalent bond.
- The element that will have the greatest attraction for a bonding pair of electrons is related to its electronegativity.
- Electronegativity values increase from left to right on the periodic table and decrease from top to bottom.
- The $N - A = S$ rule can be used to help draw the Lewis structure of a molecule.
- Molecular geometry, the arrangement of atoms in three-dimensional space, can be predicted using the VSEPR theory. This theory says the electron pairs around a central atom will try to get as far as possible from each other to minimize the repulsive forces.
- In using the VSEPR theory, first determine the electron-group geometry, then the molecular geometry.
- The valence bond theory describes covalent bonding as the overlap of atomic orbitals to form a new kind of orbital, a hybrid orbital.
- The number of hybrid orbitals is the same as the number of atomic orbitals that were combined.

- There are several types of hybrid orbital, such as sp, $sp^2$, and $sp^3$.
- In the valence bond theory, sigma ($\sigma$) bonds overlap on a line drawn between the two nuclei, while pi ($\pi$) bonds result from the overlap of atomic orbitals above and below a line connecting the two atomic nuclei.
- A double or triple bond is always composed of one sigma bond and the rest pi bonds.
- Resonance occurs when more than one Lewis structure can be written for a molecule.
- The actual structure of the molecule is an average of the Lewis resonance structures.
- The higher the bond order, the shorter and stronger the bond.
- Paramagnetism, the attraction of a molecule to a magnetic field, is due to the presence of unpaired electrons. Diamagnetism, the repulsion of a molecule from a magnetic field, is due to the presence of paired electrons.

# CHAPTER 9

# Solids, Liquids, and Intermolecular Forces

**IN THIS CHAPTER**

In this chapter, the following AP topics are covered:

2.2 Intramolecular Force and Potential Energy
2.3 Structure of Ionic Solids
3.1 Intermolecular Forces
3.2 Properties of Solids

**Summary:** In the chapter on gases, we discuss the gaseous state. In this chapter, we will discuss the liquid and solid states and the forces that exist between the particles—the intermolecular forces. A substance's state of matter depends on two factors: the average kinetic energy of the particles and the intermolecular forces between the particles. The kinetic energy tends to move the particles away from each other. The temperature of the substance is a measure of the average kinetic energy of the molecules. As the temperature increases, the average kinetic energy increases, and the particles tend to move farther apart. This is consistent with our experience of heating ice, for example, and watching it move from the solid state to the liquid state and finally to the gaseous state. For this to happen, the kinetic energy overcomes the forces between the particles, the intermolecular forces.

In the solid state, the kinetic energy of the particles cannot overcome the intermolecular forces; the particles are held close together by the intermolecular forces. As the temperature increases, the kinetic energy increases and begins to overcome the attractive intermolecular forces. The substance will eventually melt, going from the solid to the liquid state. As this melting takes place, the temperature remains constant even though energy is being added. The temperature at which the solid converts into the liquid state is called the **melting point (m.p.)** of the solid.

After all the solid has been converted into a liquid, the temperature again starts to rise as energy is added. The particles are still relatively close together and possess enough kinetic energy to move with respect to each other. Finally, if enough energy is added, the particles start to break free of the intermolecular forces, keeping them relatively close together and they escape the liquid as essentially independent gas particles. This process of going from the liquid state to the gaseous state is called boiling, and the temperature at which this occurs is called the **boiling point (b.p.)** of the liquid. Sometimes, however, a solid can go directly from the solid state to the gaseous state without ever having become a liquid. This process is called **sublimation**. Dry ice, solid carbon dioxide, readily sublimes.

These changes of state, called **phase changes** or changes in state, are related to temperature, but pressure changes will also influence the changes in state. We will see how these relationships can be diagrammed later in this chapter.

Remember these phase changes are due to changes in the average kinetic energy of the particles. The intermolecular forces remain the same.

KEY IDEA

### Keywords and Equations

No specific keywords or equations are listed on the AP Exam for this topic.

## Structures and Intermolecular Forces

**Intermolecular forces** are attractive or repulsive forces between particles, caused by partial charges. These attractive forces are the ones that work to overcome the randomizing forces of kinetic energy. The structure and type of bonding of a specific substance have quite a bit to do with the type of interaction and the strength of that interaction. Before we start examining the different types of intermolecular forces, recall from the Chapter 8, Bonding, that those molecules that have polar covalent bonding (unequal sharing of the bonding electron pair) may possess dipoles (having positive and negative ends due to charge separation within the molecule). Dipoles are often involved in intermolecular forces. Collectively, all of these are often referred to as van der Waals forces. Do not use this term to refer to any individual force. For large molecules, often biomolecules, the intermolecular forces may be between different regions of the same molecule.

The following discussion introduces the different intermolecular forces, and with one exception, it is in order of decreasing strength.

### Ionic, Covalent, and Metallic Bonds

These bonds were introduced in Chapter 8, and while they are not true intermolecular forces, there are many situations where the intermolecular forces discussed in the section much compete with these bonds. For example, when an ionic solid dissolves in water, it is necessary to relate the ionic bonds in the solid with the ion–dipole forces that form. Therefore, a few observations concerning these bonds need to be made.

When dealing with ionic bonds, the magnitude of the charges and the sizes of the ions are important. Coulomb's law is important and is the structure of the solid. The greater the charge, the stronger the ionic bond. The smaller the size of the ion, the stronger the ionic bond. The effect of structure is normally small. For example, there are two forms of ZnS with one being 0.2% more stable than the other even though the charges and sizes are identical.

For covalent bonds, both the strength and the lengths of the bonds depend upon the atoms involved and the bond order. Smaller atoms tend to form stronger and shorter bonds than larger atoms do, but comparisons must deal with comparing bonds with the same bond order. For the representative elements, the bonds may be single, double, or triple (bond orders 1, 2, and 3, respectively). Other possibilities are known for the transition metals; however, these will not appear on the AP Exam. The higher the bond order, the stronger and shorter the bond.

Predictions involving metallic bonds are beyond the AP Exam.

### Ion–Dipole Intermolecular Forces

These forces are due to the attraction of an ion and one end of a polar molecule (dipole). This type of attraction is especially important in aqueous salt solutions, where the ion attracts water molecules and may form a hydrated ion, such as $Al(H_2O)_6^{3+}$. This is one of the strongest of the intermolecular forces.

It is also important to realize that this intermolecular force requires two different species—an ion and a polar molecule. This type of intermolecular force is especially important in aqueous solutions containing an electrolyte.

### Dipole–Dipole Intermolecular Forces

These forces result from the attraction of the positive end of one dipole to the negative end of another dipole. For example, in gaseous hydrogen chloride, HCl(g), the hydrogen end has a partial positive charge, and the chlorine end has a partial negative charge, due to chlorine's higher electronegativity. Dipole–dipole attractions are especially important in polar liquids. They tend to be a rather strong force, although not as strong as ion–dipole attractions. These forces may be present in a single substance or in a solution.

Dipole–dipole forces are always present in diatomic molecules containing atoms with differing electronegativities. If a molecule contains more than two atoms, it is necessary to consider the molecular geometry in addition to the electronegativity.

### Hydrogen Bond Intermolecular Forces

**Hydrogen bonding** is a special type of dipole–dipole attraction in which a hydrogen atom is polar-covalently bonded to one of the following extremely electronegative elements: N, O, or F. These hydrogen bonds are extremely polar bonds by nature, so there is a great degree of charge separation within the molecule. Therefore, the attraction of the positively charged hydrogen of one molecule and the negatively charged N, O, or F of another molecule is extremely strong. These hydrogen bonds are, in general, stronger than the typical dipole–dipole interaction. This is the only intermolecular force in this discussion that is out of order, as it is stronger than the preceding intermolecular force.

Hydrogen bonding explains why HF(aq) is a weak acid, while HCl(aq), HBr(aq), and HI(aq) are strong acids. The hydrogen bond between the hydrogen of one HF molecule and the fluorine of another "traps" the hydrogen, so it is much harder to break its bonds and free the hydrogen to be donated as an $H^+$. Hydrogen bonding also explains why water has such unusual properties—for example, its unusually high boiling point and the fact that its solid phase is less dense than its liquid phase. The hydrogen bonds tend to stabilize the water molecules and keep them from readily escaping into the gas phase. When water freezes, the hydrogen bonds are stabilized and lock the water molecules into a framework with a lot of open space. Therefore, ice floats in liquid water. Hydrogen bonding also holds the strands of DNA together.

### Ion-Induced Dipole and Dipole-Induced Dipole Intermolecular Forces

These types of attraction occur when the charge on an ion or a dipole distorts the electron cloud of a nonpolar molecule and induces a temporary dipole in the nonpolar molecule. Like ion–dipole intermolecular forces, these also require two different species, which means they are important in solutions. They are relatively weak interactions. Increasing the charge on an ion or the polarity of a dipole will increase the strength of these types of interactions.

### London (Dispersion) Intermolecular Force

This intermolecular attraction occurs in all substances; however, London dispersion forces are only significant when the other types of intermolecular forces are absent. It arises from a momentary distortion of the electron cloud, with the creation of a very weak dipole. The weak dipole induces a dipole in another nonpolar molecule. This is an extremely weak interaction, but it is strong enough to allow us to liquefy nonpolar gases such as hydrogen, $H_2$, and nitrogen, $N_2$, and the noble gases like helium, He. If there were no intermolecular forces attracting these molecules, it would be impossible to liquefy them. The nitrogen molecule has more electrons than either the hydrogen molecule or the helium atom, and consequently $N_2$ has the highest boiling point of the three. In general, the greater the number of electrons, the greater the London dispersion force (polarizability of the electrons), and for very large molecules the combination may result in a total attraction greater than from the other intermolecular forces. In addition, the presence of $\pi$ bonds increases the polarizability of the electron cloud. An increase in the contact area between the molecules enhances the strength of London dispersion forces.

## The Liquid State

At the microscopic level, liquid particles are in constant flux. They may exhibit short-range areas of order, but these do not last very long. Clumps of particles may form and then break apart. At the macroscopic level, a liquid has a specific volume but no fixed shape. Three other macroscopic properties deserve discussion: surface tension, viscosity, and capillary action. In the body of a liquid, the molecules are pulled in all different ways by the intermolecular forces between them. At the surface of the liquid, the molecules are only being pulled into the body of the liquid from the sides and below, not from above. The effect of this unequal attraction is that the liquid tries to minimize its surface area by forming a sphere. In a large pool of liquid, where this is not possible, the surface behaves as if it had a thin "skin" over it. It requires force to break the attractive forces at the surface. The amount of force required to break through this molecular layer at the surface is called the liquid's **surface tension**. The greater the intermolecular forces, the greater the surface tension. Polar liquids, especially those that contain hydrogen bonds, have a much higher surface tension than nonpolar liquids.

**Viscosity**, the resistance of liquids to flow, is affected by intermolecular forces, temperature, and molecular shape. Liquids with strong intermolecular forces tend to have a higher viscosity than those with weak intermolecular forces. Again, polar liquids tend to have a higher viscosity than nonpolar liquids. As the temperature increases, the kinetic energy of the particles becomes greater, overcoming the intermolecular attractive forces. This causes a lower viscosity. Finally, the longer and more complex the molecules, the more contact the particles will have as they slip by each other, increasing the viscosity. The change in viscosity with a change in temperature is illustrated by the difference in behavior of cold honey versus warm honey.

**Capillary action** is the spontaneous rising of a liquid through a narrow tube, against the force of gravity. It is caused by competition between the intermolecular forces in the liquid and those attractive forces between the liquid and the tube wall. The stronger the attraction between the liquid and the walls, the higher the level will be. Liquids that have weak attractions to the walls, like mercury in a glass tube, have a low capillary action. Liquids like water in a glass tube have strong attractions to the walls and will have a high capillary action.

As we have noted before, water, because of its very strong intermolecular forces (hydrogen bonding) has some unusual properties. It will dissolve a great number of substances, both ionic and polar covalent, because of its polarity and ability to form hydrogen bonds. It is sometimes called the "universal solvent." Water has a high **heat capacity**, the heat absorbed to cause the temperature to rise, and a high **heat of vaporization**, the heat needed to transform the liquid into a gas. These thermal properties are due to the strong hydrogen bonding between the water molecules. Water has a high surface tension for the same reason. The fact that the solid form of water (ice) is less dense than liquid water is because water molecules in ice are held in a rigid, open, crystalline framework by the hydrogen bonds. As the ice starts melting, the crystal structure breaks and water molecules fill the holes in the structure, increasing the density. The density reaches a maximum at around 4°C; then the increasing kinetic energy of the particles causes the density to begin to decrease.

# The Solid State

At the macroscopic level, a **solid** is defined as a substance that has both a definite volume and a definite shape. At the microscopic level, solids may be one of two types—amorphous or crystalline. **Amorphous solids** lack extensive ordering of the particles. There is a lack of regularity of the structure. There may be small regions of order separated by large areas of disordered particles. They resemble liquids more than solids in this characteristic. Amorphous solids have no distinct melting point. They simply get softer and softer as the temperature rises, leading to a decrease in viscosity. Glass, rubber, and charcoal are examples of amorphous solids.

When a solid melts, energy must be added (this same energy would be released upon freezing). This energy is not as great as the energy required to boil a liquid, because, unlike melting, vaporization leaves the constituents no longer in contact. In general, sublimation is the sum of the energy required for melting and the energy required for vaporization. The magnitudes of these energies depend upon the strengths of the bonds and/or intermolecular forces in the substance.

**Crystalline solids** display a very regular ordering of the particles in a three-dimensional structure called the **crystal lattice**. In this crystal lattice there are repeating units called **unit cells**. Figure 9.1 shows the relationship of the unit cells to the crystal lattice.

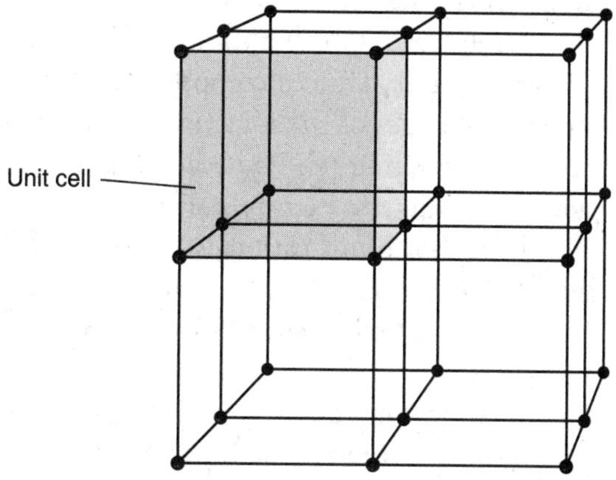


**Figure 9.1 The crystal lattice for a simple cubic unit cell.**

Several types of unit cells are found in solids. The cubic system is a common type. Three types of unit cells are found in the cubic system:

1. The **simple cubic unit cell** has particles located at the corners of a simple cube.
2. The **body-centered unit cell** has particles located at the corners of the cube and in the center of the cube.
3. The **face-centered unit cell** has particles at the corners and one in the center of each face of the cube, but not in the center of the cube itself.

Figure 9.2 shows three types of cubic unit cells.

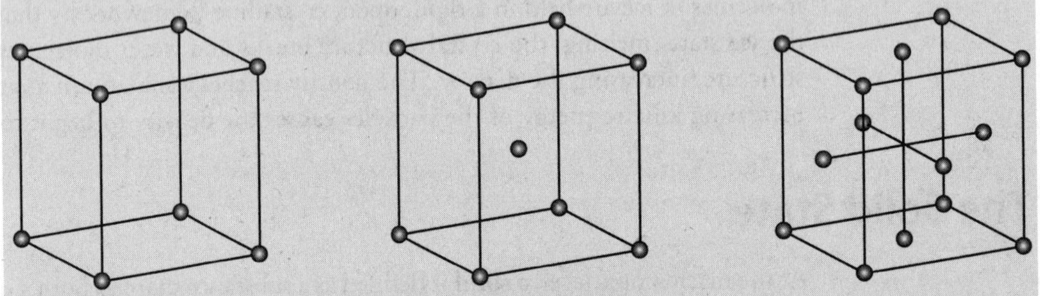


**Figure 9.2 The three types of unit cell of the cubic lattice.**

Five types of crystalline solid are known:

1. In **atomic solids,** individual atoms are held in place by London forces. The noble gases are the only substances known to form atomic solids; therefore, atomic solids are often grouped with molecular solids.
2. In **molecular solids,** lattices composed of separate molecules are held in place by London forces, dipole–dipole forces, and hydrogen bonding. Solid methane and water (ice) are examples of molecular solids. As the forces holding the molecules together are relatively weak, molecular solids tend to be soft nonconductors with low melting and boiling points. Some molecular solids may contain extremely large polymer molecules or biomolecules that have stronger interactions as a cumulative results of the London dispersion forces or other van der Waals forces.
3. In **ionic solids,** lattices composed of ions are held together by the attraction of the opposite charges of the ions (ionic bonding). These crystalline solids tend to be hard, with high melting points because of the strength of the intermolecular forces. NaCl and other salts are examples of ionic solids. Figure 9.3 shows the lattice structure of NaCl. Each sodium cation is surrounded by six chloride anions, and each chloride anion is surrounded by six sodium cations. The ions adjust to maximize the attraction between oppositely charged ions and to minimize the repulsion between ions with like charges.

   The strong interactions in ionic solids lead to low vapor pressure, high melting points, and, indirectly, high boiling points. Even though ions are present, ionic solids will not conduct electricity unless the ions become mobile, which occurs in the molten state and in solution. Most ionic solids are relatively brittle.

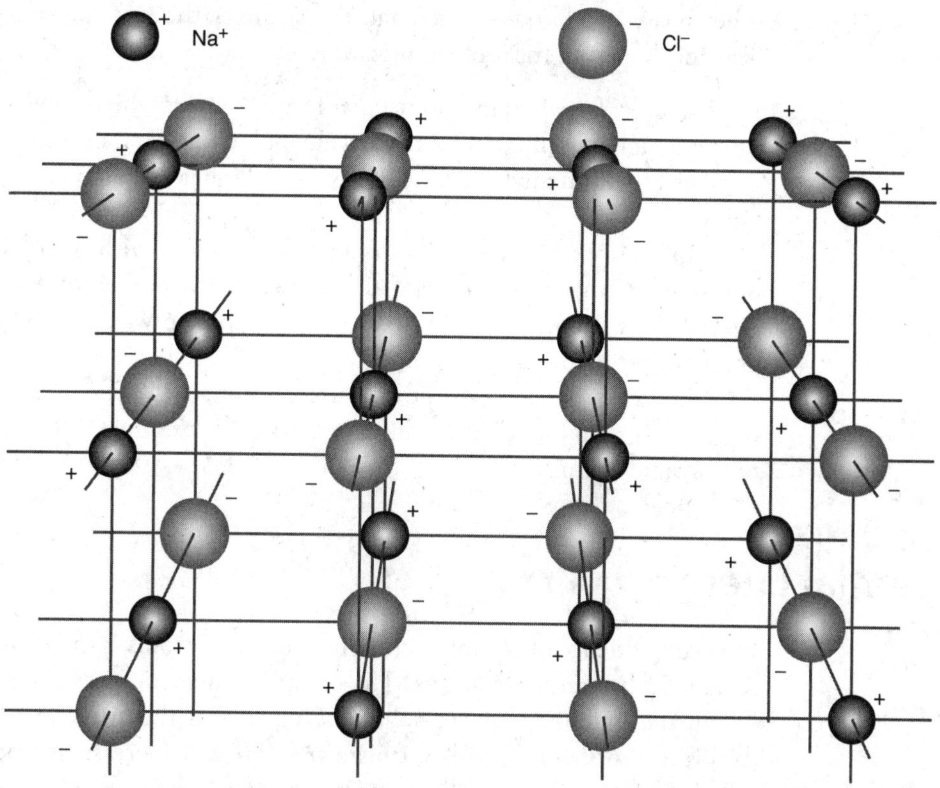


**Figure 9.3 Sodium chloride crystal lattice.**

4. In **metallic solids**, metal atoms occupying the crystal lattice are held together by metallic bonding. In **metallic bonding**, the electrons of the atoms are delocalized and are free to move throughout the entire solid. This explains electrical and thermal conductivity, as well as many other properties of metals. Compared to other types of bonds, metallic bonds can be easily deformed, which results in metals being malleable and ductile.
5. In **covalent network solids**, covalent bonds join atoms together in the crystal lattice, which is quite large. There are not too many examples in this category. Graphite, diamond, and silicon dioxide ($SiO_2$) are examples of network solids. The crystal is one giant molecule. In general, covalent network solids are hard nonconductors with high melting and boiling points. In most cases, the covalent network is a three-dimensional one. Graphite is a well-known exception as the network is only two dimensional, it is soft, and it is a conductor of electricity.

## Relationship of Intermolecular Forces to Phase Changes

The intermolecular forces can affect phase changes to a great degree. The stronger the intermolecular forces present in a liquid, the more kinetic energy must be added to convert it into a gas. Conversely, the stronger the intermolecular forces between the gas particles, the easier it will be to condense the gas into a liquid. In general, the weaker the intermolecular forces, the higher the vapor pressure. The same type of reasoning can be used about the other phase equilibria—in general, the stronger the intermolecular forces, the higher the heats of transition (heat of vaporization, etc.).

Example: Based on intermolecular forces, predict which will have the higher vapor pressure and higher boiling point: methyl alcohol, $CH_3$–OH, or dimethyl ether, $CH_3$–O–$CH_3$.

Answer: Dimethyl ether will have the higher vapor pressure and the lower boiling point.

Explanation: Methyl alcohol is a polar substance with strong intermolecular hydrogen bonds. Dimethyl ether is a polar material with weaker intermolecular forces (dipole–dipole). It will take much more energy to vaporize water; thus, water has a lower vapor pressure and higher boiling point.

Note: Even though organic chemistry is not an AP Chemistry topic, questions containing organic compounds may still appear. In this example, the key is intermolecular force, not organic chemistry.

## Potential Energy

One consequence of the interaction between two atoms is the "bond length" or most stable separation between two atoms. The complex interactions are illustrated in Figure 9.4.

In the graph, the lower solid line represents the attraction between the two atoms. According to Coulomb's law, this attraction will increase as opposite charges get closer together. The upper solid line represents the repulsion resulting when the electron clouds of the atoms begin to penetrate each other. This repulsion also follows Coulomb's law; however, now it is the repulsion between like charges. The result of these two factors is the dotted line. The minimum in the dotted-line curve is the equilibrium "bond length." This minimum also indicates the energy necessary to separate the atoms.

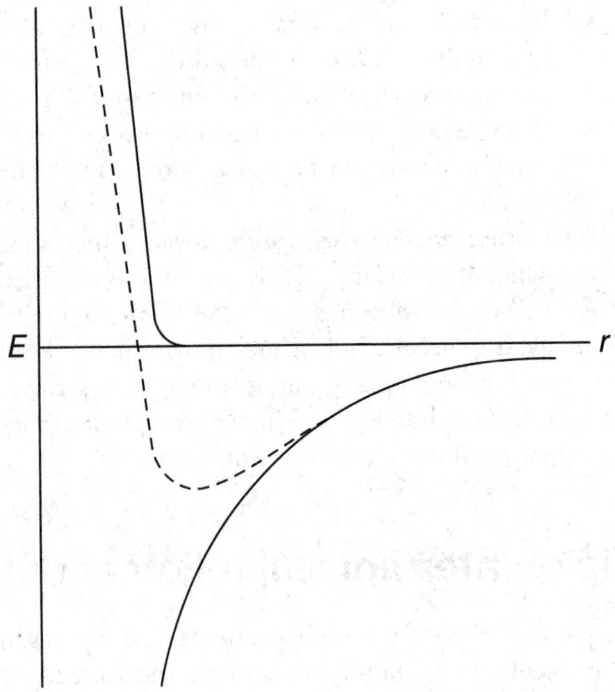


**Figure 9.4 The potential energy, *E*, between two atoms as a function of the distance between the two atoms, *r*. See the text for an explanation.**

## Experiments

STRATEGY

The concept of intermolecular forces is important in the separation of the components of a mixture. For example, you are given a sample containing sand and salt and wish to determine the percentage of sand present.

## Common Mistakes to Avoid

TIP

1. Don't confuse the various types of intermolecular forces.
2. The melting point and the freezing point for a substance are identical.
3. Hydrogen bonding can occur only when a hydrogen atom is directly bonded to an N, O, or F atom.
4. In looking at crystal lattice diagrams, be sure to count all the particles, in all three dimensions, that surround another particle.

## ❯ Review Questions

Use these questions to review the content of this chapter and practice for the AP Chemistry Exam. Below are 20 multiple-choice questions similar to what you will encounter in Section I of the AP Chemistry Exam. This set of questions includes some questions to test your recollection of prior knowledge. To make these questions an even more authentic practice for the actual exam, time yourself following the instructions provided.

### Multiple-Choice Questions

Answer the following questions in 30 minutes. You may not use a calculator. You may use the periodic table and the equation sheet at the back of this book.

**1.** Which of the following best describes Fe(s)?

(A) Iron is composed of macromolecules held together by strong bonds.
(B) Iron is composed of atoms held together by delocalized electrons.
(C) Iron is composed of positive and negative ions held together by electrostatic attractions.
(D) Iron is composed of molecules held together by intermolecular dipole–dipole interactions.

**2.** The best description of the interactions in $KNO_3$(s) is which of the following?

(A) $KNO_3$ is composed of macromolecules held together by strong bonds.
(B) $KNO_3$ is composed of atoms by delocalized electrons.
(C) $KNO_3$ is composed of positive and negative ions held together by electrostatic attractions.
(D) $KNO_3$ is composed of molecules held together by intermolecular dipole–dipole interactions.

3. Sand is primarily $SiO_2(s)$. Which of the following best describes the interactions inside a grain of sand?

(A) Sand is composed of macromolecules held together by strong bonds.
(B) Sand is composed of atoms held together by delocalized electrons.
(C) Sand is composed of positive and negative ions held together by electrostatic attractions.
(D) Sand is composed of molecules held together by intermolecular dipole–dipole interactions.

4. At sufficiently low temperatures, it is possible to form HCl(s). What best describes the interactions in this solid?

(A) HCl(s) is composed of macromolecules held together by strong bonds.
(B) HCl(s) is composed of atoms held together by delocalized electrons.
(C) HCl(s) is composed of positive and negative ions held together by electrostatic attractions.
(D) HCl(s) is composed of molecules held together by intermolecular dipole–dipole interactions.

5. Which of the following best describes diamond, C(s)?

(A) Diamond is an ionic solid.
(B) Diamond is a metallic solid.
(C) Diamond is a molecular solid containing polar molecules.
(D) Diamond is a covalent network solid.

6. What type of solid is solid sulfur dioxide, $SO_2(s)$?

(A) Sulfur dioxide is an ionic solid.
(B) Sulfur dioxide is a metallic solid.
(C) Sulfur dioxide is a molecular solid containing polar molecules.
(D) Sulfur dioxide is a covalent network solid.

7. The approximate boiling points for hydrogen compounds of some elements in the nitrogen family are ($SbH_3$ –15°C), ($AsH_3$ –62°C), ($PH_3$ –87°C), and ($NH_3$ –33°C). Which of the following is the best explanation for the fact that $NH_3$ does NOT follow the trend of the other hydrogen compounds?

(A) $NH_3$ is the only one to exhibit hydrogen bonding.
(B) $NH_3$ is the only one that is water soluble.
(C) $NH_3$ is the only one that is nearly ideal in the gas phase.
(D) $NH_3$ is the only one that is a base.

8. Why is it possible to solidify argon at a sufficiently low temperature?

(A) London dispersion forces are present.
(B) Covalent bonds form.
(C) Hydrogen bonds form.
(D) Metallic bonds form.

9. Which of the following best describes why diamond is so hard?

(A) London dispersion forces are present.
(B) Covalent bonds are present.
(C) Hydrogen bonds are present.
(D) Metallic bonds are present.

10. A sample of a pure liquid is placed in an open container and heated to the boiling point. Which of the following may increase the boiling point of the liquid?

(A) The moles of liquid are increased.
(B) The size of the container is increased.
(C) A vacuum is created over the liquid.
(D) The container is sealed.

**11.** The compounds 1-butanol, $CH_3CH_2CH_2CH_2OH$, and diethyl ether, $CH_3CH_2OCH_2CH_3$, are isomers (have the same chemical formula, $C_4H_{10}O$). However, the surface tension of 1-butanol is higher than that of diethyl ether. Which of the following best explains the higher surface tension of 1-butanol than that of diethyl ether?

(A) the higher density of 1-butanol
(B) the lower specific heat of 1-butanol
(C) the lack of hydrogen bonding in 1-butanol
(D) the presence of hydrogen bonding in 1-butanol

**12.** The compounds propanol, $CH_3CH_2CH_2OH$, ethylene glycol, $HOCH_2CH_2OH$, and butane, $CH_3CH_2CH_2CH_3$, are all similar in size. Which of the following most likely represents the relative solubilities of these compounds in water?

(A) $CH_3CH_2CH_2OH < HOCH_2CH_2OH < CH_3CH_2CH_2CH_3$
(B) $CH_3CH_2CH_2CH_3 < HOCH_2CH_2OH < CH_3CH_2CH_2OH$
(C) $CH_3CH_2CH_2CH_3 < CH_3CH_2CH_2OH < HOCH_2CH_2OH$
(D) $CH_3CH_2CH_2OH < CH_3CH_2CH_2CH_3 < HOCH_2CH_2OH$

**13.** Each of the following compounds has a similar structure, and the interionic distances are about the same. Which compound is expected to have the highest lattice energy?

(A) LiCl
(B) MgO
(C) AlN
(D) NaF

**14.** The melting point of sodium fluoride, NaF, is 993°C, and the melting point of calcium fluoride, $CaF_2$, is 1,423°C. Which of the following best explains why the melting point of calcium fluoride is higher?

(A) Sodium is a more reactive element than calcium is.
(B) The sodium ion is smaller than the calcium ion.
(C) The sodium ion has a lower charge than the calcium ion.
(D) There are fewer fluoride ions in the formula of sodium fluoride.

**15.** Pure phosphoric acid, $H_3PO_4$, freezes at about 42°C. Which of the following best describes the interactions in solid phosphoric acid?

(A) The solid consists of a collection of molecules held together by London dispersion forces.
(B) The solid consists of a collection of atoms held together by delocalized electrons.
(C) The solid consists of positive and negative ions held together by ionic bonding.
(D) The solid consists of molecules held together by intermolecular dipole–dipole interactions

**16.** Which of the following liquids will probably have the highest viscosity at a given temperature?

(A) $CH_3CH_2CH_2OH$
(B) $PCl_3$
(C) $CCl_4$
(D) $CH_3CH_2CH_2CH_3$

**17.** Most molecular species vaporize as simple molecules. However, acetic acid, $CH_3COOH$, is an exception. In the gaseous state, acetic acid molecules exist as pairs known as dimers. What is the most probable cause of this behavior?

(A) London dispersion forces
(B) covalent bonding
(C) hydrogen bonding
(D) metallic bonding

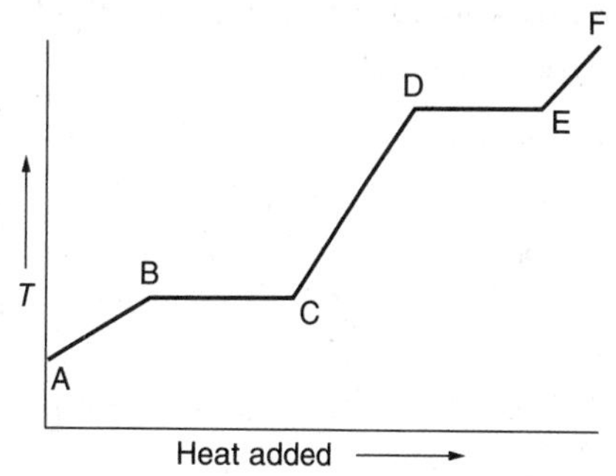


**18.** The above diagram represents the heating curve for a pure crystalline substance. Both solid and liquid are present in which region of the heating curve?

(A) between points A and B
(B) between points B and C
(C) between points C and D
(D) between points D and E

**19.** What is the strongest type of intermolar force present in an aqueous solution of sodium nitrate, $NaNO_3$?

(A) Ionic bonding
(B) Ion-dipole forces
(C) Dipole-dipole forces
(D) Hydrogen bonding

**20.** Fish and many other life-forms living in water survive by "breathing" the oxygen dissolved in the water. What type of intermolecular forces are present in $O_2(aq)$ that are not present in the separated $O_2(g)$ and $H_2O(l)$?

(A) Hydrogen bonding
(B) Covalent bonding
(C) Dipole-induced dipole forces
(D) Dipole-dipole forces

## › Answers and Explanations

**1. B**—Iron is a metal, and this answer describes a metallic solid.

**2. C**—Potassium nitrate is an ionic solid, and this answer describes an ionic solid.

**3. A**—Silicon dioxide is a covalent network solid, and this answer describes a covalent network solid.

**4. D**—Hydrogen chloride is a polar molecule, and this answer describes a solid consisting of discrete polar molecules. Even though HCl(aq) is a strong acid with ions in solution, there is no water here to lead to ionization.

**5. D**—Each of the carbon atoms is covalently bonded to four other carbon atoms.

**6. C**—Sulfur dioxide exists as molecules (molecular solid) that are polar.

**7. A**—The trend is the lighter the molecule, the lower the melting point, except for $NH_3$. For $NH_3$ to be an exception, its intermolecular forces must be different. Hydrogen bonding occurs when hydrogen is directly bonded to F, O, and in this case, N. The other three molecules have only dipole–dipole forces.

**8. A**—Argon is a noble gas; none of the other bonding choices is an option. Everything has London dispersion forces.

**9. B**—Diamond is a covalent network solid with many strong covalent bonds between the carbon atoms.

**10. D**—The size of the container and the number of moles are irrelevant, which eliminates answers A and B. Sealing the container will cause an increase in pressure that will increase the boiling point. A decrease in pressure will lower the boiling point, which eliminates answer C.

**11. D**—The compound with the higher surface tension is the one with the stronger intermolecular force. The –OH groups can form hydrogen bonds. The hydrogen bonding in 1-butanol is stronger than the dipole–dipole attractions in diethyl ether.

**12. C**—Butane is nonpolar, whereas the other two compounds can form hydrogen bonds through the –OH groups. This means that the butane should be listed first, which eliminates answers A and D. The more –OH groups, the more hydrogen bonding, and the more soluble in water (where hydrogen bonding also occurs). Ethylene glycol, with two –OH groups, should be more soluble (listed last) because propanol only has one –OH.

**13. C**—If the structures are similar and the interionic distances are about the same, then the only factor remaining that will influence the lattice energy is the magnitude of the charges. The ionic charges are $Li^+$, $Cl^-$, $Mg^{2+}$, $O^{2-}$, $Al^{3+}$, $N^{3-}$, $Na^+$, and $F^-$. The largest magnitude charges are in AlN, which will lead to the greatest attraction between the ions, which leads to the highest lattice energy.

**14. C**—For ionic compounds, the key factors are the sizes and the charges on the ions. Smaller ions lead to higher melting points. Higher charges lead to higher melting points. Answer B deals with size; however, if this were the key factor, the melting point of sodium fluoride would be higher, which is not the case. This leads to C being the correct answer. The higher charge on calcium (+2 versus +1) leads to a higher lattice energy, which results in a higher melting point.

**15. D**—This answer describes a solid consisting of discrete polar molecules. Answer A refers to a nonpolar molecule. Answer B refers to a metallic solid. Answer C might apply; however, even though phosphoric acid is an acid that forms ions in aqueous solution, there is no water present for ionization. The actual "strongest" interactions in solid $H_3PO_4$ are hydrogen bonds, which are a special type of dipole–dipole force.

**16. A**—Compound A can form hydrogen bonds. Compound B has dipole–dipole interactions. Compounds C and D are both nonpolar; therefore, their strongest intermolecular force is London dispersion force. For relatively small molecules such as these, the stronger the intermolecular force, the higher the viscosity. Hydrogen bonding in the strongest of the three intermolecular forces present in these molecules.

**17. C**—The carbonyl, C=O, and –OH groups can participate in hydrogen bonds, as illustrated by the dotted lines in the following diagram:

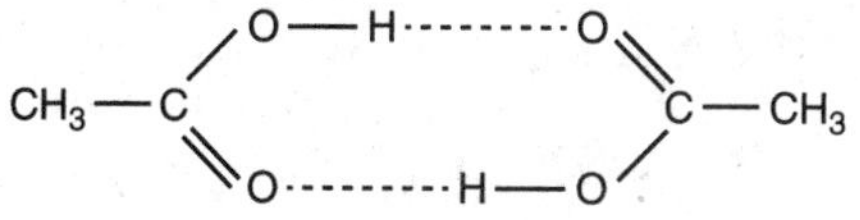


The hydrogen bonds hold the two molecules together as a dimer.

**18. B**—The solid begins to melt at B and finishes melting at C. Once the solid begins to melt, both solid and liquid are present.

**19. B**—Sodium nitrate is an ionic solid with ionic bonding; however, these ionic bonds are broken when the compound dissolves in water. The fact that this ionic compound dissolves to form an aqueous solution implies that it is a strong electrolyte. Water, the solvent, has hydrogen bonding, some of the hydrogen bonds are broken as the $NaNO_3$ dissolves. New intermolecular forces form as the $NaNO_3$ dissolves and forms $Na^+(aq)$ and $NO_3^-(aq)$. The sodium and nitrate hydrated ions are held together by strong ion-dipole forces, which, in general are stronger than hydrogen bonding.

**20. C**—Oxygen gas exists as discrete nonpolar molecules, which means that isolated $O_2$ molecules only have London dispersion forces. Water has hydrogen bonding (a type of dipole-dipole force). When $O_2$ dissolves in water the nonpolar $O_2$ interacts with polar $H_2O$ which leads to the $H_2O$ inducing a dipole in the $O_2$. This interaction leads to the formation of dipole-induced dipole forces.

## ❯ Free-Response Question

You have 15 minutes to answer the following question. You may use a calculator and the tables in the back of the book.

**Question**

Write a brief explanation concerning each of the following observations.

(a) An aqueous solution in a glass buret has a meniscus that is concave, whereas in a plastic buret, the meniscus is convex.
(b) The surface tension of liquid $CBr_4$ is greater than the surface tension of liquid $CCl_4$.
(c) At the same temperature, liquid HF has a higher viscosity than liquid HCl.
(d) When heated, glass does not melt; it becomes soft.

## › Answer and Explanation

(a) The concave surface results from capillary action, and the convex surface results from surface tension. Surface tension is the result of strong intermolecular forces between the solution and the glass; these forces are greater than those within the solution, causing a convex surface. The convex surface results from a stronger interaction within the solution than between the solution and the plastic.

Give yourself 1 point for this answer.

(b) The greater surface tension results from stronger intermolecular forces in $CBr_4$. Both $CCl_4$ and $CBr_4$ are nonpolar molecules; therefore, the intermolecular forces are London dispersion forces. For simple molecules, such as these, the one with more electrons, $CBr_4$, will have the stronger London dispersion forces and hence the greater surface tension.

Give yourself 1 point for this answer.

(c) Viscosity, the resistance to flow, is related to the strength of attraction between the molecules. Both HF and HCl are polar molecules with dipole–dipole forces; however, HF exhibits an especially strong form of dipole–dipole force known as hydrogen bonding. Since hydrogen bonding is stronger than normal dipole–dipole forces, HF has a higher viscosity.

Give yourself 1 point for this answer.

(d) Glass is a liquid with very high viscosity (amorphous solid). Heating any liquid gives the molecules more kinetic energy, which lowers the viscosity. In the case of glass, the decrease in viscosity begins with the material becoming softer and softer until it flows freely.

Give yourself 1 point for this answer.

Total your points. There are 4 points possible.

## › Rapid Review

- The state of matter in which a substance exists depends on the competition between the kinetic energy of the particles (proportional to temperature) and the strength of the intermolecular forces between the particles.
- The melting point is the temperature at which a substance goes from the solid to the liquid state and is the same as the freezing point.
- The boiling point is the temperature at which a substance goes from the liquid to the gaseous state. This takes place within the body of the liquid, unlike evaporation, which takes place only at the surface of the liquid.
- Sublimation is the conversion of a solid to a gas without ever having become a liquid. Deposition is the reverse process.
- Phase changes are changes of state.
- Intermolecular forces are the attractive forces between atoms, molecules, or ions due to full or partial charges. Be careful not to confuse intermolecular forces with intramolecular forces, the forces within the molecule.

- Ion–dipole intermolecular forces occur between ions and polar molecules.
- Dipole–dipole intermolecular forces occur between polar molecules.
- Hydrogen bonds are intermolecular forces between dipoles in which there is a hydrogen atom attached *directly* to an N, O, or F atom.
- Ion-induced dipole intermolecular forces occur between an ion and a nonpolar molecule.
- London (dispersion) forces are intermolecular forces between nonpolar molecules.
- Liquids possess surface tension (liquids behaving as if they had a thin "skin" on their surface, due to unequal attraction of molecules at the surface of the liquid), viscosity (resistance to flow), and capillary action (flow up a small tube).
- Amorphous solids have very little structure, like liquids.
- Crystalline solids are defined by their well-ordered structure.
- The crystal lattice of a crystalline solid is the regular ordering of the unit cells.
- Know the five types of crystalline solid: atomic, molecular, ionic, metallic, and network.
- Phase changes can be related to the strength of intermolecular forces.

# CHAPTER 10

# Gases

**IN THIS CHAPTER**

In this chapter, the following AP topics are covered:

3.4 Ideal Gas Law
3.5 Kinetic Molecular Theory
3.6 Deviation from Ideal Gas Law

**Summary:** Of the three states of matter—gases, liquids, and solids—gases are probably the best understood and have the best descriptive model. While studying gases in this chapter you will consider four main physical properties—volume, pressure, temperature, and amount—and their interrelationships. These relationships, commonly called gas laws, show up quite often on the AP Exam, so you will spend quite a bit of time working problems in this chapter. But before we start looking at the gas laws, let's look at the Kinetic Molecular Theory of Gases, the extremely useful model that scientists use to represent the gaseous state. Much of the introductory material in this chapter is considered "prior knowledge" for the AP Exam. As prior knowledge, it is the background material you need to know to understand the AP material.

KEY IDEA

**Keywords and Equations**

Gas constant, $R = 0.08206$ L atm mol$^{-1}$ K$^{-1}$
STP = 273.15 K and 1.0 atm
1 atm = 760 mm Hg = 760 torr

$PV = nRT$

$P_A = P_{total} \times X_A$, where $X_A = \dfrac{\text{moles A}}{\text{total moles}}$

$P_{total} = P_A + P_B + P_C + \ldots$

$KE_{molecule} = 1/2\ mv^2$

$n = \dfrac{m}{\boldsymbol{M}}$

$P$ = pressure  $M$ = molar mass  $V$ = volume  $D$ = density
$T$ = temperature  $KE$ = kinetic energy  $n$ = number of moles  $v$ = velocity
$m$ = mass

Ideal gas at STP = 22.4 L mol$^{-1}$

$R$ = 62.36 L torr mol$^{-1}$ K$^{-1}$

K = °C + 273

$D = \frac{m}{V}$

## Kinetic Molecular Theory

KEY IDEA

The **Kinetic Molecular Theory** attempts to represent the properties of gases by modeling the gas particles themselves at the microscopic level. There are five main postulates of the Kinetic Molecular Theory:

1. Gases are composed of very small particles, either molecules or atoms.
2. The gas particles are tiny in comparison to the distances between them, so we assume that the volume of the gas particles themselves is negligible.
3. These gas particles are in constant motion, moving in straight lines in a random fashion and colliding with each other and the inside walls of the container. The collisions with the inside container walls comprise the pressure of the gas.
4. The gas particles are assumed to neither attract nor repel each other. They may collide with each other, but if they do, the collisions are assumed to be elastic. No kinetic energy is lost, only transferred from one gas molecule to another.
5. The *average* kinetic energy of the gas is proportional to the Kelvin temperature.

A gas that obeys these five postulates is an **ideal gas**. However, just as there are no ideal students, there are no ideal gases, only gases that approach ideal behavior. We know that real gas particles do occupy a certain finite volume, and we know that there are interactions between real gas particles. These factors cause real gases to deviate a little from the ideal behavior of the Kinetic Molecular Theory. But a nonpolar gas at a low pressure and high temperature would come very close to ideal behavior. Later in this chapter, we'll show how to modify our equations to account for nonideal behavior.

Before we leave the Kinetic Molecular Theory (KMT) and start examining the gas law relationships, let's quantify a couple of the postulates of the KMT. Postulate 3 qualitatively describes the motion of the gas particles. The average velocity of the gas particles is called the **root-mean-square speed** and is given the symbol $u_{rms}$. This is a special type of average speed. It is the speed of a gas particle having the average kinetic energy of the gas particles. Mathematically it can be represented as:

$$u_{rms} = \sqrt{\frac{3kT}{m}} = \sqrt{\frac{3RT}{M}}$$

where $R$ is the molar gas constant (we'll talk more about it in the section dealing with the ideal gas equation), $T$ is the **Kelvin** temperature, and $M$ is the molar mass of the gas. The root-mean-square speeds are very high. Hydrogen gas, $H_2$, at 20°C has a value of approximately 2,000 m/s.

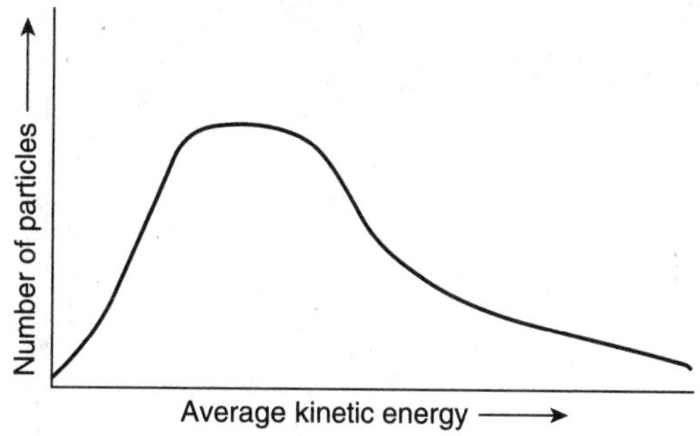


**Figure 10.1 A typical Maxwell–Boltzmann distribution of a gas.**

Postulate 5 relates the average kinetic energy of the gas particles to the Kelvin temperature. Mathematically we can represent the average kinetic energy per molecule as:

$$KE_{\text{molecule}} = 1/2\ mv^2$$

where $m$ is the mass of the molecule and $v$ is its velocity.

A plot of the number of particles versus the average kinetic energy of the particles exhibits a Maxwell–Boltzmann distribution. Figure 10.1 shows such a distribution for a gas at a certain temperature. Any gas at the same temperature will give the same distribution. At higher temperatures, the maximum will shift to higher kinetic energy, and at lower temperatures, the maximum will shift to lower kinetic energy. The average can only reach zero at absolute zero; however, gases liquify before reaching absolute zero. Note: a Maxwell–Boltzmann distribution is also present in the liquid and solid state; however, it is not as obvious since the particles are not freely moving.

The average kinetic energy per mole of gas is represented by:

$$KE \text{ per mol} = 3/2\ RT$$

where $R$ again is the ideal gas constant and $T$ is the Kelvin temperature. This shows the direct relationship between the average kinetic energy of the gas particles and the Kelvin temperature.

## Gas Law Relationships

The gas laws relate the physical properties of volume, pressure, temperature, and moles (amount) to each other. First, we will examine the individual gas law relationships. You will need to know these relationships for the AP Exam, but the use of the individual equations is not required. Then we will combine the relationships into a single equation that you will need to be able to apply. But first we need to describe a few things concerning pressure.

### Pressure

When we use the word **pressure**, we may be referring to the pressure of a gas inside a container or to atmospheric pressure, the pressure due to the weight of the atmosphere above us. These two different types of pressure are measured in slightly different ways. Atmospheric pressure is measured using a **barometer** (Figure 10.2).

An evacuated hollow tube sealed at one end is filled with mercury, and then the open end is immersed in a pool of mercury. Gravity will tend to pull the liquid level inside the

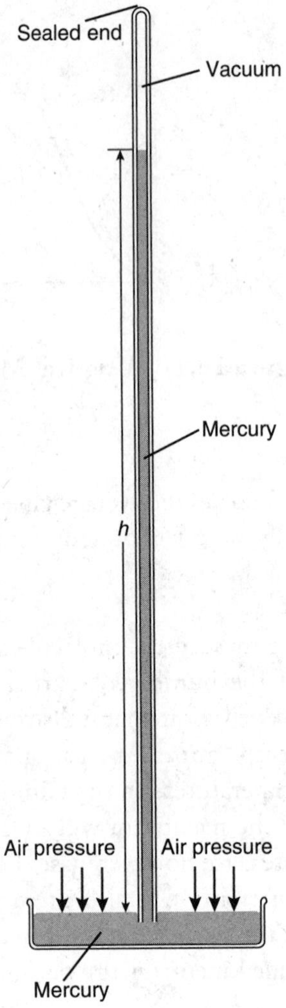


**Figure 10.2 The mercury barometer.**

tube down, while the weight of the atmospheric gases on the surface of the mercury pool will tend to force the liquid up into the tube. These two opposing forces will quickly balance each other, and the column of mercury inside the tube will stabilize. The height of the column of mercury above the surface of the mercury pool is called the atmospheric pressure. At sea level, the column averages 760 mm high. This pressure is also called 1 atmosphere (atm). Commonly, the unit torr is used for pressure, where 1 torr = 1 mm Hg, so that atmospheric pressure at sea level equals 760 torr. The SI unit of pressure is the pascal (Pa), so that 1 atm = 760 mm Hg = 760 torr = 101,325 Pa (101.325 kPa). In the United States pounds per square inch (psi) is sometimes used, so 1 atm = 14.69 psi.

To measure the gas pressure inside a container, a **manometer** (Figure 10.3) is used. As in the barometer, the pressure of the gas is balanced against a column of mercury.

## Volume–Pressure Relationship: Boyle's Law

KEY IDEA

**Boyle's law** describes the relationship between the volume and the pressure of a gas when the temperature and amount are constant. If you have a container like the one shown in Figure 10.4 and you decrease the volume of the container, the pressure of the gas increases because the number of collisions of gas particles with the container's inside walls increases.

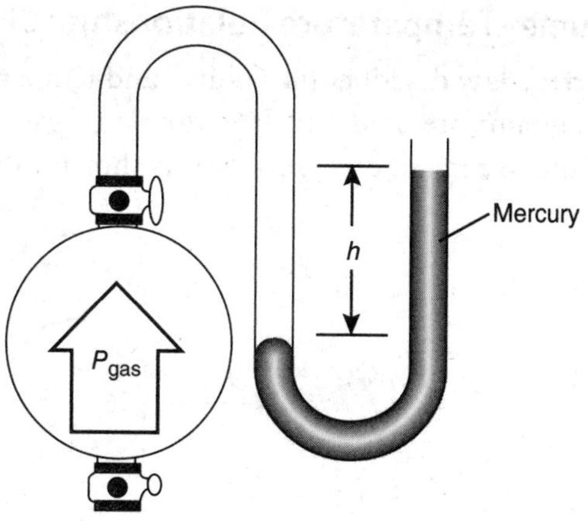


**Figure 10.3 The manometer.**

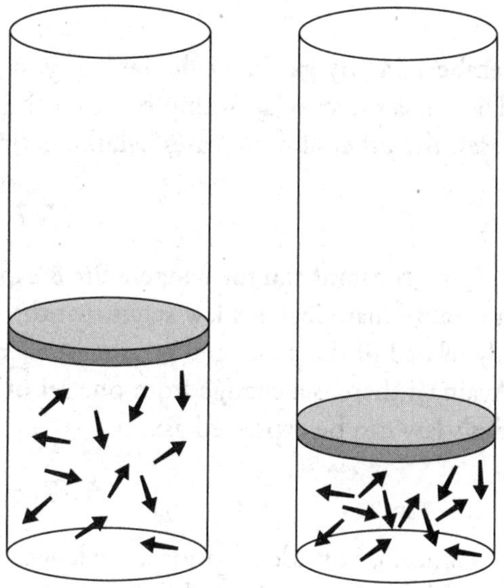

**Figure 10.4 Volume–pressure relationship for gases. As the volume decreases, the number of collisions increases.**

Mathematically this is an inverse relationship, so the product of the pressure and volume is a constant: $PV = k_b$. For the AP Exam, it is important to realize that Boyle's law states that the volume and pressure of a gas are inversely related (if the moles and temperature remain constant).

If you take a gas at an initial volume ($V_1$) and pressure ($P_1$) (amount and temperature constant) and change the volume ($V_2$) and pressure ($P_2$), you can relate the two sets of conditions to each other by the equation:

$$P_1V_1 = P_2V_2$$

In this mathematical statement of Boyle's law, if you know any three quantities, you can calculate the fourth. This equation is considered prior knowledge and will not appear directly on the AP Exam; however, the concept behind the equation is important.

## Volume–Temperature Relationship: Charles's Law

**Charles's law** describes the volume and temperature relationship of a gas when the pressure and amount are constant. If a sample of gas is heated, the volume must increase for the pressure to remain constant. This is shown in Figure 10.5.

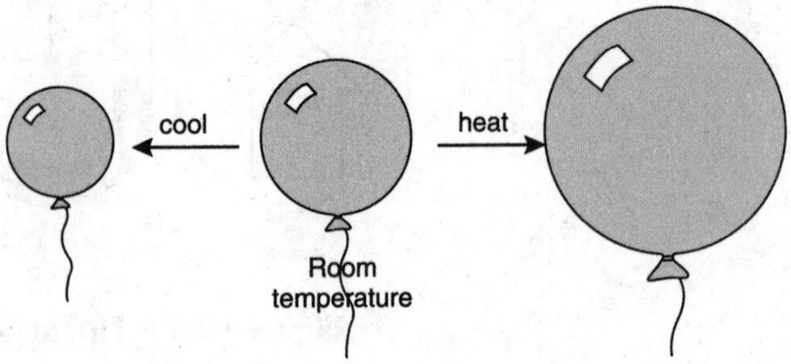


**Figure 10.5 Volume–temperature relationship for gases.**

**Remember: In any gas law calculation, you must express the temperature in kelvin.**

There is a direct relationship between the Kelvin temperature and the volume: as one increases, the other also increases. Mathematically, Charles's law can be represented as:

$$V/T = k_c$$

where $k_c$ is a constant and the temperature is expressed in kelvin. For the AP Exam, it is important to realize that Charles's law states that the volume and absolute temperature of a gas are directly related (if the moles and pressure remain constant).

Again, if there is a change from one set of volume–temperature conditions to another, Charles's law can be expressed as:

$$V_1/T_1 = V_2/T_2$$

This equation is considered prior knowledge and will not appear directly on the AP Exam; however, the concept behind the equation is important.

## Pressure–Temperature Relationship: Gay-Lussac's Law

**Gay-Lussac's law** describes the relationship between the pressure of a gas and its Kelvin temperature if the volume and amount are held constant. Figure 10.6 represents the process of heating a given amount of gas at a constant volume.

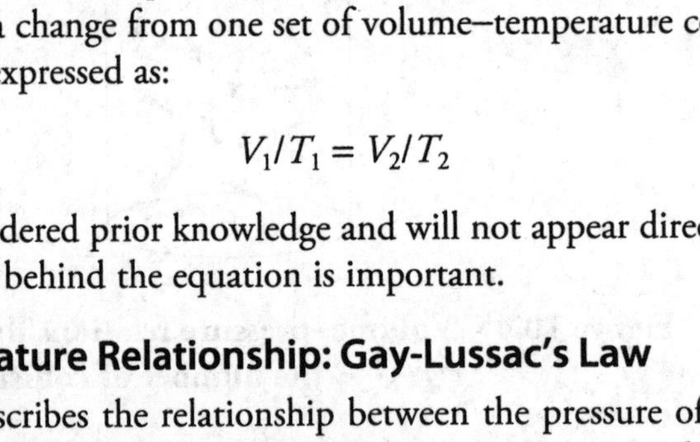


**Figure 10.6 Pressure–temperature relationship for gases. As the temperature increases, the gas particles have greater kinetic energy (longer arrows) and collisions are more frequent and forceful.**

As the gas is heated, the particles move with greater kinetic energy, striking the inside walls of the container more often and with greater force. This causes the pressure of the gas to increase. The relationship between the Kelvin temperature and the pressure is a direct one:

$$P/T = k_g \qquad \text{or} \qquad P_1/T_1 = P_2/T_2$$

For the AP Exam, it is important to realize that Gay-Lussac's law states that the pressure and absolute temperature of a gas are directly related (if the moles and volume remain constant). The equation is considered prior knowledge and will not appear directly on the AP Exam; however, the concept behind the equation is important.

### Combined Gas Law

KEY IDEA

In the discussion of Boyle's, Charles's, and Gay-Lussac's laws, we held two of the four variables constant, changed the third, and looked at its effect on the fourth variable. If we keep the number of moles of gas constant—that is, no gas can get in or out—then we can combine these three gas laws into one, the **combined gas law**, which can be expressed as:

$$(P_1V_1)/T_1 = (P_2V_2)/T_2$$

KEY IDEA

**Again, remember: in any gas law calculation, you must express the temperature in kelvin.**

In this equation, there are six unknowns; given any five, you should be able to solve for the sixth. This equation combines the concepts of the other gas laws.

For example, suppose a 3.00 L bottle of gas with a pressure of 2.25 atm at 25°C is heated to 75°C. We can calculate the new pressure using the combined gas law. Before we start working mathematically, however, let's do some reasoning. The volume of the bottle hasn't changed ($V_1 = V_2$), and neither has the number of moles of gas inside ($n_1 = n_2$). Only the temperature and pressure have changed, so this is really a Gay-Lussac's law problem. From Gay-Lussac's law you know that if you increase the temperature, the pressure should increase if the amount and volume are constant. This means that when you calculate the new pressure, it should be greater than 2.25 atm; if it is less, you've made an error. Also, **remember that the temperatures must be expressed in kelvin**. 25°C = 298 K (K = °C + 273) and 75°C = 348 K.

We will be solving for $P_2$, so we will take the combined gas law and rearrange for $P_2$:

$$\frac{T_2P_1V_1}{T_1V_2} = P_2$$

Substituting in the values:

$$\frac{(348\text{ K})(2.25\text{ atm})(3.00\text{ L})}{(298\text{ K})(3.00\text{ L})} = P_2$$

$$2.63\text{ atm} = P_2$$

The new pressure is greater than the original pressure, making the answer a reasonable one. Note that all the units canceled except atm, which is the unit that you wanted. We have deducted innumerable points when grading AP Exams because the students did not watch their units. The units not only tell you that you have rearranged the equation correctly but also tell you that you have entered the appropriate quantities. Gay-Lussac's law tells you that an increase in temperature must be accompanied by an increase in pressure. While you will probably not see a calculation problem like this on the AP Exam, this does illustrate the fact that you need to be careful with units.

Let's look at a situation in which two conditions change. Suppose a balloon has a volume at sea level of 10.0 L at 760.0 torr and 20°C (293 K). The pressure is then decreased to 725.0 torr, and the temperature is changed until the volume of the balloon is 11.5 L. What is the new temperature of the gas in the balloon? You want to calculate the new temperature of the balloon. You know that you must express the temperature in K in the calculations. It is perfectly fine to leave the pressures in torr (or any other pressure unit if they match). The pressure is decreasing, so that should cause the temperature to decrease (Gay-Lussac's law). The volume is increasing, which indicates the temperature is increasing (Charles's law). Here you have two competing factors, so it is difficult to predict the result. You'll simply have to do the calculations and see. Before reading on, try to solve this problem and compare your results with the answer (no peeking).

Using the combined gas equation, solve for the new temperature ($T_2$):

$$\frac{P_1V_1}{T_1} = \frac{P_2V_2}{T_2}$$

$$T_2 = \frac{(T_1)(P_2)(V_2)}{(P_1)(V_1)}$$

Now substitute the known quantities into the equation. (You could substitute the knowns into the combined gas equation first, and then solve for the temperature. Do it whichever way is easier for you.)

$$T_2 = \frac{(293\text{ K})(725.0\text{ torr})(11.5\text{ L})}{(760.0\text{ torr})(10.0\text{ L})}$$

$$321\text{ K} = T_2$$

Note that the units canceled, leaving the temperature unit of kelvin. However, this is the not the final answer because the problem wants the temperature in °C. The final answer is 321 K − 273 = 48°C. Overall, the temperature did increase, so in this case the volume increase had a greater effect than the pressure decrease has.

### Volume–Amount Relationship: Avogadro's Law

KEY IDEA

In all the gas law problems so far, the amount of gas has been constant. But what if the amount changes? That is where Avogadro's law comes into play.

If a container is kept at constant pressure and temperature, and you increase the number of gas particles in that container, the volume will have to increase to keep the pressure constant. This means that there is a direct relationship between the volume and the number of moles of gas ($n$). This is **Avogadro's law** and mathematically it looks like this:

$$V/n = k_a \quad \text{or} \quad V_1/n_1 = V_2/n_2$$

We could work this into the combined gas law, but more commonly the amount of gas is related to the other physical properties, most commonly to the molar volume of a gas at STP. For any ideal gas at STP:

$$\text{Ideal gas at STP} = 22.4\text{ L mol}^{-1}$$

$$\text{STP} = 273.15\text{ K and } 1.0\text{ atm}$$

The value 22.4 L mol$^{-1}$ has led us to deduct many points when we grade AP exams. Students often insist on using this value under conditions other than STP, and they even try to use this value when there is no gas involved. Your best bet is to never use this value unless you are absolutely sure that you are dealing with a GAS at STP.

The combined gas law and Avogadro's relationship can then be combined into the ideal gas equation, which incorporates the pressure, volume, temperature, and amount relationships of a gas.

## Ideal Gas Equation

KEY IDEA

The **ideal gas equation** has the mathematical form of $PV = nRT$, where:

$P$ = pressure of the gas in atm, torr, mm Hg, Pa, etc.
$V$ = volume of the gas in L, mL, etc.
$n$ = number of moles of gas
$R$ = ideal gas constant: 0.08206 L atm mol$^{-1}$ K$^{-1}$ = 62.36 L torr mol$^{-1}$ K$^{-1}$
$T$ = Kelvin temperature

This is the value for $R$ if the volume is expressed in liters, the pressure in atmospheres or torr, and the temperature in kelvin (naturally). You could calculate another ideal gas constant based on different units of pressure and volume, but the simplest thing to do is to use the 0.08206 or 62.36 and convert the given volume to liters and the pressure to atm or torr. And remember that you **must express the temperature in kelvin**. While two different pressure units are possible here, it will probably be to your advantage to pick one or the other. Our recommendation is that you pick atmospheres.

Let's see how we might use the ideal gas equation. Suppose you want to know what volume 16.0 g of oxygen gas would occupy at 27°C and 1.050 atm. You have the pressure in atm, you can get the temperature in kelvin (27°C + 273 = 300 K), but you will need to convert the grams of oxygen gas to moles of oxygen gas before you can use the ideal gas equation. Also, remember that oxygen gas is diatomic, $O_2$ (prior knowledge). On the AP Exam, if you forgot that oxygen was diatomic, you would lose points.

First, you'll convert the 16.0 g to moles:

$$(16.0 \text{ g } O_2)\left(\frac{1 \text{ mol } O_2}{32.00 \text{ g } O_2}\right) = 0.500 \text{ mol } O_2$$

(We're not worried about significant figures at this point, since this is an intermediate calculation.)

Now you can solve the ideal gas equation for the unknown quantity, the volume:

$$PV = nRT$$

$$V = \frac{nRT}{P}$$

Finally, plug in the numerical values for the different known quantities:

$$V = \frac{(0.500 \text{ mol } O_2)(0.08206 \text{ L atm mol}^{-1}\text{K}^{-1})(300.\text{ K})}{(1.050 \text{ atm})}$$

$$V = 11.7 \text{ L}$$

Is the answer reasonable? You have 1/2 mol of gas. It would occupy about 11.2 L at STP (0.5 mol × 22.4 L/mol). The pressure is slightly more than standard pressure of 1 atm, which would tend to decrease the volume (Boyle's law), and temperature is greater than standard temperature of 0°C, which would increase the volume (Charles's law). So you might expect a volume greater near 11.4 L, and that is exactly what you found.

KEY IDEA

Remember, the final thing you do when working any type of chemistry problem is to answer this question: Is the answer reasonable?

## Dalton's Law of Partial Pressures

KEY IDEA

**Dalton's law** says that in a mixture of gases (A + B + C···) the total pressure is simply the sum of the partial pressures (the pressures associated with each individual gas). Mathematically, Dalton's law looks like this:

$$P_{Total} = P_A + P_B + P_C + \cdots$$

This equation works because the gases act independently.

Commonly Dalton's law is used in calculations involving the collection of a gas over water, as in the displacement of water by oxygen gas. In this situation, there is a gas mixture: $O_2$ and water vapor, $H_2O(g)$. The total pressure in this case is usually atmospheric pressure, and the partial pressure of the water vapor is determined by looking up the vapor pressure of water at the temperature of the water in a reference book. Simple subtraction generates the partial pressure of the oxygen. (Note: you cannot measure the partial pressure of oxygen in this situation; you must calculate the value.)

If you know how many moles of each gas are in the mixture and the total pressure, you can calculate the partial pressure of each gas by multiplying the total pressure by the mole fraction of each gas:

$$P_A = (P_{Total})(X_A)$$

where $X_A$ = mole fraction of gas A. The mole fraction of gas A would be equal to the moles of gas A divided by the total moles of gas in the mixture. Recall that the mole fraction of A is defined as: $X_A = \frac{n_A}{n_{Total}}$.

## Graham's Law of Diffusion

KEY IDEA

**Graham's law** defines the relationship of the speed of gas diffusion (mixing of gases due to their kinetic energy) or effusion (movement of a gas through a tiny opening) and the gases' molecular mass. The lighter the gas, the faster is its rate of effusion or diffusion. Normally this is set up as the comparison of the rates of two gases, and the specific mathematical relationship is:

$$\frac{r_1}{r_2} = \sqrt{\frac{M_2}{M_1}}$$

where $r_1$ and $r_2$ are the rates of effusion or diffusion of gases 1 and 2, respectively, and $M_2$ and $M_1$ are the molecular masses of gases 2 and 1, respectively. **Note that this is an inverse relationship.**

Figure 10.7 shows the Graham's law experimental setup for $NH_3$/HCl versus $ND_3$/HCl. In the first experiment, cotton balls saturated with $NH_3(aq)$ and HCl(aq) are inserted into a glass tube. The vapors travel through the tube and $NH_4Cl(s)$ forms where they meet.

This combination forms the white cloud indicated in the figure. The experiment is repeated with $ND_3(aq)$, which is the form of ammonia where the normal hydrogen atoms have been replaced with deuterium atoms. The molar mass of this compound is greater than ammonia, and thus the vapors travel slower according to Graham's law. Therefore, the white cloud forms closer to the $ND_3$ end than in the first experiment.

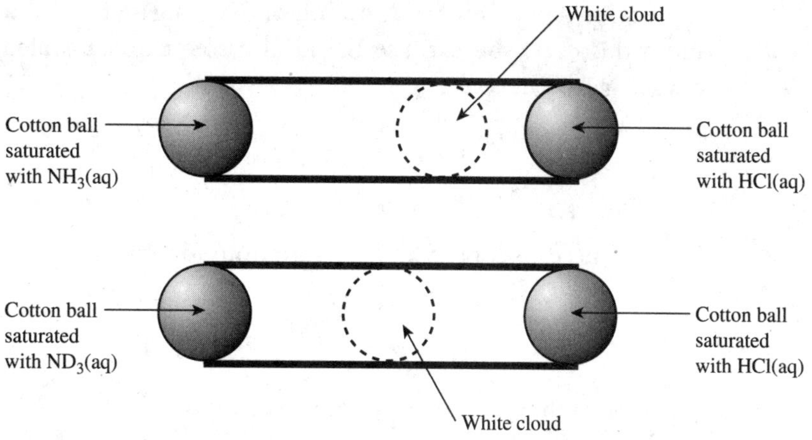


**Figure 10.7 Graham's law of diffusion setup.**

Suppose you wanted to calculate the ratio of effusion rates for $NH_3$ and $ND_3$. The molar mass for $NH_3$ is 17.04 g/mol, and the molar mass for $ND_3$ is 20.04 g/mol. Substituting into the Graham's law equation:

$$\frac{r_{NH_3}}{r_{ND_3}} = \sqrt{\frac{\boldsymbol{M}_{ND_3}}{\boldsymbol{M}_{NH_3}}}$$

$$\frac{r_{NH_3}}{r_{ND_3}} = \sqrt{\frac{20.04\ \text{g/mol}}{17.04\ \text{g/mol}}} = (1.176)^{1/2} = 1.084$$

$NH_3$ gas would effuse through a pinhole 1.084 times as fast as $ND_3$ gas. The answer is reasonable, since the lower the molecular mass, the faster the gas is moving.

## Gas Stoichiometry

KEY IDEA

The gas law relationships can be used in reaction stoichiometry problems. For example, suppose you have a mixture of $KClO_3$ and NaCl and you want to determine how many grams of $KClO_3$ are present. You take the mixture and heat it. The $KClO_3$ decomposes according to the equation:

$$2\ KClO_3(s) \rightarrow 2\ KCl(s) + 3\ O_2(g)$$

The oxygen gas that is formed is collected by displacement of water. It occupies a volume of 347 mL at 25°C. The atmospheric pressure is 765.0 torr. The vapor pressure of water at 25°C is 23.8 torr.

First, you need to determine the pressure of just the oxygen gas. It was collected over water, so the total pressure of 765.0 torr is the sum of the partial pressures of the oxygen and the water vapor:

$$P_{\text{Total}} = P_{O_2} + P_{H_2O} \text{ (Dalton's law)}$$

The partial pressure of water vapor at 25°C is 23.8 torr, so the partial pressure of the oxygen can be calculated by:

$$P_{O_2} = P_{\text{Total}} - P_{H_2O} = 765.0 \text{ torr} - 23.8 \text{ torr} = 741.2 \text{ torr}$$

At this point, you have 347 mL of oxygen gas at 741.2 torr and 298 K (25°C + 273). From this data, you can use the ideal gas equation to calculate the number of moles of oxygen gas produced:

$$PV = nRT$$

$$n = \frac{PV}{RT}$$

You will need to convert the pressure from torr to atm:

$$(741.2 \text{ torr})\left(\frac{1 \text{ atm}}{760.0 \text{ torr}}\right) = 0.9753 \text{ atm}$$

and express the volume in liters: 347 mL = 0.347 L.

Now you can substitute the quantities into the ideal gas equation:

$$n = \frac{(0.9753 \text{ atm})(0.347 \text{ L})}{(0.08206 \text{ L atm mol}^{-1} \text{ K}^{-1})(298 \text{ K})}$$

$$n = 0.0138 \text{ mol O}_2$$

Now you can use the reaction stoichiometry to convert from moles $O_2$ to moles $KClO_3$ and then to grams $KClO_3$:

$$(0.0138 \text{ mol O}_2)\left(\frac{2 \text{ mol KClO}_3}{3 \text{ mol O}_2}\right)\left(\frac{122.55 \text{ g KClO}_3}{1 \text{ mol KClO}_3}\right) = 1.13 \text{ g KClO}_3$$

If you used 22.4 L $mol^{-1}$ in the calculation, you would not only get the wrong answer but also no credit on the exam.

## Nonideal Gases

We have been considering ideal gases, that is, gases that obey the postulates of the Kinetic Molecular Theory (KMT). But remember—a couple of those postulates were on shaky ground. KMT assumes the volume of the gas molecules was negligible, and there were no attractive forces between the gas particles. In most situations, these approximations are acceptable, and the ideal gas equation works. However, there are situations where these approximations will not work, and an alternative approach is needed. In 1873, Johannes van der Waals introduced a modification of the ideal gas equation that adjusted for these two factors by introducing two constants—$a$ and $b$—into the ideal gas equation. Van der Waals realized that the actual volume of the gas is less than the ideal gas because gas molecules have a finite volume. He also realized that the more moles of gas present, the greater the real volume. He compensated for the volume of the gas particles mathematically with:

$$\text{corrected volume} = V - nb$$

where $n$ is the number of moles of gas and $b$ is a different constant for each gas. The larger the gas particles, the more volume they occupy and the larger the $b$ value.

The attraction of the gas particles for each other tends to lessen the pressure of the gas because the attraction slightly reduces the force of gas particle collisions with the container walls. The amount of attraction depends on the concentration of gas particles and the magnitude of the particles' intermolecular force. The greater the intermolecular forces of the gas, the higher the attraction is, and the less the real pressure. Van der Waals compensated for the attractive force with:

$$\text{corrected pressure} = P + an^2/V^2$$

where $a$ is a constant for individual gases. The greater the attractive force between the molecules, the larger the value of $a$. The $n^2/V^2$ term corrects for the concentration. Substituting these corrections into the ideal gas equation gives the **van der Waals equation**:

$$(P + an^2/V^2)(V - nb) = nRT$$

The larger, more concentrated, and stronger the intermolecular forces of the gas, the more deviation from the ideal gas equation one can expect and the more useful the van der Waals equation becomes.

Deviations from ideal behavior become more apparent at high pressures and low temperatures. At high pressures, the particles of a gas are pressed very close together, which results in a significant fraction of the volume being occupied by the particles. At low temperatures, the average kinetic energy of the particle is low; therefore, the particles are moving more slowly, allowing them to interact with each other. What constitutes a high pressure or a low temperature depends upon the size and strength of the intermolecular forces of the gas particles.

# Experiments

STRATEGY

Gas law experiments generally involve pressure, volume, and temperature measurements. In a few cases, other measurements such as mass and time are necessary. You should remember that $\Delta P$, for example, is NOT a measurement; the initial and final pressure measurements are the actual measurements made in the laboratory. Another common error is the application of gas law type information and calculations for nongaseous materials. Do not expect to use 22.4 L $mol^{-1}$ at any time.

A common consideration is the presence of water vapor, $H_2O(g)$. Water generates a vapor pressure, which varies with the temperature. Dalton's law is used in these cases to adjust the pressure of a gas sample for the presence of water vapor. The setup for such an experiment is shown in Figure 10.8. As the substance in the test tube is heated, a gas is generated. That gas travels to the water-filled inverted test tube, it displaces the water, and the gas is collected. However, the gas inside the test tube is a mixture of gas from the decomposed substance and water vapor. The total pressure (normally atmospheric pressure) is the pressure of the gas or gases being collected and the water vapor. When the pressure of

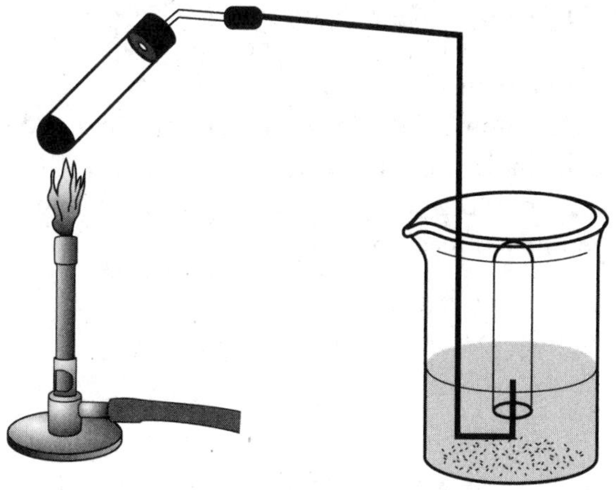

**Figure 10.8 Dalton's law collection of a gas over water.**

an individual gas is needed, the vapor pressure of water is subtracted from the total pressure. Finding the vapor pressure of water requires measuring the temperature and using a table showing vapor pressure of water versus temperature.

In experiments on Graham's law, time is measured. The amount of time required for a sample to effuse is the measurement. The amount of material effusing divided by the time elapsed is the rate of effusion.

Most gas law experiments use either the combined gas law or the ideal gas equation. Moles of gas are a major factor in many of these experiments. The combined gas law can generate the moles of a gas by adjusting the volume to STP (many students forget to make this adjustment) and using Avogadro's relationship of 22.4 L/mol at STP. The ideal gas equation gives moles from the relationship $n = PV/RT$.

*HINT: Make sure the conditions are STP before using 22.4 L/mol.*

Two common gas law experiments are "Determination of Molar Mass by Vapor Density" and "Determination of the Molar Volume of a Gas." While it is possible to use the combined gas law (through 22.4 L/mol at STP) for either of these, the ideal gas equation is easier to use. The values for $P$, $V$, $T$, and $n$ must be determined.

The temperature may be determined easily using a thermometer. The temperature measurement is normally in °C. The °C must then be converted to a Kelvin temperature (K = °C + 273).

Pressure is measured using a barometer. If water vapor is present, a correction is needed in the pressure to compensate for its presence. The vapor pressure of water is found in a table of vapor pressure versus temperature. Subtract the value found in this table from the measured pressure (Dalton's law). Values from tables are not considered to be measurements for an experiment. If you are going to use 0.08206 L atm $mol^{-1}$ $K^{-1}$ for $R$, convert the pressure to atmospheres.

The value of $V$ may be measured or calculated. A simple measurement of the volume of a container may be made, or a measurement of the volume of displaced water may be required. Calculating the volume requires knowing the number of moles of gas present. No matter how you get the volume, don't forget to convert it to liters when using $PV = nRT$ or STP.

The values of $P$, $T$, and $V$ discussed above may be used, with the ideal gas equation, to determine the number of moles present in a gaseous sample. Stoichiometry is the alternative method of determining the number of moles present. A quantity of a substance is converted to a gas. This conversion may be accomplished in a variety of ways. The most common stoichiometric methods are through volatilization or reaction. The volatilization method is the simplest. A weighed quantity (<u>measure</u> the mass) of a substance is converted to moles (<u>calculate</u> the moles) by using the molar mass (molecular weight). If a reaction is taking place, the quantity of one of the substances must be determined (normally with the mass and molar mass), and then, using the mole-to-mole ratio, this value is converted to moles (a calculation not a measurement).

Combining the value of $n$ with the measured mass of a sample will allow you to calculate the molar mass of the gas.

Do not forget: values found in tables and conversions from one unit to another are not experimental measurements.

## Common Mistakes to Avoid

1. When using any of the gas laws, be sure you are dealing with gases, not liquids or solids. We've lost track of how many times we've seen people apply gas laws in situations in which no gases were involved.
2. In any of the gas laws, be sure to express the **temperature in kelvin**. Failure to do so is a quite common mistake.
3. Be sure, especially in stoichiometry problems involving gases, that you are calculating the volume, pressure, etc., of the correct gas. You can avoid this mistake by clearly labeling your quantities (*moles of* $O_2$ instead of just *moles*).
4. Make sure your **answer is reasonable**. Analyze the problem; don't just write a number down from your calculator. Be sure to check your number of significant figures.
5. If you have a gas at a certain set of volume/temperature/pressure conditions and the conditions change, you will probably use the combined gas equation. If moles of gas are involved, the ideal gas equation will probably be useful.
6. Make sure your **units cancel**.
7. In using the combined gas equation, make sure you group all initial-condition quantities on one side of the equals sign and all final-condition quantities on the other side.
8. Be sure to use the correct molecular mass for those gases that exist as diatomic molecules—$H_2$, $N_2$, $O_2$, $F_2$, $Cl_2$, and $Br_2$ and $I_2$ vapors.
9. If the value 22.4 L/mol is to be used, make absolutely sure that it is applied to a **gas** at **STP**.
10. It is not possible to have a negative Kelvin temperature.

# › Review Questions

Use these questions to review the content of this chapter and practice for the AP Chemistry Exam. First are 20 multiple-choice questions similar to what you will encounter in Section I of the AP Chemistry Exam. This set also includes some questions meant to help you review prior knowledge. Following those is a long free-response question like the ones in Section II of the exam. To make these questions an even more authentic practice for the actual exam, time yourself following the instructions provided.

## Multiple-Choice Questions

Answer the following questions in 30 minutes. You may not use a calculator. You may use the periodic table and the equation sheet at the back of this book.

**1.** A sample of argon gas is sealed in a container. The volume of the container is doubled. If the pressure remains constant, what happens to the absolute temperature?

(A) The temperature does not change.
(B) The temperature is halved.
(C) The temperature is doubled.
(D) The temperature is squared.

**2.** A sealed, rigid container is filled with three ideal gases: A, B, and C. The partial pressure of each gas is known. The temperature and volume of the system are known. What additional information is necessary to determine the masses of the gases in the container?

(A) the average distance traveled between molecular collisions
(B) the intermolecular forces
(C) the molar masses of the gases
(D) the total pressure

**3.** Two balloons are at the same temperature and pressure. One contains 14 g of nitrogen, and the other contains 20.0 g of argon. Which of the following is true?

(A) The density of the nitrogen sample is greater than the density of the argon sample.
(B) The average speed of the nitrogen molecules is greater than the average speed of the argon molecules.
(C) The average kinetic energy of the nitrogen molecules is greater than the average kinetic energy of the argon molecules.
(D) The volume of the nitrogen container is less than the volume of the argon container.

**4.** An experiment to determine the molar mass of a gas begins by heating a solid to produce a gaseous product. The gas passes through a tube and displaces water in an inverted, water-filled bottle. Which of the following may be determined **after** the experiment is completed?

(A) vapor pressure of water
(B) temperature of the displaced water
(C) barometric pressure in the room
(D) mass of the solid used

**5.** The true volume of a real gas is smaller than that calculated from the ideal gas equation. This occurs because the ideal gas equation does NOT consider which of the following?

(A) the attraction between the molecules
(B) the shape of the molecules
(C) the volume of the molecules
(D) the mass of the molecules

**6.** A 1.00-mole sample of ammonia gas, $NH_3$, is placed in a flask. Ammonia will be most nearly ideal under which of the following sets of conditions?

(A) 250 K and 0.1 atm
(B) 350 K and 0.1 atm
(C) 350 K and 1 atm
(D) Ammonia will behave the same under all conditions.

7. A reaction produces a gaseous mixture of carbon dioxide, carbon monoxide, and water vapor. After one experiment, the mixture was analyzed and found to contain 0.60 mole of carbon dioxide, 0.30 mole of carbon monoxide, and 0.10 mole of water vapor. If the total pressure of the mixture was 0.80 atm, what was the partial pressure of the carbon monoxide?

(A) 0.080 atm
(B) 0.34 atm
(C) 0.13 atm
(D) 0.24 atm

8. A sample of methane gas was collected over water at 35°C. The sample had a total pressure of 756 mm Hg. Determine the partial pressure of the methane gas in the sample. The vapor pressure of water at 35°C is 41 mm Hg.

(A) 760 mm Hg
(B) 41 mm Hg
(C) 715 mm Hg
(D) 797 mm Hg

9. A student has three identical 2.0 L flasks (A, B, and C) all at 298 K. Each flask has an 8.0-g sample of gas sealed inside. Flask A contains methane, $CH_4$; flask B contains hydrogen, $H_2$; and flask C contains helium, He. Rank the three flasks in order of decreasing pressure.

(A) A > B > C
(B) B > C > A
(C) C > A > B
(D) All three flasks are at the same pressure.

10. An ideal gas sample weighing 1.28 g at 127°C and 1.00 atm has a volume of 0.250 L. Determine the molar mass of the gas.

(A) 322 g $mol^{-1}$
(B) 168 g $mol^{-1}$
(C) 0.00621 g $mol^{-1}$
(D) 53.4 g $mol^{-1}$

11. Increasing the temperature of an ideal gas from 50°C to 75°C at constant volume will cause which of the following to increase for the gas?

(A) the average molecular mass of the gas
(B) the average distance between the molecules
(C) the average speed of the molecules
(D) the density of the gas

12. If a sample of $CH_4$ effuses at a rate of 9.0 moles per hour at 35°C, which of the following gases will effuse at approximately twice the rate under the same conditions?

(A) CO
(B) He
(C) $O_2$
(D) $F_2$

13. A steel tank containing argon gas has additional argon gas pumped into it at constant temperature. Which of the following is true for the gas in the tank?

(A) There is no change in the number of gas atoms.
(B) There is an increase in the volume of the gas.
(C) There is a decrease in the pressure exerted by the gas.
(D) The gas atoms travel with the same average speed.

14. Choose the gas that probably shows the greatest deviation from ideal gas behavior under a given set of conditions.

(A) He
(B) $O_2$
(C) $SF_4$
(D) $SiH_4$

15. Determine the formula for a gaseous silane ($Si_nH_{2n+2}$) if it has a density of 4.02 g $L^{-1}$ at 77°C and 0.950 atm.

(A) $SiH_4$
(B) $Si_2H_6$
(C) $Si_3H_8$
(D) $Si_4H_{10}$

16. Which of the following best explains why a hot-air balloon rises?

(A) The heating of the air causes the pressure inside the balloon to increase.
(B) The moving outside air pushes higher.
(C) The temperature difference between the inside and outside air causes convection currents.
(D) Hot air has a lower density than cold air.

17. Three identical steel containers at the same temperature are filled with gas samples. One container has 16 g of methane, $CH_4$; another has 44.0 g of carbon dioxide, $CO_2$; and the third has 146 g of sulfur hexafluoride, $SF_6$. Pick the FALSE statement from the following list:

(A) The densities decrease in the following order: sulfur hexafluoride > carbon dioxide > methane.
(B) Each container has the same number of molecules.
(C) The pressure in each container is the same.
(D) The molecules in each container have the same average speed.

18. Which of the following places the gases in order of increasing deviation from ideal behavior?

(A) $He < SO_2 < CH_4 < O_2$
(B) $He < O_2 < CH_4 < SO_2$
(C) $He < CH_4 < O_2 < SO_2$
(D) $CH_4 < O_2 < He < SO_2$

19. Each of four 10.0 L containers is filled with a different noble gas (He, Ne, Ar, and Kr). Each container contains 0.5 mole of gas at 298 K. Assuming all four gases are behaving ideally, which of the following is the same for all four samples?

(A) average speed of the atoms
(B) density of the gas in the container
(C) all properties
(D) average kinetic energy of the atoms

20. Each of four 5.0 L containers is filled with a different gas (He, $CH_4$, $O_2$, and $CO_2$). Each container contains 0.75 mole of gas at 273 K. If one of the containers springs a small leak, which of the following will change in that container?

(A) moles, temperature, and pressure
(B) moles and pressure
(C) temperature and pressure
(D) moles and temperature

## › Answers and Explanations

1. **C**—This question relates to the combined gas law: $\frac{P_1V_1}{T_1} = \frac{P_2V_2}{T_2}$. Since the pressure remains constant, the pressures may be removed from the combined gas law to produce Charles's law: $\frac{V_1}{T_1} = \frac{V_2}{T_2}$. This equation may be rearranged to $T_2 = \frac{T_1V_2}{V_1}$. The doubling of the volume means $V_2 = 2V_1$. On substituting, $T_2 = \frac{T_1 2V_1}{V_1}$, giving $T_2 = 2T_1$. The identity of the gas is irrelevant in this problem.

2. **C**—This problem depends on the ideal gas equation: $PV = nRT$. $R$, $V$, and $T$ are known, and by using the partial pressure for a gas, the number of moles ($n$) of that gas may be determined. To convert from moles to mass, the molar mass of each gas is necessary.

3. **B**—Since $T$ and $P$ are known, and since the moles ($n$) can be determined from the masses given, this question could use the ideal gas equation. There are 0.50 mole of each gas. Equal moles of gases, at the same $T$ and $P$, have equal volumes, which eliminates answer D. Equal volume also means that the greater mass has the greater density, eliminating answer A. The average kinetic energy of a gas depends on the temperature. If the temperatures are the same, then the average kinetic energy is the same, eliminating C. Finally, at the same temperature, heavier gases travel slower than lighter gases. Nitrogen molecules are lighter than argon atoms, so nitrogen molecules travel at a faster average speed, making B the correct answer. You may find this type of reasoning process beneficial on any question to which you do not immediately know the answer.

4. **A**—This experiment requires the ideal gas equation. The mass of the solid is needed (to convert to moles); this eliminates answer D. The volume, temperature, and pressure must be measured during the experiment, eliminating answers B and C. The measured pressure is the total pressure. Eventually the total pressure must be converted to the partial pressure of the gas using Dalton's law. The total pressure is the sum

of the pressure of the gas plus the vapor pressure of water. The vapor pressure of water can be found in a table when the calculations are performed (only the temperature is needed to find the vapor pressure in a table). Answer A is correct because it is possible to delay looking up the vapor pressure of water. There will always be questions on the AP Exam concerning laboratory experiments.

**5. C**—Real gases are different from ideal gases because of two basic factors (see nonideal gases): molecules have a volume, and molecules attract each other. The molecules' volume is subtracted from the observed volume for a real gas (giving a smaller volume), and the pressure has a term added to compensate for the attraction of the molecules (correcting for a smaller pressure). Since these are the only two directly related factors, answers B and D are eliminated. The question is asking about volume; thus, the answer is C. The volume calculated from the ideal gas equation is the ideal volume plus the volume of the gas atoms or molecules.

**6. B**—A real gas approaches ideal behavior at higher temperatures and lower pressures.

**7. D**—The partial pressure of any gas is equal to its mole fraction of the gas times the total pressure. The mole fraction of carbon monoxide is

$$\left[\frac{0.30}{(0.60+0.30+0.10)}\right]=\left[\frac{0.30}{1.00}\right]=0.30\text{, and the}$$

partial pressure of CO is $0.30 \times 0.80\text{ atm} = 0.24\text{ atm}$.

**8. C**—Using Dalton's law ($P_{Total} = P_A + P_B + \cdots$), where $P_A$ is unknown and $P_B$ is the vapor pressure of water, the partial pressure may be found by 756 mm Hg − 41 mm Hg = 715 mm Hg.

**9. B**—The molar masses of the gases are 2.0 g/mole for $H_2$, 4.0 g/mole for He, and 16 g/mole for $CH_4$. Therefore, an 8.0-g sample means 4.0 moles of $H_2$, 2.0 moles of He, and 0.50 mole of $CH_4$. The greater the number of moles present, with volume and temperature being the same, the greater the pressure in the flask.

**10. B**—The molar mass may be obtained by dividing the grams of the gas by the number of moles (calculated from the ideal gas equation). The mole calculation is $n = \frac{PV}{RT} =$

$$\frac{(1.00\text{ atm})(0.250\text{ L})}{\left(0.08206\,\frac{\text{L atm}}{\text{mol K}}\right)(400\text{ K})} = 7.62\times10^{-3}\text{ mol,}$$

which leads to $\frac{1.28\text{ g}}{7.62\times10^{-3}\text{ mol}} = 168\text{ g mol}^{-1}$.

Simplify the problem by estimating. Do not forget to convert the temperature to kelvin. If you forgot to change to K, you got answer D. Answer C is an impossible molar mass.

**11. C**—Answer B requires an increase in volume, not allowed by the problem. Answer C requires an increase in temperature. Answer A requires a change in the composition of the gas. Answer D requires a decrease in the volume.

**12. B**—Lighter gases effuse faster. The only gas among the choices that is lighter than methane is helium. To calculate the molar mass, you would begin with the molar mass of methane and divide by the rate ratio squared.

**13. D**—A steel tank will have a constant volume, and the problem states that the temperature is constant. Adding gas to the tank will increase the number of moles of the gas and the pressure (forcing the argon atoms closer together). A constant temperature means there will be a constant.

**14. C**—Deviations from ideal behavior depend on the size of the molecules and the intermolecular forces between the molecules. The greatest deviation would be for a large polar molecule. Sulfur tetrafluoride is the largest molecule listed, and it is the only polar molecule listed.

**15. D**—The molar mass may also be determined using the ideal gas equation (with the volume being 1.00 L), which gives the moles per liter or

$$n = \frac{PV}{RT} = \frac{(0.950\text{ atm})(1.00\text{ L})}{\left(0.08206\,\frac{\text{L atm}}{\text{mol K}}\right)(350\text{ K})} =$$

$3.31 \times 10^{-2}$ mol. Simplify the problem by estimating. A sample of 1.00 L of a gas with a density of 4.02 g $L^{-1}$ weighs 4.02 grams. The mass given divided by the moles calculated from the ideal gas equation gives the molar mass or $\frac{4.02 \text{ g}}{3.31 \times 10^{-2} \text{ mol}} = 121 \text{ g mol}^{-1}$. The correct answer is the gas with the molar mass closest to 121 g mol$^{-1}$. If you incorrectly used 22.4 L mol$^{-1}$, you got 90 g mol$^{-1}$, which is answer C and wrong. The conditions are not STP, so 22.4 L mol$^{-1}$ does not apply.

**16. D**—The hot-air balloon rises because it has a lower density than the surrounding air. Less dense objects will float on more dense objects. In other words, "lighter" objects will float on "heavier" objects.

**17. D**—The densities come from the mass of gas divided by identical volumes; therefore, the container with the greatest mass of gas will have the greatest density. Each container holds one mole of gas, which means that each container has the same number of molecules of gas. The pressure in each container will be the same because the number of moles, the temperature, and the volume are the same. Ideal gases at the same temperature will have the same average kinetic energy. However, the heavier molecules do not need to travel as fast as the lighter molecules to attain equal kinetic energy. For this reason, the speeds are not identical.

**18. C**—The smaller the gas particle and the less polar (more nonpolar) the gas is, the smaller the deviation from ideal gas behavior. Sulfur dioxide, $SO_2$, is the only polar gas; therefore, it will most likely show the greatest deviation (be the last one in the list). The remaining species (nonpolar) should be in order of increasing molar mass.

**19. D**—This behavior is due to kinetic molecular theory. The average kinetic energy depends only on the absolute temperature. The average speed changes with the atomic mass, with the heavier gas moving more slowly. Since the volumes are all the same, the higher the atomic mass, the higher the density.

**20. A**—All three variables will change, which makes this the best answer. The escaping gas would lead to a decrease in the number of moles. If there are fewer moles present, the pressure would decrease. The slower-moving gas molecules would tend to remain in the container, while the faster-moving molecules would escape. This would result in a lower average velocity of those species. The molar mass may also be determined by dividing the mass of the gas by the moles in the container. If there is a lower average velocity, then there will be a lower temperature.

## › Free-Response Question

You have 20 minutes to answer the following question. You may use a calculator and the tables in the back of the book.

**Question**

A sample containing 2/3 mol of potassium chlorate, $KClO_3$, is heated until it decomposes to potassium chloride, KCl, and oxygen gas, $O_2$. The oxygen released is collected in an inverted bottle through the displacement of water. Answer the following questions using this information.

(a) Write a balanced chemical equation for the reaction.
(b) Calculate the number of moles of oxygen gas produced.
(c) The temperature and pressure of the sample are adjusted to STP. The volume of the sample is slightly greater than 22.4 L. Explain.
(d) An excess of sulfur, S, is burned in 1 mole of oxygen, in the presence of a catalyst, to form gaseous sulfur trioxide, $SO_3$. Write a balanced chemical equation, and then calculate the number of moles of gas formed.
(e) After the sulfur had completely reacted it was cooled, and a sample of the residual water was removed from the bottle and found to be acidic. Explain with a balanced chemical equation.

## Answer and Explanation

(a) $2\ KClO_3(s) \rightarrow 2\ KCl(s) + 3\ O_2(g)$

You get 1 point if you have the correct setup of reactant and products. You get 1 more point if the equation is balanced correctly.

(b) $$\left(\frac{2}{3}\text{ mol KClO}_3\right)\left(\frac{3\text{ mol O}_2}{2\text{ mol KClO}_3}\right) = 1\text{ mol O}_2$$

You get 1 point for the correct answer and 1 point for the work. You can get these points if you correctly use information from an incorrect equation in part **a.**

(c) At STP, the volume of 1 mole of $O_2$ should be 22.4 L. The volume is greater because oxygen was not the only gas in the sample. Water vapor was also present. The presence of the additional gas leads to a larger volume.

You get 1 point for discussing STP and 22.4 L, and you get 1 point for discussing the presence of water vapor (extra gas gives a greater volume).

(d) The equation is:

(a) $2\ S(s) + 3\ O_2(g) \rightarrow 2\ SO_3(g)$

According to this equation,

(b) $$(1\text{ mol O}_2)\left(\frac{2\text{ mol SO}_3}{3\text{ mol O}_2}\right) = 2/3\text{ mol SO}_3$$

You get 1 point for the equation and 1 point for the math. You can still get 1 total point if you used an incorrect number of moles of $O_2$ from an incorrectly balanced equation.

(e) A nonmetal oxide, such as sulfur trioxide, will dissolve in water to produce an acid. This will get you 1 point (even if you predict the wrong acid). The following balanced chemical equation is worth 1 additional point, even if you used the wrong acid that you predicted):

(c) $SO_3(g) + H_2O(l) \rightarrow H_2SO_4(aq)$

Total your points. There are 10 possible points.

## › Rapid Review

- Kinetic Molecular Theory (KMT)—Gases are small particles of negligible volume moving in a random straight-line motion, colliding with the container walls (that is the gas pressure) and with each other. During these collisions, no energy is lost, but energy may be transferred from one particle to another; the Kelvin temperature is proportional to the average kinetic energy. There is assumed to be no attraction between the particles.
- Pressure—Know the different units used in atmospheric pressure.
- Boyle's law—The volume and pressure of a gas are inversely proportional if the temperature and amount are constant.
- Charles's law—The volume and temperature of a gas are directly proportional if the amount and pressure are constant.
- Gay-Lussac's law—The pressure and temperature of a gas are directly proportional if the amount and volume are constant.
- Combined gas law—Know how to use the combined gas equation: $P_1V_1/T_1 = P_2V_2/T_2$.
- Avogadro's law—The number of moles and volume of a gas are directly proportional if the pressure and temperature are constant. Remember that 1 mol of an ideal gas at STP (1 atm and 0°C) occupies a volume of 22.4 L. Remember to not use this value unless the gas is at STP.
- Ideal gas equation—Know how to use the ideal gas equation: $PV = nRT$.
- Dalton's law—The sum of the partial pressures of the individual gases in a gas mixture is equal to the total pressure: $P_{Total} = P_A + P_B + P_C + ...$
- Gas stoichiometry—Know how to apply the gas laws to reaction stoichiometry problems.
- Nonideal gases—Know how the van der Waals equation accounts for the nonideal behavior of real gases. Understand how the equation works, not how to calculate answers.
- Tips—Make sure the **temperature is in kelvin**; gas laws are being applied to gases only; the **units cancel**; and the **answer is reasonable.**
- Gas laws are very useful for gases, but not for liquids and solids. Before applying a gas law, be sure you are dealing with a gas.

# CHAPTER 11

# Solutions

**IN THIS CHAPTER**

In this chapter, the following AP topics are covered:

1.4 Composition of Mixtures
3.7 Solutions and Mixtures
3.9 Separation of Solutions and Mixtures Chromatography
3.10 Solubility
4.3 Representations of Reactions

**Summary:** A **solution** is a homogeneous mixture composed of a solvent and one or more solutes. The **solvent** is the substance that acts as the dissolving medium and is normally present in the greatest amount. Commonly the solvent is a liquid, but it doesn't have to be. Our atmosphere is a solution with nitrogen as the solvent; it is the gas present in the largest amount (79%). Steel is a solution where iron is the solvent. Many times you will be dealing with a solution in which water is the solvent, an **aqueous solution**. The **solute** is the substance that the solvent dissolves and is normally present in the smaller amount. You may have more than one solute in a solution. For example, if you dissolved table salt (sodium chloride) and table sugar (sucrose) in water, you would have one solvent (water) and two solutes (sodium chloride and sucrose).

Some substances will dissolve in a particular solvent and others will not. There is a general rule in chemistry that states that "*like dissolves like.*" This general statement may serve as an answer in the multiple-choice questions; however, this simplified approach does not serve as an explanation in the free-response questions. This simply means that polar substances (salts, alcohols, etc.) will dissolve in polar solvents such as water, and nonpolar solutes, such as iodine, will dissolve in nonpolar solvents such as carbon tetrachloride. The solubility of a specific solute is normally expressed in terms of grams solute per 100 mL of solvent (g/mL) at a specified temperature. The temperature must be specified because the solubility of a substance will vary with the temperature. Normally, the solubility of solids dissolving in liquids increases with increasing temperature, while the reverse is true for gases dissolving in liquids. Pressure is important when gases are involved.

A solution in which one has dissolved the maximum amount of solute per given amount of solvent at a given temperature is called a **saturated solution**.

An **unsaturated solution** has less than the maximum amount of solute dissolved. Sometimes if the temperature, purity of the solute and solvent, and other factors are just right, you might be able to dissolve more than the maximum amount of solute, resulting in a **supersaturated solution**. Supersaturated solutions are unstable, and sooner or later separation of the excess solute will occur, until a saturated solution and separated solute remain.

The formation of a solution depends on many factors, such as the nature of the solvent, the nature of the solute, the temperature, and the pressure. Some of these factors were addressed in the Reactions and Periodicity chapter. In general, the solubility of a solid or liquid will increase with temperature and be unaffected by pressure changes. The solubility of a gas will decrease with increasing temperature and will increase with increasing partial pressure of the gas **(Henry's law)**.

Solutions will also be important in the next several chapters of this book. This is especially true of Chapter 15, Equilibrium, where many of the equilibrium constants apply to aqueous solutions.

KEY IDEA

**Keywords and Equations**

molarity, $M$ = moles solute per liter solution molality

## Concentration Units

There are many ways of expressing the relative amounts of solute(s) and solvent in a solution. The terms *saturated, unsaturated,* and *supersaturated* give a qualitative measure, as do the terms *dilute* and *concentrated.* The term **dilute** refers to a solution that has a relatively small amount of solute in comparison to the amount of solvent. **Concentrated**, on the other hand, refers to a solution that has a relatively large amount of solute in comparison to the solvent. However, these terms are very subjective. If you dissolve 0.1 g of sucrose per liter of water, that solution would probably be considered dilute; 100 g of sucrose per liter would probably be considered concentrated. But what about 25 g per liter—dilute or concentrated? In order to communicate effectively, chemists use quantitative ways of expressing the concentration of solutions. Several concentration units are useful, including percentage, molarity, and molality; however, only molarity appears on the AP Chemistry Exam.

ENRICHMENT

### Percentage

One common way of expressing the relative amount of solute and solvent is through percentage, amount per hundred. Percentage can be expressed in three ways:

- mass percent
- mass/volume percent
- volume/volume percent

**Mass (Sometimes Called Weight) Percentage**

The mass percentage of a solution is the mass of the solute divided by the mass of the solution, multiplied by 100% to get percentage. The mass is commonly measured in grams.

$$\text{mass \%} = (\text{grams of solute/grams solution}) \times 100\%$$

For example, a solution is prepared by dissolving 25.2 g of sodium chloride in 250.0 g of water. Calculate the mass percent of the solution.

Answer:

$$\text{mass \%} = \frac{25.2 \text{ g solute}}{(25.2 + 250.0) \text{ g solution}} \times 100\% = 9.16\%$$

A common error is forgetting to add the solute and solvent masses together in the denominator.

When solutions of this type are prepared, the solute and solvent are weighed out separately and then mixed to form a solution. The final volume of the solution is unknown.

Mass/volume and volume/volume percentage are done in much the same fashion.

## Molarity

Percentage concentration is common in everyday life (3% hydrogen peroxide, 5% acetic acid, commonly called vinegar, etc.). The concentration unit most commonly used by chemists is molarity. **Molarity ($M$)** is the number of moles of solute per liter of solution:

$$M = \text{moles solute/liter solution}$$

In preparing a molar solution, the correct number of moles of solute (commonly converted to grams using the molar mass) is dissolved and diluted to the required volume.

Determine the molarity of ethanol, $C_2H_5OH$, in a solution produced by dissolving 25.0 g of this compound in enough water to produce 500.0 mL of solution:

$$\text{molarity} = \frac{25.0 \text{ g } C_2H_5OH}{500.0 \text{ mL}} \times \frac{1 \text{ mol } C_2H_5OH}{46.08 \text{ g } C_2H_5OH} \times \frac{1{,}000 \text{ mL}}{1 \text{ L}} = 1.08\ M$$

STRATEGY

The most common error is not being careful with the units. Grams must be converted to moles, and milliliters must be converted to liters.

Another way to prepare a molar solution is by dilution of a more concentrated solution to a more dilute one by adding solvent. The following equation can be used:

$$(M_{\text{before}})(V_{\text{before}}) = (M_{\text{after}})(V_{\text{after}})$$

In the preceding equation, *before* refers to before dilution and *after* refers to after dilution. Let's see how to apply this relationship. Determine the final concentration when 300.0 mL of water is added to 200.0 mL of a 0.1250 $M$ solution of HCl. Assume the volumes are additive.

$$M_{\text{before}} = 0.1250\ M \qquad M_{\text{after}} = ?$$

$$V_{\text{before}} = 200.0 \text{ mL} \qquad V_{\text{before}} = (200.0 + 300.0) \text{ mL}$$

$$M_{\text{after}} = \frac{(M_{\text{before}})(V_{\text{before}})}{(V_{\text{after}})} = \frac{(0.1250\ M)(200.0 \text{ mL})}{(500.0 \text{ mL})} = 0.05000\ M \text{ HCl}$$

The most common error is forgetting to add the two volumes.

ENRICHMENT

**Molality**

Sometimes the varying volumes of a solution's liquid component(s) due to changes in temperature present a problem. Many times volumes are not additive, but mass is additive. The chemist then resorts to defining concentration in terms of the molality. **Molality ($m$)** is defined as the moles of solute per kilogram of solvent:

$$m = \frac{\text{moles solute}}{\text{kilograms solvent}}$$

Notice that this equation uses kilograms of solvent, not solution. The other concentration units use mass or volume of the entire solution. Molal solutions use only the mass of the *solvent*. For dilute aqueous solutions, the molarity and the molality will be close to the same numerical value.

Molality is important when determining the efficiency of antifreeze.

For example, methanol, $CH_3OH$, was used in antifreeze at one time. Determine the molality of methanol in a solution prepared by adding 25.00 g of methanol to 150.0 g of water.

$$\text{molality} = \frac{25.00\text{ g } CH_3OH}{150.0\text{ g } H_2O} \times \frac{1{,}000\text{ g}}{1\text{ kg}} \times \frac{1\text{ mol } CH_3OH}{32.05\text{ g } CH_3OH} = 5.200\ m\ CH_3OH$$

The most common error is to use the total grams in the denominator instead of just the grams of solvent.

# Electrolytes and Nonelectrolytes

An **electrolyte** is a substance that, when dissolved in a solvent or melted, conducts an electrical current. A **nonelectrolyte** does not conduct a current when dissolved. The conduction of the electrical current is often determined using a light bulb connected to a power source and two electrodes. The electrodes are placed in the solution or melt, and if a conducting medium is present, such as ions, the light bulb will light, indicating the substance is an electrolyte.

The ions that conduct the electrical current can result from a couple of sources. They may result from the dissociation of a soluble ionically bonded substance (a salt). If sodium chloride (NaCl) is dissolved in water, it dissolves into sodium cations ($Na^+$) and chloride anions ($Cl^-$). But certain covalently bonded substances may also produce ions if dissolved in water, a process called ionization. For example, acids, both inorganic and organic, will produce ions when dissolved in water. Some acids, such as hydrochloric acid (HCl), will completely ionize. Other acids, such as acetic acid ($CH_3COOH$), will only partially ionize. They establish an equilibrium with the ions and unionized species (see Chapter 15 for more on chemical equilibrium). Solutions of electrolytes (strong or weak) have strong ion–dipole forces.

$$HCl(aq) \rightarrow H^+(aq) + Cl^-(aq) \qquad \text{100\% ionization}$$

$$CH_3COOH(aq) \rightleftarrows H^+(aq) + CH_3COO^-(aq) \qquad \text{partial ionization}$$

Species such as HCl that completely ionize in water are called **strong electrolytes**, and those that only partially ionize are called **weak electrolytes**. Most soluble salts also fall into the strong electrolyte category.

ENRICHMENT

## Colligative Properties

Some of the properties of solutions depend on the chemical and physical nature of the individual solute. The blue color of a copper(II) sulfate solution and the sweetness of a sucrose solution are related to the properties of those solutes. However, some solution properties simply depend on the *number* of solute particles, not the type of solute. These properties are called **colligative properties** and include:

- Vapor pressure lowering
- Freezing-point depression
- Boiling-point elevation
- Osmotic pressure

### Vapor Pressure Lowering

If a liquid is placed in a sealed container, molecules will evaporate from the surface of the liquid and eventually establish a gas phase over the liquid that is in equilibrium with the liquid phase. The pressure generated by this gas is the **vapor pressure** of the liquid. Vapor pressure is temperature dependent; the higher the temperature, the higher the vapor pressure. If the liquid is made a solvent by adding a nonvolatile solute, the vapor pressure of the resulting solution is always less than that of the pure liquid. The vapor pressure has been lowered by the addition of the solute; the amount of lowering is proportional to the number of solute particles added and is thus a colligative property. When the vapor pressure equals the external pressure, the liquid or solution will boil.

Solute particles are evenly distributed throughout a solution, even at the surface. Thus, there are fewer solvent particles at the gas–liquid interface where evaporation takes place. Fewer solvent particles escape into the gas phase, and so the vapor pressure is lower. The higher the concentration of solute particles, the less solvent at the interface and the lower the vapor pressure. This relationship is referred to as **Raoult's law**.

### Freezing-Point Depression

The freezing point of a solution of a nonvolatile solute is always lower than the freezing point of the pure solvent. It is the number of solute particles that determines the amount of the lowering of the freezing point. The amount of lowering of the freezing point is proportional to the molality of the solute and is given by the equation:

$$\Delta T_f = iK_f \text{ molality}$$

where $\Delta T_f$ is the number of degrees that the freezing point has been lowered (the difference in the freezing point of the pure solvent and the solution); $K_f$ is the freezing-point depression constant (a constant of the solvent); the molality is the molality of the solute; and $i$ is the van 't Hoff factor—the ratio of the number of moles of particles released into solution per mole of solute dissolved. For a nonelectrolyte, such as ethylene glycol (antifreeze), the van 't Hoff factor would be 1. For a strong electrolyte, such as sodium chloride, you must take into consideration that if 1 mol of NaCl dissolves, 2 mol of particles would result (1 mol $Na^+$, 1 mol $Cl^-$). Therefore, the van 't Hoff factor should be 2. Let's learn to apply the preceding equation. Determine the freezing point of an aqueous solution containing 20.50 g of calcium chloride in 250.0 g of water. The value of $K_f$ for aqueous solutions is 1.86 K kg mol$^{-1}$. In northern states, calcium chloride is sometimes used to de-ice roads and sidewalks.

$$\Delta T = iK_f m = 3(1.86 \text{ K kg mol}^{-1})\left[\frac{(20.50 \text{ g CaCl}_2)\dfrac{(1 \text{ mol CaCl}_2)}{110.78 \text{ g CaCl}_2}}{(250.0 \text{ g})\left(\dfrac{1 \text{ kg}}{1{,}000 \text{ g}}\right)}\right]$$

$$= 4.13 \text{ K}$$

$$T_{fp} = (273.15 - 4.13)\text{K} = 269.02 \text{ K } (= -4.13°\text{C})$$

The most common mistake is to forget to subtract the $\Delta T$ value from the normal freezing point.

The freezing-point depression technique is also used to calculate the molar mass of a solute.

For example, a solution is prepared by dissolving 0.490 g of an unknown compound in 50.00 mL of water. The freezing point of the solution is –0.201°C. Assuming the compound is a nonelectrolyte, what is the molecular mass of the compound? Use 1.00 g/mL as the density of water.

$$m = \frac{\Delta T}{K_f} = \frac{0.201 \text{ K}}{1.86 \text{ K kg mol}^{-1}} = 0.108 \text{ mol kg}^{-1}$$

$$50.00 \text{ mL } (1.00 \text{ g/mL})\left(\frac{1 \text{ kg}}{1{,}000 \text{ g}}\right) = 0.0500 \text{ kg}$$

$$(0.108 \text{ mol kg}^{-1})(0.0500 \text{ kg}) = 0.00540 \text{ mol}$$

$$\frac{0.490 \text{ g}}{0.00540 \text{ mol}} = 90.7 \text{ g mol}^{-1}$$

Many students make the mistake of stopping before they complete this problem. If you get an answer less than 1 g mol$^{-1}$, you have made an error (that is, it is impossible to get a molar mass less than that of a hydrogen ion, $H^+$).

## Boiling-Point Elevation

Just as the freezing point of a solution of a nonvolatile solute is always lower than that of the pure solvent, the boiling point of a solution is always higher than the pure solvent. Again, only the number of solute particles affects the boiling point. The mathematical relationship is similar to the one for the freezing-point depression above and is:

$$\Delta T_b = iK_b \text{ molality}$$

where $\Delta T_b$ is the number of degrees the boiling point has been elevated (the difference between the boiling point of the pure solvent and the solution); $K_b$ is the boiling-point elevation constant; the molality is the molality of the solute; and $i$ is the van 't Hoff factor. You can calculate a solution's boiling point if you know the molality of the solution. If you know the amount of the boiling-point elevation and the molality of the solution, you can calculate the value of the van 't Hoff factor, $i$. Calculations involving boiling-point elevation are like those for freezing point depression.

### Osmotic Pressure

If you were to place a solution and a pure solvent in the same container (such as the one in Figure 11.1) but separate them by a **semipermeable membrane** (which allows the passage of some particles, but not all particles), you would observe that the level of the solvent side would decrease while the solution side would increase. This indicates that the solvent molecules are passing through the semipermeable membrane, a process called **osmosis**. Eventually the system would reach equilibrium, and the difference in levels would remain constant. The difference in the two levels is related to the **osmotic pressure**. In fact, one could exert a pressure on the solution side exceeding the osmotic pressure, and solvent molecules could be forced back through the semipermeable membrane into the solvent side. This process is called **reverse osmosis** and is the basis of the desalination of seawater for drinking purposes. Cell membranes are common examples of semipermeable membranes.

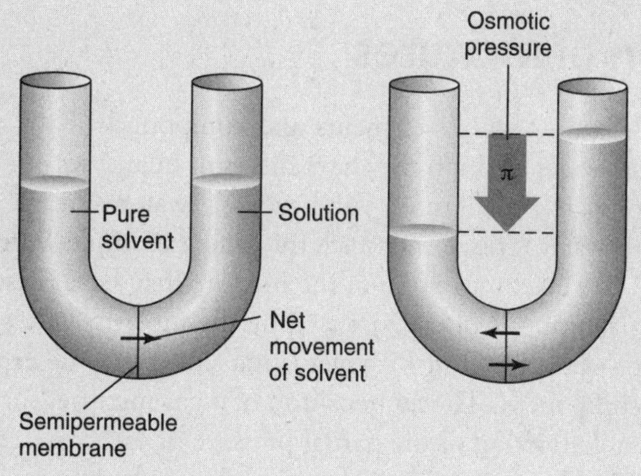


**Figure 11.1 Osmotic pressure.**

## Colloids

KEY IDEA

If you watch a glass of muddy water, you will see particles in the water settling out. This is a heterogeneous mixture where the particles are large (in excess of 1,000 nm), and it is called a **suspension**. In contrast, dissolving sodium chloride in water results in a true homogeneous **solution**, with solute particles less than 1 nm in diameter. True solutions do not settle out because of the very small particle size. However, there are mixtures whose particle diameters fall in between solutions and suspensions. These are called **colloids** and have solute particles in the range of 1 to 1,000 nm diameter. Table 11.1 shows some representative colloids.

Many times it is difficult to distinguish a colloid from a true solution. The most common method is to shine a light through the mixture under investigation. A light shone through a true solution is invisible, but a light shone through a colloid is visible because the light reflects off the larger colloid particles. This is called the **Tyndall effect**.

**Table 11.1 Common Colloid Types**

| COLLOID TYPE | SUBSTANCE DISPERSED | DISPERSING MEDIUM | EXAMPLES |
|---|---|---|---|
| aerosol | solid | gas | smoke |
| aerosol | liquid | gas | fog |
| solid foam | gas | solid | marshmallow |
| foam | gas | liquid | whipped cream |
| emulsion | liquid | liquid | milk, mayonnaise |
| solid emulsion | liquid | solid | cheese, butter |
| sol | solid | liquid | paint, gelatin |

## Composition of Mixtures

Mixtures, unlike elements and compounds, have a variable composition. For example, a saltwater solution may have different quantities of table salt dissolved in different quantities of water. In all cases, you have a saltwater solution; however, samples with a very low salt-to-water ratio do not taste the same as sample with a significantly higher ratio.

The composition of the mixture may be expressed in several ways. The composition of a solution is often expressed by the molarity of a solution. The composition of a mixture of elemental iron with elemental sulfur may be expressed by the mass percentages of each component. The composition of a gas mixture, such as air, may be expressed by either the mole fraction or the partial pressure of each gas. These are only a few examples.

The composition of a mixture may be known because the person creating the mixture may have carefully measured the quantity of each component before mixing the different components. However, a mixture of unknown composition will need to be analyzed. In many cases, physical processes may be involved in the analysis, while in other cases, the analysis may require a chemical process.

In the following examples, we will focus on determining the mass percentages of the components of the mixture. In each case, this begins with the determination of the masses of the component. Once the mass of a component is known, the mass may be converted to moles, atoms, and with the aid of density, the mass may be determined to the volume.

The composition of the saltwater may be determined by weighing a sample of the solution and then allowing the water to evaporate to leave the salt behind. The mass of the salt divided by the mass of the solution times 100% gives the mass percent of the salt and 100% minus the mass percent of the salt gives the mass percent of water.

The composition of the iron-sulfur mixture may be determined by weighing a quantity of the mixture and then using a magnet to remove the iron. Once the iron is removed, simply weigh the remaining sulfur and determine the percentages of the two components. However, what if the mixture was elemental iron mixed with elemental nickel? Magnetic separation will not work as both metals are attracted to a magnet.

On the other hand, what about determining the percentages of iron, manganese, and chromium in a sample of stainless steel? In this case, physical process will not work. The normal procedure is to weigh a sample of the steel into a container and to dissolve the sample in acid. Once the components are in solution, it is possible to determine the quantities of each component using a variety of titration or instrumental techniques.

## Separation of Solutions and Mixtures Chromatography

The components of a solution may be separated by several techniques. Two of these techniques will be discussed here. These two techniques are chromatography and distillation. These methods are necessary in the case of a liquid mixture as filtration will not work.

There are numerous types of chromatography, each designed to deal with a specific type of solution. Chromatography will work for both liquid and gaseous solutions. In all chromatography techniques, there is a mobile phase and a stationary phase. Separation is brought about because of a competition between the intermolecular forces between the components of the sample with the mobile phase versus the stationary phase.

The types of chromatography discussed here are paper, thin-layer, and column. In paper chromatography, the stationary phase is paper. Thin-layer chromatography employs a thin layer of silica or some other solid on a glass plate as the stationary phase. In column chromatography, a glass tube is filled with silica or some other solid substance as the stationary phase. In all three cases, a solvent is used as the mobile phase. The solvent may be a pure liquid or another solution.

An example of a paper chromatography experiment is the separation of the components present in a sample of ink. Most colors of ink contain a variety of components to produce a particular color. For example, a sample of green ink will most likely contain a blue component and a yellow component. There may be other components to produce different shades of green. The separation begins by placing a small drop of the ink near the bottom of a piece of chromatography paper. Additional drops of other samples or of possible components may be placed in a line alongside the first. The paper is then placed into a container containing a small quantity of a solvent (mobile phase). The ink dots must be above the surface of this solvent. The solvent will slowly "wet" the paper. That is, the solvent will soak into the paper and slowly creep higher on the paper. As the solvent front moves past the ink dots, some of the components will be more soluble in the solvent than the others. This solubility is related to the strength of the intermolecular forces. The component will readhere to the stationary phase after traveling a short distance further along and the dissolving-readhere process will repeat over and over. The component with the weakest intermolecular attraction to the stationary phase versus the mobile phase will move farther before readhering than a component with a greater attraction. Thus, over time the one component will separate from the others because of this difference in attraction. After a certain time, there will be a series of new dots representing each component above the original dot. These may be identified by comparing the distance traveled to the distance a standard has traveled.

All other chromatography techniques may be related to this procedure. In some cases, the time required to travel a fixed distance may be measured instead of the distance traveled. Any type of intermolecular force or combination of intermolecular forces may be responsible for the separation.

Another method of separation of the components of a solution is distillation. If a volatile solvent and a nonvolatile solute are present in the solution, a simple distillation will work. However, if both the solvent and solute are volatile, fractional distillation is necessary. In both cases, the volatile components are first vaporized and then condensed back to the liquid state. This is all that is necessary in a simple distillation. The solvent is vaporized and then condensed into another container, leaving the nonvolatile phase in the first container. The setup for a simple distillation is shown in Figure 11.2.

In fractional distillation, more than one component is volatile. Therefore, when heated each component will volatilize. The vapor phase will be enriched in the volatile component with the weaker intermolecular forces. Thus, when the vapor condenses,

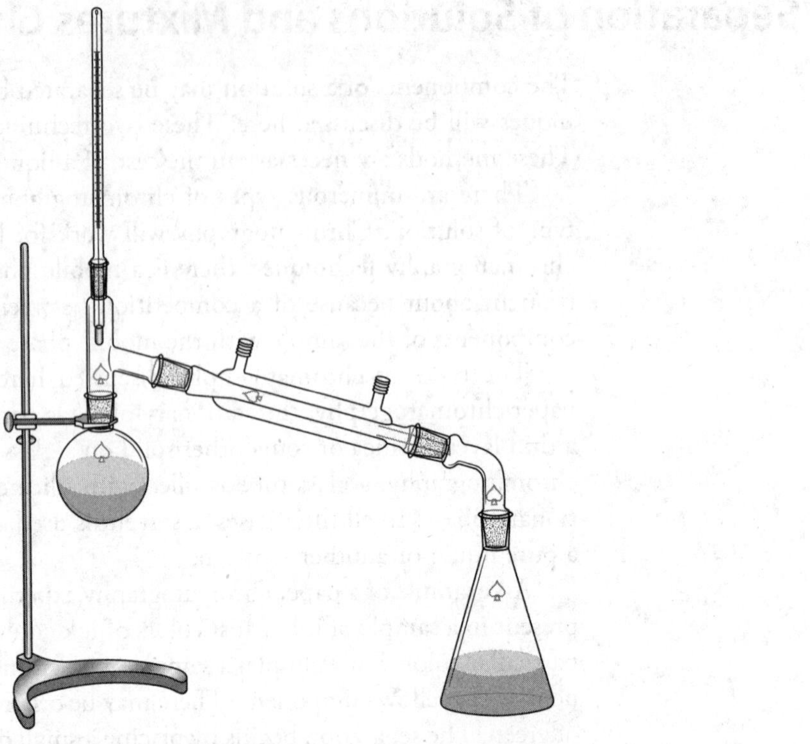

**Figure 11.2 The setup for a simple distillation minus the heat source to be placed below the flask on the left and the tubing for the cooling water to enter and leave the condenser.**

the resultant solution will be enriched in the more volatile component. This process may be repeated multiple times with each step producing a solution with a higher percentage of the more volatile component until the pure component is isolated. While the simple distillation apparatus shown in Figure 11.2 may be used for this, it is not practical because of the time involved. To do fractional distillation efficiently, a fractionating column is added to the simple distillation apparatus. A fractionating column provides numerous places for the components to condense and revaporize. In this way, by the time the vapor reaches the top of the column, several simple distillations have taken place; therefore, one pass through the system will accomplish a number of simple distillations and do so in much less time than repeated simple distillation. This method is used to separate the components of crude oil into its components, one of which is gasoline.

## Experiments

STRATEGY

Experimental procedures for solutions involve concentration units. Keeping close track of the units may simplify the problem. Titrations, which appear in Chapter 16, Acids and Bases, involve the concentrations of solutions.

## Common Mistakes to Avoid

TIP

1. In molarity problems, be sure to use liters of **solution**.
2. Make sure your units cancel, leaving you with the units desired in your final answer.
3. Round off your final numerical answers to the correct number of significant figures.
4. Remember, most molecular compounds—compounds containing only nonmetals—do not ionize in solution. Acids are the most common exceptions.

## › Review Questions

Use these questions to review the content of this chapter and practice for the AP Chemistry Exam. First are 20 multiple-choice questions similar to what you will encounter in Section I of the AP Chemistry Exam. There are a few questions designed to help you recall some prior knowledge. Following those are two long free-response questions like the ones in Section II of the exam. To make these questions an even more authentic practice for the actual exam, time yourself following the instructions provided.

### Multiple-Choice Questions

Answer the following questions in 30 minutes. You may not use a calculator. You may use the periodic table and the equation sheet at the back of this book.

**1.** A solution is prepared by dissolving 1.25 g of an unknown substance in 100.0 mL of water. Which of the following procedures could be used to determine whether the solute is an electrolyte?

(A) Measure the specific heat of the solution.
(B) Measure the volume of the solution.
(C) Measure the conductivity of the solution.
(D) Determine the specific heat of the solution.

**2.** What is the final $K^+$ concentration in a solution made by mixing 300.0 mL of 1.0 $M$ $KNO_3$ and 700.0 mL of 2.0 $M$ $K_3PO_4$?

(A) 4.5 $M$
(B) 5.0 $M$
(C) 3.0 $M$
(D) 2.0 $M$

**3.** Strontium sulfate, $SrSO_4$, will precipitate when a solution of sodium sulfate is added to a strontium nitrate solution. What will be the strontium ion, $Sr^{2+}$, concentration remaining after 30.0 mL of 0.10 $M$ $Na_2SO_4$ solution are added to 70.0 mL of 0.20 $M$ $Sr(NO_3)_2$ solution?

(A) 0.14 $M$
(B) 0.15 $M$
(C) 0.11 $M$
(D) 0.20 $M$

**4.** Which of the following is a strong electrolyte when it is mixed with water?

(A) $HNO_2$
(B) $KNO_3$
(C) $C_2H_5OH$
(D) $CH_3COOH$

**5.** A solution with a total chloride ion, $Cl^-$, concentration of 1.0 $M$ is needed. Initially, the solution is 0.30 $M$ in $MgCl_2$. How many moles of solid $CaCl_2$ must be added to 400.0 mL of the $MgCl_2$ solution to achieve the desired concentration of chloride ion?

(A) 0.10 mole
(B) 0.080 mole
(C) 0.20 mole
(D) 0.15 mole

**6.** Assuming the volumes are additive, what is the final $H^+(aq)$ concentration produced by adding 30.0 mL of 0.50 $M$ $HNO_3$ to 70.0 mL of 1.00 $M$ HCl?

(A) 0.75 $M$
(B) 1.50 $M$
(C) 1.25 $M$
(D) 0.85 $M$

7. To prepare 3.0 L of a 0.20 molar $K_3PO_4$ solution (molecular weight 212 g/mole), a student should follow which of the following procedures?

(A) The student should weigh 42 g of solute and add sufficient water to obtain a final volume of 3.0 L.
(B) The student should weigh 42 g of solute and add 3.0 kg of water.
(C) The student should weigh 130 g of solute and add sufficient water to obtain a final volume of 3.0 L.
(D) The student should weigh 42 g of solute and add 3.0 L of water.

8. How many grams of $MgSO_4$ (molecular weight 120.4 g/mol) are in 100.0 mL of a 5.00 molar solution?

(A) 602.0 g
(B) 5.00 g
(C) 12.0 g
(D) 60.2 g

9. How many milliliters of concentrated nitric acid (16.0 molar $HNO_3$) are needed to prepare 0.500 L of 6.0 molar $HNO_3$?

(A) 0.19 mL
(B) 250 mL
(C) 375 mL
(D) 190 mL

10. A solution has 10 g of urea in 100 g of solution. Which of the following are needed to calculate the molarity of this solution?

(A) the density of the solution and the molecular weight of urea
(B) the density of urea and the molecular weight of urea
(C) the density of the solvent and the density of the solute
(D) the molecular weight of urea and the density of the solvent

11. Which of the following aqueous solutions would have the greatest conductivity?

(A) 0.2 *M* NaOH
(B) 0.2 *M* RbCl
(C) 0.2 *M* $K_3PO_4$
(D) 0.2 *M* $H_2SO_3$

12. How many milliliters of water must be added to 50.0 mL of 10.0 *M* $HNO_3$ to prepare 4.00 *M* $HNO_3$, assuming that the volumes of nitric acid and water are additive?

(A) 50.0 mL
(B) 125 mL
(C) 500 mL
(D) 75.0 mL

13. The best method to isolate pure $MgSO_4$ from an aqueous solution of $MgSO_4$ is to:

(A) evaporate the solution to dryness
(B) titrate the solution
(C) electrolyze the solution
(D) use paper chromatography

14. Pick the conditions that would yield the highest concentration of $N_2(g)$ in water.

(A) partial pressure of $N_2$ = 1.0 atm; temperature of water = 25°C
(B) partial pressure of $N_2$ = 0.50 atm; temperature of water = 55°C
(C) partial pressure of $N_2$ = 2.0 atm; temperature of water = 25°C
(D) partial pressure of $N_2$ = 2.0 atm; temperature of water = 85°C

15. A student prepares 100 mL of each of the following solutions by dissolving the appropriate solute in water. He then proceeds to measure the electrical conductivity of each solution. Which of the following aqueous solutions has the greatest electrical conductivity?

(A) 0.01 *M* $Ba(OH)_2$
(B) 0.01 *M* KCl
(C) 0.01 *M* $Na_3PO_4$
(D) 0.01 *M* $HC_2H_3O_2$

16.

| ION | IONIC RADIUS (pm) (CUBIC ENVIRONMENT) |
|---|---|
| $Na^+$ | 132 |
| $Cd^{2+}$ | 124 |
| $La^{3+}$ | 130 |

The energy change in the following reaction is the heat of hydration:

$$M^{n+}(g) + x\,H_2O(l) \rightarrow M(H_2O)_x^{n+}(aq)$$
$$\Delta H = \text{Heat of hydration}$$

In general, the heat of hydration is exothermic. Assuming the value of $x$ is the same in all cases, which of the following correctly predicts the relative order of the heats of hydration for the ions listed in the table and gives a correct explanation?

(A) $Na^+ > Cd^{2+} > La^{3+}$ because ions of elements lower on the periodic table have lower hydration energies.
(B) $Cd^{2+} > La^{3+} > Na^+$ because smaller radii lead to higher hydration energies.
(C) $La^{3+} > Cd^{2+} > Na^+$ because higher charges lead to higher hydration energies.
(D) All are about the same because their ionic radii are similar.

17. Bronze is an alloy of copper and tin. What would be the most likely first step required to determine the mass percentage of tin in a sample of bronze?

(A) Distill the bronze to separate the two metals.
(B) Use paper chromatography to separate the two metals.
(C) React the bronze with an acid.
(D) Once mixed to form bronze, it is no longer possible to separate the components.

18. The separation of the components in a mixture by paper chromatography depends on what property?

(A) Intermolecular forces
(B) Melting point
(C) Molar mass
(D) Boiling point

19. Mercury(II) chloride, $HgCl_2$, dissolves in water as discrete molecules. What is a simple procedure for determining that this is true?

(A) Observe the presence of molecules with an optical microscope.
(B) Use paper chromatography.
(C) Measure the electrical conductivity of the solution.
(D) Add silver nitrate solution to precipitate the chloride ion as AgCl.

$$3\,Ba(OH)_2(aq) + 2\,H_3PO_4(aq) \rightarrow Ba_3(PO_4)_2(s) + 6\,H_2O(l)$$

20. Which of the following techniques will allow you to determine if the above reaction is complete (with no excess of either reactant)?

(A) Determine the density of the solution.
(B) Determine the electrical conductivity of the solution.
(C) Determine volume of the solution.
(D) Determine the mass of the solution.

## › Answers and Explanations

To simplify some of the calculations, molarity will be expressed as $\left(\frac{\text{mol}}{1{,}000\text{ mL}}\right)$ instead of $\left(\frac{\text{mol}}{\text{L}}\right)$. This eliminates one or two conversions in the problems where this conversion is used.

**1. C**—If the solute is an electrolyte, the solution will conduct electricity. Nonelectrolytes do not conduct electricity. Strong electrolytes conduct electricity extremely well. Weak electrolytes also conduct electricity, but not as well as a strong electrolyte.

**2. A**—The potassium ion contribution from the $KNO_3$ is:

$$(300.0\text{ mL})\left(\frac{1.0\text{ mol }KNO_3}{1{,}000\text{ mL}}\right)\left(\frac{1\text{ mol }K^+}{1\text{ mol }KNO_3}\right)$$

$$= 0.30\text{ mole }K^+$$

The potassium ion contribution from $K_3PO_4$ is:

$$(700.0\text{ mL})\left(\frac{2.0\text{ mol }K_3PO_4}{1{,}000\text{ mL}}\right)\left(\frac{3\text{ mol }K^+}{1\text{ mol }K_3PO_4}\right)$$

$$= 4.2\text{ moles }K^+$$

The total potassium is 4.5 moles in a total volume of 1.000 L. Thus, the potassium concentration is 4.5 *M*.

**3. C**—The net ionic equation for the reaction is $Sr^{2+}(aq) + SO_4^{2-}(aq) \rightarrow SrSO_4(s)$. (You do not need to worry about solubility rules since you are specifically told that strontium sulfate precipitates.) Two reactants are given; therefore, you need to determine which is the limiting reactant. The strontium nitrate solution contains:

$$(70.0\text{ mL})\left(\frac{0.20\text{ mol }Sr(NO_3)_2}{1{,}000\text{ mL}}\right)\left(\frac{1\text{ mol }Sr^{2+}}{1\text{ mol }Sr(NO_3)_2}\right)$$

$$= 0.014\text{ mole }Sr^{2+}$$

The sodium sulfate solution contains:

$$(30.0\text{ mL})\left(\frac{0.10\text{ mol }Na_2SO_4}{1{,}000\text{ mL}}\right)\times\left(\frac{1\text{ mol }SO_4^{2-}}{1\text{ mol }Na_2SO_4(NO_3)_2}\right)$$

$$= 0.0030\text{ mole }SO_4^{2-}$$

The sulfate ion is the limiting reactant. The strontium and sulfate ions react in a 1:1 ratio, so 0.0030 mole of sulfate ion will combine with 0.0030 mole of strontium ion, leaving 0.011 mole of strontium in a total volume of 100.0 mL. The final strontium ion concentration is:

$$\left(\frac{0.011\text{ mole }Sr^{2+}}{100.0\text{ mL}}\right)\left(\frac{1\text{ mL}}{0.001\text{ L}}\right) = 0.11\ M\ Sr^{2+}$$

**4. B**—A (nitrous acid) and D (acetic acid) are weak acids. Weak acids and bases are weak electrolytes. C (ethanol) is a nonelectrolyte. Potassium nitrate is a water-soluble ionic compound; such compounds are normally strong electrolytes.

**5. B**—The number of moles of chloride ion needed is

$$(400.0\text{ mL})\left(\frac{1.0\text{ mol }Cl^-}{1{,}000\text{ mL}}\right) = 0.40\text{ mole }Cl^-$$

The initial number of moles of chloride ion in the solution is:

$$(400.0\text{ mL})\left(\frac{0.30\text{ mol }MgCl_2}{1{,}000\text{ mL}}\right)\left(\frac{2\text{ mol }Cl^-}{1\text{ mol }MgCl_2}\right)$$

$$= 0.24\text{ mol }Cl^-$$

The number of moles needed

$$\left[(0.40 - 0.24)\text{ mol }Cl^-\right]\left(\frac{1\text{ mol }CaCl_2}{2\text{ mol }Cl^-}\right)$$

$$= 0.080\text{ mol }CaCl_2$$

**6. D**—Both acids are strong acids and yield 1 mole of $H^+$ each. Calculate the number of moles of $H^+$ produced by each acid. Divide the total number of moles by the final volume (100.0 mL). The calculation is:

$$\left[(30.0\text{ mL})\left(\frac{0.50\text{ mol }H^+}{1{,}000\text{ mL}}\right)\right] + \left[(70.0\text{ mL})\left(\frac{1.00\text{ mol }H^+}{1{,}000\text{ mL}}\right)\right]$$

$$= \left(\frac{0.085\text{ mol }H^+}{100.0\text{ mL}}\right)\left(\frac{1\text{ mL}}{0.001\text{ L}}\right) = 0.85\ M\ H^+$$

**7. C**—To produce a molar solution of any type, the final volume must be the desired volume. This eliminates answer D. B involves mass of water instead of volume. A calculation of the required mass will allow a decision between A and C:

$$(3.0\text{ L})\left(\frac{0.20\text{ mol K}_3\text{PO}_4}{\text{L}}\right)\left(\frac{212\text{ g K}_3\text{PO}_4}{1\text{ mol K}_3\text{PO}_4}\right)$$

$$= 130\text{ g K}_3\text{PO}_4$$

**8. D**—The calculation is:

$$\left(\frac{5.00\text{ mol MgSO}_4}{1{,}000\text{ mL}}\right)(100.0\text{ mL})\left(\frac{120.4\text{ g MgSO}_4}{1\text{ mol MgSO}_4}\right)$$

$$= 60.2\text{ g MgSO}_4$$

**9. D**—This is a dilution problem:

$$V_{\text{before}} = \frac{(M_{\text{after}})(V_{\text{after}})}{(M_{\text{before}})}$$

$$= \frac{(6.0\ M\ \text{HNO}_3)(0.500\text{ L})}{(16.0\ M\ \text{HNO}_3)}\left(\frac{1{,}000\text{ mL}}{1\text{ L}}\right)$$

$$= 190\text{ mL (2 significant figures)}$$

**10. A**—To calculate the molarity, the moles of urea and the volume of the solution are necessary. The density of the solution and the mass of the solution give the volume of the solution (it may be necessary to convert to liters). The mass of urea and the molar mass of urea give the moles of urea.

**11. C**—The strong electrolyte with the greatest concentration of ions is the best conductor. D is a weak electrolyte, not a strong electrolyte. The number of ions for the strong electrolytes may be found by simply counting the ions: A, 2; B, 2; C, 4. The best conductor has the greatest value when the molarity is multiplied by the number of ions. Also, since A and B both produce the same number of ions, they both cannot be right; therefore, neither can be right.

**12. D**—This is a dilution problem:

$$V_{\text{after}} = \frac{(M_{\text{before}})(V_{\text{before}})}{(M_{\text{after}})}$$

$$= \frac{(10.0\ M\ \text{HNO}_3)(50.0\text{ mL})}{(4.00\ M\ \text{HNO}_3)} = 125\text{ mL}$$

This is the final volume; since you already had 50.0 mL, you need an additional 75.0 mL.

**13. A**—Solutions cannot be separated by titrations or filtrations. Electrolysis of the solution would produce hydrogen and oxygen gas. Chromatography might achieve a minimal separation (so it cannot be the best method).

**14. C**—The solubility of a gas is increased by increasing the partial pressure of the gas and by lowering the temperature. Pick the answer with the highest nitrogen pressure and the lowest temperature.

**15. C**—Three of the compounds are strong electrolytes and one is a weak electrolyte. The weak electrolyte, $HC_2H_3O_2$, will not be as good a conductor as are the strong electrolytes (eliminating D). The strong electrolyte that produces the highest concentration of ions will be the best conductor. The number of ions produced by the strong electrolytes may be found by simply counting the ions: A, 3 ($Ba^{2+}$ + 2 $OH^-$); B, 2 ($K^+$ + $Cl^-$); C, 4 (3 $Na^+$ + $PO_4^{3-}$). The ion concentration for the strong electrolytes is the molarity of the solution times the number of ions present (van't Hoff factor). Answer C gives the highest concentration.

**16. C**—The ionic radii are too alike to make a significant difference; therefore, it is necessary to focus on the charge differences. The greater the charge, the greater the attraction of the ion for the polar water molecules (ion–dipole forces). The greater the attraction is, the greater the energy change is.

**17. C**—To begin the analysis it is necessary to place at least one of the two components in solution. Reacting with acid is one way of doing this. Distillation requires an unreasonably high temperature. Paper chromatography depends upon the ability of at least one of the components to be at least partially soluble in the mobile phase, which requires the bronze be dissolved in acid or some other substance first. There is always a method of separating the components.

**18. A**—Intermolecular forces are the key. The separation depends upon the relative strengths of the intermolecular forces of the components and the stationary phase (paper) and the relative intermolecular forces between the components and the mobile phase. The component held more strongly to the stationary phase moves more slowly than the component held less strongly. Intermolecular forces between the components and the mobile phase aids in this separation.

**19. C**—If the $HgCl_2$ dissolves as discrete molecules, it is a nonelectrolyte, which means there are no ions in solution. If ions are present in solution, the solution will conduct electricity, which is easily determined by measuring the electrical conductivity of the solution. Molecules are far too small to be observed by an optical isotope. Paper chromatography will not separate the cations from the anions as electrical neutrality must be maintained. A reaction to precipitate the chloride ions does not necessarily mean that they were initially present as separate ions before the reaction.

Note there are a variety of other techniques involving colligative properties (freezing point depression, boiling point depression, and osmosis) these topics only appear in college general chemistry courses and not on the AP Exam.

**20. B**—The reactants are electrolytes ($Ba(OH)_2(aq)$ is a strong electrolyte and $H_3PO_4(aq)$ is a weak electrolyte), and neither of the products is an electrolyte. Any excess reactant will yield ions making the solution conducting, while the lack of an excess reactant will leave a nonconducting mixture (note, no aqueous solution has absolutely no conductivity). Measuring the electrical conductivity of the solution is a simple method of determining if there is no excess reactant. The other methods present will not distinguish an incomplete reaction from a complete reaction.

## › Free-Response Questions

**Question 1**

You have 5 minutes to answer the following two-part question. You may use a calculator and the tables in the back of the book.

Five beakers each containing 100.0 mL of an aqueous solution are on a lab bench. The solutions are all at 25°C. Solution 1 contains 0.20 *M* $KNO_3$. Solution 2 contains 0.10 *M* $BaCl_2$. Solution 3 contains 0.15 *M* $C_2H_4(OH)_2$. Solution 4 contains 0.20 *M* $(NH_4)_2SO_4$. Solution 5 contains 0.25 *M* $KMnO_4$.

(a) Which solution has the lowest pH? Explain.

(b) Which solution would be the poorest conductor of electricity? Explain.

**Question 2**

You have 15 minutes to answer the following four-part question. You may use a calculator and the tables in the back of the book.

Five beakers are placed in a row on a countertop. Each beaker is half-filled with a 0.20 *M* aqueous solution. The solutes, in order, are (1) potassium sulfate, $K_2SO_4$; (2) methyl alcohol, $CH_3OH$; (3) sodium carbonate, $Na_2CO_3$; (4) ammonium chromate, $(NH_4)_2CrO_4$; and (5) barium chloride, $BaCl_2$. The solutions are all at 25°C. Answer the following questions with respect to the five solutions.

(a) Which solution will form a precipitate when ammonium chromate is added to it?

(b) Which solution is the most basic? Explain.

(c) Which solution would be the poorest conductor of electricity? Explain.

(d) Which solution is colored?

# ❯ Answers and Explanations

**Question 1**

(a) Solution 4, because the ammonium ion is a weak acid.
You get 1 point for picking solution 4 and 1 point for saying the ammonium ion ($NH_4^+$) is a weak acid or that it undergoes hydrolysis.

(b) Solution 3, because the solute is a nonelectrolyte.
Give yourself 1 point for picking solution 3 and 1 point for saying it is a nonelectrolyte or that it does not ionize.

Total your points. There are 4 points possible.

**Question 2**

(a) The ammonium ion, from the ammonium chromate, will not form a precipitate since most ammonium compounds are water soluble. Therefore, the precipitate must contain the chromate ion combined with a cation from one of the solutions. Solution (2) is a nonelectrolyte; therefore, there are no cations present to combine with the chromate ion. The potassium and sodium ions, from solutions (1) and (3), give soluble salts like the ammonium ion. This leaves only solution (5), barium chloride, which will give a precipitate. The formula of the precipitate is $BaCrO_4$.
You get 1 point for picking the correct solution.

(b) Solution (3), sodium carbonate, is the most basic. Since the carbonate ion is the conjugate base of a weak acid, it will undergo significant hydrolysis to produce a basic solution.
You get 1 point for picking the correct solution and giving the correct explanation.

(c) Methyl alcohol is a nonelectrolyte, so its solutions do not conduct electricity. The remaining solutions contain ionic salts, which, in general, are electrolytes in solution.
You get 1 point for picking the correct solution and giving the correct explanation.

(d) Solution (4), ammonium chromate, is yellow. Most solutions containing a transition metal ion are colored.
You get 1 point for picking the correct solution.

Total your points. There are 4 points possible.

# ❯ Rapid Review

- A solution is a homogeneous mixture composed of a solvent and one or more solutes. A solute is a substance that dissolves in the solvent and is normally present in smaller amount.
- The general rule of solubility is "like dissolves like." This means that polar solvents dissolve polar solutes and nonpolar solvents dissolve nonpolar solutes. Remember, however, that simply quoting this rule will not be sufficient as an explanation in the free-response section.
- A saturated solution is one in which the maximum amount of solute is dissolved for a given amount of solvent at a given temperature. Any solution with less than the maximum solute is called unsaturated. A solution with greater than maximum solute is supersaturated (an unstable state).

- For the chemist, the most useful unit of concentration is molarity ($M$), which is the moles of solute per liter of solution. Know how to work molarity problems. Be careful not to confuse molarity, $M$ or [ ], with moles, $n$ or mol.
- Electrolytes conduct an electrical current when melted or dissolved in a solvent, whereas nonelectrolytes do not.
- A colloid is a mixture in which the solute particle size is intermediate between a true solution and a suspension. If a light is shone through a colloid, the light beam is visible. This is the Tyndall effect.

# CHAPTER 12

# Reactions and Periodicity

**IN THIS CHAPTER**

In this chapter, the following AP topics are covered:

1.8 Valence Electrons and Ionic Compounds
3.7 Solutions and Mixtures
4.2 Net Ionic Equations
4.4 Physical and Chemical Changes
4.6 Introduction to Titration
4.7 Types of Chemical Reactions
4.8 Introduction to Acid–Base Reactions

**Summary:** Chemistry is the world of chemical reactions. Chemical reactions power our society, our environment, and our bodies. Some chemical species called **reactants** are converted into different substances called **products**. During this process, there are energy changes that take place. It takes energy to break old bonds. Energy is released when new bonds are formed. Does it take more energy to break the bonds than is released in the formation of the new bonds? If so, energy will have to be constantly supplied to convert the reactants into products. This type of reaction is said to be **endothermic**, absorbing energy. If more energy is released than is needed to break the old bonds, then the reaction is said to be **exothermic**, releasing energy. The chemical reactions that provide the energy for our world are exothermic reactions. In Chapter 14, Thermodynamics, you can read in more depth about the energy changes that occur during reactions.

Reactions occur because of collisions. One chemical species collides with another at the right place and transfers enough energy, and a chemical reaction occurs. Such reactions can be very fast or very slow. In Chapter 13, Kinetics, you can study how reactions occur and the factors that affect the speed of reactions.

In Chapter 15, Equilibrium, you will review the fact that reactions tend to go to equilibrium instead of completion. When the reaction is "over" both reactants and products will remain.

In Chapter 17, Electrochemistry, we will see how electricity may interact with reactions.

However, in this chapter, we will review the balancing of chemical equations, discuss the general types of chemical reactions, and describe why these reactions occur.

KEY IDEA

**Keywords and Equations**

There are no keywords or equations listed on the AP Exam that are specific to this chapter.

---

TIP

Reaction questions will always appear in the free-response section of the AP Exam.

# AP Exam Format

You are expected to write a balanced chemical equation for every reaction given and answer one or more questions about each reaction. If the reaction occurs in aqueous solution, you will have to write the net ionic equation for the process. For the reactions question of the AP Exam, you will be expected not only to balance the equation but also to have an understanding of why the reaction occurs. The reactions and concepts described may also appear in other parts of the AP Exam, such as the multiple-choice sections. Again, you will need to understand why a particular reaction occurs. As you study this chapter, pay particular attention to the explanations that accompany the reactions and equations. You will be expected to demonstrate your understanding on the AP Exam.

# General Aspects of Chemical Reactions and Equations

## Physical and Chemical Changes

Chemistry investigates two types of changes in chemical systems. These are **physical changes** and **chemical changes**. Physical changes involve a change in one of more physical properties with no change in composition. An example is boiling water where a liquid is converted to a gas. Even though the liquid and gas phases have different physical properties, each is composed of identical $H_2O$ molecules. Physical changes are normally accompanied by changes in intermolecular interactions. The physical change may be endothermic or exothermic. Normally, a physical change is reversible. However, this is not always true. For example, crushing a rock is a physical change that is hard to reverse.

During a chemical change there is a change in composition. There may be a change in the physical properties. Burning charcoal is an example of a chemical change. Solid charcoal (mostly carbon) combines with gaseous oxygen to produce gaseous carbon dioxide. The chemical change is accompanied by the breaking and forming of chemical bonds. All chemical changes may be described with a chemical equation. Chemical changes may be endothermic or exothermic. Normally, a chemical change is not reversible. In the charcoal example, it is not possible to "unburn" the charcoal. Equilibrium processes, Chapter 15, bend this rule to a certain extent.

Some processes have characteristics of both physical and chemical changes. An example is dissolving sodium chloride in water. This is usually characterized as a physical change even though ionic bonds in the sodium chloride are broken and ion–dipole interactions between the ions and water molecules form. However, simply heating the solution until all the water evaporates reverses the process and allows the isolation of the original sodium chloride and water.

In all chemical and physical changes the Law of Conservation of Mass is obeyed.

## Balancing Chemical Equations

We hope that, because you are preparing to take the AP Exam, you have already been exposed to the balancing of chemical equations. We will quickly review this topic and point out some specific aspects of balancing equations as the different types of chemical reactions are discussed. We have seen many students get into trouble because they did not pay close enough attention to the chemical equation.

A balanced chemical equation provides many types of information. It shows which chemical species are the reactants and which species are the products. It may also indicate in which state of matter the reactants and products exist. Special conditions of temperature, catalysts, etc., may be placed over or under the reaction arrow. And, very important, the coefficients (the integers in front of the chemical species) indicate the number of each reactant that is used and the number of each product that is formed. These coefficients may stand for individual atoms/molecules, or they may represent large numbers of them called moles (see Chapter 6, Stoichiometry, for a review of moles). The basic idea behind the balancing of equations is the **Law of Conservation of Matter**, which says that in ordinary chemical reactions matter is neither created nor destroyed. The number of each type of reactant atom must equal the number of each type of product atom. This requires adjusting the reactant and product coefficients—balancing the equation. When finished, the coefficients should be in the lowest possible whole-number ratio.

Most equations are balanced by inspection. This means basically a trial-and-error, methodical approach to adjusting the coefficients. One procedure that works well is to balance the homonuclear (same nucleus) molecule last. Chemical species that fall into this category include the diatomic elements, which you should know: $H_2$, $O_2$, $N_2$, $F_2$, $Cl_2$, $Br_2$, and $I_2$. This is especially useful when you are balancing combustion reactions. If a problem states that oxygen gas was used, then knowing that oxygen exists as the diatomic element is absolutely necessary in balancing the equation correctly.

## Periodic Relationships

The periodic table can give us many clues as to the type of reaction that is taking place. One general rule, covered in more detail in Chapter 8, Bonding, is that nonmetals react with other nonmetals to form covalent compounds, and that metals react with nonmetals to form ionic compounds. If the reaction that is producing the ionic compound is occurring in solution, you probably will be expected to write the net ionic equation for the reaction. Also, because of the wonderful arrangement of the periodic table, the members of a family or group (a vertical grouping) all react essentially in the same fashion. Many times, in reactions involving the loss of electrons (oxidation), as we proceed from top to bottom in a family, the reaction rate (speed) increases. Conversely, in reactions involving the gain of electrons (reduction), the reaction rate increases as we move from the bottom of a family to the top. Recall also that the noble gases (8A or 18) undergo very few reactions. Other specific periodic aspects will be discussed in the various reaction sections.

## General Properties of Aqueous Solutions

Many of the reactions that you will study occur in aqueous solution. Water is called the universal solvent because it dissolves so many substances. It readily dissolves ionic compounds as well as polar covalent compounds because of its polar nature. Ionic compounds that dissolve in water (dissociate) form **electrolyte** solutions, which conduct electrical current owing to the presence of ions. The ions can attract the polar water molecules and form a bound layer of water molecules around themselves. This process is called **solvation**. Refer to Chapter 11, Solutions, for an in-depth discussion of solvation.

Even though many ionic compounds dissolve in water, many others do not. If the attraction of the oppositely charged ions in the solid for each other is greater than the attraction of the polar water molecules for the ions, then the salt will not dissolve to an appreciable amount. If solutions containing ions such as these are mixed, precipitation will occur, because the strong attraction of the ions for each other overcomes the weaker attraction for the water molecules.

As mentioned, certain covalent compounds, like alcohols, readily dissolve in water because they are polar. Since water is polar, and these covalent compounds are also polar, water will act as a solvent for them (general rule of solubility: "like dissolves like"). Compounds like alcohols are **nonelectrolytes**—substances that do not conduct an electrical current when dissolved in water. However, certain covalent compounds, like acids, will **ionize** in water, that is, form ions:

$$HCl(aq) \rightarrow H^+(aq) + Cl^-(aq)$$

There are several ways of representing reactions that occur in water. Suppose, for example, that we were writing the equation to describe the mixing of a lead(II) nitrate solution with a sodium sulfate solution and showing the resulting formation of solid lead(II) sulfate. One type of equation that can be written is the **molecular equation**, in which both the reactants and products are shown in the undissociated form:

$$Pb(NO_3)_2(aq) + Na_2SO_4(aq) \rightarrow PbSO_4(s) + 2\ NaNO_3(aq)$$

Molecular equations are quite useful when you are doing reaction stoichiometry problems (see Chapter 6).

Showing the soluble reactants and products in the form of ions yields the **ionic equation** (sometimes called the total ionic equation):

$$Pb^{2+}(aq) + 2\ NO_3^-(aq) + 2\ Na^+(aq) + SO_4^{2-}(aq) \rightarrow PbSO_4(s) + 2\ Na^+(aq) + 2\ NO_3^-(aq)$$

Writing the equation in the ionic form shows clearly which species are really reacting and which are not. In the example above, $Na^+$ and $NO_3^-$ appear on both sides of the equation. These ions do not react and are simply there to maintain electrical neutrality of the solution. Ions like this, which are not actually involved in the chemical reaction taking place, are called **spectator ions**. We have seen students do this step incorrectly by separating the polyatomic ions ($NO_3^-$ and $SO_4^{2-}$) or by not including the ionic charges. Review your nomenclature to learn the polyatomic ions and the ionic charges. In an ionic equation, all strong electrolytes are written as separate ions. In water, the strong electrolytes are the strong acids, strong bases, and water-soluble ionic compounds. Any substance that is not a strong electrolyte is left in its original form.

The **net ionic equation** is written by dropping out the spectator ions and showing only those chemical species that are involved in the chemical reaction:

$$Pb^{2+}(aq) + SO_4^{2-}(aq) \rightarrow PbSO_4(s)$$

This net ionic equation focuses only on the substances that are actually involved in the reaction. It indicates that an aqueous solution containing $Pb^{2+}$ (any solution, not just $Pb(NO_3)_2(aq)$) will react with any solution containing the sulfate ion to form insoluble lead(II) sulfate. If this equation form is used, the spectator ions involved will not be known, but in most cases, this is not a problem, since the focus is really the general reaction, and not the specific one. You will be expected to write the balanced net ionic equation for many of the reactions on the test. Note, you will be given hints as to what type of reaction will occur without memorizing things like solubility rules.

## Precipitation Reactions

**Precipitation reactions** involve the formation of an insoluble compound, a **precipitate**, from the mixing of two soluble compounds. Precipitation reactions normally occur in aqueous solution. The example above that was used to illustrate molecular equations, ionic equations, etc., was a precipitation reaction. A solid, lead(II) sulfate, was formed from the mixing of the two aqueous solutions.

In order to predict whether or not precipitation will occur if two solutions are mixed, you must:

1. Learn to write the correct chemical formulas from the names; on the AP Exam, names are frequently given instead of formulas in the reaction section.
2. Be able to write the reactants and products in their ionic form, as in the ionic equation example above. Be sure, however, that you do not try to break apart molecular compounds such as most organic compounds, or insoluble species.
3. Know and be able to apply the following solubility rules by combining the cation of one reactant with the anion of the other in the correct formula ratio and determining the solubility of the proposed product. Then do the same thing for the other anion/cation combination.
4. On the AP Exam, you will be expected to explain why a substance is soluble/insoluble. Simply quoting the solubility rule is not sufficient.

Learn the following solubility rule:

All sodium, potassium, ammonium, and nitrate salts are soluble in water.

It is also possible to use hints to write the equation. For example, if you are given a solution, the substance is soluble. A soluble ionic compound is normally a strong electrolyte (you will be told if it is an exception). A soluble molecular compound usually is a nonelectrolyte unless it is an acid.

Although not required for the AP Exam, the following solubility rules are very useful.

- All salts containing acetate ($CH_3COO^-$) and perchlorates ($ClO_4^-$) are *soluble*.
- All chlorides ($Cl^-$), bromides ($Br^-$), and iodides ($I^-$) are *soluble*, except those of $Cu^+$, $Ag^+$, $Pb^{2+}$, and $Hg_2^{2+}$.
- All salts containing sulfate ($SO_4^{2-}$) are *soluble*, except those of $Pb^{2+}$, $Ca^{2+}$, $Sr^{2+}$, and $Ba^{2+}$.

Salts containing the following ions are normally **insoluble:**

- Most carbonates ($CO_3^{2-}$) and phosphates ($PO_4^{3-}$) are *insoluble,* except those of Group 1A (or Group 1) and the ammonium ion.
- Most sulfides ($S^{2-}$) are *insoluble,* except those of Groups 1A and 2A (or Groups 1 and 2) and the ammonium ion.
- Most hydroxides ($OH^-$) are *insoluble,* except those of Group 1A (Group 1), calcium, strontium, and barium.
- Most oxides ($O^{2-}$) are insoluble, except for those of Group 1A and Group 2A (Groups 1 and 2), which react with water to form the corresponding soluble hydroxides.

Let's see how one might apply these rules. Suppose a solution of lead(II) nitrate is mixed with a solution of sodium iodide. Predict what will happen.

Write the formulas:

$$Pb(NO_3)_2\,(aq) + NaI(aq) \rightarrow$$

Convert to the ionic form:

$$Pb^{2+}(aq) + 2\ NO_3^-(aq) + Na^+(aq) + I^-(aq) \rightarrow$$

Predict the possible products by combining the cation of one reactant with the anion of the other and vice versa:

$$PbI_2 + NaNO_3$$

Apply the solubility rules to the two possible products:

| | |
|---|---|
| $PbI_2(s)$ | *Insoluble*; therefore, a precipitate will form. |
| $NaNO_3(aq)$ | *Soluble*; no precipitate will form. |

Complete the chemical equation and balance it:

$$Pb(NO_3)_2(aq) + 2\ NaI(aq) \rightarrow PbI_2(s) + 2\ NaNO_3(aq)$$

$$Pb^{2+}(aq) + 2\ I^-(aq) \rightarrow PbI_2(s)$$

If both possible products are soluble, then the reaction would be listed as NR (no reaction). In the reaction question part of the AP Exam, there will be a possible reaction for every part of the question. If at least one insoluble product is formed, the reaction is sometimes classified as a **double displacement (replacement) or metathesis reaction.**

## Oxidation–Reduction Reactions

Oxidation–reduction reactions, commonly called **redox reactions**, are an extremely important category of reaction. Redox reactions include combustion, corrosion, respiration, photosynthesis, and the reactions involved in electrochemical cells (batteries). The driving force involved in redox reactions is the exchange of electrons from a more active species to a less active one. You can predict the relative activities from a table of activities or a half-reaction table. Chapter 17, Electrochemistry, goes into depth about electrochemistry and redox reactions.

TIP

The AP free-response booklet includes a table of half-reactions, which you may use for help during this part of the exam. A similar table can be found in the back of this book. Alternatively, you may wish to memorize the common oxidizing and reducing agents.

*Redox* is a term that stands for **red**uction and **ox**idation. **Reduction** is the gain of electrons, and **oxidation** is the loss of electrons. For example, suppose a piece of zinc metal is placed in a solution containing the blue $Cu^{2+}(aq)$ cation. Very quickly, a reddish solid forms on the surface of the zinc metal. That substance is copper metal. As the copper metal is deposited, the blue color of the solution begins to fade. At the molecular level, the more active zinc metal is losing electrons to form the $Zn^{2+}(aq)$ cation, and the $Cu^{2+}(aq)$ ion is gaining electrons to form the less active copper metal. These two processes can be shown as:

$$Zn(s) \rightarrow Zn^{2+}(aq) + 2e^{-} \quad \text{(oxidation)}$$

$$Cu^{2+}(aq) + 2e^{-} \rightarrow Cu(s) \quad \text{(reduction)}$$

The electrons that are being lost by the zinc metal are the same electrons that are being gained by the copper(II) ion. The zinc metal is being oxidized and the copper(II) ion is being reduced. Further discussions on why reactions such as these occur can be found in the section on single displacement reactions later in this chapter.

Something must cause the oxidation (taking the electrons), and that substance is called the **oxidizing agent** (the reactant being reduced). In the example above, the oxidizing agent is the $Cu^{2+}(aq)$ ion. The reactant undergoing oxidation is called the **reducing agent** because it is furnishing the electrons that are being used in the reduction half-reaction. Zinc metal is the reducing agent above. The two half-reactions, oxidation and reduction, can be added together to give you the overall redox reaction. When doing this, the electrons must cancel—that is, there must be the same number of electrons lost as electrons gained:

$$Zn(s) + Cu^{2+}(aq) + 2\,e^{-} \rightarrow Zn^{2+}(aq) + 2\,e^{-} + Cu(s)$$

$$\textit{or} \quad Zn(s) + Cu^{2+}(aq) \rightarrow Zn^{2+}(aq) + Cu(s)$$

In these redox reactions, there is a simultaneous loss and gain of electrons. In the oxidation reaction (commonly called a half-reaction) electrons are being lost, but in the reduction half-reaction those very same electrons are being gained. So, in redox reactions electrons being exchanged as reactants are being converted into products. This electron exchange may be direct, as when copper metal plates out on a piece of zinc, or it may be indirect, as in an electrochemical cell (battery).

Another way to determine what is being oxidized and what is being reduced is by looking at the change in oxidation numbers of the reactant species. (See Chapter 5, Basics, for a discussion of oxidation numbers and how to calculate them.) Oxidation is indicated by an increase in oxidation number. In the example above, the Zn metal went from an oxidation state of zero to +2. Reduction is indicated by a decrease in oxidation number. $Cu^{2+}(aq)$ went from an oxidation state of +2 to zero. In order to figure out whether a particular reaction is a redox reaction, write the net ionic equation. Then determine the oxidation numbers of each element in the reaction. If one or more elements have changed oxidation number, it is a redox reaction.

There are several types of redox reaction that are given specific names. In the next few pages, we will examine some of these types of redox reaction.

## Combination Reactions

**Combination reactions** are reactions in which two or more reactants (elements or compounds) combine to form one product. Although these reactions may be of several different types, some types are definitely redox reactions. These include reactions of metals with nonmetals to form ionic compounds, and the reaction of nonmetals with other nonmetals to form covalent compounds.

$$2\ K(s) + Cl_2(g) \rightarrow 2\ KCl(s)$$

$$2\ H_2(g) + O_2(g) \rightarrow 2\ H_2O(l)$$

In the first reaction, we have the combination of an active metal with an active nonmetal to form a stable ionic compound. The very active oxygen reacts with hydrogen to form the stable compound water. The hydrogen and potassium are undergoing oxidation, while the oxygen and chlorine are undergoing reduction.

### Decomposition Reactions

**Decomposition reactions** are reactions in which a compound breaks down into two or more simpler substances. Although not all decomposition reactions are redox reactions, many are. For example, the thermal decomposition reactions, such as the common laboratory experiment of generating oxygen by heating potassium chlorate, are decomposition reactions:

$$2\,KClO_3(s) \xrightarrow[\Delta]{} 2\,KCl(s) + 3\,O_2(g)$$

In this reaction the chlorine is going from the less stable +5 oxidation state to the more stable −1 oxidation state. While this is occurring, oxygen is being oxidized from −2 to 0.

Another example is **electrolysis**, in which an electrical current is used to decompose a compound into its elements:

$$2\,H_2O(l) \xrightarrow[\text{electricity}]{} 2\,H_2(g) + O_2(g)$$

The spontaneous reaction would be the opposite one; therefore, we must supply energy (in the form of electricity) in order to force the nonspontaneous reaction to occur. This type of reaction will be discussed in more detail in Chapter 17, Electrochemistry.

### Single Displacement Reactions

STRATEGY

**Single displacement (replacement) reactions** are reactions in which atoms of an element replace the atoms of another element in a compound. All the single replacement reactions are redox reactions since the element (in a zero-oxidation state) becomes an ion. Most single displacement reactions can be categorized into one of three types of reaction:

TIP

- A metal displacing a metal ion from solution
- A metal displacing hydrogen gas ($H_2$) from an acid or from water
- One halogen replacing another halogen in a compound

Remember: it is an **element** displacing another atom from a compound. The displaced atom appears as an element on the product side of the equation.

Reactions will always appear in the free-response section of the AP Chemistry Exam.

For the first two types, a table of metals relating their ease of oxidation to each other is useful in being able to predict what displaces what. Table 12.1 shows the **activity series for metals**, which lists the metal and its oxidation in order of decreasing ease of oxidation. An alternative to the activity series is a table of half-cell potentials, as discussed in Chapter 17, Electrochemistry. In general, the more active the metal, the lower its potential.

TIP

Elements on this activity series can displace ions of metals *lower* than themselves on the list. If, for example, one placed a piece of tin metal into a solution containing $Cu(NO_3)_2(aq)$, the Sn would replace the $Cu^{2+}(aq)$ cation:

$$Sn(s) + Cu(NO_3)_2\ (aq) \rightarrow Sn(NO_3)_2\ (aq) + Cu(s)$$

$$Sn(s) + Cu^{2+}(aq) \rightarrow Sn^{2+}(aq) + Cu(s)$$

**Table 12.1 Activity Series of Metals in Aqueous Solution**

| | | | | | |
|---|---|---|---|---|---|
| Li(s) | $\rightarrow$ | $Li^+(aq)$ | + | $e^-$ | Most easily oxidized |
| K(s) | $\rightarrow$ | $K^+(aq)$ | + | $e^-$ | |
| Ba(s) | $\rightarrow$ | $Ba^{2+}(aq)$ | + | $2\ e^-$ | |
| Sr(s) | $\rightarrow$ | $Sr^{2+}(aq)$ | + | $2\ e^-$ | |
| Ca(s) | $\rightarrow$ | $Ca^{2+}(aq)$ | + | $2\ e^-$ | |
| Na(s) | $\rightarrow$ | $Na^+(aq)$ | + | $e^-$ | |
| Al(s) | $\rightarrow$ | $Al^{3+}(aq)$ | + | $3\ e^-$ | |
| Mn(s) | $\rightarrow$ | $Mn^{2+}(aq)$ | + | $2\ e^-$ | |
| Zn(s) | $\rightarrow$ | $Zn^{2+}(aq)$ | + | $2\ e^-$ | |
| Cr(s) | $\rightarrow$ | $Cr^{2+}(aq)$ | + | $2\ e^-$ | |
| Fe(s) | $\rightarrow$ | $Fe^{2+}(aq)$ | + | $2\ e^-$ | |
| Cd(s) | $\rightarrow$ | $Cd^{2+}(aq)$ | + | $2\ e^-$ | |
| Co(s) | $\rightarrow$ | $Co^{2+}(aq)$ | + | $2\ e^-$ | |
| V(s) | $\rightarrow$ | $V^{3+}(aq)$ | + | $3\ e^-$ | |
| Ni(s) | $\rightarrow$ | $Ni^{2+}(aq)$ | + | $2\ e^-$ | |
| Sn(s) | $\rightarrow$ | $Sn^{2+}(aq)$ | + | $2\ e^-$ | |
| Pb(s) | $\rightarrow$ | $Pb^{2+}(aq)$ | + | $2\ e^-$ | |
| $H_2(g)$ | $\rightarrow$ | $2\ H^+(aq)$ | + | $2\ e^-$ | |
| Cu(s) | $\rightarrow$ | $Cu^{2+}(aq)$ | + | $2\ e^-$ | |
| Ag(s) | $\rightarrow$ | $Ag^+(aq)$ | + | $e^-$ | |
| Hg(l) | $\rightarrow$ | $Hg^{2+}(aq)$ | + | $2\ e^-$ | |
| Pd(s) | $\rightarrow$ | $Pd^{2+}(aq)$ | + | $2\ e^-$ | |
| Pt(s) | $\rightarrow$ | $Pt^{2+}(aq)$ | + | $2\ e^-$ | |
| Au(s) | $\rightarrow$ | $Au^{3+}(aq)$ | + | $3\ e^-$ | Least easily oxidized |

The second equation is the net ionic form that is often required on the AP Exam.

If a piece of copper metal were placed in a solution of $Sn(NO_3)_2(aq)$, there would be no reaction since copper is lower than tin on the activity series. This table allows us to also predict that if sodium metal is placed in water, it will displace hydrogen, forming hydrogen gas:

$$2\ Na(s) + 2\ H_2O(l) \rightarrow 2\ NaOH(aq) + H_2(g)$$

$$2\ Na(s) + 2\ H_2O(l) \rightarrow 2\ Na^+(aq) + 2\ OH^-(aq) + H_2(g)$$

The Group 1A and 2A (or Group 1 and 2) elements on the activity table will displace hydrogen from water, but not the other metals shown. All the metals above hydrogen will react with acidic solutions to produce hydrogen gas:

$$Co(s) + 2\ HCl(aq) \rightarrow CoCl_2(aq) + H_2(g)$$

$$Co(s) + 2\ H^+(aq) \rightarrow Co^{2+}(aq) + H_2(g)$$

Halogen reactivity decreases as one goes from top to bottom in the periodic table, because of the decreasing electronegativity. Therefore, a separate activity series for the halogens can be developed:

$F_2$

$Cl_2$

$Br_2$

$I_2$

The above series indicates that if chlorine gas were dissolved in a KI(aq) solution, the elemental chlorine would displace the iodide ion:

$$Cl_2(aq) + 2\ KI(aq) \rightarrow 2\ KCl(aq) + I_2(s)$$

$$Cl_2(aq) + 2\ I^-(aq) \rightarrow 2\ Cl^-(aq) + I_2(s)$$

As noted previously, you will not be expected to memorize these reactions. However, you may be expected to reaction based on information given in the question.

### Combustion Reactions

**Combustion reactions** are redox reactions in which the chemical species rapidly combines with oxygen and usually emits heat and light. Reactions of this type are extremely important in our society as the sources of heat energy. Complete combustion of carbon yields carbon dioxide, and complete combustion of hydrogen yields water. The complete combustion of **hydrocarbons**, organic compounds containing only carbon and hydrogen, yields carbon dioxide and water:

$$2\ C_2H_6(g) + 7\ O_2(g) \rightarrow 4\ CO_2(g) + 6\ H_2O(g)$$

If the compound also contains oxygen, such as in alcohols, ethers, etc., the products are still carbon dioxide and water:

$$2\ CH_3OH(l) + 3\ O_2(g) \rightarrow 2\ CO_2(g) + 4\ H_2O(g)$$

If the compound contains sulfur, the complete combustion produces sulfur dioxide, $SO_2$:

$$2\ C_2H_6S(g) + 9\ O_2(g) \rightarrow 4\ CO_2(g) + 6\ H_2O(g) + 2\ SO_2(g)$$

If nitrogen is present, it will normally form the very stable nitrogen gas, $N_2$.

In these reactions, the driving force is the highly reactive oxygen forming a very stable compound(s). This is shown by the exothermic nature of the reaction.

TIP: In balancing any of these combustion reactions, it is helpful to balance the oxygen last.

## Coordination Compounds

When a salt is dissolved in water, the metal ions, especially transition metal ions, form a complex ion with water molecules and/or other species. A **complex ion** is composed of a metal ion bonded to two or more molecules or ions called **ligands**. These are Lewis acid–base reactions. For example, suppose $Cr(NO_3)_3$ is dissolved in water. The $Cr^{3+}(aq)$ cation attracts water molecules to form the complex ion $Cr(H_2O)_6^{\ 3+}(aq)$. In this complex ion, water acts as the ligand. If ammonia is added to this solution, the ammonia can displace the water molecules from the complex:

$$[Cr(H_2O)_6]^{3+}(aq) + 6\ NH_3(aq) \leftrightarrows [Cr(NH_3)_6]^{3+}(aq) + 6\ H_2O(l)$$

In reactions involving coordination compounds, the metal acts as the Lewis acid (electron-pair acceptor), while the ligand acts as a Lewis base (electron-pair donor). In the reaction above, the ammonia ligand displaces the water ligand from the chromium complex because nitrogen is a better electron-pair donor (less electronegative) than oxygen.

The nitrogen in the ammonia and the oxygen in the water are the donor atoms. They are the atoms that actually donate the electrons to the Lewis acid. The **coordination number** is the number of donor atoms that surround the central atom. As seen above, the coordination number for $Cr^{3+}$ is 6. Coordination numbers are usually 2, 4, or 6, but other values can be possible. Silver ($Ag^{+}$) commonly forms complexes with a coordination number of 2; zinc ($Zn^{2+}$), copper ($Cu^{2+}$), nickel ($Ni^{2+}$), and platinum ($Pt^{2+}$) commonly form complexes with a coordination number of 4; most other central ions have a coordination number of 6. (Again, you are not expected to memorize these; however, knowing the possibilities may help you get the correct answer sooner.)

$$AgCl(s) + 2\ NH_3(aq) \rightarrow [Ag(NH)_2]^{+}(aq) + Cl^{-}(aq)$$

$$Zn(OH)_2(s) + 2\ OH^{-}(aq) \rightarrow [Zn(OH)_4]^{2-}(aq)$$

$$Fe^{3+}(aq) + 6\ CN^{-}(aq) \rightarrow [Fe(CN)_6]^{3-}(aq)$$

# Acid–Base Reactions

Acids and bases are extremely common, as are the reactions between acids and bases. The driving force is often the hydronium ion reacting with the hydroxide ion to form water. Chapter 16, Acids and Bases, describes the equilibrium reactions of acids and bases, as well as some information concerning acid–base titrations. After you finish this section, you may want to review the acid–base part of the Equilibrium chapter.

## Properties of Acids, Bases, and Salts

At the macroscopic level, acids taste sour, may be damaging to the skin, and react with bases to yield salts. Bases taste bitter, feel slippery, and react with acids to form salts.

At the microscopic level, **acids** are defined as proton ($H^{+}$) donors (Brønsted–Lowry theory) or electron-pair acceptors (Lewis theory). **Bases** are defined as proton ($H^{+}$) acceptors (Brønsted–Lowry theory) or electron-pair donors (Lewis theory). Consider the gas-phase reaction between hydrogen chloride and ammonia:

$$HCl(g) + {:}NH_3(g) \rightarrow HNH_3^{+}Cl^{-}(s)\ (\text{or } NH_4^{+}Cl^{-}(s))$$

HCl is the acid, because it is donating an $H^{+}$ and the $H^{+}$ will accept an electron pair from ammonia. Ammonia is the base, accepting the $H^{+}$ and furnishing an electron pair that the $H^{+}$ will bond via coordinate covalent bonding. **Coordinate covalent bonds** are covalent bonds in which one of the atoms furnishes both electrons for the bond. After the bond is formed, it is identical to a covalent bond formed by donation of one electron by both bonding atoms.

Acids and bases may be **strong**, dissociating completely, or **weak**, partially dissociating and forming an equilibrium system. (See Chapter 16 for the details on weak acids and bases.) Strong acids include:

STRATEGY

1. Hydrochloric, HCl
2. Hydrobromic, HBr
3. Hydroiodic, HI
4. Nitric, $HNO_3$
5. Chloric, $HClO_3$
6. Perchloric, $HClO_4$
7. Sulfuric, $H_2SO_4$

The strong acids above are all compounds that ionize completely in aqueous solution, yielding hydrogen ions and the anions from the acid.

Strong bases include:

STRATEGY

1. Alkali metal (Group IA) hydroxides (LiOH, NaOH, KOH, RbOH, CsOH)
2. $Ca(OH)_2$, $Sr(OH)_2$, and $Ba(OH)_2$

The strong bases listed above are all compounds that dissociate completely, yielding the hydroxide ion (which is really the base, not the compound).

Unless told otherwise, assume that acids and bases not on the lists above are weak and will establish an equilibrium system when placed into water.

Some salts have acid–base properties. For example, ammonium chloride, $NH_4Cl$, when dissolved in water will dissociate and the ammonium ion will act as a weak acid, donating a proton. We will examine these acid–base properties in more detail in the next section.

Certain oxides can have acidic or basic properties. These properties often become evident when the oxides are dissolved in water. In most case, reactions of this type are not redox reactions.

Many oxides of metals are called basic oxides (basic anhydrides) because they will react with acids.

$$Fe_2O_3(s) + 6\ HCl(aq) \rightarrow 2\ FeCl_3(aq) + 3\ H_2O(l)$$
$$Fe_2O_3(s) + 6\ H^+(aq) \rightarrow 2\ Fe^{3+}(aq) + 3\ H_2O(l)$$

Many oxides of metals that have a +1 or +2 charge will react with water to form a basic solution:

$$Na_2O(s) + H_2O(l) \rightarrow 2\ NaOH(aq)$$
$$Na_2O(s) + H_2O(l) \rightarrow 2\ Na^+(aq) + 2OH^-(aq)$$

Many nonmetal oxides are called acidic oxides (acidic anhydrides) because they react with water to form an acidic solution:

$$CO_2(g) + H_2O(l) \rightarrow H_2CO_3(aq)$$

$H_2CO_3(aq)$ is named carbonic acid and is the reason that most carbonated beverages are slightly acidic. It is also the reason that soft drinks have fizz, because carbonic acid will decompose to form carbon dioxide and water.

## Acid–Base Reactions

In general, acids react with bases to form a salt and, usually, water. The salt will depend upon which acid and base are used:

$$HCl(aq) + NaOH(aq) \rightarrow H_2O(l) + NaCl(aq)$$
$$HNO_3(aq) + KOH(aq) \rightarrow H_2O(l) + KNO_3(aq)$$
$$HBr(aq) + NH_3(aq) \rightarrow NH_4Br(aq)$$

Reactions of this type are called **neutralization reactions.**

The first two neutralization equations are represented by the same net ionic equation:

$$H^+(aq) + OH^-(aq) \rightarrow H_2O(l)$$

In the third case, the net ionic equation is different:

$$H^+(aq) + NH_3(aq) \rightarrow NH_4^+(aq)$$

As mentioned previously, certain salts have acid–base properties. In general, salts containing cations of strong bases and anions of strong acids are neither acidic nor basic. They are neutral, reacting with neither acids nor bases. An example would be potassium nitrate, $KNO_3$. The potassium comes from the strong base KOH and the nitrate from the strong acid $HNO_3$.

Salts containing cations not of strong bases but with anions of strong acids behave as acidic salts. An example would be ammonium chloride, $NH_4Cl$:

$$2\ NH_4Cl(aq) + Ba(OH)_2(aq) \rightarrow BaCl_2(aq) + 2\ NH_3(aq) + 2\ H_2O(l)$$

$$NH_4^+(aq) + OH^-(aq) \rightarrow NH_3(aq) + H_2O(l)$$

Cations of strong bases and anions not of strong acids are basic salts. An example would be sodium carbonate, $Na_2CO_3$. It reacts with an acid to form carbonic acid, which would then decompose to carbon dioxide and water:

$$2\ HCl(aq) + Na_2CO_3(aq) \rightarrow 2\ NaCl(aq) + H_2CO_3(aq)$$

$$\downarrow$$

$$CO_2(g) + H_2O(l)$$

$$2\ H^+(aq) + CO_3^{2-}(aq) \rightarrow H_2CO_3(aq) \rightarrow CO_2(g) + H_2O(l)$$

The same type of reaction would be true for acid carbonates, such as sodium bicarbonate, $NaHCO_3$.

Another group of compounds that have acid–base properties are the hydrides of the alkali metals and of calcium, strontium, and barium. These hydrides will react with water to form the hydroxide ion and hydrogen gas:

$$NaH(s) + H_2O(l) \rightarrow NaOH(aq) + H_2(g)$$

$$NaH(s) + H_2O(l) \rightarrow Na^+(aq) + OH^-(aq) + H_2(g)$$

Note that in this case, water is behaving as $H^+OH^-$.

## Acid–Base Titrations

A common laboratory application of acid–base reactions is a titration. (Note, there are other types of titrations.) A **titration** is a laboratory procedure in which a solution of known concentration is used to determine the concentration of an unknown solution. For strong acid/strong base titration systems, the net ionic equation is:

$$H^+(aq) + OH^-(aq) \rightarrow H_2O(l)$$

In a titration, the **titrant** is added to the **analyte**. The titrant is normally added from a buret.

For example, suppose you wanted to determine the molarity of an HCl solution. You would pipette a known volume of the acid into a flask and add a couple of drops of a suitable acid–base indicator. An indicator that is commonly used is phenolphthalein, which is colorless in an acidic solution and pink in a basic solution. You would then fill a buret with a strong base solution (NaOH is commonly used) of known concentration. The buret allows you to add small amounts of the base solution to the acid solution in the flask. See Figure 12.1 for the experimental setup for a titration. The course of the titration can also be followed using a pH meter. Initially the pH of the solution will be low since it is an acid solution. As the base is added and neutralization of the acid takes place, the pH will slowly rise. Small amounts of the base are added until one reaches the equivalence point.

The **equivalence point** is that point in the titration where the number of moles of $H^+$ in the acid solution has been exactly neutralized with the same number of moles of $OH^-$:

$$\text{moles } H^+ = \text{moles } OH^- \text{ at the equivalence point}$$

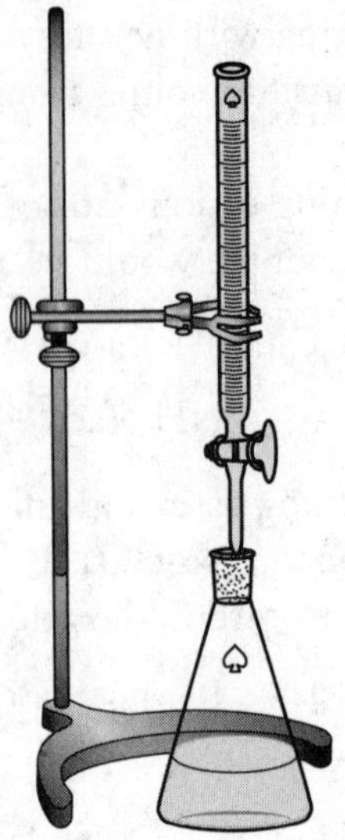

**Figure 12.1 Titration setup.**

For the titration of a strong acid with a strong base, the pH rapidly rises in the vicinity of the equivalence point. Then, as the tiniest amount of base is added in excess, the indicator turns pink. This is called the **endpoint** of the titration. In an accurate titration, the endpoint will be as close to the equivalence point as possible. For simple titrations that do not use a pH meter, it is assumed that the endpoint and the equivalence point are the same, so that:

$$\text{moles } H^+ = \text{moles } OH^- \text{ at the endpoint}$$

After the equivalence point has been passed, the pH is greater than 7 (basic solution) and begins to level out somewhat. Figure 12.2 shows the shape of the curve for this titration.

Reaction stoichiometry can then be used to solve for the molarity of the acid solution.

See Chapter 6, Stoichiometry, for a discussion of solution stoichiometry. In addition, you will see more on titrations in Chapter 20, Experimental Investigations.

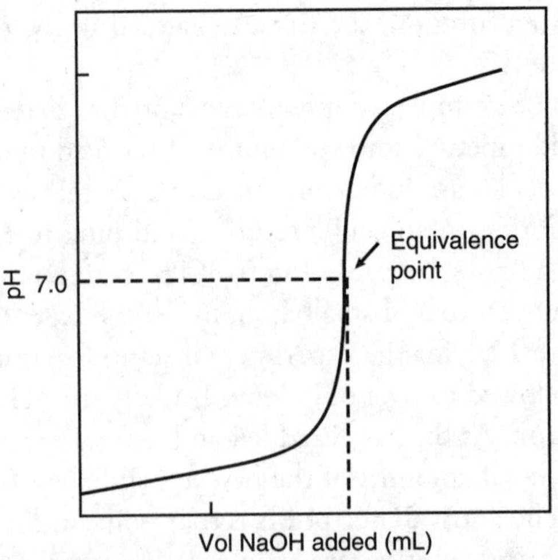


**Figure 12.2 Titration of a strong acid with a strong base.**

An unknown base can be titrated with an acid solution of known concentration. One major difference is that the pH will be greater than 7 initially and will decrease as the titration proceeds. The other major difference is that the indicator will start pink, and the color will vanish at the endpoint.

## Experiments

STRATEGY

Laboratory experiments involving reactions are usually concerned with both the reaction and the stoichiometry. You need some idea of the balanced chemical equation. In the case of an acid–base reaction, an acid reacts with a base. The acid supplies $H^+$ and the base accepts the $H^+$. If the acid is diprotic, such as $H_2SO_4$, it can donate two $H^+$.

The key to any reaction experiment is moles. The numbers of moles may be calculated from various measurements. A sample may be weighed on a balance to give the mass, and the moles calculated with the formula weight. Or the mass of a substance may be determined using a volume measurement combined with the density. The volume of a solution may be measured with a pipette or calculated (NOT measured) from the final and initial readings from a buret. This volume, along with the molarity, can be used to calculate the moles present. The volume, temperature, and pressure of a gas can be measured and used to calculate the moles of a gas. You must be extremely careful on the AP Exam to distinguish between those values that you measure and those that you calculate.

The moles of any substance in a reaction may be converted to the moles of any other substance through a calculation using the balanced chemical equation. Other calculations are presented in Chapter 6, Stoichiometry.

## Common Mistakes to Avoid

TIP

1. In balancing chemical equations **don't** change the subscripts in the chemical formula, just the coefficients.
2. Molecular compounds ionize as do ionic compounds.
3. In writing ionic and net ionic equations, show the chemical species as they actually exist in solution (i.e., strong electrolytes as ions, etc.).
4. In writing ionic and net ionic equations, don't break apart covalently bonded compounds unless they are strong acids that are ionizing.
5. Know the solubility rules as guidelines.
6. Oxidizing and reducing agents are reactants, not products.
7. The products of the complete combustion of a hydrocarbon are carbon dioxide and water. This is also true if oxygen is present as well; but if some other element, like sulfur, is present you will also have something else in addition to carbon dioxide and water.
8. If a substance that does not contain carbon, like elemental sulfur, undergoes complete combustion, no carbon dioxide can be formed.
9. If an alcohol like methanol, $CH_3OH$, is dissolved in water, no hydroxide ion, $OH^-$, will be formed.
10. Know the strong acids and bases; assume all other acids and bases are weak.
11. HF is not a strong acid.
12. In titration calculations, you must consider the reaction stoichiometry.
13. Be sure to indicate the charges on ions correctly.
14. The common coordination numbers of complex ions are 2, 4, and 6.
15. Do not confuse measured values and calculated values.

# › Review Questions

Here are questions you can use to review the content of this chapter and practice for the AP Chemistry Exam. First are 20 multiple-choice questions similar to what you will encounter in Section I of the AP Chemistry Exam. Following those is a short free-response question like ones in Section II of the exam. To make these review questions an even more authentic practice for the actual exam, time yourself following the instructions provided.

## Multiple-Choice Questions

Answer the following questions in 30 minutes. You may not use a calculator. You may use the periodic table and the equation sheet at the back of this book.

**1.** ____ $Fe(OH)_2(s)$ + ____ $H_3PO_4(aq) \rightarrow$ ____ $Fe_3(PO_4)_2(s)$ + ____ $H_2O(l)$

After the above chemical equation is balanced, the lowest whole-number coefficient for water is:

(A) 3
(B) 1
(C) 9
(D) 6

**2.** This ion will generate gas bubbles upon the addition of hydrochloric acid.

(A) $Cu^{2+}$
(B) $CO_3^{2-}$
(C) $Fe^{3+}$
(D) $Al^{3+}$

**3.** Aqueous solutions of this ion are blue.

(A) $Cu^{2+}$
(B) $CO_3^{2-}$
(C) $Fe^{3+}$
(D) $Al^{3+}$

**4.** Which of the following best represents the balanced net ionic equation for the reaction of lead(II) carbonate with concentrated hydrochloric acid? In this reaction, all lead compounds are insoluble.

(A) $Pb_2CO_3(s) + 2\ H^+(aq) + Cl^-(aq) \rightarrow Pb_2Cl(s) + CO_2(g) + H_2O(l)$
(B) $PbCO_3(s) + 2\ H^+(aq) + 2\ Cl^-(aq) \rightarrow PbCl_2(s) + CO_2(g) + H_2O(l)$
(C) $PbCO_3(s) + 2\ H^+(aq) \rightarrow Pb^{2+}(aq) + CO_2(g) + H_2O(l)$
(D) $PbCO_3(s) + 2\ Cl^-(aq) \rightarrow PbCl_2(s) + CO_3^{2-}(aq)$

**5.** A sample of copper metal is reacted with concentrated nitric acid in the absence of air. After the reaction, which of these final products are present?

(A) $CuNO_3$ and $H_2O$
(B) $Cu(NO_3)_3$, NO, and $H_2O$
(C) $Cu(NO_3)_2$, NO, and $H_2O$
(D) $CuNO_3$, $H_2O$, and $H_2$

**6.** Which of the following is the correct net ionic equation for the reaction of acetic acid with potassium hydroxide?

(A) $HC_2H_3O_2(aq) + OH^-(aq) \rightarrow C_2H_3O_2^-(aq) + H_2O(l)$
(B) $HC_2H_3O_2(aq) + K^+(aq) \rightarrow KC_2H_3O_2(aq) + H^+(l)$
(C) $HC_2H_3O_2(aq) + KOH(aq) \rightarrow KC_2H_3O_2(s) + H_2O(l)$
(D) $H^+(aq) + OH^-(aq) \rightarrow H_2O(l)$

**7.** Which of the following is the correct net ionic equation for the addition of aqueous ammonia to a precipitate of silver chloride?

(A) $AgCl(s) + 2\ NH_3(aq) \rightarrow [Ag(NH_3)_2]^+(aq) + Cl^-(aq)$
(B) $AgCl(s) + 2\ NH_4^+(aq) \rightarrow [Ag(NH_4)_2]^{3+}(aq) + Cl^-(aq)$
(C) $AgCl(s) + NH_4^+(aq) \rightarrow Ag^+(aq) + NH_4Cl(s)$
(D) $AgCl(s) + NH_3(aq) \rightarrow Ag^+(aq) + NH_3Cl(aq)$

**8.** Potassium metal will react with water to release a gas and form a potassium compound. Which of the following is true?

(A) The final solution is basic.
(B) The gas is oxygen.
(C) The potassium compound precipitates.
(D) The potassium compound will react with strong bases.

**9.** It is possible to analyze an iron sample for percent iron by dissolving the sample in sulfuric acid and titrating the solution with standard potassium dichromate solution. The balanced molecular equation for the titration is:

$$K_2Cr_2O_7(aq) + 6\ FeSO_4(aq) + 7\ H_2SO_4(aq) \rightarrow Cr_2(SO_4)_3(aq) + 3\ Fe_2(SO_4)_3(aq) + K_2SO_4(aq) + 7\ H_2O(l)$$

Which of the following is the correct net ionic equation for this reaction?

(A) $2\ Cr^{6+}(aq) + 6\ Fe^{2+}(aq) \rightarrow 2\ Cr^{3+}(aq) + 6\ Fe^{3+}(aq)$
(B) $Cr_2O_7^{2-}(aq) + 6\ Fe^{2+}(aq) + 14\ H^+(aq) \rightarrow 2\ Cr^{3+}(aq) + 6\ Fe^{3+}(aq) + 7\ H_2O(l)$
(C) $Cr_2O_7^{2-}(aq) + 6\ FeSO_4(aq) + 14\ H^+(aq) + 6\ SO_4^{2-}(aq) \rightarrow Cr_2(SO_4)_3(aq) + 3\ Fe_2(SO_4)_3(aq) + 7\ H_2O(l)$
(D) $K_2Cr_2O_7(aq) + 6\ FeSO_4(aq) + 7\ H_2SO_4(aq) \rightarrow Cr_2(SO_4)_3(aq) + 3\ Fe_2(SO_4)_3(aq) + K_2SO_4(aq) + 7\ H_2O(l)$

**10.** How many moles of $Pb(NO_3)_2$ must be added to 0.10 L of a solution that is 1.0 *M* in $MgCl_2$ and 1.0 *M* in KCl to precipitate all the chloride ion? The compound $PbCl_2$ precipitates.

(A) 1.0 mole
(B) 0.20 mole
(C) 0.50 mole
(D) 0.15 mole

**11.** When 50.0 mL of 1.0 *M* $AgNO_3$ is added to 50.0 mL of 0.50 *M* HCl, a precipitate of AgCl forms. After the reaction is complete, what is the concentration of silver ions in the solution?

(A) 0.50 *M*
(B) 0.0 *M*
(C) 1.0 *M*
(D) 0.25 *M*

**12.** A student mixes 50.0 mL of 0.10 *M* $Pb(NO_3)_2$ solution with 50.0 mL of 0.10 *M* KCl. A white precipitate forms, and the concentration of the chloride ion becomes very small. Which of the following correctly places the concentrations of the remaining ions in order of decreasing concentration?

(A) $[NO_3^-] > [Pb^{2+}] > [K^+]$
(B) $[NO_3^-] > [K^+] > [Pb^{2+}]$
(C) $[K^+] > [NO_3^-] > [Pb^{2+}]$
(D) $[Pb^{2+}] > [NO_3^-] > [K^+]$

**13.** A solution is prepared for qualitative analysis. The solution contains the following ions: $Co^{2+}$, $Pb^{2+}$, and $Al^{3+}$. Which of the following will cause no observable reaction?

(A) Dilute $NH_3(aq)$ is added.
(B) Dilute $K_2CrO_4(aq)$ is added.
(C) Dilute $HNO_3(aq)$ is added.
(D) Dilute $K_2S(aq)$ is added.

**14.** Chlorine gas is bubbled through a colorless solution, and the solution turns reddish. Adding a little methylene chloride to the solution extracts the color into the methylene chloride layer. Which of the following ions may be present in the original solution?

(A) $Cl^-$
(B) $I^-$
(C) $SO_4^{2-}$
(D) $Br^-$

**15.** The addition of excess concentrated NaOH(aq) to a 1.0 *M* $(NH_4)_2SO_4$ solution will result in which of the following observations?

(A) The solution becomes neutral.
(B) The formation of a brown precipitate takes place.
(C) Nothing happens because the two solutions are immiscible.
(D) The odor of ammonia will be detected.

**16.** $\_\_\_\_\ C_4H_{11}N(l) + \_\_\_\_\ O_2(g) \rightarrow \_\_\_\_\ CO_2(g) + \_\_\_\_\ H_2O(l) + \_\_\_\_\ N_2(g)$

When the above equation is balanced, the lowest whole number coefficient for $CO_2$ is:

(A) 4
(B) 16
(C) 27
(D) 32

$$Pb^{2+}(aq) + SO_4^{2-}(aq) \rightarrow PbSO_4(s)$$

**17.** A student mixes 50.00 mL of a 0.1000 M $Pb(NO_3)_2(aq)$ solution with 50.00 mL of a 0.1000 M $Na_2SO_4(aq)$ solution. The net ionic equation for the reaction that occurs is given above. After the reaction has gone to completion and all the precipitate has settled, the student tests the solution with an electrical conductivity meter. Which of the following results does the student observe?

(A) The solution is conducting because not all of the $Pb^{2+}(aq)$ has precipitated.
(B) The solution is nonconducting because all the ions have precipitated.
(C) The solution is nonconducting because $PbSO_4(s)$ is not an electrical conductor.
(D) The solution is conducting because of the spectator ions remaining.

$$2\ CuI_2(s) \rightarrow 2\ CuI(s) + Cu(s) + I_2(s)$$

**18.** Which of the following best describes what type of reaction the above equation represents?

(A) It is a precipitation reaction.
(B) It is an oxidation–reduction reaction.
(C) It is a neutralization reaction.
(D) It is a combination reaction.

**19.** It is possible to represent the formula of any strong acid as HX and to represent the formula of any strong base as MOH. Using these two representations, which of the following is the net ionic equation for strong acid–strong base reactions in aqueous solution?

(A) $HX(aq) + MOH(aq) \rightarrow MX(aq) + H_2O(l)$
(B) $H^+(aq) + OH^-(aq) \rightarrow H_2O(l)$
(C) $HX(aq) + MOH(aq) \rightarrow XOH(aq) + MH(aq)$
(D) $H^+(aq) + X(aq) + M^+(aq) + OH^-(aq) \rightarrow X^-(aq) + M^+(aq) + H_2O(l)$

**20.** A chemist titrates a $Ba(OH)_2$ solution with an HF solution. $BaF_2$ precipitates during the titration. Which of the following is the net ionic equation for the titration reaction?

(A) $2\ H^+(aq) + 2\ F^-(aq) + Ba^{2+}(aq) + 2\ OH^-(aq) \rightarrow BaF_2(s) + 2\ H_2O(l)$
(B) $2\ HF(aq) + Ba(OH)_2(aq) \rightarrow BaF_2(s) + 2\ H_2O(l)$
(C) $2\ HF(aq) + Ba^{2+}(aq) + 2\ OH^-(aq) \rightarrow BaF_2(s) + 2\ H_2O(l)$
(D) $H^+(aq) + OH^-(aq) \rightarrow H_2O(l)$

## › Answers and Explanations

**1. D**—The balanced equation is $3\ Fe(OH)_2(s) + 2\ H_3PO_4(aq) \rightarrow Fe_3(PO_4)_2(s) + 6\ H_2O(l)$. If you had trouble balancing this equation, you need more practice.

**2. B**—Carbonates produce carbon dioxide gas in the presence of an acid. None of the other ions will react with hydrochloric acid to produce a gas.

**3. A**—Aqueous solutions of $Cu^{2+}$ are normally blue. Iron ions give a variety of colors but are normally colorless, or nearly so, in the absence of complexing agents. The other ions are colorless.

**4. B**—Lead(II) carbonate is insoluble (given), so its formula should be written as $PbCO_3$. Hydrochloric acid is a strong acid, so it should be written as separate $H^+$ and $Cl^-$ ions. Lead(II) chloride, $PbCl_2$, is insoluble (given), and carbonic acid, $H_2CO_3$, quickly decomposes to $CO_2$ and $H_2O$. Also notice that A cannot be correct because the charges do not balance. For practice, analyze the other answers and determine why they are wrong.

**5. C**—The balanced chemical equation is $3\ Cu(s) + 8\ HNO_3(aq) \rightarrow 3\ Cu(NO_3)_2(aq) + 2\ NO(g) + 4\ H_2O(l)$. The copper is below hydrogen on the activity series, so $H_2$ cannot form by this acid–metal reaction. Nitric acid causes oxidation, which will oxidize copper to $Cu^{2+}$, giving $Cu(NO_3)_2$. Some of the nitric acid reduces to NO. An oxidation and a reduction must ALWAYS be together, so if Cu is oxidized, $HNO_3$ must be reduced. If air had been present, the NO would be converted to $NO_2$.

**6. A**—Acetic acid is a weak acid; as such, it should be written as $HC_2H_3O_2$. Potassium hydroxide is a strong base, so it will separate into $K^+$ and $OH^-$ ions. Any potassium compound that might form is soluble and will yield $K^+$ ions. The potassium ions are spectator ions and are left out of the net ionic equation.

**7. A**—Aqueous ammonia contains primarily $NH_3$, which eliminates answers B and C. Ammonia is $NH_3$ not $NH_4^+$. $NH_3Cl$ does not exist, which eliminates answer D. The reaction produces the silver–ammonia complex, $[Ag(NH_3)_2]^+$. Notice that the key here is not knowing what the reaction is but being able to eliminate impossible answers because of the nomenclature.

**8. A**—The reaction of potassium to produce a potassium compound is an oxidation; therefore, there must be a reduction, and the only species available for reduction is hydrogen. The reaction is $2\ K(s) + 2\ H_2O(l) \rightarrow 2\ KOH(aq) + H_2(g)$. KOH is a water-soluble strong base, which will not react with other strong bases.

**9. B**—All the compounds in the molecular equation except $H_2O$ ionize in aqueous solution. [We know they are in aqueous solution because their chemical formulas are followed by (aq).] Answer (A) incorrectly breaks up the dichromate ion ($Cr_2O_7^{2-}$). Answer (C) incorrectly leaves the $FeSO_4(aq)$, $Cr_2(SO_4)_3(aq)$, and $Fe_2(SO_4)_3(aq)$ undissociated. Answer (D) does not separate any of the strong electrolytes [everything but $H_2O(l)$] in solution, which is an error.

**10. D**—The magnesium chloride gives 0.20 mole of chloride ion, and the potassium chloride gives 0.10 mole of chloride ion. A total of 0.30 mole of chloride will react with 0.15 mole of lead, because two $Cl^-$ require one $Pb^{2+}$. You may wish to do the actual calculations to see how the moles were determined.

**11. D**—The HCl is the limiting reagent. The HCl will react with one-half the silver to halve the concentration. The doubling of the volume (50 mL + 50 mL) halves the concentration a second time.

**12. B**—Since the $Cl^-$ became very small, it must have combined with a cation and precipitated. You have a KCl solution, so KCl will not precipitate This leaves $PbCl_2$ as the only possible precipitate. Equal volumes of equal concentrations give the same number of moles of reactants; however, two nitrate ions are produced per solute formula as opposed to only one potassium ion. Initially, the lead and potassium would be equal, but some of the lead is precipitated as $PbCl_2$.

**13. C**—Ammonia, as a base, will precipitate the metal hydroxides since the only soluble hydroxides are the strong bases. Chromate, sulfide, and chloride ions might precipitate one or more of the ions. Nitrates, from nitric acid, are soluble; therefore, this is the solution that is least likely to cause an observable change.

**14. D**—Chlorine causes oxidation. It is capable of oxidizing both B and D. Answer B gives $I_2$, which is brownish in water and purplish in methylene chloride. Bromine solutions are reddish in both.

**15. D**—Excess strong base will ensure the solution is basic and not neutral. Both ammonium and sodium salts are soluble; therefore, no precipitate will form. One aqueous solution will mix with another aqueous solution. The following acid–base reaction occurs to release ammonia gas: $NH_4^+(aq) + OH^-(aq) \rightarrow NH_3(g) + H_2O(l)$.

**16. B**—The balanced equation is $4\ C_4H_{11}N(l) + 27\ O_2(g) \rightarrow 16\ CO_2(g) + 22\ H_2O(l) + 2\ N_2(g)$. While organic chemistry is not part of the AP curriculum, you should know how to balance any equation given to you.

**17. D**—The solutions have equal volumes with equal molarities; therefore, they contain equal moles (no need to calculate this). The reaction has 1:1 stoichiometry, so equal moles of $Pb^{2+}$ and $SO_4^{2-}$ will react, and since they have equal moles, both are limiting, which means all the $Pb^{2+}$ and $SO_4^{2-}$ has precipitated. This means that any answer with either of these ions in solution cannot be correct. In general, ionic solids, such as $PbSO_4(s)$, are nonconductors; however, since the $PbSO_4(s)$ is no longer in solution, this has nothing to do with the solution being conducting or nonconducting. While the net ionic equation shows that everything should precipitate, it is better to examine the complete ionic equation which is:

$$Pb^{2+}(aq) + 2\,NO_3^-(aq) + 2\,Na^+(aq) + SO_4^{2-}(aq) \rightarrow PbSO_4(s) + 2\,NO_3^-(aq) + 2\,Na^+(aq)$$

The $NO_3^-(aq)$ + $Na^+(aq)$ are the spectator ions and remain in solution to conduct electricity.

**18. B**—One substance going to more than one product is a decomposition reaction; however, since this is not one of the choices, it is necessary to remember that decomposition reactions are a subcategory of oxidation–reduction reactions. The type of reaction could be determined by determining the oxidation number of the elements (actually only Cu or I needs to be determined). On the reactant side, the oxidation numbers are Cu = +2 and I = −1. On the product side, the oxidation numbers are Cu = +1 and 0, while I = −1 and 0. Any change in the oxidation states makes this an oxidation reduction reaction. A precipitation reaction requires a sold forming from a solution, and there is no solution present. A neutralization reaction requires an acid and a base, acids contain $H^+$, and there is no hydrogen present. A combination reaction (also a subcategory of oxidation–reduction reactions) requires multiple reactants producing a single product.

**19. B**—If the symbolism (HX and MOH) confuses you, pick a specific strong acid and strong base, such as HCl and NaOH. Do not confuse the issue by choosing more complicated acids or bases, such as $H_2SO_4$ and $Ba(OH)_2$. Both net ionic and complete ionic equations require ions to be present on at least one side of the reaction arrow. Equations containing either of the spectator ions ($M^+$ and $X^-$) on both sides of the reaction arrow are not net ionic equations. Note, the compounds XOH and MH could not possibly exist since each contains only ions with like charges (not + and −).

**20. C**—An ionic equation must have ions on at least one side of the reaction arrow. Since hydrofluoric acid, HF, is a weak acid, it is a weak electrolyte, which means it is not ionized in an ionic equation. Barium hydroxide, $Ba(OH)_2$, is a strong base; therefore it is completely ionized in an ionic equation. The reaction $H^+(aq) + OH^-(aq) \rightarrow H_2O(l)$ applies only to strong acids reacting with strong bases, which is not the case here.

## › Free-Response Question

On the AP Exam, there will be both long-answer and short-answer free-response questions. The following is an example of a short-answer question.

You have 5 minutes to answer the following question. You may use a calculator and the tables in the back of the book.

**Question**

An iron(III) nitrate, $Fe(NO_3)_3$, solution is mixed with a potassium phosphate, $K_3PO_4$, solution, and a precipitate forms. What is the precipitate, and which ions, if any, are spectator ions in this reaction? Explain how you arrived at your answers.

## ❯ Answer and Explanation

There are four ions present. These ions are $K^+$, $PO_4^{3-}$, $Fe^{3+}$, and $NO_3^-$. The starting materials are in solution; therefore, they are soluble. The compounds that might form in the reaction are $KNO_3$ and $FePO_4$. Since potassium (and nitrate) salts are normally soluble, the precipitate must be $FePO_4$. The spectator ions are the nitrate ions ($NO_3^-$) and the potassium ions ($K^+$), the ions not in the precipitate.

Total your points. There are 4 points possible. You get 1 point for correctly identifying the precipitate. You get an additional 1 point for identifying the spectator ions and 2 points for the explanation.

## ❯ Rapid Review

- Reaction questions will always appear in the free-response section of the AP Exam. This may not be true in the multiple-choice part.
- Energy will be released in a reaction (exothermic) or absorbed (endothermic).
- Chemical equations are balanced by adding coefficients in front of the chemical species until the number of each type of atom is the same on both the right and left sides of the arrow.
- The coefficients in the balanced equation must be in the lowest whole-number ratio.
- Water is the universal solvent, dissolving a wide variety of both ionic and polar substances.
- Electrolytes are substances that conduct an electrical current when dissolved in water; nonelectrolytes do not.
- Most ions in solution attract and bind a layer of water molecules in a process called solvation.
- Some molecular compounds, like acids, ionize in water, forming ions.
- In the molecular equation, the reactants and products are shown in their undissociated/un-ionized form; the ionic equation shows the strong electrolytes in the form of ions; the net ionic equation drops out all spectator ions and shows only those species that are undergoing chemical change.
- Precipitation reactions form an insoluble compound, a precipitate, from the mixing of two soluble compounds.
- It will help if you have some idea of which ionic compounds are soluble.
- Redox reactions are reactions where oxidation and reduction take place simultaneously.
- Oxidation is the loss of electrons, and reduction is the gain of electrons.
- Combination reactions are usually redox reactions in which two or more reactants (elements or compounds) combine to form one product.

- Decomposition reactions are usually redox reactions in which a compound breaks down into two or more simpler substances.
- Single displacement reactions are redox reactions in which atoms of an element replace the atoms of another element in a compound.
- Combustion reactions are redox reactions in which the chemical species rapidly combine with diatomic oxygen gas, emitting heat and light. The products of the complete combustion of a hydrocarbon are carbon dioxide and water.
- Indicators are substances that exhibit different colors under acidic or basic conditions.
- Acids are proton donors (electron-pair acceptors).
- Bases are proton acceptors (electron-pair donors).
- Coordinate covalent bonds are covalent bonds in which one atom furnishes both electrons for the bond.

# CHAPTER 13

# Kinetics

**IN THIS CHAPTER**

In this chapter, the following AP topics are covered:

5.1 Reaction Rates
5.2 Introduction to Rate Law
5.3 Concentration Changes Over Time
5.4 Elementary Reactions
5.5 Collision Model
5.6 Reaction Energy Profile
5.7 Introduction to Reaction Mechanisms
5.8 Reaction Mechanism and Rate Law
5.9 Steady-State Approximation
5.10 Multistep Reaction Energy Profile
5.11 Catalysis

**Summary:** Thermodynamics often can be used to predict whether a reaction will occur spontaneously, but it gives very little information about the speed at which a reaction occurs. **Kinetics** is the study of the speed of reactions and is largely an experimental science. Some general qualitative ideas about reaction speed may be developed, but accurate quantitative relationships require experimental data to be collected.

For a chemical reaction to occur, there must be a collision between the reactant particles. That collision is necessary to transfer kinetic energy, to break reactant chemical bonds and form new bonds in the product. If the collision doesn't transfer enough energy, no reaction will occur. And the collision must take place with the proper orientation at the correct place on the molecule, the reactive site.

**Five factors affect the rates of a chemical reaction:**

1. **Nature of the reactants**—Large, complex molecules tend to react more slowly than smaller ones because statistically there is a greater chance of collisions occurring in the wrong place on the molecule, that is, not at the reactive site.
2. **The temperature**—Temperature is a measure of the average kinetic energy of the molecules. The higher the temperature, the higher the kinetic energy and the greater the chance that enough energy will be transferred to cause the reaction. Also, the higher the temperature, the greater the number of collisions and the greater the chance of a collision at the reactive site.
3. **The concentration of reactants**—The higher the concentration of reactants, the greater the chance of collision and (normally) the greater the reaction rate. For gaseous reactants, the pressure is directly related to the concentration; the greater the pressure, the greater the reaction rate.
4. **Physical state of reactants**—When reactants are mixed in the same physical state, the reaction rates should be higher than if they are in different states, because there is a greater chance of collision. Also, gases and liquids tend to react faster than solids because of the increase in surface area. The more chance for collision, the faster the reaction rate.
5. **Catalysts**—A **catalyst** is a substance that speeds up the reaction rate and is (at least theoretically) recoverable at the end of the reaction in an unchanged form. Catalysts accomplish this by reducing the activation energy of the reaction. **Activation energy** is that minimum amount of energy that must be supplied to the reactants in order to initiate or start the reaction. Many times the activation energy is supplied by the kinetic energy of the reactants.

KEY IDEA

**Keywords and Equations**

$k$ = rate constant $\quad$ $t$ = time $\quad$ $t_{1/2}$ = half-life

$$[A]_t - [A]_0 = -kt \qquad \frac{1}{[A]_t} - \frac{1}{[A]_0} = kt$$

$$\ln [A]_t - \ln [A]_0 = -kt \qquad t_{1/2} = \frac{0.693}{k}$$

# How Reactions Occur—Collision Model

For two molecules to react, they must come into contact. However, simply coming into contact is not enough. Two conditions must be met for a collision to be effective. An **effective collision** occurs when the molecules collide with sufficient energy to react and with the proper orientation. The minimum energy necessary for an effective collision is the **activation energy**. This energy comes from the kinetic energy of the molecules, which have a Maxwell–Boltzmann distribution of energies. The "proper orientation" requires the reactive parts of the molecules coming into contact.

Let's use the reaction $NO_2(g) + CO(g) \rightarrow NO(g) + CO_2(g)$ to illustrate what it means to have the proper orientation. Examples of the collision of the reactant molecules both with and without the proper orientation are illustrated in Figure 13.1. In the reaction, an oxygen atom is transferred from a nitrogen dioxide molecule to a carbon dioxide molecule. For this transfer to occur, one of the oxygen atoms from the $NO_2$ must come into contact with the carbon atom of the CO. In the figure, only the first collision has

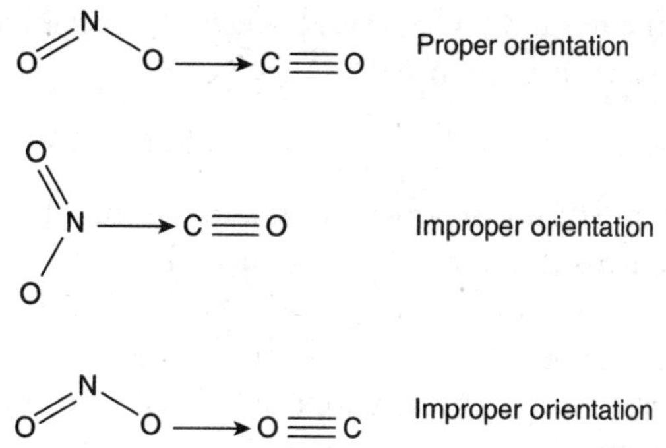


**Figure 13.1 Some examples of collisions between $NO_2(g)$ molecules and CO(g) molecules. The arrow indicates the relative motion of the $NO_2$ molecule relative to the CO molecule.**

the proper orientation (the O from $NO_2$ coming in contact with the C of the CO). The second collision has the N from $NO_2$ coming with the C of the CO. The last example in the figure has two oxygen atoms coming together. To make the first collision in the figure effective, the molecules would need to collide with sufficient kinetic energy to initiate the breaking of the nitrogen–oxygen bond and the formation of a carbon–oxygen bond.

The two requirements for an effective collision mean that only a small fraction of all collisions are effective.

# Rates of Reaction

The rate (or speed) of reaction is related to the change in concentration of either a reactant or product with time. Consider the general reaction: $2A + B \rightarrow C + 3D$. As the reaction proceeds, the concentrations of reactants A and B will decrease, and the concentrations of products C and D will increase. Thus, the rate can be expressed in the following ways:

$$\text{Rate} = -\frac{1}{2}\frac{\Delta[A]}{\Delta t} = -\frac{\Delta[B]}{\Delta t} = \frac{\Delta[C]}{\Delta t} = \frac{1}{3}\frac{\Delta[D]}{\Delta t}$$

The first two expressions involving the reactants are negative because their concentrations will decrease with time (the reactants are disappearing). The square brackets represent moles per liter concentration (molarity). The deltas (Δ) indicate change (final – initial).

The rate of reaction decreases during the course of the reaction. The rate that is calculated above can be expressed as the average rate of reaction over a given time frame or, more commonly, as the initial reaction rate—the rate of reaction at the instant the reactants are first mixed.

## The Rate Equation

The rate of reaction may depend upon reactant concentration, product concentration, and temperature. Cases in which the product concentration affects the rate of reaction are rare and are not covered on the AP Exam. Therefore, we will not address those situations. We will discuss temperature effects on the reaction later in this chapter. For the time being, let's just consider those cases in which the reactant concentration may affect the speed of reaction. For the general reaction: $a\,A + b\,B + \ldots \rightarrow c\,C + d\,D + \ldots$ where the lowercase letters are the coefficients in the balanced chemical equation, the uppercase letters stand for the reactant, and product chemical species and initial rates are used, the rate equation (rate law) is written as:

$$\text{Rate} = k[\text{A}]^m[\text{B}]^n \ldots$$

It is important to remember that any similarity between the coefficients (*a*, *b*, etc.) and the exponents (*m*, *n*, etc.) is coincidental.

KEY IDEA

In this expression, *k* is the **rate constant**—a constant for each chemical reaction at a given temperature. The exponents *m* and *n*, called the **orders of reaction**, indicate what effect a change in concentration of that reactant species will have on the reaction rate. Say, for example, $m = 1$ and $n = 2$. That means that if the concentration of reactant A is doubled, then the rate will also double ($[2]^1 = 2$), and if the concentration of reactant B is doubled, then the rate will increase fourfold ($[2]^2 = 4$). We say that it is first order with respect to A and second order with respect to B. If the concentration of a reactant is doubled and that has no effect on the rate of reaction, then the reaction is zero order with respect to that reactant ($[2]^0 = 1$). Many times the overall order of reaction is calculated; it is simply the sum of the individual coefficients, third order in this example. The rate equation would then be shown as:

$$\text{Rate} = k[\text{A}][\text{B}]^2 \text{ (If an exponent is 1, it is generally not shown.)}$$

TIP

It is important to realize that the rate law (the rate, the rate constant, and the orders of reaction) is determined experimentally. Do not use the balanced chemical equation to determine the rate law.

The rate of reaction may be measured in a variety of ways, including taking the slope of the concentration versus time plot for the reaction. Once the rate has been determined, the orders of reaction can be determined by conducting a series of reactions in which the reactant species concentrations are changed one at a time, and then mathematically determining the effect on the reaction rate. Once the orders of reaction have been determined, it is easy to calculate the rate constant.

For example, consider the reaction:

$$2\ ClO_2(aq) + 2\ OH^-(aq) \rightarrow ClO_2^-(aq) + ClO_3^-(aq) + H_2O(l)$$

The following kinetics data were collected:

| **Experiment** | **Initial [$ClO_2$]** | **Initial [$OH^-$]** | **Rate of $ClO_2^-$ formation (*M*/s)** |
|---|---|---|---|
| 1 | 0.0200 | 0.0200 | 0.00184 |
| 2 | 0.0400 | 0.0200 | 0.00736 |
| 3 | 0.0200 | 0.0400 | 0.00368 |

There are a couple of ways to interpret the data to generate the rate equation. If the numbers involved are simple (as above and on most tests, including the AP Exam), you can reason out the orders of reaction. You can see that in going from experiment 1 to experiment 2, the [$ClO_2$] was doubled, [$OH^-$] held constant, and the rate increased fourfold $\left(\frac{0.00736}{0.00184} = 4\right)$. This means that the reaction is second order ($2^2 = 4$) with respect to $ClO_2$. Comparing experiments 1 and 3, you see that the [$OH^-$] was doubled, [$ClO_2$] was held constant, and the rate doubled $\left(\frac{0.00736}{0.00368} = 2\right)$. Therefore, the reaction is first order ($2^1 = 2$) with respect to $OH^-$ and the rate equation can be written as:

$$\text{Rate} = k[ClO_2]^2[OH^-]$$

The rate constant can be determined by substituting the values of the concentrations of $ClO_2$ and $OH^-$ from any of the experiments into the rate equation above and solving for $k$.

Using experiment 1:

$$0.00184\ M/\text{s} = k\,(0.0200\ M)^2(0.0200\ M)$$

$$k = \frac{0.00184\ M/\text{s}}{(0.0200\ M)^2(0.0200\ N)}$$

$$k = 230\ M^{-2}\text{s}^{-1}$$

Sometimes because of the numbers' complexity, you must set up the equations mathematically. The ratio of the rate expressions of two experiments will be used in determining the reaction orders. The equations will be chosen so that the concentration of only one reactant has changed while the others remain constant. In the example above, the ratio of experiments 1 and 2 will be used to determine the effect of a change of the concentration of $ClO_2$ on the rate, and then experiments 1 and 3 will be used to determine the effect of $O_2$. Experiments 2 and 3 cannot be used because both chemical species have changed concentration.

KEY IDEA

Remember: in choosing experiments to compare, choose two in which the concentration of only one reactant has changed while the others have remained constant.

Compare experiments 1 and 2:

$$\frac{0.00184\frac{M}{s} = k[0.0200]^m[0.0200]^n}{0.00736\frac{M}{s} = k[0.0400]^m[0.0200]^n}$$

Cancel the rate constants and the $[0.0200]^n$ and simplify:

$$\frac{1}{4} = \left(\frac{1}{2}\right)^m$$

$$m = 2 \text{ (use logarithms to solve for } m\text{)}$$

(To solve using logarithms begin with: $[0.250 = 0.500^m]$ and take the logs of both sides to get $[\log 0.250 = m \log 0.500]$; this leads to $[-0.602 = m\,(-0.301)]$, and finally $m = \frac{-0.602}{-0.301} = 2$)

Compare experiments 1 and 3:

$$\frac{0.00184\frac{M}{s} = k[0.0200]^m[0.0200]^n}{0.00368\frac{M}{s} = k[0.0200]^m[0.0400]^n}$$

Cancel the rate constants, units, and the $[0.0200]^m$ and simplify:

$$\frac{1}{2} = \left(\frac{1}{2}\right)^m$$

$$n = 1$$

Write the rate equation:

$$\text{Rate} = k[ClO_2]^2[OH^-]$$

Again, the rate constant $k$ could be determined by choosing any of the three experiments, substituting the concentrations, rate, and orders into the rate expression, and then solving for $k$.

## Integrated Rate Laws

Thus far, only cases in which instantaneous data are used in the rate expression have been shown. These expressions allow us to answer questions concerning the speed of the reaction at a specific moment, but not questions about how long it might take to use up a certain reactant, etc. If changes in the concentration of reactants or products over time are taken into account, as in the **integrated rate laws**, these questions can be answered. Consider the following reaction:

$$A \rightarrow B$$

If this reaction is first order, then the rate of reaction can be expressed as the change in concentration of reactant A with time:

$$\text{Rate} = -\frac{\Delta[A]}{\Delta t}$$

and as the rate law:

$$\text{Rate} = k[A]$$

Setting these terms equal to each other gives:

$$-\frac{\Delta[A]}{\Delta t} = k[A]$$

and integrating over time gives:

$$\ln [A]_t - \ln [A]_0 = -kt$$

where "ln" is the natural logarithm, $[A]_0$ is the concentration of reactant A at time = 0, and $[A]_t$ is the concentration of reactant A at some later time $t$. (Radioactive decay processes are the best examples of first-order kinetics.)

If the reaction is second order in A, then the following equation can be derived using the same procedure:

$$\frac{1}{[A]_t} - \frac{1}{[A]_0} = kt$$

The only other integrated rate law that you may see on the AP Exam is a zero-order integrated rate law, which is:

$$[A]_t - [A]_0 = -kt$$

Consider the following problem: carbon-14, $^{14}C$, decays through a first-order process to form nitrogen-14, $^{14}N$. The rate constant is $1.21 \times 10^{-4}\ \text{yr}^{-1}$ at 25°C. How long will it take for the concentration of $^{14}C$ to drop from 0.200 $M$ to 0.190 $M$ at 25°C?

Answer: $4.24 \times 10^2$ yr.

In this problem, $k = 1.21 \times 10^{-4}\ \text{yr}^{-1}$, $[A]_0 = 0.200\ M$, and $[A]_t = 0.190\ M$. You can simply insert the values and solve for $t$, or you first can rearrange the equation to give $t = \frac{\ln [A]_t - \ln [A]_0}{k}$. You will get the same answer in either case. If you get a negative answer, you interchanged $[A]_t$ and $[A]_0$. A common mistake is to use the wrong integrated rate equation. The problem will always give you the information needed to determine whether the first-order or second-order equation or zero-order equation is required.

The order of reaction can be determined graphically. If a plot of the ln [A] versus time yields a straight line, then the reaction is first order with respect to reactant A. If a plot of $\frac{1}{[A]}$ versus time yields a straight line, then the reaction is second order with respect to reactant A. Finally, if a plot of [A] versus time yields a straight line, the reaction is zero order with respect to reactant A. These plots are shown in Figure 13.2.

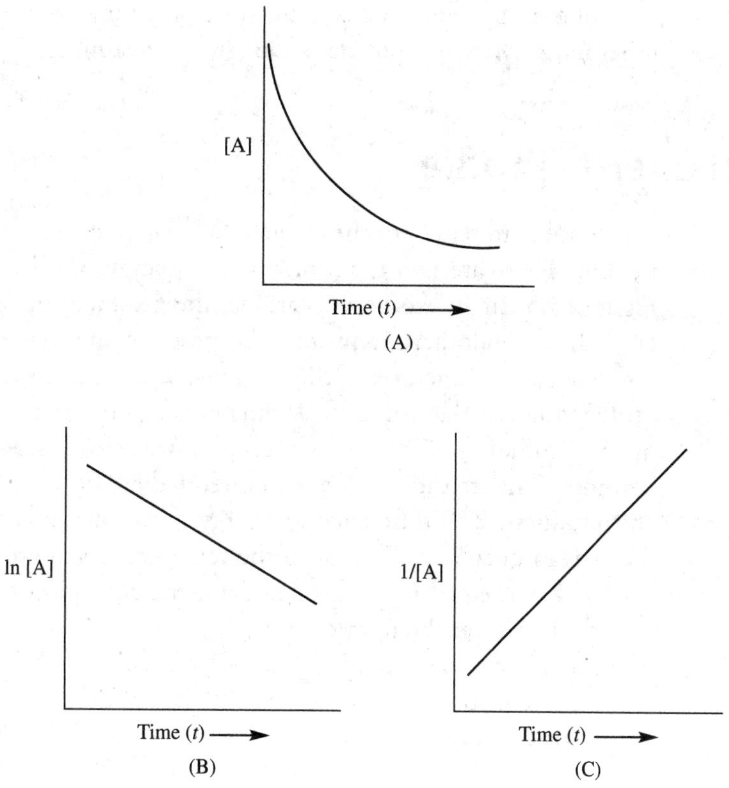


**Figure 13.2 Integrated rate law plots.**

The reaction **half-life**, $t_{1/2}$, is the amount of time that it takes for a reactant concentration to decrease to one-half its initial concentration. For a first-order reaction, the half-life is a constant, independent of reactant concentration, and can be shown to have the following mathematical relationship:

$$t_{1/2} = \frac{\ln 2}{k} = \frac{0.693}{k}$$

For second-order reactions, the half-life does depend on the reactant concentration and can be calculated using the following formula:

$$t_{1/2} = \frac{1}{k[A]_0}$$

For zero-order reactions, the half-life equation is:

$$t_{1/2} = \frac{[A]_0}{2k}$$

This means that as a second-order or a zero-order reaction proceeds, the half-life changes. However, neither second-order nor zero-order half-life equations are required for the AP Exam.

As mentioned previously, radioactive decay is a first-order process, and the half-lives of the radioisotopes are well documented (see Chapter 18, Nuclear Chemistry, for further discussion of half-lives with respect to nuclear reactions).

If you are unsure about your work in any kinetics problems, just follow your units. For example, you are asked for time, so your answer must have time units only and no other units. Many people make the error of assuming $s^{-1}$ or $min^{-1}$ are time units.

## Reaction Energy Profile

It is possible to represent the progress of a chemical reaction by plotting a **reaction energy profile**. There are two types of reaction energy profiles, both of which are illustrated in Figure 13.3. In an exothermic profile, the products are lower in energy than are the reactants. In an endothermic profile, the products are higher energy than the reactants. The difference in the energies of the reactants and products is the heat of reaction. The energy profile indicates that for the reactants to get to the products (progressing from left to right on the profile) they must pass through a **transition state**, sometimes called an **activated complex**. The transition state is an intermediate form with both characteristics of reactants and products. The difference in energy between the reactants and the transition state is the activation energy, $E_a$. One of the requirements of an effective collision is that it has an energy that is equal to, or greater than, the activation energy. The greater the activation energy, the slower the reaction.

The activation energy may be related to the rate constant for the reaction by the Arrhenius equation. However, the AP Exam does not assess calculations involving the Arrhenius equation.

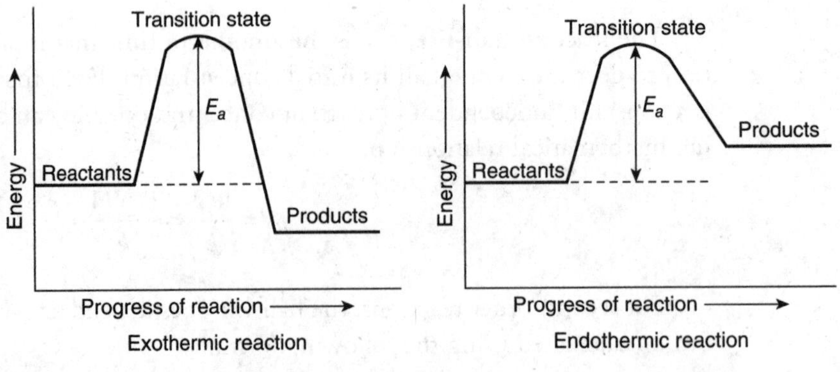


**Figure 13.3 Two different reaction energy profiles.**

# Activation Energy

A change in the temperature at which a reaction is taking place will affect the rate constant $k$. As the temperature increases, the value of the rate constant increases and the reaction goes faster. (A rate constant is only constant if the temperature is constant.) The Swedish scientist Arrhenius derived a relationship in 1889 that related the rate constant and temperature. The Arrhenius equation has the form: $k = Ae^{-E_a/RT}$ where $k$ is the rate constant, $A$ is a term called the frequency factor that accounts for molecular orientation, $e$ is the natural logarithm base, $R$ is the universal gas constant 8.314 J mol $K^{-1}$, $T$ is the Kelvin temperature, and $E_a$ is the **activation energy**, the minimum amount of energy that is needed to initiate or start a chemical reaction.

The Arrhenius equation is most commonly used to calculate the activation energy of a reaction. One way this can be done is to plot the ln $k$ versus $1/T$. This gives a straight line whose slope is $-E_a/R$. Knowing the value of $R$ allows the calculation of the value of $E_a$.

Normally, high activation energies are associated with slow reactions. Anything that can be done to lower the activation energy of a reaction will tend to speed up the reaction.

# Reaction Mechanisms

In the introduction to this chapter, we discussed how chemical reactions occurred. Recall that before a reaction can occur there must be a collision between one reactant with the proper orientation at the reactive site of another reactant that transfers enough energy to provide the activation energy. However, many reactions do not take place in quite this simple a way. Many reactions proceed from reactants to products through a sequence of reactions. This sequence of reactions is called the **reaction mechanism**. For example, consider the reaction:

$$A + 2B \rightarrow E + F$$

Most likely, E and F are not formed from the simple collision of an A and two B molecules. This reaction might follow this reaction sequence:

$$A + B \rightarrow C$$

$$C + B \rightarrow D$$

$$D \rightarrow E + F$$

If you add together the three equations above, you will get the overall equation A + 2B → E + F. C and D are called **reaction intermediates**, chemical species that are produced and consumed during the reaction but that do not appear in the overall reaction.

Each individual reaction in the mechanism is called an **elementary step** or **elementary reaction**. Each reaction step has its own rate of reaction. One of the reaction steps is slower than the rest and is the **rate-determining step**. The rate-determining step limits how fast the overall reaction can occur. Therefore, the rate law of the rate-determining step is the rate law of the overall reaction.

The rate equation for an elementary step can be determined from the reaction stoichiometry, unlike the overall reaction. The reactant coefficients in the elementary step become the reaction orders in the rate equation for that elementary step.

Many times a study of the kinetics of a reaction gives clues to the reaction mechanism. For example, consider the following reaction:

$$NO_2(g) + CO(g) \rightarrow NO(g) + CO_2(g)$$

It has been determined experimentally that the rate law for this reaction is: Rate = $k[NO_2]^2$. This rate law indicates that the reaction does not occur with a simple collision between $NO_2$ and CO. A simple collision of this type would have a rate law of Rate = $k[NO_2][CO]$. The following mechanism has been proposed for this reaction:

$$NO_2(g) + NO_2(g) \rightarrow NO_3(g) + NO(g)$$

$$NO_3(g) + CO(g) \rightarrow NO_2(g) + CO_2(g)$$

Notice that if you add these two steps together, you get the overall reaction. The first step has been shown to be the slow step in the mechanism, the rate-determining step. If we write the rate law for this elementary step, it is: Rate = $k[NO_2]^2$, which is identical to the experimentally determined rate law for the overall reaction.

Also note that both steps in the mechanism are **bimolecular reactions**, reactions that involve the collision of two chemical species. In **unimolecular reactions**, a single chemical species decomposes or rearranges. Both bimolecular and unimolecular reactions are common, but the collision of three or more chemical species is quite rare. Therefore, in developing or assessing a mechanism, it is best to consider only unimolecular or bimolecular elementary steps.

## Steady-State Approximation

In multistep reactions it is not always easy to determine the rate law. This is especially true when the first step in the mechanism is not the rate-determining step. In these cases, the **steady-state approximation** may be used to derive the rate law. This method assumes that one of the intermediates in the mechanism reacts as quickly as it was generated, thus its concentration remains constant throughout the reaction.

## Multistep Reaction Energy Profile

The reaction energy profiles shown in Figure 13.3 are for single-step reactions. However, some reactions require more than one step. The reaction energy profiles for multistep reactions are different than those for single-step reactions. Figure 13.4 shows the energy profile for a three-step exothermic reaction. Each step has its own transition state and activation energy, which are labelled in the figure. Notice that in the figure, one activation energy ($E_{a2}$) is greater than the other two, which means that this is the rate-determining step.

## Catalysts

A **catalyst** is a substance that speeds up the rate of reaction without being consumed in the reaction. A catalyst may take part in the reaction and even be changed during the reaction, but at the end of the reaction, it is at least theoretically recoverable in its original form. It will not produce more of the product, but it allows the reaction to proceed more quickly. In equilibrium reactions (see Chapter 15, Equilibrium), the catalyst speeds up both the

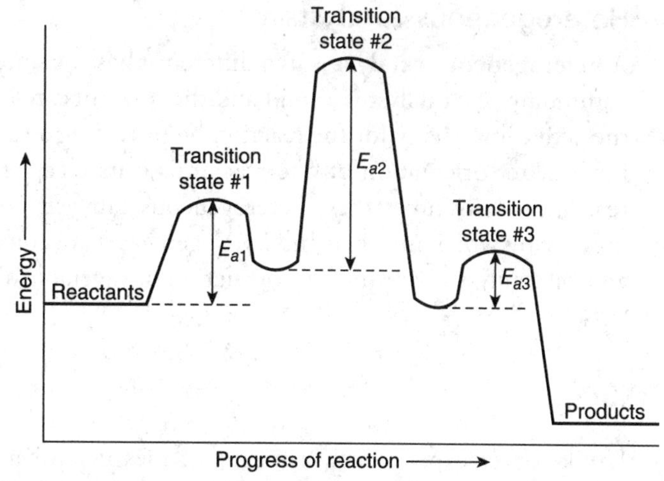


**Figure 13.4 A reaction energy profile for a three-step reaction. Each step has its own transition state and activation energy.**

forward and reverse reactions. Catalysts speed up the rates of reaction by providing a different mechanism that has a lower activation energy or by increasing the number of effective collisions. The higher the activation energy of a reaction, the slower the reaction will proceed. Catalysts provide an alternative pathway that has a lower activation energy and thus will be faster. In general, there are two distinct types of catalyst: homogeneous catalysts and heterogeneous catalysts. Often the catalyst forms a bond to one or more reactants. If no bond forms, the binding is due to intermolecular forces. The formation of the bond or the interactions from intermolecular forces often distort a reactant to increase the probability of an effective collision or lowering the activation energy.

## Homogeneous Catalysts

**Homogeneous catalysts** are catalysts that are in the same phase or state of matter as the reactants. They provide an alternative reaction pathway (mechanism) with a lower activation energy.

The decomposition of hydrogen peroxide is a slow, one-step reaction, especially if the solution is kept cool and in a dark bottle:

$$2\ H_2O_2(aq) \rightarrow 2\ H_2O(l) + O_2(g)$$

However, if ferric ion is added, the reaction speeds up tremendously. The proposed reaction sequence for this new reaction is:

$$2\ Fe^{3+}(aq) + H_2O_2(aq) \rightarrow 2\ Fe^{2+}(aq) + O_2(g) + 2\ H^+(aq)$$

$$2\ Fe^{2+}(aq) + H_2O_2(aq) + 2\ H^+(aq) \rightarrow 2\ Fe^{3+}(aq) + 2\ H_2O(l)$$

Notice that in the reaction the catalyst, $Fe^{3+}$, was reduced to the ferrous ion, $Fe^{2+}$, in the first step of the mechanism, but in the second step it was oxidized back to the ferric ion. Overall, the catalyst remained unchanged. Notice also that although the catalyzed reaction is a two-step reaction, it is significantly faster than the original uncatalyzed one-step reaction. You should also note that this is the "proposed mechanism"; experimental evidence suggests what a mechanism may be, but such evidence can never prove a mechanism.

### Heterogeneous Catalysts

A **heterogeneous catalyst** is in a different phase or state of matter from the reactants. Most commonly, the catalyst is a solid and the reactants are liquids or gases. These catalysts lower the activation energy for the reaction by providing a surface for the reaction and by providing a better orientation of one reactant, so its reactive site is more easily hit by the other reactant. Many times these heterogeneous catalysts are finely divided metals. The Haber process, by which nitrogen and hydrogen gases are converted into ammonia, depends upon an iron catalyst, while the hydrogenation of vegetable oil to margarine uses a nickel catalyst.

## Experiments

STRATEGY

Unlike other experiments, a means of measuring time is essential to all kinetics experiments. This may be done with a clock or a timer. The initial concentration of each reactant must be determined. Often this is done through a simple dilution of a stock solution. The experimenter must then determine the concentration of one or more substances later or record some measurable change in the solution. Unless there will be an attempt to measure the activation energy, the temperature should be kept constant. A thermometer is needed to confirm this.

"Clock" experiments are common kinetics experiments. They do not require a separate experiment to determine the concentration of a substance in the reaction mixture. In clock experiments, after a certain amount of time, the solution suddenly changes color. This occurs when one of the reactants has disappeared, and another reaction involving a color change can begin.

In other kinetics experiments, the volume or pressure of a gaseous product is monitored. Again, it is not necessary to analyze the reaction mixture. Color changes in a solution may be monitored with a spectrophotometer. Finally, as a last resort, a sample of the reaction mixture may be removed at intervals and analyzed.

The initial measurement and one or more later measurements are required. (Remember, you measure times; you calculate changes in time [$\Delta t$]). Glassware, for mixing and diluting solutions, and a thermometer are the equipment needed for a clock experiment. Other kinetics experiments will use additional equipment to measure volume, temperature, etc. Do not forget: in all cases, you measure a property and then calculate a change. You never measure a change.

## Common Mistakes to Avoid

TIP

1. When working mathematical problems, be sure your units cancel to give you the desired unit in your answer.
2. Be sure to round your answer off to the correct number of significant figures.
3. In working rate law problems, be sure to use molarity for your concentration unit.
4. In writing integrated rate laws, be sure to include the negative sign with the change in *reactant* concentration since it will be decreasing with time.
5. Remember that the rate law for an overall reaction must be derived from experimental data.
6. In mathematically determining the rate law, be sure to set up the ratio of two experiments such that the concentration of only one reactant has changed.
7. Remember that in most of these calculations the base e logarithm (ln) is used and not the base 10 logarithm (log).

## ❯ Review Questions

Use these questions to review the content of this chapter and practice for the AP Chemistry Exam. First are 20 multiple-choice questions similar to what you will encounter in Section I of the AP Chemistry Exam. There are some questions present to help you review prior knowledge. Following those is a long free-response question like the ones in Section II of the exam. To make these questions an even more authentic practice for the actual exam, time yourself following the instructions provided.

### Multiple-Choice Questions

Answer the following questions in 30 minutes. You may not use a calculator. You may use the periodic table and the equation sheet at the back of this book.

**1.** A reaction follows the rate law Rate = $k[A]^2$. Which of the following plots will give a straight line?

(A) 1/[A] versus 1/time
(B) $[A]^2$ versus time
(C) 1/[A] versus time
(D) ln [A] versus time

**2.** For the reaction $NO_2(g) + CO(g) \rightarrow NO(g) + CO_2(g)$, the rate law is Rate = $k[NO_2]^2$. If a small amount of gaseous carbon monoxide (CO) is added to a reaction mixture that was 0.10 molar in $NO_2$ and 0.20 molar in CO, which of the following statements is true?

(A) Both *k* and the reaction rate remain the same.
(B) Both *k* and the reaction rate increase.
(C) Both *k* and the reaction rate decrease.
(D) Only *k* increases; the reaction rate will remain the same.

**3.** The specific rate constant, *k*, for radioactive beryllium-11 is 0.049 $s^{-1}$. What mass of a 0.500-mg sample of beryllium-11 remains after 28 seconds?

(A) 0.250 mg
(B) 0.125 mg
(C) 0.0625 mg
(D) 0.375 mg

**4.** The rate of reaction for a certain chemical is slow. A possible cause of the slow rate might be which of the following?

(A) The activation energy is low.
(B) The activation energy is high.
(C) There is a catalyst present.
(D) There was an increase in the temperature.

**5.** The steps below represent a proposed mechanism for the catalyzed oxidation of CO by $O_3$.

Step 1: $NO_2(g) + CO(g) \rightarrow NO(g) + CO_2(g)$
Step 2: $NO(g) + O_3(g) \rightarrow NO_2(g) + O_2(g)$

What are the overall products of the catalyzed reaction?

(A) $CO_2$ and $O_2$
(B) NO and $CO_2$
(C) $NO_2$ and $O_2$
(D) NO and $O_2$

**6.** The decomposition of ammonia to the elements is a first-order reaction with a half-life of 200 s at a certain temperature. How long will it take the partial pressure of ammonia to decrease from 0.100 atm to 0.00625 atm?

(A) 200 s
(B) 400 s
(C) 800 s
(D) 1,000 s

**7.** The energy difference between the reactants and the transition state is:

(A) the free energy
(B) the heat of reaction
(C) the activation energy
(D) the kinetic energy

**8.** Which of the following is the reason it is necessary to strike a match against the side of a box to light the match?

(A) It is necessary to supply the free energy for the reaction.
(B) It is necessary to supply the activation energy for the reaction.
(C) It is necessary to supply the heat of reaction for an endothermic reaction.
(D) It is necessary to supply the heat of reaction for an exothermic reaction.

**9.** The following table gives the initial concentrations and rate for three experiments.

| EXPERIMENT | INITIAL [CO] ($mol\ L^{-1}$) | INITIAL $[Cl_2]$ ($mol\ L^{-1}$) | INITIAL RATE OF FORMATION OF $COCl_2$ ($mol\ L^{-1}\ min^{-1}$) |
|---|---|---|---|
| 1 | 0.200 | 0.100 | $3.9 \times 10^{-25}$ |
| 2 | 0.100 | 0.200 | $3.9 \times 10^{-25}$ |
| 3 | 0.200 | 0.200 | $7.8 \times 10^{-25}$ |

The reaction is $CO(g) + Cl_2(g) \rightarrow COCl_2(g)$. What is the rate law for this reaction?

(A) Rate = $k[CO]$
(B) Rate = $k[CO]^2\ [Cl_2]$
(C) Rate = $k[CO][Cl_2]$
(D) Rate = $k[CO][Cl_2]^2$

**10.** The reaction $(CH_3)_3CBr(aq) + H_2O(l) \rightarrow (CH_3)_3COH(aq) + HBr(aq)$ follows the rate law Rate = $k[(CH_3)_3CBr]$. What will be the effect of decreasing the concentration of $(CH_3)_3CBr$?

(A) The rate of the reaction will increase.
(B) More HBr will form.
(C) The rate of the reaction will decrease.
(D) The reaction will shift to the left.

**11.** When the concentration of $H^+(aq)$ is doubled for the reaction $H_2O_2(aq) + 2\ Fe^{2+}(aq) + 2\ H^+(aq) \rightarrow 2\ Fe^{3+}(aq) + 2\ H_2O(g)$, there is no change in the reaction rate. This indicates that:

(A) the $H^+$ is a spectator ion
(B) the rate-determining step does not involve $H^+$
(C) the reaction mechanism does not involve $H^+$
(D) the $H^+$ is a catalyst

**12.** The following mechanism has been proposed for the reaction of $CHCl_3$ with $Cl_2$:

| | | |
|---|---|---|
| Step 1 | $Cl_2(g) \rightarrow 2\ Cl(g)$ | fast |
| Step 2 | $Cl(g) + CHCl_3(g) \rightarrow CCl_3(g) + HCl(g)$ | slow |
| Step 3 | $CCl_3(g) + Cl(g) \rightarrow CCl_4(g)$ | fast |

Which of the following rate laws is consistent with this mechanism?

(A) Rate = $k[Cl_2]$
(B) Rate = $k[CHCl_3][Cl_2]$
(C) Rate = $k[CHCl_3]$
(D) Rate = $k[CHCl_3][Cl_2]^{1/2}$

**13.** The reaction $NO_2(g) + CO(g) \rightarrow NO(g) + CO_2(g)$ has the rate law Rate = $k[NO_2]^2$. In one experiment, the initial amounts of $NO_2$ and CO were both 0.100 *M*. In another experiment, the initial concentration of CO was doubled to 0.200 *M*, and the concentration of $NO_2$ remained the same (0.100 *M*). All other variables remained unchanged. Which of the following expresses how the rate of the second experiment compares to that of the first experiment?

(A) The rate of both experiments is the same.
(B) The rate of the second experiment is double the first.
(C) The rate of the second experiment is one-half the first.
(D) There is insufficient information to make a conclusion.

**14.** The rate law for the following reaction is Rate = $k[H_2][I_2]$. The reaction is $H_2(g) + I_2(g) \rightarrow 2\ HI(g)$. A chemist studying this reaction prepared what he thought was a mixture that was 0.10 *M* in $H_2$ and 0.20 *M* in $I_2$. In reality, the mixture had a slightly higher $I_2$ concentration. All other reaction conditions were correct. Because of the error, the experiment did not proceed exactly as expected. Which of the following statements is true about the actual experiment (higher $I_2$) relative to the experiment the chemist thought he was performing (expected $I_2$)?

(A) The values of *k* and the reaction rate both decreased.
(B) The values of *k* and the reaction rate both increased.
(C) The value of the rate increased, but *k* remained the same.
(D) The value of *k* increased, but the reaction rate remained the same.

**15.** Step 1: $2\ NO_2(g) \rightarrow N_2(g) + 2\ O_2(g)$
Step 2: $2\ CO(g) + O_2(g) \rightarrow 2\ CO_2(g)$
Step 3: $N_2(g) + O_2(g) \rightarrow 2\ NO(g)$

The above is a proposed mechanism for the reaction of $NO_2$ and CO. What are the overall products of the reaction?

(A) NO and $CO_2$
(B) $O_2$ and $CO_2$
(C) $N_2$ and NO
(D) NO and $O_2$

**16.** The reaction of bromine, $Br_2$, with nitrogen oxide, NO, is $Br_2(g) + 2\ NO(g) \rightarrow 2\ NOBr(g)$.

For this reaction, the observed rate law is Rate = $k\ [Br_2]\ [NO]^2$. Why is the following step unlikely to be in the mechanism?

$$Br_2(g) + 2\ NO(g) \rightarrow 2\ NOBr(g)$$

(A) NO is an unstable molecule.
(B) $Br_2$ is too stable to react.
(C) This is a ternary step.
(D) This could be a step in the mechanism.

Use the following information to answer Question 17.

| Time (s) | $[O_2]$ (mole $L^{-1}$) |
|---|---|
| 0.00 | 0.210 |
| 1.00 | 0.165 |
| 2.00 | 0.150 |
| 3.00 | 0.135 |
| 4.00 | 0.100 |

$$2\ NO(g) + O_2(g) \rightarrow 2\ NO_2(g)$$

**17.** An environmental chemist investigates the above reaction and obtains the data listed in the above table. Which of the following is the rate between 1.00 and 3.00 seconds?

(A) $-0.0450\ M\ s^{-1}$
(B) $-0.0217\ M\ s^{-1}$
(C) $-0.0150\ M\ s^{-1}$
(D) $-0.0275\ M\ s^{-1}$

Use the following information to answer Questions 18 and 19.

$$CHCl_3(g) + Cl_2(g) \rightarrow CCl_4(g) + HCl(g)$$

The proposed mechanism for the above reaction is as follows:

Step 1: $Cl_2(g) \rightarrow 2\ Cl(g)$ (fast)
Step 2: $CHCl_3(g) + Cl(g) \rightarrow CCl_3(g) + HCl(g)$ (slow)
Step 3: $CCl_3(g) + Cl(g) \rightarrow CCl_4(g)$ (fast)

**18.** The reaction energy profile for the above reaction will have how many peaks?

(A) 3
(B) 1
(C) 2
(D) 4

**19.** What are possible units for the rate constant for the above reaction?

(A) It would have no units.
(B) $\left(\frac{\text{min}}{M}\right)^{1/2}$
(C) $\left(\frac{M}{\text{min}}\right)^{1/2}$
(D) $\left(\frac{\text{min}}{M}\right)^{3/2}$

**20.** The decomposition reaction of $KClO_3(s)$ is catalyzed by $MnO_2(s)$. The reaction produces KCl(s) and $O_2(g)$. In one experiment 12.24 g of $KClO_3(s)$ and 0.87 g of $MnO_2(s)$ are used, and 9.60 g of $O_2(g)$ are produced. In second experiment, the mass of $KClO_3(s)$ is halved and the mass of $MnO_2(s)$ is kept the same (0.87 g). In the second experiment, the mass of $O_2(g)$ produced is one-half that in the first experiment. In a third experiment, 12.24 g of $KClO_3(s)$ and one-half the grams of $MnO_2(s)$ are used, how does the mass of $O_2(g)$ produced in the third experiment compare to the mass of $O_2(g)$ in the first experiment?

Molar masses (in g $mol^{-1}$)
$KClO_3$ = 122.4, $MnO_2$ = 86.94, $O_2$ = 32.00, KCl = 74.55

(A) 4.80 g $O_2(g)$
(B) 9.60 g $O_2(g)$
(C) 19.20 g $O_2(g)$
(D) 9.26 g $O_2(g)$

## › Answers and Explanations

**1. C**—The exponent 2 means this is a second-order rate law. Second-order rate laws give a straight-line plot for 1/[A] versus *t*. D applies to first-order reactions. A and B do not apply to any reaction.

**2. A**—The value of *k* remains the same unless the temperature is changed or a catalyst is added. Only materials that appear in the rate law, in this case $NO_2$, will affect the rate. Adding $NO_2$ would increase the rate and removing $NO_2$ would decrease the rate. CO has no effect on the rate.

**3. B**—The half-life is $\frac{0.693}{k} = \frac{0.693}{0.049\ s^{-1}} = 14$ s. (It is possible to get this answer by rounding the values to 0.7/0.05 $s^{-1}$.) The time given, 28 s, represents two half-lives. The first half-life uses one-half of the beryllium, and the second half-life uses one-half of the remaining material, so only one-fourth of the original material remains (0.500 mg)$\left(\frac{1}{4}\right)$ = 0.125 mg. The relationship $\frac{0.693}{k}$ is given on the AP Exam. This may be mistaken for a nuclear chemistry problem. Remember, radioactive decay processes are amongst the best examples of first-order kinetics, and all first-order kinetics equation apply.

**4. B**—Slow reactions have high activation energies. Low activation energies (A) are typical of fast reactions. A catalyst (C) will increase the rate of a reaction. Increasing the temperature (D) will increase the rate of a reaction.

**5. A**—Add the two equations together:

$$NO_2(g) + CO(g) + NO(g) + O_3(g) \rightarrow NO(g) + CO_2(g) + NO_2(g) + O_2(g)$$

Then cancel identical species that appear on opposite sides:

$$CO(g) + O_3(g) \rightarrow CO_2(g) + O_2(g)$$

The $NO_2(g)$ cancels because it is the catalyst.

**6. C**—The value will be decreased by one-half for each half-life. Using the following table:

| HALF-LIVES | REMAINING |
|---|---|
| 0 | 0.100 |
| 1 | 0.0500 |
| 2 | 0.0250 |
| 3 | 0.0125 |
| 4 | 0.00625 |

Four half-lives = 4(200 s) = 800 s

This answer may also be determined using the following two equations that are given on the AP Exam: $\ln [A]_t - \ln [A]_0 = -kt$ and $t_{1/2} = \frac{\ln 2}{k} = \frac{0.693}{k}$.

**7. C**—This is the definition of the activation energy.

**8. B**—The friction supplies the energy necessary to start the reaction. This energy is the activation energy. The free energy and the heat of reaction for the reaction deal with the reactants and products. It is necessary to deal with the reactants and transition state (activated complex), which are separated by the activation energy.

**9. C**—Beginning with the generic rate law, Rate = $k[CO]^m [Cl_2]^n$, it is necessary to determine the values of $m$ and $n$ (the orders). Comparing experiments 2 and 3, note that the rate doubles when the concentration of CO is doubled. This direct change means the reaction is first order with respect to CO. Comparing experiments 1 and 3, note that the rate doubles when the concentration of $Cl_2$ is doubled. Again, this direct change means the reaction is first order. This gives Rate = $k$[CO] [$Cl_2$].

**10. C**—The compound appears in the rate law, so a change in its concentration will change the rate. The reaction is first order in $(CH_3)_3CBr$, so the rate will change directly with the change in concentration of this reactant. Do not be distracted because this is an organic compound.

**11. B**—All substances involved, directly or indirectly, in the rate-determining step will change the rate when their concentrations are changed. The ion is required in the balanced chemical equation, so it cannot be a spectator ion, and it must appear in the mechanism. Catalysts will change the rate of a reaction. Since $H^+$ does not affect the rate, the reaction is zero order with respect to this ion.

**12. D**—The rate law depends on the slow step of the mechanism. The reactants in the slow step are Cl and $CHCl_3$ (one of each). The rate law is first order with respect to each of these. The Cl is half of the original reactant molecule $Cl_2$. This replaces the [Cl] in the rate law with $[Cl_2]^{1/2}$. Do not make the mistake of using the overall reaction to predict the rate law.

**13. A**—Carbon monoxide, CO, does not appear in the rate law. Since it does not appear in the rate law, changing the concentration of CO will not change the rate of the reaction.

**14. B**—The higher $I_2$ concentration will increase the value of the rate and give a higher apparent $k$. This $k$ is higher than the true $k$.

**15. A**—Add the equations and cancel anything that appears on both sides of the reaction arrows.

Total: $2\,NO_2(g) + \cancel{N_2(g)} + 2\,CO(g) + \cancel{2\,O_2(g)}$
$\rightarrow \cancel{N_2(g)} + \cancel{2\,O_2(g)} + 2\,CO_2(g) + 2\,NO(g)$

Leaving: $2\,NO_2(g) + 2\,CO(g) \rightarrow$
$2\,CO_2(g) + 2\,NO(g)$

Or: $NO_2(g) + CO(g) \rightarrow CO_2(g) + NO(g)$

**16. C**—Ternary steps, steps involving three molecules, are very unlikely in mechanisms.

**17. C**—The rate of the reaction is equal to the slope of the line between the times selected. The slope is $\Delta M/\Delta t$, which for a reactant, like $O_2$, must be negative. As an example, the slope between the 1.00 and 3.00 seconds is:

$$\text{slope} = \frac{(0.135-0.165)\ M}{(3.00-1.00)\ \text{s}} = -0.0150\ M\ \text{s}^{-1}.$$

The other answers result when the slope is determined between the wrong two points. The slope between the first and last point is $-0.0275\ M\,\text{s}^{-1}$. The slope between the first and second point is $-0.0450\ M\,\text{s}^{-1}$. The slope between the second and last point is $-0.0217\ M\,\text{s}^{-1}$.

We have seen the students picking the wrong two points in a calculation such as this.

**18. A**—There should be one peak for each step in the mechanism.

**19. B**—Note that unlike many rate constants which use seconds as the time unit, the rate constants here use minutes as the time unit, which is acceptable.

To begin solving the problem you will need the rate law for the reaction. The rate law comes from the rate determining (slow) step and is: Rate = $k\,[CHCl_3][Cl] = k\,[CHCl_3][Cl_2]^{1/2}$. The first choice comes directly from the slow step, which must be changed to the second as the rate law must use the reactants from the overall reaction and not an equation containing any reaction intermediates (Cl). Adding units to the rate law gives:

$$\text{Rate} = k\,[CHCl_3][Cl_2]^{1/2} \rightarrow \left(\frac{M}{\text{min}}\right) =$$

$$(k)\left(\frac{M}{\text{min}}\right)\left(\frac{M}{\text{min}}\right)^{1/2} = (k)\left(\frac{M}{\text{min}}\right)^{3/2}$$

The units on both sides of the rate law equation must be identical, and if they are not, the units on the rate constant will correct the inconsistency. Therefore:

$$\left(\frac{M}{\text{min}}\right) = \left(\frac{\text{min}}{M}\right)^{1/2}\left(\frac{M}{\text{min}}\right)^{3/2} = \left(\frac{M}{\text{min}}\right)$$

**20. B**—Catalysts change the rate of the reaction not the overall yield. So changing the quantity of catalyst (other than to 0) will not alter the yield.

## › Free-Response Question

You have 15 minutes to answer the following long question. You may use a calculator and the tables in the back of the book.

**Question**

$$2\ ClO_2(aq) + 2\ OH^-(aq) \rightarrow ClO_3^-(aq) + ClO_2^-(aq) + H_2O(l)$$

A series of experiments were conducted to study the above reaction. The following table provides the initial concentrations and rates.

| | INITIAL CONCENTRATIONS (mol/L) | | |
|---|---|---|---|
| **EXPERIMENT** | **$[OH^-]$** | **$[ClO_2]$** | **INITIAL RATE OF FORMATION OF $ClO_3^-$ (mol/L min)** |
| 1 | 0.030 | 0.020 | 0.166 |
| 2 | 0.060 | 0.020 | 0.331 |
| 3 | 0.030 | 0.040 | 0.661 |

(a) (i) Determine the order of the reaction with respect to each reactant. Make sure to explain your reasoning.
(ii) Give the rate law for the reaction.

(b) Determine the value of the rate constant, making sure to include the units.

(c) Calculate the initial rate of disappearance of $ClO_2$ in experiment 1.

(d) The following is the proposed mechanism for this reaction:

Step 1: $ClO_2(aq) + ClO_2(aq) \rightarrow Cl_2O_4(aq)$

Step 2: $Cl_2O_4(aq) + OH^-(aq) \rightarrow ClO_3^-(aq) + HClO_2(aq)$

Step 3: $HClO_2(aq) + OH^-(aq) \rightarrow ClO_2^-(aq) + H_2O(l)$

Which step is the rate-determining step? Show that this mechanism is consistent with both the rate law for the reaction and with the overall stoichiometry.

## Answer and Explanation

(a) (i) This part of the problem begins with a generic rate equation: Rate = $k[ClO_2]^m[OH^-]^n$. The values of the exponents, the orders, must be determined. It does not matter which exponent is done first. If you want to begin with $ClO_2$, you must pick two experiments from the table in which the concentration of $ClO_2$ changes but the $OH^-$ concentration does not change. These are experiments 1 and 3. Experiment 3 has twice the concentration of $ClO_2$ as experiment 1. This doubling of the $ClO_2$ concentration has quadrupled the rate. The relationship between the concentration (× 2) and the rate (× 4 = × $2^2$) indicates that the order for $ClO_2$ is 2 (= $m$). Using experiments 1 and 2 (in which only the $OH^-$ concentration changes), we see that doubling the concentration simply doubles the rate. Thus, the order for $OH^-$ is 1 (= $n$).

Give yourself 1 point for each order you got correct, for a maximum of 2 points.

(ii) Inserting the orders into the generic rate law gives Rate = $k[ClO_2]^2[OH^-]^1$, which is usually simplified to Rate = $k[ClO_2]^2[OH^-]$.

Give yourself 1 point if you got this equation correct. If you got the wrong answer for part (a) (i) but used it correctly here, you still get 1 point.

(b) Any one of the three experiments may be used to calculate the rate constant. If the problem asked for an average rate constant, you would need to calculate a value for each of the experiments and then average the values.

The rate law should be rearranged to $k = \dfrac{\text{Rate}}{[ClO_2]^2[OH^-]}$. Then, the appropriate values are entered into the equation. Using experiment 1 as an example,

$$k = \frac{\text{Rate}}{[ClO_2]^2[OH^-]} = \frac{\dfrac{0.166\ \text{mol}}{\text{L mol}}}{[0.020\ M]^2[0.030\ M]}$$

$$= 1.3833 \times 10^4\ M/M^3\ \text{min} = 1.4 \times 10^4/M^2\ \text{min}$$

The answer could also be reported as $1.4 \times 10^4\ \text{L}^2/\text{mol}^2$ min. You should not forget that $M$ = mol/L.

Give yourself 1 point for the correct numerical value. Give yourself 1 point for the correct units. If you had the wrong rate law in part (a) (ii) but used it correctly in part (b), you can still get one or both points.

(c) The coefficients from the equation say that for every mole of $ClO_3^-$ that forms, 2 moles of $ClO_2$ react. Thus, the rate of $ClO_2$ is twice the rate of $ClO_3^-$. Do not forget that since $ClO_3^-$ is forming, it has a positive rate, and since $ClO_2$ is reacting, it has a negative rate. Rearranging and inserting the rate from experiment 1 gives $\dfrac{\Delta[ClO_2]}{\Delta t}$ = −2(0.166 mol/L min)] = −0.332 mol/L min.

Give yourself 2 points if you got the entire answer correct. You get only 1 point if the sign or units are missing or incorrect.

(d) The rate-determining step must match the rate law. One approach is to determine the rate law for each step in the mechanism. This gives the following:

Step 1: Rate = $k[ClO_2]^2$
Step 2: Rate = $k[Cl_2O_4]\ [OH^-] = k[ClO_2]^2\ [OH^-]$
Step 3: Rate = $k[HClO_2]\ [OH^-] = k[ClO_2]\ [OH^-]^2$

For steps 2 and 3, it is necessary to replace the intermediates with reactants. Step 2 gives a rate law matching the one derived in part (a).

To see if the stoichiometry is correct, simply add the three steps together and cancel the intermediates (materials that appear on both sides of the reaction arrow).

Step 1: $ClO_2(aq) + ClO_2(aq) \rightarrow Cl_2O_4(aq)$
Step 2: $Cl_2O_4(aq) + OH^-(aq) \rightarrow ClO_3^-(aq) + HClO_2(aq)$
Step 3: $HClO_2(aq) + OH^-(aq) \rightarrow ClO_2^-(aq) + H_2O(l)$
Total: $2\ ClO_2(aq) + Cl_2O_4(aq) + 2\ OH^-(aq) + HClO_2(aq) \rightarrow$
$Cl_2O_4(aq) + ClO_3^-(aq) + HClO_2(aq) + ClO_2^-(aq) + H_2O(l)$

After removing the intermediates ($Cl_2O_4$ and $HClO_2$):

$$2\ ClO_2(aq) + 2\ OH^-(aq) \rightarrow ClO_3^-(aq) + ClO_2^-(aq) + H_2O(l)$$

As this matches the original reaction equation, the mechanism fulfills the overall stoichiometry requirement.

Give yourself 1 point if you picked step 2, or if you picked a step with a rate law that matches your wrong answer for part (a). Give yourself 1 more point if you explained the substitution of reactants for intermediates. Give yourself 1 point for summing the equations and proving the overall equation is consistent.

Total your points. There are 10 points possible. Subtract 1 point if any numerical answer has an incorrect number of significant figures.

## › Rapid Review

- Kinetics is the study of the speed of a chemical reaction.
- The five factors that can affect the rates of chemical reaction are the nature of the reactants, the temperature, the concentration of the reactants, the physical state of the reactants, and the presence/absence of a catalyst.
- The rate equation relates the speed of reaction to the concentration of reactants and has the form: Rate = $k[A]^m[B]^n$ . . . where $k$ is the rate constant and $m$ and $n$ are the orders of reaction with respect to that specific reactant.
- The rate law must be determined from experimental data. Review how to determine the rate law from kinetics data.
- When mathematically comparing two experiments in the determination of the rate equation, be sure to choose two in which all reactant concentrations except one remain constant.
- Rate laws can be written in the integrated form.

- If a reaction is first order, it has the rate law of Rate = $k$[A]; $\ln [A]_t - \ln [A]_0 = -kt$; a plot of ln [A] versus time gives a straight line. If a reaction is second order, it has the form of Rate = $k[A]^2$; $\frac{1}{[A]_t} - \frac{1}{[A]_0} = kt$ (integrated rate law); a plot of $\frac{1}{[A]}$ versus time gives a straight line.
- If a reaction is zero order, it has the rate law of Rate = $k[A]^0$; $[A]_t - [A]_0 = -kt$; a plot of [A] versus time gives a straight line.
- The reaction half-life is the amount of time that it takes the reactant concentration to decrease to one-half its initial concentration.
- The half-life for a first-order reaction can be determined by the equation: $t_{1/2} = \frac{\ln 2}{k} = \frac{0.693}{k}$. If the reaction is not first order, a different equation must be given to you.
- The activation energy is the minimum amount of energy needed to initiate or start a chemical reaction.
- Many reactions proceed from reactants to products by a series of steps called elementary steps. All these steps together describe the reaction mechanism, the pathway by which the reaction occurs.
- The slowest step in a reaction mechanism is the rate-determining step. It determines the rate law.
- A catalyst is a substance that speeds up a reaction without being consumed in the reaction.
- A homogeneous catalyst is in the same phase as the reactants, whereas a heterogeneous catalyst is in a different phase from the reactants.

CHAPTER 14

# Thermodynamics

**IN THIS CHAPTER**

In this chapter, the following AP topics are covered:

6.1 Endothermic and Exothermic Processes
6.2 Energy Diagrams
6.3 Heat Transfer and Thermal Equilibrium
6.4 Heat Capacity and Calorimetry
6.5 Energy of Phase Changes
6.6 Introduction to Enthalpy of Reaction
6.7 Bond Enthalpies
6.8 Enthalpy of Formation
6.9 Hess's Law
9.1 Introduction to Entropy
9.2 Absolute Entropy and Entropy Change
9.3 Gibbs Free Energy and Thermodynamic Favorability
9.4 Thermodynamic and Kinetic Control
9.5 Free Energy and Equilibrium
9.6 Coupled Reactions

**Summary: Thermodynamics** is the study of heat and its transformations. **Thermochemistry** is the part of thermodynamics that deals with changes in heat that take place during chemical processes. We will be describing energy changes in this chapter. Energy can be of two types: kinetic or potential. **Kinetic energy** is energy of motion, while **potential energy** is stored energy. Energy can be converted from one form to another but, unless a nuclear reaction occurs, energy cannot be created or destroyed (Law of Conservation of Energy). We will discuss energy exchanges between a system and the surroundings. The **system** is that part of the universe that we are studying. The system may be a beaker, or it may be Earth, or any other region. The **surroundings** are the rest of the universe.

The most common units of energy used in the study of thermodynamics are the joule and the calorie. The **joule (J)** is defined as:

$$1\ \text{J} = 1\ \text{kg m}^2/\text{s}^2$$

The **calorie** was originally defined as the amount of energy needed to raise the temperature of 1 g of water 1°C. Now it is defined in terms of its relationship to the joule:

$$1\ \text{cal} = 4.184\ \text{J}$$

KEY IDEA

It is important to realize that this is not the same calorie that is commonly associated with food and diets. That is the nutritional Calorie, Cal, which is really a kilocalorie (1 Cal = 1,000 cal).

Most of the variables discussed in this chapter are reported under standard conditions. For thermodynamics, the standard state is the value of the variable when the pressure is 1 atmosphere (1 bar) and, if a solution is involved, the concentration is 1 *M*. While not required, a temperature of 25°C (298 K) is often assumed. A degree symbol (°) is normally added to the variable to indicate that it is standard.

**Keywords and Equations**

$S°$ = standard entropy  $H°$ = standard enthalpy
$G°$ = standard Gibbs free energy  $q$ = heat
$c$ = specific heat capacity
Gas constant, $R = 8.314\ \text{J mol}^{-1}\ \text{K}^{-1}$
$KE$ = kinetic energy  $T$ = temperature
$n$ = moles  $m$ = mass
$\mathbf{M}$ = molar mass

$\Delta S° = \Sigma\, S°\ \text{products} - \Sigma\, S°\ \text{reactants}$

$\Delta H° = \Sigma\, \Delta H_f°\ \text{products} + \Sigma\, \Delta H_f°\ \text{reactants}$

$\Delta G° = \Sigma\, \Delta G_f°\ \text{products} + \Sigma\, \Delta G_f°\ \text{reactants}$

$\Delta G° = \Delta H° - T\Delta S°$

$= -RT \ln K$

$= -nFE°$

$q = mc\Delta T$

## Energy Diagrams

The energy changes for any process may be represented with an energy diagram. Simple processes require simple diagrams and complicated processes require complicated diagrams. The complicated diagrams are only several simple diagrams stacked together. Do not be intimidated by a diagram. A simple diagram is shown in Figure 14.1. If the process involved in this figure is water melting or freezing, State 1 would be ice and State 2 would be liquid water, and the endothermic process would be melting and the exothermic process would be freezing.

## Heat Transfer and Thermal Equilibrium

One fundamental process of thermodynamics is that heat will spontaneously flow from a hot object to a cold object. For example, an ice cube taken from a freezer and placed in a glass will spontaneously warm until it melts, and eventually reach the same temperature as the room where the glass is located.

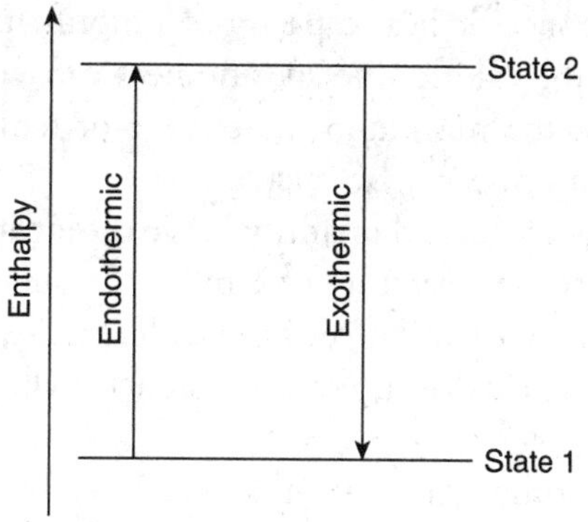


**Figure 14.1 A simplified energy diagram showing an endothermic and an exothermic process.**

At the particle level, there is an exchange in kinetic energy between the particles. Particles at a higher temperature will have a higher average kinetic energy than particles at a lower temperature. No matter what the temperature or the state of matter, the particles present will display a Maxwell–Boltzmann distribution of energies.

Let's reexamine the ice cube in a glass example. When the ice cube is first placed in the glass, the bottom of the ice cube touches the inside bottom of the glass (and possibly one or more sides). This results in glass particles encountering ice particles. The glass particles have a higher average kinetic energy than the water particles. (The form of the matter each is in limits the amount of motion, but not the average kinetic energy.) Glass particles collide with ice particles at the interface of the two with the higher-energy particles transferring some of their kinetic energies to the lower-kinetic-energy particles. This process is known by many names such as "heat transfer," "heat exchange," or "transfer of energy as heat." These higher-energy ice particles transfer some of this energy to ice particles in the interior of the ice. This process continues until the ice begins to melt, and after all the ice has melted, the process will continue with the liquid formed until the water and the glass are at the same temperature. When the water and the glass are at the same temperature, they are said to be in **thermal equilibrium**.

# Calorimetry

**Calorimetry** is the laboratory technique used to measure the heat released or absorbed during a chemical or physical change. The quantity of heat absorbed or released during a chemical or physical change (chemical reaction or phase transition) is represented as $q$ and is proportional to the change in temperature of the system being studied. This system has what is called a **heat capacity**, which is the quantity of heat needed to change the temperature 1 K. It has the form:

$$\text{heat capacity} = q/\Delta T$$

Heat capacity most commonly has units of J/K. The **specific heat capacity (or specific heat)** ($c$) is the quantity of heat needed to raise the temperature of 1 g of a substance 1 K:

$$c = q/(m \times \Delta T) \text{ or } q = cm\Delta T$$

where $m$ is the mass of the substance.

The specific heat capacity commonly has units of J/g K. Because of the original definition of the calorie, the specific heat capacity of water is 4.184 J/g K. If the specific heat capacity, the mass, and the change of temperature are all known, the amount of energy absorbed can easily be calculated.

Another related quantity is the **molar heat capacity** ($C$), the amount of heat needed to change the temperature of 1 mole of a substance by 1 K.

Different substances have different heat capacities. Therefore, adding equal amounts of energy to two different substances will not necessarily produce the same temperature change.

Calorimetry involves the use of a laboratory instrument called a calorimeter. Two types of calorimeter, a simple coffee-cup calorimeter, and a more sophisticated bomb calorimeter, are shown in Figure 14.2. In both, a process is carried out with known amounts of substances and the change in temperature is measured.

The coffee-cup calorimeter can be used to measure the heat changes in reactions or processes that are open to the atmosphere: $q_p$, constant-pressure reactions. These might be reactions that occur in open beakers and the like. This type of calorimeter is also commonly used to measure the specific heats of solids (the system). A known mass of solid is heated to a certain temperature (initial temperature of the solid) and then is added to the calorimeter containing a known mass of water at a known temperature (initial temperature of the water). The final temperature is then measured, allowing us to calculate two $\Delta T$ values, one for the solid ($\Delta T_{solid}$) and one for the water ($\Delta T_{water}$). (Remember, you cannot measure the change in temperature.) We know that the heat lost by the solid (the system) is equal to the heat gained by the surroundings (the water and calorimeter, although for simple coffee-cup calorimetry, the heat gained by the calorimeter is small and is normally ignored):

$$-q_{solid} = q_{water}$$

This is a simple expression of the First Law of Thermodynamics.

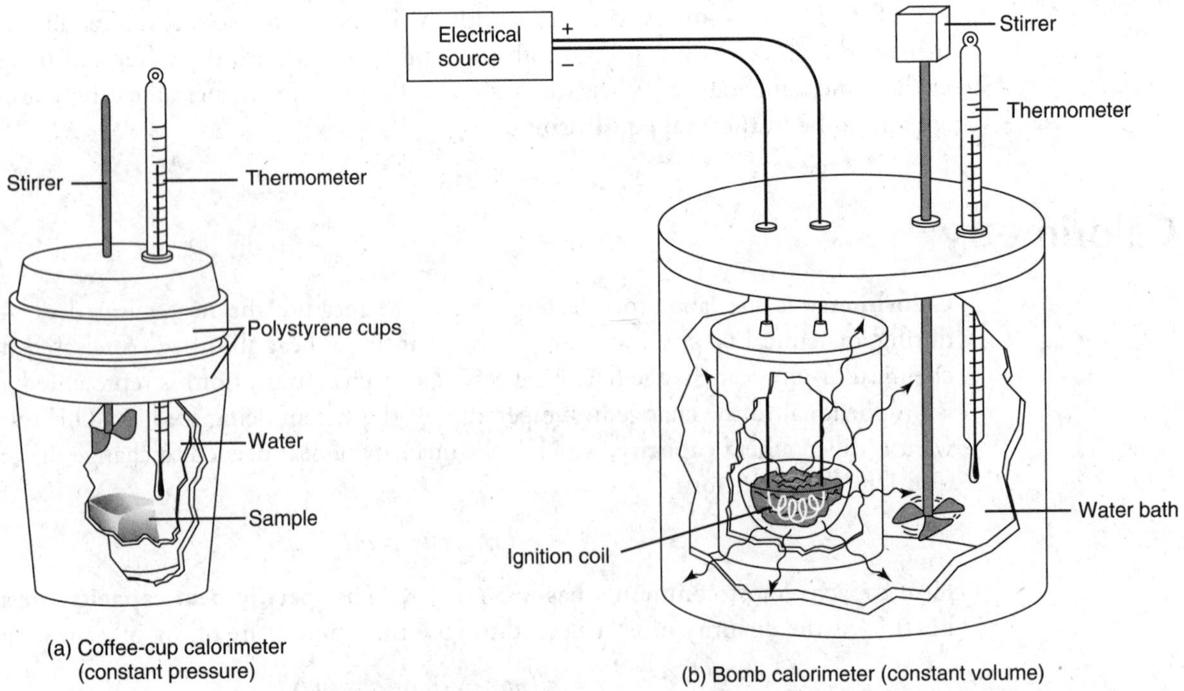


**Figure 14.2 Two types of calorimeters.**

Substituting the mathematical relationship for $q$ gives:

$$-(c_{solid} \times m_{solid} \times \Delta T_{solid}) = c_{water} \times m_{water} \times \Delta T_{water}$$

This equation can then be solved for the specific heat capacity of the solid.

The constant-volume bomb calorimeter is used to measure the energy changes that occur during combustion reactions. A weighed sample of the substance being investigated is placed in the calorimeter and compressed oxygen is added. The sample is ignited by a hot wire, and the temperature change of the calorimeter and a known mass of water is measured. The heat capacity of the calorimeter/water system is sometimes known.

For example, a 1.0155-g sample of ethanol ($C_2H_6O$) was ignited in a bomb calorimeter. The temperature increased by 3.889°C. The heat capacity of the calorimeter was 3.562 kJ/°C, and the calorimeter contained 1.000 kg of water (specific heat capacity = 4.184 J $g^{-1}$ $°C^{-1}$). Find the molar heat of reaction (i.e., kJ/mole) for:

$$2\ C_2H_6O(l) + 7\ O_2(g) \rightarrow 4\ CO_2(g) + 6\ H_2O(l)$$

$$\frac{(3.562\ \text{kJ})}{(°\text{C})}(3.889°\text{C}) = 13.85\ \text{kJ}$$

$$(1.000\ \text{kg})\left(\frac{1{,}000\ \text{g}}{1\ \text{kg}}\right)\left(\frac{4.184\ \text{J}}{\text{g}°\text{C}}\right)\left(\frac{1\ \text{kJ}}{1{,}000\ \text{J}}\right)(3.889°\text{C}) = 16.27\ \text{kJ}$$

$$\text{Total heat} = 13.85\ \text{kJ} + 16.27\ \text{kJ} = 30.12\ \text{kJ}$$

**Note:** The temperature increased so the reaction was exothermic (–).

$$\rightarrow -30.12\ \text{kJ}$$

This is not molar (yet); one more conversion is needed:

$$(1.0155\ \text{g})\frac{(1\ \text{mol})}{(46.08\ \text{g})} = 2.204 \times 10^{-2}\ \text{mol}$$

Answer:

$$\frac{-30.12\ \text{kJ}}{2.204 \times 10^{-2}\ \text{mol}} = -1367\ \text{kJ/mol}$$

Heating increases the energy of the system and cooling lowers the energy of a system. The energy of the system may also be changed by phase transitions or chemical reactions.

## Energy of Phase Changes

Any physical or chemical process will involve energy. The amount of energy and whether the energy enters or leaves the system depends on the process. One category of physical changes includes the phase changes. The most common phase changes are **fusion** (melting), **vaporization**, **sublimation**, **solidification** (freezing), **condensation**, and **deposition**. The processes involved are listed in the Table 14.1.

There are other phase changes, such as the conversion of one solid phase into another; however, they are normally not covered on the AP Exam.

The first three processes in Table 14.1 are endothermic, and the last three processes are exothermic. The endothermic processes are usually listed in tables, while the exothermic

**Table 14.1 Common Types of Phase Changes**

| TYPE | TRANSITION | EXAMPLE |
|---|---|---|
| Fusion | Solid to Liquid | Ice melting |
| Vaporization | Liquid to Gas | Water boiling |
| Sublimation | Solid to Gas | Dry ice "disappearing" |
| Solidification | Liquid to Solid | Water freezing |
| Condensation | Gas to Liquid | Water forming on the side of a glass of ice |
| Deposition | Gas to Solid | The formation of frost on a window |

processes are usually not tabulated. For example, it requires 0.334 kJ of energy to melt a gram of water. The energy released to freeze that same gram of water is 0.334 kJ. The two processes are simply the reverse of each other, and, as with other substances, a simple reversal of a processes only reverses the sign of the energy change. Thus, tables of the endothermic processes become tables of the exothermic processes simply by changing the signs of the values.

The energies associated with each of these processes are normally referred to as the "heat of . . ." or the "enthalpy of . . . ." Thus when water melts, the energy change is known as the heat of fusion or the enthalpy of fusion and symbolizes as $q_{\text{fusion}}$ or $\Delta H_{\text{fusion}}$. The values listed may be per gram or per mole.

In general, the amount of energy involved in a phase transition depends upon the strength of the intermolecular forces involved. For example, the very strong hydrogen bonds in water makes phase changes involving water involve much more energy than phase changes involving other substances. For example, while the heat of fusion of water is 0.334 kJ $g^{-1}$, the heat of fusion of nonpolar nitrogen is 0.0129 kJ $g^{-1}$. Overcoming the intermolecular forces requires energy and reforming these intermolecular forces releases that quantity of energy.

Using water as an example, when ices melts, it requires 6.01 kJ $mol^{-1}$. When water vaporizes, it requires 44.0 kJ $mol^{-1}$. When ice sublimes, it requires 51.1 kJ $mol^{-1}$. These values will vary with temperature. Even though all of the processes involve overcoming hydrogen bonding, the value for fusion is the smallest of the three because only sufficient hydrogen bonds are overcome to break down the structure of ice; some of the hydrogen bonds are still present in water. Vaporization completely overcomes the remaining hydrogen bonds. Sublimation is the sum of these two processes.

## Introduction to Enthalpy of Reaction

Any chemical reaction involves energy. This energy is referred to as the Heat of Reaction or the Enthalpy of Reaction (normally in molar terms). The quantity of energy involved is often determined using a calorimeter. It is possible to add this information to a chemical reaction to generate a thermochemical equation such as:

$$N_2(g) + 3\ H_2(g) \rightarrow 2\ NH_3(g) \qquad \Delta H^{\circ}_{\text{reaction}} = 91.8 \text{ kJ mol}^{-1}$$

Thermochemical equations may be written for any reaction and are often used in Hess's law problems.

## Bond Enthalpies

The formation of a covalent bond releases energy and breaking that bond requires an equal quantity of energy. These energies are referred to as **bond enthalpies** or bond energies. The energy involved depends upon the elements involved in the bond and upon whether the bond is single, double, or triple. Note: a double bond does not necessarily involve double the energy of a single bond, and a triple bond is not necessarily triple the energy of a single bond. Other factors, such a resonance, will also alter the values. Table 14.2 is a table of average bond enthalpies.

**Table 14.2 Some Average Bond Enthalpies in kJ mol$^{-1}$**

| | | | | | | | | | |
|---|---|---|---|---|---|---|---|---|---|
| Br–Br | 192.5 | C–O | 351 | F–Si | 540. | N–O | 176 |
| Br–C | 276 | C=O* | 781 | H–H | 436.4 | N=O | 607 |
| Br–H | 366.1 | C≡O | 1072 | H–I | 298.3 | O–O | 142 |
| C–C | 347 | C–S | 255 | H–N | 393 | O=O | 498.7 |
| C=C | 615 | C=S | 477 | H–O | 464 | O–P | 350. |
| | | | | | | | |
| C≡C | 812 | Cl–Cl | 242.7 | H–P | 326 | O=P | 502 |
| C–Cl | 331 | Cl–H | 431.9 | H–S | 340. | O–S | 347 |
| C–F | 439 | Cl–O | 205 | I–I | 151.0 | O=S | 469 |
| C–H | 414 | Cl–P | 330. | I–P | 215 | O–Si | 370. |
| C–I | 240. | Cl–S | 250. | I–O | 200. | P–P | 215 |
| | | | | | | | |
| C–N | 293 | F–F | 150.6 | N–N | 159 | P=P | 489 |
| C=N | 615 | F–H | 568.2 | N=N | 418 | P–S | 230. |
| C≡N | 891 | F–N | 272 | N≡N | 941.4 | S–S | 215 |
| F–O | 185 | | | | | | |

*C=O 799 in $CO_2$

To determine the enthalpy change from bond enthalpies, use the following equation:

$$\Delta H_{\text{reaction}} = \Sigma \text{ bonds broken} - \Sigma \text{ bonds formed}$$

Let's use bond enthalpies in the following example.

What is the enthalpy change for the following reaction, which is used in the Born–Haber process?

$$N_2(g) + 3\,H_2(g) \rightarrow 2\,NH_3(g)$$

Solution:

Rewriting the reaction emphasizing the bonds gives:

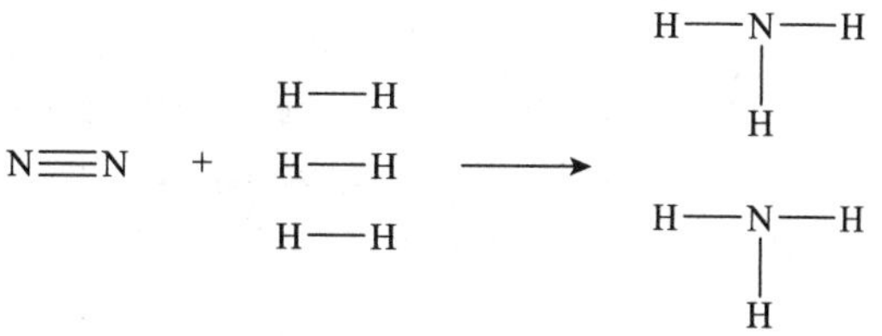

From Table 14.2 the bond enthalpies needed are: N≡N = 941.4, H–H = 436.4, and H–N = 393, all values are in kJ mol$^{-1}$. Using these values in ($\Delta H_{reaction} = \Sigma$ bonds broken – $\Sigma$ bonds formed) gives:

$$\Delta H_{reaction} = [(941.4) + 3\,(436.4)] - \{2\,[3(393)]\} = -107 \text{ kJ mol}^{-1}$$

In this calculation, the first 3 and the 2 are the coefficients from the balanced chemical equation. The second 3 is the number of N–H bonds in each ammonia molecule.

The enthalpy change for this reaction using standard heats of formation is –91.8 kJ mol$^{-1}$. This value is different from the value calculated from the bond enthalpies. A discrepancy is not unusual. Values in bond enthalpy tables are average values, and the bonds in a particular substance may be above or below average. Also, while not present here, resonance will yield a discrepancy with resonance increasing the stability. So why use bond enthalpies to determine the enthalpy of reaction? One reason is that heat of reaction data may be lacking for one or more substances involved in a reaction; therefore, bond enthalpies are the only option. Data is often lacking for newly discovered materials.

## Laws of Thermodynamics

The **First Law of Thermodynamics** states that the total energy of the universe is constant. This is simply the Law of Conservation of Energy. This can be mathematically stated as:

$$\Delta E_{universe} = \Delta E_{system} + \Delta E_{surroundings} = 0$$

The Second Law of Thermodynamics involves a term called entropy. **Entropy (*S*)** is related to the disorder of a system. The **Second Law of Thermodynamics** states that all processes that occur spontaneously move in the direction of an increase in entropy of the universe (system + surroundings). Mathematically, this can be stated as:

$$\Delta S_{universe} = \Delta S_{system} = \Delta S_{surroundings} > 0 \qquad \text{for a spontaneous process}$$

For a reversible process, $\Delta S_{universe} = 0$. The qualitative entropy change (increase or decrease of entropy) for a system can sometimes be determined using a few simple rules:

1. Entropy increases when the number of molecules increases during a reaction.
2. Entropy increases with an increase in temperature.
3. Entropy increases when a gas is formed from a liquid or solid.
4. Entropy increases when a liquid is formed from a solid.
5. Entropy increases when the volume increases.
6. Entropy increases when a chemical reaction increases the number of moles of gas.

Reversing any of these processes results in a decrease in entropy.

Let us now look at some applications of these first two laws of thermodynamics.

## Hess's Law

### Enthalpies

KEY IDEA

Chemists study reactions under a variety of conditions, such as reactions that occur at constant pressure. During the discussion of the coffee-cup calorimeter, the heat change at constant pressure was defined as $q_p$. Because this constant-pressure situation is so common in chemistry, a special thermodynamic term is used to describe this energy: enthalpy. The **enthalpy change**, $\Delta H$, is equal to the heat gained or lost by the system under constant-pressure conditions. The following sign conventions apply:

If $\Delta H > 0$, the reaction is endothermic.

If $\Delta H < 0$, the reaction is exothermic.

If a reaction is involved, $\Delta H$ is sometimes indicated as $\Delta H_{reaction}$. $\Delta H$ is often given in association with a specific process. For example, the enthalpy change associated with the formation of water from hydrogen and oxygen gases can be shown in this fashion:

$$H_2(g) + 1/2\ O_2(g) \rightarrow H_2O(g) \qquad \Delta H = -241.8\ kJ$$

The negative sign indicates that this reaction for the formation of water is exothermic. This value of $\Delta H$ is for the formation of 1 mol of water. If 2 mol were produced, $\Delta H$ would be twice this value or –483.6 kJ. The techniques developed in working reaction stoichiometry problems (see Chapter 6, Stoichiometry) also apply here. In addition, thermochemical equations, such as this one, may contain fractions because these equations are restricted to moles and never molecules. A fraction of a molecule is not possible, but a fraction of a mole is allowed.

If the previous reaction for the formation of water were reversed, the sign of $\Delta H$ would be reversed. That would indicate that it would take 483.6 kJ of energy to decompose 2 moles of water. This would then become an endothermic process.

$\Delta H$ is dependent upon the state of matter. The enthalpy change would be different for the formation of liquid water instead of gaseous water and a third value would apply if ice were formed instead of liquid or gaseous water.

$\Delta H$ can also indicate whether a reaction will be spontaneous. A negative (exothermic) value of $\Delta H$ is associated with a spontaneous reaction. However, in many reactions this is not the case. There is another factor to consider in predicting a reaction's spontaneity. We will cover this other factor a little later in this chapter.

Enthalpies of reaction can be measured using a calorimeter. However, they can also be calculated in other ways. **Hess's law** states that if a reaction occurs in a series of steps, then the enthalpy change for the overall reaction is simply the sum of the enthalpy changes of the individual steps. If, in adding the equations of the steps together, it is necessary to reverse one of the given reactions, then the sign of $\Delta H$ must also be reversed. Also, be very careful of the reaction stoichiometry. The value of an individual $\Delta H$ may need to be adjusted.

It doesn't matter whether the steps used are the actual steps in the mechanism of the reaction, because $\Delta H_{reaction}$ ($\Delta H_{rxn}$) is a **state function**, a function that doesn't depend on the pathway, but only on the initial and final states.

Let's see how Hess's law can be applied, given the following information:

One step in the Ostwald process to produce nitric acid is the combustion of ammonia in the presence of a platinum catalyst. The reaction is:

$$4\ NH_3(g) + 5\ O_2(g) \rightarrow 4\ NO(g) + 6\ H_2O(g)$$

Use the following thermodynamic equations and Hess's law to determine the heat of reaction for this process.

$$1/2\ N_2(g) + 1/2\ O_2 \rightarrow NO(g) \qquad \Delta H = 90.3\ kJ$$

$$1/2\ N_2(g) + 3/2\ H_2(g) \rightarrow NH_3(g) \qquad \Delta H = -45.9\ kJ$$

$$2\ H_2(g) + O_2(g) \rightarrow 2\ H_2O(g) \qquad \Delta H = -483.6\ kJ$$

Answer:
It is necessary to manipulate the three given equations so that they sum to the desired equation. To do this, the first equation must be multiplied by 4, which will also multiply the enthalpy change by 4. The second equation will need to be reversed (reversing the sign of its $\Delta H$), and it will also be necessary to multiply the reaction and enthalpy change by 4. Finally, multiply the third equation and its enthalpy change by 3. In terms of the reactions, these steps are:

$$4[1/2\ N_2(g) + 1/2\ O_2 \rightarrow NO(g)] \qquad \Delta H = 4[90.3\ kJ]$$

$$4[NH_3(g) \rightarrow 1/2\ N_2(g) + 3/2\ H_2(g)] \qquad \Delta H = 4[-(-45.9\ kJ)]$$

$$3[2\ H_2(g) + O_2(g) \rightarrow 2\ H_2O(g)] \qquad \Delta H = 3[-483.6\ kJ]$$

Or

$$2\ N_2(g) + 2\ O_2 \rightarrow 4\ NO(g)] \qquad \Delta H = 361.2\ kJ$$

$$4\ NH_3(g) \rightarrow 2\ N_2(g) + 6\ H_2(g) \qquad \Delta H = 183.6\ kJ$$

$$6\ H_2(g) + 3\ O_2(g) \rightarrow 6\ H_2O(g)] \qquad \Delta H = -1450.8\ kJ$$

Equal amounts of anything appearing on opposites sides of the reaction arrow will cancel, and if they are on the side, they will sum. This gives:

$$\cancel{2\ N_2(g)} + 2\ O_2 \rightarrow 4\ NO(g)] \qquad \Delta H = 361.2\ kJ$$

$$4\ NH_3(g) \rightarrow \cancel{2\ N_2(g)} + \cancel{6\ H_2(g)} \qquad \Delta H = 183.6\ kJ$$

$$\cancel{6\ H_2(g)} + 3\ O_2(g) \rightarrow 6\ H_2O(g)] \qquad \Delta H = -1450.8\ kJ$$

Summing the equations and the enthalpy values leaves:

$$4\ NH_3(g) + 5\ O_2(g) \rightarrow 4\ NO(g) + 6\ H_2O(g) \qquad \Delta H = -906.0\ kJ$$

## Enthalpies of Formation

KEY IDEA

Enthalpies of reaction can also be calculated from individual enthalpies of formation (or heats of formation), $\Delta H_f$ for the reactants and products. Because the temperature, pressure, and state of the substance will cause these enthalpies to vary, it is common to use a standard state convention. For gases, the standard state is 1 atm pressure. For a substance in an aqueous solution, the standard state is 1 molar concentration. And, for a pure substance (compound or element), the standard state is the most stable form at 1 atm pressure and 25°C. A degree symbol to the right of the $H$ indicates a standard state, $\Delta H°$. The **standard enthalpy of formation** of a substance ($\Delta H_f^\circ$) is the change in enthalpy when 1 mole of the substance is formed from its elements when all substances are in their standard states. There are tables containing this information in the form of standard heats of formation ($\Delta H_f^\circ$). These values are for the formation of ONE mole of a substance from the ELEMENTS under standard conditions. In a table of $\Delta H_f^\circ$ values, there would be an entry such as $H_2O(g) = -241.8$ kJ. If the conditions are not standard, the enthalpy will be different than the standard value.

$\Delta H_f^\circ$ of an element in its standard state is zero.

$\Delta H_{f\ rxn}^\circ$ can be determined from the tabulated $\Delta H_f^\circ$ of the individual reactants and products. It is the sum of the $\Delta H_f^\circ$ of the products minus the sum of the $\Delta H_f^\circ$ of the reactants:

$$\Delta H°_{rxn} = \Sigma\ \Delta H_f^\circ \text{ products} + \Sigma\ \Delta H_f^\circ \text{ reactants}$$

In using this equation be sure to consider the number of moles of each, because $\Delta H_f^\circ$ for the individual compounds refers to the formation of 1 mole.

For example, let's use standard enthalpies of formation to calculate $\Delta H_{rxn}$ for:

$$4\ NH_3(g) + 5\ O_2(g) \rightarrow 4\ NO(g) + 6\ H_2O(g)$$

Answer:

$$\Delta H_{rxn} = \{4[\Delta H_f^\circ\ NO(g)] + 6[\Delta H_f^\circ\ H_2O(g)]\} - \{[4\ \Delta H_f^\circ\ NH_3(g)] + 5[\Delta H_f^\circ\ O_2(g)]\}$$

Using tabulated standard enthalpies of formation gives:

$$\Delta H_{rxn} = [4(90.3\ kJ) + 6(-241.8\ kJ)] - [4(-45.9\ kJ) + 5(0.0)] = -906.0\ kJ$$

TIP

People commonly forget to subtract *all* the reactants from the products.

The values of $\Delta H_f^\circ$ will be given to you on the AP Exam, or you will be asked to stop before putting the numbers into the problem. To save time, the value for all elements in their standard states is defined as zero.

An alternative means of estimating the heat of reaction is to take the sum of the average bond energies of the reactant molecules and subtract the sum of the average bond energies of the product molecules.

## Entropies

In much the same way as $\Delta Hf$ was determined, the **standard molar entropies ($S^\circ$)** of elements and compounds can be tabulated. The standard molar entropy is the entropy associated with 1 mole of a substance in its standard state. Entropies are also tabulated, but unlike enthalpies, the entropies of elements are not zero. For a reaction, the standard entropy change is calculated in the same way as the enthalpies of reaction:

$$\Delta S^\circ \text{ reaction} = \Sigma\ S^\circ \text{ products} - \Sigma\ S^\circ \text{ reactants}$$

TIP

Calculate $\Delta S^\circ$ for the following reaction. If you do not have a table of $S^\circ$ values, just set up the problems.

**Note: these are thermochemical equations, so fractions are allowed.**

$$2\ NH_3(g) + 5/2\ O_2(g) \rightarrow 2\ NO(g) + 3\ H_2O(g)$$

Answer:

$$2\ NH_3(g) + 5/2\ O_2(g) \rightarrow 2\ NO(g) + 3\ H_2O(g)$$

$$[192.7 \qquad 205.0 \qquad 210.6 \qquad 188.7]\ J\ mol^{-1}\ K^{-1}$$

$$\Delta S^\circ = \{2[S^\circ\ NO(g)] + 3[S^\circ\ H_2O(g)]\} - \{2[S^\circ\ NH_3(g)] + 5/2[S^\circ\ O_2(g)]\}$$

$$\Delta S^\circ = \{2[210.6\ J\ mol^{-1}\ K^{-1}] + 3[188.7\ J\ mol^{-1}\ K^{-1}]\} - \{2[192.7\ J\ mol^{-1}\ K^{-1}] + 5/2[205.0\ J\ mol^{-1}\ K^{-1}]\}$$

$$\Delta S^\circ = 89.4\ J\ mol^{-1}\ K^{-1}$$

One of the goals of chemists is to be able to predict if a reaction will be spontaneous or nonspontaneous. Some general guidelines for a spontaneous reaction have already been presented (negative $\Delta H$ and positive $\Delta S$), but neither is a reliable predictor by itself. Temperature also plays a part. A thermodynamic factor that combines the entropy, enthalpy, and temperature of a process is the best indicator of spontaneity. This factor is called the Gibbs free energy.

## Gibbs Free Energy

The **Gibbs free energy** (***G***) is a thermodynamic function that combines the enthalpy, entropy, and temperature:

$$G = H - TS, \text{ where } T \text{ is the Kelvin temperature}$$

Like most thermodynamic functions, only the change in Gibbs free energy can be measured, so the relationship becomes:

$$\Delta G = \Delta H - T\Delta S$$

KEY IDEA

- If $\Delta G > 0$, the reaction is not spontaneous (thermodynamically unfavored); energy must be supplied to cause the reaction to occur.
- If $\Delta G < 0$, the reaction is spontaneous (thermodynamically favored).
- If $\Delta G = 0$, the reaction is at equilibrium (neither spontaneous nor nonspontaneous).

Thermodynamic favorability may also be predicted by using the following table.

| $\Delta H^\circ$ | $\Delta S^\circ$ | SYMBOLS | $\Delta G^\circ < 0$ (favorable at) |
|---|---|---|---|
| $< 0$ | $> 0$ | $< >$ | Any $T$ |
| $> 0$ | $< 0$ | $> <$ | No $T$ |
| $> 0$ | $> 0$ | $> >$ | High $T$ |
| $< 0$ | $< 0$ | $< <$ | Low $T$ |

If there is a $\Delta G$ associated with a reaction and that reaction is then reversed, the sign of $\Delta G$ also reverses.

Just like with the enthalpy and entropy, the standard Gibbs free energy change, $\Delta G^\circ$, is calculated:

$$\Delta G^\circ = \Sigma\, \Delta G_f^\circ \text{ products} + \Sigma\, \Delta G_f^\circ \text{ reactants}$$

$\Delta G_f^\circ$ of an element in its standard state is zero.

$\Delta G^\circ$ for a reaction may also be calculated by using the standard enthalpy and standard entropy of reaction:

$$\Delta G^\circ = \Delta H^\circ_{rxn} - T\Delta S^\circ_{rxn}$$

Calculate $\Delta G^\circ$ for:

$$2\ NH_3(g) + 5/2\ O_2(g) \rightarrow 2\ NO(g) + 3\ H_2O(g)$$

(If you do not have a table of $\Delta G^\circ$ values, just set up the problems.)

Answer:

$$2\ NH_3(g) + 5/2\ O_2(g) \rightarrow 2\ NO(g) + 3\ H_2O(g)$$

$$[-16.4 \qquad 0.0 \qquad 86.6 \qquad -288.6]\ \text{kJ mol}^{-1}$$

$$\Delta G^\circ = \{2[\Delta G_f^\circ\ NO(g)] + 3[\Delta G_f^\circ\ H_2O(g)]\} - \{2[\Delta G_f^\circ\ NH_3(g)] + 5/2[\Delta G_f^\circ\ O_2(g)]\}$$

$$\Delta G^\circ = \{2[86.6\ \text{kJ mol}^{-1}] + 3[-288.6\ \text{kJ mol}^{-1}]\} - \{2[-16.4\ \text{kJ mol}^{-1}] + 5/2[0.0\ \text{kJ mol}^{-1}]\}$$

$$\Delta G^\circ = -659.8\ \text{J mol}^{-1}\ \text{K}^{-1}$$

## Thermodynamics and Equilibrium

Thus far, we have considered only situations under standard conditions. But how do we cope with nonstandard conditions? The change in Gibbs free energy under nonstandard conditions is:

$$\Delta G = \Delta G^\circ + RT \ln Q = \Delta G^\circ + 2.303\ RT \log Q$$

$Q$ is the activity quotient, products over reactants (see Chapter 15, Equilibrium). This equation allows the calculation of $\Delta G$ in those situations in which the concentrations or pressures are not 1.

Note that $Q$, when at equilibrium, becomes $K$, and $\Delta G = 0$. This equation gives us a way to calculate the equilibrium constant, $K$, from a knowledge of the standard Gibbs free energy of the reaction and the temperature. Substituting $K$ for $Q$, entering $\Delta G = 0$, and rearranging converts the preceding equation to:

$$\Delta G^\circ = -RT \ln K = -2.303\ RT \log K$$

This equation sometimes appears in another form:

$$K = e^{-\Delta G^\circ / RT}$$

For example, calculate $\Delta G^\circ$ for:

$$HOCN(aq) \leftrightarrows H^+(aq) + OCN^-(aq) \qquad K = 3.5 \times 10^{-4}$$

Note: ° = 298 K

Answer:

$$\begin{aligned}\Delta G^\circ &= -RT \ln K \\ &= \frac{-(8.314\ J)}{(mol\ K)}(298\ K) \ln 3.5 \times 10^{-4} \\ &= 2.0 \times 10^4\ J/mol\end{aligned}$$

## Thermodynamic and Kinetic Control

Why do some reactions not occur when they are thermodynamically favored? The energy diagram in Figure 13.3 for an exothermic reaction offers an explanation. This reaction is thermodynamically favored; however, the reactants must get over the barrier (activation energy) to reach the products. The higher the barrier is, the slower the reaction will be. An extremely high barrier will lead to an extremely slow reaction. A reaction with an extremely high activation energy is considered to be under kinetic control.

A high activation energy is the primary reason for a reaction to be under kinetic control. It is improper to assume the system is in equilibrium simply because there is no noticeable change in a reasonable time.

## Coupled Reactions

A thermodynamically unfavorable process may be forced to occur through coupled reactions. There are many examples of coupled reactions in biological systems.

The following example illustrates coupled reactions.

The decomposition of $PbCO_3(s)$ has a positive $\Delta G^\circ_{reaction}$; therefore, it is not thermodynamically favored.

$$PbCO_3(s) \leftrightarrows PbO(s) + CO_2(g) \qquad \Delta G^\circ_{reaction} = 43.1 \text{ kJ mol}^{-1}$$

The combustion of carbon has a negative $\Delta G^\circ_{reaction}$; therefore, it is a thermodynamically favored process.

$$C(s) + O_2(g) \leftrightarrows CO_2(g) \qquad \Delta G^\circ_{reaction} = -394.4 \text{ kJ mol}^{-1}$$

If these two processes are coupled, a thermodynamically favored reaction results.

$$PbCO_3(s) + C(s) + O_2(g) \leftrightarrows PbO(g) + 2\,CO_2(g) \qquad \Delta G^\circ_{reaction} = -351.3 \text{ kJ mol}^{-1}$$

A coupled reaction may also come from combining a thermodynamically unfavored process with some other energy source. Examples are using an external power source to charge a battery or using sunlight to drive photosynthesis.

## Experiments

The most common thermodynamic experiment is a calorimetry experiment. In this experiment, the heat of transition or heat of reaction is determined.

The experiment will require a balance to determine the mass of a sample and possibly a pipet to measure a volume, from which a mass may be calculated using the density. A calorimeter, usually a polystyrene (Styrofoam) cup, is needed to contain the reaction. Finally, a thermometer is required. Tables of heat capacities or specific heats may be provided.

Mass and possible volume measurements, along with the initial and final temperatures, are needed. Remember: you *measure* the initial and final temperature so you can *calculate* the change in temperature.

After the temperature change is calculated, there are several ways to proceed. If the calorimeter contains water, the heat may be calculated by multiplying the specific heat of water (normally given) by the mass of water by the calculated temperature change. The heat capacity of the calorimeter may be calculated by dividing the heat by the temperature change. If a reaction is carried out in the same calorimeter, the heat from that reaction is the difference between the heat with and without a reaction.

Do not forget, the thermometer is part of the surroundings, so if the temperature increases, heat has gone from the system to the thermometer (surroundings), making the process exothermic, and the heat has a negative sign. The opposite is true if the temperature drops.

## Common Mistakes to Avoid

1. Be sure your units cancel, giving you the unit desired in the final answer.
2. Check your significant figures.
3. Don't mix energy units, joules, and calories.
4. Watch your signs in all the thermodynamic calculations. They are extremely important.
5. Don't confuse enthalpy, $\Delta H$, entropy, $\Delta S$, and $\Delta G$.
6. Pay close attention to the state of matter for your reactants and products and choose the appropriate value for use in your calculated entropies and enthalpies.

7. Remember: **products minus reactants.**
8. $\Delta H_f$ and $\Delta G_f$ are for 1 mol of substance. Use appropriate multipliers if needed.
9. $\Delta G_f$ and $\Delta H_f$ for an element in its standard state are zero.
10. All temperatures are in kelvin.
11. When using $\Delta G° = \Delta H°_{rxn} - T\,\Delta S°_{rxn}$, pay attention to your enthalpy and entropy units. Commonly, enthalpies will use kJ and entropies J. This means you will be required to make a J to kJ conversion or a kJ to J conversion.
12. $\Delta T$ is numerically the same in °C and in K. For example, $\Delta T$ going from 0°C (273 K) to 25°C (298 K) is 25°C (25 K).

# ❯ Review Questions

Use these questions to review the content of this chapter and practice for the AP Chemistry Exam. First are 24 multiple-choice questions similar to what you will encounter in Section I of the AP Chemistry Exam. This list includes questions to help you review prior knowledge. Following those is a long free-response question like the ones in Section II of the exam. To make these questions an even more authentic practice for the actual exam, time yourself following the instructions provided.

## Multiple-Choice Questions

Answer the following questions in 35 minutes. You may not use a calculator. You may use the periodic table and the equation sheet at the back of this book.

1. Which of the following is the minimum energy required to initiate a reaction?

(A) free energy
(B) lattice energy
(C) kinetic energy
(D) activation energy

2. What is the minimum energy required to force a nonspontaneous reaction to occur?

(A) free energy
(B) lattice energy
(C) kinetic energy
(D) activation energy

3. A student heats a 25-g sample of lead metal to 65°C. This sample is immediately clamped in contact with a 47-g sample of magnesium metal. The original temperature of the magnesium was 25°C. No heat was lost to the surroundings during the experiment. The specific heat of lead metal is 0.127 J/g °C, and the specific heat of magnesium metal is 1.024 J/g °C. The final temperature of both metals was 27°C. What is one possible conclusion the student might postulate from this experiment?

(A) The lead lost more heat than the magnesium gained.
(B) The lead lost the same amount of heat as the magnesium gained.
(C) The lead lost less heat than the magnesium gained.
(D) The student made an error because the final temperature should be the average (45°C).

4. What is the energy released when gaseous ions combine to form an ionic solid?

(A) free energy
(B) lattice energy
(C) kinetic energy
(D) activation energy

5. $C(s) + O_2(g) \rightarrow CO_2(g)$ $\Delta H = -393.5$ kJ

$H_2(g) + (1/2)\ O_2(g) \rightarrow H_2O(l)$

$\Delta H = -285.8$ kJ

$C_2H_2(g) + (5/2)\ O_2(g) \rightarrow 2\ CO_2(g) + H_2O(l)$

$\Delta H = -1{,}299.8$ kJ

Given this information, find the enthalpy change for $2\ C(s) + H_2(g) \rightarrow C_2H_2(g)$.

(A) 454.0 kJ
(B) –227.0 kJ
(C) 0.0 kJ
(D) 227.0 kJ

6. A 10-g sample of solid mercury metal is sealed inside a well-insulated, rigid container. The temperature inside the container is at the melting point of mercury metal (–38.8°C). The system is well insulated, so it is possible to assume the insulation prevents any energy change with the surroundings. Which of the following is true about the total energy and the entropy of the system after equilibrium has been established in the system?

(A) The total energy increases. The total entropy will increase.
(B) The total energy is constant. The total entropy is constant.
(C) The total energy is constant. The total entropy will decrease.
(D) The total energy is constant. The total entropy will increase.

7. When ammonium chloride dissolves in water, the temperature drops. Which of the following conclusions may be related to this?

(A) Ammonium chloride is more soluble in hot water.
(B) Ammonium chloride produces an ideal solution in water.
(C) The heat of solution for ammonium chloride is exothermic.
(D) Ammonium chloride has a low lattice energy.

8. Which of the following reactions is expected to have the greatest increase in entropy?

(A) $H_2O(g) \rightarrow H_2O(l)$
(B) $2\ KClO_3(s) \rightarrow 2\ KCl(s) + 3\ O_2(g)$
(C) $Ca(s) + H_2(g) \rightarrow CaH_2(s)$
(D) $N_2(g) + 3\ H_2(g) \rightarrow 2\ NH_3(g)$

9. Magnesium metal reacts readily with liquid bromine under standard conditions. Which of the following conclusions may be drawn from this fact?

(A) $K_{eq} < 1$ and $\Delta G° > 0$
(B) $K_{eq} > 1$ and $\Delta G° = 0$
(C) $K_{eq} < 1$ and $\Delta G° < 0$
(D) $K_{eq} > 1$ and $\Delta G° < 0$

10. Which of the following combinations is true when sodium chloride melts?

(A) $\Delta H > 0$ and $\Delta S > 0$
(B) $\Delta H = 0$ and $\Delta S > 0$
(C) $\Delta H > 0$ and $\Delta S < 0$
(D) $\Delta H < 0$ and $\Delta S < 0$

11. Which of the following reactions has a negative entropy change?

(A) $2\ C_2H_6(g) + 7\ O_2(g) \rightarrow 4\ CO_2(g) + 6\ H_2O(g)$
(B) $2\ NH_3(g) \rightarrow N_2(g) + 3\ H_2(g)$
(C) $CaCl_2(s) \rightarrow Ca(s) + Cl_2(g)$
(D) $2\ H_2(g) + O_2(g) \rightarrow 2\ H_2O(l)$

12. A certain reaction is nonspontaneous under standard conditions but becomes spontaneous at higher temperatures. What conclusions may be drawn under standard conditions?

(A) $\Delta H < 0$, $\Delta S > 0$, and $\Delta G > 0$
(B) $\Delta H > 0$, $\Delta S < 0$, and $\Delta G > 0$
(C) $\Delta H > 0$, $\Delta S > 0$, and $\Delta G > 0$
(D) $\Delta H < 0$, $\Delta S < 0$, and $\Delta G > 0$

13. $2\ H_2(g) + O_2(g) \rightarrow 2\ H_2O(l)$

From the table below, determine the enthalpy change for the above reaction.

| BOND | AVERAGE BOND ENERGY (kJ/mol) |
|---|---|
| H–H | 436 |
| O=O | 499 |
| H–O | 464 |

(A) 0 kJ
(B) 485 kJ
(C) –485 kJ
(D) 464 kJ

14. Which of the following reactions is accompanied by the greatest increase in entropy?

(A) $2\ H_2(g) + O_2(g) \rightarrow 2\ H_2O(g)$
(B) $2\ Mn_2O_7(l) \rightarrow 4\ MnO_2(s) + 3\ O_2(g)$
(C) $2\ C(s) + O_2(g) \rightarrow 2\ CO(g)$
(D) $2\ Mg(s) + O_2(g) \rightarrow 2\ MgO(s)$

15. Hydrogen gas burns in oxygen gas according to the following reaction:

$$2\ H_2(g) + O_2(g) \rightarrow 2\ H_2O(l)\ \Delta H = -572\ \text{kJ}$$

What is the energy change when 2.00 moles of water decompose to the elements at constant pressure?

(A) –286 kJ
(B) –572 kJ
(C) +572 kJ
(D) +286 kJ

16. A solution is prepared by dissolving solid ammonium nitrate, $NH_4NO_3$, in water. The initial temperature of the water was 25°C, but after the solid had dissolved, the temperature fell to 20°C. What conclusions may be made about $\Delta H$ and $\Delta S$?

(A) $\Delta H < 0$ and $\Delta S > 0$
(B) $\Delta H > 0$ and $\Delta S > 0$
(C) $\Delta H > 0$ and $\Delta S < 0$
(D) $\Delta H < 0$ and $\Delta S < 0$

17. The temperature increases when lithium sulfate, $Li_2SO_4$, dissolves in water. Which of the following conclusions may be related to this?

(A) Lithium sulfate is less soluble in hot water.
(B) The hydration energies of lithium ions and sulfate ions are very low.
(C) The heat of solution for lithium sulfate is endothermic.
(D) Lithium sulfate solutions are not ideal solutions.

18. Calcium carbonate, $CaCO_3$, decomposes when heated according to the following reaction:

$$CaCO_3(s) \leftrightarrows CaO(s) + CO_2(g)$$

Increasing the temperature shifts the equilibrium to the right. Which of the following is applicable to this reaction?

(A) The reaction is faster at higher temperatures.
(B) The process is enthalpy and entropy driven.
(C) The process is enthalpy driven.
(D) The process is entropy driven.

19. Which of the following combinations is true when ethanol, $C_2H_5OH$, boils?

(A) $\Delta H > 0$ and $\Delta S > 0$
(B) $\Delta H = 0$ and $\Delta S > 0$
(C) $\Delta H > 0$ and $\Delta S < 0$
(D) $\Delta H < 0$ and $\Delta S < 0$

**Use the following information to answer questions 20–23:**

$Xe(g) + 2\ F_2(g) \leftrightarrows XeF_4(g)$ $\Delta H° = -262$ kJ mol$^{-1}$

The above reaction is the standard heat of formation reaction for xenon tetrafluoride.

**20.** For this reaction, what can be said about the value of $\Delta S°$?

(A) $\Delta S°$ is near zero.
(B) $\Delta S°$ is positive.
(C) $\Delta S°$ is negative.
(D) The reaction does not involve $\Delta S°$.

**21.** This reaction is spontaneous under standard conditions. What will happen to the value of $\Delta G$ for this reaction when the temperature increases if you assume $\Delta S$ is negative?

(A) $\Delta G$ will decrease.
(B) $\Delta G$ will increase.
(C) $\Delta G$ will remain the same.
(D) Only $\Delta H_f°$ is important; $\Delta G$ does not matter.

**22.** What will happen to the value of *K* for this reaction as the temperature increases? Assume that $\Delta G$ for this reaction is increasing.

(A) *K* will decrease.
(B) *K* will increase.
(C) *K* will approach 1.
(D) *K* is a constant and will not change

**23.** If you have a table of standard thermodynamic values for the substances involved in the reaction, how might the temperature at which the reaction changes from spontaneous to nonspontaneous be predicted?

(A) It is impossible to predict the temperature.
(B) The change will occur at 298 K (25°C).
(C) $\Delta G$ cannot change from spontaneous to nonspontaneous.
(D) At this point, $\Delta G = 0$, which leads to $T = \Delta H/\Delta S$.

**24.** Both carbon monoxide, CO, and nitrogen, $N_2$, have about the same molar mass (28 g mol$^{-1}$). Both molecules have a triple bond between the two atoms. At absolute zero, the entropy of CO(s) is greater than 4 J mol$^{-1}$ K$^{-1}$, and that of $N_2$(s) is 0 J mol$^{-1}$ K$^{-1}$. Why is the standard entropy of CO(g) greater than that of $N_2$(g)?

(A) CO is more disordered than $N_2$.
(B) The presence of carbon leads to greater entropy.
(C) Oxygen is more electronegative than nitrogen.
(D) The triple bond in CO is polar, whereas the triple bond in $N_2$ is nonpolar.

## › Answers and Explanations

**1. D**—You may wish to review the Kinetics chapter if you have forgotten what the activation energy is.

**2. A**—The free energy is the minimum energy required for a nonspontaneous reaction to occur and the maximum energy available from a spontaneous reaction.

**3. B**—The Law of Conservation of Energy (First Law of Thermodynamics) says the amount of heat lost must be equal to the heat gained. For each metal, the heat (*q*) involved is determined from $q = mc\Delta T$. The hot metal will lose heat ($-q$), and the cold metal will gain heat ($+q$).

**4. B**—This process is the reverse of the lattice energy definition.

**5. D**—This is a Hess's law problem. Double the first equation given (and $\Delta H$). Use the second equation as is. Reverse the third equation (changing the sign of $\Delta H$). Cancel equal amounts of each substance that appears on each side of the reaction arrow and add the results. If the sum exactly matches the desired equation, the sum of the $\Delta H$ values is the answer. If you do not get an exact match, you made an error.

$2[C(s) + O_2(g) \rightarrow CO_2(g)]$ $2\ (-393.5\ kJ)$
$H_2(g) + (1/2)\ O_2(g) \rightarrow H_2O(l)$ $-285.8$ kJ
$2\ CO_2(g) + H_2O(l) \rightarrow C_2H_2(g) + (5/2)\ O_2(g)$ $-(-1{,}299.8\ kJ)$

$2\ C(s) + H_2(g) \rightarrow C_2H_2(g)$ 227.0 kJ

Simple rounding to the nearest 100 kJ gives 200 kJ.

**6. D**—The system is insulated, and no work can be done on or by the system (rigid container); thus, the energy is constant. At the melting point, some of the mercury will spontaneously melt; changing from a solid to a liquid increases the entropy.

**7. A**—The process is endothermic (the ammonium chloride is absorbing heat to cool the water). Endothermic processes are "helped" by higher temperatures. C and possibly D would give an increase in temperature. There is insufficient information about B. Do not forget, the thermometer measuring the temperature is part of the surroundings and not part of the system.

**8. B**—The reaction showing the greatest increase in the number of moles of gas will show the greatest entropy increase. If no gases are present, then the greatest increase in the number of moles of liquid would yield the greatest increase.

**9. D**—The reaction occurs readily; therefore, it must be a spontaneous reaction. If the reaction is spontaneous, then $\Delta G° < 0$. If the free energy is negative free energy, then $K$ must be large ($> 1$). (The calculation would be $\Delta G = -RT \ln K_{eq}$.)

**10. A**—Heat is required to melt something ($\Delta H > 0$). A transformation from a solid to a liquid gives an increase in entropy ($\Delta S > 0$).

**11. D**—This equation has an overall decrease in the amount of gas present (decreases entropy). The other answers produce more gas (increasing entropy).

**12. C**—Nonspontaneous means that $\Delta G > 0$. Since the reaction becomes spontaneous, the sign must change. Recall: $\Delta G = \Delta H - T\Delta S$ (given in the exam booklet). The sign change at higher temperature means that the entropy term (with $\Delta S > 0$) must become more negative than the enthalpy term ($\Delta H > 0$).

**13. C**—The calculation is [2(436 kJ) + 499 kJ] – {2[2(464 kJ)]} = –485 kJ. (Using bond energies $\Delta H = \Sigma$ bonds broken – $\Sigma$ bonds formed.)

**14. B**—This is the reaction that has the greatest increase in the number of moles of gas.

**15. C**—The decomposition of water is the reverse of the reaction shown; therefore, the enthalpy change is reversed (positive instead of negative). The amount of water decomposing is 2.00 moles, which is the same amount of water in the reaction.

**16. B**—Dissolving almost always has $\Delta S > 0$. A decrease in temperature means the process has $\Delta H > 0$ (the system is absorbing energy from the surroundings). The thermometer measuring the temperature is part of the surroundings.

**17. A**—The increase in temperature of the solution indicates that the process is exothermic. An exothermic process will shift toward the starting materials (solid lithium sulfate and water) when heated.

**18. D**—This is a thermodynamic problem, so a kinetics answer (A) is not applicable. For the reaction to occur, $\Delta G$ must be negative. It is possible to determine $\Delta G$ from $\Delta G = \Delta H - T\Delta S$. Since heating causes the equilibrium to shift to the right, $\Delta H$ must be positive. A positive $\Delta H$ will not lead to a negative $\Delta G$; therefore, enthalpy cannot be the driving force (eliminating B and C). Thus, the reaction must be entropy driven because $\Delta S$ is positive owing to the release of the carbon dioxide gas.

**19. A**—Heat is required to boil a substance; therefore, $\Delta H$ is greater than 0. A transformation from a liquid to a gas gives an increase in entropy ($\Delta S > 0$).

**20. C**—The value is negative because there is a decrease in the number of moles of gas during the reaction.

**21. B**—The key relationship is $\Delta G = \Delta H - T\Delta S$. From this relationship, it is apparent that the value of $\Delta G$ will increase (become less negative) as the temperature increases. In general, both $\Delta H$ and $\Delta S$ are relatively constant with respect to small temperature changes. As the temperature increases, the value of the entropy term, $T\Delta S$, becomes more negative. The negative sign in front of this term leads to a positive contribution. The value of $\Delta G$ will first become less negative (more positive) and eventually become positive (no longer spontaneous).

**22. A**—Recall that $\Delta G = -RT \ln K$. As the value of $\Delta G$ increases, the value of $K$ will decrease.

23. D—Recalling $\Delta G = \Delta H - T\Delta S$, it is possible to determine $\Delta G$, $\Delta H$, and $\Delta S$ from the standard thermodynamic values. The change from spontaneous to nonspontaneous occurs when $\Delta G = 0$. Rearranging this equation and setting $\Delta G = 0$ gives $T = \Delta H/\Delta S$, which will allow the temperature to be estimated.

24. A—Carbon monoxide exhibits two molecular orientations, CO and OC, while the orientations of $N_2$ both appear the same. For this reason, there are more states (disorder and higher entropy) present in solid CO.

## › Free-Response Question

You have 10 minutes to answer the following question. You may use a calculator and the tables in the back of the book.

### Question

$$Xe(g) + 3\ F_2(g) \leftrightarrows XeF_6(g)$$

Under standard conditions, the enthalpy change for the above reaction going from left to right (forward reaction) is $\Delta H° = -294$ kJ.

(a) In the above reaction, is the value of $\Delta S°$ positive or negative? Justify your conclusion.

(b) The above reaction is spontaneous under standard conditions. Predict what will happen to $\Delta G$ for this reaction as the temperature is increased. Justify your prediction.

(c) Will the value of $K$ remain the same, increase, or decrease as the temperature increases? Justify your prediction.

(d) Show how the temperature at which the reaction changes from spontaneous to nonspontaneous can be predicted. What additional information is necessary?

(e) Draw the Lewis structure of $XeF_6$.

## › Answer and Explanation

(a) The value is negative. The decrease in the number of moles of gas (from 4 to 1) during the reaction means there is a decrease in entropy.

Give yourself 1 point if you predicted negative. Give yourself 1 point for discussing the decreasing number of moles of gas. You may get this point even if you did not get the first point.

(b) Recall that $\Delta G = \Delta H - T\Delta S$. (This equation is given on the equation page of the AP Exam.) The value of $\Delta G$ will increase (become less negative) as the temperature is increased.

Give yourself 1 point for this answer if it is obvious that increasing means less negative.

In general, both $\Delta H$ and $\Delta S$ are relatively constant with respect to small temperature changes. As the temperature increases, the value of the entropy term, $T\Delta S$, becomes more negative. The negative sign in front of this term leads to a positive contribution. The value of $\Delta G$ will first become less negative (more positive) and eventually become positive (no longer spontaneous).

Give yourself 1 point for the $\Delta G = \Delta H - T\Delta S$ argument even if you did not get the first point.

(c) Recall that $\Delta G = -RT \ln K$. (This equation is given on the equation page of the AP Exam.) The value of $K$ will decrease as the temperature increases (due to the negative sign).

You get 1 point for this answer.

As the value of $\Delta G$ increases [see part (b)], the value of $K$ will decrease. You get 1 point for using $\Delta G = -RT \ln K$ in your discussion.

If you got the justification for part (b) wrong, and you used the same argument here, you will not be penalized twice. You still get your point here.

(d) The reaction changes from spontaneous to nonspontaneous when $\Delta G = 0$.

Recall that $\Delta G = \Delta H - T\Delta S$ (given on exam).

Rearranging this equation to $T = -\Delta H/\Delta S$ allows the temperature to be estimated.

This rearranged equation is worth 1 point. To do the calculation, the value of $\Delta S$ is the additional information needed. Give yourself 1 point for this.

(e) The Lewis structure is

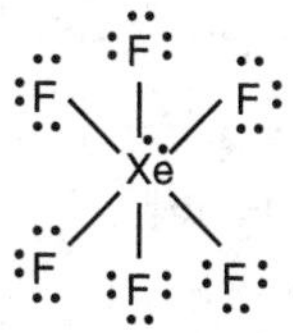


The complete Lewis structure, with all fluorine atoms attached to the xenon atom, is worth 2 points. If all the fluorine atoms do not have an octet of electrons, the structure is worth only 1 point. Even if you have not worked a Lewis structure of this type, you should know that fluorine will follow the octet rule. This illustrates the diversity of the free-response questions on the AP Exam.

## ❯ Rapid Review

- Thermodynamics is the study of heat and its transformations.
- Kinetic energy is energy of motion, while potential energy is stored energy.
- The common units of energy are the joule, J, and the calorie, cal.
- A calorimeter is used to measure the heat released or absorbed during a chemical or physical change. Know how a calorimeter works.
- The specific heat capacity is the amount of heat needed to change the temperature of 1 g of a substance by 1 K, while the molar heat capacity is the heat capacity per mole.
- The heat lost by the system in calorimetry is equal to the heat gained by the surroundings.
- The specific heat ($c$) of a solid can be calculated by: $-(c_{\text{solid}} \times m_{\text{solid}} \times \Delta T_{\text{solid}}) = c_{\text{water}} \times m_{\text{water}} \times \Delta T_{\text{water}}$ or by $q = cm\Delta T$.
- The First Law of Thermodynamics states that the total energy of the universe is constant. (Energy is neither created nor destroyed.)
- The Second Law of Thermodynamics states that all spontaneous processes move in a way that increases the entropy (disorder) of the universe.

- The enthalpy change, $\Delta H$, is equal to the heat lost or gained by the system under constant-pressure conditions.
- $\Delta H$ values are associated with a specific reaction. If that reaction is reversed, the sign of $\Delta H$ changes. If one must use a multiplier on the reaction, the multiplier must also be applied to the $\Delta H$ value.
- The standard enthalpy of formation of a compound, $\Delta H_f^\circ$, is the enthalpy change when 1 mole of the substance is formed from its elements and all substances are in their standard states.
- The standard enthalpy of formation of an element in its standard state is zero.
- $\Delta H^\circ_{rxn} = \Sigma\, \Delta H_f^\circ$ products $- \Sigma\, \Delta H_f^\circ$ reactants. Know how to apply this equation.
- $\Delta H^\circ_{rxn}$ is usually negative for a spontaneous reaction.
- $\Delta S^\circ = \Sigma\, S^\circ$ products $- \Sigma\, S^\circ$ reactants. Know how to apply this equation.
- $\Delta S^\circ$ is usually positive for a spontaneous reaction.
- The Gibbs free energy is a thermodynamic quantity that relates the enthalpy, entropy, and temperature and is the best indicator if a reaction is spontaneous, nonspontaneous, or at equilibrium.
- If $\Delta G^\circ > 0$, the reaction is not spontaneous; if $\Delta G^\circ < 0$, the reaction is spontaneous; and if $\Delta G^\circ = 0$, the reaction is at equilibrium.
- $\Delta G^\circ = \Sigma\, \Delta G_f^\circ$ products $- \Sigma\, \Delta G_f^\circ$ reactants. Know how to apply this equation.
- $\Delta G^\circ = \Delta H^\circ_{rxn} - T\Delta S^\circ_{rxn}$. Know how to apply this equation.
- For a system at equilibrium: $\Delta G^\circ = -RT \ln K = -2.303\, RT \log K$. Know how to apply this equation to calculate equilibrium constants.

CHAPTER 15

# Equilibrium

**IN THIS CHAPTER**

In this chapter, the following AP topics are covered:

- 7.1 Introduction to Equilibrium
- 7.2 Direction of Reversible Reactions
- 7.3 Reaction Quotient and Equilibrium Constant
- 7.4 Calculating the Equilibrium Constant
- 7.5 Magnitude of the Equilibrium Constant
- 7.6 Properties of the Equilibrium Constant
- 7.7 Calculating Equilibrium Concentrations
- 7.8 Representations of Equilibrium
- 7.9 Introduction to Le Châtelier's Principle
- 7.10 Reaction Quotient and Le Châtelier's Principle
- 7.11 Introduction to Solubility Equilibria
- 7.12 Common-Ion Effect
- 7.13 pH and Solubility
- 7.14 Free Energy of Dissolution

**Summary:** We've been discussing chemical reactions for several chapters. In the Kinetics chapter you saw how chemical reactions take place and some of the factors that affect the reactions' speed. In this chapter, we will discuss another aspect of chemical reactions: equilibrium.

A few chemical reactions proceed to completion, using up one or more of the reactants and then stopping. However, most reactions behave in a different way. Consider the general reaction:

$$a\,A + b\,B \rightarrow c\,C + d\,D$$

Reactants A and B are forming C and D. Then C and D start to react to form A and B:

$$c\,C + d\,D \rightarrow a\,A + b\,B$$

These two reactions proceed until the two rates of reaction become equal. That is, the speed of production of C and D in the first reaction is equal to the speed of production of A and B in the second reaction. Since these two reactions are occurring simultaneously in the same container, the amounts of A, B, C, and D become constant. A **chemical equilibrium** has been reached, in which two exactly opposite reactions are occurring at the same place, at the same time, and with the same rates of reaction. When a system reaches the equilibrium state, the reactions do not stop. A and B are still reacting to form C and D; C and D are still reacting to form A and B. But because the reactions proceed at the same rate, the amounts of each chemical species are constant. This state is sometimes called a **dynamic** equilibrium state to emphasize the fact that the reactions are still occurring—it is a dynamic, not a static, state. An equilibrium state is indicated by a double arrow instead of a single arrow. For the reaction above it would be shown as:

$$\mathrm{a\,A + b\,B \leftrightarrows c\,C + d\,D}$$

KEY IDEA

**It is important to remember that at equilibrium the concentrations of the chemical species are constant, not necessarily equal.** There may be a lot of C and D and a little A and B, or vice versa. The concentrations are constant, unchanging, but not necessarily equal.

At any point during the preceding reaction, a relationship may be defined called the **reaction quotient,** *Q*. It has the following form:

$$Q = \frac{[\mathrm{C}]^c\,[\mathrm{D}]^d}{[\mathrm{A}]^a\,[\mathrm{B}]^b}$$

The reaction quotient is a fraction. In the numerator is the product of the chemical species on the right-hand side of the equilibrium arrow, each raised to the power of that species' coefficient in the balanced chemical equation. It is called the $Q_c$ in this case because molar concentrations are being used. If this were a gas-phase reaction, gas pressures could be used, and it would become a $Q_p$.

KEY IDEA

**Remember: products over reactants**

KEY IDEA

**Keywords and Equations**

Equilibrium Constants

| | | |
|---|---|---|
| $K_c$ (molar concentrations) | $K_p$ (gas pressures) | |
| $K_a$ (weak acid) | $K_b$ (weak base) | $K_w$ (water) |

$$K_c = \frac{[\mathrm{C}]^c\,[\mathrm{D}]^d}{[\mathrm{A}]^a\,[\mathrm{B}]^b},\ \text{where } \mathrm{a\,A + b\,B \leftrightarrows c\,C + d\,D}$$

$$K_p = \frac{(P_\mathrm{C})^c(P_\mathrm{D})^d}{(P_\mathrm{A})^a(P_\mathrm{B})^b}$$

## Equilibrium Expressions

The reactant quotient can be written at any point during the reaction, but the most useful point is when the reaction has reached equilibrium. At equilibrium, the reaction quotient becomes the **equilibrium constant**, $K_c$ (or $K_p$ if gas pressures are being used). Usually this equilibrium constant is expressed simply as a number without units. In addition, the concentrations of solids or pure liquids (not in solution) that appear in the equilibrium expression are assumed to be 1, since their concentrations do not change. (The use of concentrations or pressures is only an approximation; equilibrium constants are based upon something called activities. Activities are, by definition, unitless, which makes the equilibrium constants unitless.) (Note: the equilibrium constant is constant as long as the temperature is constant. However, if the temperature is only slightly changed, it may be assumed that the change in the constant is negligible.)

Consider the Haber process for producing ammonia:

$$N_2(g) + 3H_2(g) \leftrightarrows 2NH_3(g)$$

The equilibrium constant expression would be written as:

$$K_c = \frac{[NH_3]^2}{[N_2][H_2]^3}$$

If the partial pressures of the gases were used, then $K_p$ would be written in the following form:

$$K_p = \frac{\left(P_{NH_3}\right)^2}{\left(P_{N_2}\right)\left(P_{H_2}\right)^3}$$

KEY IDEA

There is a relationship between $K_c$ and $K_p$: $K_p = K_c(RT)^{\Delta n}$, where $R$ is the ideal gas constant (0.08206 L atm mol$^{-1}$ K$^{-1}$) and $\Delta n$ is the change in the number of moles of gas in the reaction. However, this topic will not appear on the AP Exam.

## Magnitude of the Equilibrium Constant

The numerical value of the equilibrium constant can give an indication of the extent of the reaction after equilibrium has been reached. If the value of $K$ is large, that means the numerator is much larger than the denominator and the reaction has produced a relatively large quantity of products (reaction lies far to the right). If $K$ is small, then the numerator is much smaller than the denominator and not much product has been formed (reaction lies far to the left).

There is a wide range of values for the equilibrium constant. The magnitude of the equilibrium not only says something about the degree of reaction but also says something about how to solve a problem involving equilibrium.

Very large equilibrium constants mean that nearly everything to the left of the equilibrium arrow will be converted to the substances to the right of the arrow. Very small equilibrium constants mean that nearly everything to the right of the equilibrium arrow will be converted to the substances to the left of the arrow. Identifying the constants as very large or very small is a subjective judgment.

The following example will illustrate how a problem may or may not be simplified. If you have not covered ICE tables yet, you may wish to return to this later.

Given the following general equilibrium and equilibrium constant expression:

$$a\,\mathrm{A} \leftrightarrows c\,\mathrm{C} + d\,\mathrm{D}$$

$$K_c = \frac{[\mathrm{C}]^c[\mathrm{D}]^d}{[\mathrm{A}]^a}$$

This also applies if a $K_p$ was used. If the original concentrations of the reactant and products are expressed as [A], [C], and [D]. A table for this equilibrium would look like the following.

| | A | C | D |
|---|---|---|---|
| Initial | [A] | [C] | [D] |
| Change | $\pm ax$ | $\pm cx$ | $\pm dx$ |
| Equilibrium | $[\mathrm{A}] \pm ax$ | $[\mathrm{C}] \pm cx$ | $[\mathrm{D}] \pm dx$ |

The ± will be + in some cases and – in others; it depends upon the original concentrations and the value of the equilibrium constant. The general solution will require a quadratic formula. However, a very small equilibrium constant means that [C] and/or [D] must be small. If the initial are equal to 0, then $[\mathrm{C}] \pm cx \approx cx$ and/or $[\mathrm{D}] \pm dx \approx dx$, and $[\mathrm{A}] \pm ax \approx [\mathrm{A}]$, it is no longer be necessary to do a quadratic.

## Properties of the Equilibrium Constant

The general reaction quotient is written as:

$$Q = \frac{[\mathrm{C}]^c\,[\mathrm{D}]^d}{[\mathrm{A}]^a\,[\mathrm{B}]^b}$$

$$a\,\mathrm{A} + b\,\mathrm{B} \leftrightarrows c\,\mathrm{C} + d\,\mathrm{D}$$

If concentrations are used, this is a $Q_c$, and if pressures are used, this is a $Q_p$. (Do not mix concentrations and pressures.) If the values used in the expression are the equilibrium values, then $Q$ becomes $K$.

Note: using concentrations or pressures is only an approximation. True reaction quotients and equilibrium constants require a concept from beyond AP Chemistry, notable activities. The activity of a substance is a unitless quantity, which may be approximated by the concentration or partial pressure.

If the above equilibrium were written as:

$$c\,\mathrm{C} + d\,\mathrm{D} \leftrightarrows a\,\mathrm{A} + b\,\mathrm{B}$$

Then the reaction quotient would change to:

$$Q' = \frac{[\mathrm{A}]^a\,[\mathrm{B}]^b}{[\mathrm{C}]^c\,[\mathrm{D}]^d}$$

The relationship between $Q$ and $Q'$: $Q' = \frac{1}{Q}$, which should be apparent if one compares the two reaction quotient expressions. This relationship applies to equilibrium constants also. That is, if the equilibrium reaction is reversed, the reaction quotient or equilibrium constant for the reversed reaction is the reciprocal of the initial.

Consider the following two equilibria:

$$2\ SO_2(g) + O_2(g) \leftrightarrows 2\ SO_3(g) \qquad (1)$$

$$4\ SO_2(g) + 2\ O_2(g) \leftrightarrows 4\ SO_3(g) \qquad (2)$$

Equation (2) is simply equation (1) doubled. The equilibrium constant expressions for these two equilibria are (subscripts indicate to which equilibrium the constant applies):

$$K_1 = \frac{[SO_3]^2}{[SO_2]^2[O_2]}$$

$$K_2 = \frac{[SO_3]^4}{[SO_2]^4[O_2]^2}$$

Comparing the two equilibrium constant expressions shows that $K_2 = K_1^{\,2}$ or $K_1 = \sqrt{K_2}$. This is a property of equilibria. Doubling a reaction squares the constant and halving an equation gives the square root of the original constant. Similarly, tripling the reaction cubes the constant, and so on. This applies to all equilibria.

Consider the following two equilibria and their sum:

$$H_2C_2O_4(aq) \leftrightarrows H^+(aq) + HC_2O_4^-(aq) \qquad K_1 = \frac{[H^+][HC_2O_4^-]}{[H_2C_2O_4]}$$

$$HC_2O_4^-(aq) \leftrightarrows H^+(aq) + C_2O_4^{2-}(aq) \qquad K_2 = \frac{[H^+][C_2O_4^{2-}]}{[HC_2O_4^-]}$$

$$\text{Sum} \qquad H_2C_2O_4(aq) \leftrightarrows 2\ H^+(aq) + C_2O_4^{2-}(aq) \qquad K_{sum} = \frac{[H^+]^2[C_2O_4^{2-}]}{[H_2C_2O_4]}$$

The sum is determined by a procedure similar to a Hess's law problem.

Let's explore the relationship between the three equilibrium constants. What happens if we multiply $K_1$ by $K_2$? Let's begin by writing the individual expressions:

$$K_1 \times K_2 = \frac{[H^+][\cancel{HC_2O_4^-}]}{[H_2C_2O_4]} \times \frac{[H^+][C_2O_4^{2-}]}{[\cancel{HC_2O_4^-}]} = \frac{[H^+]^2[C_2O_4^{2-}]}{[H_2C_2O_4]} = K_{sum}$$

This illustrates another general property of equilibria. The constant for the sum of any number of separate equilibria is equal to the product of the separate equilibrium constants.

These relationships apply to any $K$ (both $K_c$ and $K_p$) or $Q$ (both $Q_c$ and $Q_p$).

## Calculating Equilibrium Concentrations

The following example will illustrate a common method that may be used to solve equilibrium problems:

Gaseous BrCl will decompose to the elements when heated. At 500 K, the equilibrium constant for this decomposition reaction is $K_c = 33$. What are the equilibrium concentrations of the three substances involved in this equilibrium if the initial concentration of BrCl(g) is 1.0 $M$?

The first step is to write the reaction and the equilibrium constant expression.

$$2\ BrCl(g) \leftrightarrows Br_2(g) + Cl_2(g) \qquad K_c = \frac{[Br_2][Cl_2]}{[BrCl]^2} = 33$$

Sometimes one or both of these is given, which will save you some work.

The next step is to begin a table. The headings of the columns are the substances involved in the equilibrium. It will help to list them in the order they appear in the reaction.

| BrCl | $Br_2$ | $Cl_2$ |
|---|---|---|

Below each substance in a row labelled "Initial" are the initial values of the concentration for each substance (0 if none of the substance was given). This gives:

| | BrCl | $Br_2$ | $Cl_2$ |
|---|---|---|---|
| Initial | 1.0 | 0 | 0 |

While an initial value may be 0, no equilibrium value will ever be 0 (it may be close). Therefore, for any substance that is 0, some must be produced, and the expense of any substances on the opposite of the equilibrium arrow. The values are normally assigned to be *x*, with every *x* multiplied by the coefficient from the equilibrium reaction. In this case, we get a "Change" row as shown here:

| | BrCl | $Br_2$ | $Cl_2$ |
|---|---|---|---|
| Initial | 1.0 | 0 | 0 |
| Change | $-2\,x$ | $+x$ | $+x$ |

The final row of the table is the "Equilibrium" row, which is the sum of the Initial and Change rows. This gives the following complete table:

| | BrCl | $Br_2$ | $Cl_2$ |
|---|---|---|---|
| Initial | 1.0 | 0 | 0 |
| Change | $-2\,x$ | $+x$ | $+x$ |
| Equilibrium | $1.0 - 2\,x$ | $+x$ | $+x$ |

This table is sometimes called an "ICE" table from the first letter in the label of each of the three lines.

The next step is to enter the values from the Equilibrium line into the equilibrium constant:

$$K_c = \frac{[Br_2][Cl_2]}{[BrCl]^2} = \frac{[x][x]}{[1.0-2x]^2} = 33$$

Solving this equation for *x* will allow you to determine the equilibrium concentrations of the substances involved. Since the key concept for this section is the construction of an ICE table, we will not solve this problem for the concentrations at this point.

Let's look at two variations on this problem and see what the ICE table will look like.

Variation 1

Instead of the initial being 1.0 M BrCl, the initial is 1.0 M $Br_2$ and 1.0 M in $Cl_2$.

| | BrCl | $Br_2$ | $Cl_2$ |
|---|---|---|---|
| I | 0 | 1.0 | 1.0 |
| C | $+2x$ | $-x$ | $-x$ |
| E | $2x$ | $1.0 - x$ | $1.0 - x$ |

$$K_c = \frac{[Br_2][Cl_2]}{[BrCl]^2} = \frac{[1.0 - x][1.0 - x]}{[2x]^2} = 33$$

Variation 2

Now use the initial BrCl = 1.0 *M*, and the initial $Br_2$ = 1.0 *M*.

| | BrCl | $Br_2$ | $Cl_2$ |
|---|---|---|---|
| I | 1.0 | 1.0 | 0 |
| C | $-2x$ | $+x$ | $+x$ |
| E | $1.0 + 2x$ | $1.0 + x$ | $+x$ |

$$K_c = \frac{[Br_2][Cl_2]}{[BrCl]^2} = \frac{[1.0 + x][x]}{[1.0 + 2x]^2} = 33$$

Since the initial chlorine concentration was 0, the equilibrium must shift to the right to alleviate the problem of having a 0 concentration.

If none of the initial values was 0, then a $Q$ calculation would be needed to predict which direction the equilibrium would shift. If it shifts to the right, substances on the left would have a negative change and substances on the right would have a positive change. If it shifts to the left, substances on the right would have a negative change and substances on the left would have a positive change. Finally, if $Q_c = K_c$, the system is already at equilibrium, and the concentrations given are the equilibrium concentrations.

If the problem dealt with a $K_p$ instead of a $K_c$, the procedure would be the same except partial pressures would replace the concentrations.

Once you have an equilibrium expression with the appropriate values entered from the Equilibrium line of the ICE table, the problem becomes a math problem where it is necessary to solve for $x$. Some of these problems will be more of a challenge than others to solve. You will find that in many cases, there will be a simplifying assumption to make the solution easy to find. In general, the simplifying assumptions can be made if $K$ is very large or very small.

## Representations of Equilibrium

There are many ways to represent a system moving to equilibrium. Figure 15.1 shows two of these methods. Reaction A illustrates the reaction A(g) + B(g) ⟶ AB(g), from pure A + B to equilibrium. Reaction B illustrates the reaction AB(g) ⟶ A(g) + B(g), from pure AB to equilibrium. Together, these two reaction schemes show the same equilibrium being achieved by two methods. The equilibrium is A(g) + B(g) ⇆ AB(g).

You should prove for yourself that each of the reaction schemes do achieve the same equilibrium. In addition, you should calculate the equilibrium constant before going on to the solution.

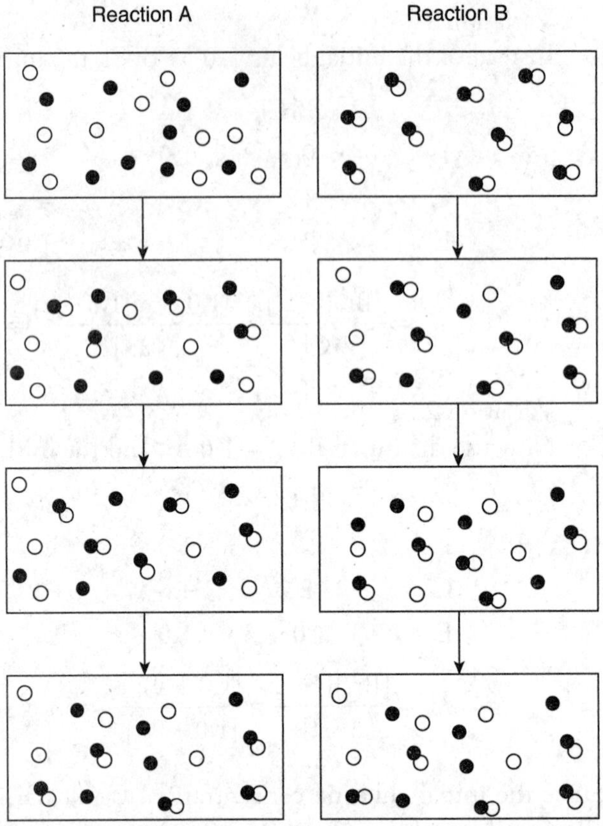


**Figure 15.1 Two reaction schemes (A and B) to represent the reaction A + B → AB reaching equilibrium. The dark circles represent atoms of A, and the open circles represent atoms of B. All species are in the gas phase.**

### Solution:

Begin by writing the equilibrium constant expression. Then enter the number of A, B, and AB you count in the box representing equilibrium.

$$K = \frac{[AB]}{[A][B]} = \frac{[5]}{[5][5]} = 0.2$$

The last box in each reaction scheme is at equilibrium. You may recognize this because the number of atoms/molecules has not changed from the preceding box.

# Le Châtelier's Principle

At a given temperature, a reaction will reach equilibrium with the production of a certain amount of product. If the equilibrium constant is small, that means that not much product will be formed. But is there anything that can be done to produce more? Yes, there is—through the application of **Le Châtelier's principle**. Le Châtelier, a French scientist, discovered that if a chemical system at equilibrium is stressed (disturbed), it will reestablish equilibrium by shifting the reactions involved. This means that the amounts of the reactants and products will change, but the final ratio will remain the same. The equilibrium may be stressed in numerous ways: changes in concentration, pressure, and temperature. Many times the use of a catalyst is mentioned. However, a catalyst will have no effect on the equilibrium amounts because it affects both the forward and reverse reactions equally. It will, however, cause the reaction to reach equilibrium faster.

### Changes in Concentration

If the equilibrium system is stressed by a change in concentration of one of the reactants or products, the equilibrium will react to remove that stress. If the concentration of a chemical species is decreased, the equilibrium will shift to produce more of it. In doing so, the concentration of chemical species on the other side of the reaction arrows will be decreased. If the concentration of a chemical species is increased, the equilibrium will shift to consume it, increasing the concentration of chemical species on the other side of the reaction arrows.

For example, again consider the Haber process:

$$N_2(g) + 3H_2(g) \leftrightarrows 2NH_3(g)$$

If one increases the concentration of hydrogen gas, then the equilibrium shifts to the right to consume some of the added hydrogen. In doing so, the concentration of ammonia ($NH_3$) will increase, and the concentration of nitrogen gas will decrease. On the other hand, if the concentration of nitrogen gas was decreased, the equilibrium would shift to the left to form more, the concentration of ammonia would decrease, and the concentration of hydrogen would increase.

Again, remember that the concentrations may change, but the value of $K_c$ or $K_p$ would remain the same. Changes in concentration never change the value of the equilibrium constant.

### Changes in Pressure

Changes in pressure are significant only if gases are involved. The pressure may be changed by changing the volume of the container or by changing the concentration of a gaseous species (although this is really a change in concentration and can be treated as a concentration effect, as above). If the container becomes smaller, the pressure increases because there is an increased number of collisions on the inside walls of the container. This stresses the equilibrium system, and it will shift to reduce the pressure. This can be accomplished by shifting the equilibrium toward the side of the equation that has the lesser number of moles of gas. If the container size is increased, the pressure decreases, and the equilibrium will shift to the side containing more moles of gas to increase the pressure. If the number of moles of gas is the same on both sides, changing the pressure will not affect the equilibrium.

Once again, consider the Haber reaction:

$$N_2(g) + 3H_2(g) \leftrightarrows 2NH_3(g)$$

KEY IDEA

Note that there are 4 moles of gas (1 of nitrogen and 3 of hydrogen) on the left side and 2 moles on the right. If the container is made smaller, the pressure will increase, and the equilibrium will shift to the right because 4 moles would be converted to 2 moles. The concentrations of nitrogen and hydrogen gases would decrease, and the concentration of ammonia would increase. Changes in pressure never change the value of the equilibrium constant. It is important to use the partial pressures of the gases involved as a gas that is not part of the equilibrium does not count.

**Remember: pressure effects are only important for gases.**

### Changes in Temperature

Changing the temperature changes the value of the equilibrium constant. It also changes the amount of heat in the system and can be treated as a concentration effect. To treat it this way, one must know which reaction, forward or reverse, is exothermic (releasing heat).

One last time, let's consider the Haber reaction:

$$N_2(g) + 3H_2(g) \leftrightarrows 2NH_3(g)$$

The formation of ammonia is exothermic (liberating heat), so the reaction could be written as:

$$N_2(g) + 3H_2(g) \leftrightarrows 2NH_3(g) + \text{heat}$$

If the temperature of the reaction mixture were increased, the amount of heat would be increased, and the equilibrium would shift to the left to consume the added heat. In doing so, the concentration of nitrogen and hydrogen gases would increase, and the concentration of ammonia gas would decrease. If you were in the business of selling ammonia, you would probably want to operate at a reduced temperature, to shift the reaction to the right.

Remember, unlike concentration and pressure, changes in temperature will change the value of the equilibrium constant.

Consider the following equilibrium (endothermic as written), and predict what changes, if any, would occur if the following stresses were applied after equilibrium was established:

$$2\ NaHCO_3(s) \leftrightarrows Na_2CO_3(s) + H_2O(g)$$

a. Add $H_2O(g)$
b. Remove $H_2O(g)$
c. Add $Na_2CO_3(s)$
d. Increase $T$
e. Decrease $V$
f. Add a catalyst

Answers:

a. Left—The equilibrium shifts to remove some of the excess $H_2O(g)$.
b. Right—The equilibrium shifts to replace some of the $H_2O(g)$.
c. No change—Solids do not shift equilibria unless they are totally removed.
d. Right—Endothermic reactions shift to the right when heated.
e. Left—A decrease in volume, or an increase in pressure, will shift the equilibrium toward the side with less gas.
f. No change—Catalysts do not affect the position of an equilibrium.

## Reaction Quotient and Le Châtelier's Principle

If a system at equilibrium is disturbed, Le Châtelier's principle governs what will happen. Predictions may also be made by comparing the value of the reaction quotient to the value of the equilibrium constant.

For this discussion, we will consider the following equilibrium:

$$N_2(g) + 3\ H_2(g) \leftrightarrows 2\ NH_3(g)$$

Two reaction quotients may be written for this reaction:

$$Q_c = \frac{[NH_3]^2}{[N_2][H_2]^3} \qquad Q_p = \frac{\left(P_{NH_3}\right)^2}{\left(P_{N_2}\right)\left(P_{H_2}\right)^3}$$

If the system is in equilibrium, $Q_c = K_c$ and $Q_p = K_p$. However, if the system is disturbed, one or more of the concentrations or pressures in these expression will be changed. Once the equilibrium has been changed, according to Le Châtelier's principle, it will return. For example, a simple increase in the ammonia will result in a shift to the left (reactants). However, how will the reaction shift if nitrogen is increased and hydrogen is decreased? In this case, the new values should be entered into the reaction quotient expression. Once the values are entered, a reaction quotient may be calculated. There are three possible outcomes (for either *Q* and its respective *K*):

$$K > Q$$
$$K < Q$$
$$K = Q$$

If *K* is greater than *Q*, the reaction must shift to the right to increase *Q* until it equals *K*. If *K* is less than *Q*, the reaction must shift to the left to decrease *Q* until it equals *K*. If $Q = K$, the system is still in equilibrium, so no change will occur.

## Solubility Equilibria

Many salts are soluble in water, but some are only slightly soluble. These salts, when placed in water, quickly reach their solubility limit and the ions establish an equilibrium system with the undissolved solid. For example, $PbSO_4$, when added to water, establishes the following equilibrium:

$$PbSO_4(s) \leftrightarrows Pb^{2+}(aq) + SO_4^{2-}(aq)$$

The equilibrium constant expression for systems of slightly soluble salts is called the **solubility product constant, $K_{sp}$**. It is the product of the ionic concentrations, each one raised to the power of the coefficient in the balanced chemical equation. It contains no denominator since the concentration of a solid is, by convention, 1 and does not appear in the equilibrium constant expressions. (Some textbooks will say that the concentrations of solids, liquids, and solvents are included in the equilibrium constant.) The $K_{sp}$ expression for the $PbSO_4$ system would be:

$$K_{sp} = [Pb^{2+}][SO_4^{2-}]$$

Never place any terms in the denominator of a $K_{sp}$ expression.

For this salt, the numerical value of $K_{sp}$ is $1.6 \times 10^{-8}$ at 25°C. Note that the $Pb^{2+}$ and $SO_4^{2-}$ ions are formed in equal amounts, so the right-hand side of the equation could be represented as $[x]$. If the numerical value of the solubility product constant is known, then the concentration of the ions can be determined. And if one of the ion concentrations can be determined, then $K_{sp}$ can be calculated.

Here is an example of a $K_{sp}$ problem. The $K_{sp}$ of lead(II) fluoride in water is $3.6 \times 10^{-8}$. How many grams of lead(II) fluoride will dissolve in 0.500 L of water?

$$\begin{array}{ccc} PbF_2(s) \leftrightarrows & Pb^{2+}(aq) + & 2\,F^-(aq) \\ — & x & 2x \end{array}$$

$$K_{sp} = [Pb^{2+}][F^-]^2 = 3.6 \times 10^{-8}$$
$$= (x)(2x)^2 = 4x^3 = 3.6 \times 10^{-8}$$
$$x = 2.1 \times 10^{-3} = [Pb^{2+}]$$

$$\left(\frac{2.1 \times 10^{-3}\ Pb^{2+}}{L}\right)(0.500\ L)\left(\frac{1\ mol\ PbF_2}{1\ mol\ Pb^{2+}}\right)\left(\frac{245.2\ g\ PbF_2}{1\ mol\ PbF_2}\right) = 0.26\ g\ PbF_2$$

The mass (grams) dissolved in a solution is known as the **solubility**. The line immediately below the equilibrium equation is the Equilibrium line from the ICE table.

If a slightly soluble salt solution is at equilibrium and a solution containing one of the ions involved in the equilibrium is added, the solubility of the slightly soluble salt is decreased. For example, let's again consider the $PbSO_4$ equilibrium:

$$PbSO_4(s) \leftrightarrows Pb^{2+}(aq) + SO_4^{2-}(aq)$$

Suppose a solution of $Na_2SO_4$ is added to this equilibrium system. The additional sulfate ion will disrupt the equilibrium, by Le Châtelier's principle, and shift it to the left, decreasing the solubility. The same would be true if you tried to dissolve $Na_2SO_4$ in a solution of $Na_2SO_4$ instead of pure water—the solubility would be lower. This application of Le Châtelier's principle to equilibrium systems of slightly soluble salts is called the **common-ion effect** (buffer solutions are another example of the common-ion effect). Calculations like the ones above involving finding concentrations and $K_{sp}$ can still be done, but the concentration of the additional common ion will have to be inserted into the solubility product constant expression. Sometimes, if $K_{sp}$ is very small and the common ion concentration is large, the concentration of the common ion can simply be approximated by the concentration of the ion added.

For example, calculate the silver ion concentration in each of the following solutions:

**a.** $Ag_2CO_3(s)$ + water $\quad K_{sp}\ Ag_2CO_3 = 8.1 \times 10^{-12}$
**b.** $Ag_2CO_3(s) + 1.00\ M\ Na_2CO_3$

**a.** $Ag_2CO_3(s) \leftrightarrows 2\ Ag^+(aq) + CO_3^{2-}(aq)$

$$2x \qquad x$$

$$K_{sp} = (2x)^2(x) = 8.1 \times 10^{-12} = 4x^3$$

$$x = 1.3 \times 10^{-4}$$

$$[Ag^+] = 2x = 2.6 \times 10^{-4}\ M$$

**b.** $1.00\ M\ Na_2CO_3 \rightarrow 1.00\ M\ CO_3^{2-}$ (common ion)

$$Ag_2CO_3(s) \leftrightarrows 2Ag^+(aq) + CO_3^{2-}(aq)$$

$$2x \qquad 1.00 + x$$

$$K_{sp} = (2x)^2(1.00 + x) = 8.1 \times 10^{-12} = 4x^2 \text{ (neglect } x\text{)}$$

$$x = 1.4 \times 10^{-6}\ M$$

$$[Ag^+] = 2x = 2.8 \times 10^{-6}\ M$$

The molarity of the dissolved solid is known as the **molar solubility**. Knowing the value of the solubility product constant can also allow us to predict whether a precipitate will form if two solutions, each containing an ion component of a slightly soluble salt, are mixed. The **ion-product**, sometimes represented as $Q$ (same form as the solubility product constant), is calculated taking into consideration the mixing of the volumes of the two solutions, and this ion-product is compared to $K_{sp}$. If it is greater than $K_{sp}$, precipitation will occur until the ion concentrations have been reduced to the solubility level.

If 10.0 mL of a 0.100 $M$ $CaCl_2$ solution is added to 40.0 mL of a 0.0250 $M$ $Pb(NO_3)_2$ solution, will $PbCl_2$ precipitate? $K_{sp}$ for $PbCl_2 = 1.7 \times 10^{-5}$.

To answer this question, the concentrations of the chloride ion and the lead(II) ion *before* precipitation must be used. These may be determined simply from $M_{dil} = M_{con}V_{con}/V_{dil}$. (You should recall this dilution formula from prior knowledge.) For both ions, $V_{dil}$ = (10.0 + 40.0) = 50.0 mL. $V_{con}$ for $CaCl_2$ is 10.0 mL and for $Pb(NO_3)_2$ it is 40.0 mL. The values of $M_{con}$ are 2(0.100) = 0.200 $M$ $Cl^-$ and 0.0250 $M$ $Pb^{2+}$. It is now necessary to calculate $M_{dil}$ for each ion. (The $Ca^{2+}$ and $NO_3^-$ ions are ignored because they are not part of the $K_{sp}$ equilibrium.)

$$\text{For } Pb^{2+}\text{: } M_{dil} = \frac{(M_{con})(V_{con})}{(V_{dil})} = \frac{(0.0250\ M\ Pb^{2+})(40.0\ mL)}{(50.0\ mL)} = 0.0200\ M\ Pb^{2+}$$

$$\text{For } Cl^-\text{: } M_{dil} = \frac{(M_{con})(V_{con})}{(V_{dil})} = \frac{(0.0200\ M\ Cl^-)(10.0\ mL)}{(50.0\ mL)} = 0.00400\ M\ Cl^-$$

(Note: no volume conversions were necessary because all the volumes are in milliliters.)

Entering these values into the following relation produces:

$$Q = [Pb^{2+}][Cl^-]^2 = (0.0200)(0.00400)^2 = 3.2 \times 10^{-7}$$

Since $Q$ is smaller than $K_{sp}$, no precipitation will occur.

# Common-Ion Effect

Consider the following equilibrium:

$$KIO_4(s) \leftrightarrows K^+(aq) + IO_4^-(aq) \qquad K_{sp} = [K^+][IO_4^-] = [x][x] = 8.3 \times 10^{-4}$$

At equilibrium $[K^+] = [IO_4^-] = 2.9 \times 10^{-2}$. Now assume that 1.0 mole of $KNO_3$ is added to 1.0 liter of a solution where the $KIO_4$ equilibrium has been established. The additional $KNO_3$ will generate $[K^+] = [NO_3^-] = 1.0\ M$. The added $NO_3^-(aq)$ will not influence the established equilibrium as it does not appear in the equilibrium constant expression; however, the $K^+(aq)$ does appear, so it will influence the equilibrium. This changes the equilibrium constant expression to:

$$K_{sp} = [K^+][IO_4^-] = [1.0 + x][x] = 8.3 \times 10^{-4}$$

Solving for the concentrations gives $[K^+] = 1.0\ M$ and $[IO_4^-] = 8.3 \times 10^{-4}\ M$. These values are different from the concentrations determined before the $KNO_3$ was added. Since $K^+(aq)$ was added, the change in $K^+(aq)$ would be obvious; however, the $IO_4^-(aq)$ change is a different matter. This example illustrates the common-ion effect. The **common-ion effect** is the changing of an equilibrium by the addition of one of the equilibrium ions from an outside source. This is an application of Le Châtelier's ionic equilibria.

The common-ion effect applies to all ionic equilibria. It will appear again in Chapter 16 in the discussion of buffer solutions.

# pH and Solubility

You may wish to come back to this topic after Chapter 16.

Acids and bases can alter the solubility of an ionic salt. Acids will alter the solubility of salts of weak acids, and bases will alter the solubility of salts of weak bases. The solubility of salts of strong acids with strong bases are not altered. Examples are $BaCO_3$ (salt of a weak acid), $K_{sp} = 5.1 \times 10^{-9}$, $(NH_4)_2PtCl_6$ (salt of a weak base), $K_{sp} = 9 \times 10^{-6}$, $BaSO_4$ (salt of a strong acid and a strong base), $K_{sp} = 1.1 \times 10^{-10}$. (Both acids and bases will affect the pH of a solution.) This is related to Le Châtelier's principle.

Let's use AgCN ($K_{sp} = 1.4 \times 10^{-16}$) as an example of a salt of a weak acid. In this case, the weak acid is HCN ($K_a = 6.2 \times 10^{-10}$). The equilibrium expressions for these two reactions are:

$$AgCN(s) \leftrightarrows Ag^+(aq) + CN^-(aq) \qquad K_{sp} = 1.4 \times 10^{-16}$$

$$HCN(aq) \leftrightarrows H^+(aq) + CN^-(aq) \qquad K_a = 6.2 \times 10^{-10}$$

Reversing the $K_a$ equilibrium requires the reciprocal of the equilibrium constant (this procedure may be applied to any equilibrium, as both situations are occurring simultaneously).

$$H^+(aq) + CN^-(aq) \leftrightarrows HCN(aq) \qquad K_{rev} = \frac{1}{K_a} = 1.6 \times 10^9$$

If solid AgCN is added to an HCN solution, or HCN is added to a solution where the AgCN has been established, then one equilibrium is being added to the other. In this example, we will add the $K_{sp}$ to the $K_{rev}$:

$$AgCN(s) \leftrightarrows Ag^+(aq) + CN^-(aq) \qquad K_{sp} = [Ag^+]\,[CN^-] = 1.4 \times 10^{-16}$$

$$H^+(aq) + CN^-(aq) \leftrightarrows HCN(aq) \qquad K_{rev} = \frac{[HCN]}{[H^+]\,[CN^-]} = 1.6 \times 10^9$$

Summing these two equilibria and calculating a new constant gives:

$$H^+(aq) + \cancel{CN^-(aq)} + AgCN(s) \leftrightarrows Ag^+(aq) + \cancel{CN^-(aq)} + HCN(aq)$$

$$K_{combined} = K_{sp} \times K_{rev} = [Ag^+]\,\cancel{[CN^-]} \times \frac{[HCN]}{[H^+]\,\cancel{[CN^-]}}$$

$$= (1.4 \times 10^{-16}) \times (1.6 \times 10^9) = 2.2 \times 10^{-7}$$

The new $K$ for the dissolution of AgCN is much larger than the original $K_{sp}$, which means the AgCN is more soluble in the acid solution.

In most cases, you will not be required to do this type of calculation; you will only need to be able to predict the change in solubility. To make a correct prediction, you will need to recognize what type of salt you are considering.

## Free Energy of Dissolution

Solubility constants, like all equilibrium constants, may be related to the Gibbs free energy by the following relationship:

$$\Delta G = -RT \ln K$$

For soluble materials, $\Delta G$ is negative (thermodynamically favorable), and for "insoluble" materials, $\Delta G$ is positive (thermodynamically unfavorable).

The Gibbs free energy may be defined by the relationship $\Delta G = \Delta H - T\,\Delta S$. The enthalpy, $\Delta H$, relates to the breaking and forming of interactions between the solvent molecules and the solute ions. The magnitude of these interactions depends upon the number and strength of the intermolecular forces. Breaking these interactions leads to a positive contribution, and forming new interactions leads to a negative contribution. To dissolve an ionic solid, it is necessary to break the ionic bonds in the solid. To make room for the ions in the solution, some of the interactions between the solvent molecules must be broken. New interactions (ion–dipole forces) can then form.

The entropy, $\Delta S$, relates to the breakdown of the ordered crystalline structure of the solid (a positive contribution) and the ordering of the solvent molecules around the ions (ion–dipole forces), which leads to a negative contribution. The combination of these contributions yields the entropy of solution.

The enthalpy of solution and the entropy of solution lead to the Gibbs free energy of solution, the value, and more importantly the sign, of which dictates how soluble a substance is in a particular solvent.

## Other Equilibria

Other types of equilibria can be treated in much the same way as the ones discussed above. For example, there is an equilibrium constant associated with the formation of complex ions. This equilibrium constant is called the **formation constant, $K_f$.** $Zn(H_2O)_4^{2+}$ reacts with cyanide ion to form the $Zn(CN)_4^{2-}$ complex ion according to the following equation:

$$Zn(H_2O)_4^{2+}(aq) + 4\ CN^-(aq) \leftrightarrows Zn(CN)_4^{2-}(aq) + 4H_2O(l)$$

The $K_f$ of $Zn(CN)_4^{2-}(aq)$ is $4.2 \times 10^{19}$, indicating that the equilibrium lies to the right. The actual equilibrium process is more complicated than shown.

## Experiments

KEY IDEA

Equilibrium experiments such as 10, 11, and 13 in Chapter 20, Experimental Investigations, directly or indirectly involve filling a table like the following:

| REACTANTS AND PRODUCTS |
| --- |
| Initial amount |
| Change |
| Equilibrium amount |

The initial amounts—concentrations or pressures—are normally zero for the products, and a measured or calculated value for the reactants. Once equilibrium has been established, the amount of at least one of the substances is determined. Based on the change in this one substance and the stoichiometry, the amounts of the other materials may be calculated (not measured).

Measurements may include the pressure, the mass (to be converted to moles), the volume (to be used in calculations), and the pH (to be converted into either the hydrogen ion or hydroxide ion concentration). Some experiments measure the color intensity (with a spectrophotometer), which may be converted to a concentration.

Do not make the mistake of "measuring" a change. Changes are never measured; they are always calculated.

## Common Mistakes to Avoid

TIP

1. Be sure to check the units and significant figures of your final answer.
2. When writing equilibrium constant expressions, use products over reactants. Each concentration is raised to the power of the coefficient in the balanced chemical equation.
3. Remember, in working Le Châtelier problems, pressure effects are important only for gases that are involved in the equilibrium.

## › Review Questions

Use these questions to review the content of this chapter and practice for the AP Chemistry Exam. First are 20 multiple-choice questions similar to what you will encounter in Section I of the AP Chemistry Exam. These questions also include ones designed to help you review prior knowledge. Following those is a long free-response question like the ones in Section II of the exam. To make these questions an even more authentic practice for the actual exam, time yourself following the instructions provided.

### Multiple-Choice Questions

Answer the following questions in 30 minutes. You may not use a calculator. You may use the periodic table and the equation sheet at the back of this book.

**1.** A student wishes to reduce the zinc ion concentration in a saturated zinc iodate solution to $1 \times 10^{-6}$ *M*. How many moles of solid $KIO_3$ must be added to 1.00 L of solution? [$Zn(IO_3)_2 = 4 \times 10^{-6}$ at 25°C]

(A) 1 mole
(B) 0.5 mole
(C) 2 moles
(D) 4 moles

**2.** At constant temperature, a change in volume will NOT affect the moles of substances present in which of the following?

(A) $H_2(g) + I_2(g) \leftrightarrows 2\ HI(g)$
(B) $CO(g) + Cl_2(g) \leftrightarrows COCl_2(g)$
(C) $PCl_5(g) \leftrightarrows PCl_3(g) + Cl_2(g)$
(D) $N_2(g) + 3\ H_2(g) \leftrightarrows 2\ NH_3(g)$

**3.** The equilibrium constant for the hydrolysis of $C_2O_4^{2-}$ is best represented by which of the following?

(A) $K = \dfrac{[OH^-][C_2O_4^{2-}]}{[HC_2O_4^-]}$

(B) $K = \dfrac{[H_3O^+][C_2O_4^{2-}]}{[HC_2O_4^-]}$

(C) $K = \dfrac{[OH^-][HC_2O_4^-]}{[C_2O_4^{2-}]}$

(D) $K = \dfrac{[C_2O_4^{2-}]}{[OH^-][HC_2O_4^-]}$

**4.** $C(s) + H_2O(g) \leftrightarrows CO(g) + H_2(g)$ endothermic

An equilibrium mixture of the reactants is placed in a sealed container at 150°C. The amount of the products may be increased by which of the following changes?

(A) decreasing the volume of the container
(B) raising the temperature of the container and increasing the volume of the container
(C) lowering the temperature of the container
(D) adding 1 mole of C(s) to the container

**5.** $CH_4(g) + CO_2(g) \leftrightarrows 2\ CO(g) + 2\ H_2(g)$

A 1.00 L flask is filled with 0.30 mole of $CH_4$ and 0.40 mole of $CO_2$ and allowed to come to equilibrium. At equilibrium, there are 0.20 mole of CO in the flask. What is the value of $K_c$, the equilibrium constant, for the reaction?

(A) 1.2
(B) 0.027
(C) 0.30
(D) 0.060

**6.** $2\ NO_2(g) \leftrightarrows 2\ NO(g) + O_2(g)$

The above materials were sealed in a flask and allowed to come to equilibrium at a certain temperature. A small quantity of $O_2(g)$ was added to the flask, and the mixture was allowed to return to equilibrium at the same temperature. Which of the following has increased over its original equilibrium value?

(A) the quantity of $NO_2(g)$ present
(B) the quantity of NO(g) present
(C) the equilibrium constant, *K*
(D) the rate of the reaction

7. $2\ CH_4(g) + O_2(g) \leftrightarrows 2\ CO(g) + 4\ H_2(g)\ \Delta H < 0$

To increase the value of the equilibrium constant, $K$, which of the following changes must be made to the above?

(A) increase the temperature
(B) increase the volume
(C) decrease the temperature
(D) add CO(g)

8. At constant temperature, a change in the volume of the system will NOT affect the moles of the substances present in which of the following?

(A) $C(s) + H_2O(g) \leftrightarrows H_2(g) + CO(g)$
(B) $3\ O_2(g) \leftrightarrows 2\ O_3(g)$
(C) $Xe(g) + 2\ F_2(g) \leftrightarrows XeF_4(g)$
(D) $6\ CO_2(g) + 6\ H_2O(l) \leftrightarrows 6\ O_2(g) + C_6H_{12}O_6(aq)$

9. A chemistry student adds some dilute ammonia solution to some insoluble silver chloride. The solid dissolves. Which of the following is the correct net ionic equation for the reaction?

(A) $AgCl(s) + 2\ NH_3(aq) \rightarrow [Ag(NH_3)_2]^+(aq) + Cl^-(aq)$
(B) $AgCl(s) + 2\ NH_4^+(aq) \rightarrow [Ag(NH_4)_2]^{3+}(aq) + Cl^-(aq)$
(C) $AgCl(s) + NH_4^+(aq) \rightarrow Ag^+(aq) + NH_4Cl(aq)$
(D) $AgCl(s) + NH_3(aq) \rightarrow Ag^+(aq) + NH_3Cl(aq)$

10. Which of the following contains only equilibria that are normally always homogeneous?

(A) $K_a$, $K_b$, and $K_{sp}$
(B) $K_a$, $K_{sp}$, and $K_f$
(C) $K_a$, $K_b$, and $K_f$
(D) $K_{sp}$, $K_b$, and $K_f$

11. For which of the following equilibriums will $K_c = K_p$?

(A) $H_2(g) + I_2(g) \leftrightarrows 2\ HI(g)$
(B) $CO(g) + Cl_2(g) \leftrightarrows COCl_2(g)$
(C) $PCl_5(g) \leftrightarrows PCl_3(g) + Cl_2(g)$
(D) $N_2(g) + 3\ H_2(g) \leftrightarrows 2\ NH_3(g)$

12. $CaCO_3(s) \leftrightarrows CaO(s) + CO_2(g)$

Which of the following is the correct $K_p$ expression for the above reaction?

(A) $K_p = \dfrac{P_{CaO}\ P_{CO_2}}{P_{CaCO_3}}$

(B) $K_p = [CO_2]$

(C) $K_p = \dfrac{[CaO]\ [CO_2]}{[CaCO_3]}$

(D) $K_p = P_{CO_2}$

13. Which of the following has the lower molar solubility in water $CaCO_3$ or $SrF_2$?

$K_{sp}(CaCO_3) = 4.0 \times 10^{-9}$, $K_{sp}(SrF_2) = 8.0 \times 10^{-9}$

(A) $CaCO_3$
(B) $SrF_2$
(C) Both are nearly equal.
(D) There is insufficient information.

14. Altering the pH of a solution of which of the following will change the solubility of that substance?

(A) $PbSO_4(s) K_{sp} = 1.6 \times 10^{-8}$
(B) $PbF_2(s) K_{sp} = 3.6 \times 10^{-8}$
(C) $PbCl_2(s) K_{sp} = 1.7 \times 10^{-5}$
(D) $PbI_2(s) K_{sp} = 7.9 \times 10^{-9}$

15. Potassium perchlorate, $KClO_4$, has $K_{sp} = 1.1 \times 10^{-2}$. Adding which of the following to a saturated solution of $KClO_4$ will decrease its solubility.

(A) HCl(aq)
(B) $HClO_4(aq)$
(C) NaOH(aq)
(D) $Ca(C_2H_3O_2)_2(aq)$

16. The $K_{sp}$ for silver nitrite, $AgNO_2(s)$, is $1.6 \times 10^{-4}$. A sample containing $1.0 \times 10^{-3}$ moles of $Ca(NO_2)_2$ and $8.0 \times 10^{-3}$ moles of $AgNO_3$ is added to a 1 liter volumetric flask and distilled water is added to dilute to the mark on the flask and both solids dissolve completely. Will $AgNO_2$ precipitate.

(A) Yes
(B) No
(C) Impossible to determine
(D) Insufficient information

**17.** A petroleum chemists is investigating the equilibrium:

$$2\,CO(g) + 2\,H_2(g) \rightleftharpoons CH_4(g) + CO_2(g)$$

For one experiment, she finds that at equilibrium the reaction mixture has the following composition:

| | $CO(g)$ | $H_2(g)$ | $CH_4(g)$ | $CO_2(g)$ |
|---|---|---|---|---|
| Moles | 0.20 | 0.20 | 0.10 | 0.30 |
| Partial pressure (atm) | 5.0 | 5.0 | 3.0 | 8.0 |

The container had a volume of 1.00 L and was at 298 K. What is the approximate value of $K_p$?

(A) 0.038
(B) 19
(C) 26
(D) 0.053

**18.** In determining the solubility of a substance, a substance with a large positive $\Delta G$ of dissolution is likely to be

(A) Soluble
(B) Slightly soluble
(C) Insoluble
(D) Not predictable

**19.** In an aqueous solution of $H_2S$, there are two equilibria directly related to the $H_2S$. These equilibria are:

$$H_2S(aq) \rightleftharpoons H^+(aq) + HS^-(aq) \qquad K_1$$
$$HS^-(aq) \rightleftharpoons H^+(aq) + S^{2-}(aq) \qquad K_2$$

One way to simplify problems dealing with these two equilibria is:

(A) Add the two equations and add the constants.
(B) Ignore the first equilibrium.
(C) Both equation must always be dealt with separately.
(D) Add the two equations and multiply the constants.

**20.** An inorganic chemist was investigating the following equilibrium in aqueous solution:

$$[Ag(H_2O)_2]^+(aq) + 2\,OH^-(aq) \rightleftharpoons [Ag(OH)_2]^+(aq) + 2\,H_2O(l)$$

In one experiment he found that the equilibrium concentrations of the substances in the equilibrium were:

$[Ag(H_2O)_2]^+(aq) = 1.0 \times 10^{-4}$  $OH^-(aq) = 1.0\ M$
$[Ag(OH)_2]^-(aq) = 1.0\ M$  $H_2O(l) = 55\ M$

What is the value of $K_f$?

(A) $1.0 \times 10^4$
(B) $1.0 \times 10^{-4}$
(C) $3.0 \times 10^7$
(D) $1.0 \times 10^{-7}$

## › Answers and Explanations

**1. C**—The solubility-product constant expression is $K_{sp} = [Zn^{2+}][IO_3^-]^2 = 4 \times 10$. This may be rearranged to $[IO_3^-]^2 = \dfrac{4 \times 10^{-6}}{[Zn^{2+}]}$. Inserting the desired zinc ion concentration gives $[IO_3^-]^2 = \dfrac{4 \times 10^{-6}}{1 \times 10^{-6}} = 4$. Taking the square root of each side leaves a desired $IO_3^-$ concentration of 2 *M*. Two moles of $KIO_3$ must be added to 1.00 L of solution to produce this concentration. Since you can estimate the answer, no calculator is needed.

**2. A**—When dealing with gaseous equilibriums, volume changes are important when there is a difference in the total number of moles of gas on opposite sides of the equilibrium arrow. All the answers, except A, have differing numbers of moles of gas on opposite sides of the equilibrium arrow.

**3. C**—The hydrolysis of any ion begins with the interaction of that ion with water. Thus, both the ion and water must be on the left side of equilibrium arrow and hence in the denominator of the equilibrium constant expression (water, like all solvents, will be left out of the expression). The oxalate ion is the conjugate base of a weak acid. As a base, it will produce $OH^-$ in solution along with the conjugate acid, $HC_2O_4^-$, of the base. The equilibrium reaction is $C_2O_4^{2-}(aq) + H_2O(l) \leftrightarrows OH^-(aq) + HC_2O_4^-(aq)$.

**4. B**—The addition or removal of some solid, as long as some remains present, will not change the equilibrium. An increase in volume will cause the equilibrium to shift toward the side with more moles of gas (right). Raising the temperature of an endothermic process will shift the equilibrium to the right. Any shift to the right will increase the amounts of the products.

**5. B**—Using the following table:

| | $[CH_4]$ | $[CO_2]$ | $[CO]$ | $[H_2]$ |
|---|---|---|---|---|
| Initial | 0.30 | 0.40 | 0 | 0 |
| Change | $-x$ | $-x$ | $+2x$ | $+2x$ |
| Equilibrium | $0.30 - x$ | $0.40 - x$ | $2x$ | $2x$ |

The presence of 0.20 mole of CO (0.20 *M*) at equilibrium means that $2x = 0.20$ and that $x = 0.10$. Using this value for *x*, the bottom line of the table becomes

| | $[CH_4]$ | $[CO_2]$ | $[CO]$ | $[H_2]$ |
|---|---|---|---|---|
| Equilibrium | 0.20 | 0.30 | 0.20 | 0.20 |

The equilibrium expression is $K = \dfrac{[CO]^2\,[H_2]^2}{[CH_4]\,[CO_2]}$.

Entering the equilibrium values into the equilibrium expression gives $K = \dfrac{[0.20]^2\,[0.20]^2}{[0.20]\,[0.30]}$. As usual, you do not need to do an exact calculation as estimation will work.

**6. A**—The addition of a product will cause the equilibrium to shift to the left. The amounts of all the reactants will increase, and the amounts of all the products will decrease (the $O_2$ will not go below its earlier equilibrium value since excess was added). The value of *K* is constant unless the temperature is changed. The rates of the forward and reverse reactions are equal at equilibrium.

**7. C**—The only way to change the value of *K* is to change the temperature. For an exothermic process ($\Delta H < 0$), *K* increases with a decrease in temperature.

**8. D**—If there are equal numbers of moles of gas on each side of the equilibrium arrow, then volume or pressure changes will not affect the equilibrium. The presence of solids, liquids, or aqueous phases does not make any difference as long as some of the phase is present.

**9. A**—Aqueous ammonia contains primarily $NH_3$, which eliminates B and C. $NH_3Cl$ does not exist, which eliminates D. The reaction produces the silver-ammonia complex, $[Ag(NH_3)_2]^+$.

**10. A**—A *K* is never homogeneous; all the others are always homogeneous.

**11. A**—$K_c = K_p$ occurs whenever there are equal moles of gaseous molecules on each side of the equilibrium arrow.

**12. D**—This is a heterogeneous equilibrium; therefore, the solids ($CaCO_3$ and CaO) will not appear in the equilibrium expression. B is the $K_c$ expression, not the $K_p$ expression.

**13. A**—Lower molar solubility means which one will have the lower concentration (*M*) in solution. We can start by writing the equilibrium equations and the equilibrium constant expressions:

$$CaCO_3(s) \rightleftharpoons Ca^{2+}(aq) + CO_3^{2-}(aq)$$
$$K_{sp} = [Ca^{2+}][CO_3^{2-}] = 4.0 \times 10^{-9}$$
$$SrF_2(s) \rightleftharpoons Sr^{2+}(aq) = 2\ F^-(aq)$$
$$K_{sp} = [Sr^{2+}][F^-]^2 = 8.0 \times 10^{-9}$$

Replacing the concentrations with *x* values (if this is not obvious, create and ICE table):

$$K_{sp} = [x][x] = x^2 = 4.0 \times 10^{-9}$$

$$K_{sp} = [x][2\,x]^2 = 4\,x^3 = 8.0 \times 10^{-9}$$

If the stoichiometries were the same (both $x^2$ or both $4\,x^3$), the smaller $K_{sp}$ is the less soluble; however since the stoichiometries are not the same, it is necessary to solve for *x*.

For $CaCO_3$: $x = \sqrt{4.0 \times 10^{-9}}$

For $SrF_2$: $x^3 = 8.0 \times 10^{-9}/4 = 2.0 = 10^{-9}$

$x = \sqrt[3]{2.0 \times 10^{-9}}$

Solving these without a calculator is challenging; however, it is not necessary to solve these to answer the question. Both values are $10^{-9}$ and the square root of this value ($\approx 10^{-4.5}$) will be smaller than the cube root ($\approx 10^{-3}$). Thus, $CaCO_3$ is less soluble.

**14. A**—The lead(II) is a constant; therefore, it cannot be a factor. The anions are $F^-$, $SO_4^{2-}$, $Cl^-$, and $I^-$. Since changing the pH is what causes the change, we will examine the parent acid of these anions. The parent acids are HF, $H_2SO_4$, HCl, and HI. All these acids except HF are strong acids, so the solubility of the fluoride salt, $PbF_2$, is pH dependent.

**15. B**—The equilibrium reaction equation is: $KClO_4(s) \rightleftharpoons K^+(aq) + ClO_4^-(aq)$.

Any substance that increase the $K^+$ or $ClO_4^-$ from this equilibrium will decrease the solubility. The ions are from KOH and $HClO_4$ which are a strong base and a strong acid, respectively. Since the parents are both strong, pH will not be a factor; thus adding an acid of a base will not alter the solubility. The calcium acetate, $Ca(C_2H_3O_2)_2(aq)$, has nothing in common with the $KClO_4$ equilibrium. The strong acid, $HClO_4$, will decrease the solubility, not because it is an acid, but because it supplies $ClO_4^-$ ions to the solution. This supplied $ClO_4^-$ will decrease the solubility of $KClO_4$ by the common-ion effect.

**16. B**—The question is asking if something will happen, in general, this means that a reaction quotient, *Q*, will need to be calculated. The first step in this calculation will be to determine the concentrations of the $Ag^+$ and $NO_2^-$ ion (the remaining ions are spectator ions).

$8.0 \times 10^{-3}$ mol of $AgNO_3 = 8.0 \times 10^{-3}$ mol of $Ag^+$

$1.0 \times 10^{-3}$ mol of $Ca(NO_2)_2 = 2(1.0 \times 10^{-3})$ mol of $NO_2^- = 2.0 \times 10^{-3}$ mol of $NO_2^-$

The volume of the solution is 1.00 L (a volumetric flask is very accurate, so a 1 liter flask holds 1.00 L of solution—some volumetric flasks are even more accurate). Therefore, the concentrations of the ions are the moles just determined divided by 1.00 L to give: $8.0 \times 10^{-3}$ *M* $Ag^+ = [Ag^+]$ and $2.0 \times 10^{-3}$ *M* $NO_2^- = [NO_2^-]$

The equilibrium reaction and the reaction quotient relationship for $AgNO_2$ are

$$AgNO_2(s) \rightleftharpoons Ag^+(aq) + NO_2^-(aq)$$

$$Q = [Ag^+]\,[NO_2^-] = [8.0 \times 10^{-3}]\,[2.0 \times 10^{-3}]$$
$$= 1.6 \times 10^{-5} < 1.6 \times 10^{-4} = K_{sp}$$

Since $Q < K_{sp}$ no precipitate will form.

**17. A**—First, set up the $K_p$ equilibrium constant expression: $K_p = \frac{P_{CH4}\,P_{CO2}}{P_{CO}^2\,P_{H2}^2}$. Hopefully, you did not make the error of setting up a $K_c = \frac{[CH_4]\,[CO_2]}{[CO]^2\,[H_2]^2}$. Entering the values from partial pressure line of the data table gives: $K_p = \frac{(3.0)\,(8.0)}{(5.0)^2\,(5.0)^2} = 0.038$ (you can round to simplify the final calculation and pick the nearest answer). The value of 26 is the inverse of the correct answer, which means that you wrote the $K_p$ expression upside-down. The value of 19 means that you used the $K_c$ expression instead of the correct $K_p$. The value of 0.053 is the inverse of the $K_c$ answer, which means that you wrote the $K_c$ expression upside-down.

**18. C**—Dissolution is related to $\Delta G$ by the relationship: $\Delta G = -RT \ln K$. If you remember this equation, fine; however, if you do not, it is in the equation information supplied with the exam. Note, the negative sign in the equation means that there is a sign change and a positive $\Delta G$ leads to a negative exponent for *K*. A negative exponent indicates low solubility with the larger the positive value of $\Delta G$, the lower the value of *K*. A small positive value of $\Delta G$ leads to a slightly soluble substance and a large positive value indicates an insoluble substance. Soluble materials have a negative $\Delta G$.

**19. D**—One common way of dealing with multiple related equilibria is to add the equilibrium reactions, which requires that the equilibrium constants be multiplied NOT added. In a series of related equilibria, the first one is probably the largest, and the largest *K* should not be ignored.

**20. A**—As is the case with most equilibrium calculations it is useful begin by writing the correct equilibrium constant expression ($K$). For a $K_f$ reaction, such as this one, the expression is:

$$K_f = \frac{\left[Ag(OH)_2^-\right]}{\left[Ag(H_2O)_2^+\right]\left[OH^-\right]^2}$$

The next step is to enter the values from the table into the equilibrium expression:

$$K_f = \frac{[1.0]}{\left[1.0 \times 10^{-4}\right][1.0]^2} = \frac{1}{\left[1.0 \times 10^{-4}\right]}$$

$$= 1.0 \times 10^4$$

The answer $1.0 \times 10^{-4}$ comes from setting the equilibrium constant expression up incorrectly (inverted). The answer $3.0 \times 10^7$ comes from incorrectly including the solvent ($H_2O$) in the equilibrium constant expression. The answer $1.0 \times 10^{-7}$ comes from incorrectly including the solvent ($H_2O$) in the inverse of the equilibrium constant expression.

## › Free-Response Question

You have 20 minutes to answer the following long question. You may use a calculator and the tables in the back of the book.

### Question

An aqueous solution is prepared that is initially 0.100 $M$ in $CdI_4^{2-}$. After equilibrium is established, the solution is found to be 0.013 $M$ in $Cd^{2+}$. The products of the equilibrium are $Cd^{2+}(aq)$ and $I^-(aq)$.

(a) Derive the expression for the dissociation equilibrium constant, $K_d$, for the equilibrium, and determine the value of the constant.

(b) What will be the cadmium ion concentration arising when 0.400 mol of KI is added to 1.00 L of the solution in part (a)?

(c) A solution is prepared by mixing 0.500 L of the solution from part (b) and 0.500 L of $2.0 \times 10^{-5}$ $M$ NaOH. Will cadmium hydroxide, $Cd(OH)_2$, precipitate? The $K_{sp}$ for cadmium hydroxide is $2.2 \times 10^{-14}$.

(d) When the initial solution is heated, the cadmium ion concentration increases. Is the equilibrium an exothermic or an endothermic process? Explain how you arrived at your conclusion.

(e) Complete the Lewis structure below for the cyanate ion and determine the formal charge for each atom. If resonance is possible, you only need to show one resonance form.

$$[O\ C\ N]^-$$

## › Answer and Explanation

(a) The equilibrium is: $[CdI_4]^{2-}(aq) \leftrightarrows Cd^{2+}(aq) + 4\,I^-(aq)$.

$$K_d = \frac{[Cd^{2+}]\,[I^-]^4}{[CdI_4^{2-}]}$$

Give yourself 1 point for this expression (the "d" subscript is unnecessary).
Using the following table:

| | $CdI_4^{2-}$(aq) | $Cd^{2+}$(aq) | $I^-$(aq) |
|---|---|---|---|
| Initial | 0.100 *M* | 0 | 0 |
| Change | $-x$ | $+x$ | $+4x$ |
| Equilibrium | $0.100 - x$ | $x$ | $4x$ |

The value of $[Cd^{2+}]$ is given (= 0.013), and this is $x$. This changes the last line of the table to:

| | $CdI_4^{2-}$(aq) | $Cd^{2+}$(aq) | $I^-$(aq) |
|---|---|---|---|
| Equilibrium | $0.100 - x = 0.087$ | 0.013 | $4x = 0.052$ |

Entering these values into the $K_d$ expression gives $\dfrac{[0.013]\,[0.052]^4}{[0.087]} = 1.1 \times 10^{-6}$.

Give yourself 1 point for this answer. You can also get 1 point if you correctly put your values into the wrong $K_d$ equation.

(b) The table in part (a) changes to the following:

| | $CdI_4^{2-}$(aq) | $Cd^{2+}$(aq) | $I^-$(aq) |
|---|---|---|---|
| Initial | 0.100 *M* | 0 | 0.400 |
| Change | $-x$ | $+x$ | $+4x$ |
| Equilibrium | $0.100 - x$ | $x$ | $0.400 + 4x$ |

(Since the initial $[Cd^{2+}] = 0$, the equilibrium must shift to the right, which also changes the $[I^-]$.)

$$K_d = \frac{[Cd^{2+}]\,[I^-]^4}{[CdI_4^{2-}]} = 1.1 \times 10^{-6} = \frac{[x]\,[0.400 + 4x]^4}{[0.100 - x]} = \frac{[x]\,[0.400]^4}{[0.100]}$$

$$x = 4.3 \times 10^{-6}\ M = [Cd^{2+}]$$

Give yourself 1 point for the correct setup and 1 point for the correct answer. If you got the wrong value for *K* in part (a), you can still get one or both points for using the value correctly in this calculation.

(c) The $K_{sp}$ equilibrium is: $Cd(OH)_2(s) \leftrightarrows Cd^{2+}(aq) + 2\,OH^-(aq)$
The dilution reduces both the $Cd^{2+}$ ($4.3 \times 10^{-6}$ *M*) and $OH^-$ ($2.0 \times 10^{-5}$ *M*) concentrations by a factor of 2. This gives:

$$[Cd^{2+}] = \frac{4.3 \times 10^{-6}}{2} = 2.2 \times 10^{-6}\ M \text{ and } [OH^-] = \frac{2.0 \times 10^{-5}}{2} = 1.0 \times 10^{-5}\ M.$$

The reaction quotient is $Q = [Cd^{2+}][OH^-]^2 = (2.2 \times 10^{-6})\,(1.0 \times 10^{-5})^2 = 2.2 \times 10^{-16}$. This value is less than the $K_{sp}$, so no precipitate will form. (We have seen students lose points by incorrectly saying that $2.2 \times 10^{-14} < 2.2 \times 10^{-16}$, so be careful.)

Give yourself 1 point for the correct setup and 1 point for the correct answer. If you got the wrong value for $K$ in part (a), you can still get 1 or both points for using the value correctly in this calculation.

(d) Since the cadmium ion concentration increases, the equilibrium must shift to the right. Endothermic processes shift to the right when they are heated. This is in accordance with Le Châtelier's principle.

Give yourself 1 point for endothermic. Give yourself 1 point for correctly mentioning Le Châtelier's principle.

(e) There are three acceptable resonance forms. It is only necessary for you to draw one of them correctly. For an atom, the formal charge = valence electrons – nonbonding electrons – ½ (bonding electrons).

Each of the resonance forms is shown below with the formal charge for each atom calculated:

| | 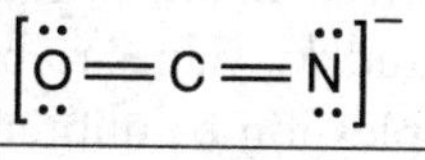 | 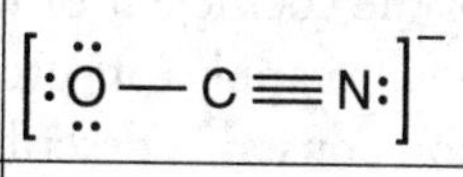 | 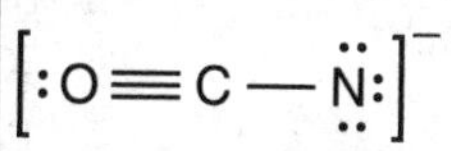 |
|---|---|---|---|
| O | 6 – 4 – ½ (4) = 0 | 6 – 6 – ½ (2) = –1 | 6 – 2 – ½ (6) = +1 |
| C | 4 – 0 – ½ (8) = 0 | 4 – 0 – ½ (8) = 0 | 4 – 0 – ½ (8) = 0 |
| N | 5 – 4 – ½ (4) = –1 | 5 – 2 – ½ (6) = 0 | 5 – 6 – ½ (2) = –2 |
| Total | –1 | –1 | –1 |

The total is a check in case of a calculation error. The total must equal the charge on the ion (0 for a molecule).

You get 1 point for a correct Lewis structure and 1 point for a correct set of formal charges. You will get no more points for drawing more than one Lewis structure. If you draw more than one Lewis structure, you may not get the point for this part if the additional structure is incorrect.

Total your points. There are 10 points possible. Subtract 1 point if any numerical answer has an incorrect number of significant figures.

## › Rapid Review

A chemical equilibrium is established when two exactly opposite reactions occur in the same container at the same time and with the same rates of reaction. At equilibrium, the concentrations of the chemical species become constant, but not necessarily equal.

For the reaction $a\,\text{A} + b\,\text{B} \leftrightarrows c\,\text{C} + d\,\text{D}$, the equilibrium constant expression would be: $K_c = \dfrac{[\text{C}]^c\,[\text{D}]^d}{[\text{A}]^a\,[\text{B}]^b}$. Know how to apply this equation.

Le Châtelier's principle says that if an equilibrium system is stressed, it will reestablish equilibrium by shifting the reactions involved. A change in concentration of a species will cause the equilibrium to shift to reverse that change. A change in pressure or temperature will cause the equilibrium to shift to reverse that change.

The solubility product constant, $K_{sp}$, is the equilibrium constant expression for sparingly soluble salts. It is the product of the ionic concentration of the ions, each raised to the power of the coefficient of the balanced chemical equation.

Know how to apply ion-products and $K_{sp}$ values to predict precipitation.

Formation constants describe complex ion equilibria.

# CHAPTER 16

# Acids and Bases

**IN THIS CHAPTER**


8.1 Introduction to Acids and Bases
8.2 pH and pOH of Strong Acids and Bases
8.3 Weak Acid and Base Equilibria
8.4 Acid–Base Reactions and Buffers
8.5 Acid–Base Titrations
8.6 Molecular Structure of Acids and Bases
8.7 pH and p$K_a$
8.8 Properties of Buffers
8.9 Henderson–Hasselbalch Equation
8.10 Buffer Capacity



**Summary:** In Chapter 12, Reactions and Periodicity, we introduced the concept of acids and bases. Recall that acids are proton ($H^+$) donors and bases are proton acceptors. Also, recall that acids and bases may be strong or weak. **Strong acids** completely dissociate in water (strong electrolytes); **weak acids** only partially dissociate (weak electrolytes). There are generally only two strong bases (strong electrolytes) to consider: the hydroxide and the oxide ion ($OH^-$ and $O^{2-}$, respectively). All other common bases are weak (weak electrolytes). In Chapter 12, our discussion focused on strong acids and bases and their reactions. In this chapter we will concentrate on weak acids and bases, their equilibria and reactions.

It is important to be able to recognize the strong acids and the strong bases. You should assume all other acids and bases are weak unless told otherwise. As a reminder, the strong acids are: HCl, HBr, HI, $HNO_3$, $H_2SO_4$, $HClO_3$, and $HClO_4$. The strong bases are the hydroxides of Li, Na, K, Rb, Cs, Ca, Sr, and Ba.

In this chapter we will also cover pH and pOH, alternate ways of expressing the concentration of weak acids and bases. We will also cover buffers and how they react to control the pH of solutions. In addition we will present the topic of the acid–base properties of salts. Finally, we will address the topic of acid–base titrations involving weak acids and weak bases.

It is important to remember equilibria is equilibria—the general techniques that you learned to handle general equilibrium situations still apply with regards to acid–base equilibria.

**Keywords and Equations**

$K_a$ (weak acid)  $K_b$ (weak base)  $K_w$ (water)

$$K_a = \frac{[H^+][A^-]}{[HA]} \qquad K_b = \frac{[OH^-][HB^+]}{[B]}$$

$K_w = [H^+][OH^-] = 1.0 \times 10^{-14}$ at 25°C

$K_w = K_a \times K_b$

$pH = -\log [H^+]$  $pK_a = -\log K_a$

$pOH = -\log [OH^-]$  $pK_b = -\log K_b$

$14 = pH + pOH$  $pH = pK_a + \log\frac{[A^-]}{[HA]}$

## Acid–Base Equilibrium

Consider two acids: HCl (strong) and $CH_3COOH$ (weak). If each is added to water to form aqueous solutions, the following reactions take place:

$$HCl(aq) + H_2O(l) \rightarrow H_3O^+(aq) + Cl^-(aq)$$

$$CH_3COOH(aq) + H_2O(l) \leftrightarrows H_3O^+(aq) + CH_3COO^-(aq)$$

These reactions are sometimes simplified to:

$$HCl(aq) \rightarrow H^+(aq) + Cl^-(aq)$$

$$CH_3COOH(aq) \leftrightarrows H^+(aq) + CH_3COO^-(aq)$$

In these latter two equations, $H^+(aq)$ is equal to $H_3O^+(aq)$. However, even though acids donate $H^+$, using $H^+$ in the equation for an aqueous solution is not correct. It should be noted that both $H_3O^+(aq)$ and $H^+(aq)$ are simplifications, as the "true" formula of the hydrogen ion in solution is between $H_9O_4^+(aq)$ and $H_{11}O_5^+(aq)$.

The first reaction essentially goes to completion—there is no HCl left in solution. The second reaction is an equilibrium reaction—there are appreciable amounts of both reactants and products left in solution.

There are generally only two strong bases (strong electrolytes) to consider: the hydroxide and the oxide ion ($OH^-$ and $O^{2-}$, respectively). All other common bases are weak (weak electrolytes). **Weak bases**, like weak acids, also establish an equilibrium system, as in aqueous solutions of ammonia:

$$NH_3(aq) + H_2O(l) \leftrightarrows OH^-(aq) + NH_4^+(aq)$$

In the Brønsted–Lowry acid–base theory, there is competition for an $H^+$. Consider the acid–base reaction between acetic acid, a weak acid, and ammonia, a weak base:

$$CH_3COOH(aq) + NH_3(aq) \leftrightarrows CH_3COO^-(aq) + NH_4^+(aq)$$

Acetic acid donates a proton ($H^+$) to ammonia in the forward (left-to-right) reaction of the equilibrium to form the acetate and ammonium ions. But in the reverse (right-to-left) reaction, the ammonium ion donates a proton to the acetate ion to form ammonia and acetic acid. The ammonium ion is acting as an acid and the acetate ion as a base. Under the Brønsted–Lowry system, acetic acid ($CH_3COOH$) and the acetate ion ($CH_3COO^-$) are called a conjugate acid–base pair. **Conjugate acid–base pairs** differ by only a single $H^+$. Ammonia ($NH_3$) and the ammonium ion ($NH_4^+$) are also a conjugate acid–base pair. In this reaction, there is a competition for the $H^+$ between the acetic acid and the ammonium ion. To predict on which side the equilibrium will lie, this general rule applies: *the equilibrium will favor the side in which the weaker acid and base are present.* Figure 16.1 shows the relative strengths of the conjugate acid–base pairs.

In Figure 16.1, you can see that acetic acid is a stronger acid than the ammonium ion and ammonia is a stronger base than the acetate ion. Therefore, the equilibrium will lie to the right.

The reasoning above allows us to find good qualitative answers, but to be able to do quantitative problems (how much is present, etc.), the extent of the dissociation of the weak acids and bases must be known. That is where a modification of the equilibrium constant is useful.

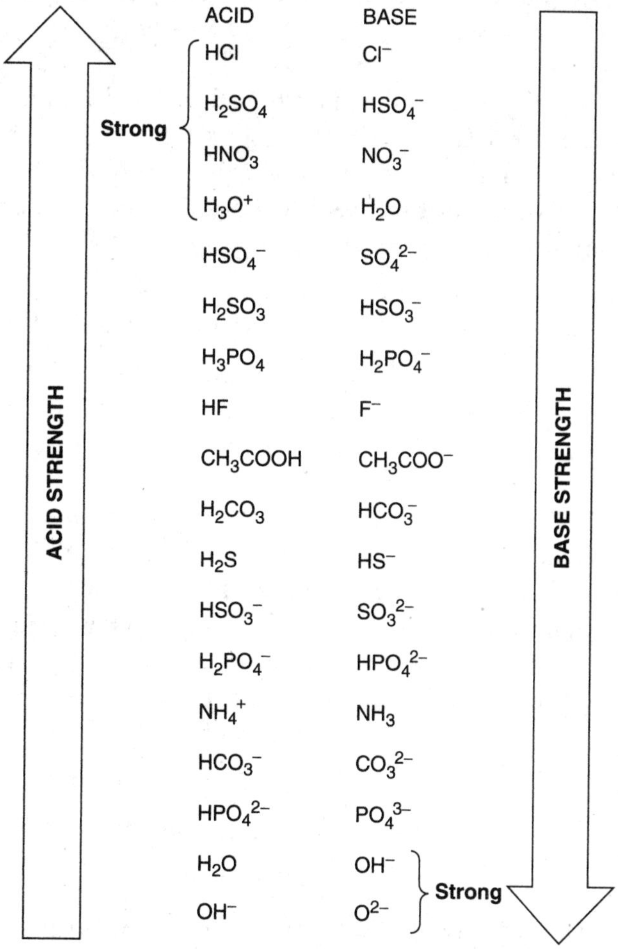


**Figure 16.1 Conjugate acid–base pair strengths.**

# $K_a$—the Acid Dissociation Constant

Strong acids completely dissociate (ionize) in water. Weak acids partially dissociate and establish an equilibrium system. But as shown in Figure 16.1, there is a large range of weak acids based upon their ability to donate protons. Consider the general weak acid, HA, and its reaction when placed in water:

$$HA(aq) + H_2O(l) \leftrightarrows H_3O^+(aq) + A^-(aq)$$

An equilibrium constant expression can be written for this system:

$$K_a = \frac{[H^+][A^-]}{[HA]}$$

The $[H_2O]$ is assumed to be a constant and is incorporated into the $K_a$ value. It is not shown in the equilibrium constant expression.

Since this is the equilibrium constant associated with a weak acid dissociation, this specific $K_c$ is most commonly called the **acid dissociation constant**, $K_a$. The $K_a$ expression is then:

$$K_a = \frac{[H^+][A^-]}{[HA]}$$

In some cases, the $pK_a$ is needed. The $pK_a$ is calculated using the following relationship:

$$pK_a = -\log K_a$$

In general, if the $pH < pK_a$, there will be more of the acid form, HA, in solution than the base form, $A^-$. Also if $pH > pK_a$, then the base form will predominate. If $pH = pK_a$ the concentrations of the two forms will be equal.

Many times the weak acid dissociation reaction will be shown in a shortened notation, omitting the water:

$$HA(aq) \leftrightarrows H^+(aq) + A^-(aq) \qquad \text{with} \qquad K_a = \frac{[H^+][A^-]}{[HA]}$$

The greater the amount of dissociation is, the larger the value of $K_a$. Table 16.1 shows the $K_a$ values of some common weak acids. Strong acids do not have a $K_a$.

TIP

The [HA] is the equilibrium molar concentration of the undissociated weak acid, not its initial concentration. The exact expression would then be $[HA] = M_{\text{initial}} - [H^+]$, where $M_{\text{initial}}$ is the initial concentration of the weak acid. This is true because for every $H^+$ that is formed, an HA must have dissociated. However, many times if $K_a$ is small, you can approximate the equilibrium concentration of the weak acid by its initial concentration, $[HA] = M_{\text{initial}}$.

If the initial molarity and $K_a$ of the weak acid are known, the $[H^+]$ (or $[A^-]$) can be calculated easily. And if the initial molarity and $[H^+]$ are known, $K_a$ can be calculated. For example, calculate the $[H^+]$ of a 0.250 $M$ benzoic acid solution.

$$K_a = 6.3 \times 10^{-5}$$

$$\begin{array}{ccccc} HC_7H_5O_2(aq) & \leftrightarrows & H^+(aq) & + & C_7H_5O_2^-(aq) \\ 0.250 - x & & x & & x \end{array}$$

The quantity of acid that dissociated is $x$, which must be subtracted from the initial concentration (0.250 $M$) to give $(0.250 - x)M$. Each acid molecule that dissociates produces a hydrogen ion ($H^+$) and a benzoate ion ($C_7H_5O_2^-$), so $x$ dissociated molecules produces $x$

$H^+$ and $x$ $C_7H_5O_2^-$. These equilibrium amounts are listed below the respective formulas in the equilibrium reaction and substituted for the formulas in the $K_a$ expression.

$$K_a = \frac{[H^+][C_7H_5O_2^-]}{[HC_7H_5O_2]} = 6.3 \times 10^{-5}$$

$$\frac{[x][x]}{[0.250 - x]} = 6.3 \times 10^{-5}$$

$$x = [H^+] = 4.0 \times 10^{-3}\ M$$

Strong acids are 100% dissociated, and weak acids are less than 100% ionized. In the problem just completed, we can calculate the percent dissociation of the acid by:

$$\%\ \text{dissociation} = \frac{[\text{dissociated acid}]}{[\text{original acid}]} \times 100\%$$

$$= \frac{[x]}{[0.250]} \times 100\% = \frac{[4.0 \times 10^{-3}]}{[0.250]} \times 100\% = 1.6\%$$

For **polyprotic acids**, acids that can donate more than one proton, the $K_a$ for the first dissociation is much larger than the $K_a$ for the second dissociation. If there is a third $K_a$, it is much smaller still. For most practical purposes, you can simply use the first $K_a$.

Remember: $K_a$ expressions are for weak acids. Never ever use a $K_a$ for a strong acid.

# $K_w$—the Water Dissociation Constant

Before examining the equilibrium behavior of aqueous solutions of weak bases, let's look at the behavior of water itself. In the initial discussion of acid–base equilibrium above, we showed water acting both as an acid (proton donor when put with a base) and a base (proton acceptor when put with an acid). Water is **amphoteric**; it will act as either an acid or a base, depending on whether the other species is a base or acid. But in pure water the same amphoteric nature is noted. In pure water, an exceedingly small amount of proton transfer is taking place:

$$H_2O(l) + H_2O(l) \leftrightarrows H_3O^+(aq) + OH^-(aq)$$

This is commonly written as:

$$H_2O(l) \leftrightarrows H^+(aq) + OH^-(aq)$$

There is an equilibrium constant, called the **water dissociation constant, $K_w$**, which has the form:

$$K_w = [H^+][OH^-] = 1.0 \times 10^{-14} \text{ at } 25°C$$

Again, the concentration of water is a constant and is incorporated into $K_w$.

The numerical value of $K_w$ of $1.0 \times 10^{-14}$ is true for the product of the $[H^+]$ and $[OH^-]$ in pure water and for aqueous solutions of acids and bases. This equilibrium is always present any time $H_2O(l)$ is present.

In the discussion of weak acids, we indicated that the $[H^+] = [A^-]$. However, there are two sources of $H^+$ in the system: the weak acid and water. The amount of $H^+$ that is due to the water dissociation is exceedingly small and can be easily ignored.

# Molecular Structure of Acids and Bases

The structures of some acids are shown in Table 16.1. The key to the strength of an acid is how easy it is for the acid to donate an $H^+$. There are many factors influencing this, and while some of these are complimentary, others work against each other. One factor allowing an acid to donate an $H^+$ in aqueous solution is the ability of $H_2O$ to hydrogen bond to an H atom before it is donated. The greater the strength of this hydrogen bond relative to the bond holding the H to the acid, the stronger the acid. The presence of very electronegative elements tends to stabilize the $A^-$ ions formed, and thus increase the strength of the acid. Multiple electronegative atoms are usually better than one.

If we compare the halogen acids HF(aq), HCl(aq), HBr(aq), and HI(aq), HF(aq) is weak and the other three are strong. The three strong acids are strong because the hydrogen–halogen bond is weak relative to the hydrogen bonding present. In the case of HF(aq), the acid is weak because fluorine forms a stronger hydrogen bond than oxygen.

Three of the acids in Table 16.1 are carboxylic acids. If you examine their structures, you will see a common feature of all carboxylic acids. The acidic hydrogen in these structures is the hydrogen to the far right of the structure. Carboxylic acids are a common category of weak acids. Even though these are organic acids, they may appear on the AP Exam in acid–base problems or Lewis structure problems. The organic chemistry of these compounds will not appear on the exam.

**Table 16.1 The Formulas, Structures, and $K_a$ Values for Some Acids.** (Acids in Order of Decreasing $K_a$)

| NAME (FORMULA) | LEWIS STRUCTURE | $K_a$ |
|---|---|---|
| Iodic acid ($HIO_3$) | 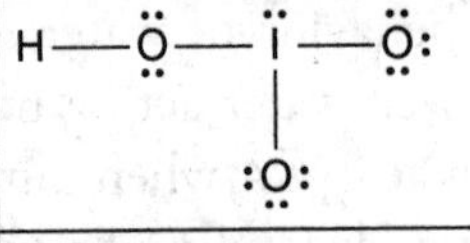 | $1.6 \times 10^{-1}$ |
| Chlorous acid ($HClO_2$) | 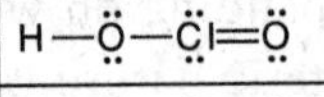 | $1.12 \times 10^{-2}$ |
| Nitrous acid ($HNO_2$) | 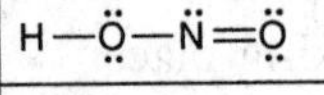 | $7.1 \times 10^{-4}$ |
| Hydrofluoric acid (HF) | 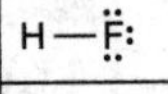 | $6.8 \times 10^{-4}$ |
| Benzoic acid ($C_6H_5COOH$) | 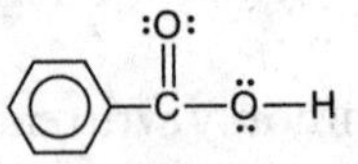 | $6.3 \times 10^{-5}$ |
| Acetic acid ($CH_3COOH$) | 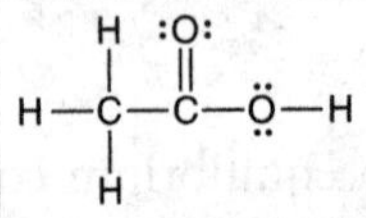 | $1.8 \times 10^{-5}$ |
| Propanoic acid ($CH_3CH_2COOH$) | 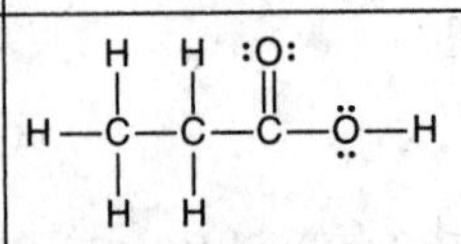 | $1.3 \times 10^{-5}$ |
| Hypochlorous acid (HClO) | 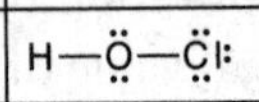 | $2.9 \times 10^{-9}$ |
| Hypobromous acid (HBrO) | 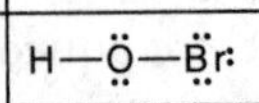 | $2.3 \times 10^{-9}$ |
| Phenol ($C_6H_5OH$) | 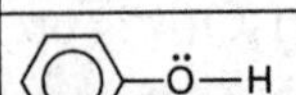 | $1.0 \times 10^{-10}$ |
| Hypoiodous acid (HIO) | 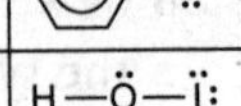 | $2.3 \times 10^{-11}$ |

The conjugate bases of the carboxylic acids are the carboxylate ions, which are common weak bases. For example, the carboxylate ion derived from acetic acid, $CH_3COOH$, is the acetate ion, $CH_3COO^-$. Other common weak bases are nitrogenous bases, the simplest of which is ammonia, $NH_3$. Consider the following representation of the structure of the nitrogenous bases and their acceptance of an $H^+$:

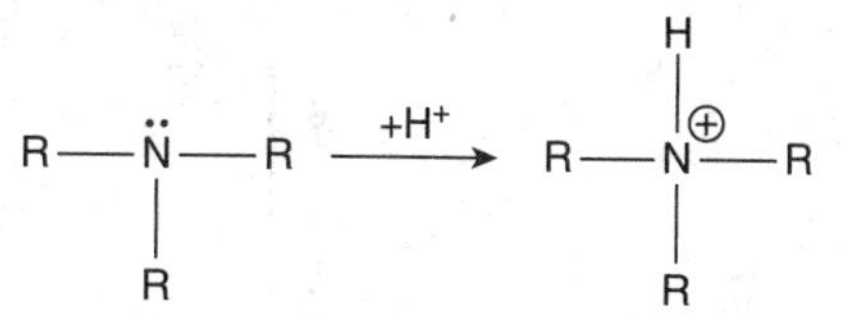

If all three R groups are hydrogen, the reaction is ammonia changing to the ammonium ion. If one or more of the R groups is an organic group, such a $CH_3^-$, the compound is an amine, which are the common organic bases. As with the carboxylic acids, the organic chemistry of amines is not an AP topic; however the acid–base chemistry of these compounds is an AP topic.

## pH

Because the concentration of the hydronium ion, $H_3O^+$, can vary tremendously in solutions of acids and bases, a scale to easily represent the acidity of a solution was developed. It is called the pH scale and is related to the $[H_3O^+]$:

$$pH = -\log [H_3O^+] \text{ or } -\log [H^+] \text{ using the shorthand notation}$$

Remember that in pure water $K_w = [H^+][OH^-] = 10^{-14}$, at 25°C. This value will change if the temperature is not 25°C; however, in most cases, the difference is not too large. This equilibrium is present whenever water is present, but in many cases, $K_w$ is too small to make a difference. Since both the hydrogen ion and hydroxide ions are formed in equal amounts (both $x$), the $K_w$ expression can be expressed as:

$$[H^+][OH^-] = [x][x] = x^2 = 1.0 \times 10^{-14}$$

Solving for $[H^+]$ gives us $[H^+] = 1.0 \times 10^{-7}$. If you then calculate the pH of pure water:

$$pH = -\log [H^+] = -\log [1.0 \times 10^{-7}] = -(-7.00) = 7.00$$

The pH of pure water is 7.00 (at 25°C), slightly different at different temperatures. On the pH scale, this is called **neutral**. A solution whose $[H^+]$ is greater than in pure water will have a pH less than 7.00 and is called **acidic**. A solution whose $[H^+]$ is less than in pure water will have a pH greater than 7.00 and is called **basic**. Figure 16.2, on the next page, shows the pH scale and the pH values of some common substances. In this figure, all solutions below 7 contain an acid, and solutions above 7 contain a base.

The pOH of a solution can also be calculated. It is defined as $pOH = -\log[OH^-]$. The pH and the pOH are related:

$$pH + pOH = pK_w = 14.00 \text{ at } 25°C$$

In any of the problems above in which $[H^+]$ or $[OH^-]$ was calculated, you can now calculate the pH or pOH of the solution.

You can estimate the pH of a solution by looking at its $[H^+]$. For example, if a solution has an $[H^+] = 1 \times 10^{-5}$, its pH would be 5. This value was determined from the value of the exponent in the $[H^+]$. This is why determining the pH of a solution of a strong acid or base is usually much simpler than calculations involving weak acid or bases. For example,

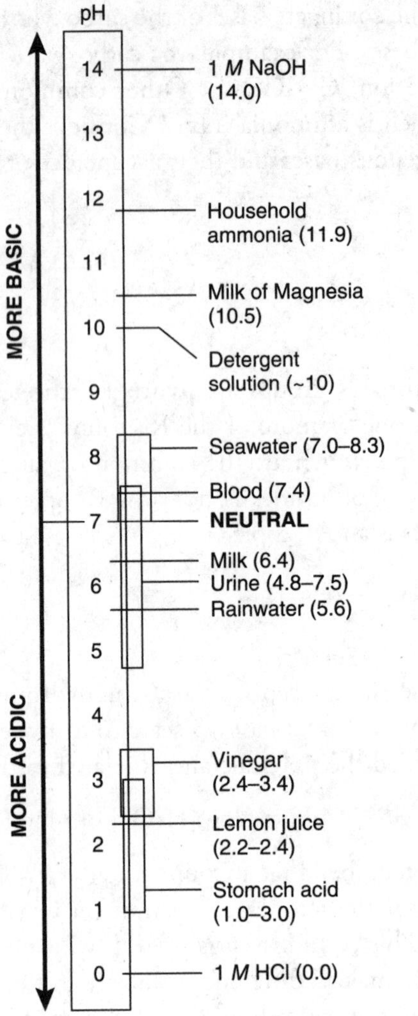


**Figure 16.2 The pH scale.**

the pH of a 0.015 $M$ nitric acid solution is simply pH = – log (0.015) = 1.82, while the pH of a 0.015 $M$ barium hydroxide solution may be found as pOH = – log (2 × 0.015) = 1.52 and pH = p$K_w$ – pH = 14.00 – 1.52 = 12.48 [the 2 is because each $Ba(OH)_2$ has 2 hydroxide ions]. Care must be taken when using this approach. For example, what is the pH of a $1.0 \times 10^{-8}$ $M$ hydrochloric acid solution? If you get an answer of 8.0, and that does not immediately strike you as impossible, you have obviously missed something in the previous discussion, and you need to review the material again.

## $K_b$—the Base Dissociation Constant

Weak bases (B), when placed into water, also establish an equilibrium system much like weak acids:

$$B(aq) + H_2O(l) \leftrightarrows HB^+(aq) + OH^-(aq)$$

Ammonia is a common example of a weak base. The $K_b$ reaction for ammonia is:

$$NH_3 + H_2O \leftrightarrows NH_4^+ + OH^-$$

Many other weak bases substitute hydrocarbon (C + H) groups for one or more of the hydrogen atoms bonded to the nitrogen in ammonia.

The equilibrium constant expression is called the weak **base dissociation constant,** $K_b$, and has the form:

$$K_b = \frac{[HB^+][OH^-]}{[B]}$$

The same reasoning that was used in dealing with weak acids is also true here: $[HB^+] = [OH^-]$; $[B] \approx M$ initially. Calculations involving $K_b$ are like those involving $K_a$.

As with $K_a$ and p$K_a$, the p$K_b$ is sometimes useful. The p$K_b$ is found by the following relationship:

$$pK_b = -\log K_b$$

For example, a 0.500 *M* solution of methylamine, $CH_3NH_2$, has a pH of 12.17. What is the $K_b$ of methylamine? (Note that methylamine is an ammonia molecule with one H replaced by a $CH_3$.)

$$pH = 12.17$$

$$[H^+] = 10^{-12.17}$$

$$[H^+] = 6.8 \times 10^{-13}\ M$$

$$K_w = [H^+][OH^-] = [6.8 \times 10^{-13}][OH^-] = 1.0 \times 10^{-14}$$

$$[OH^-] = 1.5 \times 10^{-2}\ M$$

$$CH_3NH_2(aq) + H_2O(l) \leftrightarrows CH_3NH_3^+(aq) + OH^-(aq)$$

$$0.500 - x \qquad\qquad x \qquad\qquad x$$

$$K_b = \frac{[CH_3NH_3^+][OH^-]}{[CH_3NH_2]}$$

$$[OH^-] = [CH_3NH_3^+] = 1.5 \times 10^{-2}\ M$$

$$[CH_3NH_2] = 0.500 - 1.5 \times 10^{-2} = 0.485\ M$$

$$K_b = \frac{(1.5 \times 10^{-2})(1.5 \times 10^{-2})}{(0.485)} = 4.6 \times 10^{-4}$$

The percent ionization of a base may be calculated by a procedure similar to the calculation of the percent ionization of an acid. Strong bases, like strong acids, are 100% dissociated.

The $K_a$ and $K_b$ of conjugate acid–base pairs are related through the $K_w$ expressions:

$$K_a \times K_b = K_w$$

$$pK_a + pK_b = pK_w = 14.00$$

This equation shows an inverse relationship between $K_a$ and $K_b$ for any conjugate acid–base pair.

This relationship may be used in problems such as: Determine the pH of a solution made by adding 0.400 mol of strontium nitrite to enough water to produce 2.000 L of solution.

Solution:

The initial molarity is 0.400 mol/2.000 L = 0.200 *M*.

When a salt is added to water dissolution will occur:

$$Ca(NO_2)_2 \rightarrow Ca^{2+}(aq) + 2NO_2^-(aq)$$

The resultant solution, since calcium nitrite is soluble, has 0.200 *M* $Ca^{2+}$ and 0.400 *M* $NO_2^-$.

Ions such as $Cl^-$ and $Ca^{2+}$, which come from strong acids or strong bases, may be ignored in this type of problem. Ions such as $NH_4^+$ and $NO_2^-$, from weak acids or bases, will undergo hydrolysis. The nitrite ion is the conjugate *base* of nitrous acid ($K_a = 4.5 \times 10^{-4}$). Since nitrite is not a strong base, this will be a $K_b$ problem, and $OH^-$ will be produced. The equilibrium is:

$$NO_2^-(aq) + H_2O(l) \leftrightarrows OH^-(aq) + HNO_2(aq)$$

$$0.400 - x \qquad\qquad x \qquad\qquad x$$

$$K_b = \frac{[OH^-][HNO_2]}{[NO_2^-]}$$

Determining $K_b$ it from $K_a$ (using $K_w = K_aK_b = 1.0 \times 10^{-14}$) gives:

$$K_b = \frac{K_w}{K_a} = \frac{1.0 \times 10^{-14}}{4.5 \times 10^{-4}} = 2.2 \times 10^{-11}$$

Entering the equilibrium ($x$) values into the $K_b$ expression:

$$\frac{[x][x]}{0.400 - x} = K_b = 2.2 \times 10^{-11}$$

Solving for $x$ gives $x = 3.0 \times 10^{-6} = [OH^-]$.

Using $K_w = [H^+][OH^-] = 1.0 \times 10^{-14}$ to solve for $[H^+]$:

$$[H^+] = \frac{K_w}{[OH^-]} = \frac{1.0 \times 10^{-14}}{3.0 \times 10^{-6}} = 3.3 \times 10^{-9}\ M$$

Finally:

$$pH = -\log [H^+] = -\log (3.3 \times 10^{-9}) = 8.48$$

## Acidic/Basic Properties of Salts

The behavior of a salt will depend upon the acid–base properties of the ions present in the salt. The ions may lead to solutions of the salt being acidic, basic, or neutral. The pH of a solution depends on hydrolysis, a generic term for a variety of reactions with water. Some ions will undergo hydrolysis, and this changes the pH.

The reaction of an acid and a base will produce a salt. The salt will contain the cation from the base and the anion from the acid. In principle, the cation of the base is the conjugate acid of the base, and the anion from the acid is the conjugate base of the acid. Thus, the salt contains a conjugate acid and a conjugate base. This is always true in principle. In some cases, one or the other of these ions is not a true conjugate base or a conjugate acid. Just because the ion is not a true conjugate acid or base does not mean that we cannot use the ion as if it were. The conjugate base of any strong acid is so weak that it will not undergo any significant hydrolysis; the conjugate acid of any strong base is so weak that it, too, will not undergo any significant hydrolysis. Ions that do not undergo any significant hydrolysis will have no effect upon the pH of a solution and will leave the solution neutral. The presence of the following conjugate bases $Cl^-$, $Br^-$, $I^-$, $NO_3^-$, $ClO_3^-$, and $ClO_4^-$ will leave the solution neutral. The cations from the strong bases, $Li^+$, $Na^+$, $K^+$, $Rb^+$, $Cs^+$, $Ca^{2+}$, $Sr^{2+}$, and $Ba^{2+}$, while not true conjugate acids, will also leave the solution neutral. Salts containing only these cations and anions are neutral.

The conjugate base from any weak acid is a "strong" base and will undergo hydrolysis in aqueous solution to produce a basic solution. If the conjugate base (anion) of a weak acid is in a salt with the conjugate of a strong base (cation), the solution will be basic because only the anion will undergo any significant hydrolysis. Salts of this type are basic salts. All salts containing the cation of a strong base and the anion of a weak acid are basic salts.

The conjugate acid of a weak base is a "strong" acid, and it will undergo hydrolysis in an aqueous solution to make the solution acidic. If the conjugate acid (cation) of a weak base is in a salt with the conjugate base of a strong acid (anion), the solution will be acidic because only the cation will undergo any significant hydrolysis. Salts of this type are acidic salts. All salts containing the cation of a weak base and the anion of a strong acid are acidic salts.

There is a fourth category that consists of salts that contain the cation of a weak base with the anion of a weak acid. Prediction of the acid–base character of these salts is less obvious because both ions undergo hydrolysis. The two equilibria not only alter the pH of the solution but also interfere with each other. Predictions require a comparison of the $K$ values for the two ions. The larger $K$ value predominates. If the larger value is $K_a$, the solution is acidic. If the larger value is $K_b$, the solution is basic. In the rare case where the two values are equal, the solution would be neutral.

The following table summarizes this information:

| CATION FROM | ANION FROM | SOLUTION |
|---|---|---|
| Strong base | Strong acid | Neutral |
| Strong base | Weak acid | Basic |
| Weak base | Strong acid | Acidic |
| Weak base | Weak acid | Must be determined by comparing $K$ values |

For example, suppose you are asked to determine if a solution of sodium carbonate, $Na_2CO_3$, is acidic, basic, or neutral. Sodium carbonate is the salt of a strong base (NaOH) and a weak acid ($HCO_3^-$). Salts of strong bases and weak acids are basic salts. As a basic salt, we know the final answer must be basic (pH above 7).

## Buffers

**Buffers** are solutions that resist a change in pH when an acid or base is added to them. The most common types of buffer are a mixture of a weak acid and its conjugate base or a mixture of a weak base and its conjugate acid. The weak acid will neutralize any base added, and the weak base of the buffer will neutralize any acid added to the solution. Thus, the presence of the conjugate acid–base pair will stabilize the pH of the solution. The hydronium ion concentration of a buffer can be calculated using an equation derived by rearranging the $K_a$ expression:

$$[H^+] = K_a \times \frac{[HA]}{[A^-]}$$

Taking the negative log of both sides yields the **Henderson–Hasselbalch equation,** which can be used to calculate the pH of a buffer:

$$pH = pK_a + \log \frac{[A^-]}{[HA]}$$

The weak base $K_b$ expression can also be used, giving:

$$[OH^-] = K_b \times \frac{[B]}{[HB^+]} \quad \text{and} \quad pOH = pK_b + \log \frac{[HB^+]}{[B]}$$

These equations allow us to calculate the pH or pOH of the buffer solution knowing *K* of the weak acid or base and the concentrations of the conjugate weak acid and its conjugate base. Also, if the desired pH is known, along with *K*, the ratio of base to acid can be calculated. The more concentrated these species are, the more acid or base can be neutralized and the less the change in buffer pH. This is a measure of the **buffer capacity,** the ability to resist a change in pH. When the buffer capacity of the buffer is exceeded by the addition of too much acid or base, the solution will cease to be a buffer.

Let's calculate the pH of a buffer. What is the pH of a solution containing 2.50 mol of ammonia and 2.50 mol of ammonium chloride in a volume of 1.00 L?

$$K_b = 1.81 \times 10^{-5}$$

$$NH_3(aq) + H_2O(l) \leftrightarrows NH_4^+(aq) + OH^-(aq)$$

There are two ways to solve this problem.

$$K_b = \frac{[NH_4^+][OH^-]}{[NH_3]} = \frac{(2.50+x)(x)}{(2.50-x)} = 1.81 \times 10^{-5}$$

Assume $x$ is small:

$$1.81 \times 10^{-5} = \frac{2.50\ x}{2.50}$$

$$x = 1.81 \times 10^{-5}$$

$$pOH = -\log [OH^-] = -\log [1.81 \times 10^{-5}] = 4.742$$

$$pH = 14.000 - pOH = 14.000 - 4.742 = 9.258$$

Alternative (shorter) solution:

$$pOH = -\log 1.81 \times 10^{-5} + \log \frac{[NH_4^+]}{[NH_3]}$$

$$= 4.742 + \log \frac{[2.50]}{[2.50]}$$

$$= 4.742 \qquad pH = 9.258$$

This example also illustrates that when the concentrations of the conjugates are the same, $pH = pK_a$.

## Acid–Base Reactions and Buffers

Acid–base reactions were first introduced in Chapter 12. At this time it would be helpful to review the Chapter 12 information in light of the new information that appears in this chapter.

The net ionic equation for the reaction of any strong acid with any strong base is:

$$H^+(aq) + OH^-(aq) \rightarrow H_2O(l)$$

Since this reaction occurs in every strong acid–strong base reaction, problems dealing with this type of reactions are relatively simple. For example, the pH at the equivalence point of such a titration is always 7. At points other than the equivalence point, either the acid or the base is the limiting reactant, and the concentration of the excess reactant controls the pH.

The net ionic equation for the reaction of any weak acid with any strong base may be written as:

$$HA(aq) + OH^-(aq) \rightarrow A^-(aq) + H_2O(l)$$

As long as the excess reactant is the weak acid (if the base is being added to the acid, this is before the equivalence point), the resultant solution is a buffer, and it is possible to use the Henderson–Hasselbalch equation to determine the pH of the solution. (Note at halfway to the equivalence the $pH = pK_a$ of the acid.) When the strong base is in excess (if the base is being added to the acid, this is after the equivalence point), the pH is determined from the concentration of the excess hydroxide ion. At the equivalence point, the pH of the solution will be greater than 7. The pH at the equivalence point is determined by the $K_b$ equilibrium for the conjugate base of the weak acid. This equilibrium is:

$$A^-(aq) + H_2O(l) \leftrightarrows HA(aq) + OH^-(aq) \qquad K_b = \frac{K_w}{K_a}$$

The net ionic equation for the reaction of any weak base with any strong acid may be written as:

$$B(aq) + H^+(aq) \rightarrow HB^+(aq) + H_2O(l)$$

As long as the excess reactant is the weak base (if the acid is being added to the base, this is before the equivalence point), the resultant solution is a buffer, and it is possible to use the Henderson–Hasselbalch equation to determine the pH of the solution. (Note at halfway to the equivalence the $pOH = pK_b$ of the acid.) When the strong acid is in excess (if the acid is being added to the base, this is after the equivalence point), the pH is determined from the concentration of the excess hydrogen ion. At the equivalence point, the pH of the solution will be less than 7. The pH at the equivalence point is determined by the $K_a$ equilibrium for the conjugate acid of the weak base. This equilibrium is:

$$HB^+(aq) + H_2O(l) \leftrightarrows B(aq) + H_3O^+(aq) \qquad K_a = \frac{K_w}{K_b}$$

The net ionic equation for the reaction of any weak acid and any weak base may be written as:

$$HA(aq) + B(aq) \leftrightarrows A^{-}(aq) + HB^{+}(aq)$$

The presence of two conjugate acid–base pairs significantly complicates the calculation, and such calculations are normally avoided.

# Titration Equilibria

An acid–base **titration** is a common laboratory procedure used to determine the concentration of an unknown solution. A base solution of known concentration is added to an acid solution of unknown concentration (or vice versa) until an acid–base **indicator** visually signals that the **endpoint** of the titration has been reached. (A pH meter may also be used to determine the endpoint.) The **equivalence point** is the point at which a stoichiometric amount of the base has been added to the acid. Both chemists and chemistry students hope that the equivalence point (theoretical) and the endpoint (experimental) are close together. If there is an acid–base indicator, there is an additional equilibrium involving the indicator. Note: the members of the conjugate acid–base pair for the indicator are different colors.

If the acid being titrated is a weak acid, then there are equilibria that will be established and must be accounted for in the calculations. Typically, a plot of pH of the weak acid solution being titrated versus the volume of the strong base added (the **titrant**) starts at a low pH and gradually rises until close to the equivalence point, where the curve rises dramatically. After the equivalence point region, the curve returns to a gradual increase. This is shown in Figure 16.3. The titration of a polyprotic acid will contain the same type of plot with a break as indicated in the plot for each of the acidic hydrogen atoms present in the acid.

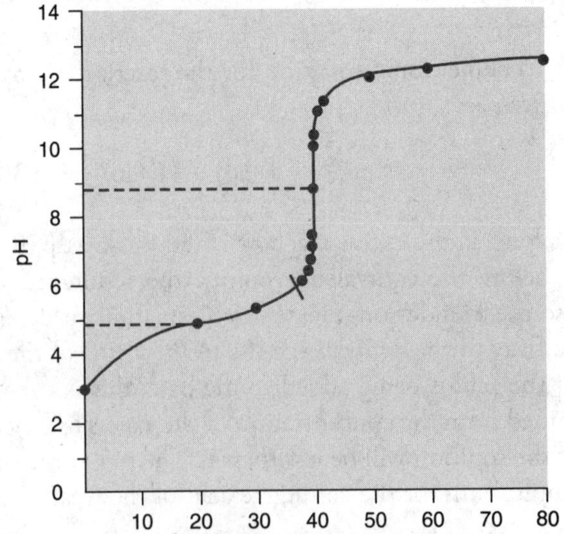


**Figure 16.3 The titration of a weak acid with a strong base.**

In many cases, one may know the initial concentration of the weak acid but may be interested in the pH changes during the titration. To study the changes, one can divide the titration curve into four distinctive areas in which the pH is calculated:

1. Calculating the initial pH of the weak acid solution is accomplished by treating it as a simple weak acid solution of known concentration and using its $K_a$.
2. As base is added, a mixture of the remaining weak acid and its conjugate base is formed. This is a buffer solution and can be treated as one in the calculations. Determine the moles of acid consumed from the moles of titrant added—that will be the moles of conjugate base formed. Then calculate the molar concentration of weak acid and conjugate base, taking into consideration the volume of titrant added. Finally, apply your buffer equations.
3. At the equivalence point, all the weak acid has been converted to its conjugate base. The conjugate base will react with water, so treat it as a weak base solution and calculate the $[OH^-]$ using $K_b$ of the conjugate base of the weak acid ($K_b = \frac{K_w}{K_a}$). Finally, calculate the pH of the solution.
4. After the equivalence point, you have primarily the excess strong base that will determine the pH.

All these steps are reversed if acid is being added to base.

Let's consider a typical titration problem. A 50.00-mL sample of 0.150 *M* formic acid, $HCHO_2$, ($pK_a = 3.74$) was titrated with 0.300 *M* sodium hydroxide. Determine the pH of the solution after the following quantities of base have been added to the acid solution:

**a.** 0.00 mL

**b.** 12.50 mL

**c.** 24.50 mL

**d.** 25.00 mL

**e.** 27.50 mL

**f.** 37.50 mL

Note that throughout this problem we will express the molarity as $\left(\frac{\text{mol}}{1{,}000\text{ mL}}\right)$ instead of $\left(\frac{\text{mol}}{1\text{ L}}\right)$, which will simplify the calculations.

**a.** 0.00 mL. Since no base has been added, only $HCHO_2$ is present. $HCHO_2$ is a weak acid, so this can only be a $K_a$ problem.

$$HCHO_2 \leftrightarrows H^+(aq) + CHO_2^-$$

$$0.150 - x \qquad x \qquad x$$

$$K_a = 10^{-3.74} = 1.8 \times 10^{-4} = \frac{(x)(x)}{0.150 - x}$$

Quadratic needed: $x^2 + 1.8 \times 10^{-4}x - 2.7 \times 10^{-5} = 0$

$$x = [H^+] = 5.1 \times 10^{-3}\text{ M} \qquad pH = 2.29$$

**b.** 12.50 mL. Since both an acid and a base are present (and they are not conjugate to each other), this must be a stoichiometry problem. Stoichiometry requires a balanced chemical equation and moles.

$$HCHO_2(aq) + NaOH(aq) \rightarrow Na^+(aq) + CHO_2^-(aq) + H_2O(l)$$

$Na^+ + CHO_2^-$ could be written as $NaCHO_2$, but the separated ions are more useful.

Initial moles acid: $\left(\frac{0.150 \text{ mol}}{1{,}000 \text{ mL}}\right)(50.00 \text{ mL}) = 0.00750 \text{ mol}$

(This number will be used in all remaining steps. It does not change because no more acid is added.)

Added moles base: $\left(\frac{0.300 \text{ mol}}{1{,}000 \text{ mL}}\right)(12.50 \text{ mL}) = 0.00375 \text{ mol}$

| | $HCHO_2(aq)$ + | $NaOH(aq)$ → | $Na^+(aq)$ + | $CHO_2^-(aq) + H_2O(l)$ |
|---|---|---|---|---|
| init. | 0.00750 | 0.00375 | 0 | 0 |
| react. | −0.00375 | −0.00375 | +0.00750 | +0.00375 |
| final | 0.00375 | 0.000 | — | 0.00375 |

The stoichiometry portion of part (b) is finished.

The solution is no longer $HCHO_2$ and NaOH, but $HCHO_2$ and $CHO_2^-$ (a conjugate acid–base pair).

Since a CA/CB pair is present, this is now a buffer problem, and the Henderson–Hasselbalch equation may be used.

$$pH + pK_a + \log (CB/CA) = 3.74 - \log (0.00375/0.00375) = 3.74$$

Note the simplification in the CB/CA concentrations. Both moles are divided by exactly the same volume (since they are in the same solution), so the identical volumes cancel.

$$\frac{\left[\frac{0.00375 \text{ mol base}}{\cancel{0.06250 \text{ L solution}}}\right]}{\left[\frac{0.00375 \text{ mol acid}}{\cancel{0.06250 \text{ L solution}}}\right]}$$

Another useful fact to remember occurs here. At the halfway point in the titration of a weak acid or a weak base, the concentration of both members of the conjugate acid–base pair are present in equal amounts. This leads to pH = p$K_a$ or pOH = p$K_b$ at this point in the titration.

**c.** 24.50 mL. Since both an acid and a base are present (and they are not conjugate to each other), this must be a stoichiometry problem again. Stoichiometry requires a balanced chemical equation and moles.

$$HCHO_2(aq) + NaOH(aq) \rightarrow Na^+(aq) + CHO_2^-(aq) + H_2O(l)$$

Base: $\left(\frac{0.300 \text{ mol}}{1{,}000 \text{ mL}}\right)(24.50 \text{ mL}) = 0.00735 \text{ mol}$

Use the previously calculated moles of acid (0.00750 mole).

Based on the stoichiometry of the problem, and on the moles of acid and base, NaOH is the limiting reagent.

| | $HCHO_2(aq)$ + | $NaOH(aq)$ → | $Na^+(aq)$ + | $CHO_2^-(aq) + H_2O(l)$ |
|---|---|---|---|---|
| init. | 0.00750 | 0.00735 | 0 | 0 |
| react. | –0.00735 | –0.00735 | +0.00735 | +0.00735 |
| final | 0.00015 | 0.000 | — | 0.00735 |

The stoichiometry portion of part (c) is finished.

The solution is no longer $HCHO_2$ and NaOH, but $HCHO_2$ and $CHO_2^-$ (a conjugate acid–base pair).

Since a CA/CB pair is present, this is now a buffer problem, and the Henderson–Hasselbalch equation may be used.

$$pH + pK_a + \log(CB/CA) = 3.75 - \log(0.00735/0.00015) = 2.1$$

**d.** 25.00 mL. Since both an acid and a base are present (and they are not conjugate to each other), this must be a stoichiometry problem. Stoichiometry requires a balanced chemical equation and moles.

$$HCHO_2(aq) + NaOH(aq) \rightarrow Na^+(aq) + CHO_2^-(aq) + H_2O(l)$$

$$\text{Base: } \left(\frac{0.300 \text{ mol}}{1{,}000 \text{ mL}}\right)(25.00 \text{ mL}) = 0.00750 \text{ mol}$$

Use the previously calculated moles of acid (0.00750 moles).

Based on the stoichiometry of the problem, and on the moles of acid and base, both are limiting reagents.

| | $HCHO_2(aq)$ + | $NaOH(aq)$ → | $Na^+(aq)$ | $+ CHO_2^-(aq) + H_2O(l)$ |
|---|---|---|---|---|
| init. | 0.00750 | 0.00750 | 0 | 0 |
| react. | –0.00750 | –0.00750 | +0.00750 | +0.00750 |
| final | 0.0000 | 0.000 | — | 0.00750 |

$$[CHO_2^-] = 0.00750 \text{ mol}/0.07500 \text{ L} = 0.100\ M$$

The stoichiometry portion of part (d) is finished.

The solution is no longer $HCHO_2$ and NaOH, but an $CHO_2^-$ solution (a conjugate base of a weak acid).

Since the CB of a weak acid is present, this is a $K_b$ problem.

$$pK_b = 14.000 - pK_a = 14.000 - 3.74 = 10.26$$

$$CHO_2^-(aq) + H_2O(l) \leftrightarrows OH^-(aq) + HCHO_2(aq)$$

$$0.100 - x \qquad x \qquad x$$

$$K_b = 10^{-10.26} = 5.50 \times 10^{-11} = \frac{(x)(x)}{0.100 - x} \qquad \text{(neglect } -x\text{)}$$

$$x = [OH^-] = 2.35 \times 10^{-6}\ M \qquad pOH = 5.63$$

$$pH = 14.00 - pOH^- = 14.00 - 5.63 = 8.37$$

**e.** 27.50 mL. Since both an acid and a base are present (and they are not conjugate to each other), this must be a stoichiometry problem. Stoichiometry requires a balanced chemical equation and moles.

$$HCHO_2(aq) + NaOH(aq) \rightarrow Na^+(aq) + CHO_2^-(aq) + H_2O(l)$$

$$\text{Base: } \left(\frac{0.300\ \text{mol}}{1{,}000\ \text{mL}}\right)(27.50\ \text{mL}) = 0.00825\ \text{mol}$$

Use the previously calculated moles of acid (0.00750 moles).

Based on the stoichiometry of the problem, and on the moles of acid and base, the acid is now the limiting reagent.

| | $HCHO_2(aq)$ + | $NaOH(aq)$ → | $Na^+(aq)$ | + $CHO_2^-(aq)$ + $H_2O(l)$ |
|---|---|---|---|---|
| init. | 0.00750 | 0.00825 | 0 | 0 |
| react. | –0.00750 | –0.00750 | +0.00750 | +0.00750 |
| final | 0.0000 | 0.00075 | — | 0.00750 |

The strong base will control the pH.

$$[OH^-] = 0.00075\ \text{mol}/0.0775\ \text{L} = 0.0097\ M$$

The stoichiometry portion of part (e) is finished.

Since this is now a solution of a strong base, it is now a simple pOH/pH problem.

$$pOH = -\log 9.7 \times 10^{-3} = 2.01$$

$$pH = 14.00 - pOH = 14.00 - 2.01 = 11.99$$

**f.** 37.50 mL. Since both an acid and a base are present (and they are not conjugate to each other), this must be a stoichiometry problem. Stoichiometry requires a balanced chemical equation and moles.

$$HCHO_2(aq) + NaOH(aq) \rightarrow Na^+(aq) + CHO_2^-(aq) + H_2O(l)$$

$$\text{Base: } \left(\frac{0.300\ \text{mol}}{1{,}000\ \text{mL}}\right)(37.50\ \text{mL}) = 0.0112\ \text{mol}$$

Use the previously calculated moles of acid (0.00750 moles).

Based on the stoichiometry of the problem, and on the moles of acid and base, the acid is again the limiting reagent.

| | $HCHO_2(aq)$ + | $NaOH(aq)$ → | $Na^+(aq)$ | + $CHO_2^-(aq)$ + $H_2O(l)$ |
|---|---|---|---|---|
| init. | 0.00750 | 0.0112 | 0 | 0 |
| react. | –0.00750 | –0.00750 | +0. 0.00750 | +0.00750 |
| final | 0.0000 | 0.0037 | — | 0.0150 |

The strong base will control the pH.

$$[OH^-] = 0.0037 \text{ mol}/0.0875 \text{ L} = 4.2 \times 10^{-2}\ M$$

The stoichiometry portion of part (f) is finished.
Since this is now a solution of a strong base, it is now a simple pOH/pH problem.

$$pOH = -\log 4.2 \times 10^{-2} = 1.38$$

$$pH = 14.00 - pOH = 14.00 - 1.37 = 12.62$$

## Experiments

STRATEGY

Equilibrium experiments such as 10, 11, and 13 in Chapter 20, Experimental Investigations, directly or indirectly involve filling a table like the following:

| REACTANTS AND PRODUCTS |
|---|
| Initial amount |
| Change |
| Equilibrium amount |

The initial amounts—concentrations or pressures—are normally zero for the products, and a measured or calculated value for the reactants. Once equilibrium has been established, the amount of at least one of the substances is determined. Based on the change in this one substance and the stoichiometry, the amounts of the other materials may be calculated (not measured).

Measurements may include the pressure, the mass (to be converted to moles), the volume (to be used in calculations), and the pH (to be converted into either the hydrogen ion or hydroxide ion concentration). Some experiments measure the color intensity (with a spectrophotometer), which may be converted to a concentration.

Do not make the mistake of "measuring" a change. Changes are never measured; they are always calculated.

## Common Mistakes to Avoid

TIP

1. Be sure to check the units and significant figures of your final answer.
2. Be sure, when working weak-base problems, to use $K_b$ and not $K_a$.
3. In titration problems, make sure you compensate for dilution when mixing two solutions together.
4. A $K_a$ expression must have $[H^+]$ in the numerator, and a $K_b$ expression must have $[OH^-]$ in the numerator. There are NO exceptions.

## › Review Questions

Use these questions to review the content of this chapter and practice for the AP Chemistry Exam. First are 20 multiple-choice questions similar to what you will encounter in Section I of the AP Chemistry Exam. These questions also include ones designed to help you review prior knowledge. Following those is a long free-response question like the ones in Section II of the exam. To make these questions an even more authentic practice for the actual exam, time yourself following the instructions provided.

### Multiple-Choice Questions

Answer the following questions in 30 minutes. You may not use a calculator. You may use the periodic table and the equation sheet at the back of this book.

**1.** A 0.1 molar solution of acetic acid, $CH_3COOH$, has a pH of about:

(A) 1
(B) 3
(C) 7
(D) 10

**2.**

| Acid | $K_a$, Acid Dissociation Constant |
|---|---|
| $H_3PO_4$ | $7.2 \times 10^{-3}$ |
| $H_2PO_4^-$ | $6.3 \times 10^{-8}$ |
| $HPO_4^{2-}$ | $4.2 \times 10^{-13}$ |

Using the given information, choose the best answer for preparing a buffer with a pH of 8.

(A) $K_2HPO_4 + KH_2PO_4$
(B) $H_3PO_4$
(C) $K_2HPO_4 + K_3PO_4$
(D) $K_3PO_4$

**Use the following information for questions 3 and 4.**

| Acid/Base | Ionization Constants |
|---|---|
| HCOOH | $K_b = 1.8 \times 10^{-4}$ |
| $CH_3NH_2$ | $K_b = 4.4 \times 10^{-4}$ |
| $H_3PO_2$ | $K_{a1} = 3 \times 10^{-2}$ |
| | $K_{a2} = 1.7 \times 10^{-7}$ |

**3.** Which of the following is a solution with an initial KCOOH concentration of 1 *M* and an initial $K_2HPO_2$ concentration of 1 *M*?

(A) a solution with a pH > 7, which is a buffer
(B) a solution with a pH < 7, which is not a buffer
(C) a solution with a pH < 7, which is a buffer
(D) a solution with a pH > 7, which is not a buffer

**4.** Which of the following is a solution with an initial $H_3PO_2$ concentration of 1 *M* and an initial $KH_2PO_2$ concentration of 1 *M*?

(A) a solution with a pH > 7, which is a buffer
(B) a solution with a pH < 7, which is not a buffer
(C) a solution with a pH < 7, which is a buffer
(D) a solution with a pH > 7, which is not a buffer

**5.** A solution of a weak base is titrated by adding a solution of a standard strong acid. The progress of the titration is followed with a pH meter. Which of the following observations would occur?

(A) The pH of the solution gradually decreases throughout the experiment.
(B) Initially the pH of the solution drops slowly, and then it drops much more rapidly.
(C) At the endpoint, the pH is 7.
(D) After the equivalence point, the pH becomes constant because this is the buffer region.

**6.** What is the ionization constant, $K_a$, for a weak monoprotic acid with a 0.10 molar solution having a pH of 3.0?

(A) $1 \times 10^{-5}$
(B) $1 \times 10^{-2}$
(C) $1 \times 10^{-6}$
(D) $1 \times 10^{-4}$

**7.** Phenol, $C_6H_5OH$, has $K_a = 1.0 \times 10^{-10}$. What is the pH of a 0.010 *M* solution of phenol?

(A) between 3 and 7
(B) 10
(C) 2
(D) between 7 and 10

**8.** You are given equimolar solutions of each of the following. Which has the lowest pH?

(A) $NH_4Cl$
(B) NaCl
(C) $K_3PO_4$
(D) $Na_2CO_3$

**9.** When sodium nitrite dissolves in water:

(A) The solution is acidic because of the hydrolysis of the sodium ion.
(B) The solution is basic because of the hydrolysis of the $NO_2^-$ ion.
(C) The solution is basic because of the hydrolysis of the sodium ion.
(D) The solution is acidic because of the hydrolysis of the $NO_2^-$ ion.

**10.** Which of the following solutions has a pH nearest 7?

(A) 1 *M* $H_2C_2O_4$ (oxalic acid) and 1 *M* $KHC_2O_4$ (potassium hydrogen oxalate)
(B) 1 *M* $KNO_3$ (potassium nitrate) and 1 *M* $HNO_3$ (nitric acid)
(C) 1 *M* $NH_3$ (ammonia) and 1 *M* $NH_4NO_3$ (ammonium nitrate)
(D) 1 *M* $CH_3NH_2$ (methylamine) and 1 *M* $HC_2H_3O_2$ (acetic acid)

**11.** Determine the $OH^-(aq)$ concentration in a 1.0 *M* aniline ($C_6H_5NH_2$) solution. The $K_b$ for aniline is $4.0 \times 10^{-10}$.

(A) $2.0 \times 10^{-5}$ *M*
(B) $4.0 \times 10^{-10}$ *M*
(C) $3.0 \times 10^{-6}$ *M*
(D) $5.0 \times 10^{-7}$ *M*

**12.** $ZnS(s) + 2\,H^+(aq) \leftrightarrows Zn^{2+}(aq) + H_2S(aq)$

What is the equilibrium constant for the above reaction? The successive acid dissociation constants for $H_2S$ are $9.5 \times 10^{-8}$ ($K_{a1}$) and $1 \times 10^{-19}$ ($K_{a2}$). The $K_{sp}$, the solubility product constant, for ZnS equals $1.6 \times 10^{-24}$.

(A) $1.7 \times 10^{-17}$
(B) $6.3 \times 10^{-56}$
(C) $1.7 \times 10^{2}$
(D) $5.9 \times 10^{16}$

**13.** The addition of nitric acid increases the solubility of which of the following compounds?

(A) KCl(s)
(B) $Pb(CN)_2(s)$
(C) $Cu(NO_3)_2(s)$
(D) $NH_4NO_3(s)$

**14.** Which of the following is the strongest Brønsted–Lowry acid?

(A) HBrO
(B) $HBrO_3$
(C) $HBrO_2$
(D) $HBrO_4$

**15.**

| **Ionization** | **Constants** |
|---|---|
| $NH_3$ | $K_b = 1.8 \times 10^{-5}$ |
| $CH_3NH_2$ | $K_b = 4.4 \times 10^{-4}$ |
| $(CH_3)_2NH$ | $K_b = 1.1 \times 10^{-3}$ |

How would a solution with an initial $NH_4Cl$ ($NH_4^+ + Cl^-$) concentration of 1 *M* and an initial concentration of $CH_3NH_3Cl$ ($CH_3NH_3^+ + Cl^-$) concentration of 1 *M* be classified?

(A) a solution with a pH > 7, which is a buffer
(B) a solution with a pH < 7, which is not a buffer
(C) a solution with a pH < 7, which is a buffer
(D) a solution with a pH > 7, which is not a buffer

**16.** Which of the following species CANNOT serve as both a Brønsted base and a Brønsted acid?

(A) $H_2PO_4^{2-}$
(B) $CO_3^{2-}$
(C) $HSeO_4^-$
(D) $HCO_3^-$

**17.** A buffer stock solution is made by mixing 2.0 moles of $NH_3$ and 3.0 moles of $NH_4Cl$ and diluting to 1.0 L. What is the buffer capacity of 100.0 mL of this solution toward NaOH?

(A) 0.20 moles NaOH
(B) 0.30 moles NaOH
(C) 3.0 moles NaOH
(D) 2.0 moles NaOH

**18.** Acetic acid, $HC_2H_3O_2$, is a commonly used weak acid, which is also an organic compound. This acid, and many other organic acids, own their acidic behavior to a specific structure of a particular group of atoms. What is the one way of writing the general formula of this particular group of atoms?

(A) –COOH
(B) $HC_2^-$
(C) $HC^-$
(D) There is no general formula.

**19.** In the titration of a weak base solution with a strong acid solution where does the $pOH = pK_b$ of the weak base?

(A) At the equivalence point
(B) At the endpoint
(C) At no point in the titration
(D) Halfway to the equivalence point

**20.** Under what circumstances will it not be a problem to add the indicator after an acid–base titration has begun?

(A) Any time if the acid and base are both strong.
(B) Any time if either the acid or base is weak.
(C) As long as it is added before the endpoint.
(D) It is never acceptable to add the indicator late.

## Answers and Explanations

1. **B**—Any acid will have a pH below 7; thus, C and D can be eliminated. A 0.1 molar solution of a strong acid would have a pH of 1. Acetic acid is not a strong acid, which eliminates A.

2. **A**—The $K$ nearest $10^{-8}$ will give a pH near 8. The answer must involve the $H_2PO_4^-$ ion. The potassium ions are spectator ions and have no effect on the pH.

3. **D**—The two substances are not a conjugate acid–base pair, so this is not a buffer, which eliminates answers A and C. Both compounds are salts of a strong base and a weak acid; such salts are basic (pH > 7).

4. **C**—The two substances constitute a conjugate acid–base pair of a weak acid, so this is a buffer. The pH should be near $-\log K_{a1}$. This is about 2 (acid).

5. **B**—Anytime an acid is added, the pH will drop. The reaction of the weak base with the acid produces the conjugate acid of the weak base. The combination of the weak base and its conjugate is a buffer, so the pH will not change very much until all the base is consumed. After all the base has reacted, the pH will drop much more rapidly. The equivalence point of a weak base–strong acid titration is always below 7 (only strong base–strong acid titrations will give a pH of 7 at the endpoint). The value of pOH is equal to $pK_b$ halfway to the equivalence point.

6. **A**—If pH = 3.0, then $[H^+] = 1 \times 10^{-3} = [A^-]$, and $[HA] = 0.10 - 1 \times 10^{-3} \approx 0.10$. The generic $K_a$ is $= \dfrac{[H^+][A^-]}{[HA]}$ and when the values are entered into this equation, $\dfrac{(1 \times 10^{-3})^2}{(0.10)} = 1 \times 10^{-5}$. Since you can estimate the answer, no actual calculations are necessary.

7. **A**—This is an acid dissociation constant; thus, the solution must be acidic (pH < 7). The pH of a 0.010 $M$ strong acid would be 2.0. This is not a strong acid, so the pH must be above 2. Even though phenol has an OH in its formula, the fact that it has a $K_a$ means that it must be an acid. Phenol is an organic compound, which is irrelevant since there is only one way to handle a $K_a$ equilibrium.

8. **A**—A is the salt of a strong acid and a weak base; therefore, this salt is acidic. B is a salt of a strong acid and a strong base; such salts are neutral. C and D are salts of a weak acid and a strong base; such salts are basic. Since A is the only acidic salt, it is the solution with the lowest pH.

9. **B**—Sodium nitrite is a salt of a weak acid and a strong base. Ions from strong bases ($Na^+$ in this case) do not undergo hydrolysis and do not affect the pH. Ions from weak acids ($NO_2^-$ in this case) undergo hydrolysis to produce basic solutions.

10. **D**—The weak acid and the weak base partially cancel each other to give a nearly neutral solution. Methylamine is related to ammonia, and like ammonia it is a weak base.

11. **A**—The equilibrium constant expression is $K_b = \dfrac{[OH^-][C_6H_5NH_3^+]}{[C_6H_5NH_2]}$ (not needed). This expression becomes $\dfrac{[x][x]}{[1.0-x]} = 4.0 \times 10^{-10}$ (needed), which simplifies to $\dfrac{[x][x]}{[1.0]} = 4.0 \times 10^{-10}$. Taking the square root of each side gives $x = 2.0 \times 10^{-5} = [OH^-]$. Since you can estimate the answer, no calculator is necessary. The formula of the compound is irrelevant since there is only one way to do a $K_b$ problem.

12. **C**—The equilibrium given is the sum of the following three equilibriums:

$$ZnS(s) \leftrightarrows Zn^{2+}(aq) + S^{2-}(aq) \quad K_{sp} = 1.6 \times 10^{-24}$$

$$S^{2-}(aq) + H^+(aq) \leftrightarrows HS^-(aq) \quad K = 1/K_{a2} = 1/1 \times 10^{-19}$$

$$HS^-(aq) + H^+(aq) \leftrightarrows H_2S(aq) \quad K' = 1/K_{a1} = 1/9.5 \times 10^{-8}$$

Summing these equations means you need to multiply the equilibrium constants: $K_{sum} = K_{sp}K\ K' = \dfrac{K_{sp}}{K_{a2}K_{a1}} = \dfrac{1.6 \times 10^{-24}}{(1 \times 10^{-19})(9.5 \times 10^{-8})}$. Estimate the answer by using the exponents to get the exponent of the correct answer (+3) and pick the closest.

**13. B**—Nitric acid, being an acid, will react with a base. In addition to obvious bases containing $OH^-$, the salts of weak acids are also bases. All the anions, except $CN^-$ are from strong acids and, as such, are not bases. The removal of the $CN^-$ ion shifts the $K_{sp}$ equilibrium for $Pb(CN)_2$ to the right (more soluble).

**14. D**—Perbromic acid, $HBrO_4$, is expected to be the strongest acid in this group because the greater number of oxygen atoms pulls more electron density from the hydrogen atom, making it easier to be lost as a hydrogen ion.

**15. B**—The two substances ($NH_4Cl$ and $CH_3NH_3Cl$) do not contain a conjugate acid–base pair, so the mixture is not a buffer, which eliminates A and C. Both compounds are salts of a weak base ($NH_3$ or $CH_3NH_2$) and a strong acid (HCl); such salts are acidic (pH < 7). Salts of a strong acid and a weak base are acidic salts. The $K_b$ values shown in the table indicate that all three compounds are weak bases.

**16. B**—All the ions can serve as Brønsted bases (accept a hydrogen ion to form $H_3PO_4$, $HCO_3^-$, $H_2SeO_4$, and $H_2CO_3$). All but B can behave as Brønsted acids (donate a hydrogen ion to form $HPO_4^{2-}$, $SeO_4^{2-}$, and $CO_3^{2-}$).

**17. B**—A 100.0 mL sample of the stock is one-tenth of the solution; therefore, it contains one-tenth of the solutes: 0.20 mole of $NH_3$ and 0.30 mole $NH_4Cl$. The added NaOH will react with the acid component of the buffer, $NH_4Cl$. The reaction is:

$$NaOH(aq) + NH_4Cl(aq) \rightarrow NaCl(aq) + NH_3(aq) + H_2O(l)$$

Since the reaction stoichiometry is 1:1, 0.30 moles of $NH_4Cl$ will react with 0.30 mole of NaOH.

**18. A**—Acetic acid is an example of a carboxylic acid. In some cases, the formula of acetic acid is written as $CH_3COOH$ to emphasize this. Two other carboxylic acids are formic acid, HCOOH, and propanoic acid, $CH_3CH_2COOH$. You may have seen or even used oxalic acid, $H_2C_2O_4$, which is a combination of two carboxylic acid groups as seen when the formula is writer as HOOCCOOH or $(COOH)_2$. Note, this question deals with the AP topic 8.6 The Molecular Structure of Acids and Bases. A similar question might deal with some of the organic bases, which have structures derived from ammonia, $NH_3$.

**19. D**—While it may seem simpler to simply memorize this fact for a multiple-choice question, free-response questions require explanations.

This may be demonstrated by using the pOH form of the Henderson–Hasselbalch equation, which may be derived from the acid form:

Acid form: $pH = pK_a + \log\frac{[A^-]}{[HA]}$ given on the exam

Alternate acid form: $pH = pK_a + \log\frac{[CB]}{[CA]}$

In this form, CA and CB being the members of a conjugate acid-base pair.

Analogous base form: $pOH = pK_b + \log\frac{[CA]}{[CB]}$

At halfway to the equivalence point, [CA] = [CB], which means $\log\frac{[CA]}{[CB]} = \log 1 = 0$

**20. C** The purpose of the indicator is to determine the endpoint; therefore, as long as the indicator is present before the endpoint is reached, the titration should work.

Expect questions involving laboratory experiments throughout the exam.

## › Free-Response Question

You have 10 minutes to answer the following short question. You may use a calculator and the tables in the back of the book.

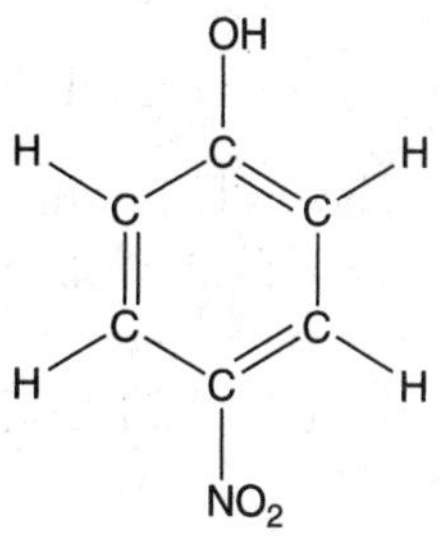


The compound p-nitrophenol (pictured above) may be used as an acid–base indicator. It is typically used as an indicator in the form of a 0.1% aqueous solution. In acid, this indicator is colorless, while in base the indicator is yellow. The maximum absorption for the colorless form is 313 nm and the maximum absorption for the yellow form is 402 nm. As an indicator, it reacts with hydroxide ions according to the following equilibrium:

$$C_6H_5NO_3(aq) + OH^-(aq) \leftrightarrows C_6H_4NO_3^-(aq) + H_2O(l)$$

colorless yellow

(a) Write the $K_{eq}$ for the above reaction.

(b) Like many acid–base indicators, p-nitrophenol is a weak acid. An indicator solution is made by adding 0.100 g of this compound to a 100-mL volumetric flask containing a little water. The sample is diluted to volume by the addition of more water. If the molar mass of this compound is 139.110 g mol$^{-1}$, what is the molarity of this solution?

(c) Several samples of p-nitrophenol are prepared by diluting the indicator solution with pH = 10 buffer to assure conversion of all the $C_6H_5NO_3(aq)$ to $C_6H_4NO_3^-(aq)$. These samples were used to create the calibration plot below at a wavelength of 402 nm.

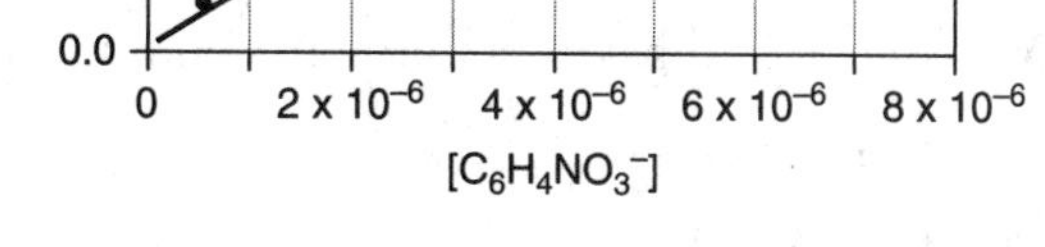


The experimental data points and the best-fit line is shown on the graph. What is the approximate absorbance of a solution with $[C_6H_4NO_3^-] = 3 \times 10^{-6}$ *M*?

(d) The color change of the indicator is in the 5.6–7.6 pH range. This indicator would work best for which of the following titrations: (i) $Na_2CO_3$ with standard HCl; (ii) HCl with standard NaOH; (iii) $NH_3$ with standard $HC_2H_3O_2$?

## › Answer and Explanation

(a) $K_{eq} = \frac{[C_6H_4NO_3^-]}{[C_6H_5NO_3][OH^-]}$

1 point for the correct equilibrium expression unless $H_2O$ is included in the expression.

(b) To determine the molarity, the moles of indicator must be divided by the liters of solution. The grams of p-nitrophenol need to be converted to moles and the volume of the solution needs to be converted to liters. These may be done as two separate calculations or as one combined calculation as shown below.

$$M = \frac{(0.100 \text{ g } C_6H_5NO_3)\left(\frac{\text{mol}}{139.110 \text{ g}}\right)}{(100.00 \text{ mL})\left(\frac{\text{L}}{1{,}000 \text{ mL}}\right)} = 7.19 \times 10^{-3}\ M$$

1 point for the correct calculation unless the answer has the wrong number of significant figures (3).

(c) 0.23
1 point for this answer. Significant figures are not important. Values from 0.21 through 0.25 are acceptable. Units are unnecessary; however, a.u. or absorbance (units) may be used.

(d) The best choice is (ii).
The midpoint of the pH range is 6.6; therefore, a titration with an equivalence point near this value would be best. The indicator works better when the pH is increasing (colorless → yellow), since it is easier to see the color appearing than disappearing (yellow → colorless). This is one reason why (ii) is a better choice than (i). The other reason why (ii) is better than (i) is that it is a strong acid–strong base titration, and as such the equivalence point is at pH = 7 (close to 6.6). (iii) is not a good choice regardless of the indicator since it is a weak base–weak acid titration.
1 point for choosing (ii) and giving either of the two reasons listed.

## › Rapid Review

- Strong acids completely dissociate in water, whereas weak acids only partially dissociate (have an equilibrium constant).
- Weak acids and bases establish an equilibrium system.
- Under the Brønsted–Lowry acid–base theory, acids are proton ($H^+$) donors and bases are proton acceptors.
- Conjugate acid–base pairs differ only in a single $H^+$; the one that has the extra $H^+$ is the acid.
- The equilibrium for a weak acid is described by $K_a$, the acid dissociation constant. It has the form: $K_a = \frac{[H^+][A^-]}{[HA]}$. Know how to apply this equation. If there is an exponent other than 1 anywhere in the equation, you have made an error.

- Most times the equilibrium concentration of the weak acid, [HA], can be approximated by the initial molarity of the weak acid.
- Knowing $K_a$ and the initial concentration of the weak acid allows the calculation of the $[H^+]$.
- Water is an amphoteric substance, acting either as an acid or a base.
- The product of the $[H^+]$ and $[OH^-]$ in a solution or in pure water is a constant, $K_w$, called the water dissociation constant, $1.0 \times 10^{-14}$. $K_w = [H^+]\,[OH^-] = 1.0 \times 10^{-14}$ at 25°C. Know how to apply this equation.
- The pH is a measure of the acidity of a solution. $pH = -\log[H^+]$. Know how to apply this equation and estimate the pH from the $[H^+]$.
- On the pH scale 7 is neutral; pH > 7 is basic; and pH < 7 is acidic.
- $pH + pOH = pK_w = 14.00$. Know how to apply this equation.
- $K_b$ is the ionization constant for a weak base. $K_b = \dfrac{[OH^-][HB^+]}{[B]}$. Know how to apply this equation. If there is an exponent other than 1 anywhere in the equation, you have made an error.
- $K_a \times K_b = K_w$ for conjugate acid–base pairs. Know how to apply this equation.
- Buffers are solutions that resist a change in pH by neutralizing either an added acid or an added base.
- The Henderson–Hasselbalch equation allows the calculation of the pH of a buffer solution: $pH = pK_a + \log \dfrac{[A^-]}{[HA]}$. Know how to apply this equation.
- The buffer capacity is a quantitative measure of the ability of a buffer to resist a change in pH. The more concentrated the acid–base components of the buffer, the higher its buffer capacity.
- A titration is a laboratory technique to determine the concentration of an acid or base solution.
- An acid–base indicator is used in a titration and changes color in the presence of an acid or base.
- The equivalence point or endpoint of a titration is the point at which an equivalent amount of acid or base has been added to the base or acid being neutralized.
- Know how to determine the pH at any point of an acid–base titration.
- If you have a solution of an acid, the pH will be below 7.
- If you have a solution of a base, the pH will be above 7.

CHAPTER 17

# Electrochemistry

**IN THIS CHAPTER**

In this chapter, the following AP topics are covered:

9.7 Galvanic (Voltaic) and Electrolytic Cells
9.8 Cell Potential and Free Energy
9.9 Cell Potential Under Nonstandard Conditions
9.10 Electrolysis and Faraday's Law

**Summary: Electrochemistry** is the study of the chemical reactions that produce electricity and chemical reactions that take place because electricity is supplied. Electrochemical reactions may be of many types. Electroplating is an electrochemical process. So are the electrolysis of water, the production of aluminum metal, and the production and storage of electricity in batteries. All these processes involve the transfer of electrons and redox reactions.

## Keywords and Equations

KEY IDEA

A table of half-reactions is given in the exam booklet and in the back of this book.

Gas constant, $R = 8.314\ \text{J mol}^{-1}\ \text{K}^{-1} = 0.08206\ \text{L atm mol}^{-1}\ \text{K}^{-1}$

$q$ = charge (coulombs) $E°$ = standard reduction potential
$t$ = time (seconds) $I$ = current (amperes)
$n$ = number of moles $T$ = temperature

Faraday's constant, $F$ = 96,485 coulombs per mole of electrons

$Q$ = reaction quotient $1\ \text{volt} = \dfrac{1\ \text{joule}}{1\ \text{coulomb}}$

$\Delta G° = \Delta H° - T\Delta S° = -RT \ln K = -nFE°$

$E_{\text{cell}} = E°_{\text{cell}} - \dfrac{RT}{nF} \ln Q \qquad I = \dfrac{q}{t}$

$K_c = \dfrac{[C]^c[D]^d}{[A]^a[B]^b}$, where $aA + bB \rightarrow cC + dD$

## Redox Reactions

Electrochemical reactions involve redox reactions. In Chapter 12, Reactions and Periodicity, we discussed redox reactions, but here is a brief review: *Redox* is a term that stands for reduction and oxidation. Reduction is the gain of electrons, and oxidation is the loss of electrons. For example, suppose a piece of zinc metal is placed in a solution containing blue $Cu^{2+}$ ions. Very quickly, a reddish solid forms on the surface of the zinc metal. That substance is copper metal. At the molecular level, the zinc metal atoms are losing electrons to form $Zn^{2+}$ and $Cu^{2+}$ ions are gaining electrons to form copper metal. These two processes can be shown as:

$$Zn(s) \rightarrow Zn^{2+}(aq) + 2e^- \qquad \text{(oxidation)}$$

$$Cu^{2+}(aq) + 2e^- \rightarrow Cu(s) \qquad \text{(reduction)}$$

The electrons that are being lost by the zinc metal are the same electrons that are being gained by the cupric ion. The zinc metal is being oxidized, and the copper(II) cation is being reduced.

Something must cause the oxidation (taking of the electrons), and that substance is called the oxidizing agent (the reactant being reduced). In the example above, the oxidizing agent is $Cu^{2+}$. The reactant undergoing oxidation is called the reducing agent because it is furnishing the electrons used in the reduction half-reaction. Zinc metal is the reducing agent above. The two half-reactions, oxidation and reduction, can be added together to give you the overall redox reaction. The electrons must cancel—that is, there must be the same number of electrons lost as electrons gained. Adding the two reactions above (oxidation and reduction) gives:

$$Zn(s) + Cu^{2+}(aq) + 2e^- \rightarrow Zn^{2+}(aq) + 2e^- + Cu(s)$$

The next step is to cancel the electrons, which leaves:

$$Zn(s) + Cu^{2+}(aq) \rightarrow Zn^{2+}(aq) + Cu(s)$$

In these redox reactions, like the electrochemical reactions we will show you, there is a simultaneous loss and gain of electrons. In the oxidation reaction (commonly called a half-reaction) electrons are being lost, but in the reduction half-reaction those very same electrons are being gained. So, in redox reactions electrons are being exchanged as reactants are being converted into products. This electron exchange may be direct, as when copper metal plates out on a piece of zinc, or it may be indirect, as in an electrochemical cell (battery). In this chapter, we will show you both processes and the calculations associated with each.

Knowing how to balance redox equations can be useful on the AP Exam, so we have included the half-reaction method of balancing redox reactions in the appendixes just in case you are having trouble with the technique in your chemistry class.

The definitions for oxidation and reduction given above are the most common and the most useful ones. A couple of others might also be useful: Oxidation is the gain of oxygen or loss of hydrogen and involves an increase in oxidation number. Reduction is the gain of hydrogen or loss of oxygen and involves a decrease in oxidation number.

## Electrochemical Cells

In the example above, the electron transfer was direct; that is, the electrons were exchanged directly from the zinc metal to the copper(II) ions. But such a direct electron transfer doesn't allow for any useful work to be done by the electrons. Therefore, in order to use these electrons, indirect electron transfer must be done. The two half-reactions are physically separated and connected by a wire. The electrons that are lost in the oxidation half-reaction flow through the wire to get to the reduction half-reaction. While those electrons are flowing through the wire, they can do useful work, like powering a calculator or a pacemaker. **Electrochemical cells** use indirect electron transfer to produce electricity by a redox reaction, or they use electricity to produce a desired redox reaction.

## Galvanic (Voltaic) Cells

**Galvanic (voltaic) cells** produce electricity by using a redox reaction. Let's take that zinc/copper redox reaction that we studied before (the direct electron-transfer reaction) and make it a galvanic cell by separating the oxidation and reduction half-reactions. (See Figure 17.1.) The reaction is a thermodynamically favorable reaction. The cell potential for a galvanic cell is positive.

Instead of one container, as before, two will be used. A piece of zinc metal will be placed in one container, and a piece of copper metal in another container. A solution of aqueous zinc sulfate (or some other water-soluble zinc compound) will be added to the container containing the zinc electrode and an aqueous solution of copper(II) sulfate [or some other water-soluble copper(II) compound] will be added to the container containing the copper metal. The zinc and copper metals will form the **electrodes** of the cell, the portion of the cell that conducts the electrons involved in the redox reaction. The solutions in which the electrodes are immersed are called the **electrode compartments**. The electrodes are connected by a wire and . . . nothing happens. If the redox reactions were to proceed, the container containing the zinc metal would build up a positive charge due to the zinc cations being produced in the oxidation half-reaction. The container containing the copper would build up a negative charge due to the loss of the copper(II) cations. The solutions (compartments) must maintain electrical neutrality. To accomplish this, a salt bridge will be used. A **salt bridge** is often an inverted U-tube that holds a gel containing a concentrated electrolyte solution, such as $KNO_3$ in this example. Any electrolyte could be used if it does not interfere with the redox reaction. The anions in the salt bridge will migrate through the gel into the beaker containing the zinc metal (to balance the excess positive charge), and the salt-bridge cations will migrate in the opposite direction (to balance the excess negative charge). In this way, electrical neutrality is maintained. In electrical terms,

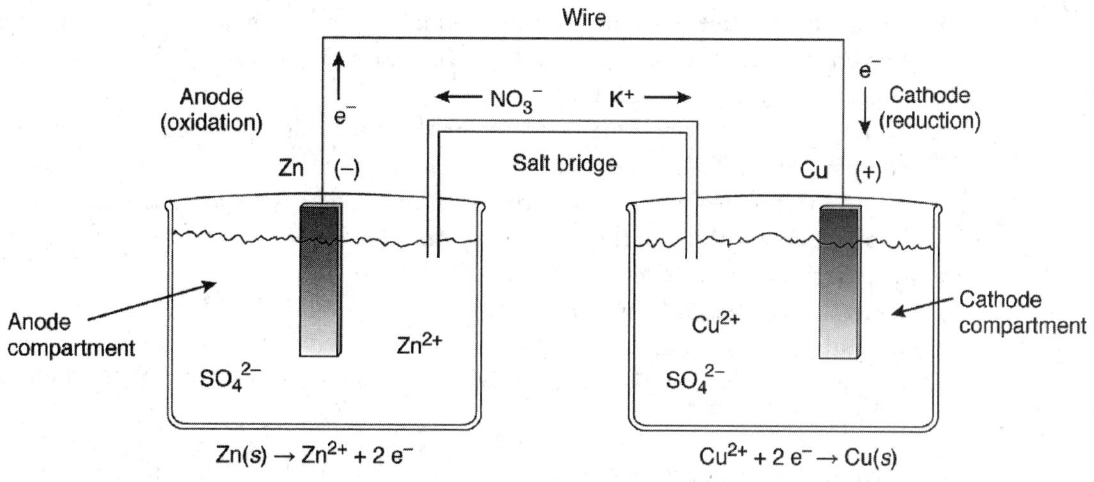


**Figure 17.1 A galvanic cell.**

the circuit has been completed and the redox reaction can occur. The zinc electrode is being oxidized in one container, and the copper(II) ions in the other container are being reduced to copper metal. The same redox reaction is happening in this indirect electron transfer as happened in the direct one:

$$Zn(s) + Cu^{2+}(aq) \rightarrow Zn^{2+}(aq) + Cu(s)$$

The difference is that the electrons are now flowing through a wire from the oxidation half-reaction to the reduction half-reaction. And electrons flowing through a wire is electricity, which can do work. If a voltmeter was connected to the wire connecting the two electrodes, a current of 1.10 V would be measured. This galvanic cell shown in Figure 17.1 is commonly called a Daniell cell.

TIP

In the Daniell cell shown in Figure 17.1, note that the compartment with the oxidation half-reaction is on the left and the compartment undergoing reduction is on the right. The electrode at which oxidation is taking place is called the **anode**, and the electrolyte solution in which it is immersed is called the **anode compartment**. The electrode at which reduction takes place is called the **cathode**, and its solution is the **cathode compartment**. The anode is labeled with a negative sign (–), while the cathode has a positive sign (+). The electrons flow from the anode to the cathode, which is – to +, the thermodynamically favored direction.

**Remember: oxidation is an anode process.**

KEY IDEA

Sometimes the half-reaction(s) involved in the cell lack a conductive part to act as the electrode, so an **inert (inactive) electrode**, a solid conducting electrode that does not take part in the redox reaction, is used. Graphite and platinum are commonly used as inert electrodes.

Note: The electrode must be a conductor onto which a wire may be attached. It can never be an ion in solution.

## Cell Notation

**Cell notation** is a shorthand notation representing a galvanic cell. To write the cell notation in Figure 17.1:

1. Write the chemical formula of the anode: **Zn(s)**
2. Draw a single vertical line to represent the phase boundary between the anode and the solution: **Zn(s)|**
3. Write the reactive part of the anode compartment with its initial concentration (if known) in parentheses (assume 1 *M* in this case): **Zn(s) | Zn$^{2+}$(1 *M*)**. (If unknown, the concentration may be left out.)
4. Draw a double vertical line to represent the salt bridge connecting the two electrode compartments: **Zn(s) | Zn$^{2+}$ (1 *M*) ||**
5. Write the reactive part of the cathode compartment with its initial concentration (if known) shown in parentheses: **Zn(s) | Zn$^{2+}$ (1 *M*) || Cu$^{2+}$ (1 *M*)**. (If unknown, the concentration may be left out.)
6. Draw a single vertical line representing the phase boundary between the solution and the cathode: **Zn(s) | Zn$^{2+}$ (1 *M*) || Cu$^{2+}$ (1 *M*) |**
7. Finally, write the chemical formula of the cathode: **Zn(s) | Zn$^{2+}$ (1 *M*) || Cu$^{2+}$ (1 *M*) | Cu(s)**

If an inert electrode is used because one or both redox half-reactions do not have a suitable conducting electrode material associated with the reaction, the inert electrode is shown with its phase boundary. If the electrode components are in the same phase, they are separated by commas; if not, a vertical phase boundary line. For example, consider the following redox reaction:

$$Ag^{+}(aq) + Fe^{2+}(aq) \rightarrow Fe^{3+}(aq) + Ag(s)$$

The oxidation of the iron(II) ion to iron(III) doesn't involve a suitable electrode material, so an inert electrode, such as platinum, would be used. The cell notation in this case would be:

$$Pt(s) \mid Fe^{2+}(aq), Fe^{3+}(aq) \parallel Ag^{+}(aq) \mid Ag(s)$$

## Cell Potential

In the discussion of the Daniell cell, we indicated that this cell produces 1.10 volts. This voltage is really the difference in potential between the two half-cells. There are half-cell potentials associated with all half-cells. A list of all possible combinations of half-cells would be tremendously long. Therefore, a way of combining desired half-cells has been developed. The cell potential (really the half-cell potentials) depends on concentration and temperature, but initially we'll simply look at the half-cell potentials at the standard temperature of 298 K (25°C) and all components in their standard states (1 *M* concentration of all solutions, 1 atmosphere pressure for any gases, and pure solid electrodes). All the half-cell potentials are tabulated as the reduction potentials, that is, the potentials associated with the reduction reaction. The hydrogen half-reaction has been defined as the standard and has been given a value of exactly 0.00 V. All the other half-reactions have been measured relative to it, some positive and some negative. The table of **standard reduction potentials** provided on the AP Exam is shown in Table 17.1.

KEY IDEA

Here are some things to be aware of in looking at this table:

- All reactions are shown in terms of the reduction reaction relative to the standard hydrogen electrode.
- The more positive the value of the voltage associated with the half-reaction ($E°$), the more readily the reaction occurs.
- The strength of the oxidizing agent increases as the value becomes more positive, and the strength of the reducing agent increases as the value becomes more negative.

This table of standard reduction potentials can be used to write the overall cell reaction and to calculate the **standard cell potential** (E°), the potential (voltage) associated with the cell at standard conditions. There are a few things to remember when using these standard reduction potentials to generate the cell reaction and cell potential:

1. The standard cell potential for a galvanic cell must be a positive value, $E° > 0$.
2. Because one half-reaction must involve oxidation, one of the half-reactions shown in the table of reduction potentials must be reversed to indicate the oxidation. If the half-reaction is reversed, the sign of the standard reduction potential must be reversed. However, this is not necessary to calculate the standard cell potential. Other than the sign, make no other change in the standard cell potential.
3. Because oxidation occurs at the anode and reduction at the cathode, the standard cell potential can be calculated from the standard reduction potentials of the two half-reactions involved in the overall reaction by using the equation:

$$E^{\circ}_{cell} = E^{\circ}_{cathode} - E^{\circ}_{anode} > 0$$

**Table 17.1 Standard Reduction Potentials in Aqueous Solution at 25°C. All Ions Are in Aqueous Solution (aq)**

| HALF-REACTION | | | E°(V) |
|---|---|---|---|
| $Li^+ + e^-$ | → | Li(s) | −3.05 |
| $Cs^+ + e^-$ | → | Cs(s) | −2.92 |
| $K^+ + e^-$ | → | K(s) | −2.92 |
| $Rb^+ + e^-$ | → | Rb(s) | −2.92 |
| $Ba^{2+} + 2\ e^-$ | → | Ba(s) | −2.90 |
| $Sr^{2+} + 2\ e^-$ | → | Sr(s) | −2.89 |
| $Ca^{2+} + 2\ e^-$ | → | Ca(s) | −2.87 |
| $Na^+ + e^-$ | → | Na(s) | −2.71 |
| $Mg^{2+} + 2\ e^-$ | → | Mg(s) | −2.37 |
| $Be^{2+} + 2\ e^-$ | → | Be(s) | −1.70 |
| $Al^{3+} + 3\ e^-$ | → | Al(s) | −1.66 |
| $Mn^{2+} + 2\ e^-$ | → | Mn(s) | −1.18 |
| $Zn^{2+} + 2\ e^-$ | → | Zn(s) | −0.76 |
| $Cr^{3+} + 3\ e^-$ | → | Cr(s) | −0.74 |
| $Fe^{2+} + 2\ e^-$ | → | Fe(s) | −0.44 |
| $Cr^{3+} + e^-$ | → | $Cr^{2+}$ | −0.41 |
| $Cd^{2+} + 2\ e^-$ | → | Cd(s) | −0.40 |
| $Tl^+ + e^-$ | → | Tl(s) | −0.34 |
| $Co^{2+} + 2\ e^-$ | → | Co(s) | −0.28 |
| $Ni^{2+} + 2\ e^-$ | → | Ni(s) | −0.25 |
| $Sn^{2+} + 2\ e^-$ | → | Sn(s) | −0.14 |
| $Pb^{2+} + 2\ e^-$ | → | Pb(s) | −0.13 |
| $2\ H^+ + 2\ e^-$ | → | $H_2(g)$ | 0.00 |
| $S(s) + 2\ H^+ + 2\ e^-$ | → | $H_2S(g)$ | 0.14 |
| $Sn^{4+} + 2\ e^-$ | → | $Sn^{2+}$ | 0.15 |
| $Cu^{2+} + e^-$ | → | $Cu^+$ | 0.15 |
| $Cu^{2+} + 2\ e^-$ | → | Cu(s) | 0.34 |

**Table 17.1 Standard Reduction Potentials in Aqueous Solution at 25°C. All Ions Are in Aqueous Solution (aq) (*Continued*)**

| HALF-REACTION | | | $E°$(V) |
|---|---|---|---|
| $Cu^{+} + e^{-}$ | → | Cu(s) | 0.52 |
| $I_2(s) + 2\ e^{-}$ | → | $2I^{-}$ | 0.53 |
| $Fe^{3+} + e^{-}$ | → | $Fe^{2+}$ | 0.77 |
| $Hg_2^{2+} + 2\ e^{-}$ | → | 2 Hg(l) | 0.79 |
| $Ag^{+} + e^{-}$ | → | Ag(s) | 0.80 |
| $Hg^{2+} + 2\ e^{-}$ | → | Hg(l) | 0.85 |
| $2\ Hg^{2+} + 2\ e^{-}$ | → | $Hg_2^{2+}$ | 0.92 |
| $Br_2(l) + 2\ e^{-}$ | → | $2Br^{-}$ | 1.07 |
| $O_2(g) + 4\ H^{+} + 4\ e^{-}$ | → | $2\ H_2O(l)$ | 1.23 |
| $Cl_2(g) + 2\ e^{-}$ | → | $2Cl^{-}$ | 1.36 |
| $Au^{3+} + 3\ e^{-}$ | → | Au(s) | 1.50 |
| $Co^{3+} + e^{-}$ | → | $Co^{2+}$ | 1.82 |
| $F_2(g) + 2\ e^{-}$ | → | $2F^{-}$ | 2.87 |

But remember, both $E°$ cathode and $E°$ anode are shown as reduction potentials, used directly from the table without reversing.

Once the standard cell potential has been calculated, the reaction can be written by reversing the half-reaction associated with the anode and adding the half-reactions together, using appropriate multipliers if needed to ensure that the numbers of electrons lost and gained are equal.

Suppose a galvanic cell was to be constructed utilizing the following two half-reactions taken from Table 17.1:

$$Ni^{2+}(aq) \rightarrow Ni(s) \qquad E° = -0.25\ V$$

$$Ag^{+}(aq) \rightarrow Ag(s) \qquad E° = 0.80\ V$$

First, the cell voltage can be calculated using:

$$E°_{cell} = E°_{cathode} - E°_{anode} > 0$$

Since the cell potential must be positive (a galvanic cell), there is only one arrangement of −0.25 and 0.80 volts than can result in a positive value (a useful check):

$$E°_{cell} = 0.80\ V - (-0.25\ V) = 1.05\ V$$

TIP

This means that the Ni electrode is the anode and must be involved in oxidation, so its reduction half-reaction must be reversed, changing the sign of the standard half-cell potential, and added to the silver half-reaction. **Note that the silver half-reaction must be**

**multiplied by 2 to equalize electron loss and gain, but the half-cell potential remains the same:**

$$Ni(s) \rightarrow Ni^{2+}(aq) + 2e^- \qquad E° = 0.25\ V$$
$$2 \times (Ag^+(aq) + e^- \rightarrow Ag(s)) \qquad E° = 0.80\ V$$
$$Ni(s) + 2Ag^+(aq) \rightarrow Ni^{2+}(aq) + 2Ag(s) \qquad E°_{cell} = 1.05\ V$$

Note that the same cell potential is obtained as using: $E°_{cell} = E°_{cathode} - E°_{anode} > 0$

If, for example, you are given the cell notation, you could use this method to determine the cell potential. In this case, the cell notation would be: Ni | $Ni^{2+}$ || $Ag^+$ | Ag.

## Electrolytic Cells

**Electrolytic cells** use electricity from an external source to produce a desired redox reaction. The reaction is a thermodynamically unfavorable reaction. Electroplating and the recharging of an automobile battery are examples of electrolytic cells. Like galvanic cells, oxidation occurs at the anode and reduction occurs at the cathode. The electrons flow from the + electrode to the – electrode, which is the thermodynamically unfavored direction. The cell potential for an electrolytic cell is negative.

Figure 17.2 shows a comparison of a galvanic cell and an electrolytic cell for the Sn/Cu system. On the left-hand side of Figure 17.2, the galvanic cell is shown for this system. Note that this reaction produces 0.48 V. But what if we wanted the reverse reaction to

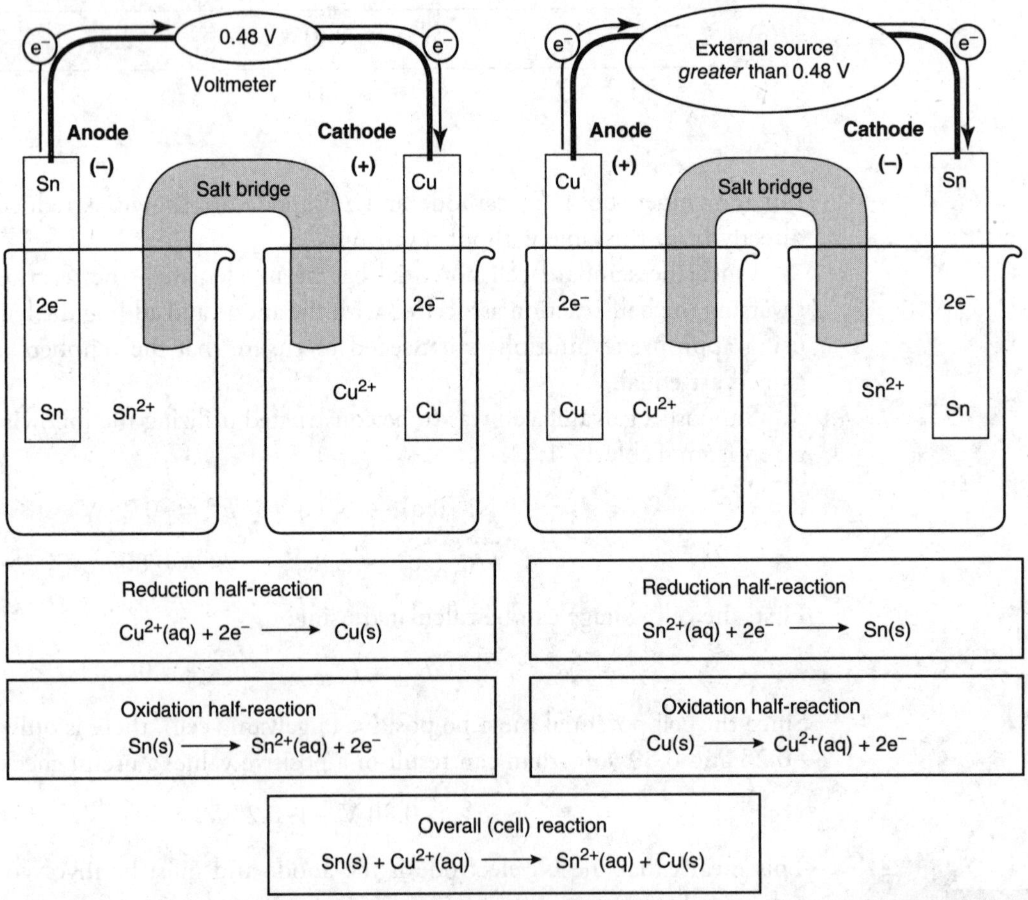


**Figure 17.2 Comparison of a galvanic cell (left) and an electrolytic cell (right).**

occur, the nonspontaneous reaction? This can be accomplished by applying a voltage in excess of 0.48 V from an external electrical source. This is shown on the right-hand side of Figure 17.2. In this electrolytic cell, electricity is being used to produce the nonspontaneous redox reaction.

## Quantitative Aspects of Electrochemistry

One of the most widely used applications of electrolytic cells is in **electrolysis**, the decomposition of a compound with electricity. Water may be decomposed into hydrogen and oxygen. Aluminum oxide may be electrolyzed to produce aluminum metal. In these situations, several questions may be asked: *How long* will it take; *how much* can be produced; *what current* must be used? Given any two of these quantities, the third may be calculated.

To answer these questions, the balanced half-reaction must be known. Then the following relationships can be applied:

$$1 \text{ Faraday} = 96{,}500 \text{ coulombs per mole of electrons}$$
$$(F = 96{,}500 \text{ C/mol e}^- \text{ or } 96{,}500 \text{ J/V mol})$$
$$1 \text{ ampere} = 1 \text{ coulomb/second (A = C/s)}$$

Knowing the amperage and how long it is being applied (seconds), the coulombs can be calculated. Then the coulombs can be converted into moles of electrons, and the moles of electrons can be related to the moles (and then grams) of material being electrolyzed through the balanced half-reaction.

For example, while not the best ion for the purpose, gold plating may be done using a solution containing $[AuCl_4]^-$ as the source of the gold. If a solution of sodium tetracyanoaurate(III), $Na[Au(Cl)_4]$, is electrolyzed by a current of 1.500 amperes for 3.000 h, how many grams of gold will be produced?

Answer:

$$2\ Na[Au(CN)_4](aq) \rightarrow 2\ Au(s) + 2\ NaCl(aq) + 3\ Cl_2(g) \text{ (not necessary)}$$

$$Au^{3+}(aq) + 3\ e^- \rightarrow Au(s) \text{ (necessary)}$$

$$(3.000\ \text{h})\left(\frac{3{,}600\ \text{s}}{\text{h}}\right)\left(\frac{1.500\ \text{C}}{\text{s}}\right)\left(\frac{1\ \text{mol e}^-}{96{,}485\ \text{C}}\right)\left(\frac{1\ \text{mol Au}}{3\ \text{mol e}^-}\right)\left(\frac{197.0\ \text{g Au}}{\text{mol Au}}\right)$$
$$= 11.03\ \text{g Au}$$

Note the change from 1.500 amperes to 1.500 coulombs per second using the definition above.

Calculation of $E^\circ_{cell}$ also allows for the calculation of two other useful quantities—the Gibbs free energy ($\Delta G^\circ$) and the equilibrium constant ($K$). The equations (given on the exam) are:

$$\Delta G^\circ = \Delta H^\circ - T\Delta S^\circ = -RT \ln K = -nFE^\circ$$

The Gibbs free energy is the best single thermodynamic indicator of whether a reaction will be spontaneous (review Chapter 14, Thermodynamics). The Gibbs free energy for a reaction can be calculated from the $E^\circ$ of the reaction using the following equation:

$$\Delta G^\circ = -nFE^\circ_{cell}$$

where $F$ is Faraday's constant of 96,485 C/mol $e^-$ = 96,485 J/V mol, and $n$ is the number of electrons transferred.

If the redox reaction is at equilibrium, the equilibrium constant may be calculated by using the given equations:

$$\Delta G° = -RT \ln K = -nFE°$$

$$RT \ln K = nFE°$$

$$\frac{RT}{nF} \ln K = E°$$

While it is perfectly acceptable to use this equation, traditionally, the values of the constants ($R$, $T$, and $F$) are combined and the logarithm base is changed from base e to base 10, which leaves these two forms:

$$E° = \frac{0.0592 \text{ V}}{n} \log K \text{ or } \log K = \frac{n E°_{cell}}{0.0592 \text{ V}}$$

Let's apply these relationships. Determine $\Delta G°$ and $K$ for the following reaction:

$$Zn(s) + 2\ Ag^+(aq) \rightarrow Zn^{2+}(aq) + Ag(s) \qquad E°_{cell} = 1.10 \text{ V}$$

Answer:

For this reaction, two electrons are transferred from the Zn to the Ag. Thus, $n$ is 2 for this reaction. The value of $F$ (96,485 J/V mol) is given on the exam, so you will not need to memorize it.

The first answer is:

$$\Delta G° = -nFE°_{cell} = -2(96{,}485 \text{ J/V mol})(1.10 \text{ V}) = -2.12 \times 10^5 \text{ J/mol}$$

The second answer is:

$$\frac{RT}{nF} \ln K = E°$$

$$\ln K = \frac{nFE°}{RT}$$

$$\ln K = \frac{(2)(96{,}485 \text{ J V}^{-1} \text{ mol}^{-1})(1.10 \text{ V})}{(8.314 \text{ J mol}^{-1} \text{ K}^{-1})(298 \text{ K})} = 85.7$$

or, using the other form of the equation:

$$\log K = \frac{n E°_{cell}}{0.0592 \text{ V}} = \frac{2(1.10 \text{ V})}{0.0592 \text{ V}} = 37.2$$

In either case, the calculation gives a $K$ of about $10^{37}$ (actually $K = 1.5 \times 10^{37}$). In many cases, the approximate value will be all you need for the AP Exam.

## Nernst Equation

So far, all the calculations have used the standard cell potential or standard half-cell potentials, which means the reaction is under standard conditions (defined previously). However, what if the conditions are not standard? When the conditions are not standard, an adjustment is necessary. The most common nonstandard condition is where the molarity is no longer 1 *M*. The nonstandard cell potential, $E_{cell}$, (no degree symbol) is calculated using the **Nernst equation**, which appears on the AP Exam as:

$$E_{cell} = E^{\circ}_{cell} - \frac{RT}{nF} \ln Q$$

where $R$ is the ideal gas constant (8.314 J mol$^{-1}$ K$^{-1}$), $T$ is the Kelvin temperature, $n$ is the number of electrons transferred, $F$ is Faraday's constant (96,485 C/mol $e^-$ = 96,485 J/V mol), and $Q$ is the reaction quotient discussed Chapter 15, Equilibrium. Note: at equilibrium $Q = K$, and $E_{cell} = 0$, which leads to:

$$E^{\circ}_{cell} = \frac{RT}{nF} \ln K$$

As seen previously, it is possible to enter the values of the constants and convert to base 10 logarithms to give:

$$E_{cell} = E^{\circ}_{cell} - \frac{0.0592}{n} \log Q$$

The second form, involving log $Q$, is the more useful form in that it is no longer necessary to enter all the constants every time. If one knows the cell reaction or half-reaction, the concentrations of ions, and $E^{\circ}$, then the actual cell potential can be calculated. Another useful application of the Nernst equation is in calculating the concentration of one of the reactants from cell-potential measurements. Knowing the actual cell potential and $E^{\circ}_{cell}$ allows calculation of $Q$, the reaction quotient. Knowing $Q$ and all but one of the concentrations allows the calculation of the unknown concentration.

Another application of the Nernst equation is in concentration cells. A **concentration cell** is an electrochemical cell in which the same chemical species is used in both cell compartments; however, the concentrations differ. Because the half-reactions are the same, $E^{\circ}_{cell}$ = 0.00 V. Simply substituting the appropriate concentrations into the reaction quotient allows calculation of the actual cell potential.

When using the Nernst equation on a cell reaction in which the overall reaction is not supplied, only the half-reactions and concentrations, there are two equivalent methods to work the problem. The first way is to write the overall redox reaction based upon $E^{\circ}$ values, and then apply the Nernst equation. The second method is to treat each half-reaction independently and then combine the two results to produce the overall potential. Let's practice the second method. Calculate the potential of a half-cell containing 0.20 *M* $K_2Cr_2O_7$(aq), 0.10 *M* $Cr^{3+}$(aq), and 1.0 × 10$^{-3}$ *M* $H^+$(aq).

Answer:

The following half-reaction is given on the AP Exam:

$$Cr_2O_7^{2-}(aq) + 14H^+(aq) + 6e^- \leftrightarrows 2Cr^{3+}(aq) + 7H_2O(l) \qquad E^{\circ} = 1.33\ V$$

$$E = E^{\circ} - \frac{0.0592}{n} \log \frac{[Cr^{3+}]^2}{[Cr_2O_7^{2-}][H^+]^{14}} \quad \text{(ignore } H_2O\text{)}$$

$$= 1.33\ V - \frac{0.0592}{6} \log \frac{[0.10]^2}{[0.20][1.0 \times 10^{-3}]^{14}}$$

$$= 0.93\ V$$

## Electrolysis and Faraday's Law

It is possible to use Faraday's law for reactions occurring in electrochemical cells. The equation (from the AP Exam) is $I = \frac{q}{t}$, where $I$ is the current, $q$ is the charge transferred, and $t$ is the elapsed time.

In general, this equation is not often used directly. You will see in the section Quantitative Aspects of Electrochemistry how this equation is applied indirectly. Schematically this process may be represented as:

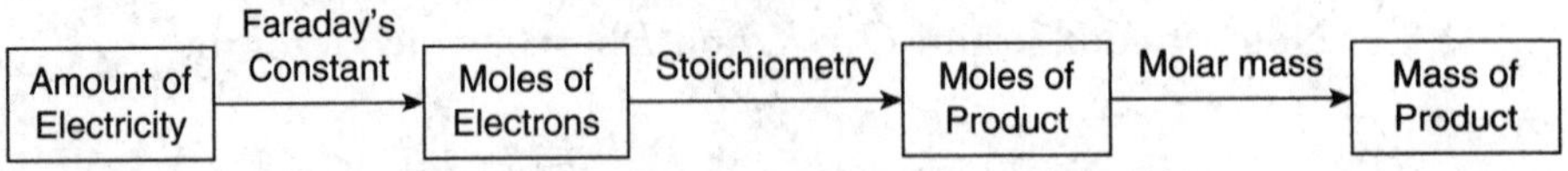


This process will work for both galvanic and electrolytic cells. For galvanic cells, the key is the electricity produced. For electrolytic cells, the key is the electricity required.

## Experiments

Electrochemical experiments are normally concerned with standard cell voltages. Measurements of the cell potential are essential and require a voltmeter (potentiometer). These measurements may be taken from different combinations of half-cells, or from measurements before and after changes of some aspect of the cell were made.

Using measurements of different half-cell combinations, a set of "standard" reduction potentials may be constructed. This set will be similar to a table of standard reduction potentials. The solutions used in the half-cells must be of known concentration. These solutions are produced by weighing reagents and diluting to volume. The measurements will require a balance and a volumetric flask. It is also possible to produce known concentrations by diluting solutions. This method requires a pipette and a volumetric flask. Review Chapter 11, Solutions, for solution techniques.

## Common Mistakes to Avoid

TIP

1. Be sure your units cancel to give the unit wanted in your final answer.
2. Be sure to round your answer off to the correct number of significant figures.
3. Remember that oxidation is the loss of electrons and reduction the gain, and that in redox reactions the same number of electrons is lost and gained.
4. When diagramming an electrochemical cell, be sure the electrons go from anode to cathode. (It will help if you follow the convention of placing the reduction [cathode] on the right.)
5. Be sure that for a galvanic cell, the cell potential is greater than 0.
6. In cell notation, be sure to write anode, anode compartment, salt bridge, cathode compartment, cathode in this specific order. (The cathode [reduction] is on the right.)
7. When using a multiplier to equalize electron loss and gain in reduction half-cell potentials, ***do not*** use the multiplier on the voltage of the half-cell.

# ❯ Review Questions

Use these questions to review the content of this chapter and practice for the AP Chemistry Exam. First are 20 multiple-choice questions similar to what you will encounter in Section I of the AP Chemistry Exam. Some of these questions are designed to review prior knowledge. Following those is a long free-response question like the ones in Section II of the exam. To make these questions an even more authentic practice for the actual exam, time yourself following the instructions provided.

**Multiple-Choice Questions**

Answer the following questions in 30 minutes. You may not use a calculator. You may use the periodic table and the equation sheet at the back of this book.

**Choose one of the following for questions 1 and 2.**

(A) There is no change in the voltage.
(B) The voltage becomes zero.
(C) The voltage increases.
(D) The voltage decreases but stays positive.

The following reaction takes place in a voltaic cell:

$$Zn(s) + Cu^{2+}(1\ M) \rightarrow Cu(s) + Zn^{2+}(1\ M)$$

The cell has a voltage that is measured and found to be +1.10 V.

1. What happens to the cell voltage when the copper electrode is made smaller?

2. What happens to the cell voltage when the salt bridge is filled with deionized water instead of 1 $M$ $KNO_3$?

3. $MnO_4^-(aq) + H^+(aq) + C_2O_4^{2-}(aq) \rightarrow Mn^{2+}(aq) + H_2O(l) + CO_2(g)$

What is the coefficient of $H^+$ when the reaction is balanced?

(A) 16
(B) 2
(C) 8
(D) 5

4. $S_2O_3^{2-}(aq) + OH^-(aq) \rightarrow SO_4^{2-}(aq) + H_2O(l) + e^-$

After the above half-reaction is balanced, which of the following are the respective coefficients of $OH^-$ and $SO_4^{2-}$?

(A) 8 and 3
(B) 6 and 2
(C) 10 and 2
(D) 5 and 2

5. How many moles of Pt may be deposited on the cathode when 0.80 F of electricity is passed through a 1.0 $M$ solution of $Pt^{4+}$?

(A) 1.0 mole
(B) 0.60 mole
(C) 0.20 mole
(D) 0.80 mole

6. A chemistry student obtains the following answer when balancing a redox equation:

$$Cr_2O_7^{2-}(aq) + 14\ H^+(aq) + 3\ S^{2-}(aq) \rightarrow 2\ Cr^{3+}(aq) + 3\ S(s) + 7\ H_2O(l)$$

Which of the following is a true statement concerning the balanced equation?

(A) The $Cr_2O_7^{2-}$ reduces the $S^{2-}$.
(B) The oxidation number of chromium changes from +7 to +3.
(C) The oxidation number of the sulfur remains −2.
(D) The $Cr_2O_7^{2-}$ oxidizes the $S^{2-}$.

7. $H^+(aq) + NO_3^-(aq) + e^- \rightarrow NO(g) + H_2O(g)$

What is the coefficient for water when the above half-reaction is balanced?

(A) 3
(B) 4
(C) 2
(D) 1

8. $Co^{2+}(aq) + 2\ e^- \rightarrow Co(s) \quad E° = -0.28\ V$

$Cd^{2+}(aq) + 2\ e^- \rightarrow Cd(s) \quad E° = -0.40\ V$

Given the above standard reduction potentials, estimate the approximate value of the equilibrium constant for the following reaction: $Cd(s) + Co^{2+}(aq) \rightarrow Cd^{2+}(aq) + Co(s)$.

(A) $e^{-4.60}$
(B) $e^{-9.35}$
(C) $e^{9.35}$
(D) $e^{36.84}$

9. A sample of silver is to be purified by electrorefining. This will separate the silver from an impurity of gold. The impure silver is made into an electrode. Which of the following is the best way to set up the electrolytic cell?

(A) an impure silver cathode and an inert anode
(B) an impure silver cathode and a pure gold anode
(C) a pure silver cathode with an impure silver anode
(D) a pure gold cathode with an impure silver anode

10. $2\ Fe^{3+}(aq) + Zn(s) \rightarrow Zn^{2+}(aq) + 2\ Fe^{2+}(aq)$

The reaction shown above was used in an electrolytic cell. The voltage measured for the cell was not equal to the calculated $E°$ for the cell. Which of the following could cause this discrepancy?

(A) The anion in the anode compartment was chloride instead of nitrate, as in the cathode compartment.
(B) One or more of the ion concentrations was not 1 *M*.
(C) Both solutions were at 25°C instead of 0°C.
(D) The solution in the salt bridge was $Na_2SO_4$ instead of $KNO_3$.

11. How many grams of metallic mercury could be produced by electrolyzing a 1.0 *M* $Hg(NO_3)_2$ solution with a current of 2.00 A for 3.00 h?

(A) 22.4 g
(B) 201 g
(C) 11.2 g
(D) 44.8 g

12. An electrolysis cell was constructed with two platinum electrodes in a 1.00 *M* aqueous solution of KCl. An odorless gas evolves from one electrode, and a gas with a distinctive odor evolves from the other electrode. Choose the correct statement from the following list.

(A) The gas with the distinctive odor was evolved at the anode.
(B) The odorless gas was oxygen.
(C) The gas with the distinctive odor was evolved at the cathode.
(D) The odorless gas was evolved at the anode.

13. $2\ BrO_3^-(aq) + 12\ H^+(aq) + 10\ e^- \rightarrow Br_2(aq) + 6\ H_2O(l)$

Which of the following statements is correct for the above reaction?

(A) The $BrO_3^-$ undergoes oxidation at the anode.
(B) Br goes from a −1 oxidation to a 0-oxidation.
(C) $Br_2$ is oxidized at the anode.
(D) The $BrO_3^-$ undergoes reduction at the cathode.

14. $2\ M(s) + 3\ Zn^{2+}(aq) \rightarrow 2\ M^{3+}(aq) + 3\ Zn^{2+}(aq) \quad E° = 0.90\ V$

$Zn^{2+}(aq) + 2e^- \rightarrow Zn(s) \quad E° = -0.76\ V$

Using the above information, determine the standard reduction potential for the following reaction: $M^{3+}(aq) + 3\ e^- \rightarrow M(s)$.

(A) 0.90 V
(B) −1.66 V
(C) 0.00 V
(D) −0.62 V

**15.** $2\ SO_4^{2-}(aq) + 10\ H^+(aq) + 8\ e^- \rightarrow S_2O_3^{2-}(aq) + 5\ H_2O(l)$

A chemistry student constructs a voltaic cell. The above half-reaction occurs in one of the cell compartments. Which of the following statements is true concerning this half-reaction?

(A) The sulfur undergoes oxidation.
(B) This half-reaction occurs at the cathode.
(C) The oxidation state of sulfur does not change.
(D) The $H^+$ serves as a catalyst.

**Use the information on standard reduction potentials in the following table to answer questions 16–18.**

| | $E^\circ$ (V) |
|---|---|
| $Cl_2(g) + 2\ e^- \rightarrow 2\ Cl^-(aq)$ | +1.36 |
| $S_2O_6^{2-}(aq) + 4\ H^+(aq) + 2\ e^- \rightarrow 2\ SO_2(g) + 2\ H_2O(l)$ | +0.56 |
| $Cu^{2+}(aq) + 2\ e^- \rightarrow Cu(s)$ | +0.34 |
| $Sn^{2+}(aq) + 2\ e^- \rightarrow Sn(s)$ | −0.14 |
| $2\ H_2O(l) + 2\ e^- \rightarrow H_2(g) + 2\ OH^-(aq)$ | −0.83 |
| $Ca^{2+}(aq) + 2\ e^- \rightarrow Ca(s)$ | −2.87 |
| $K^+(aq) + e^- \rightarrow K(s)$ | −2.92 |

**16.** A chemist constructs an electrolysis cell with two platinum electrodes in a 1.00 *M* aqueous solution of sodium chloride, NaCl. When she connects the cell to a power source, an odorless gas forms at one electrode, and a gas with a distinctive odor forms at the other electrode. Choose the correct statement from the following list.

(A) The odorless gas was oxygen.
(B) The odorless gas was the result of oxidation.
(C) The gas with the distinctive odor was the result of oxidation.
(D) The odorless gas was evolved at the positive electrode.

**17.** A student mixed an acidic 1.0 *M* sodium dithionate, $Na_2S_2O_6$, solution with a 1.0 *M* tin(II) bromide, $SnBr_2$, solution containing some tin metal, Sn, and observed a gas forming. Which of the following is the gas?

(A) $H_2(g)$
(B) $SO_2(g)$
(C) $Br_2(g)$
(D) $Sn(g)$

**18.** A chemist constructs a galvanic cell with a tin, Sn, electrode in a compartment containing a 1.0 *M* tin(II) perchlorate, $Sn(ClO_4)_2$, solution and a platinum, Pt, electrode in a compartment containing a 1.0 *M* copper(II) chloride, $CuCl_2$, solution. The salt bridge connecting the two compartments contains a 1.0 *M* potassium sulfate, $K_2SO_4$. Which of the following is the net ionic equation for the cell?

(A) $CuCl_2(aq) + Sn(s) \rightarrow SnSO_4(aq) + Cu(s)$
(B) $Sn^{2+}(aq) + Cu(s) \rightarrow Cu^{2+}(aq) + Sn(s)$
(C) $Cu^{2+}(aq) + Sn(s) \rightarrow Sn^{2+}(aq) + Cu(s)$
(D) $2\ Cl^-(aq) + 2\ H_2O(l) \rightarrow H_2(g) + 2\ OH^-(aq) + Cl_2(g)$

**19.** $Ni(s) + 2\ Ag^+(aq) \rightarrow Ni^{2+}(aq) + 2\ Ag(s)$
$E^\circ = 1.05$ V

A student builds a galvanic cell utilizing the above reaction. At 25°C, what could the student do for the cell to generate a potential greater than that of the original standard cell.

(A) Increase the $Ag^+(aq)$ concentration
(B) Increase the size of the Ni(s) electrode
(C) Decrease the size of the Ag(s) electrode
(D) Increase the pressure

**20.** $2\ Au^{3+}(aq) + 3\ Zn(s) \rightarrow 2\ Au(s) + 3\ Zn^{2+}(aq)$
$E^\circ_{cell} = 2.26$ V

The above standard cell is constructed and allowed to operate. At what point will $\Delta G_{cell} = 0$?

(A) At no point
(B) When the cell reaches equilibrium
(C) When $[Au^{3+}] = 0$
(D) When no more zinc remains

## › Answers and Explanations

**1. A**—The size of the electrode is not important when determining the cell voltage.

**2. B**—The salt bridge serves as an ion source to maintain charge neutrality. Deionized water would not be an ion source, so the cell could not operate (cell voltage = 0 V).

**3. A**—The balanced equation is:

$$2\ MnO_4^-(aq) + 16\ H^+(aq) + 5\ C_2O_4^{2-}(aq) \rightarrow 2\ Mn^{2+}(aq) + 8\ H_2O(l) + 10\ CO_2(g)$$

**4. C**—The balanced equation is:

$$S_2O_3^{2-}(aq) + 10\ OH^-(aq) \rightarrow 2\ SO_4^{2-}(aq) + 5\ H_2O(l) + 8\ e^-$$

**5. C**—It takes 4 moles of electrons (4 $F$) to change the platinum ions to platinum metal. The calculation would be $(0.80\ F)\left(\frac{1\ \text{mol Pt}}{4\ F}\right) =$ 0.20 mol Pt.

**6. D**—The dichromate ion oxidizes the sulfide ion to elemental sulfur, as the sulfide ion reduces the dichromate ion to the chromium(III) ion. Chromium goes from +6 to +3, while sulfur goes from −2 to 0. The hydrogen remains at +1 and the oxygen remains −2, so neither hydrogen nor oxygen is oxidized nor reduced.

**7. C**—The balanced chemical equation is:

$$4\ H^+(aq) + NO_3^-(aq) + 3\ e^- \rightarrow NO(g) + 2\ H_2O(l).$$

**8. C**—It is necessary to reverse the Cd half-reaction to $Cd(s) \rightarrow Cd^{2+}(aq) + 2\ e^-$ $\quad E° = +0.40$ V.

The standard cell potential is (0.40 – 0.28)V = 0.12 V

It is necessary to use two equations from the list provided on the exam:

$$\Delta G° = -RT \ln K \text{ and } \Delta G° = -nFE°$$

These may be used separately, or combined, it is faster to use the combined equation which comes from setting the two $\Delta G°$ equations equal to each other

$$-RT \ln K = -nFE°$$

and rearranging

$$\frac{-nF}{-RT}E° = \frac{nF}{RT}E° = \ln K$$

Entering values and substituting V = J/coul:

$$\ln K = \frac{(2)\left(96{,}485\ \frac{\text{coul}}{\text{mol } e^-}\right)}{\left(8.314\ \frac{\text{J}}{\text{mol K}}\right)(298\ \text{K})}\left(0.12\ \frac{\text{J}}{\text{coul}}\right)$$

Without a calculator, you will need to do some rounding; however, you should recall that calculations involving logarithms of any type are extremely sensitive to rounding.

Rounding gives:

$\ln K = \frac{(2)(100{,}000)}{(8)(300)}(0.12) = 10$ (no rounding would give 9.35)

This leads to $K = e^{10}$ (actually $e^{9.35}$).

The closest answer in the problem is $e^{9.35}$.

The actual value is $K = 1.1 \times 10^4$ (if the rounded value were used, the $K$ would be double the actual $K$ or $2.2 \times 10^4$, showing the sensitivity of logarithms to rounding).

**9. C**—The impure silver must be oxidized so it will go into solution. Oxidation occurs at the anode. Reduction is required to convert the silver ions to pure silver. Reduction occurs at the cathode. The cathode must be pure silver; otherwise, it could be contaminated with the cathode material.

**10. B**—If the voltage was not equal to $E°$, then the cell was not standard. Standard cells have 1 $M$ concentrations and operate at 25°C with a partial pressure of each gas equal to 1 atm. No gases are involved in this reaction, so the cell must be operating at a different temperature or a different concentration (or both).

**11. A**—The half-reaction is $Hg^{2+}(aq) + 2\,e^- \rightarrow Hg(l)$.

The calculation based on this half-reaction is:

$$\left(\frac{2.00\text{ C}}{\text{s}}\right)\left(\frac{3{,}600\text{ s}}{\text{h}}\right)(3.00\text{ h})\left(\frac{1\text{ F}}{96{,}485\text{ C}}\right)\left(\frac{1\text{ mol Hg}}{2\text{ F}}\right)\left(\frac{200.6\text{ g Hg}}{1\text{ mol Hg}}\right)$$

You can estimate the answer by replacing 96,485 with 100,000; 3,600 × 3 with 10,000; and 200.6 with 200, which gives:

$$\left(\frac{\cancel{2.00}\text{ C}}{\text{s}}\right)\left(\frac{10{,}000\text{ s}}{\text{h}}\right)\left(\frac{1\text{ F}}{100{,}000\text{ C}}\right)\left(\frac{1\text{ mol Hg}}{\cancel{2}\text{ F}}\right)\left(\frac{200\text{ g Hg}}{1\text{ mol Hg}}\right)$$

$$\left(\frac{1}{10}\right)\left(\frac{200\text{ g Hg}}{1}\right) \approx 20\text{ g}$$

(which is slightly low owing to the rounding).

**12. A**—The possible gases are $H_2$, $O_2$, and $Cl_2$. The only one of these three gases with a distinctive odor is $Cl_2$. The half-reaction producing $Cl_2$ is $2\,Cl^-(aq) \rightarrow Cl_2(g) + 2\,e^-$, which is an oxidation (at the anode). The cathode reaction must produce $H_2$ (producing $O_2$ requires an oxidation).

**13. D**—The bromate ion, $BrO_3^-$, is gaining electrons, so it is being reduced. Reduction always occurs at the cathode.

**14. B**—The half-reactions giving the overall reaction must be as follows:

$3\,[Zn^{2+}(aq) + 2\,e^- \rightarrow Zn(s)]$ $\qquad E° = -0.76$ V (given)

$2\,[M(s) \rightarrow M^{3+}(aq) + 3\,e^-]$ $\qquad E° = ?$

$2\,M(s) + 3\,Zn^{2+}(aq) \rightarrow 2\,M^{3+}(aq) + 2\,Zn(s)$ $\qquad E° = 0.90$ V (given)

Thus, −0.76 + ? = 0.90, giving ? = 1.66 V. The half-reaction under consideration is the reverse of the one used in this combination, so the sign of the calculated voltage must be reversed. Do not make the mistake of multiplying the voltages when the half-reactions were multiplied to equalize the electrons.

**15. B**—This is a reduction half-reaction (electrons are being gained). Reductions take place at the cathode.

**16. C**—The only gases in the table are hydrogen, sulfur dioxide, and chlorine. Of the three gases, the only odorless gas is hydrogen. The formation of hydrogen is through reduction; therefore, it is necessary to determine the oxidation half-reaction. Sulfur dioxide forms through reduction, so it cannot be the gas. The gas with the distinctive odor must be chlorine, which is produced through oxidation. (There will be a longer table given on the AP Exam.)

**17. B**—Based on the reduction potentials in the table, tin is a sufficiently strong reducing agent to reduce the dithionate ion to sulfur dioxide, a gas with a distinctive odor. Tin cannot reduce water to produce hydrogen, and tin cannot oxidize chloride ion to produce chlorine. None of the other substances is a gas.

**18. C**—Using the cell potentials, the copper(II) ions will undergo reduction (use the half-reaction from the table), and the tin metal will undergo oxidation (reverse the half-reaction from the table). Combine the resultant half-reactions and cancel electrons to get this answer. A is not a net ionic equation. B is the reverse reaction. D is nonspontaneous (according to the cell potentials).

**19. A**—For this cell, the Nernst equation is:

$$E_{cell} = E°_{cell} - \frac{RT}{nF}\ln\frac{[Ni^{2+}]}{[Ag^{+2}]}$$

For this cell $\frac{RT}{nF}$ is a constant at 25°C and therefore changing any of these is not an option. There are no gases involved, so a pressure change is unlikely to make a difference. Solids do not appear in the $Q$ expression, and as always, the amount of solid does not alter the value, which means changing the size of an electrode will not make a difference. Increasing the $Ag^+(aq)$ concentration will make $Q$ smaller, thus a smaller number is subtracted from the $E°_{cell}$.

**20. B**—The cell will cease to operate when $[Au^{3+}] = 0$ or when no more zinc remains; however, $\Delta G_{cell}$ may not equal zero under these circumstances. $\Delta G = 0$ at equilibrium.

## › Free-Response Question

You have 15 minutes to answer the following long question. You may use a calculator and the tables in the back of the book.

**Question**

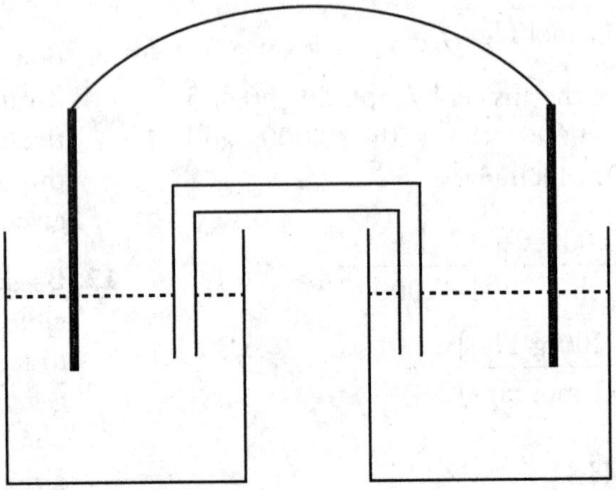

The galvanic cell pictured is constructed with a cobalt electrode in a 1.0 $M$ $Co(NO_3)_2$ solution in the left compartment and a silver electrode in a 1.0 $M$ $AgNO_3$ solution in the right compartment. The salt bridge contains a $KNO_3$ solution. The cell voltage is positive.

(a) What is the balanced net ionic equation for the reaction, and what is the cell potential?

$$Co^{2+}(aq) + 2e^- \rightarrow Co(s) \qquad E° = -0.28 \text{ V}$$

$$Ag^+(aq) + 1e^- \rightarrow Ag(s) \qquad E° = +0.80 \text{ V}$$

(b) Which electrode is the anode? Justify your answer.

(c) If some solid $Co(NO_3)_2$ is added to the cobalt compartment, what will happen to the voltage? Justify your answer.

(d) If the cell operates until equilibrium is established, what will the potential be? Justify your answer.

(e) Write the electron configurations for Co and $Co^{2+}$.

## › Answer and Explanation

(a) The cell reaction is:

$$Co(s) + 2\,Ag^+(aq) \rightarrow Co^{2+}(aq) + 2\,Ag(s)$$

The calculation of the cell potential may be done in different ways. Here is one method:

$$Co^{2+}(aq) + 2e^- \rightarrow Co(s) \qquad E° = -0.28 \text{ V}$$

$$2\,Ag^+(aq) + 1e^- \rightarrow Ag(s) \qquad E° = +0.80 \text{ V}$$

Based upon the half-reaction potentials, the cobalt half-reaction must be reversed to get an oxidation (−0.28 V changes to +0.28 V) and then the two equations added to get the correct answer.

$$Co(s) + 2\ Ag^{+}(aq) \rightarrow Co^{2+}(aq) + 2\ Ag(s) \quad E^\circ = +1.08\ V$$

Give yourself 1 point if you got the correct equation. The physical states are not necessary. Give yourself 1 point for the correct answer (1.08 V) regardless of the method used. The most common mistake is to multiply the silver voltage by 2. You do not get the point for an answer of 1 V.

(b) The cobalt is the anode. The reason Co is the anode is because the Co is oxidized.

You get 1 point for identifying the anode. You get 1 point for the explanation of why Co is the anode or if you state that the Co loses electrons (undergoes oxidation).

(c) The voltage would decrease. The excess $Co^{2+}$, from the $Co(NO_3)_2$, would impede the reactions from proceeding as written.

An alternate explanation uses the Nernst equation (given on the AP Exam).

$$E_{cell} = E^\circ_{cell} - \left(\frac{RT}{nF}\right)\ln Q = E^\circ_{cell} - \left(\frac{0.0592}{n}\right)\log Q \text{ at } 25^\circ C$$

For this cell, the Nernst equation becomes:

$$E_{cell} = E^\circ_{cell} - \left(\frac{0.0592}{n}\right)\log\frac{[Co^{2+}]}{[Ag^{+}]^2}$$

Increasing the cobalt ion concentration means a larger value will be subtracted from $E^\circ_{cell}$ to decrease $E_{cell}$.

Give yourself 1 point for saying decrease. Give yourself 1 point for the explanation.

(d) At equilibrium, the cell voltage would be 0 V. At equilibrium no work is done, so the potential must be zero.

Give yourself 1 point for saying 0 V and give yourself 1 point for the equilibrium explanation.

(e) The electron configurations are as follows:

$$Co\ 1s^2 2s^2 2p^6 3s^2 3p^6 4s^2 3d^7 \quad \text{or} \quad [Ar]\ 4s^2 3d^7$$

$$Co^{2+}\ 1s^2 2s^2 2p^6 3s^2 3p^6 3d^7 \quad \text{or} \quad [Ar]\ 3d^7$$

Give yourself 1 point for each correct electron configurations. A common error is to forget that the first electrons removed are the 4s electrons. The orbitals do not need to be in the "correct" order, but they must have the correct superscripts.

Total your points. There are 10 points possible.

## › Rapid Review

- In redox reactions, electrons are lost and gained. Oxidation is the loss of electrons, and reduction is the gain of electrons.
- The same number of electrons is lost and gained in the redox half-reactions.
- Galvanic (voltaic) cells produce electricity from a redox reaction.

- The anode is the electrode at which the oxidation half-reaction takes place. The anode compartment is the solution in which the anode is immersed.
- The cathode is the electrode at which reduction takes place, and the cathode compartment is the solution in which the cathode is immersed.
- A salt bridge is used in an electrochemical cell to maintain electrical neutrality in the cell compartments.
- Be able to diagram an electrochemical cell.
- The cell notation is a shorthand way of representing a cell. It has the form: anode | anode compartment || cathode compartment | cathode
- Standard reduction potentials are used to calculate the cell potential under standard conditions. All half-reactions are shown in the reduction form.
- For a galvanic cell, $E^\circ_{cell} > 0$.
- $E^\circ_{cell} = E^\circ_{cathode} - E^\circ_{anode} > 0$. Know how to use this equation to calculate $E^\circ_{cell}$.
- Electrolytic cells use an external source of electricity to produce a desired redox reaction.
- Review how to diagram an electrolytic cell.
- The following relationships can be used to calculate quantitative changes that occur in an electrochemical cell, especially an electrolytic one: 1 $F = 96{,}485$ C per mole of electron ($F = 96{,}485$ C/mol $e^-$ = 96,485 J/V mol) and 1 amp = 1 C/s (A = C/s).
- The standard cell potential can be used to calculate the Gibbs free energy for the reaction: $\Delta G^\circ = -nFE^\circ_{cell}$ (given on the AP Exam). Know how to use this equation.
- The standard cell potential can also be used to calculate the equilibrium constant for a reaction (from the equation given on the exam): $\Delta G^\circ = -RT \ln K = -nFE^\circ$. Know how to use this equation.

# Additional Review and Applications

CHAPTER 18 Nuclear Chemistry
CHAPTER 19 Organic Chemistry
CHAPTER 20 Experimental Investigations

CHAPTER 18

# Nuclear Chemistry

IN THIS CHAPTER

**Summary:** Radioactivity, the spontaneous decay of an unstable isotope to a more stable one, was first discovered by Henri Becquerel in 1896. Marie Curie and her husband expanded on his work and developed most of the concepts that are used today.

Nuclear chemistry is not a specific AP Chemistry topic; however, you should review parts of this chapter for two reasons. First, some of you need a review of atomic structure, a pre-AP topic that is prior knowledge, which will help you to understand the background for some AP Chemistry questions. Second, you need more practice with kinetics, and radioactivity contains the best examples of first-order kinetics.

Throughout this book, you have been studying traditional chemistry and chemical reactions. This has involved the transfer or sharing of electrons from the electron clouds, especially the valence electrons. Before you decided to take AP Chemistry, you learned information concerning atomic structure; it has been a while since you covered this material, so now is the time to make sure you remember the material.

KEY IDEA

**Keywords and Equations**

There are no specific nuclear equations provided; however, you will need to be able to use the first-order equations repeated below from Chapter 13, Kinetics.

$k$ = rate constant $t$ = time $t_{1/2}$ = half-life

$[A]_t$ = amount of radioactive material remaining after time $t$ has passed

$[A]_0$ = original amount of radioactive material

$$\ln [A]_t - \ln [A]_0 = -kt \qquad t_{1/2} = \frac{0.693}{k}$$

# Nuclear Reactions

## Balancing Nuclear Reactions

Prior to taking AP Chemistry, you learned that the nucleus of an atom contained protons and neutrons. In addition, you learned that the number of protons present is the **atomic number**. Also, you learned that the sum of the protons and neutrons is the **mass number**. Nuclear reactions involve changes in one or more atomic nuclei. During these changes, the total mass number and the total atomic number remains unchanged. Balancing nuclear equations involves balancing the atomic numbers and mass numbers.

Previously, you learned that the atomic number and mass numbers of an atom could be represented as:

$$^{A}_{Z}X$$

In this notation, *X* is the symbol for the particle (normally the chemical symbol from the periodic table), *A* is the mass number for the particle (rarely from the periodic table), and *Z* is the atomic number for the particle (normally from the periodic table). (Hopefully, you still remember this.) The values of both *A* and *Z* are <u>always</u> integers. Many people make an error by using the atomic mass (atomic weight) in place of the mass number. Do not forget, both *A* and *Z* are important when balancing nuclear reactions. In a balanced nuclear reaction, the sum of all *A* values to the left of the reaction arrow must equal the sum of all *A* values to the right of the arrow. Similarly, the sum of all the *Z* values to the left of the reaction arrow must equal the sum of all the *Z* values to the right of the reaction arrow.

As an example of how to balance a nuclear equation, we will investigate the reaction of a chlorine-35 nucleus with a neutron to form hydrogen-1 and another nucleus. This process is known as a transmutation. In a transmutation, an element is converted into one or more different elements. This is entirely unlike "normal" chemical equations where balancing requires the atoms to remain unchanged. The first step in balancing this equation is to write the symbols of the known species on either side of the reaction arrow. You should already know how to write the symbols of chlorine-35 and hydrogen-1; however, you may not remember how to write the symbol of a neutron. We will use an *X* to indicate the unknown element. This gives the following:

$$^{35}_{17}\mathrm{Cl} + {}^{1}_{0}n \rightarrow {}^{1}_{1}H + {}^{A}_{Z}X$$

In this equation, the mass numbers on the left sum to 36 = (35 + 1) and on the right they sum to 1 + *A*. This leads to 36 = 1 + *A*, which means *A* = 35. In an analogous fashion, sum of the atomic numbers on the left is 17 = (17 + 0), and 1 + *Z* on the right, which means 17 = 1 + *Z*, which means *Z* = 16. Checking the periodic table, we see the element with *Z* = 16 is sulfur. We can now include this material into the nuclear equation to produce a balanced equation:

$$^{35}_{17}\mathrm{Cl} + {}^{1}_{0}n \rightarrow {}^{1}_{1}H + {}^{35}_{16}S$$

# Natural Radioactive Decay Modes

KEY IDEA

Three common types of radioactive decay are observed in nature, and two others are occasionally observed. While you do not need to know any specifics about these, it is useful to recognize their names and for you to get more practice in recognizing atomic symbols.

## Alpha Emission

An alpha particle is a helium nucleus with two protons and two neutrons. It is represented as ${}_{2}^{4}\text{He}$ or ${}_{2}^{4}\alpha$. As this particle is expelled from the nucleus of the radioisotope that is undergoing decay, it has no electrons and thus has a 2+ charge. However, it quickly acquires two electrons from its surroundings to form the neutral atom. Most commonly, the alpha particle is shown as the neutral particle and not the cation.

Radon-222 undergoes alpha decay according to the following equation:

$$ {}_{86}^{222}\text{Rn} \rightarrow {}_{84}^{218}\text{Po} + {}_{2}^{4}\text{He} $$

Notice that in going from Rn-222 to Po-218, the atomic number has decreased by 2 and the mass number by 4.

## Beta Emission

A beta particle is an electron and can be represented as either ${}_{-1}^{0}\beta$ or ${}_{-1}^{0}e$. This electron comes from the nucleus, *not* the electron cloud, and results from the conversion of a neutron into a proton and an electron: ${}_{0}^{1}n \rightarrow {}_{1}^{1}p + {}_{-1}^{0}e$

Nickel-63 will undergo beta decay according to the following equation:

$$ {}_{28}^{63}\text{Ni} \rightarrow {}_{29}^{63}\text{Cu} + {}_{-1}^{0}e. $$

Notice that the atomic number has increased by 1 in going from Ni-63 to Cu-63, but the mass number has remained unchanged.

## Gamma Emission

Gamma emission is the giving off of high-energy, short-wavelength photons like X-rays. This radiation is commonly represented as $\gamma$. Gamma emission commonly accompanies most other types of radioactive decay but is often not shown in the balanced nuclear equation because it has neither appreciable mass nor charge.

Alpha, beta, and gamma emissions are the most common types of natural decay mode, but positron emission and electron capture are also observed occasionally.

## Positron Emission

A positron is essentially an electron that has a positive charge instead of a negative one.

It is represented as ${}_{+1}^{0}\beta$ or ${}_{+1}^{0}e$. Positron emission results from the conversion of a proton to a neutron and a positron: ${}_{1}^{1}p \rightarrow {}_{0}^{1}n + {}_{+1}^{0}e$. It is observed in the decay of some natural radioactive isotopes, such as K-40: ${}_{19}^{40}\text{K} \rightarrow {}_{18}^{40}\text{Ar} + {}_{+1}^{0}e$.

## Electron Capture

The four decay modes described above all involve the emission or giving off a particle; electron capture is the capturing of an electron from the energy level closest to the nucleus (1s) by a proton in the nucleus. This creates a neutron: ${}_{-1}^{0}e + {}_{1}^{1}p \rightarrow {}_{0}^{1}n$. Electron capture leaves a vacancy in the 1s energy level, and an electron from a higher energy level drops down to fill this vacancy. A cascading effect occurs as the electrons shift downward and, as they do so, energy is released. This energy falls in the X-ray part of the electromagnetic spectrum. These X-rays give scientists a clue that electron capture has taken place.

Polonium-204 undergoes electron capture: ${}_{19}^{40}\text{K} + {}_{-1}^{0}e \rightarrow {}_{83}^{204}\text{Bi}$ + X-rays. Notice that the atomic number has decreased by 1, but the mass number has remained the same.

TIP

Remember that electron capture is the only decay mode that involves adding a particle to the left side of the reaction arrow.

## Nuclear Stability

KEY IDEA

Predicting whether a specific isotope is stable and what type of decay mode it might undergo can be tricky. All isotopes containing 84 or more protons are unstable and will undergo nuclear decay. For these large, massive isotopes, alpha decay is observed most commonly. Alpha decay gets rid of four units of mass and two units of charge, thus helping relieve the repulsive stress found in these nuclei. For other isotopes, with atomic numbers less than 84, stability is best predicted determining the neutron-to-proton (n/p) ratio. Nuclei with a high ratio tend to undergo either positron emission or electron capture, while nuclei with a low ratio tend to undergo beta emission.

These predictions are only guidelines, and there are isotopes that utilize more than one decay mode. In addition, the isotope formed may not be stable and undergo further decay steps until a stable isotope results. For example, radioactive U-238 decays to stable Pb-206 in 14 steps, a majority of which are alpha emissions, as one might predict.

## Nuclear Decay Calculations

A radioactive isotope may be unstable, but it is impossible to predict when a certain atom will decay. However, if a statistically large enough sample is examined, some trends become obvious. The radioactive decay follows first-order kinetics (see Chapter 13, Kinetics, for a more in-depth discussion of first-order reactions and equations). If the number of radioactive atoms in a sample is monitored, it can be determined that it takes a certain amount of time for half the sample to decay; it takes the same amount of time for half the remaining sample to decay; and so on. The amount of time it takes for half the sample to decay is called the half-life of the isotope and is given the symbol $t_{1/2}$. The table below shows the percentage of radioactive isotope remaining versus half-life.

| HALF-LIFE, $t_{1/2}$ | PERCENT RADIOACTIVE ISOTOPE REMAINING |
|---|---|
| 0 | 100 |
| 1 | 50 |
| 2 | 25 |
| 3 | 12.5 |
| 4 | 6.25 |
| 5 | 3.12 |
| 6 | 1.56 |
| 7 | 0.78 |
| 8 | 0.39 |
| 9 | 0.16 |
| 10 | 0.09 |

Half-lives may be very short, $4.2 \times 10^{-6}$ seconds for Po-213, or very long, $4.5 \times 10^{9}$ years for U-238. The long half-lives of some waste products is a major problem with nuclear fission reactors.

If only multiples of half-lives are considered, the calculations are very straightforward. For example, I-131 is used in the treatment of thyroid cancer and has a $t_{1/2}$ of 8 days. How long would it take to decay to 25% of its original amount? Looking at the chart, you see that 25% decay would occur at two half-lives, or 16 days. However, radioactive decay is not a linear process; you cannot use the chart to predict how much would still be radioactive at the end of 12 days or at some time (or amount) that is not associated with a multiple of a half-life. To solve these types of problems, one must use the mathematical relationships associated with first-order kinetics that were presented in the Kinetics chapter. In general, two equations are used:

$$(1)\ \ln [A]t - \ln [A]_0 = -kt$$

$$(2)\ t_{1/2} = \frac{\ln 2}{k} = \frac{0.693}{k}$$

In these equations, the ln is the natural logarithm; $[A]t$ is the amount of isotope radioactive remaining after some time $t$; $[A]_0$ is the amount initially radioactive; and $k$ is the rate constant for the decay. If you know initial and final amounts and are looking for the half-life, you will use equation (1) to solve for the rate constant and then use equation (2) to solve for $t_{1/2}$.

For example: What is the half-life of a radioisotope that takes 45 min to decay to 80% of its original activity?

First use equation (1) to determine $k$; then use the value of $k$ in equation (2) to determine the half-life:

Using equation (1): $\ln [80] - \ln [100] = -k(45\text{ min})$

$$-0.2231 = -k(45\text{ min})$$

$$4.96 \times 10^{-3}\text{ min}^{-1} = k$$

Now equation (2):

$$t_{1/2} = \frac{0.693}{4.96 \times 10^{-3}\text{ min}^{-1}}$$

$$t_{1/2} = 140\text{ min}$$

If one knows the half-life and amount remaining radioactive, equation (2) can be used to calculate the rate constant $k$ and equation (1) can then be used to solve for the time. This is the basis of carbon-14 dating, which is used to determine the age of objects that were once alive.

For example, suppose a wooden tool is discovered and its carbon-14 activity is determined to have decreased to 73% of the original. How old is the object?

The half-life of carbon-14 is 5,730 yr. Substituting this into equation (2):

$$5{,}730\text{ yr} = \frac{0.693}{k}$$

$$k = 1.21 \times 10^{-4}\text{ yr}^{-1}$$

Substituting this rate constant into equation (1):

$$\ln [73] - \ln [100] = -(1.21 \times 10^{-4}\text{ yr}^{-1})t$$

$$-0.3147 = -(1.21 \times 10^{-4}\text{ yr}^{-1})t$$

$$t = 2{,}600\text{ yr}$$

## Mass–Energy Relationships

Like "normal" chemical reactions, nuclear reactions involve energy. In general, nuclear reactions involve much more energy than do "normal" chemical reactions. In a nuclear process, the energy results from the conversion of a very small amount of matter into energy.

(Remember that in nuclear reactions there is no conservation of matter, as in ordinary chemical reactions.) The amount of energy that is produced can be calculated by using Einstein's equation $E = mc^2$, where $E$ is the energy produced, $m$ is the mass converted into energy (the mass defect), and $c$ is the speed of light. The amount of matter that is converted into energy is normally very small, but when it is multiplied by the speed of light (a very large number) squared, the amount of energy produced is very large.

## Common Mistakes to Avoid

TIP

1. Make sure your answer is reasonable. Don't just write down the answer from your calculator.
2. Make sure your units cancel in your calculations, leaving the unit you want.
3. In half-life problems, don't omit the minus sign. Watch your units. Half-lives must be in time units.
4. In half-life problems, be sure to use the amount of isotope still radioactive as $[A]_t$ and not the amount decayed.

## › Review Questions

Use these questions to review the content of this chapter and practice for the AP Chemistry Exam. First are 10 multiple-choice questions similar to what you will encounter in Section I of the AP Chemistry Exam. Following those is a long free-response question like the ones in Section II of the exam. These questions are primarily designed to review prior knowledge and kinetics. To make these questions an even more authentic practice for the actual exam, time yourself following the instructions provided.

### Multiple-Choice Questions

Answer the following questions in 15 minutes. You may not use a calculator. You may use the periodic table and the equation sheet at the back of this book.

**1.** When $^{226}_{88}Ra$ decays, it emits 2 α particles, then a β particle, followed by another α. The resulting nucleus is:

(A) $^{212}_{83}Bi$

(B) $^{222}_{86}Rn$

(C) $^{214}_{82}Pb$

(D) $^{214}_{83}Bi$

**2.** The formation of $^{230}_{90}Th$ from $^{234}_{92}U$ occurs by:

(A) electron capture
(B) α decay
(C) β decay
(D) positron decay

**3.** Which of the following lists the types of radiation in the correct order of increasing penetrating power?

(A) α, γ, β
(B) β, α, γ
(C) α, β, γ
(D) β, γ, α

**4.** Choose the correct statement from the following that is applicable to β particles.

(A) Beta particles are electrons and have a mass number of zero and a charge of −1.
(B) Beta particles have a mass number of zero, a charge of −1, and are less penetrating than α particles.
(C) Beta particles are electrons with a charge of +1 and are less penetrating than α particles.
(D) Beta particles have a mass number of zero and a charge of +1.

**5.** An atom of $^{238}_{92}U$ undergoes radioactive decay by α emission. What is the product nuclide?

(A) $^{230}_{90}Th$

(B) $^{234}_{90}Th$

(C) $^{230}_{92}U$

(D) $^{230}_{91}Pa$

**6.** If 75% of a sample of pure $^{3}_{1}H$ decays in 24.6 years, what is the half-life of $^{3}_{1}H$?

(A) 24.6 yr
(B) 18.4 yr
(C) 12.3 yr
(D) 6.15 yr

**7.** Which of the following will have the smallest mass defect?

(A) $^{238}U$
(B) $^{12}C$
(C) $^{56}Fe$
(D) $^{1}H$

**8.** Several types of radioactive decay were mentioned in this chapter. How does electron capture differ from the other types mentioned?

(A) Electron capture is the only radioactive decay process that involves an electron.
(B) Electron capture is the only radioactive decay process in which something enters the nucleus.
(C) Electron capture is the only radioactive decay process that does not change the mass defect.
(D) Electron capture is the only radioactive decay process that involves no change in atomic number.

**9.** The age of Earth is over 4.4 billion years. This was determined by radioactive dating. Which of the following radioactive isotopes could NOT be used to determine the age of the Earth?

(A) $^{87}Rb$
(B) $^{238}U$
(C) $^{40}K$
(D) $^{14}C$

**10.** Uranium-236 undergoes spontaneous fission as indicated by the following partial equation: $^{236}_{92}U \rightarrow 4\ ^{1}_{0}n + ^{136}_{53}I +$ ______. What is the missing product?

(A) $^{90}_{39}Y$

(B) $^{96}_{38}Sr$

(C) $^{96}_{39}Y$

(D) $^{98}_{40}Zr$

## › Answers and Explanations

**1. D**—The mass of the starting nucleus is 226 and its atomic number is 88 (prior knowledge). Each $\alpha$ particle reduces the mass by 4 and each $\beta$ reduces the mass by 0. The final mass should be 226 – (4 + 4 + 0 + 4) = 214. Each $\alpha$ particle reduces the atomic number by 2 and each $\beta$ reduces the atomic number by –1. The final atomic number should be 88 – (2 + 2 – 1 + 2) = 83.

**2. B**—The calculations are as follows: mass difference = 234 – 230 = 4; atomic number difference = 92 – 90 = 2. These correspond to an $\alpha$ particle.

**3. C**—Alpha particles are the least penetrating, and gamma rays are the most penetrating (prior knowledge).

**4. A**—The complete symbol for a $\beta$ particle is ${}^{0}_{-1}\beta$ or ${}^{0}_{-1}e$ (prior knowledge). As indicated by the symbol, the mass number is zero. Beta particles are electrons, which means they have a –1 charge.

**5. B**—An $\alpha$ particle reduces the mass by 4 and reduces the atomic number by 2. The calculations are as follows: mass number = 238 – 4 = 234; atomic number = 92 – 2 = 90.

**6. C**—After one half-life, 50% would remain. After another half-life, this amount would be reduced by one-half to 25%. The total amount decayed is 75%. Thus, 24.6 years must be two half-lives of 12.3 years each. This is reviewed in Chapter 13, Kinetics.

**7. D**—${}^{1}H$ has no mass defect because there is nothing to bind to the single proton in the nucleus (prior knowledge).

**8. B**—During electron capture, an electron is absorbed into the nucleus, which will alter the mass defect and change the atomic number. Beta decay also involves electrons.

**9. D**—The half-life of carbon-14 (5,730 years) is much too short to determine an age in the billions of years.

**10. C**—It is necessary to determine both the mass number and the atomic number of the nucleus formed. The mass number difference depends on the superscripts. The total on each side of the reaction arrow must be identical. Mass difference = 236 – 4(1) – 136 = 96. The atomic number difference depends on the subscripts. The total on each side of the reaction arrow must be identical. Atomic number difference = 92 – 4(0) – 53 = 39. The mass numbers and atomic number values should all be prior knowledge, covered in your pre-AP chemistry course when you learned about the structures of atoms.

## › Free-Response Question

You have 10 minutes to answer the following question. You may use a calculator and the tables in the back of the book.

**Question**

It is possible to determine the age of a sample from a meteorite by determining the amounts of thorium-232 and lead-208 present. Thorium-232 decays to lead-208 with a half-life of $1.40 \times 10^{10}$ years. A mineral sample contains 40.2 mg of thorium-232 and 18.0 mg of lead-208. Answer the following two questions concerning this sample.

(a) How many milligrams of thorium-232 were originally in the sample?
(b) What is the age of the sample?

## ❯ Answer and Explanation

Note that, while nuclear chemistry is not an AP topic, all the materials in these questions depend on basic AP Chemistry knowledge, which is why this chapter can be valuable. It is especially important to remember that nuclear decay processes follow first-order kinetics; for this reason, this question is reviewed in Chapter 13, Kinetics.

(a) This is a stoichiometry calculation. The calculation of the original mass is the mass at present plus the mass of the thorium-232 that decayed. To simplify the mole calculation, it is useful to remember that numerically, g/mole is the same as mg/mmole.

$$\text{Mass } ^{232}\text{Th} = 40.2 \text{ mg } ^{232}\text{Th} + (18.0 \text{ mg } ^{208}\text{Pb})$$
$$\left(\frac{1 \text{ mmole } ^{208}\text{Pb}}{208 \text{ mg } ^{208}\text{Pb}}\right)\left(\frac{1 \text{ mmole } ^{232}\text{Th}}{1 \text{ mmole } ^{208}\text{Pb}}\right)\left(\frac{232 \text{ mg } ^{232}\text{Th}}{1 \text{ mmole } ^{232}\text{Th}}\right)$$
$$= 60.3 \text{ mg } ^{232}\text{Th}$$

The molar mass of $^{208}$Pb is 208 g/mole and not 207.2 g/mole (from the periodic table) because only one isotope is present. Using the molar mass from the periodic table gives an incorrect answer of 60.4 mg $^{232}$Th. If you did not convert the mass of lead-208 to mass of thorium-232, you got an incorrect answer of 58.2 mg $^{232}$Th.

The set up earns 1 point even if you incorrectly used 207.2 g/mole and 0 points if you did not convert lead to thorium. The correct answer (60.3 mg $^{232}$Th) earns a second point.

(b) The equation given in the exam booklet relating the quantities of material in a first-order reaction to time (integrated rate law) is $\ln [A]t - \ln [A]_0 = -kt$. Another equation, also given in the exam booklet, is $t_{1/2} = \ln 2/0.693 = 0.693/k$. It is possible to rearrange and combine these equations. Rearrangement gives:

$$\text{Age} = t = \frac{(\ln [A]_0 - \ln [A]_t)}{k} \text{ where } k = \frac{0.693}{t_{1/2}}$$

Entering the values $[A]_t = 40.2$ mg $^{232}$Th, $[A]_0 = 60.3$ mg $^{232}$Th, and $t_{1/2} = 1.40 \times 10^{10}$ years gives:

$$\text{Age} = t = \frac{(\ln [A]_0 - \ln [A]_t)}{k} = \frac{(\ln [A]_0 - \ln [A]_t)}{\frac{0.693}{t_{1/2}}}$$
$$= \frac{(\ln [60.3 \text{ mg}]_0 - \ln [40.2 \text{ mg}]_t)}{\frac{0.693}{1.40 \times 10^{10} \text{ yr}}} = 8.19 \times 10^9 \text{ yr}$$

Both $[A]_t$ and $[A]_0$ must be in the same units, which, in this case, are mg $^{232}$Th. Using the wrong initial mass (60.4 mg) gives $8.22 \times 10^9$ yr (an error of 30 million years). Using the mass of lead-208 instead of converting to thorium-232 gives $7.48 \times 10^9$ yr.

Give yourself 1 point for the correct setup. You still get the point if you use a wrong answer from part (a). The correct answer ($2.16 \times 10^9$ yr) earns a second point.

Total your points. There are 4 points possible. Subtract 1 point if your answers do not have the correct number of significant figures.

# › Rapid Review

- Know how to incorporate the mass number and the atomic number into a chemical symbol.
- Nuclear decay processes follow first-order kinetics. Use the appropriate equations.

# CHAPTER 19

# Organic Chemistry

**SPECIAL NOTE**

ENRICHMENT

Although organic chemistry is not specifically tested on the AP Chemistry Exam, an overview of the subject will help you recognize and understand organic structures that appear in relation to other topics on the exam. In many cases, it will be important to be able to draw a Lewis structure for a molecule that happens to be organic. Organic molecules are good examples used to illustrate intermolecular forces. In addition, this material is taught by some high school and college teachers.

**IN THIS CHAPTER**

**Summary:** Organic chemistry is the study of the chemistry of carbon. Almost all the compounds containing carbon are classified as organic compounds. Only a few—for example, carbonates and cyanides—are classified as inorganic. It used to be thought that all organic compounds had to be produced by living organisms, but this idea was proven wrong in 1828 when German chemist Friedrich Wöhler produced the first organic compound from inorganic starting materials. Since that time, chemists have synthesized many organic compounds found in nature and have also made many never found naturally. It is carbon's characteristic of bonding strongly to itself and to other elements in long, complex chains and rings that gives carbon the ability to form the many diverse and complex compounds needed to support life. It is important to remember that in organic compounds, carbon has four bonds.

KEY IDEA

### Keywords and Equations

No keywords or equations specific to this chapter are listed on the AP Exam.

# Hydrocarbons

Hydrocarbons are the simplest type of organic compound because they contain only the elements carbon and hydrogen. The electronegativities of carbon and hydrogen are similar, so these are nonpolar substances. As nonpolar substances, only London dispersion forces may be present.

There are four types of hydrocarbons; these are alkanes, alkenes, alkynes, and aromatics. **Alkanes** contain only single bonds. **Alkenes** contain at least one double bond between two carbon atoms. **Alkynes** contain at least one triple bond between two carbon atoms. **Aromatics** have ring structures with alternating single and double bonds between the carbon atoms. In all four categories, the carbon atoms have four bonds each and the hydrogen atoms have only one bond each.

The great variety of hydrocarbons is due to the ability of carbon atoms to form strong bonds to other carbon atoms. This is often seen as long chains of carbon atoms with hydrogen atoms off the side of the chain. The carbon atoms are bonded to each other with the hydrogen atoms off to the side. The number of hydrogen atoms depends on how many are needed to give each carbon atom four bonds. For example, if a carbon atom forms two single bonds to other carbon atoms, there will need to be two hydrogen atoms to bring the total to four bonds.

# Structural Isomerism

Another reason why there are some many hydrocarbons is that it is possible to arrange the carbon atoms in different ways. These different arrangements are known as isomers. Compounds with the same molecular formulas but different structural formulas are called isomers. With hydrocarbons, this applies to a different arrangement of the carbon atoms. Isomers such as these are called **structural isomers**. Figure 19.1 shows the structural isomers of $C_5H_{12}$. Note that there are the same number of carbons and hydrogens in each structure. Only the way the carbons are bonded is different.

In writing structural isomers, or any other organic compounds, remember that **carbon forms four bonds**. This should be apparent to you when inspecting Figure 19.1. One of the most common mistakes that a chemistry student makes is writing an organic structure with a carbon atom having fewer or more than four bonds.

There are additional types of isomers. One of the additional types of isomerism is optical isomerism. Optical isomers are extremely important in biological systems. If you enter a college program leading to a medical career, you will see many examples of optical isomers.

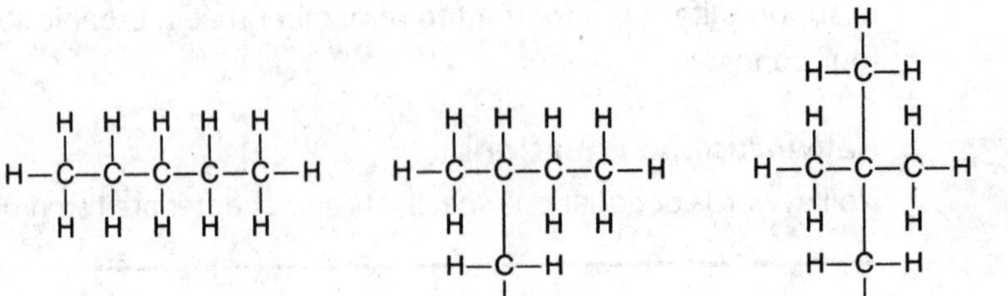


**Figure 19.1 Structural isomers of $C_5H_{12}$.**

## Common Functional Groups

Organic molecules may include functional groups. A functional group is anything in the molecule other than carbon–carbon single bonds or carbon–hydrogen bonds. The double and triple carbon–carbon bonds in alkenes and alkynes are functional groups. The presence of any atom other than carbon or hydrogen is a functional group.

The addition of other elements to hydrocarbons results in polar molecules. The intermolecular forces in polar molecules are either dipole–dipole forces or hydrogen bonding. The presence of polar molecules results in molecules that have higher melting and boiling points than hydrocarbons. (Note that if you are going to compare the melting or boiling points of molecules, the molecules you are comparing should be about the same size.)

Any of the hydrogen atoms in an organic compound may be replaced by a halogen (F, Cl, Br, or I).

The other carbon compounds that may appear on the AP Exam contain oxygen and/or nitrogen. Both oxygen and nitrogen are significantly more electronegative than either carbon or hydrogen. This significantly higher electronegativity means that oxygen and nitrogen containing organic compounds are polar. In addition, if a hydrogen atom is attached to the oxygen or nitrogen, hydrogen bonding is possible.

Oxygen containing organic compounds, with only single bonds, include ethers and alcohols. In an ether, an oxygen atom is attached to two carbon atoms, leaving a polar molecule with dipole–dipole forces. In an alcohol, an oxygen atom is attached to a carbon atom and a hydrogen atom, which leads to hydrogen bonding being the key intermolecular force.

Nitrogen containing organic compounds, with only single bonds, are the amines. In an amine, the nitrogen atom forms a single bond to one, two, or three carbon atoms. Amines are ammonia molecules with one, two, or three of the hydrogen atoms replaced by carbon-containing groups. If there are one or two hydrogen atoms attached to the nitrogen, there will be hydrogen bonding; otherwise, dipole–dipole forces are important. The key property of amines is that they are bases. As bases, they react with acids. The reaction with an acid is very much like the reaction of ammonia with an acid. Acid–base reactions of amines should be treated like reactions of ammonia with acids.

It is also possible for an oxygen atom to form a double bond to a carbon atom. Compounds containing a carbon–oxygen double bond include aldehydes, ketones, carboxylic acids, and esters. The present of oxygen makes these compounds polar with intermolecular dipole–dipole forces; in addition, carboxylic acids have hydrogen bonding. Besides recognizing the intermolecular forces, it will be important for you to deal with carboxylic acids.

Carboxylic acids are the most common organic acids. You have already dealt with one carboxylic acid—acetic acid. All other carboxylic acids behave like acetic acid, so you should not be distracted by their different formulas.

The introduction of other atoms (N, O, Cl, etc.) to organic compounds gives rise to many other functional groups. The major functional groups are shown in Table 19.1 on the next page.

## Acid–Base Chemistry

While organic chemistry is not an AP topic, acid–base chemistry is a topic. These compounds do illustrate many of the AP topics. Organic acids (carboxylic acids) and bases (amines) are weak acids or weak bases. For this reason, they will have a $K_a$ or a $K_b$ (amino acids are organic compounds that are acids *and* bases). While the structures are different,

**Table 19.1 Common Functional Groups**

| Functional Group | Compound Type | Suffix or Prefix of Name | Example | Systematic Name (Common Name) |
|---|---|---|---|---|
| C=C | alkene | -ene | $H_2C{=}CH_2$ | ethene (ethylene) |
| —C≡C— | alkyne | -yne | H—C≡C—H | ethyne (acetylene) |
| —C—Ö—H | alcohol | -ol | $H_3C$—Ö—H | methanol (methyl alcohol) |
| —C—X: (X=halogen) | haloalkane | halo- | $H_3C$—Cl: | chloromethane (methyl chloride) |
| —C—N— | amine | -amine | $H_3C$—$CH_2$—N—H (H) | ethyl amine |
| :O: ‖ —C—H | aldehyde | -al | $H_3C$—C(=O:)—H | ethanal (acetaldehyde) |
| :O: ‖ —C—C—C— | ketone | -one | $H_3C$—C(=O:)—$CH_3$ | propanone (acetone) |
| :O: ‖ —C—Ö—H | catboxylic acid | -oic acid | $H_3C$—C(=O:)—Ö—H | ethanoic acid (acetic acid) |
| :O: ‖ —C—Ö—C— | ester | -oate | $H_3C$—C(=O:)—Ö—$CH_3$ | methyl ethanoate (methyl acetate) |
| :O: ‖ —C—N— | amide | -amide | $H_3C$—C(=O:)—N—H (H) | ethanamide (acetamide) |

the acid–base equilibria are identical to the acid–base equilibria presented in Chapter 15 (Unit 8).

A typical weak-acid equilibrium is:

$$HA(aq) \leftrightarrows H^+(aq) + A^-(aq) \qquad K_a = \frac{[H^+][A^-]}{[HA]}$$

You probably have seen the acetic acid, a common weak acid, where A = $C_2H_3O_2$. Substituting for A in the above equilibrium gives:

$$HC_2H_3O_2(aq) \leftrightarrows H^+(aq) + C_2H_3O_2^-(aq) \qquad K_a = \frac{[H^+][C_2H_3O_2^-]}{[HC_2H_3O_2]}$$

It is possible to write the formula of any carboxylic acid as:

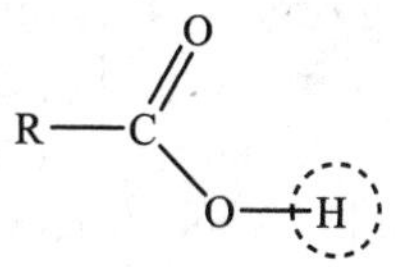

The circled hydrogen atom is the acid hydrogen. R may represent hydrogen or nearly any organic group. R = H– in formic acid, R = $CH_3$– in acetic acid, and so on. The structural formula is the reason why acetic acid is sometimes written as $CH_3COOH$ instead of $HC_2H_3O_2$. Do not let the identity of R distract you; as far as solving $K_a$ problems, R makes no difference in the procedure.

The amines (organic bases) are related to ammonia, which means all amine $K_b$ equilibria are related to the $K_b$ for ammonia.

$$NH_3(aq) + H_2O(l) \leftrightarrows OH^-(aq) + NH_4^+(aq) \qquad K_b = \frac{[OH^-][NH_4^+]}{[NH_3]}$$

The formation of the ammonium ion may be represented as:

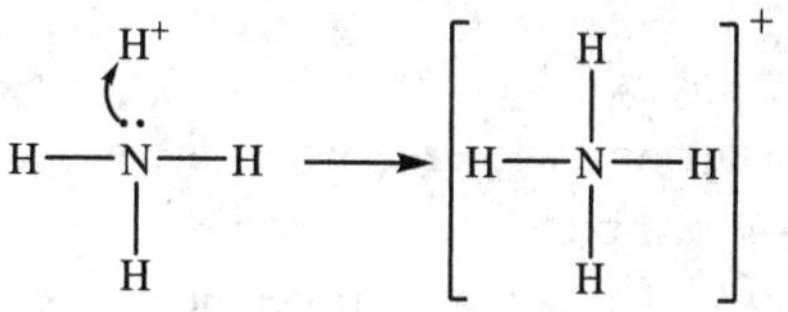

The formula of an amine may be represented as NR′R″R‴, where the different Rs may or may not be the same. For ammonia, R′ = R″ = R‴ = H. For a primary amine, one of the Rs ≠ H. For a secondary amine, two Rs ≠ H. In a tertiary amine, none of the Rs is an H. Based upon the general formula of an amine the above reaction becomes:

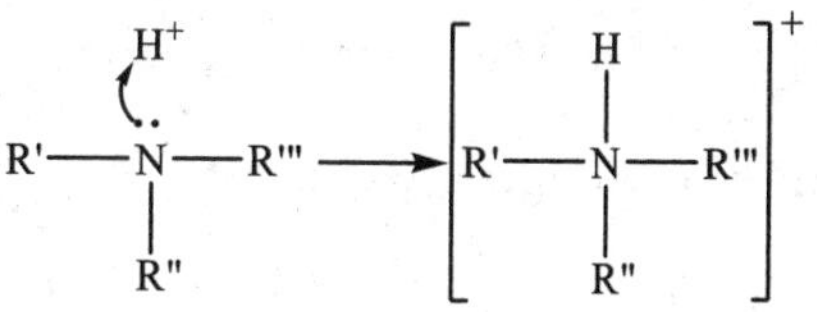

As with organic acids, do not be distracted by the identities of the Rs.

All organic acids have a hydrogen atom attached to an oxygen atom, and in all amines, except tertiary amines, there is at least one hydrogen atom attached to a nitrogen atom. This means that in all organic acids and in most amines, hydrogen bonding is present, which means that everything you learned about hydrogen bonding as an intermolecular interaction applies.

## Experiments

Many experiments involving the concepts of organic chemistry are synthesis reactions. In addition, acid–base titrations involving organic materials are important.

## Common Mistakes to Avoid

TIP

1. When writing organic formulas, make sure that every carbon has four bonds.
2. Hydrocarbons are nonpolar, and the intermolecular forces are London dispersion forces.
3. Adding other elements to a hydrocarbon may make the molecule polar. If it is polar, there are dipole–dipole forces and/or hydrogen bonding between the molecules.
4. **Be sure that every carbon has four bonds!**

## › Review Questions

Use these questions to review the content of this chapter and improve your understanding of chemistry. Although organic chemistry won't specifically be tested on the exam, this section contains questions of the same types as those found on the AP Exam. First are 9 multiple-choice questions. Following those is a long free-response question. Time yourself following the instructions provided to practice pacing yourself.

### Multiple-Choice Questions

Answer the following questions in 15 minutes. You may not use a calculator. You may use the periodic table and the equation sheet at the back of this book.

**1.** Cycloalkanes are hydrocarbons with the general formula $C_nH_{2n}$. If a 14-g sample of any alkene is combusted in excess oxygen, how many moles of water will form?

(A) 14 moles
(B) 2.0 moles
(C) 1.0 mole
(D) 28 moles

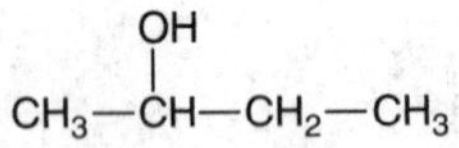


**2.** The organic compound shown above would be classified as:

(A) an organic base
(B) a hydrocarbon
(C) an alcohol
(D) a carboxylic acid

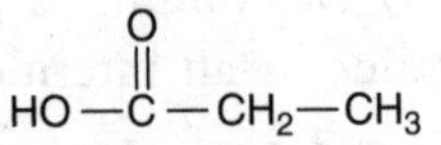


**3.** The above compound would be classified as:

(A) an organic base
(B) a hydrocarbon
(C) an alcohol
(D) a carboxylic acid

**4.** Which of the following compounds can form hydrogen bonds?

(A) $CH_3CH_2CH_2CH_2OH$
(B) $CH_3CH{=}CHCH_2CH_3$
(C) $CH_3CH_2CHClCH_2CH_3$
(D) $CH_3CHClCH_2CH_2CH_3$

**5.** A carboxylic acid may be represented as:

(A) ROH
(B) RCHO
(C) R-O-R
(D) RCOOH

**6.** Which of the following compounds will give the highest pH when dissolved in water?

(A) $CH_3CHO$
(B) $CH_3OH$
(C) HCOOH
(D) $CH_3NH_2$

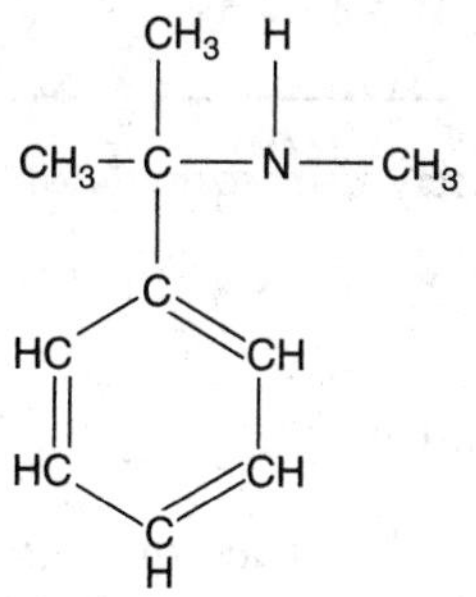

7. The organic compound shown above would be classified as:

(A) an organic base
(B) a hydrocarbon
(C) an alcohol
(D) a carboxylic acid

8. Which basic concept from Chapter 8, Bonding, best explains why carbon in stable organic compounds has four bonds?

(A) VSEPR
(B) octet rule
(C) Avogadro's hypothesis
(D) electronegativity

9. Which of the following is the one reaction that all organic compounds will undergo?

(A) neutralization
(B) precipitation
(C) combustion
(D) polymerization

## Answers and Explanations

1. C—Using the empirical formula gives the following combustion reaction:

$$C_nH_{2n}(g) + 1.5\ O_2(g) \rightarrow n\ CO_2(g) + n\ H_2O(g)$$

The general formula $C_nH_{2n}$ means that 1 mole of $H_2O$ will form per mole of empirical formula unit, regardless of the value of $n$. The moles of water formed are the mass of the alkene divided by the empirical formula mass:

$$(14\text{ g alkene})\left(\frac{1\text{ mol alkene}}{14\text{ g alkene}}\right)\left(\frac{1\text{ mol }H_2O}{1\text{ mol alkene}}\right)$$

$$= 1.0\text{ mole}$$

2. C—Organic bases are, in general, amines (contain N). A hydrocarbon only contains C and H. A carboxylic acid (like acetic acid) has one oxygen double-bonded to a carbon and an –OH bonded to a carbon atom. Alcohols have an –OH bonded to a carbon atom.

3. D—Organic bases are, in general, amines (contain N). A hydrocarbon only contains C and H. A carboxylic acid (like acetic acid) has one oxygen double-bonded to a carbon and an –OH bonded to a carbon atom. Alcohols have an –OH bonded to a carbon atom.

4. A—Just because these are organic compounds does not alter the fact that hydrogen bonding requires a hydrogen atom bonded to one of the following: N, O, or F. Answer A has an H attached to an O.

5. D—A common example of a carboxylic acid is acetic acid (often written as $CH_3COOH$), where R = $CH_3$. A is an alcohol, B is an aldehyde, and C is an ether.

6. D—Only acids and bases change the pH. The acids are RCOOH, and the bases contain N. The highest pH is the result of dissolving a base in water. A is an aldehyde, which is neutral. B is an alcohol, which is neutral (or very slightly acidic). C is a carboxylic acid, which is an acid. D is an amine, which is a base. You should be able to recognize acids and bases.

7. A—Organic bases are, in general, amines (contain N). A hydrocarbon only contains C and H. Alcohols and carboxylic acids contain O. Do not be distracted by the "complicated" structure.

8. B—A carbon atom, with four bonds, is surrounded by $4 \times 2 = 8$ electrons (an octet).

9. C—All organic compounds burn.

## › Free-Response Questions

You have 20 minutes to answer the following questions. You may use a calculator and the tables in the back of the book.

**Question 1**

The alkane hexane, $C_6H_{14}$, has a molecular mass of 86.17 g $mol^{-1}$.

(a) Like all hydrocarbons, hexane will burn. Write a balanced chemical equation for the complete combustion of hexane. This reaction produces gaseous carbon dioxide, $CO_2$, and water vapor, $H_2O$.

(b) The complete combustion of 10.0 g of hexane produces 487 kJ. What is the molar heat of combustion ($\Delta H$) of hexane?

(c) Determine the pressure exerted by the carbon dioxide formed when 5.00 g of hexane is combusted. Assume the carbon dioxide is dry and stored in a 20.0 L container at 27°C. Show all work.

(d) Hexane, like most alkanes, may exist in different isomeric forms. The structural formula of one of these isomers is pictured below. Draw the structural formula of any two other isomers of hexane. Make sure all carbon atoms and hydrogen atoms are shown.

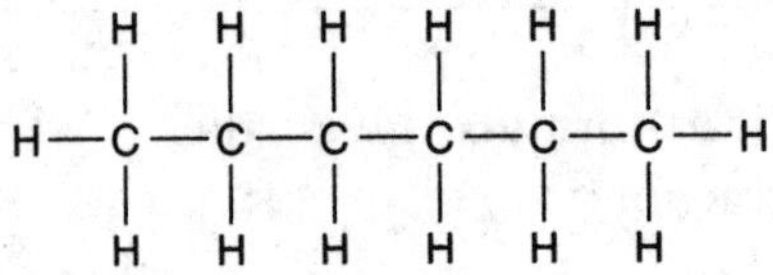

**Question 2**

Amino acids are biological molecules with an organic acid group and an organic base group present. These two groups react with each other. The simplest natural amino acid is glycine, $NH_2CH_2COOH$, which, after its internal acid–base reaction, is better formulated as [$N^+H_3CH_2COO^-$].

(a) Complete the Lewis structure below for glycine in its ionic form. If resonance is possible, you only need to show one resonance form.

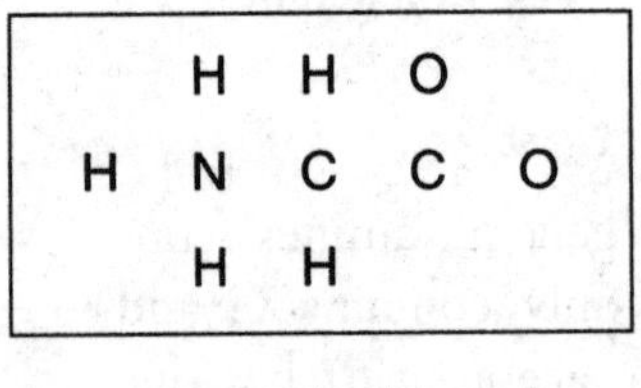


(b) Determine the formal charge for each nonhydrogen atom.

## › Answers and Explanations

Note that, while organic chemistry is not an AP topic, all the materials in these questions depend on basic AP Chemistry knowledge, which is why this chapter can be valuable.

**Question 1**

(a) $2\ C_6H_{14}(g) + 19\ O_2(g) \rightarrow 12\ CO_2(g) + 14\ H_2O(g)$

Give yourself 2 points for the answer shown above or for the coefficients 1, 9/2, 6, and 7. Give yourself 1 point if you have one or more, but not all, of the elements balanced. This question reviews balancing equations.

(b) $$\left(\frac{-487\text{ kJ}}{10.0\text{ g hexane}}\right)\left(\frac{86.17\text{ g hexane}}{1\text{ mol hexane}}\right) = -4.20 \times 10^{3}\text{ kJ mol}^{-1}$$

Give yourself 2 points for the above setup and correct answer (this requires a negative sign in the answer). If the set up is partially correct, give yourself 1 point. This question reviews thermochemistry.

(c) The ideal gas equation should be rearranged to the form $P = nRT/V$.

$$\text{Moles} = n = (5.00\text{ g } C_6H_{14})\left(\frac{1\text{ mol } C_6H_{14}}{86.17\text{ g } C_6H_{14}}\right)\left(\frac{12\text{ mol } CO_2}{2\text{ mol } C_6H_{14}}\right) = 0.3481\text{ mol } CO_2$$

This answer has an extra significant figure. The mole ratio should match the one given in your balanced equation. You will not be penalized again for an incorrectly balanced equation.

$R = 0.08206$ L atm mol$^{-1}$ K$^{-1}$ (This value is in your test booklet.)

$V = 20.0$ L

$T = 27°C + 273 = 300$ K (In this case, there is no penalty if you forget to use the Kelvin temperature.)

$$P = \frac{nRT}{V} = \frac{(0.3481\text{ mol } CO_2)(0.08206\text{ L atm mol}^{-1}\text{ K}^{-1})(300\text{ K})}{(20.0\text{ L})} = 0.429\text{ atm}$$

Give yourself 2 points for the correct setup and answer. Give yourself 1 point if you did everything correctly, except the mole ratio or the kelvin conversion. This question reviews gas stoichiometry.

(d) You may need to redraw one or more of your answers to match the answers shown below.

Give yourself 1 point for each correct answer, with a 4-point maximum. There are no bonus points for additional answers.

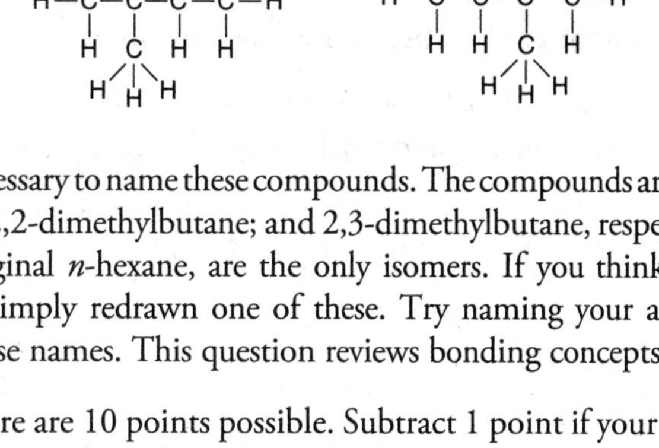

While it is unnecessary to name these compounds. The compounds are 2-methylpentane; 3-methylpentane; 2,2-dimethylbutane; and 2,3-dimethylbutane, respectively. These four, along with the original *n*-hexane, are the only isomers. If you think you have another isomer, you have simply redrawn one of these. Try naming your answer and see if it matches one of these names. This question reviews bonding concepts.

Total your points. There are 10 points possible. Subtract 1 point if your numerical answers do not have the correct number of significant figures.

**Question 2**

(a) As shown below, there are two different resonance forms. You only need to draw one of these.

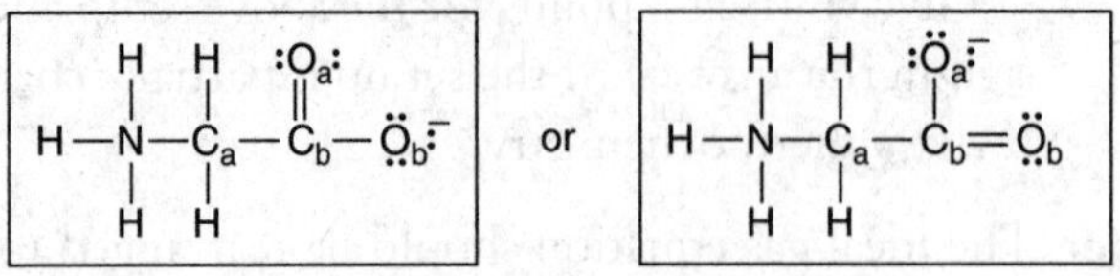


You get 1 point for a correct Lewis structure around the nitrogen and carbon atoms. You get 1 point for a correct Lewis structure around both oxygen atoms. This question reviews bonding. Since the atom placement was given to you it is irrelevant whether this is an organic compound or not.

(b) There are two acceptable resonance forms, differing only in the bonding to the oxygen atoms (and hence their formal charges). For an atom, the formal charge = valence electrons – nonbonding electrons – ½ (bonding electrons).

The formal charges for the left structure are in the following table. For the other structure, simply reverse the lines for $O_a$ and $O_b$.

| | |
|---|---|
| N | 5 – 0 – ½ (8) = +1 |
| $C_a$ | 4 – 0 – ½ (8) = 0 |
| $C_b$ | 4 – 0 – ½ (8) = 0 |
| $O_a$ | 6 – 4 – ½ (4) = 0 |
| $O_b$ | 6 – 6 – ½ (2) = –1 |

You get 1 point for a correct set of formal charges and 1 point if the total of all the formal charges is 0. This question helps review the bonding concepts.

Total your points. There are 4 points possible.

## › Rapid Review

- Organic chemistry is the chemistry of carbon and its compounds.
- Hydrocarbons are organic compounds of just carbon and hydrogen atoms.
- Alkanes are hydrocarbons in which there are only single bonds.
- Isomers are compounds that have the same molecular formulas but different structural formulas. Review the writing of the various structural isomers of alkanes. **Make sure that each carbon atom has four bonds.**
- A functional group is a group of atoms that is the reactive part of the molecule. Review the general functional groups. Especially review amines and carboxylic acids.

CHAPTER 20

# Experimental Investigations

**IN THIS CHAPTER**

**Summary:** The free-response portion of the AP Exam will contain a question concerning an experiment, and there may also be a few multiple-choice questions on one or more of these experiments. This chapter reviews the basic experiments that the AP Exam Committee believes to be important. You should look over all the experiments in this chapter and pay particular attention to any experiments you did not perform. In some cases, you may find, after reading the description, that you did a similar experiment. Not every AP class does every experiment, but any of these experiments may appear on the AP Exam.

The free-response questions on recent exams have been concerned with the equipment, measurements, and calculations required. In some cases, sources of error are considered. To answer the question completely, you will need an understanding of the chemical concepts involved.

To discuss an experiment, you must be familiar with the equipment needed. In the keywords section at the beginning of this chapter is a complete list of equipment for the experiments (see also Figure 20.1). Make sure you are familiar with each item. You may know an item by a different name, or you may need to talk to your teacher to get additional information concerning an item.

In some cases, the exam question will request a list of the equipment needed, while in other cases you will get a list from which to choose the items you need. Certain items appear in many experiments. These include the analytical balance, beakers, support stands, pipets, test tubes, and Erlenmeyer flasks. Burets, graduated cylinders, clamps, desiccators, drying ovens, pH meters, volumetric flasks, and thermometers are also commonly used. If you are not sure what equipment to choose, these serve as good guesses. Most of the remaining equipment appears in three or fewer experiments.

KEY IDEA

You will need to know the basic measurements required for the experiment. For example, you may need to measure the initial and final temperatures. Do not make the mistake of saying you measure the change in temperature. You calculate the change in temperature from your measured initial and final temperatures. You do not need to give a lot of detail when listing the required measurements, but you need to be very specific in what you measure. Many students have lost exam points for not clearly distinguishing between measured and calculated values.

The basic calculations fall into two categories. Simple calculations, such as the change in temperature or the change in volume, are the easiest to forget. Simple calculations may also include mass-to-mole conversions. The other calculations normally involve entering values into one of the equations given at the beginning of the previous chapters of this book.

**Keywords and Equations**

KEY IDEA

Pay special attention to the specific keywords and equations in the chapters associated with the individual experiments. This is especially true for experiments you did not do or if it is a name that is not familiar to you.

$A = \varepsilon bc$ ($A$ = absorbance; $\varepsilon$ = molar absorptivity; $b$ = path length; $c$ = concentration)

$q = mc\Delta T$ ($q$ = heat; $m$ = mass; $c$ = specific heat capacity; $\Delta T$ = change in temperature)

analytical balance
barometer
beaker(s)
buret
burner
calorimeter
capillary tubes
centrifuge
clamp
crucible and cover
cuvettes
desiccator
drying oven
electrodes
Erlenmeyer flask
evaporating dish
filter crucibles and adapters
filter flasks
forceps
funnel
graduated cylinder
hot plate
ice
ion exchange resin or silica gel
Meker burner
mortar and pestle
pH meter
pipet
power supply (battery)
Pt or Ni test wire
rubber tubing
spectrophotometer
stirrer
stopwatch
support stand
test-tube rack
test tube(s)
thermometer
tongs
triangle crucible support
voltmeter
volumetric flask
wash bottle
watch glass
water bath
wire gauze

# Experiment 1: Spectroscopy

## Synopsis

Specific experiments of this type are often an introduction to the field of spectroscopy. Such experiments are designed to demonstrate the relationship between the amount of light absorbed by some solutions and their concentrations. Light of a specific wavelength is passed through both the solvent and a sample, or several wavelengths are used to determine the maximum absorbance. The amount of light transmitted by the solvent is subtracted from the amount of light transmitted by the sample. If you made a number of measurements at different concentrations, you could create a graphical relationship between the amount of light absorbed and the concentration of the solution. By using this relationship, you could determine the concentration of an unknown solution.

## Equipment

Spectrophotometer (commonly a SPEC 20)
Cuvettes (sample tubes for the spectrophotometer)
Stock solutions (of known concentrations) of the solute (commonly some dye)
One or more solutions of unknown concentration (may be a household substance)
Assorted glassware, including volumetric glassware

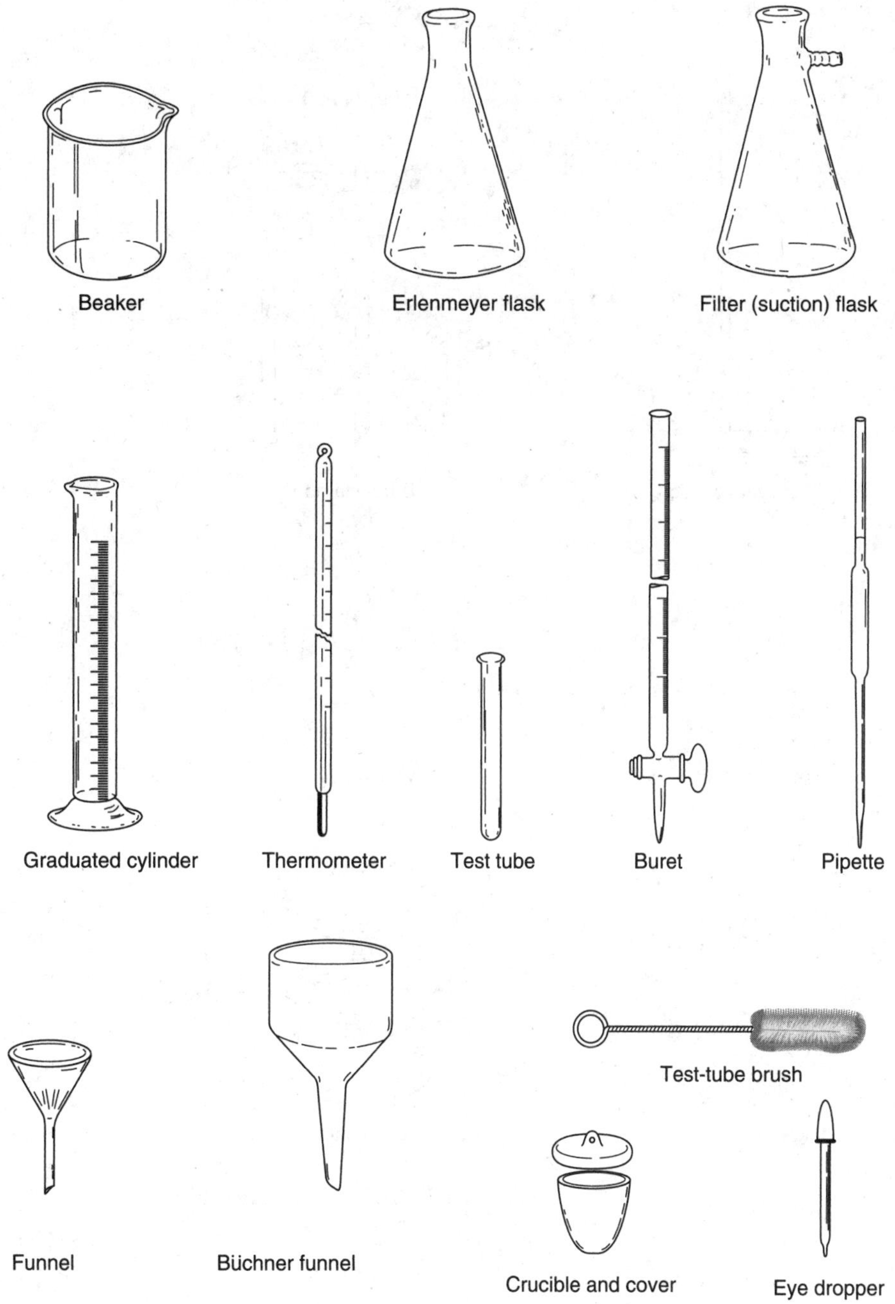


**Figure 20.1 Common laboratory equipment.**

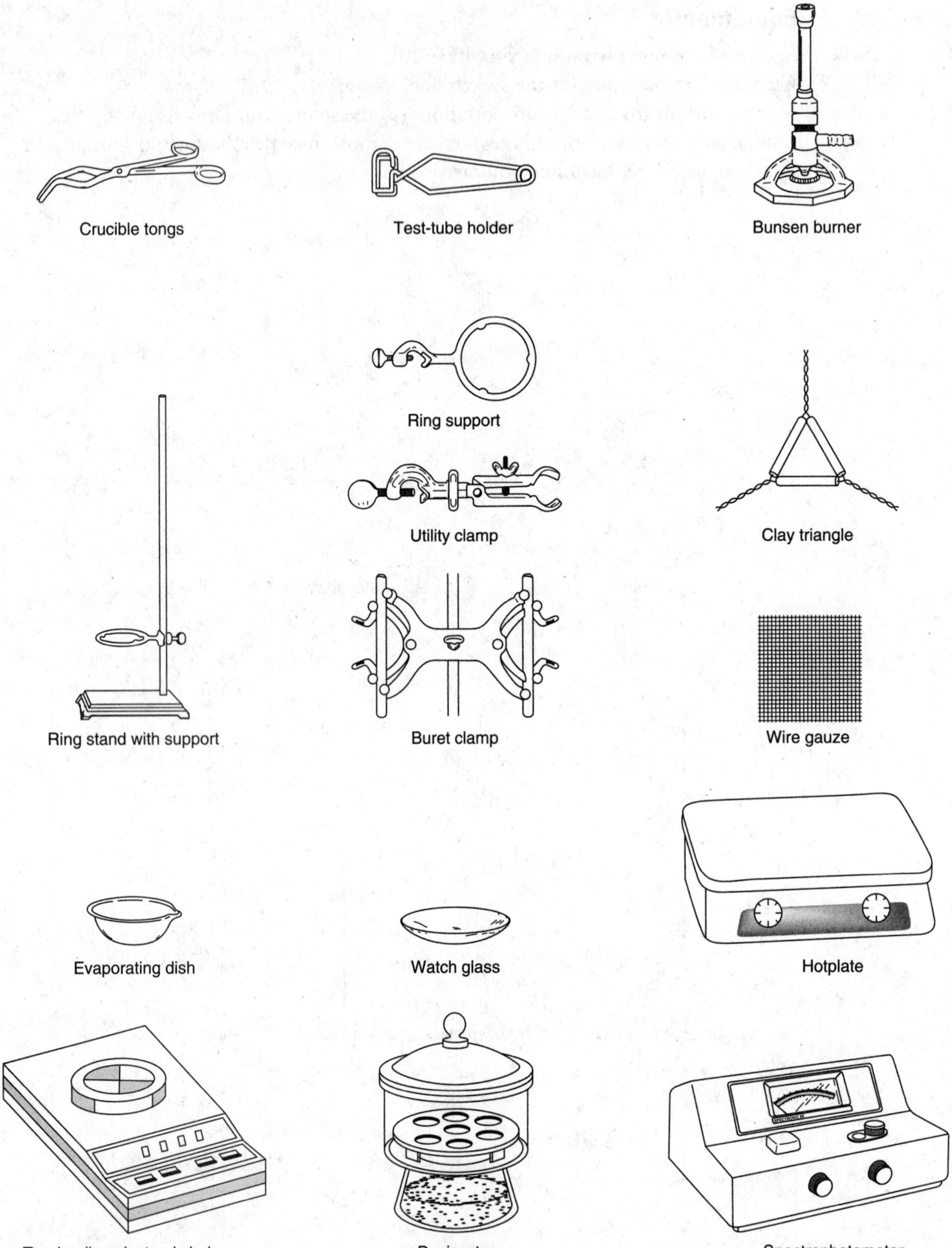


**Figure 20.1** (***Continued***)

### Measurements

The student will make several dilutions of the stock solution and will calculate the concentration of each dilution (using $M_{con}V_{con} = M_{dil}V_{dil}$ or $M_{before}\ V_{before} = M_{after}\ V_{after}$). The transmittance (%$T$) will be measured for each solution (remembering to subtract the transmittance of the solvent—this may be done by adjusting the spectrophotometer to 100% $T$ and then measuring the transmittance of the solution). You measure the volumes and calculate one or both concentrations.

### Calculations

To determine the relationship between the concentration of the solution and the transmittance, plot the molarity of the different solutions versus the transmittance (expressed as a decimal). The absorbance (Abs) of the solution (how much light is absorbed) is calculated by the formula $Abs = -\log(T)$, where $T$ is the transmittance of the solution (not the percent transmittance or temperature). On most spectrophotometers you can read absorbance directly. You may need to use Beer's law in the form of the following equation: $A = \varepsilon bc$ ($A$ = absorbance; $\varepsilon$ = molar absorptivity; $b$ = path length; $c$ = concentration).

### Comments

If you are asked for the mass of the solute in the unknown, you first determine its molar concentration ($c$, in the Beer's law equation) using your spectroscopy data. Then, using the molar concentration, the volume of the solution, and the molar mass of the solute, you can calculate the grams of solute present in the sample. Experiments of this type involve colored solutions and a spectrophotometer.

## Experiment 2: Spectrophotometry

### Synopsis

Specific experiments that are performed in this investigation use the concepts and techniques developed in Experiment 1: Spectroscopy to determine the mass percentage of a substance in a solid sample. For example, the determination of the amount of copper in a brass sample is a common experiment that is used in this category as well as the amount of iron in a vitamin pill. First, the "best" wavelength to be used is determined. The "best" wavelength is the one that gives the maximum absorbance of the chemical species being determined. Next, solutions of the solute being determined are prepared and their absorbance is measured using a spectrophotometer. A plot of absorbance versus concentration (Beer's law) is prepared. The solid sample is dissolved and diluted to a certain volume. The absorbance of a portion of this sample is measured and its concentration is determined using the graph. From this information the mass of the substance can be found. Using this mass information and the mass of the sample allows you to calculate the mass percentage of the substance in the sample.

### Equipment

Spectrophotometer (commonly SPEC 20)
Cuvettes (sample tubes for the spectrophotometer)
Stock solution (known concentration) of the solute
Sample to be analyzed
Assorted glassware, including volumetric glassware

### Measurements

The student will make several dilutions of the stock solution (solution of known concentration of the substance being determined) and will calculate the concentration of each dilution (using $M_{con}V_{con} = M_{dil}V_{dil}$). (You measure the volumes and calculate one or both concentrations.) The absorbance of one of the stock solutions is measured at several wavelengths (generally 400–700 nm in 10- to 20-nanometer increments) using a spectrophotometer. The data of absorbance versus wavelength is plotted, and the wavelength that gives the maximum absorbance is chosen to be used for the rest of the experiment. The absorbance of each of the dilutions is measured. A plot of absorbance versus concentration (Beer's law plot) is prepared either by hand or using a spreadsheet. The solid sample is dissolved (if it is copper, this will require the use of nitric acid) and diluted to a certain volume. The concentration of that solution is determined using the Beer's law plot. Using the concentration of the solution and the solution's volume, you can calculate the moles and then grams of the substance. Using the initial mass of the sample, you can finally calculate the mass percentage of the substance in the sample.

### Calculations

You can determine the concentrations of the diluted stock solution by using the dilution equation ($M_{con}V_{con} = M_{dil}V_{dil}$). The mass percentage is calculated by:

$$\text{Mass percentage} = \frac{\text{grams substance}}{\text{grams sample}} \times 100\%$$

### Comments

If you are doing a brass analysis for percentage of copper, you will dissolve the brass in concentrated nitric acid. Be extremely careful. The nitric acid is corrosive and the $NO_2$ gas that is produced is toxic. On the AP Exam be sure to stress safety if you are describing this process. The preparation of other solutions may have other hazards you should be familiar with, and you should take appropriate precautions. Experiments of this type involve colored solutions and a spectrophotometer.

## Experiment 3: Gravimetric Analysis

### Synopsis

Specific experiments that are performed in this investigation use determination of the mass of a specific substance in a sample by precipitation, drying, and weighing. A common experiment done in this category is the determination of the hardness of a water sample. The hardness of a water sample is related to the amounts of calcium, magnesium, and iron ions in solution. These ions may be precipitated as the carbonate salts. For simplicity's sake, hard-water samples are commonly prepared with only one of these ions, generally calcium. The carbonate salt is precipitated, separated from the solution by suction filtration, and dried in a drying oven. The mass of the dry salt is determined, and the water sample hardness is calculated as mg calcium carbonate per liter of water sample.

### Equipment

Various salt solutions of known concentration
Analytical balance
Drying oven
Suction filtration apparatus

Büchner funnel
Filter paper
Aspirator
Ring stands
Assorted glassware, including volumetric glassware

### Measurements

The student will make several measurements in gravimetric analysis, especially mass and volume determinations.

### Calculations

If a water hardness analysis is being done, the grams of calcium carbonate per milliliter of water sample are initially calculated. This value is then converted to milligrams of calcium carbonate per liter of water sample (hardness) using appropriate conversions.

### Comments

All measurements must be done accurately, especially the mass and volume measurements. The key to experiments of this type is mass measurements.

## Experiment 4: Titration

### Synopsis

In the titration procedure, the concentration of one solution is determined by adding small quantities at a time of another solution with known concentration until the point at which the moles of the first substance equal the moles of the other substance present (the endpoint). It is possible to do a titration by adding small amounts of a solution of a known concentration to determine the concentration of another solution. Many times this endpoint cannot be determined unaided, so an indicator or a pH meter is used. The point at which a color change happens with the indicator or an abrupt change in pH occurs with the pH meter is called the endpoint of the titration. Knowing the volume of the unknown, the concentration of the other reactant, and the number of milliliters it took to reach the endpoint, allows you to calculate the concentration of the unknown. Figure 20.2 shows a typical titrations setup.

### Equipment

Burets
Erlenmeyer flasks
Pipets
Acid–base indicators or a pH meter
Acid or base solution of known concentration

### Measurements

You will be placing a required volume of the unknown acid (or base) solution into the Erlenmeyer flask with a pipet. The buret will be filled with the other base (or acid) solution. As an alternative, a sample may be weighed directly into the flask and then dissolved in water. Be sure to record your initial volume. You will add small amounts of base drop by drop until the indicator changes color. Record the final volume. The final volume reading minus the initial volume reading is the volume of base added (this is a calculation, not a measurement).

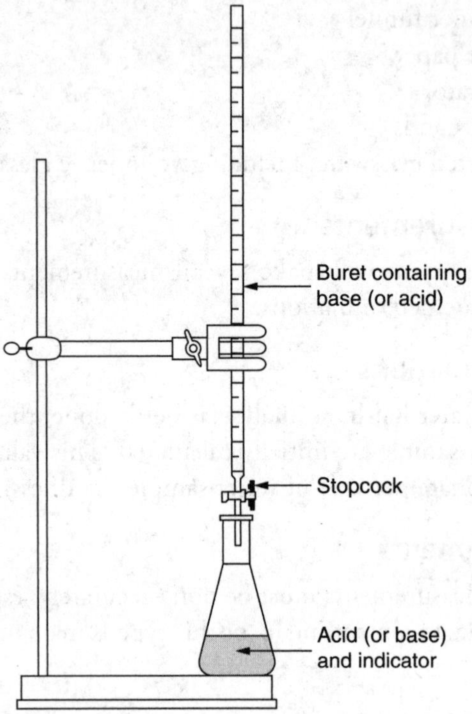


**Figure 20.2 General acid–base titration setup.**

## Calculations

If the titration involves an acid–base reaction, the calculation of the concentration of the base is essentially a stoichiometry calculation. Most of the time you will be able to generalize the process using the equation:

$$H^+(aq) + OH^-(aq) \rightarrow H_2O(l)$$

From the molarity of the base and the volume used, you can calculate the moles of base ($OH^-$). Because of the 1:1 stoichiometry that also will be the moles of acid. Dividing the moles by the liters of acid solution pipetted into the flask gives the acid's molarity.

Titrations involving other reactions are similar. You still operate the equipment the same way and make the same measurements. You will need the specific chemical for the reaction used and to account for the stoichiometry.

## Comments

If the titration involves an acid–base reaction, it may be performed with a pH meter without an indicator. The pH readings will be plotted against the volume. The endpoint is the point of inflection of the curve. A titration, either with an indicator or a pH meter, can be used to determine the acid content of household substances such as fruit juices or sodas. Nearly any type of reaction between two solutions may be utilized in a titration. Normally, one solution is added from a buret to another solution.

# Experiment 5: Chromatography

## Synopsis

Many times the components (solutes) in a solution cannot be separated by simple physical means. This is especially true of polar solutes because of their interactions with the solvent or each other. One method that is commonly used is chromatography (Figure 20.3). A very small amount of the solution is spotted onto a strip of filter paper or chromatography paper and allowed to dry. The strip is placed vertically into a jar containing a small amount of solvent. As the solvent is drawn up the strip by capillary action, it dissolves the sample. The various solutes have different affinities to the paper and to the solvent and can thus be separated as the solvent moves up the strip. Choice of the solvent is critical and can be related to its polarity; however, the choice sometimes must be done by trial and error.

## Equipment

Filter paper or chromatography paper
Chromatography jar or large beaker
Various solvents
Metric ruler
Sample to be analyzed
Assorted glassware

## Measurements

The student will make measurements of the distance that each component travels from the original spot and the distance that the solvent traveled.

## Calculations

The calculations involve determining the $R_f$ value for each component. The $R_f$ value is the distance the component travels divided by the distance the solvent traveled. Substances that interact strongly with the paper do not travel very far (low $R_f$ values), while those that interact strongly with the solvent travel much farther (high $R_f$ values).

## Comments

Chromatography is a very powerful separation technique.

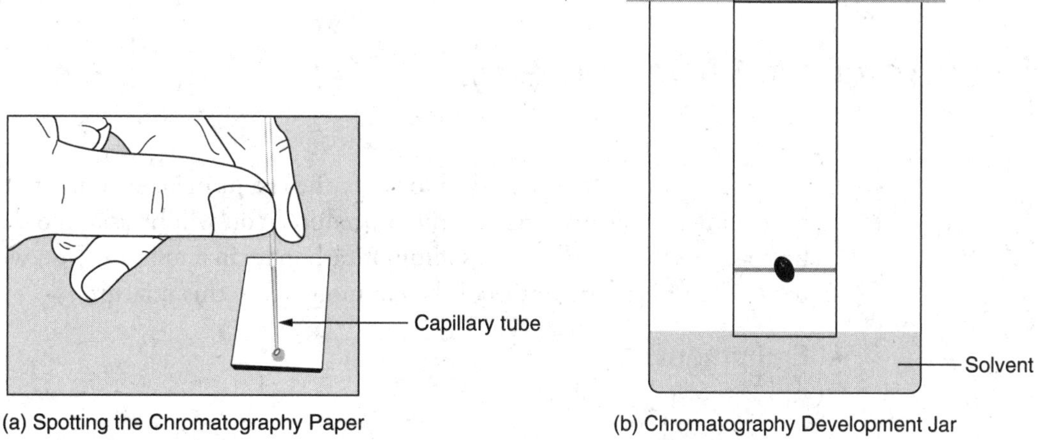


**Figure 20.3 Basic procedure for a paper chromatography experiment.**

# Experiment 6: Determination of the Type of Bonding in Solid Samples

## Synopsis

In this type of experiment, the student is given a set of bottles that contain solids with various types of bonding—ionic, covalent, or metallic. The student uses various physical and chemical tests to determine the bonding type. These tests might include melting point, conductivity, solubility, etc., along with observations of physical properties such as luster and hardness.

## Equipment

Assorted solids—ionic, covalent, metals
Assorted solvents—polar and nonpolar
Conductivity tester
pH paper
Thermometer
Assorted glassware

## Measurements

Many measurements and observations may be made. Some of these are:
**Luster:** metals tend to have a metallic luster; solid nonmetals often have a dull luster.
**Melting point:** ionic solids and metals have high melting points; covalent compounds have lower melting points.
**Solubility:** ionic compounds and polar covalent solids are generally soluble in water; metals and nonpolar covalent solids are generally insoluble or very slightly soluble in water.
**Conductivity:** aqueous solutions of ionic compounds are conductors; aqueous solutions of most polar covalent compounds are nonconductors.

## Calculations

There are generally no calculations associated with this experiment.

## Comments

Many other tests could be used: pH of the aqueous solutions, solubility on organic solvents, and so on.

# Experiment 7: Stoichiometry

## Synopsis

In this experiment, you are asked to verify the results of an experiment by checking both the stoichiometric calculations and the procedure. You will be asked to determine the percent by mass of substances such as sodium bicarbonate in a mixture. You will do this by making use of the unique properties of the components in this mixture.

## Equipment

Bunsen burners and strikers
Digital balances
Ring stands and rings

Ceramic triangles
Crucibles and lids
Assorted glassware, including volumetric glassware

### Measurements

A weighed sample mixture of sodium bicarbonate and sodium carbonate is heated to constant mass. The sodium bicarbonate decomposes to sodium carbonate, carbon dioxide (gas), and water vapor: $2\ NaHCO_3(s) \rightarrow Na_2CO_3(s) + H_2O(g) + CO_2(g)$. The loss of mass is the loss in mass of $CO_2 + H_2O$. Examining the equation for the decomposition reaction, you can see that there is a 1:1 ratio of moles of water and carbon dioxide.

### Calculations

If you let $z$ = moles $CO_2$ = moles $H_2O$, then the total grams of mass lost can be shown as the sum of the moles of each (which will be the same) times the molar mass of each substance:

$$\text{Mass lost (grams)} = (z \times 18.02\ \text{g}\ H_2O/\text{mol}) + (z \times 44.01\text{g}\ CO_2/\text{mol})$$

You can then solve for $z$, the number of moles. As you can see from the balanced equation, the moles of $NaHCO_3$ solid that decomposed is $2z$. The mass of $NaHCO_3$ that decomposed will be:

$$2z \times 84.02\text{g}\ NaHCO_3/\text{mol}$$

The percent of $NaHCO_3$ in the mixture will be the mass of the sodium bicarbonate divided by the mass of the mixture sample times 100%:

$$\text{Mass percent} = \frac{\text{g}\ NaHCO_3}{\text{g mixture}} \times 100\%$$

### Comments

In order to increase the precision (and hopefully the accuracy) of the determination, several runs should be made, and an average taken.

This same procedure may be applied to many other reactions and mixtures. These samples could also be analyzed by a titration procedure.

## Experiment 8: Redox Titration

### Synopsis

The procedure here is basically the same as that in Experiment 4. In this experiment, the concentration of a substance will be determined by using a redox titration. The titrant will need to be standardized before it can be used in the titration. Commonly, the redox titration involves the titration of hydrogen peroxide ($H_2O_2$) with potassium permanganate ($KMnO_4$), with the goal of analyzing the commercial hydrogen peroxide that can be found in a pharmacy. The $KMnO_4$ solution can be standardized against a $Fe(NH_4)_2(SO_4)_2 \times 6H_2O$ solution. You will prepare a standard (known concentration) solution of the $Fe(NH_4)_2(SO_4)_2 \times 6H_2O$, a sulfuric acid solution, and a solution of potassium permanganate. The redox half-reactions involved in the standardization are:

$$Fe^{2+}(aq) \rightarrow Fe^{3+}(aq) + 1\ e^- \text{ and}$$

$$MnO_4^-(aq) + 8\ H^+(aq) + 5\ e^- \rightarrow Mn^{2+}(aq) + 4\ H_2O(l)$$

giving an overall redox reaction of:

$$5\ Fe^{2+}(aq) + MnO_4^-(aq) + 8\ H^+(aq) \rightarrow 5\ Fe^{3+}(aq) + Mn^{2+}(aq) + 4\ H_2O(l)$$

The half-reactions involved in the titration of the hydrogen peroxide are:

$$H_2O_2(aq) \rightarrow O_2(g) + 2\ H^+(aq) + 2\ e^- \text{ and}$$

$$MnO_4^-(aq) + 8\ H^+(aq) + 5\ e^- \rightarrow Mn^{2+}(aq) + 4\ H_2O(l)$$

giving the overall redox-reaction:

$$5\ H_2O_2(aq) + 2\ MnO_4^-(aq) + 6\ H^+(aq) \rightarrow 2\ Mn^{2+}(aq) + 8\ H_2O(l) + 5\ O_2(g)$$

## Equipment

Buret
Ring stand and clamps
Pipets of assorted volumes
Pipet bulbs
Assorted glassware, including volumetric glassware

## Measurements

You will be making mass measurements of the $Fe(NH_4)_2(SO_4)_2{\cdot}6H_2O$ and the $KMnO_4$ and many volume measurements of the pipets, volumetric flasks, and the buret.

## Calculations

For the standardization: from the number of grams of $Fe(NH_4)_2(SO_4)_2{\cdot}6H_2O$ used, you can calculate the moles of $Fe^{2+}$ used. Knowing this, you can determine the moles $MnO_4^-$ used from the stoichiometry in the overall reaction ($1\ MnO_4^- : 5\ Fe^{2+}$) and then its molarity.

For the peroxide titration: from the buret volume and the molarity of the $KMnO_4$ solution, you can calculate the moles used in the titration, and by applying the overall reaction stoichiometry you can get the moles of hydrogen peroxide ($5\ H_2O_2 : 2\ MnO_4^-$). From the moles, you can get grams and finally mass percent (assuming the density of the peroxide solution is 1.00 g/mL).

A redox titration is not limited to the reactions shown here. There are many alternate combinations of oxidizing and reducing agents.

## Comments

Be very careful in making your measurements. The same general procedure can be applied to other titration systems.

# Experiment 9: Chemical and Physical Changes

### Synopsis

Commonly this experiment involves separating the components of a mixture by using the chemical and physical properties of the mixture components. This is the basis of the analysis of commercially available samples such as over-the-counter acetaminophen- or aspirin-based pain relievers. The binder (many times sucrose), aspirin, and acetaminophen can be separated by the difference in their solubility in water and organic solvents, their acidity, and the difference in the way they react with hydrochloric acid and sodium bicarbonate solutions. Any chemical or physical change may be used.

### Equipment

Büchner funnels
Vacuum filtration apparatus
Separatory funnel
Hot plate or drying oven
Assorted glassware

### Measurements

You will be making mass measurements of the sample, and every time a component is separated as a solid, it is dried, and the mass determined.

### Calculations

The overall percent recovery for the sample would be the sum of the masses of all the recovered components divided by the initial mass of the sample:

$$\text{Percent recovery} = \frac{\text{Sum of masses of all recovered components}}{\text{Mass of sample}} \times 100\%$$

The percentage of each component can be calculated by dividing the mass of a component by the total mass of all recovered components:

$$\text{Percent component} = \frac{\text{Mass of component}}{\text{Sum of masses of all recovered components}} \times 100\%$$

### Comments

Be very careful in making your measurements. The same general procedure can be applied to numerous other systems.

Be especially careful when handling the acid solutions and organic solvents. Be sure to turn the separatory funnel upside down and open the stopcock (vent) to the funnel before opening it.

# Experiment 10: Kinetics

### Synopsis

In this experiment, some of the factors involved in the speed of a chemical reaction will be explored. Commonly this experiment focuses on the decomposition of calcium carbonate—limestone, $CaCO_3(s)$, and hydrochloric acid, $HCl(aq)$. Pieces of calcium carbonate of different sizes (to test how the speed of reaction varies with surface area) and HCl solutions of different concentrations will be available. You can vary the temperature of the reaction mixture by using an ice bath or heating the mixture. In order to measure the speed of the reaction, the carbon dioxide gas product can be collected in a syringe, or a gas pressure probe can be used to monitor the production of the $CO_2(g)$ as a function of time. The mass of sample consumed (or the decrease in the total mass of the reaction flask) versus time can also be used as an indication of the speed of reaction.

### Equipment

Balance
Hotplate
Syringes
Stopwatch
Assorted glassware
Magnetic stirrer and stir bar
Gas pressure probe and data collection device

### Measurements

Measurements include the initial and final mass of the calcium carbonate sample, the volume of gas evolved, and time measurements.

### Calculations

Calculations commonly involve determining the mass of sample consumed (lost) as a function of time. The results of the mass versus time measurements are commonly plotted.

### Comments

When plotting the data, the time is commonly the horizontal axis, while the mass lost, or mL of gas produced, is the vertical axis.

Be especially careful when handling the hydrochloric acid.

Other reactions may be investigated. The only requirement is that the reaction be slow enough for you to be able to measure the time involved.

## Experiment 11: Rate Laws

### Synopsis

This is another type of kinetics experiment. In this experiment, you will determine the rate law for a specific chemical reaction. Commonly the reaction involved is the reaction of crystal violet (CV) with sodium hydroxide (NaOH). The progress of the reaction is followed with a spectrophotometer or colorimeter. You will initially create a Beer's law calibration curve by measuring the absorbance of solutions of crystal violet of varying concentrations. Then you will use the same spectrophotometer to follow the change in concentration of crystal violet as it reacts with NaOH as a function of time:

$$CV^+(aq) + OH^-(aq) \rightarrow CVOH(aq)$$

The rate expression for this reaction would be:

$$\text{Rate} = k\,[CV^+]^x\,[OH^-]^y$$

If we use a large stoichiometric excess of NaOH, then the rate equation becomes:

$$\text{Rate} = k^* \, [CV^+]^x$$

since there is so much hydroxide ion present that its concentration essentially becomes constant.

### Equipment

Spectrophotometer (commonly SPEC 20)
Cuvettes (sample tubes for the spectrophotometer)
Pipettes and bulbs
Assorted glassware, including volumetric glassware

### Measurements

You will be making measurements of absorbance and time. Be sure to use a blank containing only water and NaOH but no crystal violet.

### Calculations

You will be making different concentrations of the stock crystal violet solution by dilution, so that you will use the dilution equation $M_{con} V_{con} = M_{dil} V_{dil}$. You will be making three graphs:

(1) concentration versus time (straight line indicates zero order with respect to CV [$x = 0$ in rate expression]); (2) ln (concentration) versus time (straight line indicates first order with respect to CV [$x = 1$ in rate expression]); and (3) 1/concentration versus time (straight line indicates second order with respect to CV [$x = 2$ in rate expression]).

### Comments

Be especially careful when handling the sodium hydroxide solution.

## Experiment 12: Calorimetry

### Synopsis

In this experiment, you will be measuring the heat produced (or absorbed) during the dissolving of various ionic substances in water with the goal of determining which of the salts is most efficient (with respect to cost) in generating or absorbing heat. Substances to test might include anhydrous calcium chloride ($CaCl_2$), anhydrous sodium carbonate ($Na_2CO_3$), anhydrous ammonium nitrate ($NH_4NO_3$), anhydrous sodium acetate ($NaC_2H_3O_2$), and similar salts. You will calculate the change in enthalpy of dissolution in kJ/mol ($\Delta H_{soln}$) by using a coffee-cup calorimeter (see Figure 14.1 in Chapter 14, Thermodynamics). You may be using a magnetic stirrer instead of the stirring wire shown in the figure.

### Equipment

Thermometers or temperature probes
Polystyrene cups
Magnetic stirrers and stir bars
Assorted glassware

### Measurements

You will be making measurements of the initial and final temperatures of the solutions formed by adding a certain mass of solute to a measured amount of water. The $\Delta T$ is the final temperature minus the initial temperature. The value of $\Delta T$ is a calculated number and not a measured number.

### Calculations

You may be given or may have to calculate the calorimeter constant, $C$, for your calorimeter—the heat absorbed by the calorimeter per degree of temperature change. The energy of solution formation ($q_{rxn}$) is calculated by multiplying the mass times the specific heat of the solution (given) times the change in temperature ($q_{rxn} = mc\Delta T$), and the energy of solution ($q_{soln}$) is calculated by $q_{soln} = -(q_{rxn} + C\Delta T)$. The enthalpy of dissolution ($\Delta H_{soln}$) is calculated by dividing the $q_{soln}$ (in kJ) by the number of moles of salt used.

### Comments

Be especially careful with the ammonium nitrate—it is a strong oxidizer.

The thermometer is part of the surroundings, not the system.

## Experiment 13: Chemical Equilibrium—Le Châtelier's Principle

### Synopsis

Experiments that fall into this category examine systems that are at equilibrium and what happens when that equilibrium is disturbed. Many times this involves having a small tray of reagents and testing an equilibrium system by mixing selected reagents and making observations. You may change concentrations (adding more reagent) or change the temperature of the solutions. This may involve an acid–base equilibrium or complex-ion equilibriums. Reactions will be given, and you should be able to describe the stress that you imposed and how the system reacted to that stress.

### Equipment

Test tubes
Stirring rods
Spatula
Assorted glassware

### Measurements

This experiment normally involves no measurements, only estimations of volumes and masses.

### Calculations

This experiment usually involves no calculations. If calculations are involved, at a minimum, you will need to know the concentrations of any solutions used.

### Comments

Be very careful when working with concentrated ammonia and hydrochloric acid. Always wear goggles, gloves, and an apron, and keep these reagents in the hood.

# Experiment 14: Acid–Base Titrations

## Synopsis

The procedure here is basically the same as that in Experiment 4. Experiments that fall into this category are acid–base titrations involving weak acids or weak bases versus a strong acid or strong base. Many times the course of the titration is followed by a pH meter and the equivalence point is determined graphically. This allows you to determine not only the concentration of the weak acid or base but also its $pK_a$ or $pK_b$. Both monoprotic and polyprotic acids may be examined. From an examination of the specific reaction involving a weak acid or base, you should be able to determine whether the solution at the equivalence point will be acidic or basic.

## Equipment

Stirring rods
pH meters or pH probes
Buret
Assorted glassware

## Measurements

You will be making pH measurements and plotting them against volume of titrant added. In many cases, you will titrate various acids (strong and weak) with a NaOH solution of known concentration. The endpoint for such a titration is the point at which a dramatic increase in pH occurs; this is called the point of inflection of the curve. The pH at the volume corresponding to half the endpoint volume is the $pK_a$ of the acid. The same is true of bases, except the pH will be decreasing during the titration. A polyprotic acid or base will give you two or more points of inflection, and two or more p*K*s and *K*s may be calculated.

## Calculations

The $K_a$ of the acid can be calculated by the equation $K_a = 10^{-pK_a}$. If the $K_b$ of a weak base is to be determined, use $K_b = 10^{-pK_b}$.

## Comments

Be extremely careful when working with the acids and bases and wear personal protective equipment, especially your goggles. When making dilutions, always add the acid (or base) to water, NOT water to acid.

# Experiment 15: Buffer pH

## Synopsis

A buffer is a substance that resists a change in pH when an acid or base is added to it. It is normally a mixture of a weak acid and its conjugate base, but it can be a weak base and its conjugate acid. Experiments in this category involve examining the properties of buffers and household substances that are buffers. This will involve titrating a substance with an acid or base while following the course of the titration with a pH meter, plotting the pH versus mL of titrant added, and determining the endpoint graphically. At any point before the endpoint, you have a buffer present. Common household substances may be tested for their buffer ability. The curve of pH versus mL of a substance that has some buffering ability rises sharply initially and then levels off much more than a titration of a substance that is not a buffer. You can use this to determine whether an unknown solution exhibits any buffering capability.

### Equipment

pH meter
Burets and clamps
Magnetic stirrer
Assorted glassware

### Measurements

You will be making measurements of volume and pH for a wide variety of substances. The point in a titration involving a buffer that corresponds to halfway to the endpoint is called the point of maximum buffering.

### Calculations

The $K_a$ of the acid can be calculated by the equation $K_a = 10^{-pK_a}$. If the $K_b$ of a weak base is to be determined, then use $K_b = 10^{-pK_b}$.

### Comments

Be careful in handling the acid and base solutions.

## Experiment 16: The Capacity of a Buffer

### Synopsis

Experiments in this category are designed to explore the capacity of a buffer, which is the amount of acid or base that can be neutralized by the buffer. You can determine this by using different amounts of the conjugate acid and base components or by changing the concentration of each by the same amount. Normally, the higher the concentration of the conjugate acid and base in the buffer, the more moles of added base or acid can be neutralized and thus the higher the buffer capacity. You will also be asked to create a buffer of a specific pH.

### Equipment

Balance
Burets and clamps
Assorted glassware

### Measurements

You will be making measurements of volume and pH for a wide variety of substances. You will be making graphs of pH versus mL of titrant added.

### Calculations

You can calculate the initial pH of a conjugate acid/base buffer by using the following equations:

$$[H^+] = K_a \frac{[\text{weak acid}]}{[\text{conjugate base}]}$$

$$pH = -\log [H^+]$$

If you want a buffer of a certain pH, then put in the $K_a$ of the weak acid you want to use and the $[H^+]$ desired and solve for the ratio of acid to base. If you have a choice of several acid/base systems, then choose the one whose $pK_a$ is closest to the desired pH. It is also possible to use the $K_b$ of a weak base in your calculations.

### Comments

Be extremely careful when working with the acids and bases and wear personal protective equipment, especially your goggles. When making dilutions, always add the acid (or base) to water, NOT water to acid. The equations used may be in a different form.

## Common Mistakes to Avoid

1. You *measure* initial and final values but *calculate* the change.
2. You use an analytical balance to weigh the mass (grams), but not the moles.

## ❯ Review Questions

Use these questions to review the content of this chapter and practice for the AP Chemistry Exam. First are 20 multiple-choice questions similar to what you will encounter in Section I of the AP Chemistry Exam. Following those is a long free-response question and four short free-response questions like the ones in Section II of the exam. To make these questions an even more authentic practice for the actual exam, time yourself following the instructions provided.

### Multiple-Choice Questions

Answer the following questions in 30 minutes. You may not use a calculator. You may use the periodic table and the equation sheet at the back of this book.

**1.** You have an aqueous solution of sugar. The simplest method to separate the sugar from the solution is to:

(A) evaporate the solution to dryness
(B) centrifuge the solution
(C) filter the solution
(D) electrolyze the solution

**2.** A chemistry student adds 25.0 g of sodium hydroxide, NaOH, to 500.0 g of water. Which of the following procedures should he employ to determine the molarity of the solution?

(A) He should convert the grams of NaOH to moles and measure the volume of the solution.
(B) He should titrate the solution with standard potassium hydroxide solution.
(C) He should determine the freezing point of the solution.
(D) He should determine the vapor pressure of the solution at room temperature.

**3.** A chemistry student prepares a solution of an unknown solid with a molar mass of 78.3 g/mol. She prepares the solution by dissolving 2.50 g of the unknown substance in 100.0 g of water. Which of the following procedures could she use to determine whether the unknown substance is an electrolyte?

(A) She could measure the specific heat of the solution.
(B) She could measure the volume of the solution.
(C) She could measure the freezing point of the solution.
(D) She could determine the specific heat of the solution.

4. A chemist makes a solution by dissolving 10 g of urea in 100 g of water. What additional information does he need to calculate the molarity of this solution?

(A) He needs the density of the solution and the molar mass of urea.
(B) He needs the density of urea and the molar mass of urea.
(C) He needs the density of water and the density of the solution.
(D) He needs the molar mass of urea and the density of water.

5. A certain reaction follows the rate law Rate = $k[Br^-][BrO^-][H^+]^2$. What are the units of the rate constant, $k$?

(A) $s^{-1}M^{-3}$
(B) $M\ s^{-1}$
(C) $M^3\ s$
(D) $M\ s$

Use the following diagram for questions 6 and 7.

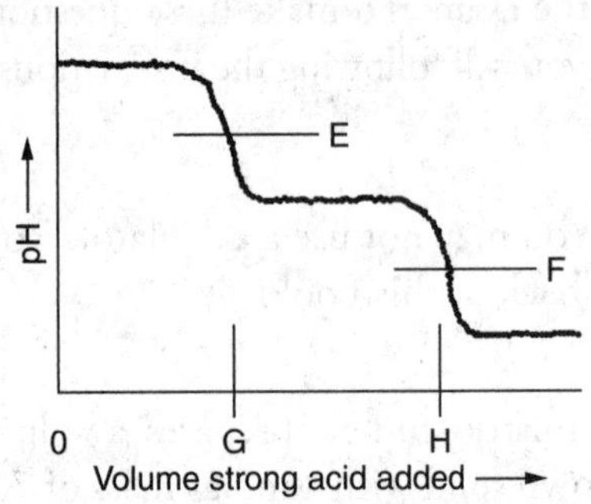


The diagram above represents the idealized titration curve for the reaction of sodium oxalate ($Na_2C_2O_4$) with a strong acid like hydrochloric acid (HCl). E and F represent the pH at the endpoints. G and H will depend on the composition of the sample with the possibility that one may not be present.

6. A trial run used a sample of pure sodium oxalate. How does the volume of acid necessary to reach G compare to the volume of acid necessary to get from G to H?

(A) The volumes required will be the same.
(B) A larger volume is necessary to reach G.
(C) A larger volume is necessary to get from G to H.
(D) It is impossible to determine.

7. In addition to water, what are the predominant species in solution at E?

(A) $Na_2C_2O_4$ and HCl
(B) $Na^+$, $Cl^-$, and $HC_2O_4^-$
(C) $C_2O_4^{2-}$ and $H^+$
(D) $Na^+$, $H^+$, and $C_2O_4^{2-}$

8. A student is attempting to prepare an electrochemical cell, which ideally should produce 1.23 V. Unfortunately, he was unable to make a salt bridge. He reasoned that a copper wire would conduct electricity like a salt bridge, so he used a copper wire in place of the salt bridge. How will the voltage of the cell with the copper wire compare to that of the ideal cell?

(A) The voltage is ideal.
(B) The voltage becomes zero.
(C) The voltage is greater than ideal.
(D) The voltage less than ideal but greater than zero.

9. A chemist constructs an electrochemical cell with an iron anode and a copper cathode. She measures the cell voltage. Next, she replaces the copper electrode with a larger copper electrode. What does she find when she measures the cell voltage of the cell with the larger copper electrode?

(A) There is no change in the voltage.
(B) The voltage becomes zero.
(C) The voltage increases.
(D) The voltage decreases but stays positive.

10. While investigating a radioactive decay process, a chemist constructs a linear graph. What information did she plot?

(A) She plotted the concentration remaining versus time.
(B) She plotted the natural logarithm of the concentration remaining versus time.
(C) She plotted the reciprocal of the concentration remaining versus time.
(D) She plotted the natural logarithm of the concentration remaining versus the inverse of the time.

**11.** The teacher gave a student a 0.10 *M* solution of an unknown indicator solution. The student was to prepare a calibration graph of the absorbance versus indicator concentration for this unknown indicator. The 0.10 *M* solution was sufficiently dilute to be used directly in a spectrophotometer. What should be the student's first step?

(A) Determine the wavelength of maximum absorbance.
(B) Make a series of dilutions to produce a set of solutions of varying concentrations.
(C) Determine the molar mass of the unknown indicator.
(D) Measure the mass and volume of the solution to determine its density.

**12.** The teacher gave another student a 0.10 *M* solution of an unknown indicator solution. The wavelength of maximum absorbance is 640 nm, the molar mass of the unknown indicator was 347 g $mol^{-1}$, and the density of the solution was 1.00 g $mL^{-1}$. To facilitate the construction of the calibration curve, the student used a standard cuvette as the reference in the spectrophotometer and placed the various dilutions in a series of test tubes. The resulting calibration curve seemed very erratic. What was the student's error?

(A) There were no precautions taken to keep the temperature constant.
(B) Test tubes should never be used as a substitute for a standard cuvette.
(C) The unknown was one of the few substances that do not produce a linear calibration curve.
(D) The concentrations of the diluted solutions were all too high.

**13.** A student is given the task of preparing a 0.10 *M* solution of $H_2SO_4$ (molar mass = 98 g $mol^{-1}$) to be used by the class in an experiment. The class needs 1.00 L of this solution. The student reasons that they will need to weigh 9.8 g of sulfuric acid and add this to a 1 L volumetric flask, add about 500 mL distilled water and swirl the flask to mix. After the solution is mixed, additional distilled water is added to bring the level to the line in the volumetric flask. Finally the flask is stoppered and inverted several times to assure the solution is well mixed. The student presents this procedure to the teacher, who rejects it because of a mistake. What was the student's mistake?

(A) The student does not allow tie for the solution to cool.
(B) The student used the wrong mass of $H_2SO_4$.
(C) The student suggests adding water to acid.
(D) The solution will not have the correct molarity.

**14.** Two students, A and B, are conducting an experiment in gravimetric analysis. They are attempting to determine the quantity of silver in a sample by precipitating the silver as silver acetate, $AgC_2H_3O_2$, which has $K_{sp} = 4 \times 10^{-3}$. Both students precipitate the silver from solution by adding an excess of 0.10 *M* sodium acetate, $NaC_2H_3O_2$ solution. Once all the silver has precipitated, student A washes the precipitate several times with sodium acetate solution, and finally once with a little distilled water while student B washes the solution several times with distilled water. Once washed, both students dry and weigh the precipitate. Based upon the masses of the dried precipitates, each student calculates the percent silver in the sample. How do the results of the student results compare to the correct percent of silver in the sample?

(A) The values are too low with student B being closer than student A.
(B) The values are too high with student B being closer than student A.
(C) The values are too high with student A being closer than student B.
(D) The values are too low with student A being closer than student B.

**15.** $2\ KMnO_4(aq) + 5\ Na_2C_2O_4(aq) + 8\ H_2SO_4(aq) \rightarrow 2\ MnSO_4(aq) + 10\ CO_2(g) + K_2SO_4(aq) + 5\ Na_2SO_4(aq) + 8\ H_2O(l)$

A student is planning on doing a redox titration involving the above chemical reaction. The first step the student must perform is to standardize the $KMnO_4$ solution (approximately 0.1 *M*) with primary standard sodium oxalate (molar mass 134.0 g $mol^{-1}$). The student carefully weighs 5.360 g of $Na_2C_2O_4$ into a flask and adds about 25 mL of distilled water to dissolve the sample and 50.00 mL of 1.000 M $H_2SO_4$ to the flask. The $Na_2C_2O_4$ solution is then titrated with the $KMnO_4$. This titration requires 40.00 mL of the $KMnO_4$ solution. From this information, the student calculates the molarity. The student carefully repeats this procedure three more times and averages the consistent results of the four titrations. However, when the standardized $KMnO_4$ solution is used to determine the amount of $Na_2C_2O_4$ in an unknown, the results are inaccurate. What did the student do wrong?

(A) The student did not add sufficient $H_2SO_4$ to the samples.
(B) The student incorrectly weighed the $Na_2C_2O_4$ for one of the solutions used for standardization.
(C) The student incorrectly recorded the volume at the endpoint of one of the samples used for standardization.
(D) The student titrated the solution in one titration too fast and missed getting and accurate endpoint.

**16.** A student adds 100.0 g of water to a "coffee-cup" calorimeter. The initial temperature of the water was 20.00°C. The student add 4.000 g of solid NaOH, and the temperature increases to 35.00°C. The heat of solution for sodium hydroxide is –44.50 kJ $mol^{-1}$. Determine the heat capacity of the solution in J $g^{-1}$ $°C^{-1}$.

(A) −2.833 J $g^{-1}$ $°C^{-1}$
(B) 2.833 J $g^{-1}$ $°C^{-1}$
(C) 73.67 J $g^{-1}$ $°C^{-1}$
(D) −73.67 J $g^{-1}$ $°C^{-1}$

**17.** A student wishes to determine the $K_a$ of an unknown weak acid, HA, with a molar mass of 140 g $mol^{-1}$. The student first accurately weighs 1.400 g of the unknown acid. The HA is dissolved in a little water, transferred to a 100 mL volumetric flask and distilled water added until the line on flask is reached. A pipette is used to transfer 50.00 mL of this solution to an Erlenmeyer flask. The solution in the Erlenmeyer flask is titrated to the endpoint with standard NaOH solution. The untitrated and titrated samples are mixed in a beaker and the pH of the mixture is determined with a pH meter. What must the student now due to determine the $K_a$ of the solution?

(A) Determine the moles of acid present in the titrated sample.
(B) Determine the value of $10^{-pH}$.
(C) Determine the final volume of the mixed solution.
(D) Determine the moles of untitrated acid present.

**18.** A student is preparing to do an experiment to determine the mass percent of copper in brass. Unfortunately, while collecting the materials for the experiment, the student learns that there is no nitric acid. The student rationalizes that if should be possible to substitute hydrochloric acid for the nitric acid since they are both strong acids. So the student sets up the experiment using hydrochloric acid. After completing the experiment, the student obtains results that are:

(A) the same as with nitric acid
(B) no results
(C) lower than with nitric acid
(D) higher than with nitric acid

Use the following graph for Question 19

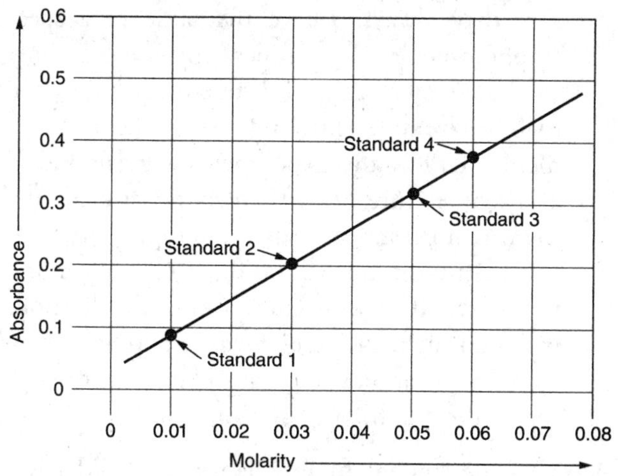


**19.** A student is studying the absorbance of an unknown indicator versus concentration. The student constructs the above graph. To test the accuracy of the calibration curve, another student prepares a different solution of the same indicator. The solution prepared by the other student has an absorbance of 0.44. Will the other student's solution be a fair test of the calibration curve?

(A) Yes, the solution will work fine.
(B) Unknown until the other student's calculations are checked.
(C) No, the absorbance is outside the range established by the standards.
(D) Unknown until the temperature is measured.

**20.** It is possible to determine the calcium in water (hardness) by titrating the water with $Na_2EDTA$ (EDTA is an abbreviation for ethylenediaminetetraacetic acid). This titration requires Eriochrome black as an indicator. This is an example of a complexometric titration as the calcium forms a complex with EDTA. To analyze a hard water sample a sample is pipetted into a flask, the indicator is added, a pH = 10 buffer and a small amount of magnesium ion are added. Theis solution is titrated as normal until the indicator changes from wine-red to blue. The net-ionic equation for the reaction is:

$$Ca^{2+}(aq) + EDTA^{4-}(aq) \rightarrow CaEDTA^{2+}(aq)$$

Historically, the concentration was reported as the titer (mg $CaCO_3$ $L^{-1}$) instead of $M$ (mole $L^{-1}$). Today ppm (parts per million) are normally used; however, ppm is numerically equal to the titer. A student conducts a titration of a hard-water sample and determines the $Ca^{2+}$ concentration to be 0.0100 $M$. What is the titer of this solution?

(A) $4.00 \times 10^2$ mg $CaCO_3$ $L^{-1}$
(B) $1.00 \times 10^3$ mg $CaCO_3$ $L^{-1}$
(C) 1.00 mg $CaCO_3$ $L^{-1}$
(D) $1.00 \times 10^{-3}$ mg $CaCO_3$ $L^{-1}$

## › Answers and Explanations

**1. A**—Separating materials in solution normally involves a physical change such as removing the solvent through evaporation. B and C will work on a heterogeneous mixture but not a solution (homogeneous mixture). D is a chemical change.

**2. A**—Molarity is moles per liter. The moles are readily determined from the grams of NaOH. Then, simply measuring the volume (and converting to liters) is all that is needed to determine the molarity. B may seem like a good option because titration is a common method for determining the molarity of a solution; however, one base (KOH) cannot be used to titrate another base (NaOH), as an acid is needed. C could be used to determine the molality of the solution; however, it is easier to determine the molality from the mass of NaOH and the mass of water; to convert to molarity, another measurement would be required. The vapor pressure would help determine the molarity, but it would not be easy to get to the molarity from the vapor pressure.

**3. C**—If the solute contains an electrolyte, the solution will conduct electricity and the van't Hoff factor, $i$, will be greater than 1. The choices do not include any conductivity measurements; therefore, it is necessary to determine the van't Hoff factor. It is possible to determine the van't Hoff by measuring the osmotic pressure, the boiling-point elevation, or the freezing-point depression. The freezing-point depression may be found by measuring the freezing point of the solution and comparing the measured freezing-point depression to that expected for a nonelectrolyte.

**4. A**—To calculate the molarity, the moles of urea and the volume of the solution are necessary. It is possible to calculate the volume of the solution from the density of the solution and the mass of the solution (110 g). The mass of urea and the molar mass of urea give the moles of urea.

**5. A**—The units on each side must match. The rate has the units of *M*/s (or $M\ s^{-1}$ or mol $L^{-1}\ s^{-1}$). Substituting units for symbols changes the rate law from Rate = $k\ [Br^-]\ [BrO^-]\ [H^+]^2$ to $M/s = k\ [M]\ [M]\ [M^2]$ or $M/s = k[M^4]$. From this, *k* must have the units $1/(s\ M^3)$ or $s^{-1}M^{-3}$.

**6. A**—At G, all the $C_2O_4^{2-}$ has been converted to $HC_2O_4^-$, and the of $HC_2O_4^-$ will equal the moles of $C_2O_4^{2-}$ originally present. It will require an equal volume of acid to titrate an equal number of moles of $HC_2O_4^-$, as required for the $C_2O_4^{2-}$.

**7. B**—The reaction with HCl converts all the $C_2O_4^{2-}$ to $HC_2O_4^-$. The $Na^+$ has not reacted, so it is still present. The $Cl^-$ is from the HCl and remains in solution because it has not reacted. The $H^+$ from the acid reacted with the $C_2O_4^{2-}$ to form $HC_2O_4^-$ and is no longer present (in a significant amount). Other than water, all species are strong electrolytes and exist as ions in solution.

**8. B**—A source of cations and anions is necessary for the operation of a cell to keep the charges in each compartment neutral. If there is no salt bridge, there is no ion source, and the cell cannot operate (zero voltage).

**9. A**—The size of the electrode is irrelevant to the cell voltage.

**10. B**—The radioactive decay process follows first-order kinetics; only B will give a linear graph for a first-order process. A applies to zero-order kinetics. C applies to second-order kinetics. D is not a kinetics graph.

**11. A**—The molar mass and the density are irrelevant to the task the student has been assigned. The dilutions are necessary to construct a calibration curve; however, it is necessary to know the wavelength of maximum absorbance first.

**12. B**—Cuvettes are carefully calibrated to make sure they always behave the same in a spectrophotometer. Test tubes are not carefully calibrated, so a series of different test tubes will each behave differently and disrupt the measurements. Unless the experiment was conducted at a temperature other than room temperature, there is no need to keep the temperature constant. An indicator will produce a linear calibration curve. If the concentrations of the dilutions were too high, the results would appear to be a straight line at maximum absorbance (across the top of the graph).

**13. C**—The student forgot than one should never add water to acid.

**14. D**—The $K_{sp}$ is too large to give good results in a gravimetric analysis experiment. The relatively large $K_{sp}$ value will lead to low results. Washing the precipitate with sodium acetate solution reduces the quantity of precipitate that dissolves through Le Châtelier's principle (a final wash with distilled water should remove any residual sodium acetate in the sample and dissolve a minimal quantity of silver acetate). Washing with distilled water several times will dissolve some silver precipitate with each washing.

**15. A**—The results were consistent; therefore, something occurring in one sample would not lead to consistent results.

To check the $H_2SO_4$ answer, you need to start by determining the moles of $Na_2C2O_4$:

$$\text{Moles } Na_2C_2O_4 = (5.360\text{ g } Na_2C_2O_4)\left(\frac{1\text{ mol } Na_2C_2O_4}{134.0\text{ g } Na_2C_2O_4}\right) = 0.04000\text{ moles } Na_2C_2O_4$$

Now calculating the moles $H_2SO_4$ required:

$$\text{Moles } H_2SO_4 = (0.04000\text{ mol } Na_2C_2O_4)\left(\frac{8\text{ mol } H_2SO_4}{5\text{ mol } Na_2C_2O_4}\right) = 0.06400\text{ moles } H_2SO_4$$

needed

The moles $H_2SO_4$ the student used was:

$$\text{Moles } H_2SO_4 = (50.00\text{ mL})\left(\frac{1.000\text{ mol } H_2SO_4}{1000\text{ mL}}\right)$$

$= 0.05000$ moles $H_2SO_4$ (supplied by student)

The moles of $H_2SO_4$ the student added was less than the moles required for the reaction to go to completion.

Note: the molarity was written as $\left(\frac{1.000 \text{ mol } H_2SO_4}{1000 \text{ mL}}\right)$ instead of as $\left(\frac{1.000 \text{ mol } H_2SO_4}{1 \text{ L}}\right)$ to eliminate a step in the calculation.

**16. B**—The equation needed for this problem is $q = mC\Delta T$. This needs to be rearranged to solve for C:

$$C = \frac{q}{m\Delta T}$$

It is now necessary to determine the value of each of the quantities use in this equation.

$$\text{Heat} = q = \left(\frac{-44.20\ kJ}{\text{mol NaOH}}\right)(4.000 \text{ g NaOH})$$

$$\left(\frac{1 \text{ mol NaOH}}{40.00 \text{ g NaOH}}\right)\left(\frac{1{,}000\ J}{1\ kJ}\right) = -4{,}420 \text{ J}$$

$\Delta T = 35.00°C - 20.00°C = 15.00°C$

Mass $= m = 100.0$ g $H_2O$ + 4.00 g NaOH = 104.0 g solution

Since the dissolving of the NaOH caused 4,450 J to be released into the solution, the solution absorbed 4,420 J.

Entering the values into the equation:

$$C = \frac{q}{m\Delta T} = \frac{(4{,}420 \text{ J})}{(104.0 \text{ g})\ (15.00°C)}$$

$$= 2.833 \text{ J g}^{-1}°C^{-1}$$

Without a calculator, round the values:

$$C = \frac{q}{m\Delta T} = \frac{(4{,}400 \text{ J})}{(100.0 \text{ g})\ (15.00°C)} = 3 \text{ J g}^{-1}°C^{-1}$$

The 73.67 J $g^{-1}°C^{-1}$ results if only the mass of NaOH is used instead of the mass of the solution

The negative answers result if you forget that the solution absorbs the heat (+).

**17. B**—The resultant solution from mixing the titrated and untitrated solution is a buffer with equal concentrations of the conjugate acid and base. Such a solution has pH = p$K_a$. Then $K_a$ = or $10^{-pH}$. (Note, such a solution also results at the midpoint of a weak acid–strong base titration.)

**18. B**—While it is true that both acids are strong, only nitric acid is an oxidizing acid. It takes an oxidizing acid to react with copper metal or any less active metal. The student could have substituted another strong oxidizing acid such as sulfuric acid.

Note, the potential required to oxidize copper must be greater than 0.34 V. Nonoxidizing acids, such as hydrochloric acid, have a potential of 0.0 V. The potential for nitric acid is 0.90 V.

**19. C**—The graph shows the absorption versus concentration of the unknown indicator is linear from Standard 1 to Standard 4. To is no indication of the relationship outside this range. The first student should not have extended the calibration curve beyond this range. There is a lower limit and an upper limit to the region on linearity for any solution. An absorbance of 0.44 is outside the known linear range; therefore, it would be improper to assume that it is.

**20. B**—This is a unit conversion problem.

$$\text{Units given} = M\ Ca^{2+} = \frac{\text{mole } Ca^{2+}}{\text{L}}$$

$$\text{Units sought} = \frac{\text{mg } CaCO_3}{\text{L}}$$

As any unit conversion problem, the conversion may be done in any order:

$$0.0100\ M\ Ca^{2+} = \left(\frac{0.0100 \text{ mole } Ca^{2+}}{\text{L}}\right)$$

$$\left(\frac{1 \text{ mole } CaCO_3}{1 \text{ mole } Ca^{2+}}\right)\left(\frac{100.09 \text{ g } CaCO_3}{1 \text{ mole } CaCO_3}\right)\left(\frac{1 \text{ mg}}{0.001 \text{ g}}\right)$$

$$= 1.00 \times 10^3 \text{ mg } CaCO_3 \text{ L}^{-1}$$

The $4.00 \times 10^2$ mg $CaCO_3$ $L^{-1}$ answer comes from using the molar mass of $Ca^{2+}$ instead of the molar mass of $CaCO_3$. The 1.00 mg $CaCO_3$ $L^{-1}$ comes from forgetting the gram to milligram conversion, we have seen this commonly when students do not write their units when working problems. The $1.00 \times 10^{-3}$ mg $CaCO_3$ $L^{-1}$ comes from doing the gram to milligram conversion incorrectly, as seen on many exams we have graded.

The use of titers and ppm illustrates that the entire world is still not metric. For example, the author's local Water Quality report from the city lists an average alkalinity for 2020 as 82.45 ppm.

# › Free-Response Questions

You have 15 minutes to answer the following long question, and 10 minutes each for each of the four short questions. You may use a calculator and the tables in the back of the book.

## Question 1

A sample of a solid weak monoprotic acid, HA, is supplied, along with solid sodium hydroxide, NaOH, a phenolphthalein solution, and primary standard potassium hydrogen phthalate (KHP).

(a) Describe how a standardized sodium hydroxide solution may be prepared for the titration.

(b) Sketch a graph of pH versus volume of base added for the titration.

(c) Sketch the titration curve if the unknown acid were really a diprotic acid.

(d) Describe the steps necessary to determine $K_a$ for HA.

(e) What factor determines which indicator should be chosen for this titration?

## Question 2

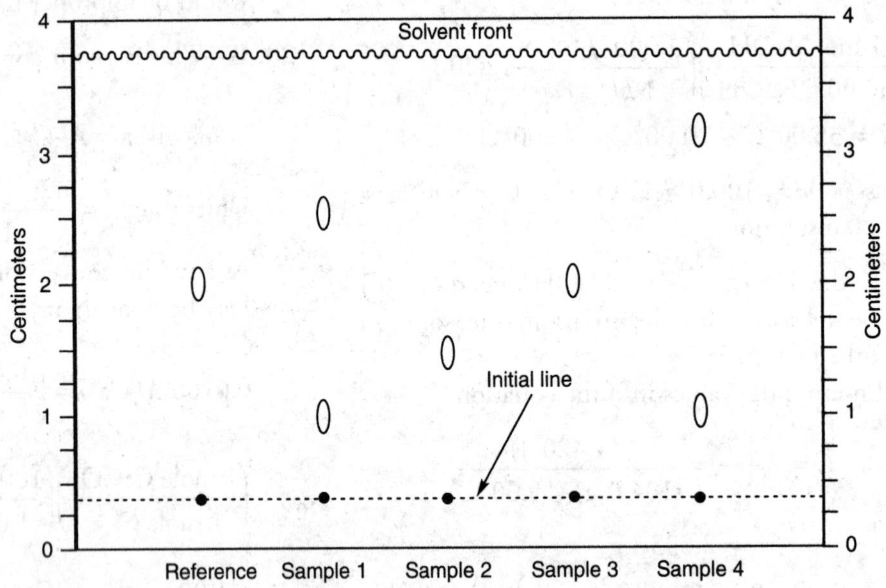


During a chemistry lab to identify the FD&C–approved dyes being used in coloring candy, a student uses paper chromatography to separate the dyes. The student obtains the chromatogram pictured above. He produced each "dot" on the initial line by moistening a piece of colored candy and rubbing it with a toothpick and repeatedly transferring some of the dye to the dot. Each of the samples was a different color of candy. The reference was FD&C–approved yellow dye #6 (the other FD&C–approved yellow dye is yellow dye #5), which causes an allergic reaction in some people. After creating all the dots, the student places the paper in a large beaker with about 0.2 cm of 0.1% aqueous NaCl. After about 20 minutes, the solvent had moved to the position indicated by the solvent front. The following table lists the colors of the candy used by this student.

| Reference | Color |
|---|---|
| Sample 1 | Green |
| Sample 2 | Red |
| Sample 3 | Yellow |
| Sample 4 | Orange |

(a) Determine the $R_f$ value for each of the spots arising from Sample 4.

(b) Assume that a green color arises from a combination a blue and a yellow dye. Is the yellow component of Sample 1 likely to be FD&C yellow dye #5 or #6? Explain why you made the choice you did.

(c) Orange is a combination of red and yellow. Sample 4 shows one way of producing orange. What is another?

(d) In paper chromatography, it is quite usual for the spots to smear while they are traveling up the paper. What could the student have done to minimize this smearing?

## Question 3

A student is performing a chemistry lab to determine the formula of a hydrate. She heats a crucible and lid over a Bunsen burner until it is red-hot, allows it to cool, and weighs the crucible and lid. The lid is kept ajar during the heating and put back on the crucible when the crucible is cooling and being weighed. She then repeats the procedure and obtains the same mass (12.125 g). Next, she adds a sample of a hydrated salt to the crucible, replaces the lid, and weighs the crucible, lid, and hydrate on a balance and finds that the combination weighs 15.245 g. In the next step, she carefully heats the crucible with the lid ajar. After a few minutes, she removes the crucible from the heat, replaces the lid on the crucible, and allows the crucible and contents to cool. After the crucible has cooled to room temperature, she weighs the crucible and contents. She then repeats the heating of the hydrate procedure two more times to get a constant mass of 13.650 g for the crucible, lid, and anhydrous salt.

The anhydrous salt was magnesium sulfate, $MgSO_4$, with a molar mass of 120.371 g $mol^{-1}$. The molar mass of water, $H_2O$, is 18.015 g $mol^{-1}$.

(a) Determine the masses of the hydrate, anhydrous salt, and the water lost by the hydrate during heating. Show your work.

(b) Determine the moles of anhydrous salt and water. Show your work.

(c) Why did the student heat the empty crucible until it was red-hot, but carefully heat the crucible plus hydrate?

(d) Why did she leave the lid of the crucible ajar while heating the hydrate and in place during cooling?

## Question 4

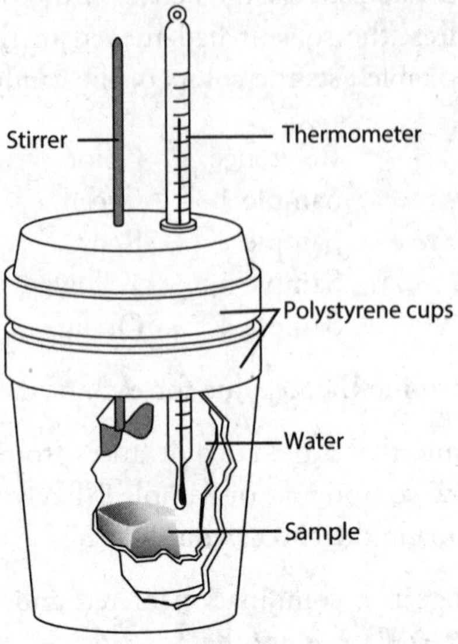


The calorimeter pictured above was used to study the enthalpy of neutralization for the reaction between sulfuric acid, $H_2SO_4$, with potassium hydroxide, KOH. A 50.0-mL sample of 0.500 *M* $H_2SO_4$ (at 22.3°C) was placed in a calorimeter. A 50.0-mL sample of 1.00 *M* KOH (at 22.3°C) was added. The temperature of the solution increased from 22.3 to 29.1°C.

(a) Assuming the reaction goes to completion, write a net ionic equation for this reaction.

(b) Determine the heat energy, *q*, produced in the reaction. The solutions are primarily water, so assume the density is 1.00 g $mL^{-1}$ and that the specific heat, *c*, is 4.18 J $g^{-1}$ $K^{-1}$. Show your work.

(c) Determine the enthalpy change, $\Delta H$, for the reaction in terms of kJ/mol $H^+$. Show your work.

(d) The theoretical value for $\Delta H$ is –55.83 kJ/mol $H^+$. Calculate the percent error in your experimental value.

## Question 5

A student wishes to determine the percent of potassium chlorate, $KClO_3$, in a sample of potassium chlorate mixed with potassium chloride, KCl. She wishes to determine the percentage through the decomposition of the $KClO_3$ in the sample. The decomposition reaction is:

$$2\ KClO_3(s) \rightarrow 2\ KCl(s) + 3\ O_2(g)$$

This decomposition is catalyzed by manganese(IV) oxide, $MnO_2$.

The experiment involves the addition of impure $KClO_3$ to a test tube containing some $MnO_2$. The mixture is then heated to decompose the $KClO_3$. The test tube and contents are cooled and weighed, then reheated, cooled, and weighed again. Depending upon the results from the second heating, there may be a third or even a fourth heating, cooling, and weighing cycle.

The chemist collected the following data:

| | |
|---|---|
| Mass of test tube + $MnO_2$ | 11.222 g |
| Mass of test tube + $MnO_2$ + impure $KClO_3$ | 12.722 g |
| Final mass of test tube + $MnO_2$ + KCl | 12.584 g |

Molar masses: $KClO_3$ 122.55 g $mol^{-1}$ KCl 74.55 g $mol^{-1}$ $MnO_2$ 86.94 g $mol^{-1}$

(a) What mass of $O_2$ was produced? Show your work.

(b) What is the percentage of $KClO_3$ in the sample? Show your work.

(c) Why is it necessary to heat the sample more than once?

(d) A separate analysis showed that the percent $KClO_3$ was incorrect. Assuming there was adequate heating, give a reason why the percentage was incorrect. Explain.

# ❯ Answers and Explanations

## Question 1

(a) A sample of sodium hydroxide is weighed and dissolved in deionized water to give a solution of the approximate concentration desired. (Alternatively, a concentrated NaOH solution with unknown concentration could be diluted.) The process is as follows:

1. Weigh samples of dried KHP into flasks and dissolve in deionized water.
2. Add a few drops of the appropriate acid–base indicator (phenolphthalein) to each sample.
3. Rinse a buret with a little of the NaOH solution; then fill the buret with the NaOH solution.
4. Take the initial buret reading.
5. Titrate the NaOH solution into the KHP samples until the first permanent pink color appears.
6. Take the final buret reading.
7. Using the molar mass of KHP, determine the moles of KHP present. This is equal to the moles of NaOH.
8. The difference in the buret readings is the volume of NaOH solution added (convert this to liters).
9. The molarity of the NaOH solution is the moles of NaOH divided by the liters of NaOH solution added.
10. (Repeat the procedure for each sample.)

Give yourself 3 points for this full list if the items are in order. If three to five items are in the wrong order or missing, you get only 2 points. If five to seven items are in the wrong order or missing, you get only 1 point. You get 0 points for three or fewer items.

(b)

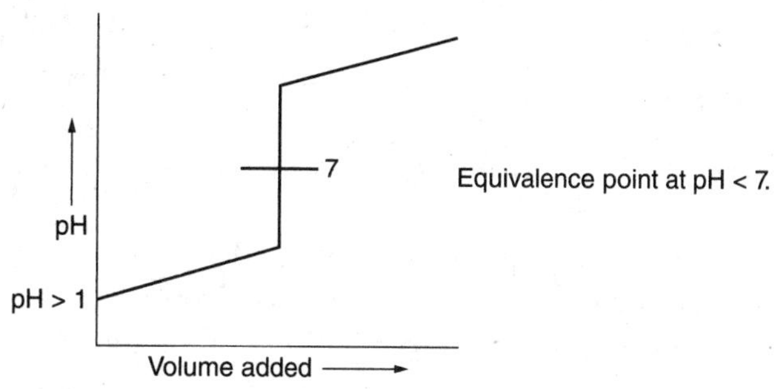

You get 1 point for this general graph. You get an additional point for noting that the equivalence point is greater than 7. The graph does not need to be perfect.

(c)

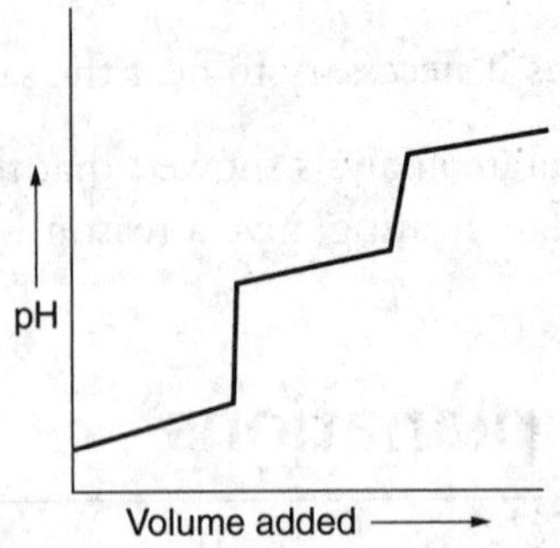


You get 2 points for this graph if you show both steps. The graph does not need to be perfect, but you need to show two steps. You get 1 point for showing only one step.

(d) There are several related ways to do this problem. One method is to split the sample into two portions. Titrate one portion to the equivalence point. Add the titrated sample to the untitrated solution and add a volume of deionized water equal to the volume of NaOH solution added. The pH of this mixture is equal to the p$K_a$ of the acid (this corresponds to a half-titrated sample).

You get 1 point for anything concerning a half-titrated sample and an additional 1 point for pH = p$K_a$ at the half-titrated point.

(e) The pH at the equivalence point must be close to the p$K_a$ of the indicator.

You get 1 point for this answer.

Total your points. There are 10 points possible.

## Question 2

(a) To determine the $R_f$ value it is necessary to determine how far a sample traveled relative to how far the solvent traveled. The distance the solvent traveled is the distance between the initial line and the solvent front.

| | |
|---|---|
| Solvent front | 3.75 cm |
| – Initial line | – 0.35 cm |
| Distance solvent traveled | 3.40 cm |

| | Top spot | Bottom spot |
|---|---|---|
| Top of spot | 3.30 cm | 1.20 |
| – Initial line | –0.35 cm | –0.35 cm |
| Distance traveled | 2.95 cm | 0.85 cm |

$R_f$ values

Top spot $$R_f = \frac{2.95 \text{ cm}}{3.40 \text{ cm}} = 0.868$$

Bottom spot $$R_f = \frac{0.85 \text{ cm}}{3.40 \text{ cm}} = 0.25$$

You get 1 point for correctly determining the two $R_f$ values. In this solution, the tops of the spots were used; however, you can still get 1 point if you consistently used the bottoms or some other position of the spot. Due to variations in reading the scale, you do not need to get the exact same numbers. We cannot count the times we have not been able to award this point because the student writes what appears to be random numbers on the test. Make sure you identify things and show your work.

(b) If green is blue plus yellow, then one of the two dots for Sample 1 must be blue and the other must be yellow. Neither of these dots matches the reference (yellow #6); therefore, this dye cannot be present. The only other choice is yellow #5, which must be one of the dots.

You get 1 point for this answer.

(c) Another way to produce orange would be to use the dyes represented by Samples 2 and 3.

You get 1 point for this answer.

(d) The smaller the dots on the initial line are, the less smearing there will be.

You get 1 point for this answer.

Total your points. There is a maximum of 4 points possible. Subtract 1 point if any calculated answer does not have the correct number of significant figures.

## Question 3

(a)

| | |
|---|---|
| Mass of crucible, lid, and hydrate | 15.245 g |
| – Mass of crucible and lid | –12.125 g |
| Mass of hydrate | 3.120 g Hydrate |
| Mass of crucible, lid, and anhydrous salt | 15.246 g |
| – Mass of crucible and lid | –13.650 g |
| Mass of anhydrous salt | 1.596 g Anhydrous salt |
| Mass of hydrate | 3.120 g |
| – Mass of anhydrous salt | –1.596 g |
| Mass of water | 1.524 g Water |

You earn 1 point total for all three answers if you show your work. All three answers are necessary to receive this point.

(b)

$$\text{Moles anhydrous salt} = (1.596\ \text{g salt})\left(\frac{1\ \text{mol salt}}{120.371\ \text{g salt}}\right) = 0.01326\ \text{mole salt}$$

$$\text{Moles water} = (1.524\ \text{g water})\left(\frac{1\ \text{mol water}}{18.015\ \text{g water}}\right) = 0.08460\ \text{mole water}$$

You earn 1 point total for both answers if you show your work. Both answers are necessary to receive this point. If you correctly used a wrong answer from part (a), you still get 1 point.

(c) It was necessary to make sure that all impurities were driven off the empty crucible; therefore, the higher the temperature the better. Heating the sample too much might lead to decomposition of the anhydrous salt.

You earn 1 point for this answer. You must explain the heating of each crucible.

(d) The lid was left ajar to allow volatile material (water vapor) to escape while heating. The lid was kept in place while cooling to minimize water vapor from air to be reabsorbed by the sample.
You earn 1 point for this answer.

Total your points. There is a maximum of 4 points possible. Subtract 1 point if any calculated answer does not have the correct number of significant figures.

## Question 4

(a) The molecular equation is:

$$H_2SO_4(aq) + 2\ KOH(aq) \rightarrow K_2SO_4(aq) + 2\ H_2O(l)$$

The total ionic equation is:

$$2\ H^+(aq) + SO_4^{2-}(aq) + 2\ K^+(aq) + 2\ OH^-(aq) \rightarrow 2\ K^+(aq) + SO_4^{2-}(aq) + 2\ H_2O(l)$$

The net ionic equation for this reaction is:

$$H^+(aq) + OH^-(aq) \rightarrow H_2O(l)$$

You get 1 point for this final answer. If you forgot to reduce the coefficients or you forgot ions have charges, you get 0 points. (The molecular and total ionic equations are only shown here to help with the explanation; they are not part of the answer required by you.)

(b) The equation you need ($q = mc\Delta T$) is given on the AP Exam and in the back of this book. The variables are:

$$m = \left[(50.0\ \text{mL})\left(\frac{1.00\ \text{g}}{\text{mL}}\right) + (50.0\ \text{mL})\left(\frac{1.00\ \text{g}}{\text{mL}}\right)\right] = 100.0\ \text{g}$$

$$q = 4.18\ \text{J g}^{-1}\ \text{K}^{-1}$$

$$\Delta T = (29.1 - 22.3)°\text{C} = 6.8°\text{C}\ (= 6.8\ \text{K})$$

Entering these values into the equation gives:

$$q = (100.0\ \text{g})\ (4.18\ \text{J g}^{-1}\ \text{K}^{-1})\ (6.8\ \text{K}) = -2.8 \times 10^3\ \text{J (or } -2.8\ \text{kJ)}$$

This is an exothermic process; therefore, the enthalpy change must be negative.
You get 1 point for this answer if you showed your work and remembered to change the sign.

(c) It is necessary to determine the moles of hydrogen ions in the reaction.

$$\text{Moles } H^+ = (50.0\ \text{mL})\left(\frac{0.500\ \text{mol } H_2SO_4}{1{,}000\ \text{mL}}\right)\left(\frac{2\ \text{mol } H^+}{1\ \text{mol } H_2SO_4}\right) = 0.0500\ \text{mole } H^+$$

The moles of $H^+$ plus your answer to part (b) gives:

$$\Delta H = \left(\frac{-2.8 \times 10^3\ \text{J}}{0.0500\ \text{mol } H^+}\right)\left(\frac{1\ \text{kJ}}{1{,}000\ \text{J}}\right) = -56\ \text{kJ/mol } H^+$$

You get 1 point for this answer if you showed your work. If you correctly used an incorrect value from part (b), you still get 1 point.

(d) The theoretical value for $\Delta H$ is –55.83 kJ/mol $H^+$. Calculate the percent error in your experimental value. Show your work.

$$\text{Percent error} = \left(\frac{|-55.83-(-56)|\ \text{kJ mol}^{-1}}{-55.83\ \text{kJ mol}^{-1}}\right) \times 100\% = 0.3\%$$

You get 1 point for this answer if you showed your work. If you correctly used an incorrect value from part (c), you still get 1 point.

Total your points. There is a maximum of 4 points. Deduct 1 point if any answer did not have the correct number of significant figures.

### Question 5

(a) The mass of the oxygen produced is determined as:

| | |
|---|---|
| Mass of test tube + $MnO_2$ + impure $KClO_3$ | 12.722 g |
| – Final mass of test tube + $MnO_2$ + KCl | −12.584 g |
| Mass of $O_2$ | 0.138 g |

You get 1 point for this answer. If you did not show your work, you get 0 points.

(b) What is the percentage of $KClO_3$ in the sample?

| | |
|---|---|
| Mass of test tube + $MnO_2$ + impure $KClO_3$ | 12.722 g |
| – Mass of test tube + $MnO_2$ | −11.222 g |
| Mass impure $KClO_3$ | 1.500 g |

| | |
|---|---|
| Final mass of test tube + $MnO_2$ + KCl | 12.584 g |
| – Mass of test tube + $MnO_2$ | −11.222 g |
| Mass KCl | 1.362 g |

| | |
|---|---|
| Mass impure $KClO_3$ | 1.500 g |
| – Mass KCl | −1.362 g |
| Mass $KClO_3$ | 0.138 g |

$$\text{Percent } KClO_3 = \frac{0.138\ \text{g } KClO_3}{1.500\ \text{g sample}} \times 100\% = 9.20\%$$

You get 1 point for this answer.

(c) The decomposition may not be complete after only one heating.
You get 1 point for this answer.

(d) One reason to get an erroneous percentage would be if the test tube and contents had not cooled completely to room temperature before weighing was done. Under these circumstances the mass would be incorrect.
You get 1 point for this answer with the explanation. If you said "experimental error," you earn 0 points.

Total your points. There is a maximum of 4 points. Deduct 1 point if any answer did not have the correct number of significant figures.

## › Rapid Review

Reviewing the experiments should include looking at the synopsis, apparatus, calculations, and comments, as well as the appropriate concept chapters, if needed.

- Pay extra attention to any experiment you did not perform.

- Be familiar with the equipment used in each experiment (in many cases beakers may substitute for flasks).
- Know the basic measurements required in each experiment.
- Know what values are measured and which are calculated.
- Pay attention to significant figures.
- Balances are used to measure the mass of a substance, not the moles.

STEP 5

# Build Your Test-Taking Confidence

AP Chemistry Practice Exam 1

AP Chemistry Practice Exam 2

# AP Chemistry Practice Exam 1—Multiple Choice

## ANSWER SHEET

1 (A) (B) (C) (D)
2 (A) (B) (C) (D)
3 (A) (B) (C) (D)
4 (A) (B) (C) (D)
5 (A) (B) (C) (D)
6 (A) (B) (C) (D)
7 (A) (B) (C) (D)
8 (A) (B) (C) (D)
9 (A) (B) (C) (D)
10 (A) (B) (C) (D)
11 (A) (B) (C) (D)
12 (A) (B) (C) (D)
13 (A) (B) (C) (D)
14 (A) (B) (C) (D)
15 (A) (B) (C) (D)
16 (A) (B) (C) (D)
17 (A) (B) (C) (D)
18 (A) (B) (C) (D)
19 (A) (B) (C) (D)
20 (A) (B) (C) (D)
21 (A) (B) (C) (D)
22 (A) (B) (C) (D)
23 (A) (B) (C) (D)
24 (A) (B) (C) (D)
25 (A) (B) (C) (D)
26 (A) (B) (C) (D)
27 (A) (B) (C) (D)
28 (A) (B) (C) (D)
29 (A) (B) (C) (D)
30 (A) (B) (C) (D)
31 (A) (B) (C) (D)
32 (A) (B) (C) (D)
33 (A) (B) (C) (D)
34 (A) (B) (C) (D)
35 (A) (B) (C) (D)
36 (A) (B) (C) (D)
37 (A) (B) (C) (D)
38 (A) (B) (C) (D)
39 (A) (B) (C) (D)
40 (A) (B) (C) (D)
41 (A) (B) (C) (D)
42 (A) (B) (C) (D)
43 (A) (B) (C) (D)
44 (A) (B) (C) (D)
45 (A) (B) (C) (D)
46 (A) (B) (C) (D)
47 (A) (B) (C) (D)
48 (A) (B) (C) (D)
49 (A) (B) (C) (D)
50 (A) (B) (C) (D)
51 (A) (B) (C) (D)
52 (A) (B) (C) (D)
53 (A) (B) (C) (D)
54 (A) (B) (C) (D)
55 (A) (B) (C) (D)
56 (A) (B) (C) (D)
57 (A) (B) (C) (D)
58 (A) (B) (C) (D)
59 (A) (B) (C) (D)
60 (A) (B) (C) (D)

*The AP Exam is a timed exam; keep this in mind as you prepare. When taking the various tests presented in this book, you should follow the AP Exam rules as closely as possible. Anyone can improve his or her score by using notes, books, or an unlimited time. You will have none of these on the AP Exam, so resist the temptation to use them on practice exams. Carefully time yourself, do not use other materials, and use a calculator only when expressly allowed to do so. After you have finished an exam, you may use other sources to go over questions you missed or skipped. We have seen many students get into trouble because the first time they attempted a test under "test conditions" was on the test itself.*

# AP Chemistry Practice Exam 1

## SECTION I
## MULTIPLE CHOICE

**Time—1 hour and 30 minutes**

**NO CALCULATOR MAY BE USED WITH SECTION I**

Answer the following questions in the time allowed. You may use the periodic table in the back of the book.

**Use the following information to answer questions 1–7.**

Sodium azide, $NaN_3$, is a component of automobile airbags. It is useful because it quickly decomposes to generate a large volume of nitrogen gas. The balanced chemical equation for the reaction is:

$$2\ NaN_3(s) \rightarrow 2\ Na(s) + 3\ N_2(g)$$

There are additional components in the airbag to react with the elemental sodium formed.

Sodium azide is an unstable compound; therefore, it is often necessary to analyze samples as a check of its purity. A chemist is attempting to develop a new analytical, which employs the following reaction:

$$NaN_3(aq) + Na_2S(aq) + 3\ H_2O(l) \rightarrow N_2(g) + NH_3(g) + S(s) + 3\ NaOH(aq)$$

The chemist weighed a small flask both with and without a sample of sodium azide and recorded the masses. Next, she connected the flask to the system shown below.

The flask in the middle and the rubber tubing leading to the beaker were completely filled with dilute acid, and then the clamp was removed. Excess sodium sulfide solution was added to the flask containing the sample. The liquid level in the second flask dropped as the generated nitrogen gas displaced the water into the beaker. The system was left intact until gas generation ceased. After the system returned to room temperature, the beaker was raised until the water in the beaker was at the same level as in the second flask. When the liquid levels were the same, the clamp was replaced to prevent further transfer. The chemist completed the following data table in her lab book.

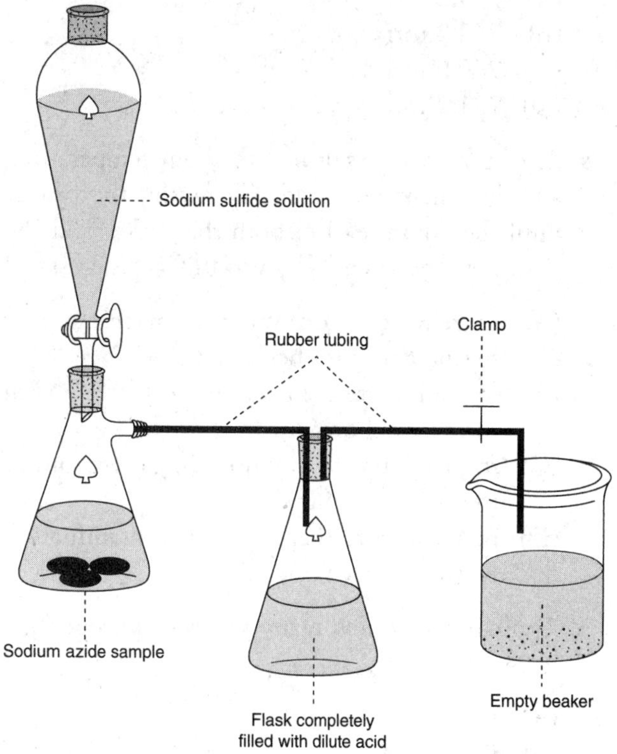


| | |
|---|---|
| Mass of empty flask | 175.245 g |
| Mass of flask plus sodium azide | 176.604 g |
| Volume of displaced water | 315 mL |
| Barometric pressure | 748.2 torr |
| Room temperature | 27.0°C |
| Vapor pressure of water at 27.0°C | 27.0 torr (assumed to be equal to that of dilute acid) |

GO ON TO THE NEXT PAGE

**1.** What type of reaction generated the nitrogen gas?

(A) oxidation–reduction
(B) combination
(C) decomposition
(D) combustion

**2.** Why must the liquid in the flask be dilute acid?

(A) Dilute acid is necessary to neutralize the sodium hydroxide formed.
(B) Dilute acid removes ammonia from the gas leaving the nitrogen behind.
(C) Dilute acid causes the reaction to go to completion.
(D) Dilute acid is easier to handle than many other liquids.

**3.** What is the partial pressure of the nitrogen gas in the flask?

(A) 775.2 torr
(B) 748.2 torr
(C) 760.0 torr
(D) 721.2 torr

**4.** After the system returned to room temperature, an adjustment was made by raising the beaker until the liquid level in both the beaker and the flask were the same. Why was this step necessary?

(A) to remove excess water from the rubber tubing and into the beaker
(B) to equilibrate the pressure in the flask with the external pressure
(C) to make sure all the nitrogen gas was out of the rubber tubing
(D) to make sure there was no contamination by the hydrochloric acid

**5.** Approximately how many moles of nitrogen gas formed?

(A) 0.1 mole
(B) 0.02 mole
(C) 0.005 mole
(D) 0.01 mole

**6.** If the sample were pure sodium azide, approximately how many moles of nitrogen gas would form?

(A) 0.04 mole
(B) 0.002 mole
(C) 0.02 mole
(D) 0.2 mole

**7.** Would it be possible to use this experimental setup to study a reaction that produced gaseous sulfur dioxide, $SO_2$? If not, why?

(A) No, because some of the sulfur dioxide gas would dissolve in the acid.
(B) No, because sulfur dioxide reacts with acids to produce solid sulfur.
(C) No, because sulfur dioxide is only a gas at very high temperatures.
(D) Yes, this apparatus could be used.

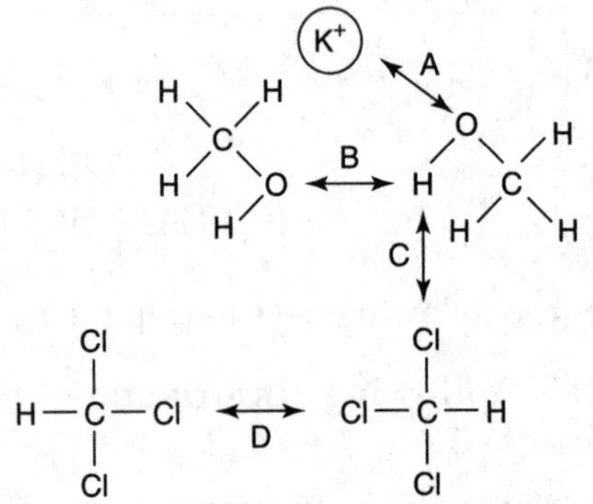


**8.** Which of the labeled arrows in the diagram above represents the strongest intermolecular force of the four indicated?

(A) arrow A
(B) arrow B
(C) arrow C
(D) arrow D

**9.** If about 88% of a sample of pure $^{131}I$ decays in 24 days, what is the approximate half-life of $^{131}I$?

(A) 24 days
(B) 16 days
(C) 8 days
(D) 90 days

**GO ON TO THE NEXT PAGE**

**Use the following information for questions 10–12.**

| Acid | $K_a$, Acid Dissociation Constant |
|---|---|
| $HIO_3$ | $1.7 \times 10^{-1}$ |
| $HIO_4$ | $2.8 \times 10^{-2}$ |
| $HNO_2$ | $4.5 \times 10^{-4}$ |
| HCN | $6.2 \times 10^{-10}$ |

**10.** A buffered solution with a pH near 5 is needed for an experiment. Using the above information, which of the combinations would be the best choice to prepare the buffer?

(A) $HIO_3 + KIO_3$
(B) HCN + KCN
(C) $HNO_2 + KNO_2$
(D) $HIO_4 + NaIO_4$

**11.** A student wishes to measure the pH of a 0.10 *M* solution of the sodium salt of each of the acids in the table. The salts chosen were $NaIO_3$, $NaIO_4$, $NaNO_2$, and NaCN, respectively. Which of the four salt solutions will have the highest pH?

(A) $NaIO_3$
(B) $NaIO_4$
(C) $NaNO_2$
(D) NaCN

**12.** Which of the acids in the table would be the easiest to titrate with a weak base like ammonia ($K_b = 1.8 \times 10^{-5}$)?

(A) $HIO_3$
(B) $HIO_4$
(C) $HNO_2$
(D) HCN

**Use the following information to answer questions 13–17.**

pH versus volume of titrant added

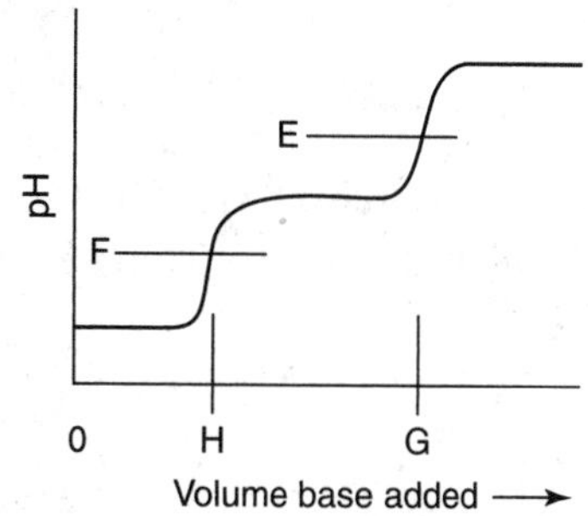


$H_2C_6O_6$ $K_{a1} = 8.0 \times 10^{-5}$ $K_{a2} = 1.6 \times 10^{-12}$

Ascorbic acid (vitamin C), $H_2C_6O_6$, is a diprotic acid used as a dietary supplement. As with all dietary supplements, it is important to analyze samples for purity. The vitamin C may be extracted from natural sources or synthesized. The extracted vitamin C may contain additional extracted ingredients to which some people are allergic. Synthetic vitamin C may contain other forms of the vitamin; however, modern synthetic methods do not generate these contaminates. The shown titration curve is an idealized graph for a diprotic acid. On this graph, E and F represent the pH at the endpoints with the possibility that E may shift slightly and either E or F may not be present. H is the volume of base required to titrate the first hydrogen ion, and G is the quantity of base necessary to titrate both hydrogen ions. G is twice H.

**13.** What is the approximate pH at ½ H?

(A) 7
(B) 4
(C) 2
(D) impossible to predict

**14.** If G were not twice H, what would this indicate?

(A) There is a contaminant that is either an acid or a base.
(B) The other form of vitamin C is present.
(C) The vitamin C was extracted from a plant.
(D) The vitamin C is synthetic.

**15.** Which of the following bases would be the best choice for the titration?

(A) $Al(OH)_3$
(B) $Na_2CO_3$
(C) $NH_3$
(D) KOH

**16.** In the titration of a sample of vitamin C with standard NaOH, what is the approximate value of F?

(A) $< 7$
(B) $> 7$
(C) $= 7$
(D) unknown

**17.** While the titration of a diprotic acid to produce a curve similar to the idealized one shown is useful in many analyses, ascorbic acid is not a good candidate for this type of analysis (determining both endpoints). Why?

(A) $K_{a2}$ and $K_{a1}$ are too close together.
(B) Ascorbic acid may occur in more than one form.
(C) Ascorbic acid is not soluble in water.
(D) $K_{a2}$ for ascorbic acid is too small.

**18.** Which of the following CANNOT behave as both a Brønsted base and a Brønsted acid?

(A) $H_2PO_4^{2-}$
(B) $CO_3^{2-}$
(C) $HSO_3^-$
(D) $HCO_3^-$

**19.** A student mixes 50.0 mL of 0.10 *M* potassium chromate, $K_2CrO_4$, solution with 50.0 mL of 0.10 *M* $AgNO_3$. A red precipitate of silver chromate forms and the concentration of the silver ion becomes very small. Correctly place the concentrations of the remaining ions in order of decreasing concentration.

(A) $[K^+] > [CrO_4^{2-}] > [NO_3^-]$
(B) $[CrO_4^{2-}] > [NO_3^-] > [K^+]$
(C) $[K^+] > [NO_3^-] > [CrO_4^{2-}]$
(D) $[NO_3^-] > [K^+] > [CrO_4^{2-}]$

**20.** There are many different experiments for the determination of the molecular mass of a gas. One method begins by heating a solid or liquid in a flask to produce a gaseous product. The gas passes through a tube and displaces water in an inverted, water-filled bottle. The mass of the starting material is determined, along with the volume of the displaced water and the temperature of the system. The pressure in the inverted water-filled bottle is equal to the external pressure. Once the barometric pressure has been recorded, what other information is needed to finish the experiment?

(A) the heat of formation of the gas
(B) the density of the water
(C) the mass of the displaced water
(D) the vapor pressure of the water

$$H_2(g) + 1/2\ O_2(g) \rightarrow H_2O(l) \quad \Delta H° = -300\ kJ$$
$$C(s) + O_2(g) \rightarrow CO_2(g) \quad \Delta H° = -400\ kJ$$
$$C_2H_2(g) + 5/2\ O_2(g) \rightarrow H_2O(l) + 2\ CO_2(g) \quad \Delta H° = -1300\ kJ$$

**21.** Using the information given above, calculate the enthalpy change for the following reaction:

$$2\ C(s) + H_2(g) \rightarrow C_2H_2(g)$$

(A) 200 kJ
(B) −200 kJ
(C) 500 kJ
(D) −500 kJ

**22.** Cerium(III) sulfate, $Ce_2(SO_4)_2$, is less soluble in hot water than it is in cold. Which of the following conclusions may be related to this?

(A) The heat of solution of cerium(III) sulfate is exothermic.
(B) The hydration energies of cerium ions and sulfate ions are very low.
(C) The heat of solution for cerium(III) sulfate is endothermic.
(D) The solution is not an ideal solution.

GO ON TO THE NEXT PAGE

**Use the information on the containers in the following diagram to answer questions 23–25.**

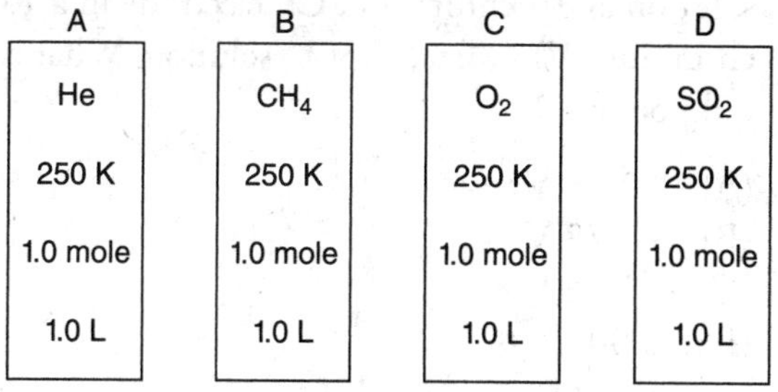


Approximate molar masses:

$He = 4\ g\ mol^{-1}$, $CH_4 = 16\ g\ mol^{-1}$,
$O_2 = 32\ g\ mol^{-1}$, $SO_2 = 64\ g\ mol^{-1}$

**23.** Under the conditions indicated, in which of the gas samples is the average velocity of the molecules half that of methane, $CH_4$?

(A) He
(B) $CH_4$
(C) $SO_2$
(D) They are all at the same temperature; therefore, they have the same average velocity.

**24.** Which of the four gases will probably show the least deviation from ideal behavior?

(A) He
(B) $CH_4$
(C) $O_2$
(D) $SO_2$

**25.** If one of the containers sprang a small leak, which of the following would change?

(A) moles, temperature, and pressure
(B) moles and pressure
(C) temperature and pressure
(D) moles and temperature

**26.** The specific rate constant, $k$, for a certain first-order reaction is 86 $h^{-1}$. What mass of a 0.0500-g sample of starting material will remain after 58 s?

(A) 0.0500 g
(B) 0.0250 g
(C) 0.0125 g
(D) 0.00625 g

**Use the information on the containers in the following diagram to answer questions 27–31 concerning the following equilibrium:**

$$CO(g) + 2\ H_2(g) \leftrightarrows CH_3OH(g)$$

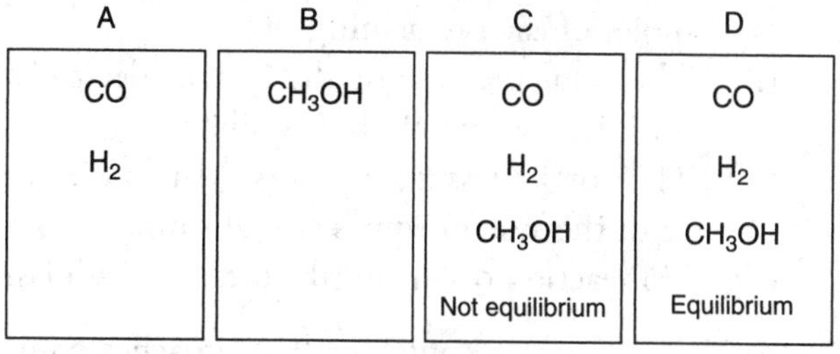


**27.** Container A initially contains 0.60 mole of $H_2$ and 0.60 mole of CO and is allowed to come to equilibrium. At equilibrium, there is 0.40 mole of CO in the flask. What is the value of $K_c$, the equilibrium constant, for the reaction?

(A) 0.40
(B) 2.5
(C) 0.080
(D) 12

**28.** A 1.00-mole sample of $CH_3OH$ is placed in container B and the system is allowed to go to equilibrium. What can be said about the relative rates of reaction with respect to the various components?

(A) The rate of CO formation is numerically equal to the rate of $CH_3OH$ loss.
(B) The rate of $H_2(g)$ formation is numerically equal to the rate of $CH_3OH$ loss.
(C) The rate of $H_2(g)$ formation is half the rate of CO(g) formation.
(D) The rate of $H_2(g)$ formation is equal to the rate of CO(g) formation.

**29.** The mixture in container D is in equilibrium. Which of the following is true?

(A) The rate of the forward and reverse reactions is equal to zero.
(B) The rate of the forward reaction is equal to the rate of the reverse reaction.
(C) The pressure in the system is increasing.
(D) The pressure in the system is decreasing.

**30.** The mixture in container A goes to equilibrium. If the initial moles of $H_2(g)$ is twice the initial moles of CO(g), which of the following is true?

(A) Both reactants are limiting; therefore, the reaction will continue until there are zero moles of each remaining.
(B) The total pressure of the system decreases until the system reaches equilibrium.
(C) The total pressure of the system increases until the system equals equilibrium.
(D) No reaction occurs until a catalyst is added.

**31.** As the mixture in container B approaches equilibrium, the partial pressure of $CH_3OH$ gas decreases by 1.5 atm. What is the net change in the total pressure of the system?

(A) +1.5 atm
(B) +3.0 atm
(C) −1.5 atm
(D) −3.0 atm

**Use the information on standard reduction potentials in the following table to answer questions 32–36.**

| | |
|---|---|
| $F_2(g) + 2\ e \rightarrow 2\ F^-(aq)$ | +2.87 |
| $Ag^+(aq) + 1\ e^- \rightarrow Ag(s)$ | +0.80 |
| $O_2(g) + 2\ H_2O(l) + 4\ e^- \rightarrow 4\ OH^-(aq)$ | +0.40 |
| $AgCl(s) + 1\ e^- \rightarrow Ag(s) + Cl^-(aq)$ | +0.22 |
| $Pb^{2+}(aq) + 2\ e^- \rightarrow Pb(s)$ | −0.13 |
| $NO_2^-(aq) + 5\ H_2O(l) + 6\ e^- \rightarrow NH_3(aq) + 7\ OH^-(aq)$ | −0.15 |
| $2\ H_2O(l) + 2\ e^- \rightarrow H_2(g) + 2\ OH^-(aq)$ | −0.83 |
| $Cr^{2+}(aq) + 2\ e^- \rightarrow Cr(s)$ | −0.91 |
| $Al^{3+}(aq) + 3\ e^- \rightarrow Al(s)$ | −1.66 |
| $Rb^+(aq) + 1\ e^- \rightarrow Rb(s)$ | −2.93 |

**32.** A student constructs an electrolysis cell with two inert electrodes in an aqueous solution that is 1.0 *M* in rubidium nitrite, $RbNO_2$, and 1.0 *M* in rubidium hydroxide, RbOH. As the cell operates, an odorless gas evolves from one electrode and a gas with a distinctive odor evolves from the other electrode. Choose the correct statement from the following list.

(A) The odorless gas is oxygen.
(B) The odorless gas is the result of reduction.
(C) The gas with the distinctive odor is the result of oxidation.
(D) The odorless gas evolves at the negative electrode.

**33.** There is a galvanic cell involving a lead, Pb, electrode in a 1.0 *M* lead(II) nitrate, $Pb(NO_3)_2$, solution and a chromium, Cr, electrode in a 1.0 *M* chromium(II) sulfate, $CrSO_4$, solution. What is the cell potential?

(A) +0.78 V
(B) −0.78 V
(C) +1.04 V
(D) 0.00 V

**34.** A student attempted to prepare an electrolysis cell to produce aluminum metal (Al) from an aqueous solution of aluminum chloride, $AlCl_3$, using a 6.0 V battery. The cathode compartment of the electrolysis contained 1.0 *M* aluminum chloride, and the anode compartment contained 1.0 *M* calcium chloride, $CaCl_2$. The student was unsuccessful. Why was the student unable to produce aluminum metal?

(A) The voltage from the battery was insufficient to force the reaction to occur.
(B) Reduction of chloride ion occurred in preference to reduction of calcium ion.
(C) Calcium chloride solutions do not conduct electricity.
(D) Reduction of water occurred in preference to reduction of calcium ion.

**35.** Which of the substances in the table would be capable of reducing the aluminum ions in solid aluminum fluoride, $AlF_3$, to aluminum metal? Assume the cell potentials in the table also apply to the solid state.

(A) Cr(s)
(B) Rb(s)
(C) $F_2(g)$
(D) none

GO ON TO THE NEXT PAGE

**36.** A student constructs a galvanic cell that has a chromium, Cr, electrode in a compartment containing a 1.0 *M* chromium(II) nitrate, $Cr(NO_3)_2$, solution and a silver, Ag, electrode in a compartment containing 1.0 *M* silver nitrate, $AgNO_3$, solution. A salt bridge containing a 1.0 *M* potassium chloride, KCl, solution connects the two compartments. When the student measures the cell potential, the value is far from the ideal predicted value. What is the cause of this discrepancy?

(A) The initial concentrations should have been lower than 1.0 *M*.
(B) The initial concentrations should have been higher than 1.0 *M*.
(C) The potassium chloride in the salt bridge interfered with the reaction.
(D) The student did not allow the cell to come to equilibrium.

**Use the information on the acids in the following diagram to answer questions 37–38.**

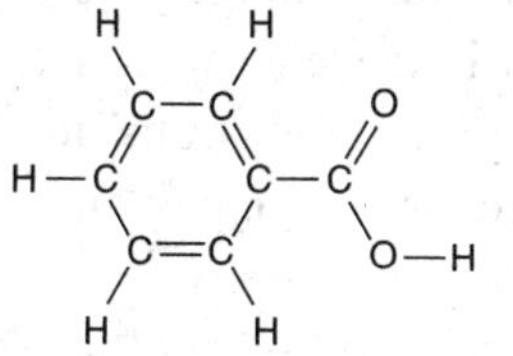
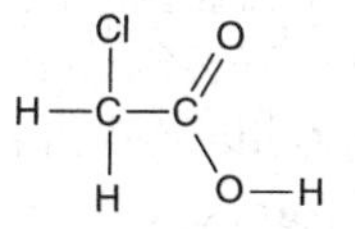
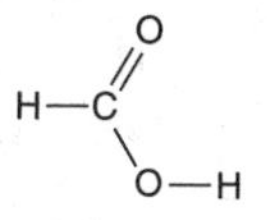

| | Benzoic acid | Chloroacetic acid | Formic acid |
|---|---|---|---|
| $K_a$ | $6.2 \times 10^{-5}$ | $1.4 \times 10^{-3}$ | $1.8 \times 10^{-4}$ |
| $pK_a$ | 4.21 | 2.86 | 3.75 |

**37.** Sample solutions of each of the three acids were titrated with 0.10 *M* sodium hydroxide, NaOH. Each of the acid solutions had a concentration of 0.10 *M*. Which of the acid titrations had the highest pH at the endpoint?

(A) formic acid
(B) benzoic acid
(C) chloroacetic acid
(D) They all had a pH of 7 at the endpoint.

**38.** A student prepares three buffer solutions. Each solution is 1.0 *M* in one of the acids in the table and 1.0 *M* in its corresponding sodium salt. Which of the solutions has the greatest buffer capacity with respect to added NaOH and why?

(A) The benzoic acid buffer because it is the strongest acid
(B) The chloroacetic acid buffer because it is the strongest acid
(C) The formic acid buffer because it donates both of its hydrogen atoms
(D) All are the same.

**39.** Hypochlorous acid is an unstable compound, and one of the decomposition products is chlorine gas, $Cl_2$. The decomposition of the acid lowers its concentration over time. What effect will the decomposition of one-fourth of the acid have on the agreement between the endpoint of the titration and the equivalence point during a titration with standard sodium hydroxide?

(A) The endpoint would remain near the ideal equivalence point.
(B) The endpoint would be after the ideal equivalence point.
(C) The endpoint would be before the ideal equivalence point.
(D) It is impossible to determine.

**40.** Three 25.00-mL samples of approximately 0.10 *M* phenol, $C_6H_5OH$, $K_a = 1.0 \times 10^{-10}$ were removed from a container and placed in separate 250-mL beakers. The samples were titrated with standard potassium hydroxide, KOH, solution. Cresol red was the acid–base indicator used in the titration. The samples required 31.75, 32.38, and 41.75 mL to reach the endpoint. Which of the following might explain why one of the samples required significantly greater amount of base to reach the endpoint?

(A) The indicator was added too late.
(B) The wrong indicator was used.
(C) There was a base contaminating the unclean beaker.
(D) There was an acid contaminating the unclean beaker.

**41.** During the study of the reaction A → 2 B, a chemist constructs several graphs. The graph of [A] versus time and the graph of ln [A] versus time both give a curved line; however, the graph of 1/[A] versus time and gives a straight line. This implies the rate law is:

(A) Rate = $k$[A]
(B) Rate = $k[A]^2$
(C) Rate = $k[A]^0$
(D) Rate = $k[A]^{-1}$

**42.** The photoelectron spectrum of carbon has three equally sized peaks. Which peak is at the lowest energy?

(A) The 1s peak has the lowest energy.
(B) The 2s peak has the lowest energy.
(C) The 2p peak has the lowest energy.
(D) The 1p peak has the lowest energy.

| COMPOUND | FORMULA | MOLAR MASS ($g\ mol^{-1}$) | BOILING POINT (°C) |
|---|---|---|---|
| Ethyl methyl ether | $C_2H_5$-O-$CH_3$ | 60.10 | 10.8 |
| Ethyl methyl amine | $C_2H_5$NH-$CH_3$ | 59.11 | 36.7 |
| Propylamine | $C_3H_7NH_2$ | 59.11 | 47.8 |
| Trimethyl amine | $N(CH_3)_3$ | 59.11 | 2.9 |

**43.** According to the data in the table above, which of the compounds has the strongest intermolecular forces?

(A) propylamine
(B) ethyl methyl ether
(C) trimethyl amine
(D) ethyl methyl amine

**Use the following information to answer questions 44 and 45.**

| METAL | ION | IONIC RADIUS (pm) (CUBIC ENVIRONMENT) | MELTING POINT OF OXIDE (°C) |
|---|---|---|---|
| Sodium | $Na^+$ | 132 | 1,275 (sublimes) |
| Cadmium | $Cd^{2+}$ | 124 | 1,500 |
| Lanthanum | $La^{3+}$ | 130 | 2,256 |

**44.** Each of the ions in the table form stable oxides ($Na_2O$, CdO, and $La_2O_3$). Lanthanum oxide, $La_2O_3$, has a melting point significantly higher than that of the other oxides. Which of the following is the best explanation of why this is true?

(A) Lanthanum is a lanthanide element, and the melting points of these elements are always high.
(B) There is more oxygen in the formula $La_2O_3$ than in the other formulas.
(C) Lanthanum had the highest charge; therefore, it has the highest lattice energy.
(D) Alkali metals like sodium and transition metals like cadmium tend to have low melting points.

**45.** The lithium ion, $Li^+$, is smaller than the sodium ion. How does the melting point of lithium oxide, $Li_2O$, compare to that of sodium oxide?

(A) It is higher because smaller ions have a higher lattice energy.
(B) It is the same because the charges are the same.
(C) It is lower because smaller ions have a smaller lattice energy.
(D) It is impossible to predict because there is insufficient information in the problem.

GO ON TO THE NEXT PAGE

**46.** During the investigation of a chemical reaction by a chemistry student, she was able to determine that the reaction was nonspontaneous at 1 atm and 298 K. However, she learned that cooling the system with dry ice (−78°C) caused the reaction to become spontaneous. Which of the following combinations must apply to this reaction?

(A) $\Delta H < 0$, $\Delta S < 0$, and $\Delta G = 0$
(B) $\Delta H > 0$, $\Delta S < 0$, and $\Delta G > 0$
(C) $\Delta H < 0$, $\Delta S < 0$, and $\Delta G > 0$
(D) $\Delta H > 0$, $\Delta S > 0$, and $\Delta G > 0$

**47.** What is the ionization constant, $K_a$, for a weak monoprotic acid if a 0.060 molar solution has a pH of 2.0?

(A) $2.0 \times 10^{-3}$
(B) $2.0 \times 10^{-1}$
(C) $1.7 \times 10^{-1}$
(D) $5.0 \times 10^{-3}$

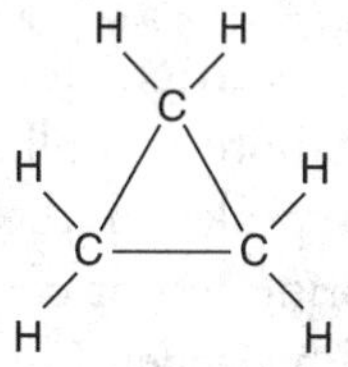

**48.** Cyclopropane, pictured above, is a relatively unstable compound. As seen in the diagram, the carbon atoms form the corners of an equilateral triangle, and each carbon atom has two hydrogen atoms attached to complete an octet of electrons around the carbon atoms. Based upon this structure, why is cyclopropane a relatively unstable compound?

(A) Hydrocarbon compounds are relatively unstable in general.
(B) Compounds that have identical atoms bonded to each other are relatively unstable.
(C) The bonds do not match the angles.
(D) There is no resonance to stabilize the compound.

**49.** A chemist has a 500-mL beaker with a small amount of mercury(II) oxide, HgO, on the bottom. Mercury(II) is insoluble in water but will dissolve in strong acid. She adds 250 mL of water and begins adding 1.0 *M* hydrochloric acid. She continues adding acid until the solid just dissolves. She then tests the solution and finds that it is nonconducting. Which of the following best represents the result for the solution just as the last of the solid dissolves?

(A)

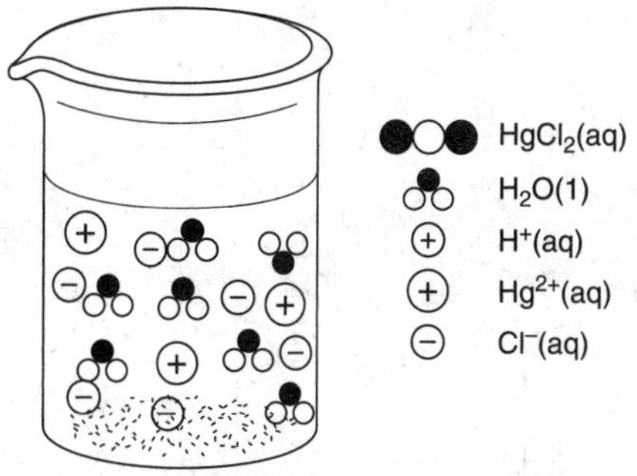


(B)

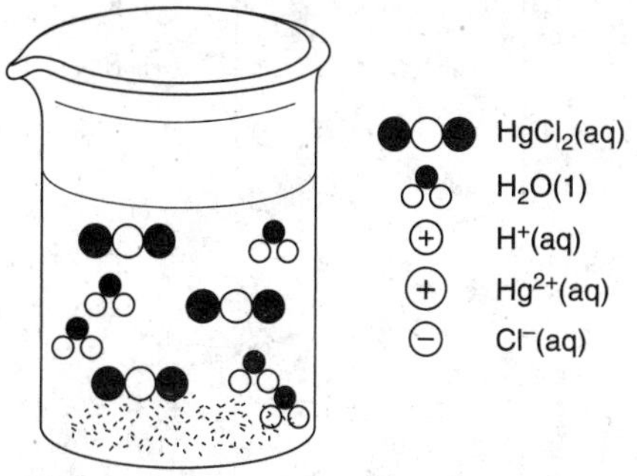


(C)

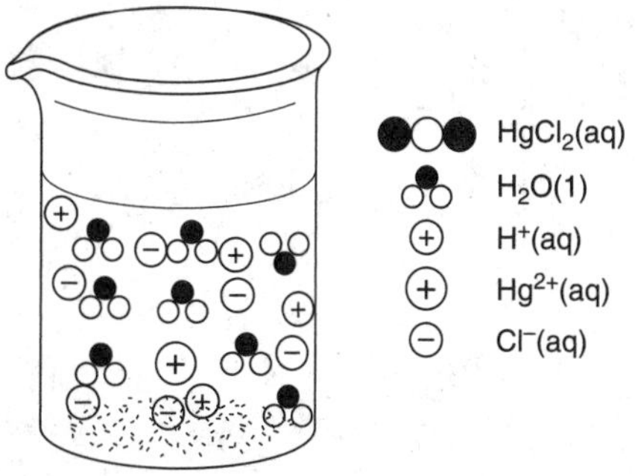


(D)

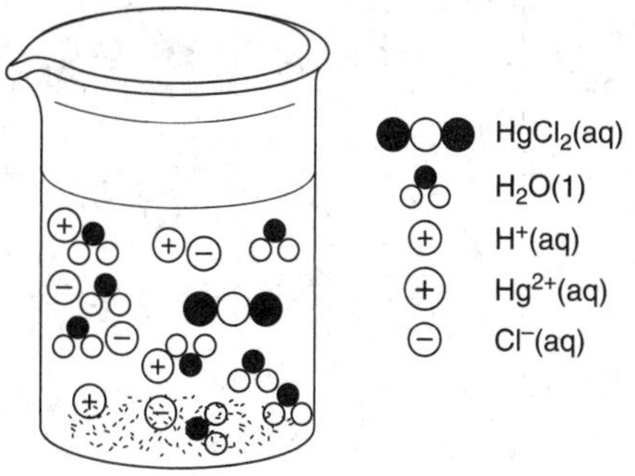

**50.** A dilute aqueous solution of potassium bromide, KBr, is heated to the boiling point. Which of the following best represents this system?

(A)

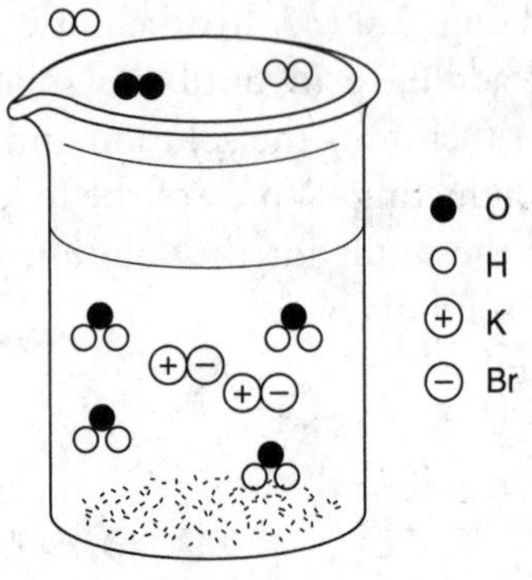


(B)

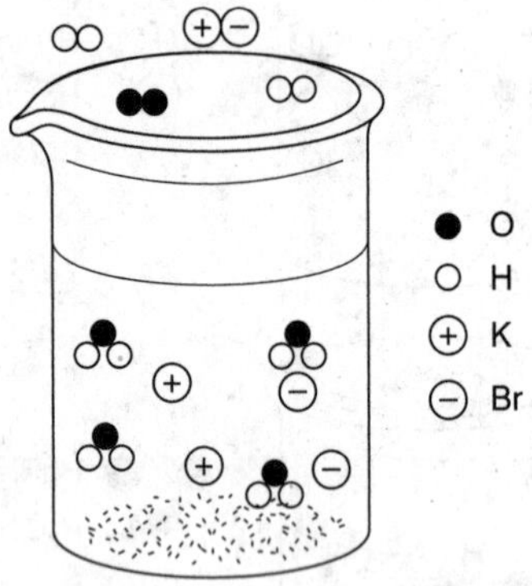


(C)

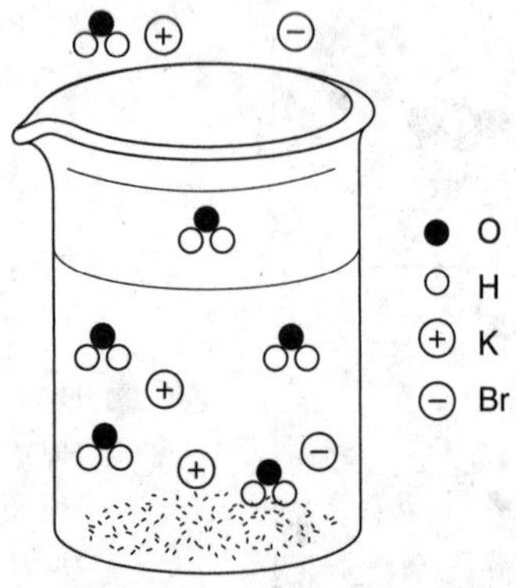


(D)

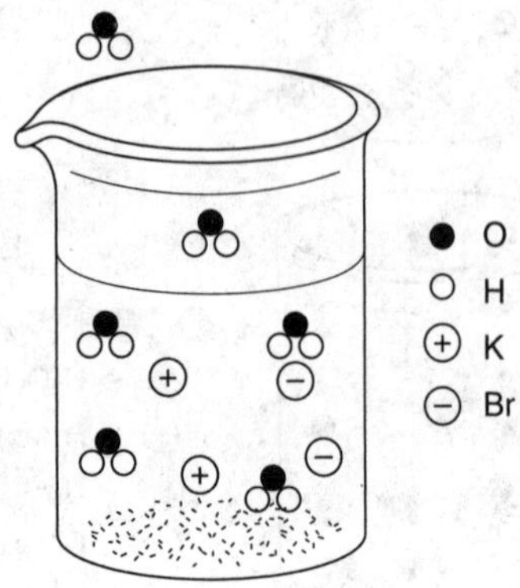


The average distribution of bromine isotopes on Earth is in the following table:

| ISOTOPE | PERCENT ABUNDANCE |
|---|---|
| $^{79}Br$ | 50.7% |
| $^{81}Br$ | 49.3% |

The highest mass peaks in the mass spectrum of methyl bromide, $CH_3Br$, are at 94 and 96 atomic mass units (there are smaller peaks corresponding to the small quantities of the less common isotopes of carbon and hydrogen). The spectrum plot shown is of this region.

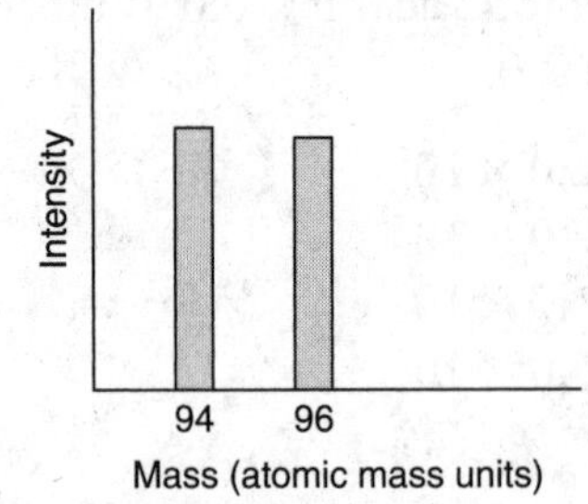


The mass spectrum for methylene bromide, $CH_2Br_2$, is more complicated in that there are three main peaks in the highest mass region (again ignoring minor contributions from other carbon and hydrogen isotopes). Methylene bromide has a mass of about 174 atomic mass units.

**51.** Which of the following is the best representation of the mass spectrum of $CH_2Br_2$ in the 174 region?

(A)

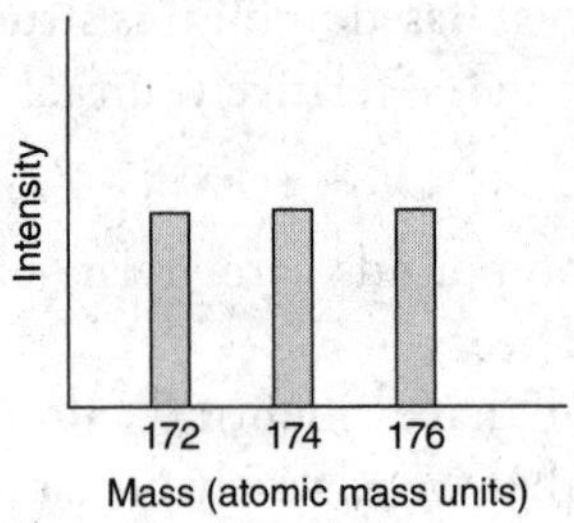


(B)

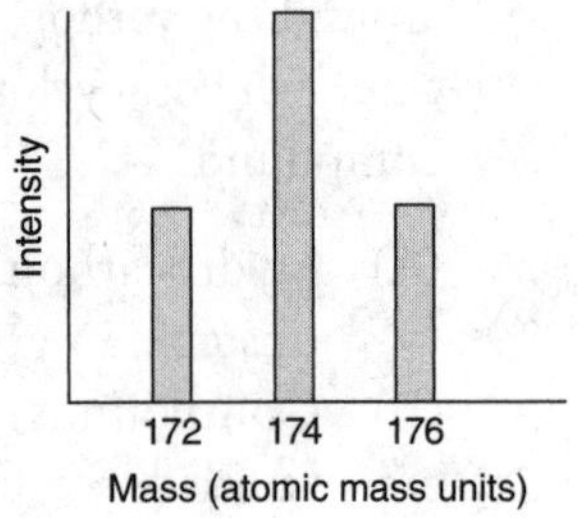


(C)

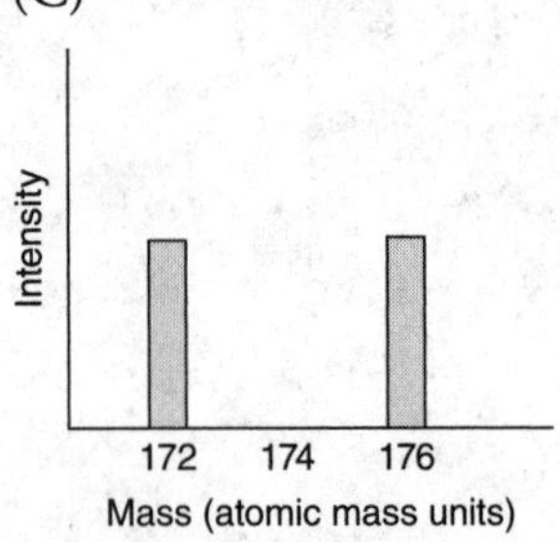


(D)

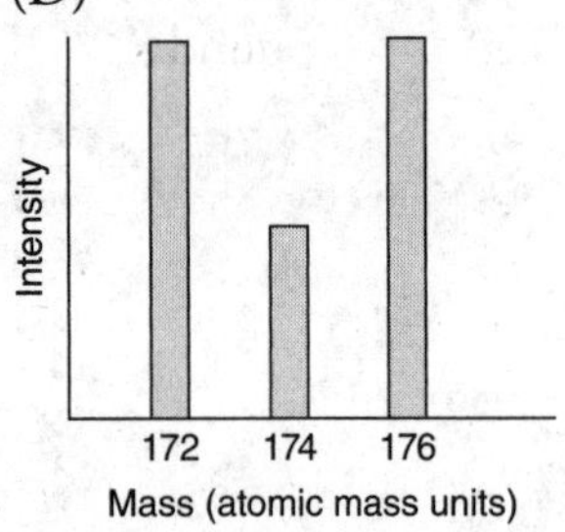


**GO ON TO THE NEXT PAGE**

52. There are three steps in the formation of a solution. It is necessary to overcome the intermolecular forces present within the solute. It is also necessary to overcome the intermolecular forces present within the solvent. Both of these steps require energy related to the strength of the intermolecular forces. The final step in the formation of a solution involves the creation of new intermolecular forces between the solute and solvent. This energy release is related to the strength of the intermolecular forces created. Which of the following illustrates a situation most likely to require the least amount of energy to overcome the intermolecular forces?

(A) $CaO(s) + H_2O(l)$
(B) $CH_3OH(l) + H_2O(l)$
(C) $CCl_4(l) + Cl_2(g)$
(D) $CCl_4(l) + CH_3OH(l)$

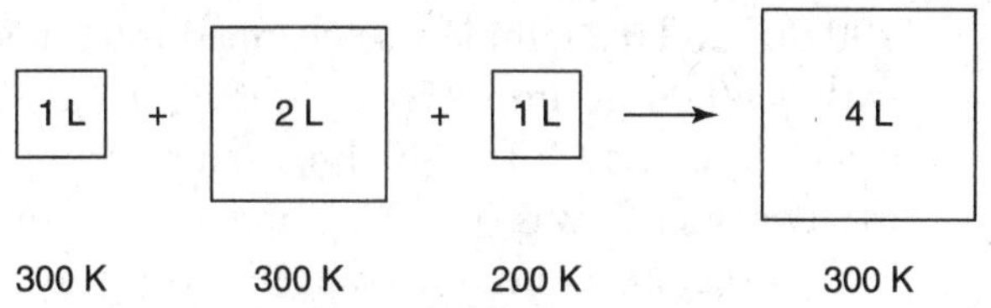


53. The contents in the three containers on the left in the diagram above are transferred to the container on the right. The volumes of the original containers are exactly the values indicated. The pressure in the first three containers is 1.0 atm. What is the pressure in the container on the right?

(A) 3.0 atm
(B) 4.0 atm
(C) 1.1 atm
(D) 0.50 atm

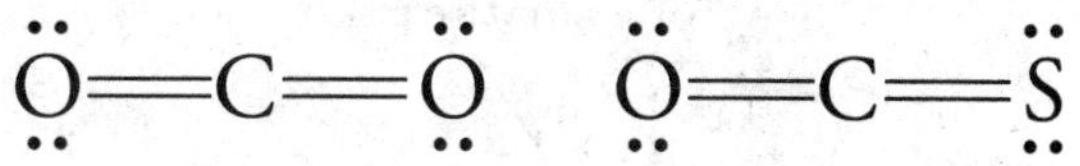

54. The diagram above shows the structure of molecules of $CS_2$ and COS. The boiling point of COS is 223 K, and the boiling point of $CS_2$ is 319 K. Which of the following is the best explanation of why the boiling point of $CS_2$ is higher?

(A) The molar mass of $CS_2$ is greater.
(B) COS has weaker covalent bonds than $CS_2$.
(C) Only $CS_2$ can form intermolecular dipole–dipole forces.
(D) COS has stronger intermolecular forces because it is polar and $CS_2$ is not.

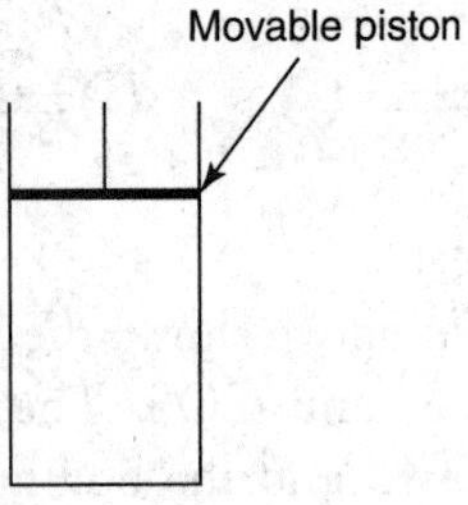


$CO(g) + Cl(g) \leftrightarrows COCl(g) \qquad \Delta H = -109$ kJ

**55.** The above equilibrium is established in a closed system with a movable piston. After establishing equilibrium, the piston is rapidly moved up (pressure change). Which of the following graphs best illustrates the rate of the reverse reaction as the system returns to equilibrium?

(A)

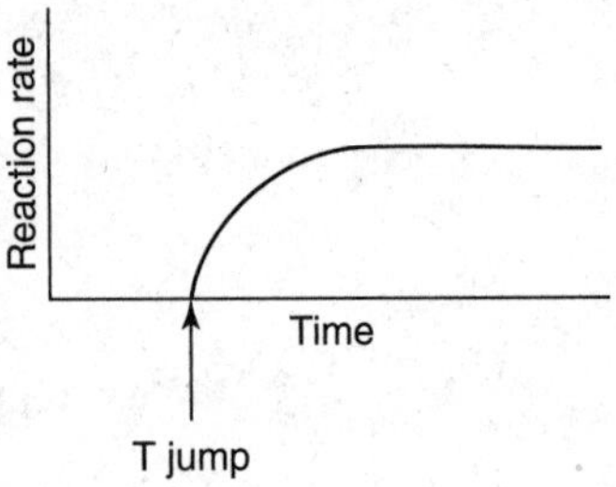


(B)

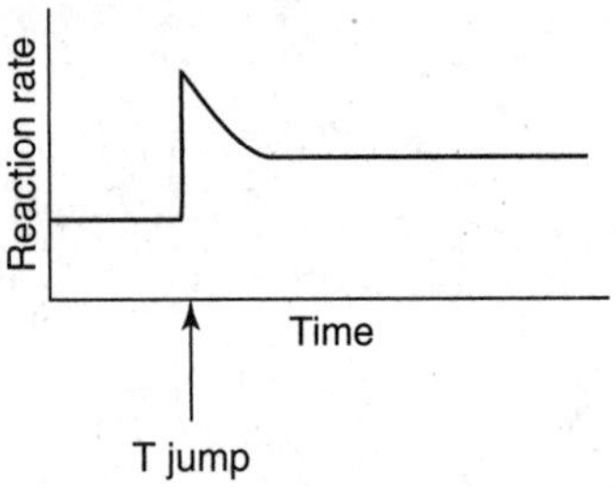


(C)

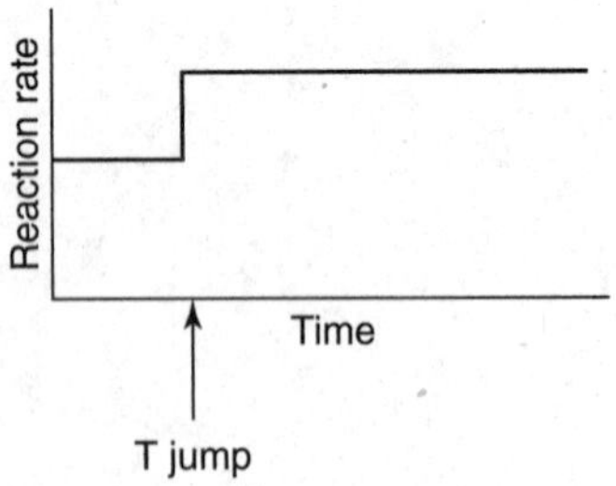


(D)

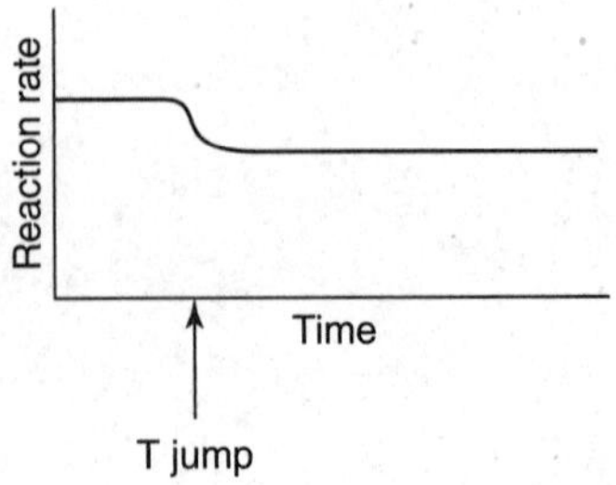


$2\ I^-(aq) + H_2O_2(aq) + 2\ H^+(aq) \rightarrow I_2(aq) + 2\ H_2O(l)$

The proposed mechanism for the above reaction is as follows:

Step 1: $H_2O_2(aq) + I^-(aq) \rightarrow HOI(aq) + OH^-(aq)$ (slow) $k_1$

Step 2: $HOI(aq) + I^-(aq) \rightarrow I_2(aq) + OH^-(aq)$ (fast) $k_2$

Step 3: $2\ OH^-(aq) + 2\ H^+(aq) \rightarrow 2\ H_2O(l)$ (fast) $k_3$

**56.** What is the rate law expression for this reaction?

(A) Rate = $k[H_2O_2][I^-]$
(B) Rate = $k[HOI][I^-]$
(C) Rate = $k[H_2O_2]$
(D) Rate = $k\dfrac{[I_2]}{[I^-]^2[H^+]^2[H_2O_2]}$

**57.** A 30.00-g sample of metal (X) was heated to 100.00°C. This sample was clamped in contact with a 40.00-g sample of a different metal (Y) originally at 25.00°C. The final temperature of the two metals was 37.30°C, and no heat was lost to the surroundings. What is one possible conclusion from this experiment?

(A) The heat lost by X was greater than the heat gained by the Y.
(B) The heat lost by X was equal to the heat gained by Y.
(C) The heat lost by X was less than the heat gained by Y.
(D) The final temperature was incorrectly determined, as it should be the average (62.50°C).

**GO ON TO THE NEXT PAGE**

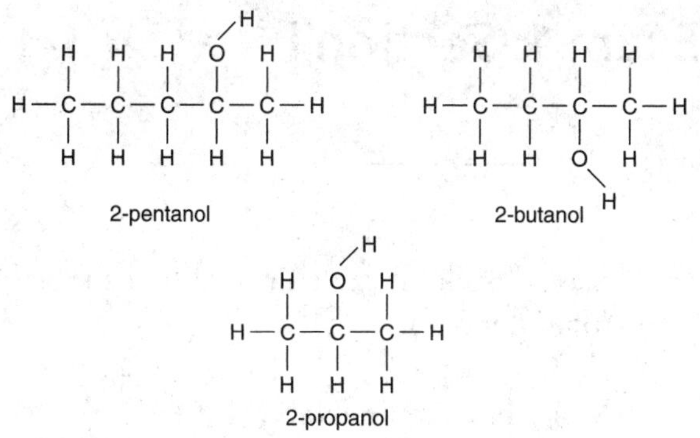


| COMPOUND | BOILING POINT (°C) | MOLAR MASS (g MOL$^{-1}$) |
|---|---|---|
| 2-pentanol | 118.9 | 88.15 |
| 2-butanol | 99.5 | 74.14 |
| 2-propanol | 82.4 | 60.11 |

**58.** Which of the following best explains why the boiling point of 2-propanol is lower than the other two compounds in the diagram and table above?

(A) Larger molecules get tangled and cannot escape each other.
(B) It has weaker hydrogen bonds.
(C) It is the lightest of the three.
(D) It is a more symmetrical molecule.

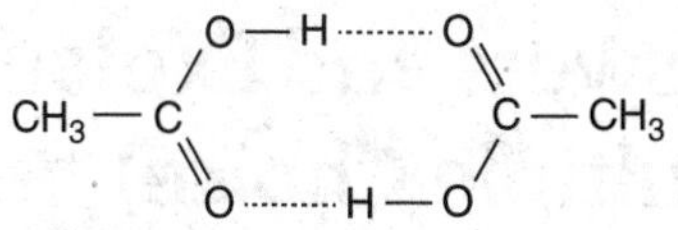

**59.** The Dumas method is a procedure for determining the molar mass of a gas. In this procedure, the mass of a gas is divided by the moles of gas determined from the ideal gas equation ($n = PV/RT$). The molar masses of some compounds, such as acetic acid, illustrated above, show significant deviations from the "correct" values. Why does the presence of dimers as illustrated make it unlikely to obtain an accurate molar mass of acids, such as acetic acid?

(A) Acetic acid, like all acids, will lose a hydrogen ion, so the molar mass is that of the acetate ion, which is less than that of acetic acid.
(B) Acetic acid is a liquid at room temperature, and its boiling point is too high to get accurate results.
(C) Acids are too reactive to give accurate results.
(D) The presence of strong intermolecular forces (hydrogen bonding) makes the gas nonideal; therefore the ideal gas law is not applicable.

**60.** In which of the following groups are the species listed correctly in order of increasing ionization energy?

(A) Sr, Ca, Ba
(B) Se, Tc, Ba
(C) Mn, Fe, Ni
(D) Cl, Br, I

**STOP. End of AP Chemistry Practice Exam 1, Section I (Multiple Choice).**

# › Answers and Explanations for Exam 1, Section I (Multiple Choice)

**1. A**—The reaction is an oxidation–reduction reaction since the sulfide ion ($S^{2-}$) undergoes oxidation to elemental sulfur and the azide ion ($N_3^-$) undergoes reduction.

**2. B**—It is necessary to remove the ammonia from the gas; otherwise the part of the volume generated would be due to the ammonia. Since ammonia is a base, it will react with the acid.

**3. D**—The pressure inside the flask is the sum of the partial pressures. Therefore, the pressure of nitrogen gas is the total pressure (748.2 torr) minus the vapor pressure of water (27.0 torr). The leveling of the water in the beaker and flask adjusted the pressure in the flask to the external (barometric) pressure.

**4. B**—When the two liquid levels are the same the pressures must be equal. In this case, both pressures are equal to the barometric pressure.

**5. D**—The ideal gas equation ($PV = nRT$) gives the moles of nitrogen gas formed.

$$\text{Moles } N_2 = n = \frac{PV}{RT}$$

$$= \frac{(721.2 \text{ torr}/760 \text{ torr})(0.315 \text{ L})}{(0.08206 \text{ L atm mol}^{-1} \text{ K}^{-1})(300.2 \text{ K})}$$

$$= 0.0121 \text{ moles } N_2$$

It is easier to approximate the answer by simple rounding as:

$$= \frac{(1 \text{ atm})(0.3 \text{ L})}{(0.08 \text{ L atm mol}^{-1} \text{ K}^{-1})(300 \text{ K})} \approx$$

$$\frac{(1)}{(0.1)}\left(\frac{0.3}{300}\right) = \left(\frac{0.3}{30.0}\right) = 0.01 \text{ mole}$$

**6. C**—The moles of nitrogen gas formed equal the moles of sodium azide reacting (see the balanced chemical equation). If the sample were pure sodium azide, the mass of sodium azide would be (176.604 – 175.245) g = 1.359-g sample (= g $NaN_3$). The moles of sodium azide are the mass of sodium azide divided by its molar mass (65.0 g $mol^{-1}$).

$$\text{Moles } N_2 = \text{moles } NaN_3 = \frac{1.359 \text{ g}}{65.0 \text{ g mol}^{-1}} \approx$$

$$\frac{1.359}{65} \approx \frac{1.3}{5(13)} \approx \frac{0.13}{5} \approx 0.026$$

Due to rounding, the actual answer must be a little smaller (0.0209 moles).

**7. A**—Sulfur dioxide gas is soluble in water and, while less soluble in dilute acid, some would still dissolve to give a smaller volume.

**8. A**—This represents an ion–dipole force, which is stronger than a hydrogen bond (B), a dipole–dipole force (C), or a London dispersion force (D).

**9. C**—The decay reaction is first order; therefore, after one half-life, 50% would remain. Another half-life would reduce this by one-half to 25% and a third half-life would reduce the remaining material by 12.5%. Thus, three half-lives = (50 + 25 + 12.5)% = 87.5% decayed. The total amount decayed is 88%. For this reason, 24 days must be three half-lives of about 8 days each. Note: this is not a nuclear chemistry problem; it is a kinetics problem.

**10. C**—The best choice to prepare the buffer is the one where the p$K_a$ is closest to the desired pH. It is possible to estimate the p$K_a$ for an acid (without a calculator) by taking the negative of the exponent for the different $K_a$ values. This gives 1 for $HIO_3$, 2 for $HIO_4$, 4 for $HNO_2$, and 10 for HCN. The $HNO_2$ has the value closest to the desired pH. It would not be a good choice since the p$K_a$ is so far from the pH; however, it is the best choice.

**11. D**—These are salts of a weak acid and a strong base. The anion in such salts undergo hydrolysis. The hydrolysis of an anion (conjugate base) yields hydroxide ion (increases the pH). This hydrolysis is a $K_b$ equilibrium. The smaller the $K_a$ of the acid, the larger the $K_b$ of the conjugate base. A larger $K_b$ means a stronger base and a higher pH.

**12. A**—In order to get good results when titrating a weak base, it is important to use as strong an acid as possible to get a sharp endpoint. $HIO_3$ is the strongest acid in the table.

**13. B**—The position ½ H is halfway to the first equivalence point. This is in the first buffer region of the titration. The pH at the halfway point is equal to p$K_a$ (= –log $K_a$). The value of $K_{a1}$ is $8.0 \times 10^{-5}$, which gives a p$K_a$ of 4.1. However, without a calculator, consider the $K_{a1} \approx 10^{-4}$, which allows you to estimate a $K_{a1}$ = 4 [the –log of a number is the negative of the power (exponent) of 10].

**14. A**—To reach H, it is necessary to convert all the ascorbic acid to the hydrogen ascorbate ion, which means the moles of hydrogen ascorbate ion formed must equal the moles of ascorbic acid originally present. The moles of hydrogen ascorbate ion formed would require the same number of moles of base as that required to convert the ascorbic acid to hydrogen ascorbate. Equal moles would mean equal volumes added. If G is not twice H, there must be some contaminant present to react with the base.

**15. D**—In any acid–base titration, it is always easier to use a strong base (and a strong acid). Potassium hydroxide, KOH, is the only strong base among the choices.

**16. B**—The titration of a weak acid with a strong base always has an equivalence point above 7. A pH = 7 occurs in the titration of a strong acid with a strong base.

**17. D**—Since $K_{a2} = 1.6 \times 10^{-12}$, the pH at the equivalence point would be greater than 12, which is too high for a simple titration.

**18. B**—All can behave as Brønsted bases (accept a hydrogen ion). Only B cannot behave as an acid (donate a hydrogen ion).

**19. C**—Initially, doubling the volume will result in halving the concentrations (0.050 *M*). Next, consider the reaction. The balanced equation is: $K_2CrO_4(aq) + 2\ AgNO_3(aq) \rightarrow Ag_2CrO_4(s) + 2\ KNO_3(aq)$. The silver ion is the limiting reagent (check this for yourself using a calculator), so very little $Ag^+(aq)$ remains in solution (due to its $K_{sp}$). The precipitation of silver chromate reduces the chromate concentration from 0.050 *M*. The nitrate does not change (soluble), remaining 0.050 *M*. Since two potassium ions (soluble) are formed per potassium chromate, after mixing, the potassium ion concentration was 0.10 *M* and does not change (soluble).

**20. D**—To determine the molar mass of the gas it is necessary to know the mass of the gas (determined) and the moles of the gas. The ideal gas equation is necessary to determine the number of moles of gas present. To use the equation, it is necessary to know the temperature (measured), volume (determined = volume of displaced water), and pressure of the gas. The pressure of the gas is equal to the barometric pressure minus the vapor pressure of water. Water, whenever present, will contribute its vapor pressure.

**21. A**—This is a Hess's law problem requiring you to manipulate the given equations to produce the desired equation. It is possible to begin with any of the given equations. Take the given equations in order. Use the first equation as is, double the second equation (doubles the $\Delta H°$), and reverse the third equation (reverses the sign of $\Delta H°$). The results are:

$H_2(g) + 1/2\ O_2(g) \rightarrow H_2O(l)$ (–300 kJ)

$2\ C(s) + 2\ O_2(g) \rightarrow 2\ CO_2(g)$ (–800 kJ)

$H_2O(l) + 2\ CO_2(g) \rightarrow C_2H_2(g) + 5/2\ O_2(g)$ (+1300 kJ)

Add the three equations together and cancel any species appearing on opposite sides of the reaction arrow. (If you get anything other than the equation sought, you made an error.)

$2\ C(s) + H_2(g) \rightarrow C_2H_2(g)$ 200 kJ

**22. A**—Since the compound is less soluble in hot water, the solution process must be exothermic. Exothermic processes shift toward the starting materials [solid cerium(III) sulfate] at higher temperatures.

**23. C**—The gases are all at the same temperature; therefore, their average kinetic energies are the same. Since kinetic energy is equal to ½ $mv^2$, ½ $m_1v_1^2$ = ½ $m_2v_2^2$; the subscripts refer to two different gases. Setting $m_1$ = 16 g $mol^{-1}$ and $v_2$ = ½ $v_1$ gives ½ $16v_1^2$ = ½ $m_2$(½ $v_1$)$^2$; this leads to $16v_1^2 = m$ (¼ $v_1^2$). Rearranging and canceling $v_1$ yields $m^2$ = 4(16) = 64 g $mol^{-1}$.

**24. A**—The smaller the molecule and the less polar (more nonpolar) the gas is, the smaller the deviation from ideal gas behavior. Helium is the smallest, and it is nonpolar. The greatest deviation would be $SO_2$, which is the largest and the only one of the gases listed that is polar.

**25. A**—Escaping gas would decrease the number of moles. Less gas remaining in the container would mean less pressure. The faster-moving gas molecules would escape faster, lowering the average velocity of those remaining in the container. A lower average velocity means a lower temperature.

**26. C**—It is necessary to use the half-life relationship for first-order kinetics. This relationship is $t_{1/2} = 0.693/k$, and $t_{1/2} = \left(\dfrac{0.693}{86\ h^{-1}}\right)\left(\dfrac{3{,}600\ s}{1\ h}\right) =$ 29 s. To save time on the exam you can approximate (no calculator) this equation as $t_{1/2} = \left(\dfrac{0.7}{90}\right)\left(\dfrac{3{,}600}{1}\right)$. Dividing 3,600 by 90 gives 40, and 40 times 0.7 is equal to 28. If the half-life is ≈ 28 s, then the time (58 s) is equivalent to about two half-lives, so one-fourth of the sample should remain. Remaining mass $= \dfrac{0.0500\ g}{4} =$ 0.0125 g.

**27. D**—The loss of 0.20 mol of CO means that 0.40 mol of $H_2$ reacted (leaving 0.20 mol) and 0.20 mol of $CH_3OH$ formed. Dividing all the moles by the volume gives the molarity, and:

$$K_c = \frac{[CH_3OH]}{[CO][H_2]^2} = \frac{[0.20]}{[0.40][0.20]^2}$$

$$= \frac{1}{[0.40][0.20]} = \frac{1}{0.080} = 12$$

**28. A**—Based upon the stoichiometry of the reaction, $H_2(g)$ will form twice as fast as $CH_3OH(g)$ disappears, while the rate of CO(g) formation will equal the rate of $CH_3OH(g)$ loss. The numerical values are the same; however, the rates have opposite signs.

**29. B**—At equilibrium, there is no net change because the forward and reverse reactions are going at the same rate. At equilibrium, the forward and reverse reactions will be going at the same rate and the pressure will not be changing.

**30. B**—As the reaction approaches equilibrium, there is a net decrease in the number of moles of gas present. A decrease in the number of moles of gas will lead to a decrease in pressure. If the system is in equilibrium, there must be some of the reactants and products present (nothing can be 0).

**31. B**—The loss of 1.5 atm of $CH_3OH(g)$, based on stoichiometry, leads to the formation of 1.5 atm of CO(g) and 3.0 atm of $H_2(g)$; therefore, the net change is $(-1.5 + 1.5 + 3.0)$ atm = 3.0 atm.

**32. A**—Oxygen (odorless) evolves at the anode (positive) and ammonia (distinctive odor) evolves at the cathode (negative). From the choices given, the only gas with a distinctive odor that could form is ammonia, $NH_3$. For this reason, the nitrite ion half-reaction must be the cathode reaction. The anode half-reaction must be the reverse of one of the reactions in the table. The only one of the half-reactions given that generates an odorless gas is the one involving oxygen, $O_2$. Do not forget that an electrolysis cell is nonspontaneous with a negative cell potential.

**33. A**—The lead electrode is the cathode (−0.13 V), and the chromium electrode is the anode (reverse sign, +0.91 V). Cell voltage = (−0.13 + 0.91) V = +0.78 V. The standard voltage of a galvanic cell is always positive, so you would know you made a mistake if you reversed the wrong half-reaction.

**34. D**—The formation of aluminum metal is a reduction and must occur in the cathode compartment. It is necessary to consider all possible half-reactions that might occur during electrolysis. Of the half-reactions listed, only the reduction of water and the reduction of aluminum ions are applicable to this experiment. For any electrolysis, the half-reaction requiring the least amount of energy will take place. So, while it is possible to reduce both water and the aluminum ion, the reduction potential for water is lower (requiring less energy), so water will reduce in preference to aluminum ion.

**35. B**—In order for substance A to reduce substance B, substance A must be a stronger reducing agent than substance B. Aluminum is a strong reducing agent as indicated by the large negative potential in the table (−1.66 V). The only substance in the table that has a more negative potential is rubidium, Rb (−2.93 V).

**36. C**—Silver appears twice in the list of half-reactions, once in the simple reduction of silver ions and once in the reduction of silver chloride, AgCl. The AgCl half-reaction clearly shows that this compound is a solid. This solid will form as the silver ion in the silver nitrate solution reacts with chloride ion from the potassium chloride in the salt bridge. The formation of solid silver chloride will alter the concentration of the silver ion, which leads to a change in the cell potential.

**37. B**—The weakest acid (smallest $K_a$) will have the highest pH at the endpoint.

**38. D**—The buffer capacity only depends on the number of moles present. All three solutions have the same number of moles.

**39. C**—Less acid would require less than the ideal amount of base to reach the endpoint. Therefore, the endpoint would occur too soon.

**40. D**—An acid contaminant must be present, and the excess acid would require additional base to titrate this acid in addition to the phenol. Do not be distracted by the "OH" in phenol. It has a $K_a$; therefore, it must be an acid.

**41. B**—Since only the plot of 1/[A] versus time yielded a straight line, this implies that the reaction is second order in A. If the reaction were first order, the graph of ln [A] versus time would have given a straight line.

**42. C**—The electron configuration of carbon is $1s^2 2s^2 2p^2$. The removal of the last electron (2p) requires the least amount of energy. Note that answer D is impossible as there is no such thing as a 1p orbital.

**43. A**—The compound with the highest boiling point has the strongest intermolecular forces. This is only valid if the molar masses are similar, which they are in the problem.

**44. C**—The melting points of ionic materials depend upon the lattice energy. The higher the lattice energy, the higher the melting point is. Lattice energies depend upon the sizes of the ions and the magnitude of the charge. All three metal ions are approximately the same size; therefore, the size factor is minimal. This leaves the magnitude of the charge, and lanthanum, with the largest charge, should have the highest lattice energy.

**45. A**—The lattice energy depends upon both the charge and the size of the ions involved. The greater the charge is, the greater the lattice energy will be (higher melting point). There is an inverse relationship between the lattice energy and the size of the ion. Therefore, the smaller the ion is, the greater the lattice energy will be (higher melting point).

**46. C**—The key relationship is $\Delta G = \Delta H - T\Delta S$. If the reaction is nonspontaneous at 1 atm and 298 K, then $\Delta G > 0$. For this reaction to become spontaneous ($\Delta G < 0$) at a lower temperature, the reaction must be impeded by entropy (entropy was negative). The enthalpy must be negative, or the reaction could never be spontaneous.

**47. A**—Enter the information into the $K_a$ expression. A pH of 2.0 means that $[H^+] = 10^{-2.0}$ M or $1.0 \times 10^{-2}$.

$$K_a = \frac{[H^+][A^-]}{[HA]};\ [H^+] = [A^-] = 1.0 \times 10^{-2}$$

$$[HA] = 0.060 - 1.0 \times 10^{-2} = 0.05;\ \text{therefore,}$$

$$K_a = \frac{[1.0\times10^{-2}][1.0\times10^{-2}]}{[0.05]} = 0.002 = 2 \times 10^{-3}.$$

As always, on the multiple-choice part of the exam (no calculator), you must estimate.

**48. C**—A carbon atom with four single bonds should be tetrahedral. Tetrahedral atoms have an ideal bond angle of 109.5°. However, the carbon atoms in cyclopropane are at the corners of an equilateral triangle, where the ideal angle is 60°. The discrepancy between the two ideal bond angles leads to the relative instability of cyclopropane. This is a VSEPR problem, not an organic chemistry problem. Organic compounds serve as many good examples, which do not involve organic chemistry.

**49. B**—The reaction is:

$HgO(s) + 2\ HCl(aq) \rightarrow HgCl_2(aq) + H_2O(l)$

When the last of the solid dissolves, we are at the stoichiometric point indicated by this reaction. No HgO remains and the chemist stopped adding HCl at this point, so there is no excess HCl present. The $HgCl_2$ must be soluble because there is no solid remaining in the beaker. Since the resultant solution is nonconducting, there must be no ions present; therefore, the products must be molecular species. The best answer should show only water molecules and $HgCl_2$ molecules.

**50. D**—This answer shows the potassium ions and bromide ions as separate ions in solution, which is a property of strong electrolytes. The water molecules are present in both the liquid and gas states. Other diagrams incorrectly show water dissociating, potassium bromide ion pairs, and potassium bromide vaporizing.

**51. B**—There are two bromine isotopes with approximately equal abundances, which is why there are two nearly equally intense peaks in the mass spectrum of $CH_3Br$. One of the peaks corresponds to $CH_3{}^{79}Br$ and the other corresponds to $CH_3{}^{81}Br$. The separation between the peaks is two mass units because the isotopic masses differ by two units. In the case of $CH_2Br_2$, the possible combinations and masses are $CH_2{}^{79}Br{}^{79}Br$ (172), $CH_2{}^{79}Br{}^{81}Br$ (174), $CH_2{}^{81}Br{}^{79}Br$ (174), and $CH_2{}^{81}Br{}^{81}Br$ (176). The four possible combinations are equally probable since the abundances of the two bromine isotopes are nearly equal. If they all had different masses, the mass spectrum would consist of four equally intense peaks. However, two of the combinations have the same mass, which results in the peak at 174 being twice as intense as the other two peaks.

**52. C**—In diagram A, the forces to overcome are ionic bonding (lattice energy) and hydrogen bonding. In diagram B, the forces to overcome are hydrogen bonding for both the solvent and the solute. In diagram C, the forces to overcome are London dispersion forces in both cases; however, since the chlorine is a gas, the London dispersion forces have already been overcome. In diagram D, the forces to overcome are London dispersion forces and hydrogen bonding. Since London dispersion forces are normally weaker than the other intermolecular forces, answer C requires the least amount of energy.

**53. C**—There are several ways of solving this problem. One way is to determine the moles present in the original containers, which must be the same as in the final container. In each case, moles $= n = PV/RT$. Numbering the containers from left to right as 1, 2, 3, and 4 gives (followed by estimating):

$$n_4 = n_1 + n_2 + n_3$$

$$n_1 + n_2 + n_3 = \left(\frac{(1.0\text{ atm})(1\text{ L})}{\left(0.08206\,\frac{\text{L atm}}{\text{mol K}}\right)(300\text{ K})}\right) + \left(\frac{(1.0\text{ atm})(2\text{ L})}{\left(0.08206\,\frac{\text{L atm}}{\text{mol K}}\right)(300\text{ K})}\right) + \left(\frac{(1.0\text{ atm})(1\text{ L})}{\left(0.08206\,\frac{\text{L atm}}{\text{mol K}}\right)(200\text{ K})}\right)$$

$$= \left(\frac{1}{(0.08206)(300)}\right) + \left(\frac{2}{(0.08206)(300)}\right) + \left(\frac{1}{(0.08206)(200)}\right)$$

$$= \left(\frac{3}{(0.08206)(300)}\right) + \left(\frac{1}{(0.08206)(200)}\right)$$

$$= \left(\frac{1}{(0.08206)(100)}\right) + \left(\frac{1}{(0.08206)(200)}\right)$$

$$= \left(\frac{1}{0.08206}\right)\left(\frac{1}{100} + \frac{1}{200}\right)\text{mol}$$

$$P_4 = n_4RT/V$$

$$= \frac{\left(\left(\frac{1}{0.08206}\right)\left(\frac{1}{100} + \frac{1}{200}\right)\right)\left(0.08206\,\frac{\text{L atm}}{\text{mol K}}\right)(300\text{ K})}{4\text{ L}}$$

$$= \frac{\left(\left(\frac{1}{100} + \frac{1}{200}\right)\text{mol}\right)(\text{atm})(300)}{4\text{ L}}$$

$$= (0.0100 + 0.0050)\text{ atm }(75.0) = 1.1\text{ atm}$$

On the exam, it is not necessary to write out all these steps. Take shortcuts.

**54. A**—Stronger intermolecular forces lead to higher boiling points. Even though COS has dipole–dipole forces, which are usually stronger than the London dispersion forces present in $CS_2$, the greater molar mass of $CS_2$ leads to a London dispersion force contribution that is sufficient to compensate for the general trend of dipole–dipole forces being stronger than London dispersion forces. This is why comparisons should only be made between molecules of similar molecular masses.

**55. B**—At equilibrium, the reverse reaction is going at a steady rate (equal to that of the forward reaction and not equal to 0). A sudden decrease in pressure will cause the rate of the reverse reaction to increase to generate more gas to increase the pressure (Le Châtelier's principle). The rate will eventually slow and become constant again (at a new equilibrium).

**56. A**—Only the slow step in a mechanism leads to the rate law. There is one $H_2O_2$ and one $I^-$ in the slow step; therefore, one of each of these will be in the rate law. Answer D contains an equilibrium constant expression, which does not apply to kinetics problems like this one.

**57. B**—This must be true according to the Law of Conservation of Energy (First Law of Thermodynamics). Answers A and C violate the Law of Conservation of Energy. For the final temperature to be the average, the metals would need to have equal masses and equal specific heats. The masses given in the problem are clearly different, and it is extremely unlikely that two different metals would have the same specific heat.

**58. C**—All three compounds are capable of hydrogen bonding; therefore, this cannot be the cause of difference. In general, all other things being equal, it takes less energy to move a lighter molecule from the liquid state to the gaseous state. The same principles apply even if the molecules happen to be organic; do not be distracted.

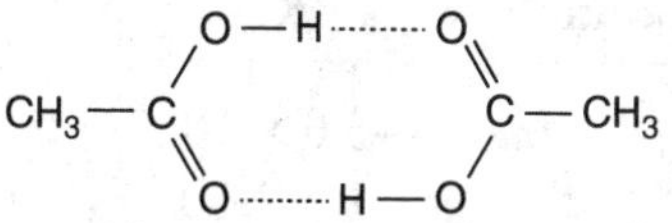


**59. D**—Strong hydrogen bonds hold two molecules of acetic acid together. Ideal gases have no intermolecular forces. Therefore, the ideal gas law used in the experiment is invalid because of the presence of strong intermolecular forces.

**60. C**—Increasing ionization energy applies to an element higher in a column on the periodic table, or in a position further to the left in a period on the periodic table. Note: this type of explanation is unacceptable on the free-response portion of the AP Exam, where your explanation would require additional information such as a discussion of radii and effective nuclear charges.

# › AP Chemistry Practice Exam 1, Section II (Free Response)

Time—1 hour and 45 minutes

Answer the following questions in the time allowed. You may use a calculator and the resources at the back of the book. Write the answers on separate sheets of paper.

| Compound | $K_{sp}$ |
|---|---|
| $AgIO_3$ | $3.0 \times 10^{-8}$ |
| $Ba(IO_3)_2$ | $1.5 \times 10^{-9}$ |
| $Cu(IO_3)_2$ | $7.4 \times 10^{-8}$ |
| $La(IO_3)_3$ | $6.2 \times 10^{-12}$ |
| $Ni(IO_3)_2$ | $1.4 \times 10^{-8}$ |
| $Zn(IO_3)_2$ | $2.0 \times 10^{-8}$ |

***Question 1***

Use the $K_{sp}$ data given above to answer the following questions.
A chemist is investigating the chemistry of metal iodate compounds. Some of her data are in the $K_{sp}$ table given above. In addition to this information, she knows that sodium iodate, $NaIO_3$, is soluble in water and that iodic acid, $HIO_3$, has $K_a = 0.16$ at 25°C.

(a) (i) Write a balanced chemical equation for the dissolution equilibrium of nickel(II) iodate, $Ni(IO_3)_2$, in water.
(ii) Write the $K_{sp}$ relationship for the dissolution equilibrium of nickel(II) iodate.
(iii) What is the concentration of iodate ions in a saturated solution of nickel(II) iodate?

(b) What is the solubility of copper(II) iodate, $Cu(IO_3)_2$, in a 0.10-*M* copper(II) nitrate, $Cu(NO_3)_2$, solution?

(c) (i) How does the solubility of silver iodate, $AgIO_3$, in 1.0 *M* nitric acid compare to its solubility in pure water?
(ii) Explain your answer to part (c) (i).

(d) Which of the following will produce a higher iodate ion concentration in solution, barium iodate, $Ba(IO_3)_2$, or lanthanum iodate, $La(IO_3)_3$? What is the iodate ion concentration for each of these two compounds?

(e) Write a balanced net ionic equation for the addition of a sodium iodate solution to a zinc nitrate, $Zn(NO_3)_2$ solution. Recall that sodium nitrate, $NaNO_3$, is very soluble in water.

*Question 2*

Selenous acid, $H_2SeO_3$, reacts with hydrogen peroxide, $H_2O_2$, in acid solution according to the following equation:

$$H_2SeO_3(aq) + H_2O_2(aq) \rightarrow HSeO_4^-(aq) + H^+(aq) + H_2O(l)$$

The following information was obtained in a series of reactions:

| EXPERIMENT | INITIAL CONCENTRATIONS (MOLARITIES) | | | RATE OF DISAPPEARANCE OF $H_2SeO_3$ ($M\ s^{-1}$) |
|---|---|---|---|---|
| | $[H_2SeO_3]$ | $[H_2O_2]$ | $[H^+]$ | |
| 1 | 0.100 | 0.100 | 0.100 | $7.4 \times 10^{-8}$ |
| 2 | 0.200 | 0.100 | 0.100 | $2.9 \times 10^{-7}$ |
| 3 | 0.100 | 0.200 | 0.100 | $1.5 \times 10^{-7}$ |
| 4 | 0.100 | 0.100 | 0.200 | $3.7 \times 10^{-8}$ |

(a) Determine the order of the reaction for $H_2SeO_3$, $H_2O_2$, and $H^+$. Justify your answers.

(b) Write the rate law for the reaction.

(c) Determine the value of the rate constant including units.

(d) (i) Is $H_2O_2$ being oxidized or reduced?
(ii) What is the oxidation state of oxygen in $H_2O_2$?
(iii) Write the balanced half-reaction for $H_2O_2$ in this reaction.

GO ON TO THE NEXT PAGE

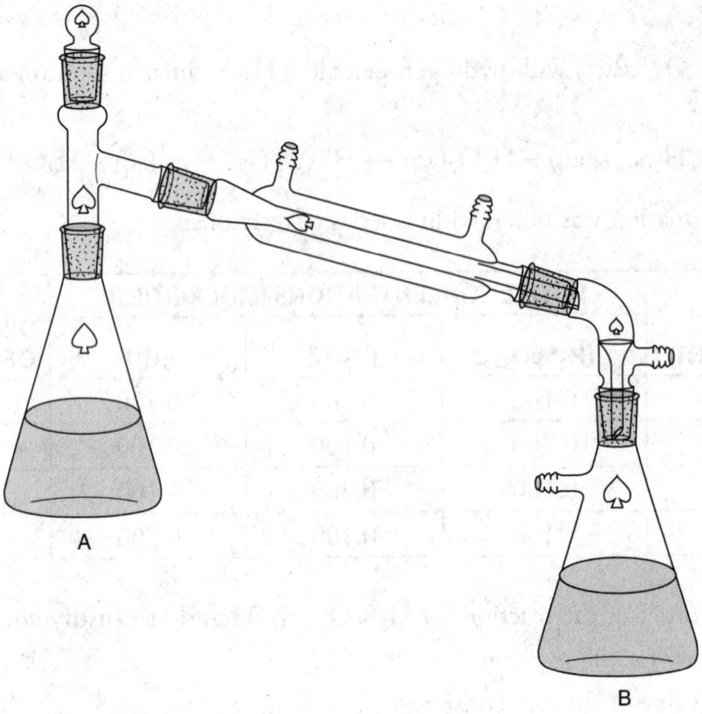


*Question 3*

A student wishes to analyze a sample of ammonium sulfate, $(NH_4)_2SO_4$, contaminated with sodium sulfate, $Na_2SO_4$. She constructs the apparatus shown above to carry out this analysis. She weighs 1.002 grams of sample into flask A and dissolves the solid in 50 mL of water. Then she adds 50.00 mL of 0.4000 *M* hydrochloric acid, HCl, to flask B. In the next step, she quickly adds an excess of concentrated sodium hydroxide, NaOH, solution to flask A and quickly seals the system. She then heats flask A to boiling and distills about 25 mL of water to flask B; during this process all the ammonia, $NH_3$, generated in flask A transfers to flask B. After the distillation is complete, she disassembles the apparatus and adds a small amount of methyl red indicator to flask B and titrates the solution in flask B with standard sodium hydroxide solution. The titration requires 35.25 mL of 0.1600 *M* sodium hydroxide solution to reach the endpoint. The reactions are:

(1) $(NH_4)_2SO_4(aq) + 2\ NaOH(aq) \rightarrow Na_2SO_4(aq) + 2\ NH_3(aq) + 2\ H_2O(l)$
(2) $NH_3(aq) + HCl(aq) \rightarrow NH_4Cl(aq)$
(3) $NaOH(aq) + HCl(aq) \rightarrow NaCl(aq) + H_2O(l)$

The first equation is for a weak acid ($pK_a\ NH_4^+ = 9.25$)/strong base reaction. The second equation is for a weak base/strong acid reaction. The third equation is for a strong base/strong acid reaction. Information on indicators:

| | pH Range | $pK_a$ | Color Change |
|---|---|---|---|
| Methyl red | 4.2–6.2 | 5.0 | Red → Yellow |
| Phenolphthalein | 8.2–10.0 | 9.3 | Colorless → Pink |

(a) (i) Calculate the moles of hydrochloric acid originally in flask B.
(ii) Calculate the moles of hydrochloric acid reacting with the sodium hydroxide solution.
(iii) Calculate the moles of ammonia that reacted with the hydrochloric acid.

**GO ON TO THE NEXT PAGE**

(b) (i) Calculate the mass of ammonium sulfate in the sample. (Molar mass of ammonium sulfate = 132.139 g $mol^{-1}$.)

(ii) Calculate the percent ammonium sulfate in the sample.

(c) (i) Strong acid–strong base titrations commonly use phenolphthalein as an indicator. Give a good reason why the student chose to use methyl red instead.

(ii) A second student used phenolphthalein in place of methyl red and got significantly different results. Was the second student's percent higher or lower than the student using methyl red? What was the cause of this discrepancy?

(d) In the box below, sketch the Lewis electron-dot structure of ammonium chloride.

***Question 4***

The following equipment, is available for the determination of the molar mass of an unknown solid monoprotic acid, HA. Assume the unknown acid is a weak acid.

| | | | |
|---|---|---|---|
| analytical balance | thermometer | beaker(s) | support stand and clamp |
| stoppers | glass tubing | hot plate | pipette(s) |
| test tube(s) | stopwatch | wire gauze | flask(s) |
| buret | pH meter | graduated cylinder | |

In addition to this equipment, there is standardized hydrochloric acid, HCl, solution and unstandardized sodium hydroxide, NaOH, solution available and a suitable acid–base indicator such as phenolphthalein.

(a) Which of the above equipment is necessary to determine the molar mass of the unknown solid?

(b) List the measurements necessary to determine the molar mass of the unknown solid.

(c) What additional equipment is necessary to determine the $K_a$ of the unknown acid?

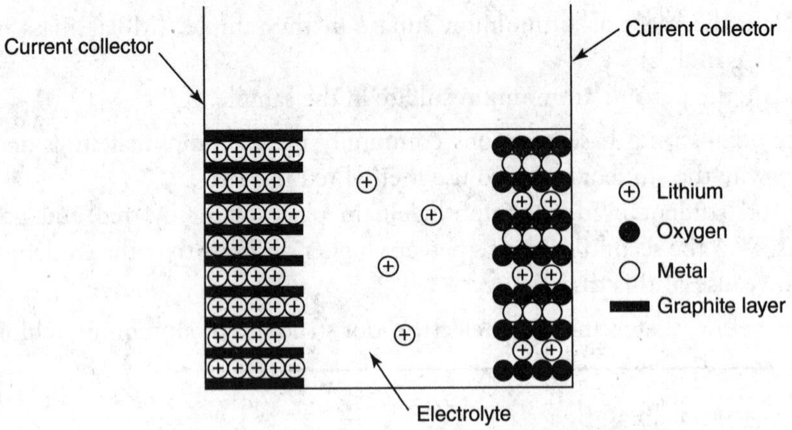


## *Question 5*

The above schematic is one form of a lithium ion battery. The negative electrode (on the left) consists of graphite with lithium ions trapped between carbon layers. The positive electrode (on the right) is a layered metal oxide that allows lithium ions to enter the solid. The electrolyte is a lithium salt dissolved in an organic solvent. The negative electrode has the approximate composition $LiC_6$, and the positive electrode can reach a composition of $LiCoO_2$ in a fully discharged battery. The half-reactions are:

$$x\mathrm{LiC_6(s)} \rightarrow x\mathrm{Li^+} + x\mathrm{e^-} + x\mathrm{C_6}$$

$$\mathrm{Li_{1-\mathit{x}}CoO_2} + x\mathrm{Li^+} + x\mathrm{e^-} \rightarrow \mathrm{LiCoO_2}$$

(a) What is the balanced net ionic equation for the reaction?
(b) Why is it necessary to use an organic solvent for the electrolyte and not water?
(c) What is the oxidation state of cobalt in $LiCoO_2$? Write the electron configuration for this cobalt ion in the ground state.

## *Question 6*

Acetylene, $C_2H_2$, will react with a limited amount of bromine vapor, $Br_2$, to form 1,2-dibromoethene, $C_2H_2Br_2$. The product of the reaction is contaminated with unreacted acetylene and 1,1,2,2-tetrabromoethane, $C_2H_2Br_4$. The key reactions are:

$$\mathrm{C_2H_2(g) + Br_2(g) \rightarrow C_2H_2Br_2(g)}$$

$$\mathrm{C_2H_2(g) + 2\ Br_2(g) \rightarrow C_2H_2Br_4(g)}$$

(a) The left box below shows the Lewis electron-dot diagram for acetylene. The box on the right has an incomplete Lewis electron-dot diagram for 1,2-dibromoethene. Complete the diagram on the right by adding all the electron pairs.

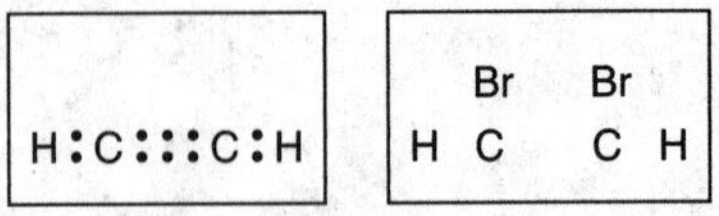


(b) In the box below, draw the complete Lewis electron-dot structure for 1,1,2,2-tetrabromoethane.

GO ON TO THE NEXT PAGE

(c) Arrange the compounds $C_2H_2$, $C_2H_2Br_2$, and $C_2H_2Br_4$ in order of decreasing H–C–C bond angle. Why did you place these compounds in the order you predicted? Your explanation should include approximate bond angles.

## *Question 7*

A student in Denver, Colorado, used the following reaction to generate oxygen gas in a gas generator:

$$2\ KClO_3(s) \rightarrow 2\ KCl(s) + 3\ O_2(g)$$

The gas generator was connected by a tube to an inverted flask, filled with water, in a water bath. The gas displaced all the water. The volume of the sample was 500.0 mL at 26°C, and the pressure in the room was 626 mm Hg. The vapor pressure of water at 26°C is 25 mm Hg.

A second student conducted a similar experiment under identical conditions beginning with the following reaction:

$$Mg_3N_2(s) + 6\ H_2O(l) \rightarrow 3\ Mg(OH)_2(s) + 2\ NH_3(g)$$

The second student's results were dramatically different from those of the first student (not as good), indicating that there was something drastically different.

(a) How many grams of oxygen are in the flask? Show all calculations.
(b) How many hydrogen atoms are in the flask after it is filled with oxygen?
(c) What is the most likely reason why the second student did not get good results? Explain your reasoning.

**STOP. End of AP Chemistry Practice Exam 1, Section II (Free Response).**

# › Answers and Explanations for Exam 1, Section II (Free Response)

*Question 1*

(a) (i) $Ni(IO_3)_2(s) \leftrightarrows Ni^{2+}(aq) + 2\ IO_3^-(aq)$

You get 1 point for this answer. The equilibrium arrow and the ionic charges must be present. We have deducted many points while grading AP exams because students incorrectly broke up polyatomic ions like the iodate ion.

(ii) $K_{sp} = [Ni^{2+}][IO_3^-]^2$

You get 1 point for this answer. The charges must be included, and the iodate ion concentration must be squared. You can still get 1 point if your expression correctly utilizes a wrong answer from part (a)(i).

(iii) $K_{sp} = [Ni^{2+}][IO_3^-]^2 = 1.4 \times 10^{-8}$

Setting $[Ni^{2+}] = x$ and $[IO_3^-] = 2x$ and inserting into the mass-action expression gives:

$$(x)(2x)^2 = 4x^3 = 1.4 \times 10^{-8}$$

Solving for $x$ gives $x = 1.5 \times 10^{-3}$, and $[IO_3^-] = 2x = 3.0 \times 10^{-3}\ M$.

You get 2 points for the correct $[IO_3^-]$. If your only mistake was forgetting to double the $IO_3^-$, you get 1 point. You can still get 1 point if you correctly used your wrong answer from part (a) (ii).

(b) Copper(II) nitrate is soluble in water (obviously because you are given a solution), which separates into copper(II) ions and nitrate ions. The copper(II) ion concentration is 0.10 $M$ and it is a common ion affecting the equilibrium.

$$K_{sp} = [Cu^{2+}][IO_3^-]^2 = 7.4 \times 10^{-8}$$

Setting $[Cu^{2+}] = 0.10 + x$ and $[IO_3^-] = 2x$ and inserting into the mass-action expression gives: $(0.10 + x)(2x)^2 = 7.4 \times 10^{-8}$. Assuming $x$ is much smaller than 0.10 allows a simplification of the calculation to $(0.10)(2x)^2 = 0.4\ x^2 = 7.4 \times 10^{-8}$.

Solving for $x$ gives $x = 4.3 \times 10^{-4}\ M$, which leads to $[IO_3^-] = 2x = 8.6 \times 10^{-4}\ M$.

You get 1 point for the correct $[IO_3^-]$.

(c) (i) Silver iodate is more soluble in nitric acid than in pure water.

You get 1 point for this answer.

(ii) Iodic acid is a weak acid ($K_a = 0.16$); therefore, according to Le Châtelier's principle, the solubility equilibrium will be displaced to the right as iodate ion combines with hydrogen ions from the nitric acid to form unionized iodic acid. The reactions are $AgIO_3(s) \leftrightarrows Ag^+(aq) + IO_3^-(aq)$ and $H^+(aq) + IO_3^-(aq) \rightarrow HIO_3(aq)$.

You get 1 point for this answer.

(d) If the two compounds have the same stoichiometry, the larger $K_{sp}$ would generate the higher iodate ion concentration. However, this is not the case, so it is necessary to calculate the iodate ion concentration for each.

$$K_{sp} = [Ba^{2+}][IO_3^-]^2 = 1.5 \times 10^{-9}$$

Setting $[Ba^{2+}] = x$ and $[IO_3^-] = 2x$, and inserting into the mass-action expression gives:

$$(x)(2x)^2 = 4x^3 = 1.5 \times 10^{-9}$$

Solving for $x$ gives $x = 7.2 \times 10^{-4}$, and $[IO_3^-] = 2x = 1.4 \times 10^{-3}$ $M$.

$$K_{sp} = [La^{3+}][IO_3^-]^3 = 6.2 \times 10^{-12}$$

Setting $[La^{3+}] = x$ and $[IO_3^-] = 3x$, and inserting into the mass-action expression gives:

$$(x)(3x)^3 = 27x^4 = 6.2 \times 10^{-12}$$

Solving for $x$ gives $x = 6.9 \times 10^{-4}$, and $[IO_3^-] = 3x = 2.0 \times 10^{-3}$ $M$.

You get 1 point for doing the calculations and showing $La(IO_3)_3$ is more soluble and 1 additional point for two correct answers.

(e) It is easier to begin with the balanced molecular equation:

$$2\ NaIO_3(aq) + Zn(NO_3)_2(aq) \rightarrow Zn(IO_3)_2(s) + 2\ NaNO_3(aq)$$

Convert the molecular equation to a complete ionic equation:

$$2\ Na^+(aq) + 2\ IO_3^-(aq) + Zn^{2+}(aq) + 2\ NO_3^-(aq) \rightarrow Zn(IO_3)_2(s) + 2\ Na^+(aq) + 2\ NO_3^-(aq)$$

The ionic compounds $NaIO_3$ and $Zn(NO_3)_2$ should be separated into their ions since you are supplied with solutions, and the sodium nitrate is also shown in the ionic form since you are told it is soluble in water. There is a $K_{sp}$ for $Zn(IO_3)_2$ given in the table; therefore, it does not separate into ions.

Removing the spectator ions ($Na^+$ and $NO_3^-$) from the complete ionic equation leaves the net ionic equation:

$$Zn^{2+}(aq) + 2\ IO_3^-(aq) \rightarrow Zn(IO_3)_2(s)$$

You get 1 point for this answer. We have deducted many points while grading AP exams because students incorrectly broke up polyatomic ions like the iodate ion.

Total your points for the different parts. There is a maximum of 10 points possible. Subtract 1 point if all answers did not have the correct number of significant figures.

### *Question 2*

(a) The order for $H_2SeO_3$ is 2. The order for $H_2O_2$ is 1. The order for $H^+$ is −1. If you get all three of these correct, you get 1 point.

The second part of part (a) is based upon comparing the rates of two experiments where only the concentration of one substance is changing.

Comparing experiments 2 and 1 (placing the larger over the smaller makes the calculations a little easier): The concentration of $H_2SeO_3$ is doubled, and the rate is quadrupled; $\frac{2.9 \times 10^{-7}}{7.4 \times 10^{-8}} \approx 4$. This leads to $H_2SeO_3$ having an order of 2.

You get 1 point for this reasoning.

Comparing experiments 3 and 1: The concentration of $H_2O_2$ is doubled, and the rate is doubled; $\frac{1.5 \times 10^{-7}}{7.4 \times 10^{-8}} \approx 2$. This leads to $H_2O_2$ having an order of 1.

You get 1 point for this reasoning.

Comparing experiments 4 and 1: The concentration of $H^+$ is doubled, and the rate is halved; $\frac{3.7 \times 10^{-8}}{7.4 \times 10^{-8}} \approx 0.5 = 2^{-1}$. This leads to $H^+$ having an order of −1.

You get 1 point for this reasoning.

(b) Rate = $k[H_2SeO_3]^2[H_2O_2][H^+]^{-1}$

This answer is worth 1 point. You will still get 1 point if you correctly use incorrect orders from part (a).

(c) Rearrange the rate law to: $k = \dfrac{\text{Rate}}{[H_2SeO_3]^2[H_2O_2][H^+]^{-1}} = \dfrac{7.4 \times 10^{-8}\ M\,s^{-1}}{[0.100\ M]^2[0.100\ M][0.100\ M]^{-1}} =$

$7.4 \times 10^{-6}\ M^{-1}\ s^{-1}$

This example uses the values from experiment 1. You could use any of the four experiments. You get 1 point for calculating the value of $k$. You get 1 additional point for the correct units. If you have trouble with the units, redo the problem with no numbers present to distract you.

(d) (i) $H_2O_2$ is being reduced. (The oxidation state of oxygen is going from −1 to −2.)

You get 1 point for this answer.

(ii) The oxidation state of oxygen in −1. (H is +1.)

You get 1 point for this answer.

(iii) $H_2O_2(aq) + 2\ H^+(aq) + 2\ e^- \rightarrow 2\ H_2O(l)$

You get 1 point for this answer.

Total your points for the different parts. There are 10 possible points. Subtract 1 point if you did not report the correct number of significant figures (2) in part (c).

***Question 3***

(a) (i) 50.00 mL 0.4000 $M$ HCl

$$\left(\frac{0.4000\text{ mol HCl}}{\text{L}}\right)(50.00\text{ mL})\left(\frac{1\text{ L}}{1{,}000\text{ mL}}\right) = 0.02000\text{ mol HCl (4 significant figures)}$$

[You can simplify this calculation as $\left(\dfrac{0.4000\text{ mol HCl}}{1{,}000\text{ mL}}\right)(50.00\text{ mL}) = 0.02000\text{ mol HCl.}$]

You get 1 point for this answer.

(ii) $HCl(aq) + NaOH(aq) \rightarrow NaCl(aq) + H_2O(l)$

35.25 mL 0.1600 $M$ NaOH

$$\left(\frac{0.1600\text{ mol NaOH}}{\text{L}}\right)(35.25\text{ mL})\left(\frac{1\text{ L}}{1{,}000\text{ mL}}\right)\left(\frac{1\text{ mol HCl}}{1\text{ mol NaOH}}\right) = 0.005640\text{ mol HCl (4 significant figures)}$$

You get 1 point for this answer.

(iii) $NH_3(aq) + HCl(aq) \rightarrow NH_4Cl(aq)$

$$(0.02000 - 0.005640)\text{ mol HCl}\left(\frac{1\text{ mol }NH_3}{1\text{ mol HCl}}\right) = 0.01436\text{ mol }NH_3\text{ (4 significant figures)}$$

You get 1 point for this answer. If you miscalculated either of the preceding two answers but used your results correctly in this step, you still earn this point.

(b) (i) $$(0.01436\text{ mol }NH_3)\left(\frac{1\text{ mol }(NH_4)_2SO_4}{2\text{ mol }NH_3}\right)\left(\frac{132.139\text{ g }(NH_4)_2SO_4}{1\text{ mol }(NH_4)_2SO_4}\right) = 0.9488\text{ g }(NH_4)_2SO_4\text{ (4 significant figures)}$$

You get 1 point for this answer.

(ii) $$\frac{0.9488\text{ g}(NH_4)_2SO_4}{1.002\text{ g sample}} \times 100\% = 94.69\%\ (NH_4)_2SO_4\text{ (4 significant figures)}$$

You get 1 point for this answer. If you got the wrong result for part (b)(i), but used it correctly here, you still get the point.

(c) (i) The sodium hydroxide solution will react with not only the hydrochloric acid (reaction 3) but also the ammonium ion (reaction 1). The methyl red endpoint is below where the ammonium ion begins to react; therefore, it is a better measure of the amount of HCl reacting than phenolphthalein, which has an endpoint after at least some of the ammonium ion has reacted.

You get 1 point for this answer.

(ii) The percent will be lower. It will be necessary to use more sodium hydroxide solution to reach the endpoint, making it appear that less ammonia reacted with the HCl. If there were less ammonia, then the percentage would be lower.

You get 1 point for predicting the percent will be lower and 1 point for the explanation.

(d)

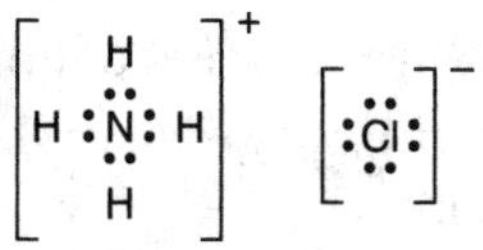

You get 1 point for having an octet on the nitrogen and an octet on the chlorine with no additional electrons shown.

You get 1 point for showing an ionic structure with no hint of a covalent bond between the ammonium ion and the chloride ion. The brackets are not essential but are present as an aid to stress that these are ions with no covalent (electron sharing).

Total your points. There is a maximum of 10 possible points. Subtract 1 point if any of your answers does not have the correct number of significant figures.

## *Question 4*

(a) Analytical balance, buret, pipette, support stand and clamp, beakers, or flasks

You must have these five items to get 1 point. There is no deduction if you have an additional item. You do not get the point if you list any item that is not on the list.

(b) **1.** It is necessary to standardize the sodium hydroxide solution.

The measurements necessary are:

Volume of standard HCl solution (from pipette)

Initial buret reading of NaOH solution

Final buret reading of NaOH solution (endpoint)

This complete list is worth 1 point. The information in parenthesis is not required.

**2.** It is possible to determine the molar mass of the unknown acid using the standard sodium hydroxide solution.

The measurements necessary are:

Mass of a sample of the unknown acid (from balance)

Initial buret reading of NaOH solution

Final buret reading of NaOH solution (endpoint)

This complete list is worth 1 point. The information in parenthesis is not required.

(c) In addition to the equipment from part (a), a pH meter is needed.

This complete list is worth 1 point.

Total your points. There are 4 possible points. We have seen students taking the AP Exam have trouble with a problem like this because they described the procedure instead of listing only the measurements.

***Question 5***

(a) Regardless of the value of *x*, it is the same in each half-reaction; therefore, it is only necessary to add the two half-reactions together.

$xLiC_6(s) \rightarrow xLi^+ + xe^- + xC_6$

$Li_{1-x}CoO_2 + xLi^+ + xe^- \rightarrow LiCoO_2$

$Li_{1-x}CoO_2 + xLiC_6(s) \rightarrow LiCoO_2 + xC_6$

You get 1 point for the correct equation.

(b) Lithium metal will react with water.

You get 1 point for this explanation.

(c) The oxidation state of cobalt is +3. This is determined by assuming the oxidation states of lithium and oxygen are +1 and −2, respectively. This leads to Li + Co + 2 (O) = 0 or (+1) + Co + 2 (−2) = 0. The ground-state electron configuration of $Co^{3+}$ is $1s^2 2s^2 2p^6 3s^2 3p^6 3d^6$ or $[Ar]3d^6$.

You get 1 point for the correct oxidation state of cobalt and 1 point for the correct electron configuration. If you did not get the correct oxidation state, you can still get the second point if you give the correct electron configuration of the ion predicted to be present. Note that no reasonable Co ion will have any 4s electrons present.

Total your points; there are 4 points possible.

***Question 6***

(a)

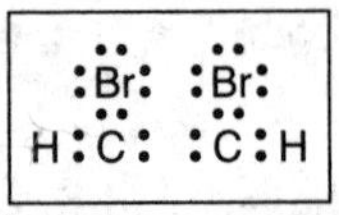

You get 1 point for the correct Lewis structure. (All carbon and bromine atoms have an octet of electrons.) Lines may be used in place of the six bonding electron pairs.

(b)

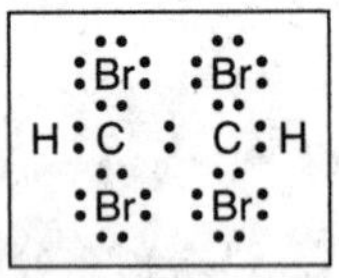

You get 1 point for the correct Lewis structure. (All carbon and bromine atoms have an octet of electrons.) Lines may be used in place of the seven bonding electron pairs.

(c) The order is $C_2H_2 > C_2H_2Br_2 > C_2H_2Br_4$.

The structure of acetylene shown in the problem indicates a linear molecule with an HCC bond angle of 180°. The correct Lewis electron-dot diagram for $C_2H_2Br_2$ indicates a trigonal planar arrangement about each carbon atom with an HCC bond angle of 120°. The correct Lewis electron-dot diagram for $C_2H_2Br_4$ indicates a tetrahedral arrangement about each carbon atom with an HCC bond angle of 109°.

You get 1 point if you list the compounds in the correct order, and you get 1 point for a correct explanation including the bond angles.

Total your points for the problem. There is a maximum of 4 possible points.

***Question 7***

(a) $P_{\text{total}} = 626$ mm Hg

$P_{\text{oxygen}} = 626 - 25 = 601$ mm Hg (Dalton's law)

$P = 601$ mm Hg/760 mm Hg $= 0.791$ atm (The 760 mm Hg = 1 atm is in the exam booklet and in the back of this book.)

$V = 500.0$ mL $= 0.5000$ L

$T = 26°C = 299$ K

$R = 0.08206$ L atm mol$^{-1}$ K$^{-1}$ (given in the exam booklet and in the back of this book)

$n = PV/RT$ (rearranged from $PV = nRT$, which is in exam booklet and in the back of this book)

$$= \frac{(0.791 \text{ atm})(0.5000 \text{ L})}{(0.08206 \text{ L atm mol}^{-1} \text{ K}^{-1})(299 \text{ K})} = 0.01612 \text{ mol } O_2 \text{ (unrounded)}$$

$$\text{Mass} = (0.01612 \text{ mol } O_2)\left(\frac{32.0 \text{ g } O_2}{1 \text{ mol } O_2}\right) = 0.516 \text{ g } O_2 \text{ (rounded to 3 significant figures)}$$

Give yourself 1 point for the correct answer (no deduction for rounding differently). You must include ALL parts of the calculation (including "="). There is no deduction for combining steps. You cannot get this point if you did not subtract the vapor pressure of water from the total pressure.

(b) The hydrogen atoms are in the water molecules present in the flask; therefore, it is necessary to calculate the moles of water present, convert moles of water to moles of hydrogen atoms, and use Avogadro's number to convert from moles to the number of atoms.

$$P_{\text{water}} = \frac{25 \text{ mm Hg}}{760 \text{ mm Hg}} = 0.0329 \text{ atm (extra significant figure). } T \text{ and } V \text{ are the same as in part (a).}$$

$$n = PV/RT = \frac{(0.0329 \text{ atm})(0.5000 \text{ L})}{(0.08206 \text{ L atm mol}^{-1} \text{ K}^{-1})(299 \text{ K})} = 6.70 \times 10^{-4} \text{ mol } H_2O$$

$$\text{Number of H atoms} = (6.70 \times 10^{-4} \text{ mol } H_2O)\left(\frac{2 \text{ mol H}}{1 \text{ mol } H_2O}\right)\left(\frac{6.022 \times 10^{23} \text{ H atoms}}{1 \text{ mol H}}\right)$$

$$= 8.1 \times 10^{20} \text{ H atoms}$$

Give yourself 1 point for the correct answer (no deduction for rounding variations).

(c) Unlike oxygen gas, ammonia gas is very soluble in water because it, like water, is capable of hydrogen bonding. The formation of hydrogen bonds between water molecules and ammonia molecules enhances the solubility of ammonia in water. Oxygen, on the other hand, is nonpolar and is only weakly attracted to water, giving oxygen a much lower solubility.

Give yourself 1 point for indicating the problem is the solubility of ammonia in water. Give yourself 1 additional point for the explanation if you invoke hydrogen bonding.

Total your points for this question. There are 4 points possible. Deduct 1 point if you reported the wrong number of significant figures in any answer.

# AP Chemistry Practice Exam 2—Multiple Choice

## ANSWER SHEET

| | | |
|---|---|---|
| 1 Ⓐ Ⓑ Ⓒ Ⓓ | 21 Ⓐ Ⓑ Ⓒ Ⓓ | 41 Ⓐ Ⓑ Ⓒ Ⓓ |
| 2 Ⓐ Ⓑ Ⓒ Ⓓ | 22 Ⓐ Ⓑ Ⓒ Ⓓ | 42 Ⓐ Ⓑ Ⓒ Ⓓ |
| 3 Ⓐ Ⓑ Ⓒ Ⓓ | 23 Ⓐ Ⓑ Ⓒ Ⓓ | 43 Ⓐ Ⓑ Ⓒ Ⓓ |
| 4 Ⓐ Ⓑ Ⓒ Ⓓ | 24 Ⓐ Ⓑ Ⓒ Ⓓ | 44 Ⓐ Ⓑ Ⓒ Ⓓ |
| 5 Ⓐ Ⓑ Ⓒ Ⓓ | 25 Ⓐ Ⓑ Ⓒ Ⓓ | 45 Ⓐ Ⓑ Ⓒ Ⓓ |
| 6 Ⓐ Ⓑ Ⓒ Ⓓ | 26 Ⓐ Ⓑ Ⓒ Ⓓ | 46 Ⓐ Ⓑ Ⓒ Ⓓ |
| 7 Ⓐ Ⓑ Ⓒ Ⓓ | 27 Ⓐ Ⓑ Ⓒ Ⓓ | 47 Ⓐ Ⓑ Ⓒ Ⓓ |
| 8 Ⓐ Ⓑ Ⓒ Ⓓ | 28 Ⓐ Ⓑ Ⓒ Ⓓ | 48 Ⓐ Ⓑ Ⓒ Ⓓ |
| 9 Ⓐ Ⓑ Ⓒ Ⓓ | 29 Ⓐ Ⓑ Ⓒ Ⓓ | 49 Ⓐ Ⓑ Ⓒ Ⓓ |
| 10 Ⓐ Ⓑ Ⓒ Ⓓ | 30 Ⓐ Ⓑ Ⓒ Ⓓ | 50 Ⓐ Ⓑ Ⓒ Ⓓ |
| 11 Ⓐ Ⓑ Ⓒ Ⓓ | 31 Ⓐ Ⓑ Ⓒ Ⓓ | 51 Ⓐ Ⓑ Ⓒ Ⓓ |
| 12 Ⓐ Ⓑ Ⓒ Ⓓ | 32 Ⓐ Ⓑ Ⓒ Ⓓ | 52 Ⓐ Ⓑ Ⓒ Ⓓ |
| 13 Ⓐ Ⓑ Ⓒ Ⓓ | 33 Ⓐ Ⓑ Ⓒ Ⓓ | 53 Ⓐ Ⓑ Ⓒ Ⓓ |
| 14 Ⓐ Ⓑ Ⓒ Ⓓ | 34 Ⓐ Ⓑ Ⓒ Ⓓ | 54 Ⓐ Ⓑ Ⓒ Ⓓ |
| 15 Ⓐ Ⓑ Ⓒ Ⓓ | 35 Ⓐ Ⓑ Ⓒ Ⓓ | 55 Ⓐ Ⓑ Ⓒ Ⓓ |
| 16 Ⓐ Ⓑ Ⓒ Ⓓ | 36 Ⓐ Ⓑ Ⓒ Ⓓ | 56 Ⓐ Ⓑ Ⓒ Ⓓ |
| 17 Ⓐ Ⓑ Ⓒ Ⓓ | 37 Ⓐ Ⓑ Ⓒ Ⓓ | 57 Ⓐ Ⓑ Ⓒ Ⓓ |
| 18 Ⓐ Ⓑ Ⓒ Ⓓ | 38 Ⓐ Ⓑ Ⓒ Ⓓ | 58 Ⓐ Ⓑ Ⓒ Ⓓ |
| 19 Ⓐ Ⓑ Ⓒ Ⓓ | 39 Ⓐ Ⓑ Ⓒ Ⓓ | 59 Ⓐ Ⓑ Ⓒ Ⓓ |
| 20 Ⓐ Ⓑ Ⓒ Ⓓ | 40 Ⓐ Ⓑ Ⓒ Ⓓ | 60 Ⓐ Ⓑ Ⓒ Ⓓ |

*The AP Exam is a timed exam; keep this in mind as you prepare. When taking the various tests presented in this book, you should follow the AP Exam rules as closely as possible. Anyone can improve his or her score by using notes, books, or an unlimited time. You will have none of these on the AP Exam, so resist the temptation to use them on practice exams. Carefully time yourself, do not use other materials, and use a calculator only when expressly allowed to do so. After you have finished an exam, you may use other sources to go over questions you missed or skipped. We have seen many students get into trouble because the first time they attempted a test under "test conditions" was on the test itself.*

# AP Chemistry Practice Exam 2

## SECTION I
## MULTIPLE CHOICE

**Time—1 hour and 30 minutes**

**NO CALCULATOR MAY BE USED WITH SECTION I**

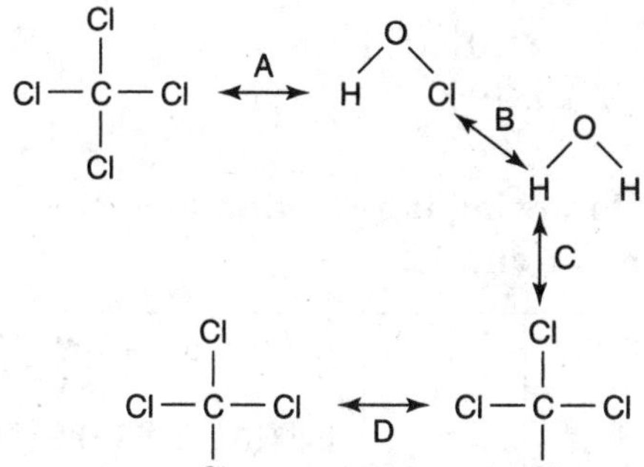


**1.** Which of the labeled arrows in the diagram above represents the strongest intermolecular force shown?

(A) A
(B) B
(C) C
(D) D

**The following information applies to questions 2–5.**

A student builds a galvanic cell to take advantage of the following reaction:

$$Zn(s) + 2\,AgNO_3(aq)(1\,M) \rightarrow 2\,Ag(s) + Zn(NO_3)_2(aq)(1\,M)$$

The cell's voltage is measured and found to be +1.56 volts.

**2.** What happens to the voltage when a small amount of silver nitrate is added to the silver compartment?

(A) There is no change in the voltage.
(B) The voltage becomes zero.
(C) The voltage increases.
(D) The voltage decreases but stays positive.

**3.** What happens to the cell voltage when the student replaces the $Zn(NO_3)_2$ solution with 1 *M* $ZnCl_2$?

(A) There is no change in the voltage.
(B) The voltage becomes zero.
(C) The voltage increases.
(D) The voltage decreases but stays positive.

**4.** If the standard reduction potential of silver is 0.80 V, what is the standard reduction potential of zinc?

(A) +0.76 V
(B) –0.76 V
(C) –0.04 V
(D) +0.04 V

**5.** What happens to the cell voltage after the cell has reached equilibrium?

(A) There is no change in the voltage.
(B) The voltage becomes zero.
(C) The voltage increases.
(D) The voltage decreases but stays positive.

**Use the following information to answer questions 6–9.**

Many metal salts crystallize from solution in the form of a hydrate. If the formula of the anhydrous salt is $A_aX_x$, then the generic formula of the hydrated form would be $A_aX_x{\bullet}xH_2O$. A student conducts an experiment to determine the formula of a hydrated metal salt by collecting the following data:

| | |
|---|---|
| Mass of crucible | 53.120 g |
| Mass of crucible plus hydrated salt | 58.677 g |
| Mass of crucible plus anhydrous salt | 57.857 g |
| Molar mass of anhydrous salt | 208.232 g $mol^{-1}$ |

The hydrated salt is finely powdered to ensure complete water loss to produce the anhydrous salt.

**6.** How many grams of water were in the hydrate?

(A) 5.557 g
(B) 4.737 g
(C) 0.987 g
(D) 0.820 g

**7.** What is the approximate percentage of water in the hydrated salt?

(A) 14%
(B) 86%
(C) 50%
(D) 28%

**8.** The student did not have time to finish the experiment during the lab period and was forced to store the anhydrous salt and crucible in his lab drawer until the next day. At the beginning of the next lab period the student weighed the anhydrous salt and crucible. After calculating the percentage of water in the sample, the student found that the percentage was lower than predicted. Assuming all weighings were done correctly, what might be the cause of the lower-than-expected percentage?

(A) The sample dried further overnight.
(B) The student performed one or more weighings before the crucible had cooled to room temperature.
(C) The sample absorbed water from the air overnight.
(D) The sample decomposed to another salt.

**9.** In another experiment on a different metal hydrate, a student found that the salt was 62.9% water. In this case, the molar mass of the anhydrous salt was 106 g $mol^{-1}$. Which of the following general formulas gives the correct value of *x*?

(A) $A_aX_x{\bullet}5H_2O$
(B) $A_aX_x{\bullet}10H_2O$
(C) $A_aX_x{\bullet}2H_2O$
(D) $A_aX_x{\bullet}6H_2O$

**10.** For the following reaction, $2\ NO(g) + O_2(g) \rightarrow 2\ NO_2(g)$, the rate law is Rate = $k[NO]^2[O_2]$. In one experiment, the rate of appearance of $NO_2$ was determined to be 0.0138 $M\ s^{-1}$ when [NO] = 0.0125 *M* and $[O_2]$ = 0.0125 *M*. What was the value of the rate constant?

(A) $7.1 \times 10^3\ M^2\ s^{-1}$
(B) $7.1 \times 10^3\ M\ s^{-1}$
(C) $7.1 \times 10^3\ M^{-2}\ s^{-1}$
(D) $7.1 \times 10^3$

**Use the following information to answer questions 11 and 12.**

| EXPERIMENT | INITIAL $[H^+]$ (M) | INITIAL $[CN_2H_4O]$ (M) | INITIAL RATE OF DISAPPEARANCE OF $CN_2H_4O$ ($M\ s^{-1}$) |
|---|---|---|---|
| 1 | 0.100 | 0.200 | $8.6 \times 10^{-5}$ |
| 2 | 0.200 | 0.100 | $4.3 \times 10^{-5}$ |
| 3 | 0.200 | 0.200 | $8.6 \times 10^{-5}$ |

**11.** The table above gives the initial concentrations and rate for three experiments involving the decomposition of urea, $CN_2H_4O$. The reaction is $H^+(aq) + 2\ H_2O(l) + CN_2H_4O(aq) \rightarrow 2\ NH_4^+(aq) + HCO_3^-(aq)$. What is the rate law for this reaction?

(A) Rate = $k[CN_2H_4O]$
(B) Rate = $k[CN_2H_4O]^2[H^+]^2$
(C) Rate = $k[H^+]$
(D) Rate = $k[CN_2H_4O]^2[H^+]$

GO ON TO THE NEXT PAGE

**12.** The chemical equation for the reaction described in the table indicates that there are three reactants ($H^+$, $H_2O$, and $CN_2H_4O$); however, only two reactants appear in the data table. Why is there no column in the table for the third reactant?

(A) The $H_2O$ behaves as a catalyst.
(B) The $H_2O$ is not a reactant; it is the solvent.
(C) The $H_2O$ concentration does not change.
(D) It is only possible to deal with two reactants.

**13.** Oxalic acid, $H_2C_2O_4$, is a useful chemical for rust removal. A student prepared five oxalic acid samples by dissolving 0.9000 grams of oxalic acid in 100.00 mL of water and pipetting 10.00 mL samples of this solution into five separate beakers. Each of the samples was diluted with deionized water, and an appropriate indicator was added as an indicator. The samples were then titrated with standard 0.05000 $M$ sodium hydroxide, NaOH, until the appearance of a permanent color change of the indicator indicated the endpoint of the titration. The following volumes were obtained. Molar mass of $H_2C_2O_4 = 90.04\ g\ mol^{-1}$.

| | VOLUME OF STANDARD NaOH |
|---|---|
| Sample 1 | 39.68 mL |
| Sample 2 | 40.27 mL |
| Sample 3 | 40.54 mL |
| Sample 4 | 36.66 mL |
| Sample 5 | 38.74 mL |

The student calculated a concentration of approximately 0.20 $M$ in each case. This is not the correct value. What is the most likely mistake that the student made?

(A) The student used the total sample volume of the acid instead of the pipetted sample volume.
(B) The student did not use the correct mole ratio in the calculation.
(C) The student did not use the correct indicator.
(D) The student contaminated the samples during preparation.

**14.** $Co^{2+}(aq) + 2\ e^- \rightarrow Co(s) \quad E° = -0.28\ V$
$Zn^{2+}(aq) + 2\ e^- \rightarrow Zn(s) \quad E° = -0.76\ V$
Given the above standard reduction potentials, estimate the approximate value of the $\Delta G°$ for the following reaction:

$$Zn(s) + Co^{2+}(aq) \rightarrow Zn^{2+}(aq) + Co(s)$$

(A) $-4.6 \times 10^4\ J\ mol^{-1}$
(B) $-9.3 \times 10^4\ J\ mol^{-1}$
(C) $+9.3 \times 10^4\ J\ mol^{-1}$
(D) $+4.6 \times 10^4\ J\ mol^{-1}$

**Use the following information to answer questions 15–19.**

pH versus volume of titrant added

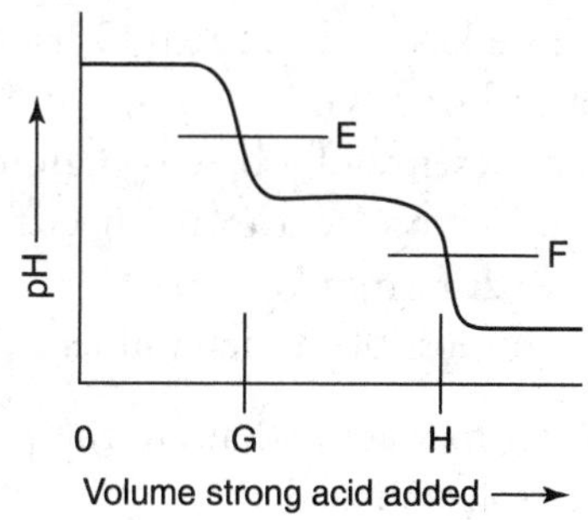


The diagram above represents the idealized titration curve for the reaction of pure sodium carbonate, $Na_2CO_3$, with a strong acid such as hydrochloric acid, HCl. E and F represent the pH at the endpoints corresponding to the formation of $HCO_3^-$ and $H_2CO_3$, respectively. G and H correspond to the quantity of acid required to reach the endpoints.

**15.** A trial run used a sample of pure sodium carbonate. How does the volume of acid necessary to reach G from 0 compare to the volume of acid necessary to get from G to H?

(A) They are the same.
(B) It takes more to reach point G.
(C) It takes more to get from G to H.
(D) It is impossible to determine.

**16.** The analysis of a sample contaminated with $NaHCO_3$ gave slightly different results. How does the volume of acid necessary to reach G from 0 compare to the volume of acid necessary to get from G to H for the second sample?

(A) It takes more to get from G to H.
(B) It takes more to reach point G.
(C) They are the same.
(D) It is impossible to determine.

**17.** How could a student determine if there was a strong acid or a strong base contaminant in the original sample?

(A) The presence of an acid contaminant would require less acid to reach H from G than to reach G from 0.
(B) The presence of a base contaminant would require less acid to reach G from 0 than to reach F from G.
(C) The presence of a base contaminant would require more acid to reach G from 0 than to reach F from G.
(D) It is impossible to determine.

**18.** In addition to water, what are the predominant species in solution at F?

(A) $Na_2CO_3$ and HCl
(B) $Na^+$, $Cl^-$, and $H_2CO_3$
(C) $HCO_3^-$ and $H^+$
(D) $Na^+$, $Cl^-$, $H^+$, and $CO_3^{2-}$

**19.** At what point on the graph for the titration of pure sodium carbonate is the pH = $pK_{a1}$ for carbonic acid?

(A) at point G
(B) halfway between the start and point G
(C) at point H
(D) halfway between points G and H

**20.** Three steel containers hold gas samples. The containers are all the same size and at the same temperature. One container has 4.0 g of helium, another has 28.0 g of nitrogen, and the third has 44.0 g of carbon dioxide. Pick the FALSE statement from the following list:

(A) The densities increase in the order helium < nitrogen < carbon dioxide.
(B) The number of molecules in all the containers is the same.
(C) The pressure in all three containers is the same.
(D) The average speed of all the molecules is the same.

**21.** When potassium perchlorate, $KClO_4$, dissolves in water, the temperature of the resultant solution is lower than the initial temperature of the components. Which of the following conclusions may be related to this?

(A) This is a spontaneous process because it is exothermic.
(B) This is a spontaneous process because of an entropy increase.
(C) This is a spontaneous process because of an entropy decrease.
(D) This is a spontaneous process because it is exothermic.

**GO ON TO THE NEXT PAGE**

**22.** The graph shows the variation of boiling point with Group number for the hydrogen compounds of the four lightest members of Group 15 on the periodic table ($NH_3$, $PH_3$, $AsH_3$ and $SbH_3$).

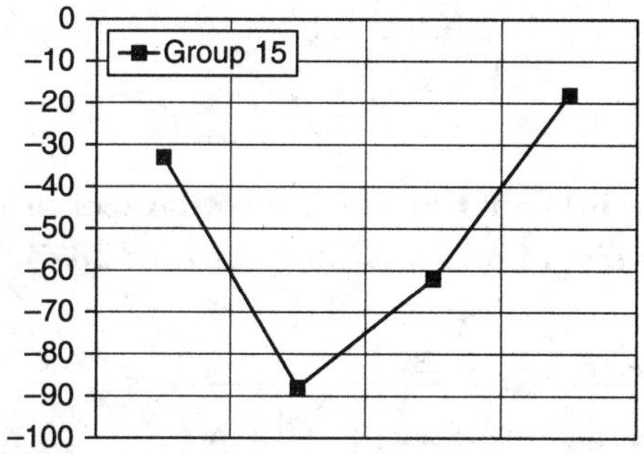


What is the reason that the lightest member of Group 15 does not follow the trend of the other members, which show that the boiling point decreases with decreasing atomic mass of the Group 15 element?

(A) ionic bonds
(B) hybrid orbitals
(C) resonance structures
(D) hydrogen bonding

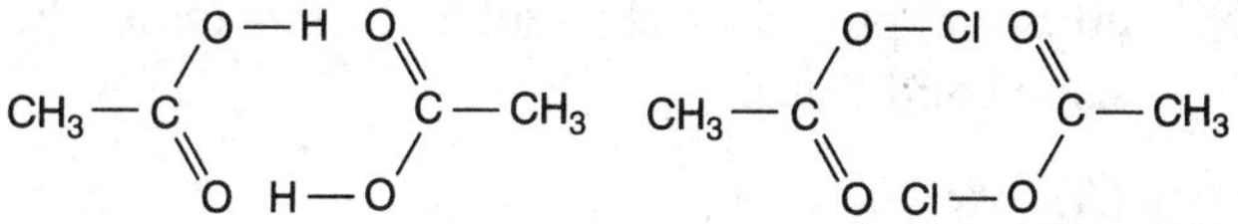

**23.** A dimer consists of two closely associated molecules. In the gas phase, acetic acid tends to form dimers as illustrated on the left in the above diagram. Acetyl chloride, on the right in the above diagram, is not very efficient in forming dimers. Why is acetic acid better able to form dimers than acetyl chloride?

(A) The molecular mass of acetyl chloride is higher than that of acetic acid, making it harder for the acetyl chloride to form dimers.
(B) It is easier to form a covalent bond between acetic acid molecules than between acetyl chloride molecules.
(C) Acetic acid can form strong hydrogen bonds, but acetyl chloride can only form weaker dipole–dipole attractions.
(D) Acetic acid is an acidic compound, but acetyl chloride is a neutral compound.

trans-1,2-dichloroethene cis-1,2-dichloroethene

**24.** Two compounds with the formula $C_2H_2Cl_2$ appear in the above diagram. These two compounds are isomers. The molecules are planar and have the approximate structures shown in the diagram. The boiling point of trans-1,2-dichloroethene is 47.5°C and the boiling point of cis-1,2-dichloroethene is 60.3°C. Which of the following best explains why cis-1,2-dichloroethene has a higher boiling point than its isomer, trans-1,2-dichloroethene?

(A) The higher boiling isomer is more polar than the other isomer.
(B) The higher boiling isomer is better able to form hydrogen bonds than the other isomer.
(C) The higher boiling isomer has a greater molar mass.
(D) The higher boiling isomer has greater London dispersion forces than the other isomer.

**Use the information on the following proposed mechanism to answer questions 25–27.**

Step 1: $N_2O_5(g) \rightarrow NO_3(g) + NO_2(g)$ Slow

Step 2: $NO_3(g) \rightarrow NO(g) + O_2(g)$ Fast

Step 3: $NO(g) + N_2O_5(g) \rightarrow N_2O_4(g) + NO_2(g)$ Fast

Step 4: $N_2O_4(g) \leftrightarrows 2\ NO_2(g)$ Fast

**25.** The above represents a proposed mechanism for the decomposition of gaseous dinitrogen pentoxide, $N_2O_5$. What are the overall products of the reaction?

(A) $N_2O_4(g) + O_2(g)$
(B) $2\ NO_2(g) + O_2(g)$
(C) $N_2O_4(g) + NO_2(g) + O_2(g)$
(D) $4\ NO_2(g) + O_2(g)$

**26.** Choose the energy profile that best describes this mechanism.

(A)

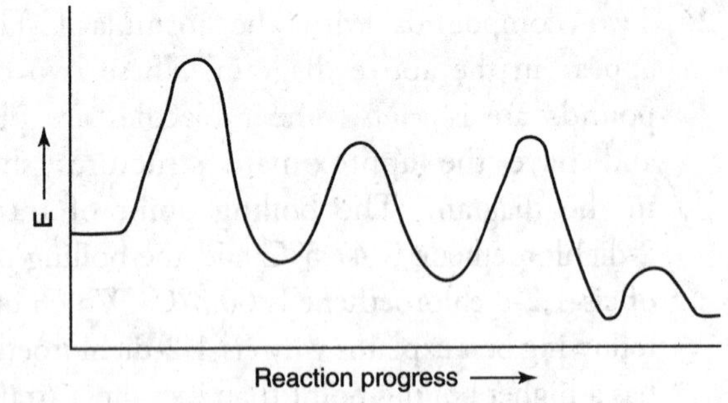


(B)

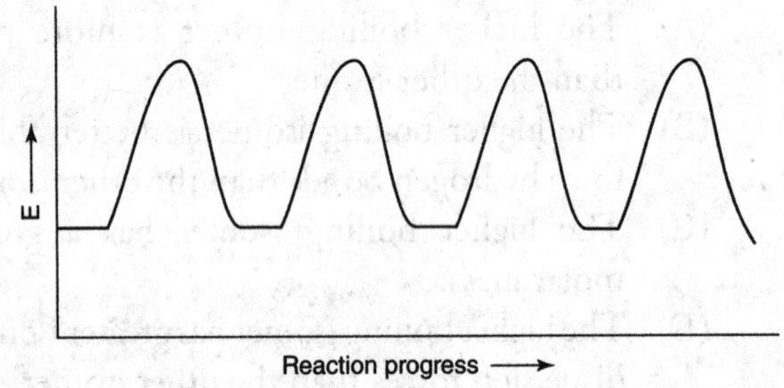


(C)

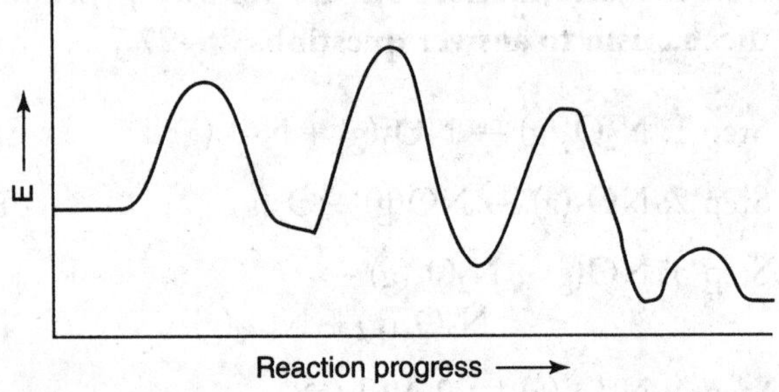


(D)

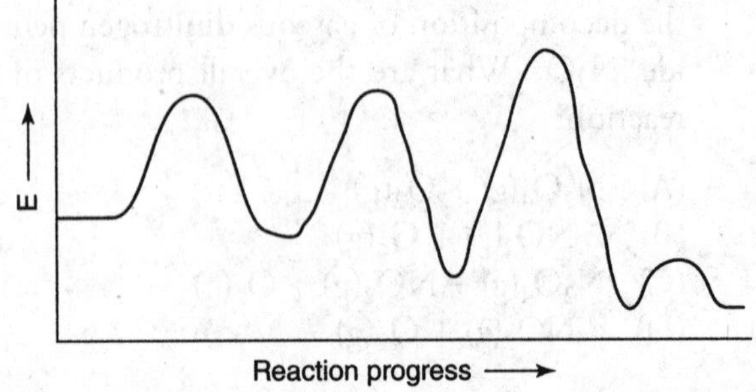


**27.** What is the rate law for the reaction?

(A) Rate = $k[N_2O_5]^2$
(B) $k = [N_2O_5]$
(C) Rate = $k[N_2O_5]$
(D) $k = \dfrac{[NO_2]^4[O_2]}{[N_2O_5]^2}$

**Use the information on the containers in the following diagram to answer questions 28–30.**

| A | B | C | D |
|---|---|---|---|
| He | Ne | Ar | Kr |
| 298 K | 298 K | 298 K | 298 K |
| 0.5 mole | 0.5 mole | 0.5 mole | 0.5 mole |
| 10.0 L | 10.0 L | 10.0 L | 10.0 L |

Approximate molar masses:

He = 4 g $mol^{-1}$, Ne = 20 g $mol^{-1}$,
Ar = 40 g $mol^{-1}$, Kr = 84 g $mol^{-1}$

**28.** If a sample of Kr effuses at a rate of 35 mL per second at 298 K, which of the gases below will effuse at approximately double the rate under the same conditions?

(A) Ar
(B) He
(C) Ne
(D) impossible to determine

**29.** Assuming all four gases are behaving ideally, which of the following is the same for all the gas samples?

(A) average kinetic energy of the atoms
(B) average speed of the atoms
(C) density of the gas in the container
(D) all properties are the same for gases behaving ideally

**30.** Which of the gases will show the greatest deviation from ideal behavior?

(A) He
(B) Ne
(C) Ar
(D) Kr

**Use the information on the containers in the following diagram to answer questions 31–34 concerning the following equilibrium.**

$$2\ Cl_2(g) + 2\ H_2O(g) \leftrightarrows 4\ HCl(g) + O_2(g)$$

$$\Delta H = +100\ \text{kJ}$$

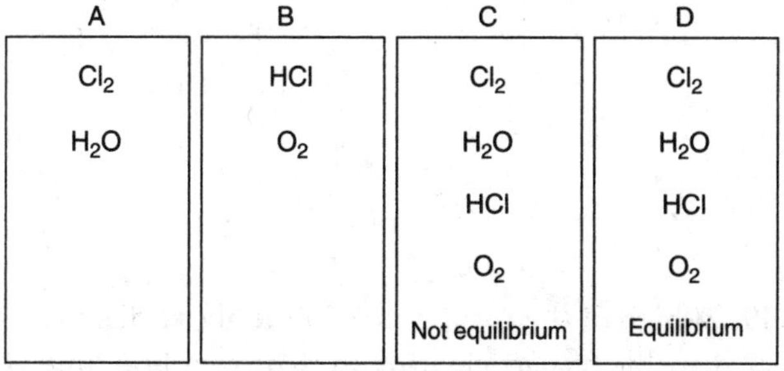


**31.** An equilibrium mixture (container D) is at 75°C. Which of the following changes may increase the amount of the HCl in the container?

(A) increasing the volume of the container
(B) decreasing the volume of the container
(C) lowering the temperature of the container
(D) adding 1 mole of He(g) to the container

**32.** Containers A, B, and C are not at equilibrium. If each container begins with equal amounts of the indicated substances present at the same temperature, which of the three will reach equilibrium first?

(A) A because producing products from reactants is faster than the reverse.
(B) B because producing reactants from products is faster than the reverse.
(C) C because there are both reactants and products already in the container.
(D) It is impossible to determine which will reach equilibrium first.

**33.** If the initial partial pressure of $Cl_2$ in container A is 1.0 atm and the initial partial pressure of $H_2O$ is also 1.0 atm, what will be the pressure at equilibrium?

(A) > 2.0 atm
(B) = 2.0 atm
(C) < 2.0 atm
(D) impossible to determine

**34.** If the moles of HCl in container B are equal to five times the $O_2$ present, what can be said about the moles of $O_2$ present at equilibrium?

(A) It will be zero because it is the limiting reagent.
(B) It will remain the same.
(C) It will be increased.
(D) It is impossible to determine.

**Use the information on the bases in the following diagram to answer questions 35–37.**

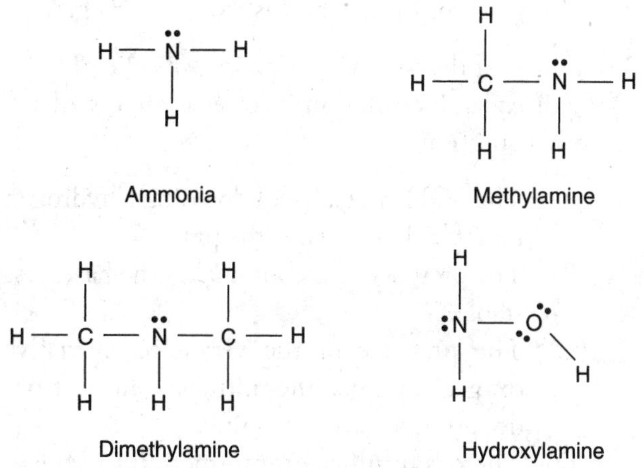


**Ammonia is only present as a reference. Questions 35–37 only refer to the other three bases.**

| | pH of a 1.0 *M* solution |
|---|---|
| Ammonia | 11.6 |
| Methylamine | 12.9 |
| Dimethylamine | 12.5 |
| Hydroxylamine | 10.0 |

**35.** Solutions of methylamine, dimethylamine, and hydroxylamine are titrated. The base concentrations were 0.1000 *M*, and 0.1000 *M* hydrochloric acid, HCl, was used for the titrations. Which of the three bases will yield the highest pH at the equivalence point?

(A) Hydroxylamine
(B) Methylamine
(C) Dimethylamine
(D) The concentrations of all the bases were the same; therefore, the pH at the equivalence point will be the same.

GO ON TO THE NEXT PAGE

**36.** All the bases in the diagram behave as Brønsted–Lowry bases in the same way; in each case, they accept a hydrogen ion to the same atom. How is this acceptance of a hydrogen ion accomplished?

(A) A hydrogen ion attaches to the lone pair on the nitrogen atom.
(B) The hydroxide ion reacts with the hydrogen ion to form water.
(C) The hydrogen ion forms a hydrogen bond to the base.
(D) The hydrogen ion combines with a hydrogen atom from the base to form $H_2$ gas.

**37.** Which of the following explains why the pH of a hydroxylamine solution is lower than any of the other solutions?

(A) The –OH is capable of donating a hydrogen ion, which will lower the pH.
(B) The presence of carbon makes the bases less stable.
(C) The presence of the very electronegative oxygen inhibits the nitrogen atom from donating its electron pair.
(D) There is insufficient information to explain this observation.

**38.** Oxidation of which of the following substances will yield a stronger acid?

(A) $HNO_2$
(B) $HNO_3$
(C) $H_2SO_4$
(D) $H_3PO_4$

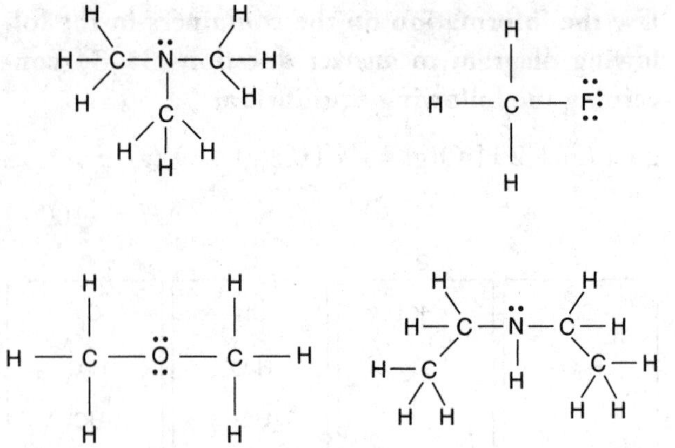

**39.** Which of the compounds in the above diagram is capable of participating in hydrogen bonding?

(A) $C_3H_9N$
(B) $CH_3F$
(C) $C_2H_6O$
(D) $C_4H_{11}N$

**40.** Choose the reaction expected to have the greatest decrease in entropy.

(A) $C(s) + CO_2(g) \rightarrow 2\ CO(g)$
(B) $2\ Na(s) + O_2(g) \rightarrow Na_2O_2(s)$
(C) $CH_4(g) + 2\ O_2(g) \rightarrow CO_2(g) + 2\ H_2O(g)$
(D) $2\ NI_3(s) \rightarrow 3\ I_2(s) + N_2(g)$

**41.** A certain reaction is nonspontaneous under standard conditions but becomes spontaneous at higher temperatures. What conclusions may be drawn under standard conditions?

(A) $\Delta H < 0$, $\Delta S < 0$, and $\Delta G = 0$
(B) $\Delta H > 0$, $\Delta S < 0$, and $\Delta G > 0$
(C) $\Delta H < 0$, $\Delta S < 0$, and $\Delta G > 0$
(D) $\Delta H > 0$, $\Delta S > 0$, and $\Delta G > 0$

**42.** Which of the following is the correct order of increasing acid strength?

(A) $H_2SeO_3 < H_2SO_3 < HClO < HBrO$
(B) $HClO < H_2SeO_3 < HBrO < H_2SO_3$
(C) $HBrO < HClO < H_2SeO_3 < H_2SO_3$
(D) $H_2SO_3 < H_2SeO_3 < HClO < HBrO$

GO ON TO THE NEXT PAGE

**Use the information on the bases in the following table to answer questions 43 and 44.**

A large number of compounds adopt the sodium chloride structure. The following table contains some examples of the compounds in this group with their respective melting points and the sum of the cation–anion radii.

| COMPOUND | FORMULA | MELTING POINT (°C) | SUM OF IONIC RADII (PM) |
|---|---|---|---|
| Sodium chloride | NaCl | 801 | 283 |
| Sodium fluoride | NaF | 996 | 235 |
| Calcium oxide | CaO | 2898 | 240 |
| Strontium oxide | SrO | 2531 | 258 |
| Barium oxide | BaO | 1972 | 275 |

**43.** Why are the melting points of the alkaline earth oxides (CaO, SrO, and BaO) so much higher than those of the other two compounds in the table?

(A) Smaller ions have lower lattice energy.
(B) Smaller ionic charges lead to higher lattice energy.
(C) Larger ions have higher lattice energy.
(D) Higher ionic charges lead to higher lattice energy.

**44.** Why do the melting points of the alkaline metal oxides decrease in the order CaO > SrO > BaO?

(A) Larger ions have higher lattice energy, which leads to lower melting points.
(B) Smaller ions have lower lattice energy, which leads to higher melting points.
(C) Larger ions have lower lattice energy, which leads to lower melting points.
(D) Smaller ions have a greater affinity for oxygen, which leads to a higher melting point.

**45.** Joseph Priestly discovered oxygen gas by the decomposition of solid mercury(II) oxide, HgO, to oxygen gas, $O_2$, and liquid mercury metal, Hg. How many moles of oxygen gas will form when 4.32 g of solid mercury(II) oxide decomposes? The formula mass of mercury(II) oxide is 216 g $mol^{-1}$.

(A) 0.100 mol
(B) 0.0100 mol
(C) 0.0200 mol
(D) 0.0150 mol

| COMPOUND | FORMULA | MOLAR MASS (g $mol^{-1}$) | MELTING POINT (°C) |
|---|---|---|---|
| Carbon tetrafluoride | $CF_4$ | 88 | −184 |
| Carbon tetrachloride | $CCl_4$ | 154 | −23 |
| Carbon tetrabromide | $CBr_4$ | 332 | 92 |
| Carbon tetraiodide | $CI_4$ | 520 | 171 |

**46.** According to the data in the table above, which of the following best explains the trend in increasing melting points?

(A) All the molecules are nonpolar, and, for such molecules, intermolecular forces increase with increasing molar mass.
(B) All the molecules are polar, and, for such molecules, intermolecular forces increase with increasing molar mass.
(C) The molecules with the lower melting points are nonpolar and the molecules with the higher molar masses are polar.
(D) The sequence is a coincidence since all the molecules have the same intermolecular forces.

**47.** Determine the $H^+(aq)$ concentration in 1.0 $M$ phenol, $C_6H_5OH$, solution. (The $K_a$ for phenol is $1 \times 10^{-10}$.)

(A) $1 \times 10^{-10}\ M$
(B) $1 \times 10^{-9}\ M$
(C) $1 \times 10^{-3}\ M$
(D) $1 \times 10^{-5}\ M$

GO ON TO THE NEXT PAGE

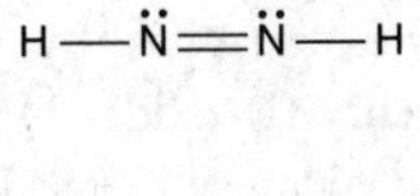

Diazene

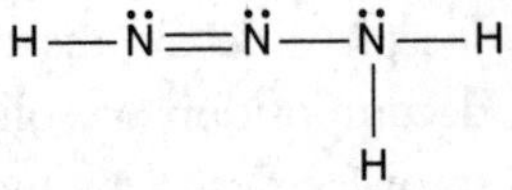

Triazene

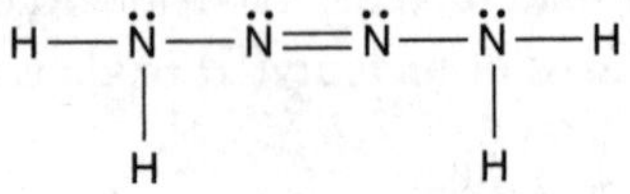

Tetrazene

**48.** Ammonia is the best-known nitrogen–hydrogen compound; however, there are a number of other nitrogen–hydrogen compounds, three of which are in the above diagram. Which of these has the longest average N-N bond length?

(A) $N_2H_2$
(B) $N_3H_3$
(C) $N_4H_4$
(D) They are all the same.

$$(NH_4)_2CO_3(s) \leftrightarrows 2\ NH_3(g) + CO_2(g) + H_2O(l)$$

**49.** The above equilibrium was established in a 1.00-L container at a certain temperature. Once the system came to equilibrium, it was found that the following amounts of materials were present in the container: $(NH_4)_2CO_3$ = 8.00 moles, $NH_3$ = 4.00 moles, $CO_2$ = 2.00 moles, and $H_2O$ = 2.00 moles.

Determine the value of $K_c$ at this temperature.

(A) 8.00
(B) 64.0
(C) 4.00
(D) 32.0

**50.** A solution of a weak base is titrated with a solution of a standard strong acid. The progress of the titration is followed with a pH meter. Which of the following observations would occur?

(A) Initially, the pH slowly decreases, then there is a rapid decrease to give a pH below 7 at the equivalence point.
(B) The pH of the solution gradually decreases throughout the experiment, and the pH at the equivalence point is below 7.
(C) Initially, the pH slowly decreases, then there is a rapid decrease to give a pH equal to 7 at the equivalence point.
(D) Initially, the pH quickly decreases, then there is a gradual decrease to the equivalence point where the pOH equals the p$K_b$ of the base.

**51.** A student mixes 100.0 mL of a 0.10 *M* hydrofluoric acid, HF, solution with 50.0 mL of a 0.10 *M* potassium hydroxide, KOH, solution. The $K_a$ for hydrofluoric acid is $6.8 \times 10^{-4}$. Which of the diagrams below best represents the species, other than $H_2O$, in the solution after the acid reacts with the base?

(A)

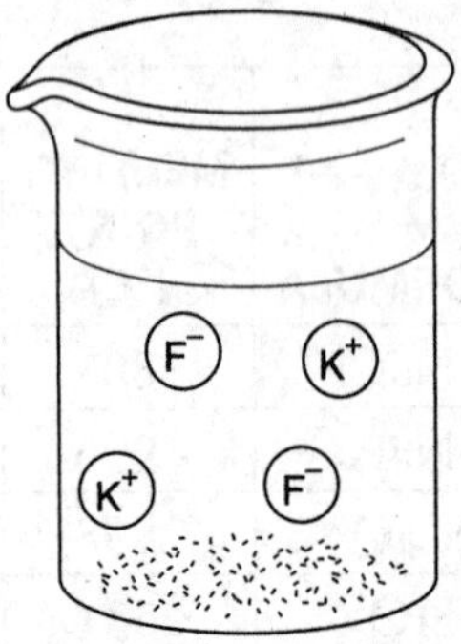


(B)

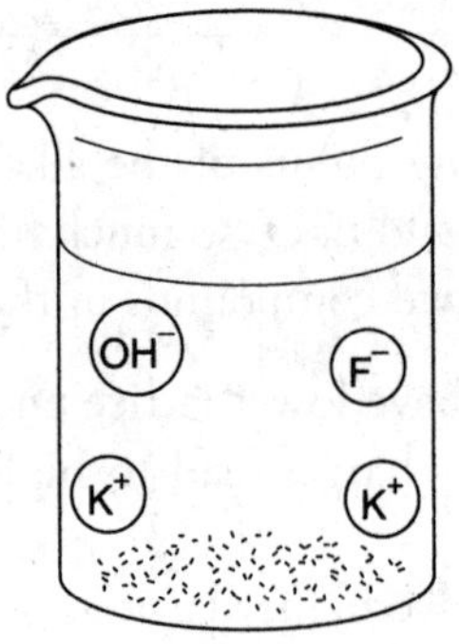


(C)

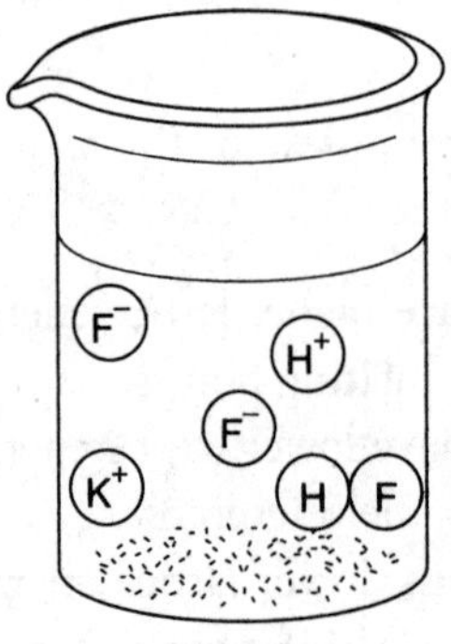


(D)

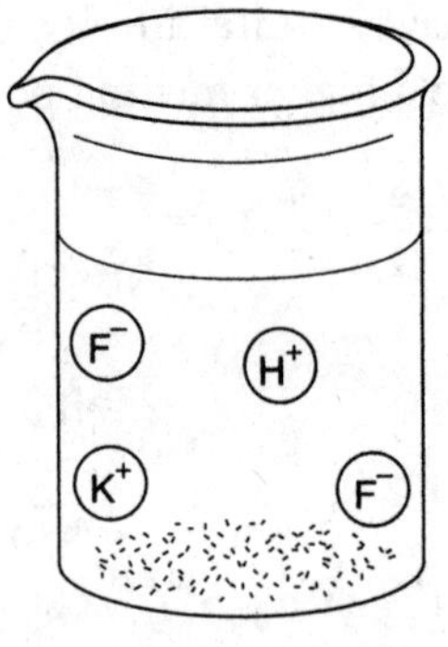


GO ON TO THE NEXT PAGE

**52.** Which of the following best represents the result for the reaction of 50.0 mL of a 0.20 *M* barium hydroxide, $Ba(OH)_2$, solution with 50.0 mL of a 0.10 *M* sulfuric acid, $H_2SO_4$, solution to form a precipitate of $BaSO_4$?

(A)

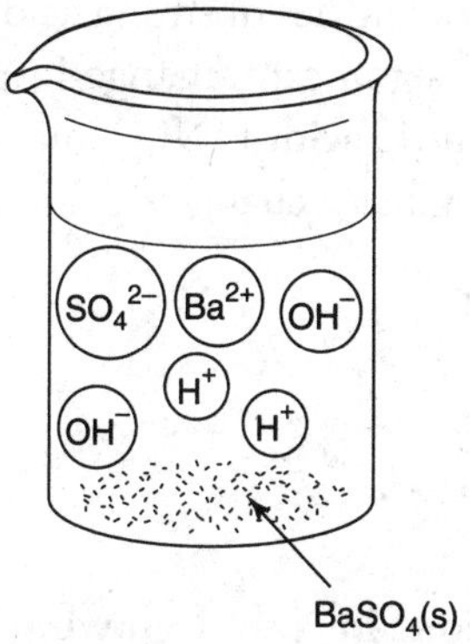


(B)

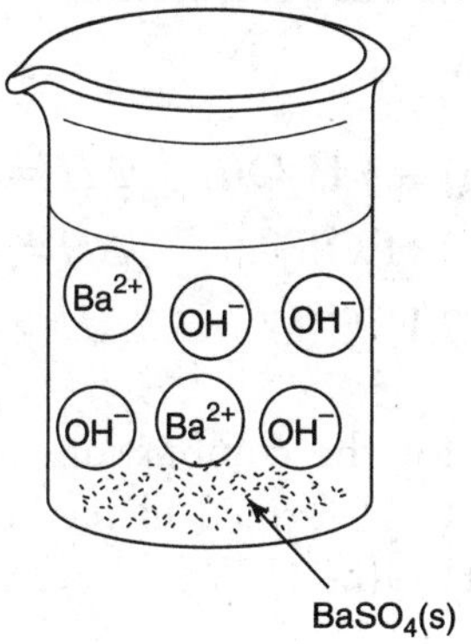


(C)

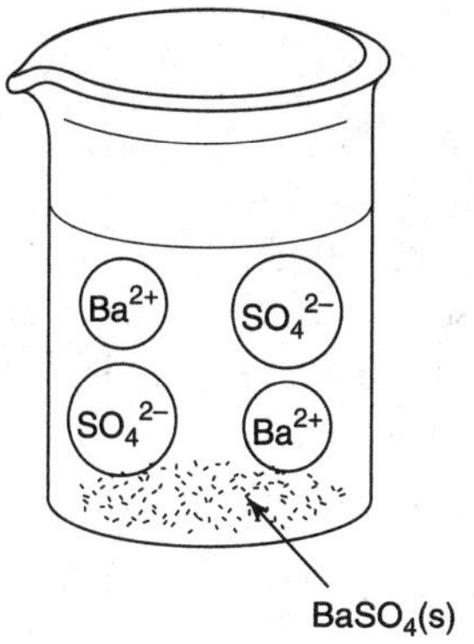


(D)

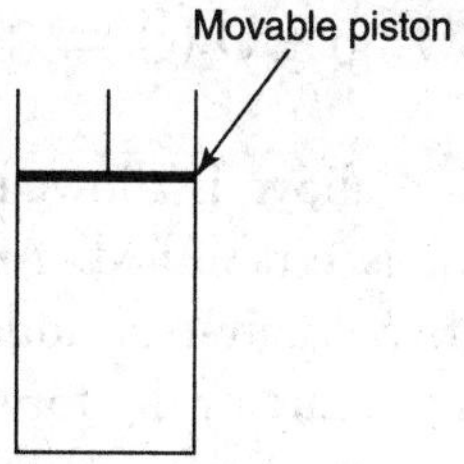


**53.** The container in the above diagram had an initial volume of 10.0 L. The container was heated until the temperature was double the original temperature. After heating, the pressure was measured, and the piston moved until the pressure was four times the original value. What was the final volume of the container?

(A) 10.0 L
(B) 1.25 L
(C) 5.00 L
(D) 20.0 L

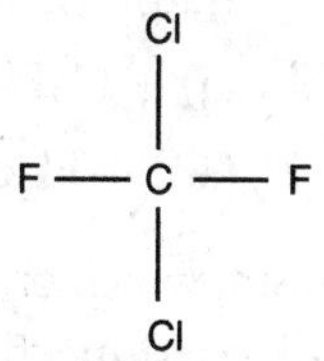


Dichlorodifluoromethane

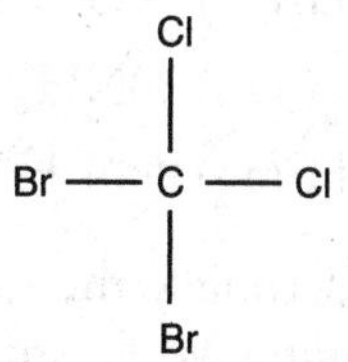


Dibromodichloromethane

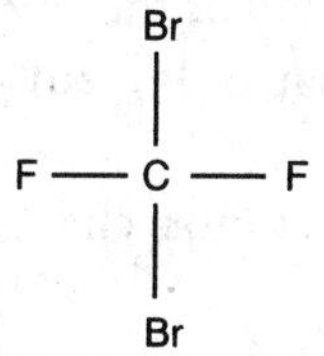


Dibromodifluoromethane

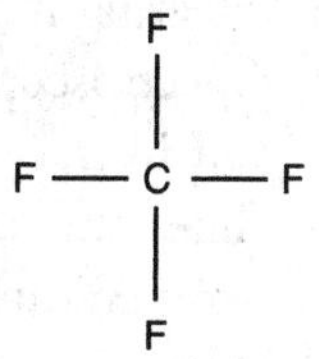


Tetrafluoromethane

| COMPOUND | BOILING POINT (°C) | MOLAR MASS ($g\ mol^{-1}$) |
|---|---|---|
| Dichlorodifluoromethane | −30 | 121 |
| Dibromodichloromethane | 150 | 243 |
| Dibromodifluoromethane | 23 | 210 |
| Tetrafluoromethane | −128 | 88 |

**54.** The diagram above shows the structure of molecules of $CCl_4$ and $CBr_4$, and the above table gives the boiling points and molar masses of the compounds. Which of the compounds is nonpolar?

(A) dichlorodifluoromethane
(B) dibromodichloromethane
(C) dibromodifluoromethane
(D) tetrafluoromethane

$$2\ SO_2(g) + O_2(g) \leftrightarrows 2\ SO_3(g)$$

**55.** The reaction above is allowed to continue until equilibrium is established. After equilibrium is established, a catalyst is added to the system. How does the rate of the forward reaction compare to the rate of the reverse reaction after the addition of the catalyst?

(A) The forward rate is faster than the reverse rate.
(B) The forward and reverse rates are the same.
(C) The reverse rate is faster than the forward rate.
(D) There is insufficient information to determine the relative rates.

A reaction has the following suggested mechanism:

1. $NH_3(aq) + OCl^-(aq) \rightarrow NH_2Cl(aq) + OH^-(aq)$
2. $NH_3(aq) + NH_2Cl(aq) \rightarrow Cl^-(aq) + N_2H_5^+(aq)$
3. $OH^-(aq) + N_2H_5^+(aq) \rightarrow N_2H_4(aq) + H_2O(l)$

**56.** Referring to the above mechanism, which of the following would support the suggested mechanism?

(A) Heating increases the rate of the reaction.
(B) Spectroscopy shows that $N_2H_5^+(aq)$ is present in trace amounts.
(C) The rate constant does not change with temperature.
(D) The first step is the rate-determining step.

**57.** Determine the final temperature, in °C, of a sample of helium gas. The sample initially occupied a volume of 5.00 L at 127°C and 875 mm Hg. The sample was heated, at constant pressure, until it occupied a volume of 10.00 L.

(A) 454°C
(B) 527°C
(C) 45°C
(D) 181°C

**58.** A solution contains 2.00 moles of acetic acid, $CH_3COOH$, and 1.00 mole of calcium acetate, $Ca(CH_3COO)_2$. The solution is able to resist the addition of a small amount of strong acid or strong base with only minor changes in the pH of the solution. Larger quantities of strong acid or strong base can cause a significant change in pH. How many moles of nitric acid, $HNO_3$, may be added before the pH begins to change significantly?

(A) 0.500 mole
(B) 1.00 mole
(C) 2.00 moles
(D) 3.00 moles

**Use the information in the following thermochemical equations to answer questions 59 and 60.**

$C_2H_5OH(l) + 3\ O_2(g) \rightarrow 2\ CO_2(g) + 3\ H_2O(l)$ $\quad \Delta H = -1370$ kJ

$2\ H_2(g) + O_2(g) \rightarrow 2\ H_2O(l)$ $\quad \Delta H = -570$ kJ

$2\ H_2(g) + O_2(g) \rightarrow 2\ H_2O(g)$ $\quad \Delta H = -480$ kJ

**59.** Determine $\Delta H$ for the combustion of ethanol, $C_2H_5OH$, if $H_2O(g)$ formed in the above reaction instead of $H_2O(l)$.

(A) +1,280 kJ
(B) –1,280 kJ
(C) +1,100 kJ
(D) –1,100 kJ

**60.** What is the energy change when 72.0 g of water vapor decomposes to the elements at constant pressure? The molar mass of $H_2O$ is 18.0 g $mol^{-1}$.

(A) –1,144 kJ
(B) –572 kJ
(C) +960 kJ
(D) +1,144 kJ

**STOP. End of AP Chemistry Practice Exam 2, Section I (Multiple Choice).**

# › Answers and Explanations for Exam 2, Section I (Multiple Choice)

1. **B**—This is a dipole–dipole force, which is stronger than a dipole-induced dipole (A and C) or a London dispersion force (D).

2. **C**—This will increase the concentration of $Ag^+$, causing a shift to the right, which will lead to an increase in the cell voltage.

3. **A**—The zinc ion concentration remains the same (1 *M*); therefore, the voltage will remain the same. The identity of the anion associated with the zinc is not important unless the compound is not soluble. Zinc chloride must be soluble; otherwise the student could not make a 1 *M* solution.

4. **B**—The cell voltage (1.56 V) is the sum of the standard reduction potential for silver (0.80 V) and the reverse of the standard reduction potential for zinc. Therefore, (1.56 – 0.80) V = 0.76 V = the reverse of the standard reduction potential for zinc. Reversing the value gives –0.76 V as the standard reduction potential for zinc.

5. **B**—As the cell begins to run, the voltage decreases until the system reaches equilibrium, where the voltage is zero.

6. **D**—The mass of water is the difference in the masses of the hydrated salt and the anhydrous salt. In this case, (mass of crucible plus hydrated salt) – (mass of crucible plus anhydrous salt) = 58.677 g – 57.857 g = 0.820 g. This assumes the mass of the crucible is constant.

7. **A**—The percent water is 100% times the grams of water divided by the mass of the hydrated salt. The mass of water is: (mass of crucible plus hydrated salt) – (mass of crucible plus anhydrous salt) = (58.677 – 57.857) g = 0.820 g water.

   The mass of the hydrated salt is: (mass of crucible plus hydrated salt) – (mass of crucible) = (58.677 – 53.120) g = 5.557 g hydrated salt.

   Finally, percent water $= \dfrac{0.820\ \text{g}\ H_2O}{5.557\ \text{g}}(100\%) =$ 14.8%. The simplified calculation would be: percent water $\approx \dfrac{0.8\ \text{g}\ H_2O}{5.6\ \text{g}}(100\%) \approx \dfrac{1}{7}(100\%) \approx 14\%$

   Remember: you will need to do this without a calculator on the exam.

8. **C**—Leaving the sample overnight in the lab drawer would cause the sample to be no longer anhydrous. The mass of the "anhydrous" salt would now be higher-indicating a smaller amount of water loss, which would lead to a lower percentage of water in the sample.

9. **B**—It is necessary to determine the empirical formula of the compound. If the sample is 63% water, then it is 37% anhydrous salt. Assuming 100 grams of compound, the masses of water and anhydrous salt are 63 g and 37 g, respectively. Converting each of these to moles gives:

   $$\text{Moles anhydrous salt} = (37\ \text{g anhydrous salt}) \times \left(\frac{1\ \text{mol anhydrous salt}}{106\ \text{g anhydrous salt}}\right) = 0.35\ \text{mole anhydrous salt}$$

   $$\text{Moles anhydrous salt} = (63\ \text{g}\ H_2O) \times \left(\frac{1\ \text{mol}\ H_2O}{18.0\ \text{g}\ H_2O}\right) = 3.5\ \text{mole}\ H_2O$$

   Since there are ten times as many moles of water as moles of the anhydrous salt, the formula must be $A_aX_x \bullet 10H_2O$. Remember, you will need to do this without a calculator on the exam.

10. **C**—No calculations are necessary as this is the only answer with the correct units.

11. **A**—Comparing experiments 1 and 3 shows that changing the hydrogen ion concentration has no effect upon the rate; therefore, the reaction is zero order in hydrogen ion (leave it out of the rate law). Comparing experiments 2 and 3 shows that doubling the urea concentration doubles the rate; therefore, the reaction is first order with respect to urea.

12. **C**—The reaction is taking place in aqueous solution. For this reason, there is no significant change in the $H_2O$ concentration. It is not possible to determine the effect of a reactant if the concentration does not change.

**13. B**—The first step is to calculate the true concentration of the sample to see how the student results compare. The balanced chemical equation is $H_2C_2O_4(aq) + 2\ NaOH(aq) \rightarrow Na_2C_2O_4(aq)$

All the volumes are similar; therefore, it is possible to use any one of them and calculate an approximate molarity using rounded numbers for simplicity.

$$M\ H_2C_2O_4 \approx (40\ \text{mL NaOH}) \times$$

$$\left(\frac{0.050\ \text{mol NaOH}}{1{,}000\ \text{mL}}\right)\left(\frac{1\ \text{mol}\ H_2C_2O_4}{2\ \text{mol NaOH}}\right)\left(\frac{1}{10\ \text{mL}}\right) \times$$

$$\left(\frac{1{,}000\ \text{mL}}{\text{L}}\right) \approx 0.1\ M$$

The calculated value should be about half what the student reported. This indicates that the student did not include the 1:2 mole ratio relating the acid to the base or that the student incorrectly used a relationship such as $M_1V_1 = M_2V_2$.

**14. B**—The relationship is: $\Delta G = -nFE°$ (given on the exam).

The number of electrons transferred = 2 = $n$, $F$ = 96,485 coulombs mol$^{-1}$, and volt = 1 joule coulomb$^{-1}$ (both given on the exam). These two relationships lead to $F$ = 96,485 J V$^{-1}$ mol$^{-1}$.

$E° = (0.76 - 0.28)\ \text{V} = 0.48\ \text{V}$

Entering this information in the equation gives

$\Delta G = -(2)(96{,}485\ \text{J V}^{-1}\ \text{mol}^{-1})(0.48\ \text{V}) \approx -(2)(100{,}000)(0.50) \approx -100{,}000\ \text{J mol}^{-1}$ (actual value = $-9.26 \times 10^4$ J mol$^{-1}$); pick the closest answer. Also, the answer must be negative. As always, estimating will help.

**15. A**—At point G, all the $CO_3^{2-}$ has been converted to $HCO_3^-$ and the moles of $HCO_3^-$ will equal the moles of $CO_3^{2-}$ originally present. It will require an equal volume of acid to titrate an equal number of moles of $HCO_3^-$ as required for the $CO_3^{2-}$. For pure sodium carbonate, F will always be 2G.

**16. A**—At point G, all the $CO_3^{2-}$ has been converted to $HCO_3^-$ and the moles of $HCO_3^-$ will equal the moles of $CO_3^{2-}$ originally present plus the quantity of $HCO_3^-$ originally present. It will require a greater volume of acid to titrate a greater number of moles of $HCO_3^-$ as required for the $CO_3^{2-}$.

**17. C**—It would be necessary to titrate the strong base and the $CO_3^{2-}$ to reach G. However, it is only necessary to titrate the $HCO_3^-$ to reach H, which means less acid is necessary.

**18. B**—At G the $CO_3^{2-}$ is now $HCO_3^-$, so no $CO_3^{2-}$ remains. The $Na^+$ did not react, so it is still present as ions. The $Cl^-$ is from the HCl and remains as separate ions in solution. After G, the $H^+$ from the acid begins to convert $HCO_3^-$ to form $H_2CO_3$, which is complete at point F, leaving no $HCO_3^-$ in the solution. Water is a nonelectrolyte. NaCl is a strong electrolyte, which exists as ions in solution. The $H_2CO_3$ will be decomposing to $H_2O$ and $CO_2(g)$.

**19. D**—The pH will equal the p$K_{a2}$ when the concentration of $HCO_3^-$ equals the concentration of $H_2CO_3$. This occurs when one-half of the $HCO_3^-$ has been converted to $H_2CO_3$. This occurs midway through the buffer region between G and H. (This is not very accurate because some of the $H_2CO_3$ has decomposed.)

**20. D**—The average kinetic energy, not the average speed, is the same if the temperatures are the same. Each container has one mole of gas, which means that at the same volume and temperature they will have the same pressure. The greater the molar mass, divided by a constant volume, the greater the density. One mole of gas will have Avogadro's number of molecules.

**21. B**—The process did happen; therefore, it is spontaneous. The decrease in temperature indicates that the system absorbed heat, meaning that this is an endothermic process. For an endothermic process to be spontaneous, the entropy must increase.

**22. D**—Hydrogen bonding may occur when hydrogen is attached directly to N, O, or F. Hydrogen bonding is a strong intermolecular force. The other compounds are polar molecules with dipole–dipole forces. $SbH_3$ is higher the $NH_3$ because of a significant London force contribution.

**23. C**—The two molecules are hydrogen bonded together. Hydrogen bonding is a relatively strong intermolecular force. Acetyl chloride cannot exhibit anything stronger than dipole–dipole forces, which are, in general, weaker than hydrogen bonds. Just because these are organic molecules does not alter the fact that they must follow the same rules as all other molecules.

**24. A**—The higher boiling isomer is more polar than the other isomer because the two very electronegative chlorine atoms are on the same side, which leads to their polar bonds working together. When the chlorine atoms are on opposite sides, their polar bonds work against each other. Hydrogen bonding is not an option for either molecule, both molecules have the same molar mass, and the London dispersion forces should be identical.

**25. D**—Add the equations together and cancel any species that appear on both sides (intermediates).

**26. A**—There are four steps in the proposed mechanism; therefore, there must be four peaks in the graph. The first step in the mechanism is the slow (rate-determining) step. It is the slowest because it has the highest activation energy. For the first step to be the slow step, the first peak must be the highest.

**27. C**—The rate law always considers the slowest step in a mechanism. There is one molecule of $N_2O_5$ as the reactant in the slow step; therefore, the rate law will only use the concentration of this reactant raised to a power equal to the number of molecules in the slow step. A cannot be correct because there is one $N_2O_5$ in the slow step instead of two as indicated. B is not a rate law. D is an equilibrium constant expression, not a rate law.

**28. C**—Use Graham's law; a molecule with one-fourth the molar mass will diffuse at double the rate. Neon is the nearest to one-fourth the molar mass of krypton.

**29. A**—This is a consequence of kinetic molecular theory. The average kinetic energy depends only on the absolute temperature.

**30. D**—Heavier nonpolar species exhibit greater London dispersion forces, and stronger attractive forces lead to greater deviation from ideal behavior under a given set of conditions.

**31. A**—An increase in volume will cause an equilibrium to shift toward the side with more gas. There are four gas molecules on the left side and five gas molecules on the right side; therefore, an increase in volume will result in a shift to the right, which increases the amount of HCl (and $O_2$). B will have the opposite effect. Cooling an endothermic equilibrium will cause a shift to the left, which will decrease the amount of HCl. D will yield no change because helium is not part of the equilibrium.

**32. D**—The amount of time necessary is a kinetics problem. There is no kinetic data presented to make the determination possible.

**33. A**—The ICE table for this equilibrium is:

| $Cl_2$ | $H_2O$ | HCl | $O_2$ |
|---|---|---|---|
| 1.0 atm | 1.0 atm | 0 | 0 |
| $-2x$ | $-2x$ | $+4x$ | $+x$ |
| $1.0 - 2x$ | $1.0 - 2x$ | $+4x$ | $+x$ |

From the equilibrium line on the table, the equilibrium pressure should be:

$(1.0 - 2x) + (1.0 - 2x) + (+4x) + (+x) = 2.0 + x$

Therefore, the equilibrium pressure will be greater than 2.0 atm by an amount equal to $x$.

**34. D**—To determine the amount, it would be necessary to know the value of the equilibrium constant. A cannot be correct because it is not possible for any of the materials to be zero at equilibrium. B and C cannot be correct because at least some of the $O_2$ would be converted to $Cl_2$ and $H_2O$, leading to a decrease in the amount.

**35. B**—The pH of a 1.0 *M* methylamine solution is the highest; therefore, it is the strongest of the bases. For this reason, the pH at the equivalence point of the methylamine titration will be the highest.

**36. A**—As in ammonia, all these compounds behave as Brønsted–Lowry bases by accepting a hydrogen ion. The reaction involves the hydrogen ion attaching to the lone pair on the nitrogen atoms. The stem says "they accept a hydrogen ion to the same atom," and only hydroxylamine contains oxygen; therefore, any answer focusing on O cannot be correct.

**37. C**—These are all bases because the nitrogen atom can react with a hydrogen ion by donating its lone pair to the hydrogen ion. The oxygen atom pulls electron density away from the nitrogen atom, causing the nitrogen atom to attract the lone pair more strongly and making it less able to donate the pair to a hydrogen ion.

**38. A**—Only A can undergo oxidation, as there are higher oxidation states of nitrogen. For example, $HNO_3$ is the most likely oxidation product and, unlike $HNO_2$, it is a strong acid.

**39. D**—Hydrogen bonding is possible when hydrogen is attached to N, O, and F. D is the only compound in the diagram where this is true. The simple presence of hydrogen and N, O, or F is insufficient.

**40. B**—In general, gases have much higher entropy than either liquids or solids. For this reason, the predictions depend primarily upon which reaction results in the greatest decrease in the number of moles of gas. A and D both result in an increase in the number of moles of gas, so there is an increase in entropy. C shows no change in the number of moles of gas; therefore, the change in entropy will be small.

**41. D**— The relationship, given on the equations page of the exam, is $\Delta G = \Delta H - T\Delta S$. Nonspontaneous under standard conditions means $\Delta G > 0$. To become spontaneous, $\Delta G$ must be less than zero ($< 0$). Increasing the temperature will change the $T\Delta S$ term (entropy). If $\Delta H$ is greater than zero and $\Delta S$ is also greater than zero, the combination will be positive if $\Delta H$ is greater than $T\Delta S$. As the temperature increases, $T\Delta S$ will eventually become larger than $\Delta H$, making the process spontaneous.

**42. C**—In general, the more oxygen atoms present not attached to hydrogen atoms, the stronger the oxyacid. If two oxyacids have the same number of oxygen atoms not attached to hydrogen atoms, the acid with the more electronegative central atom is the stronger acid. The number of oxygen atoms without hydrogen atoms attached are $HClO = 0$, $HBrO = 0$, $H_2SeO_3 = 1$, and $H_2SO_3 = 1$ (eliminating A and D). The electronegativities increase in the order Br < Cl and Se < S (making C more likely than B).

**43. D**—The melting points of ionic compounds increase with increasing lattice energy. Lattice energy increases with increasing ionic charge and with decreasing sum of ionic radii. It is apparent from comparing NaF to CaO that charge is more important than small changes in radii. The charges are $Na^+$, $Ca^{2+}$, $Sr^{2+}$, $Ba^{2+}$, $F^-$, $Cl^-$, and $O^{2-}$. If all the compounds did not have the same structure, the comparisons might not be this simple.

**44. C**—The melting points of ionic compounds increase with increasing lattice energy. Lattice energy increases with increasing ionic charge and with decreasing sum of ionic radii. The oxide ion radius is a constant for these three compounds, while the metal radii decrease in the order $Ba^{2+} > Sr^{2+} > Ca^{2+}$. The decrease in metal radii is due to the smaller ions having fewer electron shells.

**45. B**—The balanced chemical equation is:

$$2\ HgO(s) \rightarrow 2\ Hg(l) + O_2(g)$$

The calculation is:

$$(4.32\text{ g HgO})\left(\frac{1\text{ mol HgO}}{216\text{ g HgO}}\right)\left(\frac{1\text{ mol }O_2}{2\text{ mole HgO}}\right)$$

$$= (4.32)\left(\frac{1}{216}\right)\left(\frac{1\text{ mol }O_2}{2}\right)$$

$$= (2.16)\left(\frac{1}{216}\right)\left(\frac{1\text{ mol }O_2}{1}\right)$$

$$= 0.0100\text{ mole }O_2$$

Without a calculator (as required on the multiple-choice portion of the test), you should estimate the last calculation as:

$$(2)\left(\frac{1}{200}\right)\left(\frac{1\text{ mole }O_2}{1}\right) = 0.0100\text{ mole }O_2$$

**46. A**—The substance with the highest melting point has the strongest intermolecular forces. All four molecules are nonpolar; therefore, the intermolecular forces are London dispersion forces. In general, London dispersion forces, for molecules with similar structures, increase with increasing molar mass.

**47. D**—Since phenol has a $K_a$ value given, it is a weak acid; as such, the equilibrium expression can only be:

$$C_6H_5OH(aq) \leftrightarrows H^+(aq) + C_6H_5O^-(aq)$$

Use the $K_a$ expression:

$$K_a = \frac{[H^+][CB]}{[CA]} = 1.0 \times 10^{-10} = \frac{[x][x]}{[1.0]}$$

This leads to:

$$[H^+] = x = (1.0 \times 1 \times 10^{-10})^{1/2} = (1 \times 10^{-10})^{1/2} = 1 \times 10^{-5}\ M$$

The presence of the –OH on the phenol is a distractor; the key is that there is a $K_a$, not a $K_b$.

**48. C**—The higher the average number of bonds between the nitrogen atoms, the shorter the bond is. For diazene there are two bonds, for triazene the average is 1.5 bonds, and for tetrazene the average is 1.33 bonds. The length of the average bond length increases in the order 2 < 1.5 < 1.33.

**49. D**—The ammonium carbonate is a solid and the water is a liquid; therefore, neither of these will be in the calculation. Since the volume of the container is 1.00 L, the molarities of the other two substances are 4.00 $M\ NH_3$ and 2.00 $M\ CO_2$.

$$K_c = [NH_3]^2[CO_2] = (4.00)^2(2.00) = 32.0$$

**50. A**—Strong acids and strong bases have pH = 7 at the equivalence point. The presence of a weak base with a strong acid lowers this value. The pH slowly changes (add an acid means slowly decreasing) at the beginning of a titration and more rapidly near the equivalence point.

**51. C**—The reaction is:

$$HF(aq) + KOH(aq) \rightarrow KF(aq) + H_2O(l)$$

The potassium hydroxide is the limiting reagent, and all the hydroxide ions from the base combine with one-half of the hydrogen ions produced from the acid. The potassium fluoride is a strong electrolyte and is present in solution as fluoride ions and potassium ions. The hydrofluoric acid is a weak acid, as indicated by the $K_a$, and it will partially ionize in solution to form hydrogen ions and fluoride ions with the remaining acid being undissociated. C is the only answer showing unionized weak acid molecules.

**52. B**—The reaction is:

$$Ba(OH)_2(aq) + H_2SO_4(aq) \rightarrow BaSO_4(s) + 2\,H_2O(l)$$

There are 0.010 moles of barium hydroxide and 0.0050 moles of sulfuric acid. The barium hydroxide is in excess and the sulfuric acid is limiting. All the sulfate ions combine with barium ions to form the $BaSO_4$ precipitate with the excess barium ions remaining in solution. All the hydrogen ions from the acid react with the hydroxide ions from the base to produce water and leave the excess hydroxide ions in solution.

**53. C**—There are several ways of solving this problem. One way is to use the combined gas equation $\frac{(P_1V_1)}{T_1} = \frac{(P_2V_2)}{T_2}$. (It would be possible to separately apply Boyle's law and Charles's law.) In this problem, $V_1$ = 10.0 L, $T_2 = 2\ T_1$, and $P_2 = 4\ P_1$. Rearranging the combined gas equation and entering the values gives:

$$V_2 = (V_1)\left(\frac{T_2}{T_1}\right)\left(\frac{P_1}{P_2}\right) = (10.0\ \text{L})\left(\frac{2\ T_1}{T_1}\right)\left(\frac{P_1}{4\ P_1}\right)$$
$$= 5.00\ \text{L}$$

It is also possible to work this with the ideal gas equation (with no change in the moles of gas):

$$\frac{(P_1V_1)}{T_1} = nR = \frac{(P_2V_2)}{T_2}.$$

**54. D**—Tetrafluoromethane is the only nonpolar molecule in the diagram. All the other compounds are polar. Do not be distracted by the diagram; all these molecules are tetrahedral.

**55. B**—The catalyst will increase the rate of both the forward and reverse reactions. The rates will remain equal, as the presence of a catalyst does not alter the position of the equilibrium, just the time necessary to reach equilibrium. While the two rates will remain equal, they will not be the same as the rates for the uncatalyzed reaction.

**56. B**—The presence of $N_2H_5^+(aq)$ supports this mechanism because the detection of an intermediate supports a mechanism. None of the other choices support or refute the overall mechanism.

**57. B**—It is necessary to convert the temperature to kelvin (127 + 273) and back again.

$$T_2 = \frac{(T_1V_2)}{V_1} = \frac{[10.0\ \text{L} \times (127 + 273)\text{K}]}{(5.00\ \text{L})} - 273$$
$$= 527°\text{C}$$

Simplified by (10.00/5.0) = 2.00; therefore, 400 $K \times 2$ = 800 – 273 = 527°C.

**58. C**—The original solution is a buffer, which will resist changes in pH until all the acetic acid or acetate ions are reacted. The reaction of nitric acid with the acetate ion is:

$$HNO_3(aq) + CH_3COO^-(aq) \rightarrow CH_3COOH(aq) + NO_3^-(aq)$$

One mole of calcium acetate releases 2.00 moles of acetate ion into the solution. As long as any of the acetate ion remains, the solution will have some buffering ability and the pH will remain about the same. Once enough nitric acid has been added to react with all the acetate ion, it is possible to drastically lower the pH by adding more acid. The reaction will require 2.00 moles of nitric acid to completely react with the acetate ion.

**59. D**—This is a Hess's law problem requiring the manipulation of the given equations. The first equation is used directly, the second equation is reversed and tripled, and the last equation is only tripled. Adding the three resultant equations together gives the desired equation, and adding the $\Delta H$ values together gives the desired $\Delta H$.

$$C_2H_5OH(l) + 3\ O_2(g) \rightarrow 2\ CO_2(g) + 3\ H_2O(l) \quad \Delta H = -1{,}370\ kJ$$

$$3[2\ H_2O(l) \rightarrow 2\ H_2(g) + O_2(g)] \quad \Delta H = 3(+570\ kJ)$$

$$3[2\ H_2(g) + O_2(g) \rightarrow 2\ H_2O(g)] \quad \Delta H = 3(-480\ kJ)$$

$$\text{Sum } C_2H_5OH(l) + 3\ O_2(g) \rightarrow 2\ CO_2(g) + 3\ H_2O(g) \quad \Delta H = -1{,}100\ kJ$$

It is possible to simplify the problem by determining the heat of vaporization of water ($H_2O(l) \rightarrow H_2O(g)$), which is 90 kJ; this is also a Hess's law determination.

**60. C**—The decomposition of water vapor is the reverse of the last reaction shown; therefore, the enthalpy change is positive instead of negative, which eliminates answers C and D. The amount of water decomposing is 4.00 moles, which is double the amount of water in the reaction. Double the water will require double the energy.

# › AP Chemistry Practice Exam 2, Section II (Free Response)

**Time—1 hour and 45 minutes**

Answer the following questions in the time allowed. You may use a calculator and the resources at the back of the book. Write the answers on separate sheets of paper.

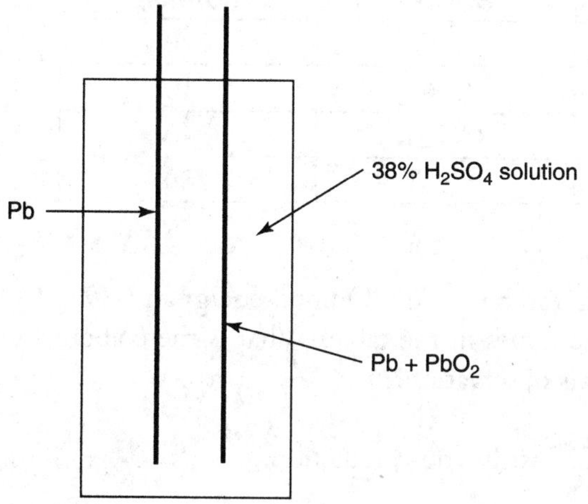


***Question 1***

A simplified diagram of one cell of a lead–acid battery as used in most automobiles is shown above. The half-reactions are:

$$PbO_2(s) + HSO_4^-(aq) + 3\ H^+(aq) + 2\ e^- \rightarrow PbSO_4(s) + 2\ H_2O(l)$$

$$Pb(s) + HSO_4^-(aq) \rightarrow PbSO_4(aq) + H^+(aq) + 2\ e^-$$

The standard cell potential is +2.04 V at 25°C. Initially the electrode on the left is pure lead, and the electrode on the right is pure lead coated with lead(IV) oxide.

(a) The standard reduction potential for the $PbO_2$ half-reaction is 1.68 V.
  (i) Write the overall reaction for the lead–acid battery.
  (ii) Calculate the value of the standard reduction potential for the Pb half-reaction.
(b) A student constructs a brand new lead–acid cell, and it is fully charged.
  (i) Calculate the initial value of $\Delta G°$ for the cell.
  (ii) Calculate the value of $K$ for the cell.
  (iii) The cell is allowed to operate until it reaches equilibrium. What is the value of $\Delta G°$ for the cell at equilibrium?
(c) In an automobile, the water from the electrolyte evaporates. Explain how this will affect the cell potential.
(d) Why is the $PbO_2$ electrode made of Pb coated with $PbO_2$ and not pure $PbO_2$?

***Question 2***

$$2\,NO(g) + Cl_2(g) \rightarrow 2\,NOCl(g)$$

Thermodynamic values related to the above reaction are given in the table below.

| SUBSTANCE | $\Delta H_f^\circ$ (kJ/mol) | S° (J/mol K) | BONDS | BOND ENERGIES (kJ/mol) |
|---|---|---|---|---|
| NO(g) | 90 | 210 | N–O | 170 |
| $Cl_2(g)$ | 0 | 220 | N=O | 610 |
| NOCl(g) | 50 | 260 | Cl–Cl | 240 |
| | | | N–Cl | 200 |

(a) Determine the enthalpy change for the above reaction.
(b) Assuming that the NO bond in NOCl is a double bond, estimate the NO bond energy in NO.
(c) Does the NO bond energy in NO agree with any of the values in the table? What is there about the electronic structure of NO that might be the cause of this observation?
(d) Calculate the entropy change for the reaction.
(e) Is this reaction spontaneous or nonspontaneous at 25°C? Justify your prediction.

***Question 3***

$$5\,Fe^{2+}(aq) + MnO_4^-(aq) + 8\,H^+(aq) \rightarrow Mn^{2+}(aq) + 5\,Fe^{3+}(aq) + 4\,H_2O(l)$$

The above reaction is to be used in the analysis of a sample containing iron metal. The sample is dissolved in acid and the iron reduced to iron(II) ions with a little solid zinc. Excess zinc is filtered from the solution and a titration with standard potassium permanganate is performed immediately before air has had time to oxidize any of the iron(II) ions. The presence of a permanent pink color of excess permanganate ion indicates the endpoint of the titration.

(a) It is possible to standardize the potassium permanganate solution using solid iron(II) ammonium sulfate hexahydrate, $Fe(NH_4)_2(SO_4)_2{\bullet}6H_2O$. You are given a potassium permanganate solution. Outline the general experimental procedure (not the calculations) for standardizing this solution.
(b) Show how to calculate the concentration of the potassium permanganate solution.
(c) Show how to calculate the percent iron in an unknown.
(d) If some of the excess zinc was not filtered from the solution, would the reported percentage of iron in the sample be higher, lower, or the same as when the zinc is completely removed? Explain.
(e) Standardization with iron(II) ammonium sulfate hexahydrate has the advantage of employing the same reaction as in the iron determination. However, there is a problem with using this compound to standardize the potassium permanganate. What might this problem be?
(f) Give the electron configuration of iron(II) ions, $Fe^{2+}$.

GO ON TO THE NEXT PAGE

*Question 4*

$$Ca(CN)_2(s) + H_2SO_4(aq) + 2\ H_2O(l) \rightarrow 2\ HCN(g) + CaSO_4{\bullet}2H_2O(s)$$

It is possible to generate HCN gas by the above reaction. The gas is extremely toxic and great care is necessary when using this compound or related cyanides in any form.

(a) Calculate the number of moles of HCN present in 1.00 L of this gas at 25°C and 1.00 atm.
(b) What volume of HCN gas would the reaction of 1.00 g of $Ca(CN)_2$ with excess $H_2SO_4$ form? The volume is measured at 298 K and 1.00 atm. The molar mass of $Ca(CN)_2$ is 92.1 g $mol^{-1}$.
(c) The reaction in (b) went to completion; however, the volume of gas generated was lower than expected. Explain why the volume was low.
(d) In the box below, draw the Lewis electron-dot structure for HCN.

*Question 5*

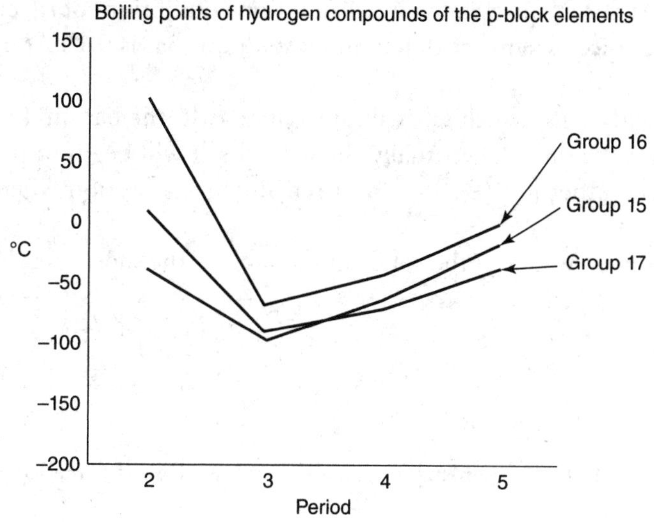


Answer each of the following with respect to the plot of the boiling points of the hydrogen compounds in the above graph. Group 15 is the nitrogen family, Group 16 is the oxygen family, and Group 17 is the halogen family.

(a) On the above plot draw a line to indicate the boiling points of the hydrogen compounds in Group 14 (carbon family).
(b) What is the cause of the upward turn in the three lines shown on the graph?
(c) Where would the compound LiH appear on this graph, and why would it appear in this position?

### *Question 6*

Five beakers (A–E) are on a countertop. Each contains 200 mL of a 0.10 *M* solution. Beaker A contains $SrCl_2$; beaker B contains $NH_4Cl$; beaker C contains $CH_3CH_2OH$; beaker D contains $Na_2C_2O_4$; and beaker E contains $Ni(NO_3)_2$.

(a) Which beaker has the lowest pH and why?
(b) Which solution is most likely to be colored?
(c) Which solution is basic?
(d) Which solution has the lowest electrical conductivity and why?

| COMPOUND | FORMULA | $K_{sp}$ |
|---|---|---|
| Silver sulfate | $Ag_2SO_4$ | $1.6 \times 10^{-5}$ |
| Barium sulfate | $BaSO_4$ | $1.1 \times 10^{-10}$ |
| Calcium sulfate | $CaSO_4$ | $9.1 \times 10^{-6}$ |
| Strontium sulfate | $SrSO_4$ | $3.2 \times 10^{-7}$ |

### *Question 7*

The solubility product constants for some insoluble sulfates are given in the table above.

(a) Write a balanced chemical equation for the dissolution equilibrium of silver sulfate, $Ag_2SO_4$, in water.
(b) A sodium sulfate solution is slowly titrated into a solution that is 0.10 *M* in $Ba(NO_3)_2$ and 0.10 *M* in $Sr(NO_3)_2$.
  (i) Show, with calculations, which salt will precipitate first, the barium salt or the strontium salt.
  (ii) If the titration is continued, eventually the second salt will begin to precipitate. What is the concentration of the other ion ($Ba^{2+}$ or $Sr^{2+}$) remaining in solution when the second salt begins to precipitate?
(c) Show, with calculations, which of the solids in the table is the most soluble.

**STOP. End of AP Chemistry Practice Exam 2, Section II (Free Response).**

# ❯ Answers and Explanations for Exam 2, Section II (Free Response)

***Question 1***

(a) (i) Add the two given half-reactions together and cancel any species appearing on both sides of the reaction arrow (the electrons must cancel).

$$PbO_2(s) + 2\ HSO_4^-(aq) + 2\ H^+(aq) + Pb(s) \rightarrow 2\ PbSO_4(aq) + 2\ H_2O(l)$$

You get 1 point for this answer.

(ii) Adding the potential information to the equations:

| | |
|---|---|
| $PbO_2(s) + HSO_4^-(aq) + 3\ H^+(aq) + 2\ e^- \rightarrow PbSO_4(s) + 2\ H_2O(l)$ | 1.68 V |
| $Pb(s) + HSO_4^-(aq) \rightarrow PbSO_4(aq) + H^+(aq) + 2\ e^-$ | ? V |
| $PbO_2(s) + 2\ HSO_4^-(aq) + 2\ H^+(aq) + Pb(s) \rightarrow 2\ PbSO_4(aq) + 2\ H_2O(l)$ | 2.04 V |

If the cell voltage is 2.04 V (given), then the two half-reaction voltages must add to this. Therefore, 2.04 V = (1.68 + ?) V, which makes the voltage for the second half-reaction equal to 0.36 V. This is the voltage for the oxidation half-reaction; to change this to a standard reduction potential it is necessary to reverse the half-reaction, which means it is necessary to reverse the sign on the voltage. Thus, the standard reduction potential for the second half-reaction is –0.36 V.

You get 1 point for calculating 0.36 V and 1 point for changing the sign to a negative value.

(b) It is necessary to use two of the equations provided on the exam to answer this problem. (If you already know the equations, it will save you the time necessary to look them up.)

(i) The exam (and the appendixes at the back of this book) provides the equation $\Delta G° = -1\ nFE°$ plus the values of the Faraday constant, $F$ = 96,485 coulombs per mole of electrons, and 1 volt $= \frac{1\text{ joule}}{1\text{ coulomb}}$. For this problem, $n$ = 2 moles of electrons (see the half-reactions) and $E°$ = + 2.04 V (given). Entering the values into the equation: $\Delta G° = -nFE° =$

$$-(2\text{ mol electrons})\left(\frac{96.485\text{ coul}}{\text{mol electrons}}\right)(2.04\text{ V})\left(\frac{\text{J}}{(\text{V})(\text{coul})}\right) = 393{,}659 = 3.94 \times 10^5\text{ J or } 394\text{ kJ}.$$

Give yourself 1 point for the correct setup of the equation including the conversion and 1 more point for the correct answer.

(ii) It is possible to get the answer by two different means by using the equations given on the test (in the back of this book). The values of the constants are also given. The important equations are $\Delta G° = -nFE°$ and $\Delta G° = -RT \ln K$. It is possible to combine these equations to $\ln K = \frac{nFE°}{RT}$. The first equation was used in part (b) (ii), and it is acceptable to use the answer from there and go directly to the second equation without recalculating the result. Using the third (combined) equation gives:

$$\ln K = \frac{nFE°}{RT} = \frac{(2\text{ mol electrons})\left(\frac{96.485\text{ coul}}{\text{mol electrons}}\right)(2.04\text{ V})\left(\frac{\text{J}}{(\text{V})(\text{coul})}\right)}{\left(\frac{8.314\text{ J}}{\text{mol K}}\right)(298\text{ K})} = 159,$$ which is the same answer you get from using the answer to part (b) (ii) and the second equation. Finally, if $\ln K = 159$, then $K = e^{159}$ (or $1.1 \times 10^{69}$).

Give yourself 1 point for the correct setup of the equation, including the conversion, and 1 more point for the correct answer.

(iii) At equilibrium $\Delta G°$ is always 0.
Give yourself 1 point for this answer.

(c) As the water evaporates, the concentration of sulfuric acid will increase, which leads to an increase in the hydrogen ion concentration (and $HSO_4^-$). An increase in the hydrogen ion concentration will alter the $PbO_2$ half-reaction more than it will change the Pb half-reaction. The result is a shift toward the right, which will increase the voltage.
Give yourself 1 point for this answer.

(d) It is necessary to have a conductor present for the transfer of electrons. Lead(IV) oxide is an ionic solid, which does not conduct electricity. Lead is a metal, which does conduct electricity.
Give yourself 1 point for this answer.

Total your points for the various parts. There are 10 possible points. Subtract 1 point if any of the answers has the wrong number of significant figures.

***Question 2***

(a) The enthalpy change is the sum of the $\Delta H_f°$ values for the products minus the sum of the $\Delta H_f°$ values for the reactants.

$$\Delta H_{rxn}° = [2(50)] - [2(90) + 1(0)] = -80 \text{ kJ}$$

The answer with appropriate units is worth 1 point. You do not need to get the exact answer, but your answer should round to this one. We have deducted many points for simple calculations such as this one because the student was in a hurry and under stress. Take your time, and do not throw away easy points.

(b) The answer from part (a) equals the bonds broken minus the bonds formed.

$[(2 \text{ NO}) + (\text{Cl–Cl})] - 2\,[(\text{N=O}) + (\text{N–Cl})] = -80 \text{ kJ}$

$[(2 \text{ NO}) + (240)] - 2\,[(610) + (200)] = -80 \text{ kJ}$

$\text{NO} = 650 \text{ kJ}$

The setup (bonds broken – bonds formed) is worth 1 point, and the answer is worth 1 point. You do not need to get the exact answer, but your answer should round to this one. If your answer from part (a) was wrong, but you used it correctly in this part, you still get your setup and answer points.

(c) The value is higher than the value given for an N=O bond. The NO molecule has an odd number of electrons and this will alter its bonding. (Drawing a Lewis dot structure might help you.)
You get 1 point for the correct observation, and 1 point for any explanation involving an odd number of electrons. If you got the wrong answer for part (a) or (b), you can still get 1 or 2 points if you used the answer correctly on this part.

(d) The entropy change is the sum of the $S°$ values for the products minus the sum of the $S°$ values for the reactants.

$$\Delta S_{rxn}° = [2(260)] - [2(210) + 1(220)] = -120 \text{ J/K}$$

The $\Delta S_{rxn}°$ should be negative since there is a decrease in the number of moles of gas.

The setup (products – reactants) is worth 1 point, and the answer is worth 1 point. You do not need to get the exact answer, but your answer should round to this one.

(e) It is necessary to calculate the free-energy change using the following equation (given on the exam and at the back of this book).

$$\Delta G_{rxn}° = \Delta H_{rxn}° - T\Delta S_{rxn}° = -80 \text{ kJ} - (298 \text{ K})(1 \text{ kJ}/1{,}000 \text{ J})(-120 \text{ J/K}) = -44 \text{ kJ}$$

The negative value means the reaction is spontaneous.

You get 1 point for the prediction that the reaction is spontaneous. The setup (plugging into the equation) is worth 1 point if you remember to change the temperature to kelvin and the joule-to-kilojoule conversion (or vice versa for an answer in J). An additional 1 point comes from the answer. If you got the wrong value in either part (a) or (b), but used it correctly, you will still get the point for the answer.

Total your points for the different parts. There is a maximum of 10 points possible. Subtract 1 point if all your answers do not have the correct number of significant figures.

***Question 3***

(a) 1. Samples of iron(II) ammonium sulfate hexahydrate are weighed into beakers, and deionized water is added to dissolve each of the samples.
2. A buret is rinsed with the potassium permanganate solution and then filled.
3. The potassium permanganate solution is titrated into the iron(II) standard until a permanent pink color from the permanganate solution appears.
4. Repeat these steps with the other samples.

Listing these will get you 2 points. Missing one or more of these will get you 1 point. Other items are not necessary and will not change the scoring.

(b) The set up for the calculation is:

[(Mass of $Fe(NH_4)_2(SO_4)_2•6H_2O$)/(Molar mass of $Fe(NH_4)_2(SO_4)_2•6H_2O$)] × (1 mol $MnO_4^-$/ 5 mol $Fe^{2+}$)/(Volume of potassium permanganate solution)

You get 2 points for this complete answer. You get 1 point if a step is missing and 0 points if two or more steps are missing.

(c) The setup for the calculation is:

(Volume permanganate solution) × (Concentration permanganate solution) × (5 mol Fe/1 mol $MnO_4^-$) × (Molar mass of iron) = grams iron

You get 1 point for this intermediate answer.

$$\text{Percent iron} = \left(\frac{\text{grams iron}}{\text{grams sample}}\right) \times 100\%$$

You get 1 point for this answer.

(d) The percent iron would be higher.

You get 1 point for this answer.

The titration would require more potassium permanganate solution to reach the endpoint because it would be necessary to titrate not only the iron but also the zinc.

You get 1 point for this answer or by saying the zinc would reduce some of the iron back to iron(II), which would require it to be retitrated.

(e) As noted in the initial comments for this question, air oxidizes iron(II) ions. For this reason, the iron(II) ions in iron(II) ammonium sulfate hexahydrate might undergo air oxidation before being used to standardize the potassium permanganate.
This answer or simply stating that the compound is unstable is worth 1 point.

(f) The electron configuration may be written as $[Ar]3d^6$ or $1s^2 2s^2 2p^6 3s^2 3p^6 3d^6$. Recall that for the transition metals the s-electrons, in this case $4s^2$, are the first electrons lost in oxidation.
This answer is worth 1 point.

Total your points for the various parts. There are 10 possible points.

***Question 4***

(a) The ideal gas equation is one way of calculating the number of moles, *n*, of a gas.

$$\text{Moles} = n = \frac{PV}{RT} = \frac{(1.00\ \text{atm})(1.00\ \text{L})}{(0.08206\ \text{L atm mol}^{-1}\ \text{K}^{-1})(298\ \text{K})} = 0.0409\ \text{mol HCN (three significant figures)}$$

If you incorrectly assumed the conditions are STP and used the molar volume relation (1 mole = 22.4 L), you got 0.0446 mole HCN, and earn 0 points. Do not expect to ever use (1 mole = 22.4 L) on the AP Exam.
This answer (0.0409 mole) is worth 1 point.

(b) Again it is possible to use the ideal gas equation to solve for the volume, *V*, of a gas.

$$\text{Volume} = V = \frac{nRT}{P}$$

$$= \frac{\left[(1.00\ \text{g Ca(CN)}_2)\left(\frac{1\ \text{mol Ca(CN)}_2}{92.1\ \text{g Ca(CN)}_2}\right)\left(\frac{2\ \text{mol HCN}}{1\ \text{mol Ca(CN)}_2}\right)\right](0.08206\ \text{L atm mol}^{-1}\ \text{K}^{-1})(298\ \text{K})}{(1.00\ \text{atm})}$$

= 0.531 L (three significant figures)

The calculation inside the square brackets [ ] gives *n*.
This answer is worth 1 point. You cannot use the molar volume of a gas because the conditions are not STP.

(c) Based upon its structure, HCN is polar and, therefore, must be soluble in water. For this reason, some product will not be in the gas phase but in the solution, which means the volume of the gas will be less than expected.
This answer, including the explanation, is worth 1 point.

(d)

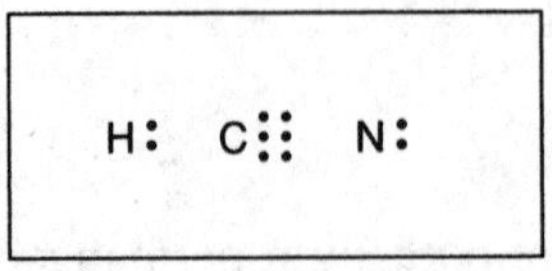

There must be a single bond between the hydrogen atom and the carbon atom and a triple bond between the carbon atom and the nitrogen atom. The lone pair on the nitrogen atom can be anywhere if it is obvious that it is only associated with the nitrogen atom. Both the carbon and the nitrogen atoms have an octet of electrons. This answer is worth 1 point. Substituting a line for the pair of electrons between the H and C, and a triple line for the three electron pairs between the C and N, is acceptable.

Total your points for each part. There are 4 possible points. Subtract 1 point if all reported answers did not have the correct number of significant figures.

*Question 5*

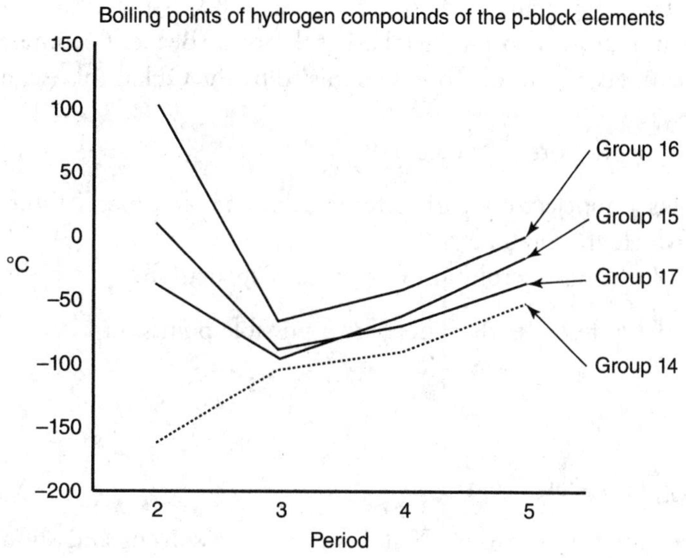


(a) The Group 14 line is the dotted line. The dotted line should always be below the other lines because the hydrogen compounds of the Group 14 elements are all nonpolar, while all the other hydrogen compounds on the graph are polar. The dotted line should not go up at the end because $CH_4$ is the only Period 2 hydrogen compound on the graph that is not capable of hydrogen bonding.
Give yourself 1 point if your line remains below all the other lines. Give yourself a second point if your line does not move up at the left end.

(b) The Period 2 compounds on the graph are, from top to bottom, $H_2O$, HF, $NH_3$, and $CH_4$. The first three of these compounds are the only compounds plotted that are capable of hydrogen bonding. Hydrogen bonding is stronger than any of the other intermolecular forces present in the compounds on the graph, which means their boiling points should be higher than those of compounds without hydrogen bonding.
Give yourself 1 point for this explanation.

(c) Li is a Period 2 element; therefore, it would appear on the left side of the graph and it would have a much higher boiling point than the other compounds because it is an ionic compound and ionic compounds, because of their high lattice energies, have very high boiling points.
You get 1 point if you give the correct approximate position and mention ionic bonding.

A total of 4 points is possible.

*Question 6*

The compounds are supplied as solutions; therefore, they must be soluble. This means any argument stating that one or more of the original substances is not soluble in water is invalid.

(a) The lowest pH will be for the solution containing an acid. Beaker B has the lowest pH. The $NH_4^+$ ion is the conjugate acid of a weak base, and as an acid (weak), it will lower the pH. There are no other acids present.

You get 1 point for choosing B with the correct explanation.

(b) Beaker E, because transition metal ions are often colored in solution.

You get 1 point for the correct choice.

(c) Solution D—solution D contains the conjugate base, $C_2O_4^{2-}$, of a weak acid. The conjugate bases of weak acids undergo hydrolysis to produce basic solutions. (Beaker C contains $CH_3CH_2OH$, which is ethyl alcohol, a neutral compound. Do not be misled by the OH as this is a molecular compound with no $OH^-$ ions present.)

You get 1 point for the correct choice.

(d) Solution C contains a nonelectrolyte; therefore, it does not conduct. All the remaining solutions contain electrolytes, which are conductors.

You get 1 point for choosing solution C with the explanation.

Total your points for the different parts. There are 4 possible points.

*Question 7*

(a) $Ag_2SO_4(s) \leftrightarrows 2\ Ag^+(aq) + SO_4^{2-}(aq)$

You get 1 point for this equation. Note: water is the solvent and should not appear directly in the equation. [Water does appear indirectly as (aq).] We have deducted many points while grading AP exams, because students incorrectly separate the polyatomic sulfate ion into S and O.

(b) (i) Since the stoichiometries of $SrSO_4$ and $BaSO_4$ are the same, the one with the lower $K_{sp}$ will precipitate first ($BaSO_4$). However, the problem states that it is necessary to show this with calculations.

Since the stoichiometries are the same, it is possible to use the generic equation and generic mass action expression with $M^{2+} = Ba^{2+}$ or $Sr^{2+}$.

$$MSO_4(s) \leftrightarrows 2\ M^{2+}(aq) + SO_4^{2-}(aq) \qquad K_{sp} = [M^{2+}][SO_4^{2-}]$$

Since both metals have the same concentration, it is only necessary to determine which requires the lower sulfate ion concentration. This is done as:

$$[SO_4^{2-}] = \frac{K_{sp}}{[M^{2+}]} = \frac{K_{sp}}{[0.10]}$$

For $BaSO_4 = 1.1 \times 10^{-9}$ M $SO_4^{2-}$ and for $SrSO_4 = 3.2 \times 10^{-6}$ M $SO_4^{2-}$

You get 1 point for determining that the sulfate ion concentration shows that $BaSO_4$ will precipitate first, if you include the appropriate calculation.

(ii) From part (i), the second ion ($Sr^{2+}$) begins to precipitate at $3.2 \times 10^{-6}$ M $SO_4^{2-}$. Using this value with the $BaSO_4$ $K_{sp}$ allows the calculation of the barium ion concentration when the $SrSO_4$ first begins to precipitate. This calculation is:

$$[Ba^{2+}] = \frac{K_{sp}}{[SO_4^{2-}]} = \frac{1.1\times10^{-10}}{3.2\times10^{-6}} = 3.4 \times 10^{-5}\ M\ Ba^{2+}$$

You get 1 point for this answer. You also get 1 point if you if you did this calculation correctly but made the wrong prediction or gave an incorrect value in part (i).

(c) For the compounds with the same stoichiometry ($BaSO_4$, $CaSO_4$, and $SrSO_4$) the one with the largest $K_{sp}$ is the most soluble; therefore, it is only necessary to compare the solubilities of $Ag_2SO_4$ and $CaSO_4$.

For $CaSO_4$:

$K_{sp} = [Ca^{2+}][SO_4^{2-}] = 9.1 \times 10^{-6}$ and $[Ca^{2+}] = [SO_4^{2-}] = x$

$K_{sp} = x^2 = 9.1 \times 10^{-6}$ so $x = 3.0 \times 10^{-3}$ $M$

For $Ag_2SO_4$:

$K_{sp} = [Ag^+]^2[SO_4^{2-}] = 1.6 \times 10^{-5}$ and $[Ag^+] = 2\ [SO_4^{2-}]$, $[Ag^+] = 2x$ and $[SO_4^{2-}] = x$

$K_{sp} = (2x)^2(x) = 4x^3 = 1.6 \times 10^{-5}$ so $x = 1.6 \times 10^{-2}$ $M$

The value for $x$ from $Ag_2SO_4$ is larger; therefore, it is more soluble.
Give yourself 1 point for this answer.

There is a total of 4 points possible. Subtract 1 point if any answer has the wrong number of significant figures.

# Appendixes

Pre-AP Diagnostic Exam
SI Units
Balancing Redox Equations Using the Ion–Electron Method
Common Ions
Bibliography
Websites
Glossary
Avoiding "Stupid" Mistakes on the Free-Response Section
Exam Resources

# PRE-AP DIAGNOSTIC EXAM

**Summary:** The AP Exam writers assume that you are bringing a certain level of knowledge to your AP Chemistry class. The AP Chemistry Exam does not test this "prior knowledge" directly, but it is still necessary to understand this material before taking the exam. For example, it is assumed that you already know that if you dissolve a strong electrolyte, such as solid $NaNO_3$, in water, then you also know that the solution contains no $NaNO_3(aq)$ but $Na^+(aq)$ and $NO_3^-(aq)$. The following sample problem is another example.

**Sample Problem:** Given the followed chemical equation:

$$AgNO_3(aq) + K_3PO_4(aq) \rightarrow Ag_3PO_4(s) + KNO_3(aq)$$

what is the $Ag^+(aq)$ concentration present after mixing 10.00 mL of a 0.1000 $M$ $AgNO_3$ solution with 5.00 mL of a 0.1000 $M$ $K_3PO_4$ solution? The $K_{sp}$ of $Ag_3PO_4$ is $1.4 \times 10^{-16}$.

The prior knowledge needed here is that you need to balance the equation before solving the problem. You should take this Pre-AP Diagnostic Exam when you first begin your study of AP Chemistry.

This Pre-AP Diagnostic Exam is for your benefit. It will test your understanding of the knowledge you should bring to your AP class. This exam will let you know where you need to spend most of your study time preparing for each topic. This does not mean you can skip the review of other topics; you should always review all topics. The exam has only multiple-choice questions and is not the mixture of multiple-choice and free-response questions that you will see on the AP Exam.

The diagnostic exam will give you an idea of where you are in terms of your preparation for your AP class and which areas you should focus on. The questions have been written to approximate the coverage of material that you will see on the AP Exam. However, there will be a few questions on content that will not be directly tested on the AP Exam; these questions refer to basic chemistry knowledge that your teacher (and the exam writers) will expect you to know and that you will need to know before taking the AP Chemistry Exam. Once you are done with the exam, check your work against the given answers, which also indicate where you can find the corresponding material in the book.

### Key Ideas

- Answer questions that approximate the coverage of topics on the AP Exam.
- Check your work against the given answers.
- Determine your areas of strength and weakness.
- Highlight the topics to which you must give special attention.

## Getting Started: The Pre-AP Diagnostic Exam

The following questions refer to different chapters in the book. Remember that it is not necessary to get the correct answer (though it would be nice). You will have time later to work on getting the correct answer. The problems you have trouble with will help direct your studying as you prepare for the AP Exam. If you have trouble (even if you got the correct answer), it indicates that you should spend additional time reviewing the topic. While answering these questions you may use a calculator and periodic table. For each question, circle the letter of your choice, and for each question you have difficulty with, circle the question number.

You may wish to repeat some or all questions on this exam before taking the AP Exam.

## Chapter 5 Basics

1. In most of its compounds, this element exists as a monatomic anion.

(A) Fe
(B) Sr
(C) Na
(D) F

2. Which of the following groups has the species correctly listed in order of increasing radius?

(A) Cu, $Cu^+$, $Cu^{2+}$
(B) $F^-$, $Br^-$, $I^-$
(C) V, $V^{2+}$, $V^{3+}$
(D) Li, Be, B

3. Which of the following elements has the highest electronegativity?

(A) Na
(B) B
(C) S
(D) Se

4. Which of the following represents the correct formula for perchloric acid?

(A) $HClO_4$
(B) $HClO_3$
(C) $HClO_2$
(D) HClO

5. Which of the following represents the correct formula for tetraamminecopper(II) chloride?

(A) $[Cu(NH_3)_4](ClO_3)_2$
(B) $(NH_3)_4Cu_2Cl$
(C) $Am_4CuCl_2$
(D) $[Cu(NH_3)_4]Cl_2$

6. The discovery that atoms have electrons in energy levels around the nucleus is credited to which of the following?

(A) Einstein
(B) Dalton
(C) Rutherford
(D) Bohr

## Chapter 6 Stoichiometry

7. $16\ H^+(aq) + 5\ C_2O_4^{2-}(aq) + 2\ MnO_4^-(aq) \rightarrow 2\ Mn^{2+}(aq) + 10\ CO_2(g) + 8\ H_2O(l)$

The above reaction is used in the titration of an oxalate solution. What is the concentration of the oxalate solution if it takes 42.20 mL of 0.1020 *M* $MnO_4^-$ solution to titrate 75.00 mL of an acidified oxalate solution?

(A) 0.05741 *M*
(B) 0.4531 *M*
(C) 0.1435 *M*
(D) 0.2296 *M*

8. Chromium, Cr, forms several oxides. A sample of one of the oxides is 61.9% by mass Cr. What is the simplest formula for this oxide?

(A) CrO
(B) $Cr_2O_3$
(C) $CrO_2$
(D) $CrO_3$

9. $7\ H_2SO_4(aq) + 6\ FeSO_4(aq) + K_2Cr_2O_7(aq) \rightarrow 3\ Fe_2(SO_4)_3(aq) + Cr_2(SO_4)_3(aq) + K_2SO_4(aq) + 7\ H_2O(l)$

In an experiment, a chemist runs the above reaction. How many moles of $Fe_2(SO_4)_3$ are produced when 1.0 mole of $K_2Cr_2O_7$, 6.0 moles of $FeSO_4$, and 6.0 moles of $H_2SO_4$ are mixed?

(A) 2.4 moles
(B) 3.0 moles
(C) 2.0 moles
(D) 3.5 moles

10. ___ $H_2O_2(aq) \rightarrow$ ___ $H_2O(l)$ + ___ $O_2(g)$

After the above equation is balanced, how many moles of $O_2$ can be produced from 1.0 mole of $H_2O_2$?

(A) 0.50 mole
(B) 1.0 mole
(C) 1.5 mole
(D) 2.0 mole

## Chapter 7 Spectroscopy, Light, and Electrons

**11.** Which of the following groups contains only atoms that are diamagnetic in their ground state?

(A) Be, O, and Ne
(B) Ca, Ne, and Rb
(C) Mg, Kr, and Cd
(D) I, As, and Br

**12.** Which of the following could be the ground-state electron configuration of a transition metal ion?

(A) $1s^2 1p^6 2s^2 2p^2$
(B) $1s^2 2s^2 2p^6 3s^2 3p^6 4s^2 3d^{10} 4p^3$
(C) $1s^2 2s^2 2p^6 3s^2 3p^6 3d^9$
(D) $1s^2 2s^2 2p^4$

**13.** Which of the following is the ground-state configuration of a noble gas?

(A) $1s^2 2s^2 2p^6 3s^2$
(B) $1s^2 2s^2 2p^6 3s^2 3p^6$
(C) $1s^2 2s^2 2p^6 3s^2 3p^6 3d^5$
(D) $1s^2 2s^1 2p^6$

**14.** Which of the following is the ground-state electron configuration of a halogen?

(A) $1s^2 2s^2 2p^6 3s^2 3p^6 4s^1 3d^{10} 4p^5$
(B) $1s^2 2s^2 2p^6 3s^2 3p^5 4s^2 3d^{10} 4p^5$
(C) $1s^2 2s^2 2p^6 3s^2 3p^6 4s^2 3d^9 4p^5$
(D) $1s^2 2s^2 2p^6 3s^2 3p^6 4s^2 3d^{10} 4p^5$

**15.** Which of the following is an impossible ground-state electron configuration?

(A) $1s^2 2s^2 2p^6 3s^3 3p^6 4s^2 3d^{10} 4p^4$
(B) $1s^2 2s^2 2p^6 3s^2 3p^6 4s^2 3d^{10} 4p^5$
(C) $1s^2 2s^2 2p^6 3s^2 3p^6 4s^2 3d^{10} 4p^6$
(D) $1s^2 2s^2 2p^6 3s^2 3p^6 4s^2 3d^{10} 4p^3$

**16.** Why is it not possible to determine the exact position of an electron in an atom?

(A) Pauli exclusion principle
(B) electron shielding
(C) Hund's rule
(D) Heisenberg uncertainty principle

**17.** In their ground state, oxygen atoms are paramagnetic. Why does this occur?

(A) This is due to the Pauli exclusion principle.
(B) This is due to electron shielding.
(C) This is due to Hund's rule.
(D) This is due to the effective nuclear charge.

**18.** Why is it NOT possible to have a $4s^3$ electron configuration?

(A) Pauli exclusion principle
(B) electron shielding
(C) Hund's rule
(D) Heisenberg uncertainty principle

**19.** Why does the 4s orbital fill before the 3d orbital?

(A) Pauli exclusion principle
(B) electron shielding
(C) Hund's rule
(D) Heisenberg uncertainty principle

**20.** Zinc reacts with element *X* to form an ionic compound. If the ground-state electron configuration of *X* is $1s^2 2s^2 2p^4$, what is the simplest formula for this compound?

(A) $ZnX_2$
(B) $Zn_2X_3$
(C) $ZnX$
(D) $Zn_3X_2$

## Chapter 8 Bonding

**21.** VSEPR predicts that an $XeF_4$ molecule will have which of the following shapes?

(A) tetrahedral
(B) trigonal bipyramidal
(C) square planar
(D) trigonal pyramidal

**22.** Which of the following does NOT have one or more π bonds?

(A) $CO_2$
(B) $SF_4$
(C) $N_2$
(D) $SO_2$

**23.** Which of the following molecules is nonpolar?

(A) $BrF_5$
(B) $NH_3$
(C) $SiF_4$
(D) $SF_4$

**24.** Which of the following substances is the only one that contains ionic, σ, and π bonds?

(A) $Na_2O$
(B) $NO_3^-$
(C) $Na_2CO_3$
(D) $PH_3$

**25.** Which of the following species has the greatest number of unshared electron pairs around the central atom?

(A) $H_2O$
(B) $NO_3^-$
(C) $KrF_2$
(D) $NF_3$

**26.** What is the hybridization of each carbon atom in the acetic acid $CH_3COOH$?

(A) $sp^3$, $sp^2$, and sp
(B) $sp^3$ only
(C) $sp^3$ and $sp^2$
(D) $sp^2$ and sp

## Chapter 9 Solids, Liquids, and Intermolecular Forces

**27.** Which of the following is the best description of the structure of diamond?

(A) It contains atoms held together by a delocalized electron cloud.
(B) It contains molecules held together by intermolecular attractions.
(C) It contains positive and negative ions held together by electrostatic attractions.
(D) It contains a giant molecule held together by covalent bonds.

**28.** Which of the following best describes the structure of Fe(s)?

(A) It contains atoms held together by a delocalized electron cloud.
(B) It contains molecules held together by intermolecular attractions.
(C) It contains positive and negative ions held together by electrostatic attractions.
(D) It contains a giant molecule held together by covalent bonds.

**29.** Which of the following categories best describes $NH_4NO_3(s)$?

(A) It contains atoms held together by a delocalized electron cloud.
(B) It contains molecules held together by intermolecular attractions.
(C) It contains positive and negative ions held together by electrostatic attractions.
(D) It contains a giant molecule held together by covalent bonds.

**30.** Which of the following is applicable to HCl(s)?

(A) It contains atoms held together by a delocalized electron cloud
(B) It contains molecules held together by intermolecular attractions.
(C) It contains positive and negative ions held together by electrostatic attractions.
(D) It contains a giant molecule held together by covalent bonds.

**31.** Which of the following best describes the critical point on a phase diagram?

(A) The critical point is the highest temperature and pressure where a substance can sublime.
(B) The critical point is the highest temperature and pressure where the substance may exist as discrete solid and gas phases.
(C) The critical point is the temperature and pressure where the substance exists in equilibrium as solid, liquid, and gas phases.
(D) The critical point is the highest temperature and pressure where the substance may exist as discrete liquid and gas phases.

**32.** Why are some substances ductile?

(A) London dispersion forces are present.
(B) Covalent bonding is present.
(C) Hydrogen bonding is present.
(D) Metallic bonding is present.

**33.** In the vapor phase, acetic acid, $CH_3COOH$, molecules exist as dimers (pairs). Why do these dimers form?

(A) London dispersion forces are present.
(B) Covalent bonding is present.
(C) Hydrogen bonding is present.
(D) Metallic bonding is present.

**34.** Which of the following is the most likely order for boiling points of the substances?

(A) $CH_3CH_2CH_2OH$ < $HOCH_2CH_2OH$ < $CH_3CH_2CH_2CH_3$
(B) $CH_3CH_2CH_2CH_3$ < $HOCH_2CH_2OH$ < $CH_3CH_2CH_2OH$
(C) $CH_3CH_2CH_2CH_3$ < $CH_3CH_2CH_2OH$ < $HOCH_2CH_2OH$
(D) $CH_3CH_2CH_2OH$ < $CH_3CH_2CH_2CH_3$ < $HOCH_2CH_2OH$

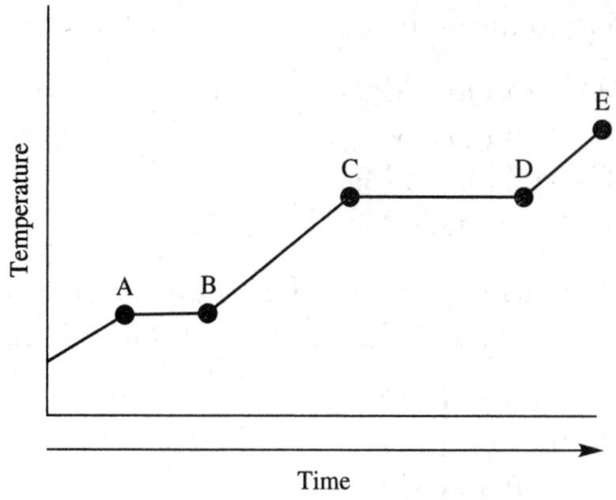


**35.** The above diagram represents the heating curve for a pure crystalline substance. The liquid is the only phase present between which two points?

(A) C and D
(B) A and B
(C) D and E
(D) B and C

**36.** For all one-component phase diagrams, choose the correct statement from the following list.

(A) The slope of the gas–liquid line may be positive or negative.
(B) The liquid–gas line terminates.
(C) The solid–liquid line has a positive slope.
(D) Sublimation occurs at temperatures higher than the triple point temperature.

## Chapter 10 Gases

**37.** $2\ Li(s) + 2\ H_2O(l) \rightarrow 2\ LiOH(aq) + H_2(g)$

Lithium reacts with water according to the above reaction. What volume of hydrogen gas, at standard temperature and pressure, is produced from 0.400 mole of lithium?

(A) 4.48 L
(B) 8.96 L
(C) 2.24 L
(D) 13.4 L

**38.** A sample of nitrogen gas is placed in a sealed container at constant pressure. The sample expands until the volume is doubled. This will also double which of the following?

(A) density
(B) number of molecules
(C) moles
(D) absolute temperature

**39.** A balloon contains 28 g of nitrogen gas. A second balloon contains 40 g of argon gas. Both balloons are at the same temperature and pressure. Which of the following statements is true?

(A) The number of nitrogen molecules is less than the number of argon atoms in each balloon.
(B) The density of the gas in each balloon is the same.
(C) The volume of the nitrogen balloon is less than that of the argon balloon.
(D) The average kinetic energy of the molecules/atoms in each balloon is the same.

**40.** The measured volume and pressure of a real gas are NOT the same as the values calculated from the ideal gas equation. Which of the following explains this discrepancy?
(A) The molecules have volume and there are attractive interactions between the molecules.
(B) The molecules have volume and the molecules have mass.
(C) There are attractive interactions between the molecules and the molecules have mass.
(D) The molecules have volume and there are variations in the absolute temperature.

**41.** Chromium metal reacts with gaseous HCl to produce chromium(III) chloride and hydrogen gas. What volume of dry hydrogen gas, at 1.00 atm and 25.0°C, is produced when 26.0 g of chromium is mixed with an excess of HCl?
(A) 12.2 L
(B) 16.8 L
(C) 36.7 L
(D) 18.3 L

**42.** A sample containing the gases methane, ethane, and propane was analyzed and found to contain 5.5 moles of methane, 3.0 moles of ethane, and 3.5 moles of propane. The mixture had a total pressure of 1.4 atm. What was the partial pressure of the ethane?
(A) 0.35 atm
(B) 0.25 atm
(C) 0.47 atm
(D) 0.30 atm

**43.** An ideal gas sample weighing 1.15 g at 100°C and 0.993 atm has a volume of 0.474 L. Determine the molar mass of the gas.
(A) 74.7 g $mol^{-1}$
(B) 54.3 g $mol^{-1}$
(C) 20.1 g $mol^{-1}$
(D) 0.0134 g $mol^{-1}$

**44.** If a sample of He effuses at a rate of 30 moles per hour at 45°C, which of the gases below will effuse at approximately 7.5 moles per hour under the same conditions?
(A) $SO_2$
(B) $NH_3$
(C) $H_2$
(D) $CH_4$

**45.** A sample of a gas has a volume of 10.0 L at 25°C and 760 torr pressure. What is the volume of this sample at STP?
(A) 9.16 L
(B) 10.9 L
(C) 7.21 L
(D) 10.0 L

## Chapter 11 Solutions

**46.** A solution is prepared by dissolving 0.500 mole of KCl in 1500.0 g of water. Which of the following would be the simplest procedure to determine the molarity of the resultant solution?

(A) Measure the volume of the solution.
(B) Titrate the solution with standard silver nitrate solution.
(C) Determine the freezing point of the solution.
(D) Determine the density of the solution.

**47.** A chemist needs 1.0 L of a 0.50 *M* iodide ion, $I^-$, solution. She has 1,000 mL of a 0.40 *M* KI solution. How many moles of solid $MgI_2$ will she need to add to increase the iodide ion concentration to the desired value?

(A) 0.25 mole $MgI_2$
(B) 0.10 mole $MgI_2$
(C) 0.025 mole $MgI_2$
(D) 0.050 mole $MgI_2$

**48.** How many grams of $H_2SO_4$ (molar mass 98.1 g $mol^{-1}$) are in 250.0 mL of a 6.00 *M* solution?

(A) 73.6 g $H_2SO_4$
(B) 98.1 g $H_2SO_4$
(C) 6.00 g $H_2SO_4$
(D) 147 g $H_2SO_4$

**49.** If a solution of chloroform, $CHCl_3$, in carbon tetrachloride, $CCl_4$, is treated as an ideal solution, what is the mole fraction of chloroform in the vapor over an equimolar solution of these two liquids? The vapor pressure of chloroform is 197 torr at 25°C, and the vapor pressure of carbon tetrachloride is 114 torr at this temperature.

(A) 0.387
(B) 0.500
(C) 0.631
(D) 1.63

## Chapter 12 Reactions and Periodicity

**50.** ___ $Fe(OH)_2(s)$ + ___ $H_3PO_4(aq) \rightarrow$ ___ $Fe_3(PO_4)_2(s)$ + ___ $H_2O(l)$

After the above chemical equation is balanced, which of the following is the lowest whole-number coefficient for water?

(A) 6
(B) 2
(C) 12
(D) 3

**51.** Which of the following best represents the net ionic equation for the reaction of the strong base barium hydroxide with an aqueous sodium sulfate solution to form a precipitate?

(A) $Ba^{2+}(aq) + Na_2SO_4(aq) \rightarrow BaSO_4(s) + 2\,Na^+(aq)$
(B) $2\,Ba(OH)(aq) + Na_2SO_4(aq) \rightarrow Ba_2SO_4(s) + 2\,NaOH(aq)$
(C) $Ba(OH)_2(aq) + SO_4^{2-}(aq) \rightarrow BaSO_4(s) + 2\,OH^-(aq)$
(D) $Ba^{2+}(aq) + SO_4^{2-}(aq) \rightarrow BaSO_4(s)$

**52.** A student mixes 50.0 mL of a 0.10 *M* $Ni(NO_3)_2$ solution with 50.0-mL solution of 0.10 *M* NaOH. A green precipitate forms, and the concentration of the hydroxide ion becomes very low. Which of the following correctly places the concentrations of the remaining ions in order of decreasing concentration?

(A) $[Ni^{2+}] > [NO_3^-] > [Na^+]$
(B) $[Ni^{2+}] > [Na^+] > [NO_3^-]$
(C) $[NO_3^-] > [Na^+] > [Ni^{2+}]$
(D) $[Na^+] > [Ni^{2+}] > [NO_3^-]$

**53.** Solutions containing this ion are blue.

(A) $Co^{2+}$
(B) $CO_3^{2-}$
(C) $Cu^{2+}$
(D) $Ca^{2+}$

## Chapter 13 Kinetics

**54.** Step 1: $Cl_2(g) \rightleftharpoons 2\,Cl(g)$
Step 2: $Cl(g) + CH_4(g) \rightarrow HCl(g) + CH_3(g)$
Step 3: $Cl(g) + CH_3(g) \rightarrow CH_3Cl(g)$

The above represents a proposed mechanism for the reaction of $Cl_2$ with $CH_4$. What are the overall products of the reaction?

(A) $CH_3Cl(g) + HCl(g)$
(B) $HCl(g) + CH_3(g)$
(C) $CH_3Cl(g)$ only
(D) $CH_3Cl(g) + Cl(g)$

**55.** The decomposition reaction of $NO_2$ to NO and $O_2$ is second order in $NO_2$. The rate constant of this reaction is 0.54 $M^{-1}s^{-1}$. In one experiment, the initial concentration of $NO_2$ was 2.50 *M*. How long will it take the $NO_2$ concentration to drop to 30% of the initial concentration?

(A) 0.32 s
(B) 1.7 s
(C) 0.65 s
(D) 1.8 s

**56.** A chemist runs a reaction ($2\,NO(g) + O_2(g) \rightarrow 2\,NO_2(g)$) three times and collects the following data:

| EXPERIMENT | INITIAL [NO] | INITIAL $[O_2]$ | INITIAL RATE |
|---|---|---|---|
| 1 | 0.0150 | 0.0150 | $2.40 \times 10^{-2}$ |
| 2 | 0.0300 | 0.0300 | $1.92 \times 10^{-1}$ |
| 3 | 0.0300 | 0.0150 | $9.59 \times 10^{-2}$ |

What is the rate law for this reaction?

(A) Rate = $k[NO_2]^2[O_2]^2$
(B) Rate = $k[NO_2]$
(C) Rate = $k[NO_2]^2[O_2]$
(D) Rate = $k[O_2]^2$

## Chapter 14 Thermodynamics

**57.** What is the term for the energy involved when a gaseous atom in its ground state adds an electron to form a gaseous anion?

(A) ionization energy
(B) free energy
(C) anion energy
(D) electron affinity

**58.** Which of the following is the same for any ideal gas at a given temperature?

(A) average free energy
(B) average electron affinity
(C) average kinetic energy
(D) average ionization energy

**59.** Which of the following is the minimum energy required to cause a nonspontaneous reaction to occur?

(A) free energy
(B) potential energy
(C) kinetic energy
(D) spontaneous energy

**60.** What is the energy necessary to separate the ions from an ionic solid to infinite separation?

(A) Gibbs free energy
(B) lattice energy
(C) kinetic energy
(D) ionization energy

**61.** Using the following thermochemical equations, calculate the standard heat of formation for $C_2H_2(g)$.

$2\ C_2H_2(g) + 5\ O_2(g) \rightarrow 4\ CO_2(g) + 2\ H_2O(l)$ $\Delta H = -2{,}547.6$ kJ

$C(s) + O_2(g) \rightarrow CO_2(g)$ $\Delta H = -393.5$ kJ

$2\ H_2(g) + O_2(g) \rightarrow 2\ H_2O(l)$ $\Delta H = -571.66$ kJ

(A) +308.6 kJ
(B) +201.0 kJ
(C) 0.0 kJ
(D) −201.0 kJ

**62.** Choose the reaction expected to have the greatest increase in entropy.

(A) $N_2(g) + 2\ O_2(g) \rightarrow 2\ NO_2(g)$
(B) $H_2O(l) \rightarrow H_2O(g)$
(C) $KrF_2(s) \rightarrow Kr(g) + F_2(g)$
(D) $Ca(s) + Cl_2(g) \rightarrow 2\ CaCl_2(s)$

**63.** A certain reaction is spontaneous under standard conditions but becomes nonspontaneous at higher temperatures. What conclusions may be drawn under standard conditions?

(A) $\Delta H > 0$, $\Delta S > 0$, and $\Delta G < 0$
(B) $\Delta H < 0$, $\Delta S > 0$, and $\Delta G = 0$
(C) $\Delta H < 0$, $\Delta S > 0$, and $\Delta G > 0$
(D) $\Delta H < 0$, $\Delta S < 0$, and $\Delta G < 0$

## Chapter 15 Equilibrium

**64.** $FeS(s) + 2\ H^+(aq) \rightleftharpoons Fe^{2+}(aq) + H_2S(aq)$

The successive acid dissociation constants for $H_2S$ are $1.0 \times 10^{-7}$ ($K_{a1}$) and $1.3 \times 10^{-13}$ ($K_{a2}$). The $K_{sp}$, the solubility product constant, for FeS equals $5.0 \times 10^{-18}$. What is the equilibrium constant for the above reaction?

(A) $6.5 \times 10^{-38}$
(B) $3.8 \times 10^{-2}$
(C) $3.8 \times 10^{2}$
(D) $1.3 \times 10^{-20}$

**65.** $2\ NO(g) + O_2(g) \rightleftharpoons 2\ NO_2(g)$ endothermic

An equilibrium mixture with each of the components is placed in a sealed container at 100°C. Which of the following changes will increase the amount of the product?

(A) lowering the temperature of the container
(B) raising the temperature of the container
(C) adding 1 mole of Ar(g) to the container
(D) removing some NO from the container

**66.** The $K_{sp}$ for $LaF_3$ is $2 \times 10^{-9}$. What term appears in the denominator of the mass action expression ($K_{sp}$ expression)?

(A) $[La^{3+}][F^-]^3$
(B) $[F^-]^3$
(C) $[LaF_3]$
(D) nothing

**67.** The $K_{sp}$ for $Ca_3(PO_4)_2$ is $1.2 \times 10^{-26}$. What is the equilibrium reaction representing the solubility product constant ($K_{sp}$) that occurs when this substance is added to water?

(A) $Ca_3(PO_4)_2(s) \rightleftharpoons 3\ Ca^{2+}(aq) + 2\ PO_4^{3-}(aq)$
(B) $Ca_3(PO_4)_2(s) \rightleftharpoons 3\ Ca^{2+}(aq) + 2\ P^{5+}(aq) + 8\ O^{2-}(aq)$
(C) $Ca_3(PO_4)_2(s) \rightleftharpoons Ca_3^{6+}(aq) + (PO_4)_2^{6-}(aq)$
(D) $Ca_3(PO_4)_2(s) + 6\ H_2O(l) \rightleftharpoons 3\ Ca^{2+}(aq) + 2\ PO_4^{3-}(aq) + 6\ H^+(aq) + 6\ OH^-(aq)$

**68.** A sample of copper(II) arsenate, $Cu_3(AsO_4)_2$, is added to water and, at equilibrium, the copper(II) ion concentration is $1.1 \times 10^{-7}$ *M*. What is the $K_{sp}$ of copper(II) arsenate?

(A) $4.2 \times 10^{-37}$
(B) $7.5 \times 10^{-36}$
(C) $4.4 \times 10^{-88}$
(D) $3.7 \times 10^{-8}$

**69.** The $K_{sp}$ for $Cr(OH)_2$ is $1.0 \times 10^{-17}$. What is the molar solubility of this compound in water?

(A) $3.2 \times 10^{-9}$ *M*
(B) $1.4 \times 10^{-6}$ *M*
(C) $1.7 \times 10^{-6}$ *M*
(D) $2.3 \times 10^{-49}$ *M*

## Chapter 16 Acids and Bases

**70.** Which of the following CANNOT behave as both a Brønsted base and a Brønsted acid?

(A) $HC_2O_4^-$
(B) $H_2PO_4^{2-}$
(C) $HSO_4^-$
(D) $SO_4^{2-}$

| Acid | $K_a$, Acid Dissociation Constant |
|---|---|
| $H_3AsO_4$ | $6.0 \times 10^{-3}$ |
| $H_2AsO_4^-$ | $1.0 \times 10^{-7}$ |
| $HAsO_4^{2-}$ | $3.0 \times 10^{-12}$ |

**71.** Using the information from the preceding table, which of the following is the best choice for preparing a pH = 7.5 buffer?

(A) $K_2HAsO_4 + K_3AsO_4$
(B) $K_2HAsO_4 + KH_2AsO_4$
(C) $K_3AsO_4$
(D) $K_2HAsO_4$

**72.** The pH of a 0.01-*M* solution of a weak monoprotic acid, HA, is 4. What is the ionization constant, $K_a$, for this acid?

(A) $10^{-4}$
(B) $10^{-6}$
(C) $10^{-8}$
(D) $10^{-2}$

**73.** Assuming all concentrations are 1 *M*, which of the following is the most basic solution (highest pH)?

(A) KBr (potassium bromide) and KOH (potassium hydroxide)
(B) $K_2C_2O_4$ (potassium oxalate) and $KHC_2O_4$ (potassium hydrogen oxalate)
(C) $NH_3$ (ammonia) and $HNO_3$ (nitric acid)
(D) $(CH_3)_2NH$ (dimethylamine) and $(CH_3)_2NH_2Cl$ (dimethylammonium chloride)

**74.** Assuming all concentrations are equal, which of the following solutions has pH nearest 7?

(A) KCl (potassium chloride) and HCl (hydrochloric acid)
(B) $H_2C_2O_4$ (oxalic acid) and NaOH (sodium hydroxide)
(C) $NH_3$ (ammonia) and $HNO_3$ (nitric acid)
(D) KOH (potassium hydroxide) and HCl (hydrochloric acid)

**75.** Which of the following yields a buffer with a pH < 7 upon mixing equal volumes of 1 *M* solutions?

(A) KCl (potassium chloride) and HCl (hydrochloric acid)
(B) $NH_3$ (ammonia) and $NH_4NO_3$ (ammonium nitrate)
(C) $H_2C_2O_4$ (oxalic acid) and $KHC_2O_4$ (potassium hydrogen oxalate)
(D) KOH (potassium hydroxide) and HCl (hydrochloric acid)

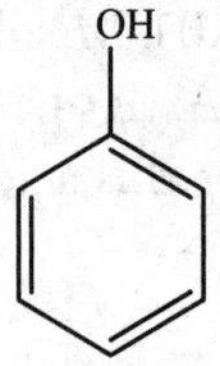

**76.** Which of the following is the $K_a$ reaction for aqueous phenol, $C_6H_5OH$? The structure of phenol is given above.

(A) $C_6H_5OH(aq) \rightleftharpoons C_6H_5O(aq) + H(aq)$
(B) $C_6H_5OH(aq) \rightleftharpoons C_6H_5O^-(aq) + H^+(aq)$
(C) $C_6H_5OH(aq) \rightleftharpoons C_6H_5(aq) + OH(aq)$
(D) $C_6H_5OH(aq) \rightleftharpoons C_6H_5^+(aq) + OH^-(aq)$

**77.** Determine the $OH^-(aq)$ concentration in 0.01 *M* aniline ($C_6H_5NH_2$) solution. (The $K_b$ for aniline is $K_b = 4 \times 10^{-10}$.)

(A) $5 \times 10^{-5}$ *M*
(B) $1 \times 10^{-2}$ *M*
(C) $2 \times 10^{-6}$ *M*
(D) $4 \times 10^{-12}$ *M*

# Chapter 17 Electrochemistry

**78.** (base) $Bi(s) + AsO_4^{3-}(aq) \rightarrow AsO_2^-(aq) + Bi_2O_3(s)$

What is the coefficient of $OH^-$ when the above reaction is balanced?

(A) 2
(B) 12
(C) 6
(D) 4

**79.** How many moles of Pt may be deposited on the cathode when 0.30 Faradays of electricity is passed through a 1.0-*M* solution of $Pt^{2+}$?

(A) 0.60 mole
(B) 0.030 mole
(C) 0.45 mole
(D) 0.15 mole

**80.** $Sn^{2+}(aq) + 2\,Hg^{2+}(aq) \rightarrow Sn^{4+}(aq) + Hg_2^{2+}(aq)$

The reaction shown above was used in an electrolytic cell. The voltage measured for the cell was not equal to the calculated E° for the cell. Which of the following could explain this discrepancy?

(A) Both solutions were at 25°C instead of 0°C.
(B) The anode and cathode were different sizes.
(C) The anion in the anode compartment was acetate, instead of nitrate as in the cathode compartment.
(D) One or more of the ion concentrations was not 1 *M*.

**Questions 81 and 82 refer to the following half-reaction in an electrolytic cell:**

$$4\,H_2O(l) + W(s) \rightarrow WO_4^{2-}(aq) + 8\,H^+(aq) + 6\,e^-$$

**81.** Choose the correct statement from the following list.

(A) The tungsten is reduced.
(B) This is the anode reaction.
(C) The oxidation state of tungsten does not change.
(D) The $H^+$ serves as a catalyst.

**82.** If a current of 0.60 amperes is passed through the electrolytic cell for 0.50 h, how many grams of tungsten metal react?

(A) 0.34 g W
(B) 0.0056 g W
(C) 2.0 g W
(D) 0.68 g W

**83.** $4\,e^- + 4\,H^+(aq) + H_2SO_3(aq) \rightarrow S(s) + 3\,H_2O(l)$

If a current of 4.0 A is passed through the electrolytic cell for 0.75 h, how many grams of S will form?

(A) 3.6 g S
(B) 0.90 g S
(C) 3.2 g S
(D) 24 g

**84.** $2\ Fe^{3+}(aq) + Fe(s) \rightleftharpoons 3\ Fe^{2+}(aq) \qquad E° = +1.2\ V$

What is the $\Delta G°$ for the above reaction under standard conditions?

(A) $+2.3 \times 10^5$ J
(B) $-4.6 \times 10^5$ J
(C) $+4.6 \times 10^5$ J
(D) $-2.3 \times 10^5$ J

## Chapter 18 Nuclear Chemistry

**85.** When $^{222}_{86}Rn$ decays, it emits two $\alpha$ particles, then two $\beta$ particles, followed by an $\alpha$ particle. What is the resulting nucleus?

(A) $^{210}_{83}Bi$
(B) $^{212}_{86}Rn$
(C) $^{214}_{82}Pb$
(D) $^{210}_{82}Pb$

**86.** Tritium, $^{3}_{1}H$, decays by beta decay with a half-life of 12.3 years. How long will it take for a sample of tritium to decay to 12.5% of its original value?

(A) 24.6 years
(B) 49.2 years
(C) 36.9 years
(D) 12.3 years

**87.** The rate constant for the beta decay of carbon-14 is $1.213 \times 10^{-4}\ yr^{-1}$. What is the half-life for the beta decay of carbon-14?

(A) 5,713 $yr^{-1}$
(B) $1.213 \times 10^{-4}\ yr^{-1}$
(C) 5,713 yr
(D) $1.213 \times 10^{-4}$ yr

**88.** If 75% of a sample of pure $^{24}_{11}Na$ decays in 30 hours, what is the half-life of $^{24}_{11}Na$?

(A) 60 hours
(B) 30 hours
(C) 15 hours
(D) 7.5 hours

## Chapter 19 Organic Chemistry

**89.** Alkenes are hydrocarbons with the general formula $C_nH_{2n}$. If a 2.80-g sample of an alkene is combusted in excess oxygen, how many moles of water will form?

(A) 0.100 mole
(B) 0.200 mole
(C) 1.50 moles
(D) 0.700 mole

**90.** What type of compound is shown?

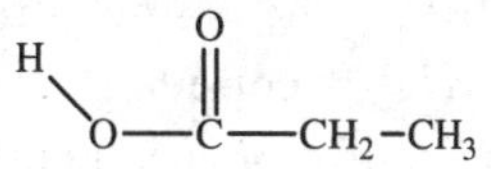


(A) an alcohol
(B) an acid
(C) a ketone
(D) an ester

## Chapter 20 Experimental Investigations

Questions on this chapter are incorporated into the chapters concerning the specific experiments.

# › Answers and Explanations

## Chapter 5 Basics

1. **D**—Fluorine is a nonmetal. Nonmetals tend to form anions. The others (metals) form cations.

2. **B**—Increasing radii is related to decreasing charges, or for going down a column (with equal charges) or moving toward the left in a period of the periodic table. This explanation will not be sufficient for the free-response portion of the test, where it is necessary to address such factors as the effective nuclear charge.

3. **C**—For the representative elements, the element that is nearest to F on the periodic table (except the noble gases) will have the highest electronegativity.

4. **A**—The others are B = chloric acid, C = chlorous acid, and D = hypochlorous acid.

5. **D**—You need to break the name into parts: tetraammine = $(NH_3)_4$; copper(II) = $Cu^{2+}$; chloride = $Cl^-$. Since ammonia is neutral, two $Cl^-$ are necessary to balance the $Cu^{2+}$ charge.

6. **D**—Bohr developed what is now known as the Bohr theory of the atom to explain the emission spectra of first hydrogen (and with less success, other elements). In this theory, energy is quantized with the electrons emitting or absorbing a quantum of energy when moving from one energy level to another. Einstein's contribution to chemistry was his explanation of the photoelectric effect. Dalton's contribution was atomic theory. Rutherford's contribution was that atoms have a nucleus.

## Chapter 6 Stoichiometry

7. **C**—This is a titration problem utilizing the given equation.

$$\left(\frac{0.1020 \text{ mol } MnO_4^-}{1{,}000 \text{ mL}}\right)(42.21 \text{ mL})$$
$$\left(\frac{5 \text{ mol } C_2O_4^{2-}}{2 \text{ mol } MnO_4^-}\right)\left(\frac{1}{75.00 \text{ mL}}\right)\left(\frac{1{,}000 \text{ mL}}{\text{L}}\right)$$
$$= 0.1435\ M\ C_2O_4^{2-}$$

Changing $M$ to mol/L and then substituting 1,000 mL for L simplifies the first calculation. The first two sets of parentheses determine the moles of permanganate ion. This is followed by a mole ratio to get moles of oxalate. Next, divide by the volume of the oxalate solution. Finally, convert milliliters to liters.

8. **C**—Either calculate the percent Cr in each oxide: (A) 76.5%; (B) 68.4%; (C) 61.9%; (D) 52.0%, or determine the empirical formula from the percent chromium and the percent oxygen (= 100.0 − 61.9). To calculate the percent Cr for C, use the following calculation:

$$\text{Percent Cr} = \frac{52.00 \dfrac{\text{g Cr}}{\text{mol Cr}}}{84.00 \text{ g} \dfrac{CrO_2}{\text{mol } CrO_2}} \times 100\%$$
$$= 69.90\ \%\ \text{Cr}$$

In this calculation, 84.00 g is the molar mass of $CrO_2$. The other percentages may be calculated in a similar manner.

9. **A**—$H_2SO_4$ is the limiting reagent, as the amount is less than the stoichiometric ratio indicates (according to the balanced equation: 1.0 mole $K_2Cr_2O_7$ and 6.0 mol $FeSO_4$ require 7.0 moles $H_2SO_4$). The calculation is:

$$(6.0 \text{ mol } H_2SO_4)\left(\frac{2 \text{ mol } Fe_2(SO_4)_3}{5 \text{ mol } H_2SO_4}\right)$$
$$= 2.4 \text{ moles } Fe_2(SO_4)_3$$

10. **A**—The coefficients in the balanced equation are 2, 2, and 1. Therefore,

$$(1.0 \text{ mol } H_2O_2)\left(\frac{1 \text{ mol } O_2}{2 \text{ mol } H_2O_2}\right) = 0.50 \text{ mole}$$

## Chapter 7 Spectroscopy, Light, and Electrons

11. **C**—Atoms with filled shells or subshells are diamagnetic; all others are paramagnetic. All odd atomic number elements are paramagnetic in their ground states (eliminating Rb, I, As, and Br). Oxygen has

a partially filled subshell, so it is also paramagnetic, which eliminates it. The paramagnetic elements eliminate answers A, B, and D.

**12.** **C**—Transition metal ions are, in general, $s^0$ and $p^0$ or $p^6$ with the possibility of having one or more electrons in the d orbitals. Answer C could be $Cu^{2+}$. Note that 1p (in answer A) is not a possible orbital.

**13.** **B**—The noble gases, except helium, are $ns^2np^6$. In this case, $n = 3$, and the gas is argon.

**14.** **D**—Halogens are $ns^2np^5$. In this case, $n = 4$, and the halogen is Br. None of the other configurations is a ground-state configuration.

**15.** **A**—It is not possible to have an $s^3$ configuration.

**16.** **D**—Heisenberg's uncertainty principle states that it is impossible to determine the exact position and momentum of an electron because any experiment to determine one of these significantly disrupts the other.

**17.** **C**—The electron configuration of a ground-state oxygen atom is $1s^22s^22p^4$. According to Hund's rule, three of the oxygen 2p electrons will enter the 2p orbitals individually (with spins parallel). The fourth will enter one of the orbitals and pair with the electron there, which leaves two unpaired electrons. The result is that the oxygen atom has two unpaired electrons, which makes it paramagnetic.

**18.** **A**—The Pauli exclusion principle limits the number of electrons that may occupy an orbital. The two electrons present in an orbital have three quantum numbers that are the same and one electron with $m_s = +1/2$ and one electron with $m_s = -1/2$.

**19.** **B**—The d orbitals are less effectively shielded than the s orbitals. Due to this difference, the s orbitals have lower energy (experience a higher effective nuclear charge, which is the result of their experiencing greater shielding).

**20.** **C**—Zn becomes $Zn^{2+}$. $X$ is O, which can become $O^{2-}$. These ions yield ZnO = Zn$X$.

# Chapter 8 Bonding

**21.** **C**—It will help if you draw the Lewis structure. The xenon has four bonding pairs and two lone pairs, which leads to a square planar molecular geometry. Answer A is four bonding pairs and no lone pairs. B has five bonding and no lone pairs. D has three bonding and one lone pair.

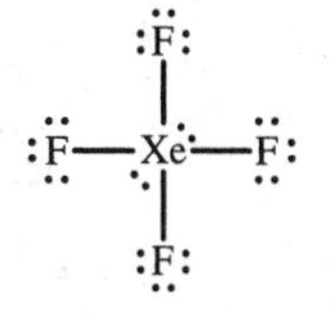


**22.** **B**—You will need to draw the Lewis structures. B is the only one with only single bonds. Single bonds are σ bonds. The other molecules have double or triple bonds. All double and triple bonds are a combination of σ and π bonds. It is not necessary to consider the different resonance forms.

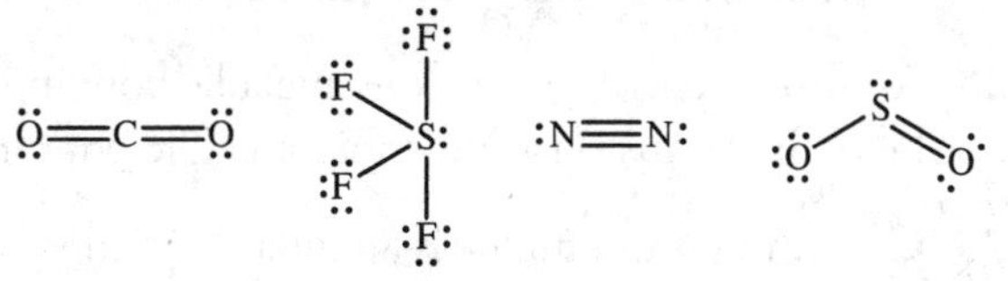


**23.** **C**—Draw the Lewis structures and use VSEPR; only the tetrahedral $SiF_4$ is nonpolar. The other materials form a square pyramidal, $BrF_5$, trigonal pyramid, $NH_3$, and irregular tetrahedral, $SF_4$, and, therefore, are polar.

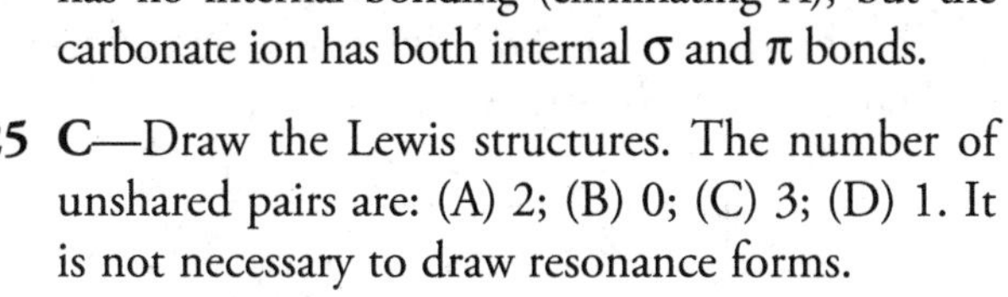


**24.** **C**—The only ionic bonds are present in the sodium compounds (eliminating B and D). The oxide ion has no internal bonding (eliminating A), but the carbonate ion has both internal σ and π bonds.

**25** **C**—Draw the Lewis structures. The number of unshared pairs are: (A) 2; (B) 0; (C) 3; (D) 1. It is not necessary to draw resonance forms.

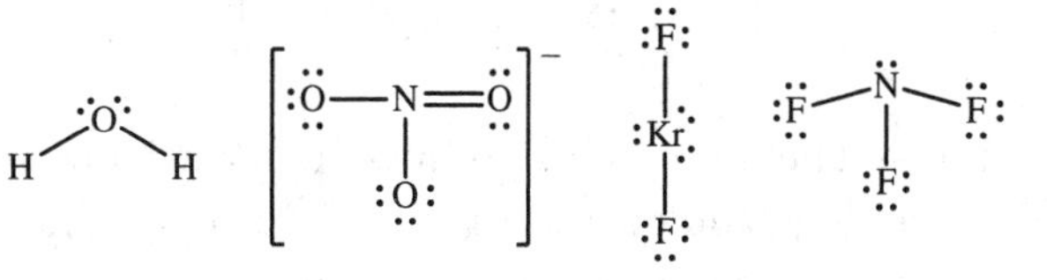

**26. C**—Draw the Lewis structure; the carbon on the left in the formula is $sp^3$ (four single bonds), and the other is $sp^2$ (two single and one double bonds). All carboxylic acids contain the same structure as the carbon atom on the right. Even though organic chemistry is not an AP topic, you should be able to deal with common chemicals such as acetic acid.

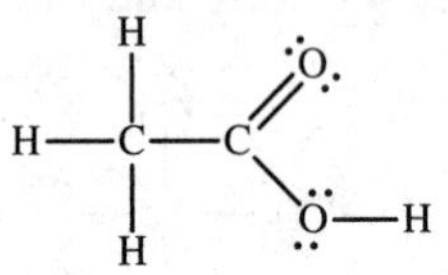

# Chapter 9 Solids, Liquids, and Intermolecular Forces

**27. D**—Diamond is a network covalent solid with each carbon atom covalently bonded to four other carbon atoms to produce a network.

**28. A**—Iron is a metal; therefore, metallic bonding will be present. Answer A describes metallic bonding.

**29. C**—Ammonium nitrate is an ionic solid containing positive ammonium ions and negative nitrate ions.

**30. B**—Hydrogen chloride consists of polar molecules, which are attracted to each other through intermolecular attractions.

**31. D**—This is the definition of the critical point.

**32. D**—Ductility is a consequence of metallic bonding, as the atoms can easily move past each other without breaking any bonds. Malleability and electrical conductivity are also consequences of metallic bonding.

**33. C**—The structure of the dimer is illustrated in the accompanying figure. The dashed lines represent hydrogen bonds. The two strong hydrogen bonds hold the two molecules together.

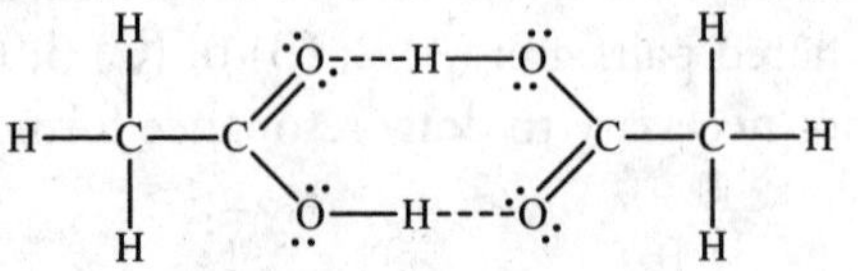

**34. C**—The more –OH groups, the more hydrogen bonding, and the more strongly the molecules are attracted to each other. The greater the attraction, the greater the boiling point. (Comparisons such as this require molecules of similar size.)

**35. D**—The solid has completely melted at point B, leaving the liquid. At point C, the liquid begins to vaporize, giving both liquid and gas.

**36. B**—The gas–liquid line always has a positive slope, which eliminates A. Answer B correctly describes the critical point, which is the end of the liquid–gas line. The slope of the solid–liquid line may be positive or negative, which eliminates C. Sublimation may occur at temperatures below the triple point.

# Chapter 10 Gases

**37. A**—$(0.400 \text{ mol Li})\left(\frac{1 \text{ mol } H_2}{2 \text{ mol Li}}\right)\left(\frac{22.4 \text{ L}}{\text{mol}}\right)$

$= 4.48 \text{ L}.$

Note that the 22.4 L $mol^{-1}$ only works at STP. It is also possible to use the ideal gas equation to get the correct answer. The conversion 22.4 L $mol^{-1}$ is not likely to be used on the AP Exam; however, it may be used to estimate an answer.

**38. D**—Charles's law applies here, as it relates volume to temperature (absolute). According to this law, volume and the absolute temperature are directly related. Thus, if either volume or temperature is doubled, the other will also double. This assumes moles and pressure remain unchanged. The container is sealed, so moles and number of molecules are constant and increasing the volume without increasing the mass will cause the density to decrease.

**39. D**—Each balloon contains 1 mole of gas; therefore, there are equal numbers of particles (atoms or molecules) present, and since the balloons are at the same temperature and pressure, the volumes will be the same. The average kinetic energy of a gas depends upon the temperature. Since the temperature of the two gases is the same, the average kinetic energy of the gases is the same. Density is mass over volume, and since the balloons have the same volume, the one with more mass will have the higher density.

**40. A**—There are two limitations with Kinetic Molecular Theory when describing an ideal gas. The volume of the molecules and the attractive interactions between the molecules are the basic differences between ideal and real gases.

**41. D**—It is necessary to first write the balanced chemical equation:

$2\ Cr(s) + 6\ HCl(g) \rightarrow 2\ CrCl_3(s) + 3\ H_2(g)$

The quickest solution is to use the ideal gas equation (rearranged to $V = nRT/P$). The calculation in the square brackets [ ] is the determination of the number of moles ($n$).

$$V = \frac{nRT}{P} = \frac{\left[(26.0\text{ g Cr})\left(\frac{1\text{ mol Cr}}{52.0\text{ g Cr}}\right)\left(\frac{3\text{ mol H}_2}{2\text{ mol Cr}}\right)\right](0.08206\text{ L atm mol}^{-1}\text{ K}^{-1})(298\text{ K})}{(1.00\text{ atm})} = 18.3\text{ L}$$

Answer A results if the chemical equation was not balanced. If you used 1 mole = 22.4 L, you got answer B, which is incorrect because this is the STP answer, and the conditions are not STP (wrong temperature).

**42. A**—The mole fraction of ethane times the total pressure yields the partial pressure. The mole fraction of ethane is the moles of ethane (3.0) divided by the total moles (5.5 + 3.0 + 3.5 = 12.0 moles). The calculation is $(1.4\text{ atm})\left(\frac{3.0\text{ mol}}{12.0\text{ mol}}\right) = 0.35\text{ atm}$. The gases are organic compounds; however, the identities of the gases are irrelevant to this calculation.

**43. A**—The molar mass is the mass of the gas divided by the moles of the gas. The mass is given (1.15 g), and the moles are calculated from the ideal gas equation.

$$n = PV/RT = \frac{(0.993\text{ atm})(0.474\text{ L})}{\left(0.08206\ \frac{\text{L atm}}{\text{mol K}}\right)(373\text{ K})}$$

$$= 1.54 \times 10^{-2}\text{ mol}$$

$$\text{Molar mass} = \frac{1.15\text{ g}}{1.54 \times 10^{-2}\text{ mol}} = 74.7\text{ g mol}^{-1}$$

This example illustrates the importance of rounding in calculations where no calculator is available. The answers are not close together; therefore, a rough calculation will lead to the correct answer. Also, you should notice answer D is impossible for any substance. In addition, since the conditions are not STP, 22.4 L mol$^{-1}$ should not appear anywhere in this calculation. If you used 22.4 L mol$^{-1}$, the answer you get is 54.3 g mol$^{-1}$ (answer B). If you did not change 100°C to 373K, you got answer C.

**44. A**—The simplest procedure is to use Graham's law: $\frac{\text{Rate}_{He}}{\text{Rate}_{unk}} = \sqrt{\frac{MM_{unk}}{MM_{He}}}$ (Note: it is acceptable to invert the Rate fraction **and** the fraction under the radical.) Entering the rates and the molar mass of helium gives $\frac{30\text{ mol/h}}{7.5\text{ mol/h}} = \sqrt{\frac{MM_{unk}}{4.0\text{ g/mol}}}$. Solving for the molar mass of the unknown gas gives $MM_{unk} = 64\text{ g mol}^{-1}$. This is reasonable since the unknown gas effuses slower than helium. The answer will be the gas with the molar mass nearest 64 g mol$^{-1}$. The molar masses are $SO_2$ = 64 g mol$^{-1}$, $NH_3$ = 17 g mol$^{-1}$, $H_2$ = 2 g mol$^{-1}$ (impossible for this problem, because a lighter gas would effuse faster than He), and $CH_4$ = 16 g mol$^{-1}$.

**45. A**—This is a Charles's law problem since it will be necessary to find the new volume of the gas due to a change in temperature. (The pressure is constant since 760 torr = 1 atm = standard pressure.) The variables are $V_1$ = 10.0 L, $T_1$ = 25°C = 298 K, $T_2$ = 273 K, and $V_2$ = ? The calculation is:

$$V_2 = \frac{V_1 T_2}{T_1} = \frac{(10.0\text{ L})(273\text{ K})}{(298\text{ K})} = 9.16\text{ L}$$

This smaller volume makes sense because there was a decrease in the temperature.

## Chapter 11 Solutions

**46. A**—While all four methods will work, A is the simplest. Molarity is moles per liter, and the moles are already known; therefore, only the volume is necessary to complete the determination.

**47. D**—Moles of $I^-$ present in the desired solution: $(1.0\ L)\left(\frac{0.50\ mol\ I^-}{L}\right) = 0.50$ mol needed. Moles of I already present: $(1.0\ L)\left(\frac{0.40\ mol\ I^-}{L}\right) =$ 0.40 mole present. Moles $MgI_2$ to be added: $[(0.50 - 0.40)\ mol\ I^-\ \text{to be added}]\left(\frac{1\ mol\ MgI_2}{2\ mol\ I^-}\right)$ $= 0.050$ mol

**48. D**—$(0.2500\ L)\left(\frac{6.00\ mol}{L}\right)\left(\frac{98.1\ g}{mol}\right) = 147\ g.$ As always, estimate the answer by rounding the values.

**49. C**—Equimolar gives a mole fraction of 0.500 for each. According to Raoult's law, the vapor pressure of a component is the mole fraction of that substance times the vapor pressure of the pure substance. The total vapor pressure of the solution is the sum of the individual vapor pressures of the components: $0.500 \times 197$ torr + $0.500 \times 114$ torr = 156 torr (total vapor pressure). The mole fraction of a substance in the vapor phase is the vapor pressure of that substance divided by the total vapor pressure: chloroform = $\frac{(0.5 \times 197\ torr)}{156\ torr} = 0.631$ mole fraction

## Chapter 12 Reactions and Periodicity

**50. A**—The balanced chemical equation is:

$$3\ Fe(OH)_2(s) + 2\ H_3PO_4(aq) \rightarrow Fe_3(PO_4)_2(s) + 6\ H_2O(l)$$

**51. D**—You are told that $Ba(OH)_2$ is a strong base; therefore, it is a strong electrolyte (totally ionized in solution). You are given a solution of $Na_2SO_4$, which means it is soluble (otherwise it would not be a solution), and, for this reason, it is also a strong electrolyte. Since all reactants are strong electrolytes, the solution contains $Ba^{2+}$, 2 $OH^-$, 2 $Na^+$, and $SO_4^{2-}$. The only potential products from these ions are NaOH and $BaSO_4$. Sodium hydroxide is not only a sodium compound but also a strong base, so it is expected to be soluble (strong electrolyte). By elimination, the only possible precipitate is $BaSO_4$. The product side of the reaction will contain 2 $Na^+$, 2 $OH^-$, and $BaSO_4$. The spectator ions (appearing on both sides of the reaction arrow) are 2 $Na^+$ and 2 $OH^-$. The final answer is what remains after canceling the spectator ions.

**52. C**—Both solutions have equal volumes and concentrations; therefore, the original concentrations of $Ni^{2+}$, $Na^+$, and $OH^-$ are equal, while the concentration of $NO_3^-$ is double the other ions [because of the 2 subscript in $Ni(NO_3)_2$]. The hydroxide becomes low because it precipitated. The only ion available to precipitate the hydroxide is $Ni^{2+}$ [the problem shows NaOH to be soluble and $OH^-$ will not combine with another anion ($NO_3^-$)]. The low $OH^-$ means that the $Ni^{2+}$ will also be low. The $Na^+$ and $NO_3^-$ concentrations remain unchanged. The results are that $NO_3^-$ remains the highest, $Na^+$ is unchanged (intermediate), and $Ni^{2+}$ will be the lowest.

**53. C**—The usual colors for these ions are: copper(II) ions, $Cu^{2+}$, are blue, cobalt(II) ions, $Co^{2+}$, are pink, and both carbonate ions, $CO_3^{2-}$, and calcium ions, $Ca^{2+}$, are colorless.

## Chapter 13 Kinetics

**54. A**—Add the equations and cancel anything that appears on both sides of the reaction arrows. The overall equation is $Cl_2(g) + CH_4(g) \rightarrow CH_3Cl(g) + HCl(g)$.

**55. B**—Begin with the integrated rate law for second-order reactions (this will be given to you on the AP Exam). Rearrange this equation to solve for the time, *t*. Finally, enter the appropriate values.

$$\frac{1}{[A]_t}-\frac{1}{[A]_0}=kt \rightarrow t=\frac{\frac{1}{[A]_t}-\frac{1}{[A]_0}}{k}$$

$$=\frac{\dfrac{1}{(2.50)\left(\dfrac{30.0\%}{100\%}\right)\text{M}}-\dfrac{1}{2.50\text{ M}}}{0.54\text{ 1/Ms}}=1.7\text{ s}$$

**56. C**—The table shows second order in nitrogen oxide (comparing experiments 1 and 3), because doubling the NO concentration quadruples ($2^2$) the rate. The reaction is first order in the oxygen (comparing experiments 2 and 3), because doubling the $O_2$ concentration doubles ($2^1$) the rate.

## Chapter 14 Thermodynamics

**57. D**—This is the definition of electron affinity.

**58. C**—This is a basic postulate of kinetic molecular theory.

**59. A**—This is one of the properties of free energy.

**60. B**—The question gives the definition of lattice energy.

**61. B**—This is an application of Hess's law. The reaction for the standard heat of formation is:

$$2\text{ C(s)} + H_2\text{(g)} \rightarrow C_2H_2\text{(g)}$$

(You should know how to write a chemical equation for any standard heat of formation.) According to Hess's law, it will be necessary to manipulate the given equations so they will sum to the standard heat of formation equation. It is necessary to reverse the first equation (which reverses the sign) and divide by 2 (which cuts the $\Delta H$ to one-half its original value). The second equation needs to be doubled (which doubles $\Delta H$). It is necessary to divide the third equation by 2 (which cuts the $\Delta H$ to one-half its original value). (You should recall that since these are thermochemical equations, it is acceptable to use fractions.) Once the equations have been manipulated, you get the three equations below; you then cancel (as shown) any species that appear on each side of the reaction arrows. Notice that $O_2$ appears twice on the reactant side. Add all uncanceled species and compare to the standard heat of formation equation; there must be an exact match. If there is not an exact match, there is an error.

$$\cancel{2\,CO_2(g)} + \cancel{H_2O(l)} \rightarrow C_2H_2(g) + \cancel{5/2\,O_2(g)}$$
$$\Delta H = ½(+2{,}547.6\text{ kJ})$$

$$2\text{ C(s)} + \cancel{2\,O_2(g)} \rightarrow \cancel{2\,CO_2(g)}$$
$$\Delta H = 2\,(-393.5\text{ kJ})$$

$$H_2(g) + \cancel{½\,O_2(g)} \rightarrow \cancel{H_2O(l)}$$
$$\Delta H = ½(-571.66\text{ kJ})$$

The sum to the standard heat of formation for $C_2H_2$:

$2\text{ C(s)} + H_2\text{(g)} \rightarrow C_2H_2\text{(g)} \quad \Delta H = 201.0\text{ kJ}$

As always, rounding and estimating will save time.

**62. C**—The equation that has the greatest increase in the number of moles of gas is the right choice. Answers A and D show a decrease in the moles of gas. Answer B has a 1-mole increase, while C has a 2-mole increase.

**63. D**—Spontaneous means $\Delta G < 0$. For a reaction to become nonspontaneous at higher temperatures, ($\Delta G > 0$) means $\Delta H < 0$ and $\Delta S < 0$.

## Chapter 15 Equilibrium

**64. C**—The three equilibria involved are:

$FeS(s) \rightarrow Fe^{2+}(aq) + S^{2-}(aq) \quad K_{sp} = 5.0 \times 10^{-18}$
$H_2S(aq) \leftrightharpoons H^+(aq) + HS^-(aq) \quad K_{a1} = 1.0 \times 10^{-7}$
$HS^-(aq) \leftrightharpoons H^+(aq) + S^{2-}(aq) \quad K_{a2} = 1.3 \times 10^{-13}$

To get the equilibrium constant for the reaction in the problem, it is necessary to combine these equilibria. The two $K_a$ equilibria need to be reversed (requiring the $K_a$ value to be inverted). Adding the $K_{sp}$ and the two reversed $K_a$ values gives the desired equation. The resultant $K$ is the product of the three $K$'s of the equations being added.

$FeS(s) \rightleftharpoons Fe^{2+}(aq) + S^{2-}(aq) \quad K_{sp} = 5.0 \times 10^{-18}$

$H^+(aq) + HS^-(aq) \rightleftharpoons H_2S(aq) \quad K'_{a1} = \left(\frac{1}{1.0\times10^{-7}}\right)$

$H^+(aq) + S^{2-}(aq) \rightleftharpoons HS^-(aq) \quad K'_{a2} = \left(\frac{1}{1.3\times10^{-13}}\right)$

Sum $FeS(s) + 2\,H^+(aq) \rightleftharpoons Fe^{2+}(aq) + H_2S(aq)$

$K = K_{sp}\,K'_{a1}\,K'_{a2} = (5.0 \times 10^{-18})\left(\frac{1}{1.0\times10^{-7}}\right) \times \left(\frac{1}{1.3 \times 10^{-13}}\right) = 3.8 \times 10^2$

You can estimate the correct answer by using the powers of ten.

**65. B**—Adding Ar yields no change, as it is not part of the equilibrium. Increasing the temperature of an endothermic equilibrium will increase the amount of product. Lowering the temperature or removing a reactant (NO) will decrease the amount of product.

**66. D**—The equilibrium reaction is ($LaF_3(s) \rightleftharpoons La^{3+}(aq) + 3\,F^-(aq)$), and the equilibrium expression is $K_{sp} = [La^{3+}][F^-]^3$. Solids ($LaF_3$) do not appear in the mass action expression.

**67. A**—All equilibrium constant expressions for the solubility of a substance have the solid (and only the solid) on the reactant side and the individual ions on the product side (which also eliminates answer D with two substances on the reactant side). The phosphate ion is a polyatomic ion and remains a polyatomic ion in solution, which eliminates answer B. $Ca_3^{6+}$ and $(PO_4)_2^{6-}$ do not exist in solution. You should know that a phosphate ion is $PO_4^{3-}$ from your nomenclature.

**68. B**—The equilibrium is:

$Cu_3(PO_4)_2(s) \rightleftharpoons 3\,Cu^{2+}(aq) + 2\,PO_4^{3-}(aq)$

The $Cu^{2+}$ concentration is $3x$ and the $PO_4^{3-}$ concentration is $2x$ and $K_{sp} = [Cu^{2+}]^3[PO_4^{3-}]^2 = (3x)^3(2x)^2 = 108x^5$. Since $[Cu^{2+}] = 3x = 1.1 \times 10^{-7}\,M$ (given), then $x = 3.7 \times 10^{-8}\,M$. Combining the above information: $K_{sp} = 108x^5 = 108\,(3.7 \times 10^{-8})^5 = 7.5 \times 10^{-36}$

**69. B**—The equilibrium is $Cr(OH)(s) \rightleftharpoons Cr^{2+}(aq) + 2\,OH^-(aq)$ $K_{sp} = [Cr^{2+}][OH^-]^2 = [x][2x]^2 = 4x^3 = 1.0 \times 10^{-17}$. Solve for $x = 1.4 \times 10^{-6}\,M$.

# Chapter 16 Acids and Bases

**70. D**—To be a Brønsted acid, the species must have an $H^+$ to donate, and to be a Brønsted base, the species must be able to accept an $H^+$. The sulfate ion has no $H^+$ to donate to be a Brønsted acid, but it can be a Brønsted base by accepting a hydrogen ion to form the hydrogen sulfate ion, $HSO_4^-$.

**71. B**—Start with the acid with a $pK_a$ as near 7.5 ($K = 10^{-7.5}$) as possible ($H_2AsO_4^-$). To go to a higher pH, add the acid (conjugate base) with the smaller $K_a$ (higher $pK_a$).

**72. B**—This is an approximation. At pH = 4, $[H^+] = 10^{-4}\,M = x$; therefore, $K_a = \frac{[H^+][A^-]}{[HA]} = \frac{[x][x]}{[HA]} = \frac{[10^{-4}][10^{-4}]}{[0.01]} = 10^{-6}$

**73. A**—KOH is a strong base, and with equal concentrations and no acid present, it will give the highest pH.

**74. D**—The strong base and the strong acid will neutralize to give a neutral solution (pH = 7). This is true because the concentrations are equal. Solutions from the neutralization involving a weak acid or base will not be neutral. A is not a neutralization reaction.

**75. C**—Only B and C are buffers. C is acidic (pH < 7), and B is basic (pH > 7).

**76. B**—The desired equilibrium is a $K_a$; therefore, $H^+(aq)$[or $H_3O^+(aq)$] MUST appear on the product side. The ions on the product side must have charges. In addition to the hydrogen ion, there must be an anion present for the equation to be balanced. This is a $K_a$, so there is only one way to write the equilibrium equation regardless of what the reacting substance is.

**77. C**—The general form of all $K_b$ relationships is: $K_b = \frac{[OH^-][CA]}{[CB]} = \frac{[x][x]}{[CB]} = \frac{[x][x]}{[0.01]} = 4 \times 10^{-10}$.

$x = [OH^-] = \sqrt[2]{0.01 \times 4 \times 10^{-10}} = \sqrt[2]{4 \times 10^{-12}} = 2 \times 10^{-6}\,M$

Estimate—the square root of $10^{-12}$ will be $10^{-6}$.

# Chapter 17 Electrochemistry

**78. C**—This is a redox equation. The balanced equation is:

$$3\ H_2O(l) + 3\ AsO_4^{3-}(aq) + 2\ Bi(s) \rightarrow Bi_2O_3(s) + 3\ AsO_2^-(aq) + 6\ OH^-(aq)$$

**79. D**—It is only necessary to know the mole ratio for the reaction $[Pt^{2+}(aq) + 2\ e^- \rightarrow Pt(s)]$, which gives $(0.30\ F)\left(\frac{1\ \text{mol Pt}}{2\ F}\right) = 0.15$ mole. Since the half-reaction has 2 $e^-$, the reaction (and calculation) requires 2 $F$.

**80. D**—The cell must be nonstandard. This could be due to a nonstandard temperature (not 25°C) or nonstandard concentrations (not 1 $M$).

**81. B**—An oxidation is shown (tungsten loses six electrons). Oxidation only occurs at the anode.

**82. A**—The calculation is (check the units):

$$\frac{\left(\frac{0.60\ \text{C}}{\text{s}}\right)(0.50\ \text{h})\left(\frac{3{,}600\ \text{s}}{\text{h}}\right)\left(\frac{184\ \text{g W}}{1\ \text{mol W}}\right)}{\left(96{,}485\ \frac{\text{C}}{F}\right)\left(\frac{6\ F}{1\ \text{mol W}}\right)} = 0.34\ \text{g W}$$

Remember: 0.60 amperes = 0.60 C/s and $F$ = Faraday.

**83. B**—Recall that 4.0 amp is 4.0 C/s. The calculation would be:

$$\frac{\left(\frac{4.0\ \text{C}}{\text{s}}\right)(0.75\ \text{h})\left(\frac{3{,}600\ \text{s}}{\text{h}}\right)\left(\frac{32.1\ \text{g S}}{1\ \text{mol S}}\right)}{\left(96{,}485\ \frac{\text{C}}{F}\right)\left(\frac{4\ F}{1\ \text{mol S}}\right)} = 0.90\ \text{g S}$$

**84. D**—The equation is $\Delta G° = -nFE°$, with $n = 2$, $F = 96{,}485\ \text{J V}^{-1}$, and $E° = +1.2$ V. The value of $n$ may be determined from either reactant, for example, $Fe(s) \rightarrow Fe^{2+}(aq) + 2\ e^-$. Entering the values into the equation gives: $-(2)(96{,}485\ \text{J V}^{-1})(+1.2\ \text{V}) = -2.3 \times 10^5$ J.

# Chapter 18 Nuclear Chemistry

**85. D**—The mass of an alpha particle is 4 and the mass of a beta particle is negligible. The mass number (superscript) for the missing product should be $222 - (4 + 4 + 0 + 0 + 4) = 210$, which eliminates answers B and C. An alpha particle has an atomic number of 2, and, due to its charge, the "atomic number" of a beta particle is −1; therefore, the atomic number (subscript) for the missing product should be $86 - (2 + 2 - 1 - 1 + 2) = 82$.

**86. C**—After one half-life, 50% would remain. After another half-life, this would be reduced by one-half to 25%. After three half-lives, it would be reduced by another half to leave 12.5%. Thus, three half-lives must have passed (3 × 12.3 yr) = 36.9 years. This is not a radioactivity problem (not covered on the AP Exam); it is a kinetics problem. All radioactive decay processes follow first-order kinetics. It is important not to be misled by the fact that this a kinetics problem. You could also have used the integrated rate law to determine the answer. The integrated rate law is $\ln [A]_t - \ln [A]_0 = -kt$.

**87. C**—A radioactive decay process follows first-order kinetics. The equation to determine the half-life of a first-order reaction is $t_{1/2} = \frac{0.693}{k}$, where $k$ is the rate constant (given). It is possible to eliminate answers A and B because the units given are not time units. Entering $k$ into the half-life equation gives the half-life.

**88. C**—After one half-life, 50% would remain. After another half-life, this would be reduced by one-half to 25%. The total amount decayed is 75%. Thus, 30 hours must be two half-lives of 15 hours each. This is not a radioactivity problem (not covered on the AP Exam); it is a kinetics problem. All radioactive decay processes follow first-order kinetics. It is important not to be misled by the fact that this a kinetics problem.

## Chapter 19 Organic Chemistry

**89. B**—The general combustion reaction is $C_nH_{2n}(g)$ + 1.5 $O_2(g) \rightarrow n\ CO_2(g) + n\ H_2O(g)$.

The general formula simplifies to $CH_2$, which has a molar mass of 14.0 g/mol. This leads to:

$$(2.80\ \text{g})\left(\frac{1\ \text{mol alkene}}{14\ \text{g}}\right)\left(\frac{1\ \text{mol H}_2\text{O}}{1\ \text{mol alkene}}\right) =$$

0.200 mole. While some people may consider this to be a question dealing with organic chemistry (not directly covered on the AP Exam), it is in reality a stoichiometry problem (covered on the exam). It is not unusual to see organic compounds on the AP Exam.

**90. B**—While organic chemistry is not an AP Exam topic, it is important to recognize some aspects of organic chemistry. The four atoms on the left side of this structure are why this compound is an acid. This collection of atoms is why acetic acid is sometimes written as $CH_3COOH$ instead of $HC_2H_3O_2$. Since acetic acid commonly appears in an AP Chemistry class, it is important to know its structure.

## Chapter 20 Experimental Investigations

All Chapter 20 questions have been incorporated into the chapter questions on this test concerning the specific experiments.

# Scoring and Interpretation

After finishing and scoring the diagnostic exam, you need to analyze your results. During this analysis, the key is not whether you got the question correct or not, but how well you understood the question. First, you should pay attention to any area where you had difficulty (even if you got the correct answer). This should not be limited to unfamiliar material, which you will no doubt see. Determine where this material is covered in the book. Plan on spending additional time on the chapters/sections in question. There may be some material that you do not recognize simply because it was not covered in your class. Save your results for comparison whenever you retake this exam.

Note: The AP Exam assumes that you brought some information into your AP class. This "prior knowledge" is not directly tested on the exam; however, this knowledge may be necessary to fully understand some of the questions. The better you know this material, the better you will do on this exam. In addition, if you know material above and beyond what is to be tested on the exam, you will be able to do better on not only the exam but future chemistry classes.

This diagnostic exam contains no free-response questions; this is because such questions are not useful at this point. You will see many examples of free-response questions elsewhere in this book. The multiple-choice question approach is the best and quickest means of estimating your level of preparation.

If you did not do as well as you would have liked, don't panic. There is plenty of time for you to prepare for the exam. This diagnostic exam is a guide to allow you to know which path you need to follow as you prepare for the AP Exam. This exam is not intended to be a predictor of your success.

As stated earlier, it may be useful for you to retake this exam before you start your final review. When doing so, focus on the areas where you did not improve as much as you would like.

You are about to begin your *5 Steps to a 5*. Remember, this test is to help you organize your study plan and not to predict your results on the exam.

Good luck!

# SI UNITS

## SI Prefixes

| PREFIX | ABBREVIATION | MEANING |
|---|---|---|
| pico- | p | 0.000000000001 or $10^{-12}$ |
| nano- | n | 0.000000001 or $10^{-9}$ |
| micro- | μ | 0.000001 or $10^{-6}$ |
| milli- | m | 0.001 or $10^{-3}$ |
| centi- | c | 0.01 or $10^{-2}$ |
| deci- | d | 0.1 or $10^{-1}$ |
| deka- | da | 10 or $10^{1}$ |
| hecto- | h | 100 or $10^{2}$ |
| kilo | k | 1,000 or $10^{3}$ |
| Mega- | M | 1,000,000 or $10^{6}$ |
| Giga- | G | 1,000,000,000 or $10^{9}$ |
| Tera- | T | 1,000,000,000,000 or $10^{12}$ |

## SI Base Units and SI/English Conversions

### Length

The base unit for length in the SI system is the *meter.*

1 kilometer (km) = 0.62 mile (mi)
1 mile (mi) = 1.61 kilometers (km)
1 yard (yd) = 0.914 meters (m)
1 inch (in) = 2.54 centimeters (cm)

### Mass

The base unit for mass in the SI system is the *kilogram* (kg).

1 pound (lb) = 454 grams (g)
1 metric ton (t) = $10^3$ kg

### Volume

The unit for volume in the SI system is the *cubic meter* ($m^3$).

1 $dm^3$ = 1 liter (L) = 1.057 quarts (qt)
1 milliliter (mL) = 1 cubic centimeter ($cm^3$)
1 quart (qt) = 0.946 liters (L)
1 fluid ounce (fl oz) = 29.6 milliliters (mL)
1 gallon (gal) = 3.78 liters (L)

### Temperature

The base unit for temperature in the SI system is *kelvin* (K).

Celsius to Fahrenheit: °F = (9/5)°C + 32
Fahrenheit to Celsius: °C = (5/9)(°F – 32)
Celsius to kelvin: K = °C + 273.15

### Pressure

The unit for pressure in the SI system is the *pascal* (Pa).

1 millimeter of mercury (mm Hg) = 1 torr
1 Pa = 1 $N/m^2$ = 1 $kg/m\ s^2$
1 atm = $1.01325 \times 10^5$ Pa = 760 torr
1 bar = $1 \times 10^5$ Pa

### Energy

The unit for energy in the SI system is the *joule* (J).

1 J = 1 $kg\ m^2/s^2$ = 1 coulomb volt
1 calorie (cal) = 4.184 joules (J)
1 food Calorie (Cal) = 1 kilocalorie (kcal) = 4,184 joules (J)
1 British thermal unit (BTU) = 252 calories (cal) = 1,053 joules (J)

# BALANCING REDOX EQUATIONS USING THE ION–ELECTRON METHOD

The following steps may be used to balance oxidation–reduction (redox) equations by the ion–electron (half-reaction) method. While other methods may be successful, none is as consistently successful as this particular method. The half-reactions used in this process will also be necessary when considering other electrochemical phenomena; thus, the usefulness of half-reactions goes beyond balancing redox equations.

The basic idea of this method is to split a "complicated" equation into two parts called half-reactions. These simpler parts are then balanced separately and recombined to produce a balanced overall equation. The splitting is done so that one of the half-reactions deals only with the oxidation portion of the redox process, whereas the other deals only with the reduction portion. What ties the two halves together is the fact that the total electrons lost by the oxidation process MUST equal the total gained by the reduction process (step 6).

It is very important that you follow each of the steps listed below completely, in order; do not try to take any shortcuts. There are many modifications of this method—for example, a modification that allows you to balance all the reactions as if they were in acidic solution followed by a step, when necessary, to convert to a basic solution. Switching to a modification before you completely understand this method very often leads to confusion and an incorrect result.

## 1. Assign Oxidation Numbers and Begin the Half-Reactions, One for Oxidation and One for Reduction

Begin with the following example (phases are omitted for simplicity):

$$CH_3OH + Cr_2O_7^{2-} + H^+ \rightarrow HCOOH + Cr^{3+} + H_2O$$

(For many reactions, the substance oxidized and the substance reduced will be obvious, so this step may be simplified. However, to be safe, at least do a partial check to confirm your predictions. Note: One substance may be both oxidized and reduced; do not let this situation surprise you—it is called disproportionation.)

Review the rules for assigning oxidation numbers, if necessary, in the Basics chapter. These numbers are only used in this step. Do not force them into step 5.

Start the half-reactions with the entire molecules or ions from the net ionic form of the reaction. Do not go back to the molecular form of the reaction or just pull out atoms from their respective molecules or ions. Thus, from the example above, the initial half-reactions should be:

$$CH_3OH \rightarrow HCOOH$$

$$Cr_2O_7^{2-} \rightarrow Cr^{3+}$$

The carbon is oxidized ($C^{2-}$ to $C^{2+}$) and the chromium is reduced ($Cr^{6+}$ to $Cr^{3+}$). Check to make sure you get the same oxidation numbers for the carbon and the chromium (hydrogen and oxygen are +1 and −2, respectively).

## 2. Balance All Atoms Except Oxygen and Hydrogen

(In many reactions this will have been done in step 1; because of this many people forget to check this step. This is a very common reason why people get the wrong result.)

In the above example, carbon (C) and chromium (Cr) are the elements to be considered. The carbon is balanced, so no change is required in the first half-reaction. The chromium needs to be balanced, and so the second half-reaction becomes:

$$Cr_2O_7^{2-} \rightarrow 2\ Cr^{3+}$$

TIP

**Note:** To carry out the next two steps correctly, it is necessary to know if the solution is acidic or basic. A basic solution is one that you are specifically told is basic, or one that contains a base of $OH^-$ anywhere within the reaction. Assume that all other solutions are acidic (even if no acid is present).

## 3. Balance Oxygen Atoms

### a. In Acidic Solutions Add 1 $H_2O$/O to the Side Needing Oxygen

### b. In Basic Solutions Add 2 $OH^-$ for Every Oxygen Needed on the Oxygen-Deficient Side, Plus 1 $H_2O$/O on the Opposite Side

Do not forget that two things ($OH^-$ and $H_2O$) must be added in a basic solution. Also, these must be added to opposite sides.

**Example acid:**

acid: $Cr_2O_7^{2-} \rightarrow 2\ Cr^{3+}$

becomes: $Cr_2O_7^{2-} \rightarrow 2\ Cr^{3+} + 7\ H_2O$

**Example base:**

base: $Cr_2O_7^{2-} \rightarrow 2\ CrO_2^-$

becomes: $3\ H_2O + Cr_2O_7^{2-} \rightarrow 2\ CrO_2^- + 6\ OH^-$

## 4. Balance Hydrogen Atoms

### a. In Acidic Solutions Add $H^+(aq)$

### b. In Basic Solutions Add 1 $H_2O$/H Needed, Plus 1 $OH^-$/H on the Opposite Side

Again, do not forget that two things must be added in basic solutions ($OH^-$ and $H_2O$). In this case, they are still added to opposite sides, but with a different ratio.

**Example acid:**

acid: $Cr_2O_7^{2-} \rightarrow 2\ Cr^{3+} + 7\ H_2O$

becomes: $14\ H^+(aq) + Cr_2O_7^{2-} \rightarrow 2\ Cr^{3+} + 7\ H_2O$

**Example base:**

base: $6\ OH^- + C_2H_5OH \rightarrow 2\ CO_2 + 3\ H_2O$

becomes: $6\ OH^- + 6\ OH^- + C_2H_5OH \rightarrow 2\ CO_2 + 3\ H_2O + 6\ H_2O$

If the basic step is done correctly, the oxygens should remain balanced. This may be used as a check at this point. Notice that in the $C_2H_5OH$ half-reaction water appears twice. The 3 $H_2O$ is from step 3 and the 6 $H_2O$ is from step 4. Temporarily keeping the two separate helps you in case you need to recheck your work.

## 5. Balance Charges by Adding Electrons

The electrons must appear on opposite sides of the two half-reactions. They will appear on the left for the reduction and on the right for the oxidation. Once added, make sure you verify that the total charge on each side is the same. Not being careful on this step is a major cause of incorrect answers. Do not forget to use both the coefficients and the overall charges on the ions (not the oxidation numbers from step 1).

**Examples:**

acid: $6\ e^- + 14\ H^+(aq) + Cr_2O_7^{2-} \rightarrow 2\ Cr^{3+} + 7\ H_2O$

base: $6\ OH^- + 6\ OH^- + C_2H_5OH \rightarrow 2\ CO_2 + 3\ H_2O + 6\ H_2O + 12\ e^-$

## 6. Adjust the Half-Reactions So That They Both Have the Same Number of Electrons

(Find the lowest common multiple and multiply each of the half-reactions by the appropriate factor to achieve this value. This is the key step, as the number of electrons lost MUST equal the number gained.)

Lowest common multiple = 12

$$3 \times (H_2O + CH_3OH \rightarrow HCOOH + 4\ H^+(aq) + 4\ e^-)$$

$$2 \times (6\ e^- + 14\ H^+(aq) + Cr_2O_7^{2-} \rightarrow 2\ Cr^{3+} + 7\ H_2O)$$

giving:

$$3\ H_2O + 3\ CH_3OH \rightarrow 3\ HCOOH + 12\ H^+(aq) + 12\ e^-$$

$$12\ e^- + 28\ H^+(aq) + 2\ Cr_2O_7^{2-} \rightarrow 4\ Cr^{3+} + 14\ H_2O$$

## 7. Add the Half-Reactions and Cancel

(The electrons must cancel.)

**Example (from step 6):**

$$12\ e^- + 3\ H_2O + 3\ CH_3OH + 28\ H^+(aq) + 2\ Cr_2O_7^{2-} \rightarrow 4\ Cr^{3+} + 14\ H_2O + 3\ HCOOH + 12\ H^+(aq) + 12\ e^-$$

becomes:

$$3\ CH_3OH(aq) + 16\ H^+(aq) + 2\ Cr_2O_7^{2-}(aq) \rightarrow 4\ Cr^{3+}(aq) + 11\ H_2O(l) + 3\ HCOOH(aq)$$

## 8. Check to See if All Atoms Balance and That the Total Charge on Each Side Is the Same

This step will let you know whether you have done everything correctly.

If all the atoms and charges do not balance, you have made a mistake. Look over your work. If you have made an obvious mistake, then you should correct it. If the mistake is not obvious, it may take less time to start over from the beginning. The most common mistakes are made in steps 2 and 5, or step 3 in a basic solution.

Make sure you learn to apply each of the preceding steps. Look over the individual examples and make sure you understand them separately. Then make sure you learn the order of these steps. Finally, balance redox reactions; this will take a lot of practice. Make sure that you reach the point of being able to consistently balance equations without looking at the rules.

# COMMON IONS

## Ions Usually with One Oxidation State

| | | | |
|---|---|---|---|
| $Li^+$ | lithium ion | $N^{3-}$ | nitride ion |
| $Na^+$ | sodium ion | $O^{2-}$ | oxide ion |
| $K^+$ | potassium ion | $S^{2-}$ | sulfide ion |
| $Mg^{2+}$ | magnesium ion | $F^-$ | fluoride ion |
| $Ca^{2+}$ | calcium ion | $Cl^-$ | chloride ion |
| $Sr^{2+}$ | strontium ion | $Br^-$ | bromide ion |
| $Ba^{2+}$ | barium ion | $I^-$ | iodide ion |
| $Ag^+$ | silver ion | | |
| $Zn^{2+}$ | zinc ion | | |
| $Cd^{2+}$ | cadmium ion | | |
| $Al^{3+}$ | aluminum ion | | |

## Cations with More Than One Oxidation State

| | **+1** | | **+2** |
|---|---|---|---|
| $Cu^+$ | copper(I) ion or cuprous ion | $Cu^{2+}$ | copper(II) ion or cupric ion |
| $Hg^{2+}$ | mercury(I) ion or mercurous ion | $Hg^{2+}$ | mercury(II) ion or mercuric ion |
| | **+2** | | **+3** |
| $Fe^{2+}$ | iron(II) ion or ferrous ion | $Fe^{3+}$ | iron(III) ion or ferric ion |
| $Cr^{2+}$ | chromium(II) ion or chromous ion | $Cr^{3+}$ | chromium(III) ion or chromic ion |
| $Mn^{2+}$ | manganese(II) ion or manganous ion | $Mn^{3+}$ | manganese(III) ion or manganic ion |
| $Co^{2+}$ | cobalt(II) ion or cobaltous ion | $Co^{3+}$ | cobalt(III) ion or cobaltic ion |
| | **+2** | | **+4** |
| $Sn^{2+}$ | tin(II) ion or stannous ion | $Sn^{4+}$ | tin(IV) ion or stannic ion |
| $Pb^{2+}$ | lead(II) ion or plumbous ion | $Pb^{4+}$ | lead(IV) ion or plumbic ion |

## Polyatomic Ions and Acids

| Formula | Name | Ion | Ion name |
|---|---|---|---|
| $H_2SO_4$ | sulfuric acid | $SO_4^{2-}$ | sulfate ion |
| $H_2SO_3$ | sulfurous acid | $SO_3^{2-}$ | sulfite ion |
| $HNO_3$ | nitric acid | $NO_3^-$ | nitrate ion |
| $HNO_2$ | nitrous acid | $NO_2^-$ | nitrite ion |

| Formula | Name | Ion | Ion name |
|---|---|---|---|
| $H_3PO_4$ | phosphoric acid | $PO_4^{3-}$ | phosphate ion |
| $H_2CO_3$ | carbonic acid | $CO_3^{2-}$ | carbonate ion |
| $HMnO_4$ | permanganic acid | $MnO_4^-$ | permanganate ion |
| HCN | hydrocyanic acid | $CN^-$ | cyanide ion |
| HOCN | cyanic acid | $OCN^-$ | cyanate ion |
| HSCN | thiocyanic acid | $SCN^-$ | thiocyanate ion |
| $HC_2H_3O_2$ | acetic acid | $C_2H_3O_2^-$ | acetate ion |
| $H_2C_2O_4$ | oxalic acid | $C_2O_4^{2-}$ | oxalate ion |
| $H_2CrO_4$ | chromic acid | $CrO_4^{2-}$ | chromate ion |
| $H_2Cr_2O_7$ | dichromic acid | $Cr_2O_7^{2-}$ | dichromate ion |
| $H_2S_2O_3$ | thiosulfuric acid | $S_2O_3^{2-}$ | thiosulfate ion |
| $H_3AsO_4$ | arsenic acid | $AsO_4^{3-}$ | arsenate ion |
| $H_3AsO_3$ | arsenous acid | $AsO_3^{3-}$ | arsenite ion |

## Oxyhalogen Acids

| Formula | Oxy name | Ion | Ion name |
|---|---|---|---|
| HClO | hypochlorous acid | $ClO^-$ | hypochlorite ion |
| $HClO_2$ | chlorous acid | $ClO_2^-$ | chlorite ion |
| $HClO_3$ | chloric acid | $ClO_3^-$ | chlorate ion |
| $HClO_4$ | perchloric acid | $ClO_4^-$ | perchlorate ion |

Br or I can be substituted for chlorine Cl. F may form hypofluorous acid and the hypofluorite ion.

## Other Ions

| Ion | Ion name |
|---|---|
| $O_2^{2-}$ | peroxide ion |
| $OH^-$ | hydroxide ion |
| $HSO_4^-$ | bisulfate ion; hydrogen sulfate ion |
| $NH_4^+$ | ammonium ion |
| $O_2^-$ | superoxide ion |
| $HCO_3^-$ | bicarbonate ion; hydrogen carbonate ion |
| $HPO_4^{2-}$ | hydrogen phosphate ion |
| $H_2PO_4^-$ | dihydrogen phosphate ion |

## Ligands

| Ligand | Formula (abbreviation) | Ligand name |
|---|---|---|
| Bromide ion | $Br^-$ | bromo |
| Carbonate ion | $CO_3^{2-}$ | carbonato |
| Chloride ion | $Cl^-$ | chloro |

| Ligand | Formula (abbreviation) | Ligand name |
|---|---|---|
| Cyanide ion | $CN^-$ | cyano |
| Fluoride ion | $F^-$ | fluoro |
| Hydride ion | $H^-$ | hydrido |
| Hydroxide ion | $OH^-$ | hydroxo |
| Iodide ion | $I^-$ | iodo |
| Nitrite ion | $NO_2^-$ | nitrito |
| Oxalate ion | $C_2O_4^{2-}$ | oxalato |
| Sulfide ion | $S^{2-}$ | thio |
| Thiocyanate ion | $SCN^-$ | thiocyanato |
| Ammonia | $NH_3$ | ammine |
| Ethylenediamine | en | ethylenediamine |
| Water | $H_2O$ | aqua |

## Colors of Common Ions in Aqueous Solution

Most common ions are colorless in solution; however, some have distinctive colors. These colors have appeared in questions on the AP Exam.

| | |
|---|---|
| $Fe^{2+}$ and $Fe^{3+}$ | various colors |
| $Cu^{2+}$ | blue to green |
| $Cr^{2+}$ | blue |
| $Cr^{3+}$ | green or violet |
| $Mn^{2+}$ | faint pink |
| $Ni^{2+}$ | green |
| $Co^{2+}$ | pink |
| $MnO_4^-$ | dark purple |
| $CrO_4^{2-}$ | yellow |
| $Cr_2O_7^{2-}$ | orange |

# BIBLIOGRAPHY


Brown, Theodore L., H. Eugene Le May, Jr., and Bruce E. Bursten. 2011. *Chemistry: The Central Science*, 12th ed. Upper Saddle Creek, NJ: Prentice Hall.

Goldberg, David E. 2006. *Fundamentals of Chemistry*, 5th ed. New York: McGraw-Hill Education.

Hostage, David, and Martin Fossett. 2005. *Laboratory Investigations: AP Chemistry.* Saddle Brook, NJ: Peoples Publishing Group.

Langley, Richard, and John T. Moore. 2020 *Atoms, Molecules and Moles,* San Diego: Cognella Publishing.

Moore, John T. 2011. *Chemistry for Dummies*. Hoboken, NJ: Wiley Publishing, Inc.

Moore, John T. 2010. *Chemistry Essentials for Dummies.* Hoboken, NJ: Wiley Publishing, Inc.

Moore, John T., and Richard Langley. 2007. *Chemistry for the Utterly Confused*. New York: McGraw-Hill Education.

Russo, Steve, and Mike Silver. 2010. *Introductory Chemistry*, 4th ed. Upper Saddle Creek, NJ: Prentice Hall.

Silberberg, Martin S. 2017. *Chemistry: The Molecular Nature of Matter and Change*, 8th ed. New York: McGraw-Hill Education.

Zumdahl, Steven S., and Susan A. Zumdahl. 2017. *Chemistry,* 10th ed. Belmont, CA: Brooks Cole.


# WEBSITES

Here is a list of websites that contain information and links that you might find useful in your preparation for the AP Chemistry Exam:

www.chemistry.about.com
www.webelements.com
www.collegeboard.com/student/testing/ap/sub_chem.html?chem
www.chemistrygeek.com/ap.htm
www.rsc.org/
www.masteringchemistry.com
www.acs.org

# GLOSSARY

**absolute zero** Absolute zero (the lowest possible temperature) is 0 K and is the point at which all molecular motion ceases.

**acid dissociation constant ($K_a$)** The acid dissociation constant is the equilibrium constant associated with a weak acid dissociation in water.

**acidic** A solution whose pH is *less* than 7.00 is said to be acidic.

**acids** These are proton ($H^+$) donors.

**activation energy** Activation energy is the minimum amount of energy that must be supplied to initiate a chemical reaction.

**activity series for metals** The activity series lists metals and hydrogen in order of decreasing ease of oxidation.

**actual yield** The actual yield is the amount of product that is actually formed in a chemical reaction.

**alkali metals** Alkali metals are elements in Group 1 on the periodic table.

**alkaline earth metals** Alkaline earth metals are elements in Group 2 on the periodic table.

**alkanes** Alkanes are hydrocarbons that contain only single covalent bonds within the molecule.

**alkenes** Alkenes are hydrocarbons that contain a carbon-to-carbon double bond.

**alkynes** Alkynes are hydrocarbons that contain a carbon-to-carbon triple bond.

**alpha particle** An alpha particle is a helium nucleus with two protons and two neutrons.

**amorphous solids** Amorphous solids are solids that lack extensive ordering of the particles.

**amphoteric** Amphoteric substances will act as either an acid or a base, depending on whether the other species is a base or acid.

**amplitude** Amplitude is the height of a wave and is related to the intensity (or brightness for visible light) of the wave.

**amu** An amu is 1/12 the mass of a carbon atom that contains 6 protons and 6 neutrons (C-12).

**angular momentum quantum number ($l$)** The angular momentum quantum number is the quantum number that describes the shape of the orbital.

**anions** Anions are negatively charged ions.

**anode** The electrode at which oxidation is taking place is called the anode.

**anode compartment** The anode compartment is the electrolyte solution in which the anode is immersed.

**aqueous solution** An aqueous solution is a solution in which water is the solvent.

**atomic number ($Z$)** The atomic number of an element is the number of protons in the nucleus.

**atomic orbital** The atomic orbital is the region of space in which it is most likely to find a specific electron in an atom.

**atomic solids** In atomic solids, individual atoms are held in place by London forces.

**Aufbau principle** The Aufbau principle states that the electrons in an atom fill the lowest energy levels first.

**Avogadro's law** Avogadro's law states that there is a direct relationship between the volume and the number of moles of gas.

**Avogadro's number** Avogadro's number is the number of particles (atoms or molecules or ions) in a mole and is numerically equal to $6.022 \times 10^{23}$ particles.

**barometer** A barometer is an instrument for measuring atmospheric pressure.

**base dissociation constant, $K_b$** The base dissociation constant is the equilibrium constant associated with the dissociation of a weak base in water.

**bases** Bases are defined as proton ($H^+$) acceptors.

**basic** A solution whose pH is *greater* than 7.00 is called basic.

**Beer–Lambert law** The amount of energy that is absorbed or transmitted by a solution is directly related to the concentration of the solute, the path length through the solution, and its molar absorptivity.

**beta particle** A beta particle is an electron.

**bimolecular reactions** Bimolecular reactions are chemical reactions that involve the collision of two chemical species.

**binary compounds** Binary compounds are compounds that consist of only two elements.

**body-centered unit cell** A body-centered unit cell has particles located at the corners of a cube and in the center of the cube.

**boiling** The process of going from the liquid state to the gaseous state is called boiling.

**boiling point** The boiling point (b.p.) is the temperature at which a liquid boils.

**bond order** The bond order relates the bonding and antibonding electrons in the molecular orbital theory (# electrons in bonding MOs – # electrons in antibonding MOs)/2.

**Boyle's law** Boyle's law states that there is an inverse relationship between the volume and pressure of a gas if the temperature and amount are kept constant.

**buffer capacity** The buffer capacity is the amount of acid or base that may be added to a buffer before it ceases to be a buffer.

**buffers** Buffers are solutions that resist a change in pH when an acid or base is added to them.

**calorie** The calorie is the amount of energy needed to raise the temperature of 1 gram of water 1°C.

**calorimetry** Calorimetry is the laboratory technique used to measure the heat released or absorbed during a chemical or physical change.

**capillary action** Capillary action is the spontaneous rising of a liquid through a narrow tube against the force of gravity.

**catalyst** A catalyst is a substance that speeds up the reaction rate and is (at least theoretically) recoverable at the end of the reaction in an unchanged form.

**cathode** The cathode is the electrode in an electrochemical cell at which reduction takes place.

**cathode compartment** The cathode compartment is the electrolyte solution in which the cathode is immersed.

**cations** Cations are positively charged ions.

**cell notation** Cell notation is a shorthand notation for representing an electrochemical cell.

**Charles's law** Charles's law states that there is a direct relationship between the volume and temperature of a gas if the pressure and amount are kept constant.

**chemical change** A chemical change is a change that occurs when one or more substances change into one or more different substances.

**chemical equilibrium** A chemical equilibrium has been reached when two exactly opposite reactions are occurring at the same place, at the same time, and with the same rates of reaction (equal rates in opposite directions).

**colligative properties** Colligative properties are solution properties that are simply dependent upon the *number* of solute particles, and not the type of solute.

**colloids** Colloids are homogeneous mixtures in which solute diameters fall in between solutions and suspensions.

**combination reactions** Combination reactions are reactions in which two or more reactants (elements or compounds) combine to form one product.

**combined gas equation** The combined gas equation relates the pressure, temperature, and volume of a gas, assuming the amount is held constant.

**combustion reactions** Combustion reactions are redox reactions in which the chemical species rapidly combines with oxygen and usually emits heat and light.

**common-ion effect** The common-ion effect is the changing of an equilibrium by the addition of one of the equilibrium ions from an outside source.

**complex** A complex is composed of a central atom, normally a metal, surrounded by atoms or groups of atoms called ligands.

**compounds** Compounds are pure substances that have a fixed proportion of two or more elements.

**concentrated** Concentrated is a qualitative way of describing a solution that has a relatively large amount of solute in comparison to the solvent.

**concentration** Concentration is a measure of the amount of solute dissolved in the solvent.

**concentration cell** A concentration cell is an electrochemical cell in which the same chemical species are used in both cell compartments but differ in concentration.

**conjugate acid–base pair** This is an acid–base pair that differs by only a single $H^+$.

**continuous spectrum** A continuous spectrum is a spectrum of light much like the rainbow.

**coordinate covalent bonds** Coordinate covalent bonds are covalent bonds in which one of the atoms furnishes both electrons for the bond.

**coordination compounds** Coordination compounds are compounds containing a complex.

**coordination number** Coordination number is the number of ligands that can covalently bond to the metal ion in the complex ion.

**covalent bonding** In covalent bonding, one or more electron pairs are shared between two atoms.

**crisscross rule** The crisscross rule can be used to help determine the formula of an ionic compound.

**critical point** The critical point of a substance is the point on the phase diagram beyond which the gas and liquid phases are indistinguishable from each other.

**crystal lattice** The crystal lattice is a three-dimensional structure that crystalline solids occupy.

**crystalline solids** Crystalline solids display a very regular ordering of the particles (atoms, molecules, or ions) in a three-dimensional structure called the crystal lattice.

**Dalton's law** Dalton's law states that in a mixture of gases ($A + B + C \ldots$) the total pressure is simply the sum of the partial pressures (the pressures associated with each individual gas).

**decomposition reactions** Decomposition reactions are reactions in which a compound breaks down into two or more simpler substances.

**diamagnetism** Diamagnetism occurs when all the electrons present in a substance are in pairs. This results in the substance being weakly repelled by a magnet.

**dilute** Dilute is a qualitative term that refers to a solution that has a relatively small amount of solute in comparison to the amount of solvent.

**dimensional analysis** Dimensional analysis, sometimes called the factor label method, is a method for generating a correct setup for a mathematical problem.

**dipole–dipole intermolecular force** Dipole–dipole intermolecular forces occur between polar molecules.

**double displacement (replacement) or metathesis reaction** A double displacement (replacement) or metathesis reaction is a chemical reaction where at least one insoluble or unionized product is formed from the mixing of two solutions.

**effective nuclear charge** The overall attraction that an electron experiences is called the effective nuclear charge. This is less than the actual nuclear charge because other electrons interfere with the attraction of the protons for the electron being considered.

**electrochemical cells** Electrochemical cells use indirect electron transfer to produce electricity by a redox reaction, or they use electricity to produce a desired redox reaction.

**electrochemistry** Electrochemistry is the study of chemical reactions involving electricity.

**electrode** The electrode is that solid part of the electrochemical cell that transfers the electrons that are involved in an electrochemical cell.

**electrode compartment** The solutions in which the electrodes are immersed are called the electrode compartments.

**electrolysis** Electrolysis is a reaction in which electricity is used to decompose a compound.

**electrolyte** An electrolyte is a substance that, when dissolved in solution or melted, conducts an electrical current.

**electrolytic cells** Electrolytic cells use electricity from an external source to force a desired redox reaction.

**electromagnetic spectrum** The electromagnetic spectrum is radiant energy, composed of gamma rays, X-rays, ultraviolet light, visible light, etc.

**electron affinity** The electron affinity is the energy change that results from adding an electron to a gaseous atom or ion.

**electron capture** Electron capture is a radioactive decay mode that involves the capturing of an electron from the energy level closest to the nucleus (1s) by a proton in the nucleus.

**electron cloud** The electron cloud is a volume of space in which the probability of finding a particular electron is high.

**electronegativity** The electronegativity (EN) is a measure of the attractive force that an atom exerts on a bonding pair of electrons in a compound.

**electronic configuration** The electronic configuration is a condensed way of representing the pattern of electrons in an atom.

**elementary step** Elementary steps are the individual reactions (unimolecular or bimolecular) in the reaction mechanism or pathway.

**empirical formula** The empirical formula is a chemical formula that tells us which elements are present in the compound and the simplest whole-number ratio of elements.

**endothermic** Endothermic reactions absorb energy (heat) from their surroundings.

**endpoint** The endpoint of a titration is the experimental point signaled by the indication that an equivalent amount of base has been added to the acid sample, or vice versa.

**enthalpy** The enthalpy change, $\Delta H$, is the heat gained or lost by the system under constant pressure conditions.

**entropy** Entropy ($S$) is a measure of the disorder of a system.

**equilibrium constant** The quantity calculated when the equilibrium concentrations of the chemical species are substituted into the reaction quotient.

**equivalence point** The equivalence point is the theoretical point in the titration where the moles of $H^+$ in the acid solution have been exactly neutralized with the same number of moles of $OH^-$.

**excited state** An excited state of an atom is an energy state where one or more electrons is not as close to the nucleus as possible.

**exothermic** An exothermic reaction releases energy (heat) to its surroundings.

**face-centered unit cell** The face-centered unit cell has particles at the corners and one in the center of each face of the cube, but not in the center of the cube.

**First Law of Thermodynamics** The First Law of Thermodynamics states that the total energy of the universe is constant.

**formation constant** The formation constant is the equilibrium constant for the formation of a complex ion from a metal ion and ligands.

**frequency** The frequency, $\nu$, is defined as the number of waves that pass a point per second.

**functional group** Functional groups are reactive groups on a compound that react in a characteristic way no matter what the structure of the rest of the molecule.

**galvanic (voltaic) cells** Galvanic (voltaic) cells are electrochemical cells that produce electricity by a redox reaction.

**gamma emission** Gamma emission is a radioactive decay process in which high-energy, short-wavelength photons that are similar to X-rays are given off.

**gas** A gas is a state of matter that has neither definite shape nor volume.

**Gay-Lussac's law** Gay-Lussac's law describes the direct relationship between the pressure of a gas and its Kelvin temperature, if the volume and amount are held constant.

**Gibbs free energy** The Gibbs free energy ($G$) is a thermodynamic function that combines the enthalpy, entropy, and temperature. $\Delta G$ is the best indicator of whether or not a reaction will be spontaneous.

**Graham's law** Graham's law says that the speed of gas diffusion (mixing of gases due to their kinetic energy) or effusion (movement of a gas through a tiny opening) is inversely proportional to the square root of the gases' molecular mass.

**ground state** The ground state is the lowest energy state where all the electrons are as near the nucleus as possible.

**groups** Groups (families) are the vertical columns on the periodic table.

**half-life** The half-life, $t_{1/2}$, is the amount of time that it takes for a reactant concentration to decrease to one-half its initial concentration.

**halogens** Halogens are elements in Group 17 on the periodic table.

**heat capacity** Heat capacity is the quantity of heat needed to change the temperature of the system by 1 K.

**heat of vaporization** The heat of vaporization is the heat needed to transform a liquid into a gas.

**Henderson–Hasselbalch equation** The Henderson–Hasselbalch equation can be used to calculate the pH or pOH of a buffer.

**Henry's law** Henry's law states the solubility of a gas will increase with increasing partial pressure of the gas.

**Hess's law** Hess's law states that if a reaction occurs in a series of steps, then the enthalpy change for the overall reaction is simply the sum of the enthalpy changes of the individual steps.

**heterogeneous catalyst** A heterogeneous catalyst is a catalyst that is in a different phase or state of matter from the reactants.

**homogeneous catalyst** A homogeneous catalyst is a catalyst that is in the same phase or state of matter as the reactants.

**Hund's rule** Hund's rule states that electrons are added to the orbitals in a set, half filling them all before any pairing occurs.

**hybrid orbitals** Hybrid orbitals are atomic orbitals formed as a result of the mixing of the atomic orbitals of the atoms involved in covalent bonding.

**hydrocarbons** Hydrocarbons are organic compounds containing only carbon and hydrogen.

**hydrogen bonding** Hydrogen bonding is a specific type of dipole–dipole attraction in which a hydrogen atom is polar-covalently bonded to one of the following extremely electronegative elements: O, N, or F.

**ideal gas** An ideal gas is a gas that obeys the five postulates of the Kinetic Molecular Theory of Gases.

**ideal gas equation** The ideal gas equation relates the temperature, volume, pressure, and amount of a gas, and has the mathematical form of $PV = nRT$.

**indicators** Indicators are substances that change their color during a titration to indicate the endpoint.

**inert (inactive) electrode** An inert (inactive) electrode is a conducting electrode in an electrochemical cell that does not take part in the redox reaction.

**inner transition elements** The inner transition elements are the elements in the two horizontal groups that have been pulled out of the main body of the periodic table.

**integrated rate law** The integrated rate law relates the change in the concentration of reactants or products over time.

**intermediates** Intermediates are chemical species that are produced and consumed during the reaction, but that do not appear in the overall reaction.

**intermolecular forces** Intermolecular forces are attractive or repulsive forces between molecules.

**ion–dipole intermolecular force** Ion–dipole intermolecular forces are attractive forces that occur between ions and polar molecules.

**ion-induced dipole intermolecular forces** Ion-induced dipole intermolecular forces are attractive forces that occur between an ion and a nonpolar molecule.

**ion-product** The ion-product has the same form as the solubility product constant but represents a system that is not at equilibrium.

**ionic bond** Ionic bonds are the result of the mutual attraction of cations and anions.

**ionic equation** The ionic equation shows the soluble reactants and products in the form of separated ions.

**ionic solids** Ionic solids have their lattices composed of ions held together by the attraction of opposite charges of the ions.

**ionization energy** The ionization energy (IE) is the energy needed to completely remove an electron from an atom in the vapor state.

**isoelectronic** Isoelectronic means having the same electronic configuration.

**isomers** Isomers are compounds that have the same molecular formulas but different structural formulas.

**isotopes** Isotopes are atoms of the same element (same number of protons) that have differing numbers of neutrons.

**joule (J)** The joule is the SI unit of energy.

**kinetic energy** Kinetic energy is energy of motion.

**Kinetic Molecular Theory** The Kinetic Molecular Theory attempts to represent the properties of gases by modeling the gas particles themselves at the microscopic level.

**kinetics** Kinetics is the study of the speed of reactions.

**Law of Conservation of Matter** The Law of Conservation of Matter says that in ordinary chemical reactions matter is neither created nor destroyed.

**Le Châtelier's principle** Le Châtelier's principle states that if a chemical system at equilibrium is stressed (disturbed), it will reestablish equilibrium by shifting the reactions involved.

**Lewis electron-dot structure** The Lewis electron-dot structure is a structural formula that represents an atom of an element and its valence electrons.

**limiting reactant** The limiting reactant is the reactant that is used up first in a chemical reaction.

**line spectrum** A line spectrum is a series of fine lines of colors representing wavelengths of photons that are characteristic of a specific element.

**liquid** A liquid is a state of matter that has a definite volume but no definite shape.

**macromolecules** Macromolecules are extremely large molecules.

**magnetic quantum number ($m_l$)** The magnetic quantum number describes the orientation of the orbital around the nucleus.

**main-group elements** Main-group elements are the groups (columns) on the periodic table that are labeled 1–2 and 13–18.

**manometer** A manometer is an instrument used to measure the gas pressure inside a container.

**mass number** The mass number (A) is the sum of the protons and neutrons in an atom.

**mass percent** The mass percentage of a solution is the mass of the solute divided by the mass of the solution and then multiplied by 100% to get percentage.

**mass spectroscopy** Mass spectroscopy is an analytical technique in which atoms or molecules are ionized by a variety of methods and then separated based on their mass-to-charge ratios (*m/z*).

**mass-volume percent** The mass-volume percent of a solution is the mass of the solute divided by the volume of the solution and then multiplied by 100% to get percentage.

**mechanism** The mechanism is the sequence of steps that a reaction undergoes in going from reactants to products.

**melting point** The temperature at which a solid converts into the liquid state is called the melting point (m.p.) of the solid.

**metallic bonding** In metallic bonding the electrons of the atoms are delocalized and are free to move throughout the entire solid.

**metallic solids** Metallic solids have metal atoms occupying the crystal lattice and held together by metallic bonding.

**metalloids** Metalloids are a group of elements that have properties of both metals and nonmetals.

**metals** Metals are normally solids (mercury being an exception), shiny, and good conductors of heat and electricity. They can be hammered into thin sheets (malleable) and extruded into wires (ductile). Chemically, metals tend to lose electrons in reactions.

**metathesis reaction** A double displacement (replacement) or metathesis reaction is a chemical reaction where at least one product is formed from the mixing of two solutions.

**molality (*m*)** Molality is defined as the moles of solute per kilogram of solvent.

**molar heat capacity** The molar heat capacity (*C*) is the amount of heat needed to change the temperature of 1 mole of a substance by 1 K.

**molar mass** The mass in grams of 1 mole of a substance.

**molarity (*M*)** or sometimes [ ] Molarity is a concentration term that represents the moles of solute per liter of solution.

**mole** The mole (mol) is defined as the amount of a substance that contains the same number of particles as atoms in exactly 12 g of carbon-12.

**molecular equation** The molecular equation is an equation in which all reactants and products are shown in the undissociated form.

**molecular formula** The molecular (actual) formula shows which elements are in the molecule and the actual number of atoms of each element.

**molecular orbital theory** The molecular orbital (MO) theory of covalent bonding proposes that atomic orbitals combine to form molecular orbitals that encompass the entire molecule.

**molecular solids** Molecular solids have their lattices composed of molecules held in place by London forces, dipole–dipole forces, and hydrogen bonding.

**molecule** A molecule is a covalently bonded species.

**monomers** Macromolecules are composed of repeating units called monomers.

**Nernst equation** The Nernst equation allows the calculation of the cell potential of a galvanic cell that is not under standard conditions.

**net ionic equation** The net ionic equation is written by dropping out the spectator ions from an ionic equation and showing only those chemical species that are involved in the chemical reaction.

**network covalent solids** Network covalent solids have covalent bonds joining the atoms together in an extremely large crystal lattice.

**neutral** Neutral is 7.00 on the pH scale.

**neutralization reactions** Neutralization reactions are acid–base reactions in which an acid reacts with a base to give a salt and usually water.

**noble gases** Noble gases are elements in Group 18 on the periodic table. They are very unreactive owing to their filled valence shell.

**nonelectrolytes** Nonelectrolytes are substances that do not conduct electricity when dissolved in water or melted.

**nonmetals** Nonmetals have properties that are generally the opposite of metals. Some are gases, are poor conductors of heat and electricity, are neither malleable nor ductile, and tend to gain or share electrons in their chemical reactions.

**nonpolar covalent bond** In a nonpolar covalent bond the electrons are shared equally by the two atoms involved in the bond.

**nuclear belt of stability** The nuclear belt of stability is a plot of the number of neutrons versus the number of protons for the known stable isotopes.

**nucleus** The nucleus is a dense core of positive charge at the center of the atom that contains most of the mass of the atom from the protons and neutrons.

**octet rule** The octet rule states that atoms lose, gain, or share electrons in order to achieve a filled valence shell, to complete their octet.

**orbital** An orbital or wave function is a quantum mechanical mathematical description of the location of electrons. The electrons in a specific subshell are distributed among these volumes of space of equal energies.

**order of reaction** The order of reaction is the exponent in the rate equation that indicates what effect a change in concentration of that particular reactant species will have on the reaction rate.

**organic chemistry** Organic chemistry is the study of the chemistry of carbon.

**osmosis** Osmosis is the passing of solvent molecules through a semipermeable membrane into a more concentrated solution.

**osmotic pressure** The osmotic pressure is the amount of pressure that must be exerted on a solution in order to prevent osmosis of solvent molecules through a semipermeable membrane.

**oxidation** Oxidation is the loss of electrons.

**oxidation numbers** Oxidation numbers are bookkeeping numbers that allow chemists to do things like balance redox equations.

**oxidizing agent** The oxidizing agent is the reactant being reduced.

**paramagnetism** Paramagnetism is the result of having one or more unpaired electrons and results is a substance that is attracted to a magnet.

**pascal** The pascal is the SI unit of pressure.

**percent yield** The percent yield (% yield) is the actual yield divided by the theoretical yield, with the result multiplied by 100.

**periods** Periods are the horizontal rows on the periodic table that have consecutive atomic numbers.

**phase changes** Phase changes are changes of state.

**phase diagram** A phase diagram is a graph representing the relationship of the states of matter of a substance to temperature and pressure.

**photoelectric effect** The photoelectric effect is the emission of electrons when electromagnetic radiation, such as light, hits a material.

**physical change** A physical change is a change in the form of a substance but not in its composition.

**pi (π) bonds** Pi bonds result from the overlap of atomic orbitals on both sides of a line connecting two atomic nuclei.

**polar covalent bonds** Polar covalent bonds are covalent bonds in which there is an unequal sharing of the bonding pair of electrons.

**polyprotic acids** Polyprotic acids are acids that can donate more than one proton.

**positron** A positron is essentially an electron that has a positive charge instead of a negative charge.

**potential energy** Potential energy is stored energy.

**precipitate** A precipitate is an insoluble product that forms in a solution.

**precipitation reactions** Precipitation reactions are reactions that involve the formation of an insoluble compound, a precipitate, from the mixing of two soluble compounds.

**pressure** Pressure is the force exerted per unit of surface area.

**principal quantum number (*n*)** The principal quantum number describes the size of the orbital and its relative distance from the nucleus.

**proof** The proof of an aqueous ethyl alcohol solution is twice the volume percent.

**quantized** Quantized means that there could be only certain distinct energies associated with a state of the atom.

**quantum numbers** Quantum numbers are used to describe each electron within an atom corresponding to the orbital size, shape, and orientation in space.

**radioactivity** Radioactivity is the spontaneous decay of an unstable isotope to a more stable one.

**rate constant (*k*)** The rate constant is a proportionality constant that appears in the rate law and relates the concentration of reactants to the speed of reaction.

**rate-determining step** The rate-determining step is the slowest of the reaction steps and controls the rate of the overall reaction.

**rate equation** The rate equation relates the speed of reaction to the concentration of reactants and has the form Rate = $k[A]^m[B]^n$. . . where $k$ is the rate constant and $m$ and $n$ are the orders of reaction with respect to that specific reactant.

**reactants** The starting materials in a chemical reaction that get converted into different substances called products.

**reaction intermediate** A reaction intermediate is a substance that is formed but then consumed during the reaction mechanism.

**reaction mechanism** The reaction mechanism is the sequence of elementary steps that occur in an overall reaction in going from reactants to products.

**reaction quotient** The reaction quotient, $Q$, is the numerical value that results when nonequilibrium concentrations are inserted into the equilibrium expression. When the system reaches equilibrium, the reaction quotient becomes the equilibrium constant.

**reactive site** The reactive site of a molecule is the place at which the reaction takes place.

**redox reactions** Redox reactions are chemical reactions in which electrons are lost and gained.

**reducing agent** The reactant undergoing oxidation in a redox reaction is called the reducing agent.

**reduction** Reduction is the gain of electrons in a redox reaction.

**resonance** Resonance is a way of describing a molecular structure that cannot be represented by a single Lewis structure. Several different Lewis structures are used, each differing only by the position of the electrons.

**reverse osmosis** Reverse osmosis takes place when the pressure on the solution side exceeds the osmotic pressure and solvent molecules are forced back through the semipermeable membrane into the solvent side.

**root-mean-square speed ($\mu_{rms}$)** The average velocity of gas particles is called the root-mean-square speed.

**salt bridge** A salt bridge is often an inverted U-tube that contains a gel containing a concentrated electrolyte solution, used in an electrochemical cell to maintain electrical neutrality in the cell compartments.

**saturated hydrocarbons** Saturated hydrocarbons are hydrocarbons where the carbon atoms are single bonded to the maximum number of other atoms.

**saturated solution** A solution in which one has dissolved the maximum amount of solute per given amount of solvent at a given temperature is called a saturated solution.

**Second Law of Thermodynamics** The Second Law of Thermodynamics states that all processes that occur spontaneously move in the direction of an increase in entropy of the universe (system + surroundings).

**semipermeable membrane** A semipermeable membrane is a thin, porous film that allows the passage of some, but not all, particles.

**shells** The electrons in an atom are located in various energy levels or shells that are located at different distances from the nucleus.

**SI system** The system of units used in science is the SI system (Système International), which is related to the metric system.

**sigma (σ) bonds** Sigma bonds have the orbital overlap on a line drawn between the two nuclei.

**simple cubic unit cell** The simple cubic unit cell has particles located at the corners of a simple cube.

**single displacement (replacement) reactions** Single displacement reactions are reactions in which atoms of an element replace the atoms of another element in a compound.

**solid** A solid is a state of matter that has both a definite shape and a definite volume.

**solubility product constant ($K_{sp}$)** The solubility product constant is the equilibrium constant associated with sparingly soluble salts and is the product of the ionic concentrations, each one raised to the power of the coefficient in the balanced chemical equation.

**solute** The solute is the component of the solution that is present in the smallest amount.

**solution** A solution is defined as a homogeneous mixture composed of solvent and one or more solutes.

**solvation** Solvation is the forming of a layer of bound solvent molecules around a solute.

**solvent** The solvent is that component of a solution that is present in the largest amount.

**specific heat capacity (or specific heat)($c$)** The specific heat capacity is the quantity of heat needed to raise the temperature of 1 g of the substance by 1 K.

**spectator ions** Spectator ions are ions that are not actually involved in the chemical reaction taking place, but simply maintain electrical neutrality.

**speed of light ($c$)** The speed of light is the speed at which all electromagnetic radiation travels in a vacuum, $3.0 \times 10^8$ m/s.

**spin quantum number ($m_s$)** The spin quantum number indicates the direction the electron is spinning.

**standard cell potential ($E°$)** The standard cell potential is the potential (voltage) associated with an electrochemical cell at standard conditions.

**standard enthalpy of formation** The standard enthalpy of formation of a compound ($\Delta H_f°$) is the change in enthalpy when 1 mole of a substance is formed from its elements and when all substances are in their standard states.

**standard molar entropies ($S°$)** Standard molar enthalpies of elements and compounds are the entropies associated with 1 mole of a substance in its standard state.

**standard reduction potentials** The standard reduction potential is the voltage associated with a half-reaction shown in the form of reduction.

**state function** A state function is a function that doesn't depend on the pathway, only the initial and final states.

**stoichiometry** Stoichiometry is the calculation of the amount (mass, moles, particles) of one substance in the chemical reaction through the use of another substance.

**strong acid** A strong acid is an acid that ionizes completely in solution.

**strong base** A strong base is a base that ionizes completely in solution.

**strong electrolytes** Strong electrolytes completely ionize or dissociate in solution.

**structural isomers** Structural isomers are compounds that have the same molecular formula but differ in how the atoms are attached to each other.

**sublimation** Sublimation is going directly from the solid state to the gaseous state without ever having become a liquid.

**subshells** Within the shells, the electrons are grouped in subshells of slightly different energies.

**supersaturated solution** A supersaturated solution has more than the maximum amount of solute dissolved in the solvent at a given temperature.

**surface tension** Surface tension is the amount of force that is required to break through the molecular layer at the surface of a liquid.

**surroundings** The surroundings is a thermodynamic term meaning the part of the universe that is not the system that is being studied.

**suspension** A suspension is a heterogeneous mixture in which the particles are large (in excess of 1,000 nm).

**system** The system is a thermodynamics term meaning the part of the universe that we are studying.

**ternary compounds** Ternary compounds are those containing three (or more) elements.

**theoretical yield** The theoretical yield is the maximum amount of product that can be formed.

**thermochemistry** Thermochemistry is the part of thermodynamics dealing with the changes in heat that take place during chemical processes, for example, $\Delta H_{\text{fusion}}$.

**thermodynamics** Thermodynamics is the study of energy and its transformations.

**titrant** The titrant is that solution in a titration that has a known concentration.

**titration** A titration is a laboratory procedure in which a solution of known concentration is used to determine the concentration of an unknown solution.

**transition elements** Groups 3–12 on the periodic table contain the transition elements.

**transmutation** Transmutation is a nuclear reaction that results in the conversion of one element into another element.

**triple point** The triple point of a substance is the combination of temperature and pressure on a phase diagram at which all three states of matter can exist in equilibrium.

**Tyndall effect** The Tyndall effect is exhibited when a light is shone through a colloid and is visible, owing to the reflection of the light off the larger colloid particles.

**unimolecular reactions** Unimolecular reactions are reactions in which a single chemical species decomposes or rearranges.

**unit cells** Unit cells are the repeating units in a crystal lattice.

**unsaturated** Unsaturated organic compounds have carbon atoms that do not have the maximum number of bonds to other atoms; there is at least one carbon-to-carbon double or triple bond present.

**unsaturated solution** An unsaturated solution has less than the maximum amount of solute dissolved in a given amount of solvent.

**valence bond theory** The valence bond theory describes covalent bonding as the overlap of atomic orbitals to form a new set of orbitals, hybrid orbitals.

**valence electrons** Valence electrons are the electrons in the outermost energy level (outermost shell). Valence electrons are normally considered to be only the s and p electrons in the outermost energy level.

**van der Waals equation** The van der Waals equation is an equation that is a modification of the ideal gas equation to compensate for the behavior of real gases.

**van't Hoff factor (*i*)** The van't Hoff factor is the ratio of moles of solute particles formed to moles of solute dissolved in solution.

**vapor pressure** The pressure exerted by the gaseous molecules that are at equilibrium with a liquid in a closed container.

**viscosity** Viscosity is the resistance to flow of a liquid.

**volume percent** The volume percent of the solution is the volume of the solute divided by the volume of the solution and then multiplied by 100% to generate the percentage.

**VSEPR theory** The VSEPR (valence-shell electron-pair repulsion) theory says that the electron pairs around a central atom will try to get as far as possible from each other in order to minimize the repulsive forces. This theory is used to predict molecular geometry.

**water dissociation constant ($K_w$)** The water dissociation constant is the equilibrium constant associated with the ionization of pure water.

**wave function** The wave function is a mathematical description of the electron's motion.

**wavelength ($\lambda$)** A wavelength is the distance between two identical points on a wave.

**weak acid** A weak acid is an acid that only partially ionizes in solution.

**weak base** A weak base is a base that only partially ionizes in solution.

**weak electrolytes** Weak electrolytes only partially ionize or dissociate in solution.

# AVOIDING "STUPID" MISTAKES ON THE FREE-RESPONSE SECTION

We have been grading the free-response part of the AP Chemistry Exam for quite a while. Between the two of us, we have almost 35 years of grading experience—that's more than 150,000 exams! Over the years, we have seen quite a number of careless mistakes made by students. These mistakes resulted from students not being careful rather than not being prepared for the exam. Here are some practical tips to avoid the most common careless errors.

- **Don't forget to state the units of measurement.** Many students would have gotten more credit if they had shown the units, both in the calculations and in the final answer. The units help you stay on the right track and help the grader determine if (or where) you went wrong.
- **Use the formula given.** If the exam gives you a chemical formula, don't use a different formula in your answer. In general, do not alter anything given to you on the exam. For example, we have seen $Ba(NO_3)_2$ become $Ba(NO_2)_2$.
- **Be careful with the math.** We have seen many errors involving the simplest math, such as 12 mL + 3 mL = 0.042 L (rather than 0.015 L).
- **Don't confuse molarity and moles.** The units *M* and [ ] are identical (molarity) and are completely different from moles.
- **Show your work for conversions.** For example, if you are changing grams to moles and make a simple mistake, showing your work (labeled) may get you partial credit.
- **Don't argue with the test.** This is an argument you cannot win. For example, if the question asks for calculations, you are unlikely to get full credit without any calculations even if you have the right answer. It won't help to write that you feel the calculations are unnecessary.
- **Be careful in applying gas laws.** Gas laws can be very useful. However, they should *never* be used when there is not a gas in the problem. Having a volume included in the question information doesn't necessarily mean you are dealing with a gas.
- **Be careful making comparisons.** We have seen many students incorrectly say that $10^{-8}$ is smaller than $10^{-12}$ and actually write $10^{-8} < 10^{-12}$. We have even seen students write the relationship correctly ($10^{-8} > 10^{-12}$) but still state that $10^{-8}$ is smaller.
- **Be careful using 22.4 L/mol.** You will probably not need to use this on the exam. But if you do want to use this value, you *must* have a gas and this gas *must* be at 0°C (273 K) and 1 atm (STP). If you forget the values for STP, they can be found on the exam. We have seen quite a few students incorrectly use this value at 298 K.
- **There are no trick questions on the exam.** If you think you have found a trick question, you need to reevaluate your thinking and reread the question.
- **Don't confuse solutions and precipitates in solution.** They are different phases and are not interchangeable. The color of one is not necessarily the color of the other.
- **Be careful describing reactions.** If the problem gives you, for example, a sodium nitrate solution, part of your answer describing a reaction cannot be "the sodium nitrate dissolves." You already have a solution, so the process of dissolving happened before you got to the problem. Furthermore, dissolving should not be treated as a reaction.

- **Be careful using positive and negative charges.** In the following equation, each reactant and product is wrong: $NH_4 + NO_3 \rightarrow NH_4^+NO_3^-$, and will not substitute for the correct $NH_4^+ + NO_3^- \rightarrow NH_4NO_3$. Remember: ionic equations, of any type, have ions (with charges) on one or both sides of the reaction arrow.
- **Don't do a calculator dump** (write down every number displayed by your calculator). For example, your final answer will not be 3.27584827 g.
- **Keep in mind the meaning of "observe."** If the problem asks about observation, tell what you would actually observe (see, hear, or smell). You will *not* see a compound separating into ions; usually you will *not* see the excess reagent, and you will *not* see the atoms forming bonds. In contrast, you might observe a compound dissolving.
- **Remember, a solvent is usually not a reactant.** Therefore, changing the grams of solvent to moles is probably wrong. (However, you will need to know the moles of solvent if you are looking for a mole fraction.)
- **Think before creating mole ratios.** Since the solvent is not a reactant, a mole ratio relating the solvent to anything else in the problem is most likely wrong. We have seen many students change the grams of water to moles and then use these moles in a mole ratio to relate to some other substance in the problem.
- **Don't go off on a tangent.** Stay focused on answering the original question.
- **Double-check the numbers you use.** We have seen many cases where the problem gave a number like $2.75 \times 10^{-18}$, and the student worked the problem with $2.75 \times 10^{-8}$. If you show your work, it will be obvious to the grader that you miscopied the value and you might pick up some points; otherwise, you just have a wrong answer.
- **Remember that sometimes not all of the information given is needed to solve the problem.** For example, in the equilibrium problem, many times the temperature is given but it is not actually part of the calculations.
- **Only round your final answer.** Don't round off the results of intermediate calculations; only use rounding after you've gotten your final answer.
- **Be careful in reading graphs.** Especially take care in reading the scales. We have seen students write down that 0.5 is between 1.0 and 2.0.
- **Don't confuse intermolecular and intramolecular forces.** These are two different concepts and are not interchangeable.

In addition to avoiding the careless mistakes mentioned above, here are some easy ways to help improve your score on the free-response questions:

- **Show your work.** In most cases, no work, no credit.
- **Use the space provided for answers.** It helps you and the grader if you answer the question in the space provided instead of crowding the answers between the questions. You will have more than enough room on the following page(s). It also helps to label the parts (a, b, etc.) and to answer the parts in order.
- **Make sure your answer can be easily read.** It will really help the grader—and your score—if you write legibly, in a normal size (not too small, please), and use a pencil or pen that writes dark enough to be easily read.
- **Don't use periodic trends and general rules as explanations.** General rules such as "like dissolves like" are never explanations. They may help you in answering the multiple-choice part of the exam but will be of little benefit by themselves in the free-response section.
- **Don't confuse "define" and "describe."** They are two different processes. If you are asked to describe or explain, simply giving a definition will earn you very few points.

- **Use only standard abbreviations.** Your instructor may understand your abbreviations, but the grader may not. If you want to use abbreviations in a response, be sure to define them.
- **Don't ramble.** Normally an explanation or justification can be done in five sentences or less. Your answers should be clear, concise, and to the point.
- **The grader cannot see your calculator display or a graph/table that you do not include in your answer.** Show all your work that you want graded; sometimes showing this will help you get a point that you might otherwise have missed.
- **In general, the graders are not "mind readers."** Show your work and your reasoning. Don't assume graders will know what you meant. They grade only what you have written down.
- **Answer the question asked, not the question you wanted.** You might have a great response to a question, but if that doesn't answer the exact question asked, it is WRONG!
- **It is usually simpler to use the units given in the problem.** It is less work on your part and less work on the grader.
- **Using extra calculation steps provides additional opportunities to make errors.** Show all your pertinent calculation steps, but extra steps are spots for potential errors. This is especially true when you are tired.

# EXAM RESOURCES

## Keywords and Equations: For Use with Free-Response Questions Only

### *Basics*

| | | | |
|---|---|---|---|
| $T$ = temperature | $n$ = moles | $m$ = mass | $P$ = pressure |
| $V$ = volume | $D$ = density | $v$ = velocity | $\boldsymbol{M}$ = molar mass |
| $KE$ = kinetic energy | $t$ = time | | |

Boltzmann's constant, $k = 1.38 \times 10^{-23}$ J K$^{-1}$
electron charge = $-1.602 \times 10^{-19}$ coulombs
1 electron volt per atom = 96.5 kJ mol$^{-1}$
Avogadro's number = $6.022 \times 10^{23}$ mol$^{-1}$
K = °C + 273 $\qquad D = m/V$

### *Gases*

STP = 0.000° C and 1.000 atm
$PV = nRT$

$$P_A = P_{total} \times X_A, \text{ where } X_A = \frac{\text{moles A}}{\text{total moles}}$$

$$P_{total} = P_A + P_B + P_C + \cdots$$

$$\frac{P_1V_1}{T_1} = \frac{P_2V_2}{T_2}$$

$KE$ per molecule = ½ $mv^2$

$r_1/r_2 = \sqrt{\boldsymbol{M}_2/\boldsymbol{M}_1}$

1 atm = 760 mm Hg
= 760 torr

Gas constant, $R$ = 8.31 J mol$^{-1}$ K$^{-1}$
= 0.0821 L atm mol$^{-1}$ K$^{-1}$
= 8.31 volt coulomb mol$^{-1}$ K$^{-1}$
= 62.36 L torr mol$^{-1}$ K$^{-1}$

### Thermodynamics

$S°$ = standard entropy
$H°$ = standard enthalpy
$G°$ = standard free energy
$q$ = heat
$c$ = specific heat capacity

$\Delta S° = \Sigma\, S°$ products $- \Sigma\, S°$ reactants
$\Delta H° = \Sigma\, \Delta H_f°$ products $- \Sigma\, \Delta H_f°$ reactants
$\Delta G° = \Sigma\, \Delta G_f°$ products $- \Sigma\, \Delta G_f°$ reactants

$$\Delta G° = \Delta H° - T\Delta S°$$
$$= -RT \text{ in } K$$
$$= -nFE°$$
$$\Delta G = \Delta G° + RT \ln Q$$
$$q = mc\,\Delta T$$

### Light and Electrons

$E$ = energy
$\nu$ = frequency
$\lambda$ = wavelength
$p$ = momentum
$v$ = velocity
$n$ = principal quantum number
$m$ = mass
$E = h\nu$
$c = \lambda\nu$

Speed of light, $c = 3.0 \times 10^{8}$ m $s^{-1}$
Planck's constant, $h = 6.63 \times 10^{-34}$ J s

### Solutions

Molarity, $M$ = moles solute per liter solution

### Kinetics

$$\ln [A]_t - \ln [A]_0 = -kt$$

$$\frac{1}{[A]_t} - \frac{1}{[A]_0} = kt$$

$E_a$ = activation energy
$k$ = rate constant
$t_{1/2} = 0.693/k$

### Electrochemistry

$I$ = current (amperes)
$q$ = charge (coulombs)
$E°$ = standard reduction potential
$K$ = equilibrium constant

Faraday's constant, $F$ = 96,500 coulombs per mole of electrons

$$I = q/t$$

### Equilibrium

$Q$ = reaction quotient

$$Q = \frac{[C]^c[D]^d}{[A]^a[B]^b},\ \text{where } aA + bB \rightarrow cC + dD$$

equilibrium constants:

$K_a$ (weak acid) $K_b$ (weak base) $K_w$ (water)

$K_p$ (gas pressure) $K_c$ (molar concentrations)

$$K_a = \frac{[H^+][A^-]}{[HA]} \qquad K_b = \frac{[OH^-][HB^+]}{[B]} \qquad K_p = \frac{(P_c)^c (P_d)^d}{(P_a)^a (P_b)^b}$$

$K_w = [OH^-][H^+] = 1.0 \times 10^{-14} = K_a \times K_b$ at 25°C

$pH = -\log [H^+]$, $pOH = -\log [OH^-]$

$14 = pH + pOH$

$$pH = pK_a + \log \frac{[A^-]}{[HA]}$$

$$pOH = pK_b + \log \frac{[HB^+]}{[B]}$$

$pK_a = -\log K_a$, $pK_b = -\log K_b$

***Experimental***

Beer's law: $A = abc$ ($A$ = absorbance; $a$ = molar absorbtivity; $b$ = path length; $c$ = concentration)

# Periodic Table of the Elements

May be used with all questions.

## The Periodic Table

Key:

| Atomic number |
|---|
| **Symbol** |
| Atomic weight (mean relative mass) |

| 1 | 2 | | 3 | 4 | 5 | 6 | 7 | 8 | 9 | 10 | 11 | 12 | 13 | 14 | 15 | 16 | 17 | 18 |
|---|---|---|---|---|---|---|---|---|---|---|---|---|---|---|---|---|---|---|
| 1 **H** 1.008 | | | | | | | | | | | | | | | | | | 2 **He** 4.002602(2) |
| 3 **Li** 6.94 | 4 **Be** 9.012182(3) | | | | | | | | | | | | 5 **B** 10.81 | 6 **C** 12.011 | 7 **N** 14.007 | 8 **O** 15.999 | 9 **F** 18.9984032(5) | 10 **Ne** 20.1797(6) |
| 11 **Na** 22.98976928(2) | 12 **Mg** 24.3050(6) | | | | | | | | | | | | 13 **Al** 26.9815386(2) | 14 **Si** 28.085 | 15 **P** 30.973762(2) | 16 **S** 32.06 | 17 **Cl** 35.45 | 18 **Ar** 39.948(1) |
| 19 **K** 39.0983(1) | 20 **Ca** 40.078(4) | | 21 **Sc** 44.955912(6) | 22 **Ti** 47.867(1) | 23 **V** 50.9415(1) | 24 **Cr** 51.9961(6) | 25 **Mn** 54.938045(5) | 26 **Fe** 55.845(2) | 27 **Co** 58.933195(5) | 28 **Ni** 58.6934(4) | 29 **Cu** 63.546(3) | 30 **Zn** 65.38(2) | 31 **Ga** 69.723(1) | 32 **Ge** 72.63(1) | 33 **As** 74.92160(2) | 34 **Se** 78.96(3) | 35 **Br** 79.904(1) | 36 **Kr** 83.798(2) |
| 37 **Rb** 85.4678(3) | 38 **Sr** 87.62(1) | | 39 **Y** 88.90585(2) | 40 **Zr** 91.224(2) | 41 **Nb** 92.90638(2) | 42 **Mo** 95.96(2) | 43 **Tc** [97.91] | 44 **Ru** 101.07(2) | 45 **Rh** 102.90550(2) | 46 **Pd** 106.42(1) | 47 **Ag** 107.8682(2) | 48 **Cd** 112.411(8) | 49 **In** 114.818(3) | 50 **Sn** 118.710(7) | 51 **Sb** 121.760(1) | 52 **Te** 127.60(3) | 53 **I** 126.90447(3) | 54 **Xe** 131.293(6) |
| 55 **Cs** 132.9054519(2) | 56 **Ba** 137.327(7) | 57–70 * | 71 **Lu** 174.9668(1) | 72 **Hf** 178.49(2) | 73 **Ta** 180.94788(2) | 74 **W** 183.84(1) | 75 **Re** 186.207(1) | 76 **Os** 190.23(3) | 77 **Ir** 192.217(3) | 78 **Pt** 195.084(9) | 79 **Au** 196.966569(4) | 80 **Hg** 200.59(2) | 81 **Tl** 204.38 | 82 **Pb** 207.2(1) | 83 **Bi** 208.98040(1) | 84 **Po** [209] | 85 **At** [210] | 86 **Rn** [222] |
| 87 **Fr** [223.02] | 88 **Ra** [226.03] | 89–102 ** | 103 **Lr** [262.11] | 104 **Rf** [265.12] | 105 **Db** [268.13] | 106 **Sg** [271.13] | 107 **Bh** [270] | 108 **Hs** [277.15] | 109 **Mt** [276.15] | 110 **Ds** [281.16] | 111 **Rg** [280.16] | 112 **Cn** [285.17] | 113 **Nh** [284.18] | 114 **Fl** [289.19] | 115 **Mc** [288.19] | 116 **Lv** [293] | 117 **Ts** [294] | 118 **Og** [294] |

| | | | | | | | | | | | | | | |
|---|---|---|---|---|---|---|---|---|---|---|---|---|---|---|
| *lanthanoids | 57 **La** 138.90547(7) | 58 **Ce** 140.116(1) | 59 **Pr** 140.90765(2) | 60 **Nd** 144.242(3) | 61 **Pm** [144.91] | 62 **Sm** 150.36(2) | 63 **Eu** 151.964(1) | 64 **Gd** 157.25(3) | 65 **Tb** 158.92535(2) | 66 **Dy** 162.500(1) | 67 **Ho** 164.93032(2) | 68 **Er** 167.259(3) | 69 **Tm** 168.93421(2) | 70 **Yb** 173.054(5) |
| **actinoids | 89 **Ac** [227.03] | 90 **Th** 232.03806(2) | 91 **Pa** 231.03588(2) | 92 **U** 238.02891(3) | 93 **Np** [237.05] | 94 **Pu** [244.06] | 95 **Am** [243.06] | 96 **Cm** [247.07] | 97 **Bk** [247.07] | 98 **Cf** [251.08] | 99 **Es** [252.08] | 100 **Fm** [257.10] | 101 **Md** [258.10] | 102 **No** [259.10] |

# NOTES

# NOTES

# NOTES

# NOTES

# NOTES

# NOTES

# NOTES

# NOTES

# 5 Steps to Teaching AP Chemistry

**TEACHER'S MANUAL**

John T. Moore, EdD
Richard H. Langley, PhD

*Thanks to Greg Jacobs, an AP physics teacher at Woodberry Forest School in Virginia, for developing the 5-step approach used in this teaching guide.*

# Introduction to the Teacher's Manual

Nowadays, teachers have no shortage of resources for the AP Chemistry class. No longer limited to just the textbook, today's teachers can utilize online simulations, apps, computer-based homework, video lectures, and so on. Even the College Board itself provides so much material related to the AP Chemistry Exam that the typical teacher—and student—can easily become overwhelmed by the excess of teaching materials and resources.

This book is a vital resource for your class because it explains in straight forward language exactly what a student needs to know for the AP Chemistry Exam and provides a review program that students can use to review for the test.

This teacher's manual will take you through the five steps of teaching AP Chemistry. These 5 steps are:

1. **Prepare a strategic plan for the course**
2. **Hold an interesting class every day**
3. **Evaluate your students' progress**
4. **Get students ready to take the AP exam**
5. **Become a better teacher every year**

We will discuss each of these steps, providing suggestions and ideas that we use in our classes. We present them here because, over the years, we have found that ***they work***. You may have developed a different course strategy, teaching activities, and evaluation techniques. That is fine; different things work for different teachers. But we hope you find in this teacher's manual something that will be useful to you.

## STEP 1

# Prepare a Strategic Plan for the Course

The Course and Exam Description (CED) from the College Board, which can be found at: **https://apcentral.collegeboard.org/courses/ap-chemistry/course**, provides a suggested scope and sequence for the AP Chemistry class. If you are a new teacher (or new to AP Chemistry), this scope and sequence will prove to be invaluable. Later on, after you have taught the course a few times and feel comfortable with the content, you may want to modify the suggested scope and sequence to better fit your style of teaching and your students.

When looking at our *5 Steps to a 5 AP Chemistry*, please note that the individual AP unit topics are not located in a single book chapter. This is because the book was designed for individual review, and we feel that our choice for grouping individual topics is better for individual review. As a teacher, please feel free to skip around to best suit your individual class. Also, we provide a diagnostic exam that is useful to determine the student's readiness for your AP course.

The chart below shows the units and pacing suggested for each unit. The number of class periods is based on a typical 45-minute class. However, if your school is on some form of block scheduling or some other type of nontraditional schedule, feel free to adjust the pacing to fit the needs of your students.

| TOPICS | PACING | 5 STEPS TO A 5 |
|---|---|---|
| **Unit 1:** Atomic Structure | 9–10 class periods | Chapter 5, pp. 74–82<br>Chapter 6, pp. 98–100<br>Chapter 7, pp. 121–124<br>Chapter 11, pp. 198–200<br>Chapter 12, pp. 209–212 |
| **Unit 2:** Molecular and Ionic Compounds Structure/Properties | 12–13 class periods | Chapter 8, pp. 131–140; 142–145<br>Chapter 9, pp. 153–161 |
| **Unit 3:** Intermolecular Forces/Properties | 14–15 class periods | Chapter 5, pp. 72; 77–78<br>Chapter 6, pp. 104<br>Chapter 7, pp. 118–121<br>Chapter 9, pp. 154–159<br>Chapter 10, pp. 170–181<br>Chapter 11, pp. 191–194; 198–200<br>Chapter 12, pp. 212–213 |
| **Unit 4:** Chemical Reactions | 14–15 class periods | Chapter 6, pp. 100–103<br>Chapter 11, pp. 191–192<br>Chapter 12, pp. 209–222 |
| **Unit 5:** Kinetics | 13–14 class periods | Chapter 13, pp. 231–242 |
| **Unit 6:** Thermodynamics | 10–11 class periods | Chapter 14, pp. 253–266 |
| **Unit 7:** Equilibrium Principles | 14–16 class periods | Chapter 15, pp. 275–289 |
| **Unit 8:** Acids and Bases | 14–15 class periods | Chapter 16, pp. 299–317 |
| **Unit 9:** Applications of Thermodynamics | 10–13 class periods | Chapter 14, pp. 253–266<br>Chapter 17, pp. 338–338 |

STEP 2

# Hold an Interesting Class Every Day

While direct instruction (sage on the stage) can be the most efficient way to deliver content, long daily lectures with copious note taking is not very effective with this age group. Make the most of lectures by trying some of the following ideas:

- **Include demonstrations to excite and engage students while making content concrete.** With a little planning and practice, this can be an easy way to encourage students to look forward to class and to visualize ideas. Demonstrations that are also discrepant events serve as great anchors for introducing new units of study.

- **Include student input in every lecture.** Ask probing questions along the way to help students open meaningful discussions about content. When possible, answer questions with more leading questions to allow the students to discover trends, processes, and answers themselves. Allow some lectures to be student-led discussions based on homework problems or reading assignments.

- **Infuse mini breakout labs within a lecture.** Get students out of their seats and moving when possible.

- **Make interesting presentations if you use them.** Chemistry is beautiful! Include well-crafted diagrams, short animations, other video clips, and pictures when possible.

In addition to weekly laboratory activities, use a variety of instructional modes each week:

- **Take advantage of technology to utilize things like Kahoot, Quizizz, Quizlet, and Sporcle for reviews and quick formative assessments.**

- **Establish traditions in class by doing one or two short activities on a regular, weekly basis.** Activities like "The Monday Molecule Minute" or "The Burning Question of the Week" give students something else interesting to anticipate.

- **Utilize cooperative working groups for skills practice, especially for new content that involves mathematics.**

- **Provide opportunities for students to draw models to represent processes throughout the course.** As students grow used to drawing dynamic models that can be manipulated to show chemical events as a function of time, their ability to reason using models will develop into a tool they can utilize to understand and visualize things they cannot see.

- **Dynamic model drawing can also be used to check for understanding when minutes count.**

Homework is an essential part of success in this course:

- **A set of homework problems is assigned at the start of each unit of study along with due dates.**
- **Students must turn in each assignment on time to receive full credit.**
- **Randomly selected problems/questions from the original set are graded, for example, at 20 points each.** This saves time on grading while holding students accountable for needed practice.
- **Ungraded problems can often be utilized for classroom discussions.**

A wealth of classroom activities and ideas may be found on the AP Central website for chemistry: **https://apcentral.collegeboard.org/courses/ap-chemistry/classroom-resources**

There you will find:

- **A list of daily videos for AP Chemistry**
- **Topic questions to help determine student understanding**
- **Progress checks to help evaluate student knowledge and skills**
- **A question bank of searchable database of real AP Chemistry questions**
- **An AP Chemistry lab manual resource**
- **Guided inquiry classroom activities**
- **A webcast describing photoelectron spectroscopy (PES)**

The *5 Steps to a 5 AP Chemistry: Elite Edition* provides additional questions that can be used in your class. It contains 180 activities and questions that require five minutes a day. While they are primarily intended to be used by students studying for the test, you can use these as daily warm-ups in your course. To do this you will need the table below that organizes these questions and activities by unit since they do not follow the course in chronological order.

| UNIT | QUESTIONS/ACTIVITIES IN THE ELITE EDITION |
|---|---|
| **Unit 1:** Atomic Structure | 6, 7, 28, 29, 31, 47, 67, 68, 69, 72, 74, 104, 173 |
| **Unit 2:** Molecular and Ionic Compounds Structure/Properties | 9, 10, 11, 25, 28, 76, 77, 79, 81, 82, 85, 88, 90, 94 |
| **Unit 3:** Intermolecular Forces/Properties | 12, 15, 40, 41, 42, 43, 45, 46, 50, 96, 97, 99, 101, 108, 142, 143 |
| **Unit 4:** Chemical Reactions | 13, 16, 18, 19, 20, 22, 34, 83, 106, 161, 178 |
| **Unit 5:** Kinetics | 110, 111, 112, 113, 114, 115, 116 |
| **Unit 6:** Thermodynamics | 53, 55, 56, 57, 58, 59, 60, 62, 63, 65 |
| **Unit 7:** Equilibrium Principles | 118, 119, 120, 122, 124, 127, 128, 130, 132, 134, 137, 143, 148 |
| **Unit 8:** Applications of Thermodynamics | 51, 52, 71, 84, 95, 154, 155,157, 158, 162, 163 |

## STEP 3

# Evaluate Your Students' Progress

The best way to prepare your students for the AP Chemistry Exam is to use AP-style questions for your own quizzes and exams. You can incorporate released AP questions from the College Board (found on AP Classroom) in your own exams. In addition, AP-style questions can be found in this book or you can use questions from your textbook or ones you make up on your own. However, there is nothing more authentic than released questions for quizzes and exams.

We highly suggest you incorporate a free-response question (FRQ) on each of your unit exams. Typically, these questions are more difficult for the students. These short-answer questions in the exam format are a great way to familiarize your students with the FRQs that they will find on the AP Chemistry Exam. The FRQs count for 40 percent of the students' grades on the AP Exam, so practicing these on every unit exam is critical to their success.

## STEP 4

# Get Students Ready to Take the AP Exam

Hopefully, you will be able to have two or even three weeks to review with your students right before they take the AP Chemistry Exam. This is the time to *review* the more difficult concepts; there isn't time to start from scratch.

Now is the time to help your students find the weak points in their knowledge in hopes that there is time to bolster their knowledge. This can be best done by utilizing the two Practice Exams found in the Build Your Test-Taking Confidence section of this book. Break each exam up into two or three class periods. They should count toward the students' grades in the class; if they are not graded, the students will not take them seriously.

## Tips for the Multiple-Choice Questions

Students have undoubtedly had many years of experience with multiple-choice exams. If on your unit exams you have used multiple-choice questions from previous AP exams, they will be familiar with the exact style of questions found on the AP exam. But there are several strategies that are important if students want to get their best score possible. Here are the most important ones that need to be reviewed to make sure all students understand them:

- **Eliminate incorrect answers and guess.** When students don't know the answer, they should eliminate the answers they know are wrong and guess among the remaining choices.

- **Mark an answer for every question.** Tell students not to leave any questions blank; there may not be time to come back. Answering every question also eliminates the possibility that they will get confused and end up putting answers on the wrong line. They want to come back to the question at the end if they have time.

- **Pace yourself.** The student's goal should be to answer every question correctly for which they know the answer. The questions on the AP exam are arranged in random order. So, the easiest question could be the last question on the test. Students need to pace themselves so that they have enough time to get to all the questions. They should not spend a lot of time thinking about difficult questions for which they don't know the answer. Make their best guess and move on.

- **There is no penalty for wrong answers.** Remind students of this. If they are running out of time, they should make sure to answer every question even if they have to guess at random.

- **Don't make stray marks on the answer sheet.** Make sure erasures are complete and that there are no marks on the page that could cause a machine to read it wrong.

## Tips for the Free-Response Questions

Students will also be familiar with the type of FRQ found on the exam if you have included at least one previously released FRQ on each unit exam. But many students do not get all the points simply because of careless mistakes. We have been grading the free-response part of the AP Chemistry Exam for quite a while. Between the two of us, we have almost 35 years of grading experience—that's more than 150,000 exams! Over the years, we have seen quite a number of careless mistakes made by students. These mistakes resulted from not being careful rather than not being prepared for the exam. Here are some practical tips to avoid the most common careless errors. (This section may also be found in the Appendix of this book, but we felt is worth repeating here.) You can incorporate a tip or so in each class period so that it becomes second nature to the students and not just something to memorize. Then during your review days, you can take a few of these tips and discuss them.

- **Don't forget to state the units of measurement.** Many students would have gotten more credit if they had shown the units, both in the calculations and in the final answer. The units help you stay on the right track and help the grader determine if (or where) you went wrong.

- **Use the formula given.** If the exam gives you a chemical formula, don't use a different formula in your answer. In general, do not alter anything given to you on the exam. For example, we have seen $Ba(NO_3)_2$ become $Ba(NO_2)_2$.

- **Be careful with the math.** We have seen many errors involving the simplest math such as 12 mL + 3 mL = 0.042 L (rather than 0.015 L).

- **Don't confuse molarity and moles.** The units *M* and [ ] are identical (molarity) and are completely different from moles.

- **Show your work for conversions.** For example, if you are changing grams to moles and make a simple mistake, showing your work (labeled) may get you partial credit.

- **Don't argue with the test.** This is an argument you cannot win. For example, if the question asks for calculations, you are unlikely to get full credit without any calculations even if you have the right answer. It won't help to write that you feel the calculations are unnecessary.

- **Be careful in applying gas laws.** Gas laws can be very useful. However, they should *never* be used when there is not a gas in the problem. Having a volume included in the question information doesn't necessarily mean you are dealing with a gas.

- **Be careful making comparisons.** We have seen many students incorrectly say that $10^{-8}$ is smaller than $10^{-12}$ and actually write $10^{-8} < 10^{-12}$. We have even seen students write the relationship correctly ($10^{-8} > 10^{-12}$) but still state that $10^{-8}$ is smaller.

- **Be careful using 22.4 L/mol.** You will probably not need to use this on the exam. But if you do want to use this value, you *must* have a gas and this gas *must* be at 0°C (273 K) and 1 atm (STP). If you forget the values for STP, they can be found on the exam. We have seen quite a few students incorrectly use this value at 298 K.

- **There are no trick questions on the exam.** If you think you have found a trick question, you need to reevaluate your thinking and reread the question.

- **Don't confuse solutions and precipitates in solution.** They are different phases and are not interchangeable. The color of one is not necessarily the color of the other.

- **Be careful describing reactions.** If the problem gives you, for example, a sodium nitrate solution, part of your answer describing a reaction cannot be "the sodium nitrate dissolves." You already have a solution, so the process of dissolving happened before you got to the problem. Furthermore, dissolving should not be treated as a reaction.

- **Be careful using positive and negative charges.** In the following equation, each reactant and product are wrong: $NH_4 + NO_3 \rightarrow NH_4^+NO_3^-$, and will not substitute for the correct $NH_4^+ + NO_3^- \rightarrow NH_4NO_3$. Remember, ionic equations, of any type, have ions (with charges) on one or both sides of the reaction arrow.

- **Don't do a calculator dump (write down every number displayed by your calculator).** For example, your final answer will not be 3.27584827 g.

- **Keep in mind the meaning of "observe."** If the problem asks about observation, tell what you would actually observe (see, hear, or smell). You will *not* see a compound separating into ions; usually you will *not* see the excess reagent, and you will *not* see the atoms forming bonds. In contrast, you might observe a compound dissolving.

- **Remember, a solvent is usually not a reactant.** Therefore, changing the grams of solvent to moles is probably wrong. (However, you will need to know the moles of solvent if you are looking for a mole fraction.)

- **Think before creating mole ratios.** Since the solvent is not a reactant, a mole ratio relating the solvent to anything else in the problem is most likely wrong. We have seen many students change the grams of water to moles and then use these moles in a mole ratio to relate to some other substance in the problem.

- **Don't go off on a tangent.** Stay focused on answering the original question.

- **Double-check the numbers you use.** We have seen many cases where the problem gave a number like $2.75 \times 10^{-18}$, and the student worked the problem with $2.75 \times 10^{-8}$. If you show your work, it will be obvious to the grader that you miscopied the value and you might pick up some points; otherwise, you just have a wrong answer.

- **Remember that sometimes not all of the information given is needed to solve the problem.** For example, in the equilibrium problem, many times the temperature is given but it is not actually part of the calculations.

- **Only round your final answer.** Don't round off the results of intermediate calculations; only use rounding after you've gotten your final answer.

- **Be careful with math.** Especially take care in reading the scales on graphs. We have seen students write down that 0.5 is between 1.0 and 2.0.

- **Don't confuse intermolecular and intramolecular forces.** These are two different concepts and are not interchangeable.

In addition to avoiding the careless mistakes mentioned above, here are some easy ways to help improve your score on the free-response questions:

- **Show your work.** In most cases, no work, no credit.
- **Use the space provided for answers.** It helps you and the grader if you answer the question in the space provided instead of crowding the answers between the questions. You will have more than enough room on the following page(s). It also helps to label the parts (a, b, etc.) and to answer the parts in order.
- **Make sure your answer can be easily read.** It will really help the grader—and your score—if you write legibly, in a normal size (not too small, please), and use a pencil or pen that writes dark enough to be easily read.
- **Don't use periodic trends and general rules as explanations.** General rules such as "like dissolves like" are never explanations. They may help you in answering the multiple-choice part of the exam but will be of little benefit by themselves in the free-response section.
- **Don't confuse "define" and "describe."** They are two different processes. If you are asked to describe or explain, simply giving a definition will earn you very few points.
- **Use only standard abbreviations.** Your instructor may understand your abbreviations, but the grader may not. If you want to use abbreviations in a response, be sure to define them.
- **Don't ramble.** Normally an explanation or justification can be done in five sentences or less. Your answers should be clear, concise, and to the point.
- **The grader cannot see your calculator display or a graph/table that you do not include in your answer.** Show all your work that you want graded; sometimes showing this will help you get a point that you might otherwise have lost.
- **In general, the graders are not "mind readers."** Show your work and your reasoning. Don't assume graders will know what you meant. They grade only what you have written down.
- **Answer the question asked, not the question you wanted.** You might have a great response to a question, but if that doesn't answer the exact question asked, it is *wrong*!
- **It is usually simpler to use the units given in the problem.** It is less work on your part and less work on the grader.
- **Using extra calculation steps provides additional opportunities to make errors.** Show all your pertinent calculation steps, but extra steps are spots for potential errors. This is especially true when you are tired.

STEP 5

# Become a Better Teacher Every Year

A good AP teacher strives to improve every year. If there is anything that didn't work as well as you had hoped this year, there's always next year to try something different. Isn't that great: a do-over every year!

How do you judge success? There is no right or wrong answer to this. We all teach at different schools with different students. You will have a few students with strong science and math skills. They could probably pass the exam without you. Most students may lack some of the skills or knowledge that is needed to do well on the AP exam. These students are the ones who need us most and when they succeed, it is because of their effort and your support.

If you are a new AP Chemistry teacher, keep the AP Central pages that are specific to chemistry bookmarked on both your school and personal computers. Take time to explore the resources available there. If there are experienced AP Chemistry teachers at your school or schools close by, reach out to them and pick their brains.

It is also very importance to attend an APSI (AP Summer Institute). This will keep you up-to-date on any changes to the AP Chemistry program. These summer institutes are a great place to meet other teachers and hear about how they teach, both as you begin to teach the course and also every few years as you continue. To get additional ideas and insights, we recommend that you take summer institutes from different instructors. There are also online workshops, free webinars and online sessions throughout the year. Links to these learning opportunities may be found here: **https://apcentral.collegeboard.org/courses/ap-chemistry/professional-learning?course=ap-chemistry**

For all AP teachers, both new and experienced, the best thing you can do to improve is to use the Instructional Planning Report you will receive after student scores are calculated. You can access this document in your AP Classroom. You will get a breakdown of scores by unit, by question type (multiple choice and FRQ), and so on. This information is what you need to adjust your course for the next school year. If you notice that students as a whole struggled with a particular unit, this is where you make changes. Maybe you will need to spend a little extra time on this unit or maybe you find new activities to use during class. Maybe you will need to be sure to review this unit in class before the next year's AP exam. What if students did really well on the multiple choice but not the FRQs? How can you get some additional professional learning to better teach them how to write? It may take a few years to see results, but with attention to the Instructional Planning Reports and with continuous adjustments to your class, your student scores will increase.

We also encourage all AP teachers to apply to be a reader for the AP Exam after they have a few years of teaching the AP class under their belts. The AP reading is the best professional learning experience you can receive, and you will meet a group of like-minded teachers who will become your friends throughout the years to come. Who knows, you might find the authors of this book there! You can apply online through the College Board's website: **https://apcentral.collegeboard.org/professional-learning/become-an-ap-reader**

## Additional Resources for Teachers

Teaching chemistry is just as much about how to teach as what to teach. The following resources can provide valuable content and pedagogy:

The **American Association of Chemistry Teachers** (AACT, teachchemistry.org) is an organization that is geared toward high school chemistry teachers. It publishes classroom resources, professional development, news, and so on. You get a lot of useful information for your dues.

The **American Chemical Society** (ACS, acs.org) is the premier organization devoted to chemistry. It has a division that is devoted to chemical education (divched.org). The ACS publishes *ChemMatters* magazine four times a year. It is devoted to clarifying chemistry for high school students and helping them see the connections between chemistry and everyday life. If you join AACT, you receive a complimentary subscription to *ChemMatters* and have access to the *ChemMatters* archive.

Another professional organization that deserves consideration is the **National Science Teaching Association** (NSTA, nsta.org). NSTA has a great deal of resources available for their members, including lesson plans, books, and so on. This organization not only covers chemistry but all the other sciences. This is invaluable for chemistry teachers who are also teaching physics, biology, and the like.

There is an online Facebook account for AP Chemistry Teachers, https://www.facebook.com/groups/866651346744793/about/. You must be an AP Chemistry teacher to join, but this would be an excellent way to remain in contact with other AP Chemistry teachers and to keep in touch with what topics are trending.

The CollegeBoard has an online resource called AP Teacher Community. It is an online presence that allows AP teachers and coordinators to connect with each other. There are discussion boards and a Resource Library to share class-ready resources. The CollegeBoard also maintains a page dedicated to online resources recommended by AP teachers at https://apcentral.collegeboard.org/courses/ap-chemistry/classroom-resources/teacher-recommended-resources.

**Flinn Scientific** (flinnsci.com) is a wonderful source for chemical supplies and chemicals. They have a real devotion for educating teachers in how to conduct safe science at the public school level. Their hard-copy catalog contains a wealth of information on chemical disposal and the safe handling of chemicals. It makes great bedtime reading!

In response to COVID-19 and the need to provide virtual instruction, many companies developed classroom instructional materials. These materials are also valuable in the face-to-face classroom. A simple Google search will generate dozens of useful hits. It is easy to get overwhelmed with the number of hits, so we suggest you specify the topic to narrow it down (i.e., teaching kinetics, teaching atomic structure). You can access a list and brief description of quite a few online resources here: https://apcentral.collegeboard.org/courses/ap-chemistry/classroom-resources/teacher-recommended-resources?course=ap-chemistry

We hope that these suggestions and tips will help you in teaching AP Chemistry and that your student scores will benefit. One final word of advice: Have fun teaching AP Chemistry! To us nerds, the content is interesting and even exciting. The students are always an interesting group. Do your best to guide them through the material. It's really rewarding to see them conquer the concepts.